THE

PRINCIPLES

OF

POLITICAL ECONOMY

APPLIED TO

THE CONDITION, THE RESOURCES, AND THE INSTITUTIONS
OF THE AMERICAN PEOPLE.

BY

FRANCIS BOWEN,

ALFORD PROFESSOR OF MORAL PHILOSOPHY AND CIVIL POLITY
IN HARVARD COLLEGE.

"It is not that a Duke has 50,000*l*. a year, but that a thousand fathers of families have 50*l*. a year, that is true national wealth and well-being." — LAING.

SECOND EDITION.

BOSTON:
LITTLE, BROWN, AND COMPANY.
1859.

UNIVERSITY PRESS, CAMBRIDGE:
WELCH, BIGELOW, & CO., ELECTROTYPERS AND PRINTERS.

TO

NATHAN APPLETON,

ONE OF THE MOST EMINENT LIVING REPRESENTATIVES

OF A HIGHLY HONORED CLASS,

THE MERCHANT PRINCES OF BOSTON,

WHO HAVE EARNED SUCCESS

BY SAGACITY, ENTERPRISE, AND UPRIGHTNESS IN ALL THEIR UNDERTAKINGS,

AND HAVE DIGNIFIED IT

BY THE MUNIFICENCE OF THEIR CHARITIES,

AND BY THEIR LIBERAL SUPPORT OF LETTERS, SCIENCE, AND THE ARTS,

THIS WORK IS RESPECTFULLY INSCRIBED.

PREFACE.

"Political Economy," says Mr. Samuel Laing, "is not a universal science, of which the principles are applicable to all men under all circumstances, and equally good and true for all nations; but every country has a Political Economy of its own, suitable to its own physical circumstances of position on the globe, climate, soil, products, and to the habits, character, and idiosyncrasy of its inhabitants, formed or modified by such physical circumstances."

I am not prepared to accept this remark in all its generality, for if it were true, it would follow, not only that Political Economy is not a universal science, but that it is no science at all, inasmuch as universal applicability, as Mr. Laing himself observes, is "the distinguishing characteristic and test of every branch of knowledge that claims the dignity of real science." But the habits and dispositions of men, as manifested in the pursuit of wealth, may be reduced to general principles, and thus become subjects of legitimate scientific classification and inquiry, just as much as those other habits and dispositions which are manifested in the constitution and conduct of organized society, and which, when generalized and classified, become the science of Politics. There is a general science of Human Nature, of which the special sciences of Ethics, Psychology, Æsthetics, Politics, and Political Economy are so many departments, all founded upon the essential unity of the human mind and character, and the consequent similarity of its manifestations under similar circumstances. These sciences may be studied either inductively or deductively; that is, either by observing the phenomena, — the conduct of men under given circumstances, — and tracing these up to their causes,

— the motives in which they must have originated; or by assuming the motives from our general knowledge of human nature, and tracing these down to the outward conduct which they cause and govern. In this sense, then, there is a universal science of Political Economy, equally applicable, not only to France, England, and America, but to China, Tartary, and New Holland, — to all nations under the sun.

But it must be admitted that these universal principles are comparatively few and unimportant, often being little more than truisms; and if the science were limited to them, it would be of rather narrow compass and limited utility. Political Economy, as it is commonly understood, embraces a great number of corollaries and deductions from these principles, and of applications of them to the analysis and explanation of complex social and commercial phenomena. It is thus that the science, or rather any particular system of it, becomes obnoxious to Mr. Laing's censure; having been suggested by the peculiar circumstances and condition of one country, relating almost exclusively to the experience of one nation, and deriving, in truth, most of its utility for them from this very fact, it is at least partially inapplicable and unsound in every other case. The Political Economy of England is even more peculiar and characteristic than her civil polity and social organization; it is conformed to that polity and organization, and it is also adapted to the physical condition and industrial pursuits of an insular people. As circumstances vary from age to age, as well as between different countries, it is continually necessary to review and modify the leading doctrines of the science, so as to preserve their conformity to the habits and the institutions of the people. If Adam Smith were living in our own day, it may be doubted whether he would be the uncompromising advocate that he was, of the principles of Free Trade. He flourished at a time when the system of monopolies and restraints was in full action and vigor; when nothing had been done to limit or reform the colonial system, the guilds of trade, the East India Company, the Universities, or the abuses of municipal corporations. It was natural that he should utter an earnest protest against these odious restrictions and monopolies, and carry his argument against them too far, by neglecting to mention the exceptions and limitations to which his own principles were liable.

I have endeavored in this work to lay the foundations at least, leaving it for others to raise the superstructure, of an American system of Political Economy, and for this purpose, have subjected to a rigorous examination the leading doctrines of the science as taught by English writers, in order not only to test their general soundness and applicability to the condition and the institutions of the American people, but to trace out and analyze the peculiar circumstances which first suggested them. Among these doctrines may be enumerated those of Adam Smith upon free trade, of Malthus upon population, of Ricardo upon rent and profits, of Torrens and Loyd upon the currency, and of McCulloch upon the laws of inheritance. It is not the light of American experience alone which has induced me to modify or reject these theories; I have attempted to show that they are indefensible even upon the principles of those who continue to support them, and to this end, have fortified my reasoning by frequent citations from English and French authorities.

The work was not designed to be wholly controversial and original; besides suggesting the doctrines which are to take the place of those which have been rejected, it was intended to contain a summary of what is most valuable in other treatises upon the subject, so as to form a convenient text-book of instruction in American colleges. Most teachers will probably accept the conclusion which I have formed, after many years' experience, that it is a wearisome and hopeless task to attempt to instruct a class of pupils from any of the English or French treatises upon the science. This volume contains the substance of a course of lectures upon Political Economy, first delivered before the Lowell Institute in Boston five years ago, and afterwards repeated, with many changes and additions, before successive classes in college. It also comprises all that was deemed worthy of preservation in a series of articles upon various topics in the science, which have been published during the last ten years in the North American Review. I have not deemed it necessary to rewrite what was at first carefully prepared for publication, when time and further reflection had not suggested any change of doctrine, or any material improvements in illustration or phraseology.

The nature of the subject has compelled me to make a kind of comparative survey of the workings and results of the social and political institutions of England and America. It is hoped that the results of this comparison, as here presented, will not seem to have been suggested by national prejudice, or to be unduly tinctured with national self-esteem.

Most of what is valuable in our civil polity has come to us by inheritance from our English ancestors, and is still the common property of the two nations; the trial by jury, the writ of *habeas corpus*, the leading forms of representative government, are still the common safeguards of English and American freedom, and the great principles of the English Common Law are still authoritative in our courts. Loyalty to the State and the Union takes the place with us of loyalty to the Crown. We have only cast off the aristocratic and monarchical appendages of these institutions, to make room for democratic ones, — a change far less important in a political than a social aspect. Whatever there is peculiar in the forms of society, the organization of industry, and the habits and dispositions of our people, which can be directly traced to this alteration, has been the subject of frequent and sharp criticism, not only by British travellers, but by British economists and statesmen. Thus, Mr. J. S. Mill, unquestionably the ablest living writer upon Political Economy and the Logic of the Inductive Sciences, and one who, from his connection with the followers of Bentham and the Radical party, might be supposed to view with some favor the workings of republican institutions, cannot speak in any more flattering terms than these of the inhabitants of the Northern and Middle States of America: "They have the six points of Chartism, and they have no poverty; and all that these advantages do for them is, that the life of the whole of one sex is devoted to dollar-hunting, and of the other to breeding dollar-hunters." And the tone of McCulloch, Tooke, and other English economists, in reference to the people of this country, is not a whit more complimentary.* Not at

* Yet Englishmen wonder and complain that the sympathies of Americans are not with them and their allies in their present contest with Russia, — a contest which, as it involves no principles of natural or popular rights, but is solely a struggle between rival governments for a preponderance of power in the Black Sea, is certainly regarded by the generality of our countrymen with unaffected indifference. The question whether Napoleon the Third has any better claim to the esteem of the people of the United States than he had to that of Englishmen only three years ago, is, perhaps, not worth discussing. But if England and America are ever to be joined in a natural alliance of spontaneous amity and mutual regard, a more conciliatory manner must be adopted by those who assume to speak the opinions of the middle and the upper classes in the former country. Disregard, if you will, all those manifestations of popular sentiment here which may be imputed to electioneering manœuvres: there still remains in the minds of the educated and reflecting portion of our peo-

all in the spirit of retaliation, but in that of self-defence, as well as for the more perfect elucidation of the principles of the science, I have compared the effects of aristocratic with those of democratic institutions upon the development of national enterprise, the growth of opulence, the security of property, the popular feeling of uneasiness or content, and the general well-being of the people in Great Britain and the United States. Too much stress is habitually laid by English economists upon the natural advantages which our countrymen are supposed to possess, especially in the broad expanse of fertile territory which still remains open for settlement by them. But surely we cannot claim superiority in this respect over England, whose colonial dominion comprises Nova Scotia and Canada, a large portion of the East and the West Indies, the southern part of Africa, and the whole of New Zealand and Australia. Besides, I have attempted to show that the causes of the increase of capital are moral rather than physical, and that there is a drawback, as well as an advantage, in the abundance and cheapness of land, which incite the people to leave behind them all the means and appliances of civilization, and to become squatters and backwoodsmen in the wilderness.

Though I have had frequent occasion to controvert the opinions of English economists, it is little to say that this work could not have been written without the aid which their writings have afforded, and that I have often borrowed from one or two of them facts and arguments which have served to confute the theories of the others. The authority of Adam Smith, Malthus, and Ricardo seems to be waning even in England; a new school has sprung up in opposition to them, whose opinions on many important points are visibly gaining ground, and have already begun to affect the legislation of the kingdom. Among these dissentients may be reckoned the eminent traveller and social economist, Mr. Samuel Laing, and the ingenious and well-informed author of "Over-Population and its Remedy," Mr. W. T. Thornton; while Mr. Tooke, the author of an admirable "History of Prices," and Mr. Fullarton, have

---

ple, who are naturally cordial well-wishers to England, a strong feeling of surprise and indignation at the insolent and domineering tone habitually assumed about everything pertaining to America by that influential journal which, even more than the British ministry, is the organ of public opinion in Great Britain, — a feeling which mere diplomacy, though conducted by persons as wise and generous as Webster and Ashburton, can never entirely eradicate.

successfully established, in opposition to the paradoxes of Ricardo and his followers, a rational theory of the currency. Mr. J. S. Mill, an avowed iconoclast and reformer, has followed or preceded these writers on some of their points of dissent from the old school, and has incorporated into his work some very bold speculations respecting the laws of inheritance and the distribution of property; but in other respects, he has followed very closely in the footsteps of Malthus and Ricardo. From the writings of all whom I have mentioned by name, and of several others, I have derived valuable aid and instruction.

Throughout the work, I have had in view the wants of learners, and have tried to incorporate into it such elementary information about banking operations, the system of disposing of the public lands, the nature of bills of exchange, the functions of the currency, the supply of the precious metals, and the course of trade both at home and with foreign countries, as might be useful not only to classes in college, but to other young men, who, with less preparatory training, are about to enter the mercantile profession.

CAMBRIDGE, December 28, 1855.

CONTENTS.

CHAPTER I.

CHAPTER II.

CHAPTER VI.

CHAPTER VII.

CHAPTER VIII.

CHAPTER IX.

CHAPTER X.

CHAPTER XI.

CHAPTER XII.

CHAPTER XIII.

CHAPTER XIV.

CHAPTER XV.

CHAPTER XVI.

CHAPTER XVII.

CHAPTER XVIII.

CHAPTER XIX.

CHAPTER XX.

CHAPTER XXI.

CHAPTER XXII.

CHAPTER XXIII.

CHAPTER XXIV.

CHAPTER XXV.

PRINCIPLES

OF

POLITICAL ECONOMY.

CHAPTER I.

WEALTH AND ITS TRANSMUTATIONS.

The most obvious, though certainly not the most important, difference between a civilized community and a nation of savages consists in the vastly greater abundance, possessed by the former, of all the means of comfort and enjoyment. These means, including the necessaries, conveniences, and luxuries of life, are chiefly *material* objects, — such as manufactured goods, articles of food and clothing, ships and buildings, the useful and the precious metals, tools and machines, and ornaments, or things designed to gratify the taste and the senses. Some, however, are *immaterial*, and yet are just as much objects of desire, just as much objects of barter and sale, as cloth and bread. The legal knowledge and acumen of a lawyer, for instance, the vocal powers of a remarkable singer, the mimetic talent of an actor, the practised hand of an ingenious and thoroughly-trained artisan, all command a price in the market quite as readily as any goods in a shop. When an occasion arises, we buy the services of a lawyer or a physician, just as we buy a ticket to a concert, or an instrument of music for a drawing-room.*

---

* Many Political Economists exclude *immaterial* products from their definition of wealth, because the labor which is devoted to such products "ends in immediate enjoyment, without any increase of the accumulated stock of permanent means of

Now, the aggregate of all these things, whether material or immaterial, which contribute to comfort and enjoyment, and which are objects of frequent barter and sale, is what we usually call WEALTH; and individuals or nations are denominated rich or poor, according to the abundance or scarcity of these articles which they possess, or have at their immediate disposal.

Two questions, we are told, may be asked respecting the production of these articles: — 1. By what mechanical processes are they manufactured or obtained? To answer this query, is the business of a man of practical science or an artisan, — of a chemist, a mechanic, or a farmer; as Political Economists, we have nothing to do with it. But (2.) we may ask, On what principles do men readily exchange these articles for each other, and what motives, what general laws, regulate their production, distribution, and consumption? Political Economy undertakes to answer this question, and is therefore properly considered as one of the Moral Sciences. It depends, quite as much as Politics and Ethics, upon the principles of the human mind. It is quite as possible to re-

enjoyment." The man who makes a fiddle, they say, is a productive laborer, because his work remains as a permanent addition to the stock of things from which men derive pleasure; but he who only plays upon the fiddle, though, like Paganini, he earns £1,000 in a single evening, adds nothing to the wealth of the community. We answer, that the characteristic of all wealth is, directly or indirectly, to satisfy some want or gratify some desire. The fiddle is but an indirect means to this end; it would gratify nobody, — it would not increase our store of valuables, — if the skill of the practised musician could not extract sweet sounds from it. The time during which the pleasure endures, or the number of occasions on which it may be repeated, is a point of no importance, except so far as it may determine the amount, or quantity, of the wealth which has been created. Food which is ready to be eaten is wealth, just as much as the knives and forks with which we eat it; though the former is devoured at once, and there is an end of it, while the latter may remain in daily use for a year or more.

"When a tailor makes a coat and sells it," argues Mr. J. S. Mill, "there is a transfer of the price from the customer to the tailor, and a coat besides, which did not previously exist; but what is gained by an actor is a mere transfer from the spectator's funds to his, leaving no article of wealth for the spectator's indemnification." We reply, that the purchaser obtains only a gratification of desire in either case. From the coat, he has moderate enjoyment prolonged for some months; but he might do without it, and work in his shirt-sleeves. From the theatre, he has keen enjoyment, that lasts only a few hours; and he may prefer such pleasure to the luxury of additional clothing. It is inconsistent to give the name of wealth to what pleases our palates for a moment, and deny it to what gives keener pleasure to our ears.

duce to general laws the habits and dispositions of men, so far as they are manifested in their efforts for the acquisition of wealth, as it is to develop, from observation and consciousness, the laws of our moral constitution. Political Economy begins with the supposition, that man is disposed to accumulate wealth beyond what is necessary for the immediate gratification of his wants, and that this disposition, in the great majority of cases, is in fact unbounded; that man's inclination to labor is mainly controlled by this desire; that he is constantly competing with his fellows in this attempt to gain wealth; and that he is sagacious enough to see what branches of industry are most profitable, and eager enough to engage in them, so that competition regularly tends to bring wages, profits, and prices to a level. The science, then, is more closely allied with the Philosophy of Mind, than with Natural History, or the physical sciences. It has been called *Catallactics*, or "the Science of Exchanges"; and, agreeably to this notion, man himself has been defined to be, *an animal* that makes exchanges; "as no other, even of those animals which, in other points, make the nearest approach to rationality, has, to all appearance, the least notion of bartering, or in any way exchanging one object for another."

With regard to the articles that constitute wealth, we observe that far the larger portion of them are perishable, or quickly consumable. Some of them, like the immaterial products, are consumed at the instant that they are produced; others, like articles of food, last a little longer, but perish if not quickly used. The fashion and the fabric of manufactured goods soon decay and pass away, the former being often more short-lived than the latter. Tools and machinery wear out; houses and other buildings need constant repair, and, at stated intervals, must be wholly renewed. Hardly anything but the solid land itself — the great God-given, food-producing machine — is permanent; and *the exchangeable value* even of the land, (the only quality of it which we have to consider in this science,) quickly diminishes, and almost wholly disappears, if it be not kept up by the constant application of labor and capital, or by the continued prosperity of the community who live upon it. The best situated land in a populous city may be worth $30 or $40 a square foot; but if the other articles which constitute the wealth of that city — the ships in her harbor and the goods in her shops — were not perpetually renewed, the land would deteriorate in value with great rapidity; and if the city should become, in respect to population and business, a small and decaying village, the land might not be worth $40 an acre.

Wealth, then, — and we may crave attention to the proposition, for it is an important one, — wealth must be perpetually renewed, or it quickly disappears. The stock of national wealth is like the flesh, blood, and bones of a man's body, which are in a state of constant flux and renovation. Physiologists tell us that our bodies are entirely renewed about once in seven years; but the riches of an opulent community are not so long-lived even as this. Let labor universally cease, let every man, woman, and child rest with folded arms, or do nothing but eat, drink, and be merry, and those riches would melt and waste like snow under a July sun. National wealth, then, may be more fitly compared to a given portion or section of the waters of a running stream, bounded by a few rods in length of the opposite banks. The water is always changing, yet in one sense is always the same, so long as the supply from above is maintained; but if the springs in the upper country should be suddenly dried up, the efflux below would drain the channel in an hour.

And here is one striking proof, among a thousand others, of the inordinate folly and ignorance of those who cry out against the institution of property, and call for an equal distribution of all the wealth of a community among all its members. "Riches have wings" in a far more immediate and practical sense than these people are at all aware of. They always talk as if the national wealth was a fixed and imperishable quantity, like the land, the sunlight, and the air; but as if, unlike these, it was monopolized by a few, though really sufficient for the wants of all. Their blunder is quite as great as would be that of an ignorant rustic, who, after visiting the well-furnished market of a populous city on the Mondays of two successive weeks, and observing that the stalls presented almost precisely the same array of meats and vegetables, in the same order, should conclude that there had been no change, and that, as here was a permanent stock of food enough for all, while some families in the city were suffering from hunger, a general and equal distribution of this stock, without compensation to the owners, should be ordered, under the idea that it would make any future want of provision impossible. The possibility that this great store might all be consumed in one day, that the dealers, deterred by this spoliation, might not supply the market at all on the next day, and that many indigent families, suddenly finding all their wants supplied without any effort on their part, would give up labor altogether, would never occur to him.*

"This perpetual consumption and reproduction of capital," says Mr. J. S. Mill, "affords the explanation of what has so often excited wonder, — the great rapidity with which countries recover from a state of devastation; the disappearance, in a short time, of all traces of the mischiefs done by earth-

* This point was admirably illustrated by the late Marshal Bugeaud, in an article published in the *Revue des deux Mondes*, soon after the French Revolution of 1848, when theories of Communism and Socialism were so rife, and were urged with so much violence, at Paris, as to menace the very existence of society. I borrow a few paragraphs from this admirable essay.

"The philanthropic dreamers, the demagogues of every age and every country, have seemed to believe that there existed somewhere a great amount of riches given by God, which might suffice for all the world, if a few aristocrats had not, with merciless selfishness, obtained possession of them. This idea is, unwittingly perhaps, the basis of all their systems, all their declamations. . . . . .

"It is matter of astonishment that all eyes are not struck by the truth written, as it were, over the whole surface of the soil, — that there are no riches but those which are produced by the industry of every day, of every year; that the riches already produced, the fruit of labor also, are almost infinitely small in comparison with the wants of a society of thirty-six millions of souls; that even if they should be taken from those who have them to be distributed to those who have nothing, or but a little, the condition of the latter would not be ameliorated; far from that, they would be impoverished. The land alone, being created by God, might appear, at first sight, as wealth existing previously to labor, and belonging to all the world. This idea was true at the moment of creation, except that the land is not, in itself, wealth in the proper acceptation of the word; it is only a vast arena for the labor of civilized man. In its primitive state, it can support only a few savages upon the fruits and roots of the forests. The value which it now has is what labor has given to it. How many ages, how much capital, how much toil, had to be buried in its bosom to produce that which we now see! . . . . . The most experienced agriculturists say, that 'the land is nothing but a matrix, a mould, or an instrument of labor. If we were to calculate all that landed estates have cost to bring them into cultivation, not ever since man has labored upon them, but during only the last two centuries, we should find that the sum was much greater than the present value of those estates.' We refer now only to the extraordinary costs, such as those of clearing the ground, draining the marshes, carrying off the rocks and stones, transport-

quakes, floods, hurricanes, and the ravages of war. An enemy lays waste a country by fire and sword, and destroys or carries away nearly all the movable wealth existing in it; all the inhabitants are ruined, and yet, in a few years after, everything is much as it was before. This *vis medicatrix naturæ* has been a subject of sterile astonishment, or has been cited to exemplify the wonderful strength of the principle of saving, which can repair such enormous losses in so brief an interval. There is nothing at all wonderful in the matter. What the enemy have destroyed would have been destroyed in a little time by the inhabitants themselves; the wealth which they so rapidly reproduce would have needed to be reproduced, and would have been reproduced, in any case, and probably in as short an interval. Nothing is changed, except that, during the reproduction, they have not now the advantage of consuming what had been produced previously. The possibility of a

---

ing soil and mineral manures, planting trees and vines, building farm-houses, and furnishing cattle and the implements of husbandry. We must leave out the expenses of the ordinary annual cultivation of the ground, as that is repaid by the crops.

"I will ask the men who have the incredible audacity to declare that property is robbery, if the ordinary laborer's wages for the week or the month are not sacred. They will answer, that certainly there is nothing more sacred in the world. Very well! The labor of months, of years, of centuries, which has made property what it is, — is not this as sacred as the labor of a week or a month? Cease your blasphemies, then, against property; instead of saying that the first person who inclosed a field and cleared it for cultivation was a fool or a rogue, bless him, honor him, respect his work; for without it, the human race would have perished, or, thinly scattered over the earth, would have lived in want and misery.

"I think I have already demonstrated that there is no such thing as primitive wealth, existing antecedently to labor, since the land itself has become an article of wealth only under the active hand of man. It is equally true, that the wealth already created is nothing; that alone which the labor of every day and every year is constantly creating, is of great importance.

"The principal articles of the wealth of a nation are, first, the products of the earth, which constitute the food of man and the raw material for his clothing; and secondly, the manufactured articles in which he is dressed, and which give him the conveniences and comforts of life.

"Now, are there any aristocrats who hold in their hands the hundred and forty millions of hectolitres of different sorts of grain, and the forty millions of hectolitres of wine, wool, hemp, flax, meat, oil, &c., which France must produce and consume in 1849? Are there other aristocrats who own the household furniture, the tools, and materials, which are consumed in a single year? No; these must be produced by the incessant labor of all, or nearly all, persons in France. If their labor should cease only for a few months, the people would be naked and would die of famine; for they have not a stock of wealth on hand large enough to keep them in supply during this respite."

rapid repair of their disasters mainly depends on whether the country has been depopulated. If its effective population have not been extirpated at the time, and are not starved afterwards, [and if their exertions are not paralyzed by the dread of a similar quickly recurring calamity,] then, with the same skill and knowledge which they had before, with their land and its permanent improvements undestroyed, and the more durable buildings probably unimpaired, or only partially injured, they have nearly all the requisites for their former amount of production. If there is as much of food left to them, or of valuables to buy food, as enables them, by any amount of privation, to remain alive and in working condition, they will in a short time have raised as great a produce, and acquired collectively as great wealth and as great a capital, as before, by the mere continuance of that ordinary amount of exertion which they are accustomed to employ in their occupations. Nor does this evince any strength in the principle of *saving*, in the popular sense of the term; since what takes place is not intentional abstinence, but involuntary privation."

This pregnant truth, that the whole stock of national wealth is in a constant and rapid process of consumption and reproduction, is generally lost sight of, because we see that the fortunes of individuals, the aggregate of which constitutes the national stock, are comparatively permanent, and, *as it seems*, do not need to be perpetually renewed. If once raised considerably above a mere competence, and then "invested," as the phrase goes, with ordinary care and judgment, a man's property will continue apparently without change, all the while yielding its regular income or increase. If its owner be not a spendthrift, an inebriate, or a simpleton, it will supply his wants and gratify his tastes, and still grow by a steady process of accumulation, the savings of income being added to the capital, without ever encroaching upon his leisure, or requiring him to superintend a change of its form. How can this fact be reconciled with the principles that have just been stated respecting the nature of all wealth? The answer to this question brings us at once to the heart of the subject.

It is the *property*, the *ownership*, that is unchanged, and thus the fortunes of individuals remain intact; the articles which are the subjects of that property — which are owned — are constantly changing; they are used up, and then renewed, without the owner's coöperation, and often even without his knowledge. Barring casualties, unlucky investments, and the like, (which, being comparatively few and infrequent, may be left out of the account,) no man's property is consumed without being replaced by the very act of consumption, unless he himself, consciously and wilfully, consumes or expends it *unproductively;* — that is, upon the gratification of his own tastes and appetites, without looking for a return or replacement. To "invest" one's savings is to *lend* them. Not having time, inclination, or perhaps ability, to use them reproductively to advantage, — that is, to superintend the constant changes of form which they *must* undergo, or quickly perish, — we lend them to others, who can and will direct their transformations, on condition of receiving a small portion of the profits of these changes. For it is also the nature of wealth, when well managed, to *grow*, or increase, by each change of form.

"Mobilitate viget, viresque acquirit eundo."

To make this clearer, we will analyze a single instance, — the simplest one that can be found. If the earnings of an artisan for a year have amounted to $ 300, he *may* expend them all upon food, clothing, and amusement. In this case, he spends them all *unproductively*, — that is, without expecting a return or replacement of them. At the year's end, all the advantage which *remains* to him from his year's labor is, that his strength, health, and spirits are renewed or replaced, so that he can now go to work and earn another year's wages.

But suppose that he is frugal and ambitious to grow rich. He will then contract his daily expenses, drink nothing but water, give up all amusements, and thus, at the end of the year, he will find that his health and spirits are even greater than before, and that he has saved perhaps $ 100, or one third of his earnings. What will he do with this $ 100? In a rude state of society, among a half-civilized people, or under the government of a Turkish pacha, property being insecure, he would probably obtain it in the form of gold or silver coin, and bury it in the corner of his cellar or garden. There, sure enough, it would remain without change, and *therefore* without income or increase. But in this country, in England, or

France, he would probably put it in the Savings' Bank; that is, he would *lend* it to the bank, which, for shortness, we will suppose to be a bank both of savings and discount. In consequence of this loan, the bank will be able to lend or discount $100 more to one of its customers. Suppose a baker wishes to extend his business, but has not capital enough of his own to buy more flour with. He borrows this $100 of the bank for four months, and with it he immediately purchases twenty barrels of flour more than he could otherwise have purchased. What he borrows of the bank is not, in fact, the $100 bill which is handed to him across the counter, but the twenty barrels of flour which he buys with it; the bank-bill being only a ticket or certificate, in which the bank directors say to the flour-dealer, "Deliver this man twenty barrels of flour, and we will pay you for it." The flour-dealer complies, and immediately carries back the bill to the bank, and is paid for it either in hard specie, or in that amount carried to his credit, or in any other form that he may prefer. We may put aside, then, in future, any consideration of the bank-bills; for they are nothing but *tickets of transfer*, or orders from the bank to any merchant, asking him to deliver the bearer a certain amount of goods, and the bank will pay him for them.

But let us follow the laborer's $100 of savings. In what form do they now exist? Evidently they have become twenty barrels of flour, which the baker gradually transforms into many loaves of bread, and sells them to his customers. Before the four months expire, the bread is all sold and eaten; so that the $100 are now fairly consumed. But has their value disappeared? By no means. The baker's customers have paid him for this bread at least $120, so that he can now repay the bank the $100 that he borrowed, with the addition of two dollars for four months' interest, and put eighteen dollars into his own pocket as the reward of his labor. The bank, being again in funds, can now lend, we will suppose, $102 worth of leather, for four months, to an enterprising cordwainer, who begins immediately to manufacture it into boots and shoes. Before *his* four months have expired, these are all sold, (half of them, perhaps, are half worn out,) and he has received, it may be, $225 for them; so that he can now repay the bank its loan of $102, besides two dollars and a fraction for interest, pay his workmen probably $ 100, for a good deal of labor was needed for the consumption of that amount of leather, and put a little more than twenty dollars into his own pocket. At the end of eight months, then, the bank has a little over $ 104 to let out for another period of four months. A paper-maker borrows this, buys rags with it, makes paper out of them, sells it, and with the proceeds he pays the bank $ 106 and a fraction.

The year has now expired, and our frugal laborer, having occasion to make a different use of his savings, goes to the bank for them, and receives $ 104.50, the bank retaining nearly two dollars as compensation for its agency in the affair. Thus the laborer finds that, by some process incomprehensible to him, the $ 100 which he deposited in the bank for a year has hatched $ 4.50, which it certainly would not have done if it had been simply locked up in the vault for safe-keeping. Could he have followed that process, he would have seen his $ 100 successively becoming, or assuming the shape of, flour, bread, leather, shoes, rags, and paper; and in each of these forms, in turn, he would have seen it entirely consumed or used up. The flour, leather, and rags have been manufactured into corresponding articles, the bread has been eaten, the shoes are half worn out, and the paper is covered with writing and printing, so that a new supply of each is called for. There has been a net gain at each stage of the transaction, and the total gain has been fairly distributed among all the parties to it, compensating each for his labor or frugality.

If any one thinks the instance here analyzed is a trivial or exceptional one, so that it throws little light on the general theory of wealth, let him look at the last annual returns made to the Legislature by all the Savings' Banks in Massachusetts, which show that the amount now deposited in those institutions exceeds $ 23,400,000; that it yields an annual average dividend of over $6\frac{2}{3}$ per cent; and that the number of depositors exceeds 117,400, so that the average amount to the credit of each depositor is a fraction less than $ 200. This aggregate of savings — made up, be it remembered, by the labor and frugality of Irish domestics, small mechanics, operatives in great manufacturing establishments, day-laborers in the country, and the like — is more than twice enough to build and keep in motion all the factories in Lowell; as the aggregate capital of all the great manufacturing establishments in that city, in 1845, fell short of eleven millions. Observe, also, that large sums are annually withdrawn from these institutions, for productive investment in other ways, and the deficit thus made is immediately supplied by fresh deposits;—so that these Savings' Banks resemble great lakes, in which the water ever remains at the same level, though they are constantly supplying running streams, which bear a fertilizing influence with them all their way towards the ocean.*

We now go back to the principle first enunciated, and which seems to be firmly established;—that the whole wealth of a civilized nation is in a state of constant flux and renovation, the apparent stability and unchangeableness of the fortunes of individuals offering no exception to this principle. The instance analyzed also proves, that a gain, a profit, an addition to the national stock, is made only at and by these successive changes of form. What is inconsumable is also necessarily unproductive. We consume in order that we may produce, and we *must* consume before we *can* produce. If Scripture may be reverently quoted on such a topic, "that which thou sowest is not quickened except it die." The wealth which is *literally* locked up or buried only rots or rusts; and we might just as well bury only stones or sand in its place. But money or wealth is *not* locked up when placed in banks, institutions for savings,—moneyed corporations, as they are called,—and the like. These institutions are nothing but contrivances for collecting it, setting it in motion, and making it circulate around us like the atmosphere which we breathe. The wealth which would otherwise be scattered in many little hoards, remaining idle because owned by those whose circumstances would not allow them to use it to advantage, or the separate sums being too small to admit of a profitable application, is, by these means, brought together and made

* The whole amount deposited in the Savings' Banks of Great Britain and Ireland, a year or two since, had risen to nearly $140,000,000, the number of individual depositors being over one million. No one can deposit more than £150 in one of these institutions, and the sum is not allowed to accumulate to more than £200; the presumption being, that, for larger sums, other safe modes of investment can be found.

as efficient as the vast accumulations of great capitalists. The aggregate thus formed is made to do its full part in supplying the lungs of industry, keeping it alive and active, and making all the parts of the body politic and social contribute to the sustenance and growth of the whole. The twenty-three millions in the Savings' Banks, and the fifty-seven millions of capital in the banks of deposit and circulation, (I speak only of Massachusetts,*) do not rest there, but are at this moment circulating around us, — driving the wheels of our factories, supplying our mechanics with tools and our tradesmen with goods, building and freighting our ships, bringing to us the productions of all habitable climes, hurrying from one task to another with indefatigable ardor, and assuming a thousand different forms and hues, according to our necessities and desires.

"Whatever a person saves from his revenue," says Adam Smith, "he adds to his capital, and either employs it himself in maintaining an additional number of productive hands, or enables some other person to do so, by lending it to him for an interest, that is, for a share of the profits." "What is annually saved is as regularly consumed as what is annually spent, and nearly in the same time too; but it is consumed by a different set of people. That portion of his revenue which a rich man annually spends is, in most cases, consumed by idle guests and menial servants, who leave nothing behind them in return for their consumption. That portion which he annually saves, as, for the sake of the profit, it is immediately employed as a capital, is consumed in the same manner, and nearly in the same time too, but by a different set of people; by laborers, manufacturers, and artificers, who reproduce, with a profit, the value of their annual consumption."

---

* The rapid increase of capital in Massachusetts, as indicated by the Bank Returns, deserves notice. The statistics to illustrate the passage in the text were first collected in 1850; and then, the amount lodged in the Savings' Banks was only about thirteen millions, and the aggregate capital in the banks of deposit and circulation was but thirty-seven millions. Hence, in five years, the savings of people of moderate means have increased seventy-seven per cent, and bank capital has received an addition of fifty-four per cent.

CHAPTER II.

THE AIMS, THE LIMITATIONS, AND THE ADVANTAGES OF THE STUDY OF POLITICAL ECONOMY: THE "LAISSEZ-FAIRE," OR "LET-ALONE" PRINCIPLE.

WE are now entitled to assume, that the theory of wealth is a large and complicated one, embracing many curious and difficult problems, and resting upon many general principles or laws, the discovery and development of which constitute a distinct and important science. One of these laws or general facts — the transmutations of capital — has been pointed out and briefly elucidated. And we perceive that it is a fruitful one, pregnant with important conclusions and inferences respecting the institution of property and the modes of favoring industry and increasing national wealth. If the science has been successfully cultivated, many more such general laws must have been discovered in it, a knowledge of which is all important to the statesman, the merchant, and the philanthropist. As Political Economy is expounded in the books, whether by Adam Smith, Ricardo, Sismondi, or Mill, it may, or may not, be well founded and trustworthy in all its parts. Authorities differ on many points. But these men have not been studying a mere chimera, or wasting their energies in a vain pursuit. There are general laws affecting the production and distribution of wealth, whether they have been discovered or not, and a knowledge of these laws is a very different thing from the practical knowledge, the acquaintance with details, and the natural shrewdness, which enable a man to acquire property, and to take good care of it when acquired.

And this leads me to remark, that Political Economy is not, as many suppose, the art of money-making, any more than meteorology is the art of predicting the weather. It is no *art* at all, but a *science;* for its immediate end is knowledge, not action, or the guidance of conduct. The meteorologist says that the phenomena of the atmosphere and the weather, irregular as they are in their occurrence, and obscure as to their immediate causes, must depend on the general principles of gravity and the equilibrium of fluids, and must be referable to general laws, which are legitimate objects of investigation. He may have studied these laws successfully, and still not be so able as an old sea-captain is, who never opened a book on meteorology in his life, to tell what the weather will be the next hour or the next day. It is a point of as much interest and importance to know *how* a storm occurs, as to know *when* it will occur. So, after one of those storms in the commercial world which are known as "commercial crises," we may reasonably seek an explanation of the phenomenon, or the cause of its occurrence, though this knowledge should not enable us to tell when another and similar disturbance will happen.

The general principles of any science are obtained only by abstraction, — by leaving out of view many of the details and particulars which actually belong to the case, and thus so far simplifying it that we can reason about it with facility. The conclusions at which we arrive by this process are very comprehensive, but do not admit of immediate application. They are true only with certain qualifications and restrictions. They are involved in all the phenomena to which they relate, and have a share in producing them; but they do not determine the whole of these phenomena.

Political Economy, Mr. Mill remarks, is a *deductive* science, so far as it reasons from assumptions, not from facts. "It supposes an arbitrary definition of a man, as a being who invariably does that by which he may obtain the greatest amount of necessaries, conveniences, and luxuries, with the smallest quantity of labor and physical self-denial with which they can be obtained in the existing state of knowledge. . . . . . It predicts only such of the phenomena of the social state as take place in consequence of the pursuit of wealth. It makes entire abstraction of every other human passion or motive, except those which may be regarded as perpetually antagonizing principles to the desire of wealth, — namely, aversion to labor, and desire of the present enjoyment of costly indulgences. These it takes, to a certain extent, into its calculations, because these do not merely, like other desires, occasionally conflict with the pursuit of wealth, but accompany it always, as a drag or impediment, and are therefore inseparably mixed up in the consideration of it. Political Economy considers mankind as occupied solely in acquiring and consuming wealth; and aims at showing what is the course of action into which mankind, living in a state of society, would be impelled, if that motive, except in the degree in which it is checked by the two perpetual counter-motives above adverted to, were absolute ruler of all their actions. Not that any one was ever so absurd as to suppose that mankind are really thus constituted, but because this is the mode in which the science must proceed.

"Political Economy, therefore, reasons from *assumed* premises,—from premises which might be totally without foundation in fact, and which are not pretended to be universally in accordance with it. The conclusions of Political Economy, consequently, like those of Geometry, are only true, as the common phrase is, *in the abstract;* that is, they are only true under certain suppositions, in which none but general causes —causes common to the whole class of cases under consideration—are taken into the account. . . . . . In proportion as the actual facts recede from the hypothesis, the Political Economist must allow a corresponding deviation from the strict letter of his conclusion; otherwise, it will be true only of things such as he has arbitrarily supposed, not of such things as really exist. That which is true in the abstract is always true in the concrete, *with proper allowances.* When a certain cause really exists, and, if left to itself, would infallibly produce a certain effect, that same effect, *modified* by all the other concurrent causes, will correctly correspond to the result really produced." *

All legislation which is designed to affect the economical interests of society, or which relates immediately to its commerce, agriculture, or manufactures, is in truth an application of the principles of *some* system of Political Economy to practice, be that system a wise or a mistaken one. It is often a very injurious application of them, because the circumstances which actually limit the principles are lost sight of, and the abstractions by which they were obtained are forgotten. Mischief results; and "practical men," seeing that the consequen-

* Mill's *Essays on some Unsettled Questions of Political Economy*, pp. 137 – 145.

ces do not square with the theory, call in question the science itself, instead of attributing the error to the faulty application of it. Hence arises an unhappy dissension between theory and practice, to the lasting detriment of both.

The Political Economists themselves are somewhat to blame for this result, by pressing too eagerly for the reduction of their favorite doctrines to practice, without regard to the particular circumstances of each case. The general doctrine of Free Trade, for instance, which may be correct when applied to two nations which are similarly situated in every respect, which have grown up under the same institutions and the same laws, and in which the profits of capital, the wages of labor, and the ratio of population to territory are nearly on a level, is extended by a hasty generalization to two countries that are contrasted with each other in all these respects, and in its application to which, to say the least, the correctness of the principle is very doubtful. We have in this country the largest extension of the system of free trade which the world has ever witnessed; we have free trade between Maine and Louisiana, between California and Massachusetts; and no one doubts that the system is equally beneficial to all these States. But before the system is carried out between England and the United States, we may reasonably inquire whether it will not necessarily tend to an equalization of profits and wages in the two countries, and whether it is desirable here to hasten the operation of the causes which are rapidly reducing the rates of both to the English standard. This subject will be considered hereafter; but I may say here, that the question does not relate to the correctness of the general principle in economical science, but only to its applicability under particular circumstances. That all terrestrial bodies gravitate to the centre of the earth, is a general law, which is not disproved by the floating of a cork in a basin of water.

Another prejudice against Political Economy has arisen from an error of an opposite character; — from too strict a limitation of it to the causes affecting the *increase* of national wealth, the other interests of a people being undervalued or left out of sight. The English Economists of Ricardo's school have most frequently fallen into this error; looking merely to the creation of material values, they have tacitly assumed that this was the only interest of society, the only end which legislation should have in view. The proposition on which they act, though they seldom directly enunciate it, is, that the augmentation of national wealth is at once the sign and the measure of national prosperity. We may admit that it is so, *if the wealth be distributed* with some approach to equality among the people. But if the vast majority of the nation is beggared, while enormous fortunes are accumulated by a few, — if pauperism increases at one end of the social scale as rapidly as wealth is heaped up at the other, — then, even though the ratio of the aggregate wealth to the aggregate population is constantly growing larger, the tendency of things is downward, and, sooner or later, if a remedy be not applied, society will rush into degradation and ruin.

In order to obtain a broader field of inquiry, the subject to be discussed in this volume will be, *the general well-being of society, so far as this is affected by the moral causes regulating the production, distribution, and consumption of wealth.* It may be doubted whether the whole of this theme is included within the limits of Political Economy, properly so called; — and therefore I propose to consider not only the science itself, but its application to a particular case, — the circumstances and institutions of the American people. Thus is opened a wide scope for investigation. The fluctuations of national prosperity; the various social condition of different communities at the same period, and of the same community at different periods; the nature, and effect upon the wealth, happiness, and numbers of the people, of the various institutions, laws, and customs which have obtained in different countries and at different times, — might all pass in review before the subject would be exhausted. Hitherto, history has been in the main a political record, — a narrative of wars, conquests, and changes in the form of government. But the social economy of different states has now become the chief object of interest even to the historian. Statesmen have been obliged to make the study of politics second to that of political economy. Monarchs now strive to guard their thrones, not so much by the number and efficiency of their standing armies, as by the prudent management of their finances, and by their successful development of the agricultural, commercial, and manufacturing resources of their people. They build railways, form Customs-Unions to relieve trade of its fetters, establish colonies to get rid of surplus population, and thus aim to acquire or regain a firm basis for that authority which formerly rested only on prescription and military force. Men now coolly count the cost, the comparative value in dollars and cents, of a monarchy and a republic. The idea of political freedom, of choosing their own governors and managing their own affairs, is no longer attractive enough to lead the people, if it be not united with some project for a new organization and a more equal enjoyment of the goods of this life. Hence the rise of so many schemes of Socialism and Communism, which gave a character to the Revolutions of 1848 wholly unlike that of any other political disturbances recorded in the previous history of the world.

Even if the disastrous consequences of the insane attempts then made to reorganize society should prevent a speedy repetition of the experiment, there is another danger, from which no civilized community is entirely free, — lest the several classes of which it is composed should cherish mutual jealousy and hate, which may finally break out into open hostilities, under the mistaken idea that their interests are opposite, and that one or more of them possess an undue advantage, which they are always ready to exercise by oppressing the others. Twenty years ago, Archbishop Whately pointed out the full extent of this danger in a single pregnant question: — "Can the laboring classes, — and that, too, in a country where they have a legal right to express practically their political opinions, — can they be safely left to suppose, as many a demagogue is ready, when it suits his purpose, to tell them, that inequality of conditions is inexpedient, and ought to be abolished; that the wealth of a man whose income is equal to that of a hundred laboring families is so much deducted from the common stock, and causes a hundred poor families the less to be sustained; and that a general spoliation of the rich, and an equal division of property, would put an end to poverty for ever?" Under these circumstances, we may ask further, Can we safely neglect to explain and teach the great truths which Political Economy has demonstrated; — that all classes of society are inseparably bound together by a community of interest; that the prosperity of each depends on the welfare of all; that the national industry must be meagre and profitless in its results, if it has not capital or concentrated wealth to coöperate with it; that an equal division of property would in fact destroy or dissipate that which was divided; and that the only equality of condition which human nature renders possible, is an equality of destitution and suffering?

I need not apologize for the science which treats of the creation of wealth, on the ground that it relates only to one of the lower interests of humanity, and that it is not of so much moment for an individual or a society to be rich, as it is to be wise, free, instructed, and virtuous. It is true that wealth is one of the lower elements or supports of civilization, and that the comparative quantity of it is but an imperfect index of national worth and national well-being. But it is also true, that wealth is that element of civilization which supports all the others, and that, without it, no progress, no refinement, no liberal art would be possible. Without property, without large accumulations of wealth, no division of labor would be possible; and without division of labor, each man must provide by his own toil for all his bodily wants. He must plant, sow, and reap for himself. He must be his own tailor, shoemaker, housewright, and cook. The scholar could no longer devote himself exclusively to his books, the man of science to the observation of nature, the artist to the canvas or marble, the physician to the cure of diseases, or the clergyman to the care of souls. All would be bound alike by the stern necessity of daily brutish toil on the most repulsive tasks. National wealth is a condition of progress, — a prerequisite of civilization. It is not in itself ennobling; but it is that which vivifies and maintains all the other elements and influences which dignify humanity and render life desirable.

Even if popular ignorance and prejudice upon this subject were not dangerous to the state, a liberal curiosity would not rest satisfied without some knowledge of the laws affecting the creation and production of wealth, — laws which are, in truth, as constant and uniform as those which bind the material universe together, and evince the wisdom and goodness of the Creator quite as clearly as any of his arrangements in the organic kingdom. Blanco White, speaking of the inattention of the ancients to the philosophy of wealth, compares their state of mind to that of children in the house of an opulent tradesman, who, finding the comforts and necessaries of life supplied to them with mechanical regularity, never inquire into the machinery by which these effects are produced, or, if they ever do think about it, suppose that breakfast, dinner, and supper succeed one another by the spontaneous bounty of nature, like spring, summer, and autumn. It is true, that men are usually selfish in the pursuit of wealth; but it is a wise and benevolent arrangement of Providence, that even those who are thinking only of their own credit and advantage are led, unconsciously but surely, to benefit others. The contrivance by which this end is effected — this reconciliation of private aims with the public advantage — is often complex, far-reaching, and intricate; and thus more strongly indicates the benevolent purpose of the Designer. In the instance already given, we have seen that the wealth of an individual, perhaps a sordid and covetous one, invested by him with a view only to his own advantage and security, and to spare himself the trouble of superintending it, still circulates through the community without his knowledge, supporting the laborer at his task, supplying means to the ingenious and the enterprising for the furtherance of their designs, and assuming with facility every shape which the necessities or the convenience of society may require.

I borrow, with some abridgment, a simple and striking illustration of the same great truth from Dr. Whately.

"Let any one propose to himself the problem of supplying with daily provisions of all kinds a city like London, containing about two millions of inhabitants. Let him imagine himself a head commissary, intrusted with the office of furnishing to this enormous host their daily rations. A failure in the supply even for a single day might produce the most frightful distress. Some, indeed, of the articles consumed might be stored up in reserve for a considerable time; but many, including most articles of animal food and many of vegetable, are of the most perishable nature. As a deficient supply of these, even for a few days, would occasion great inconvenience, so a redundancy of them would produce a corresponding waste. The city is also of vast extent, — a province covered with houses, — and it is essential that the supplies should be so distributed as to be brought almost to the doors of all the inhabitants. The supply of provisions for an army or garrison is comparatively *uniform in kind;* but here, the greatest possible variety is required, suitable to the wants of the various classes of consumers. Again, this immense population is extremely fluctuating in numbers; and the increase or diminution depends on causes of which some may, others cannot, be distinctly foreseen. Again, and above all, the daily supplies of each article must be so nicely adjusted to the stock from which it is drawn, to the scanty or abundant harvest, importation, or other source of supply, to the interval which must elapse before a fresh stock can be furnished, and to the probable abundance of the new supply, that as little distress as possible may be felt; — that, on the one hand, the population may not unnecessarily be put on short allowance of any article, and, on the other, may be preserved from the more dreadful risk of famine, which must happen if they continued to consume freely when the stock was insufficient to hold out.

"Now let any one consider this problem in all its bearings, and then reflect on the anxious toil which such a task would impose on a board of the most experienced and intelligent commissaries, — who, after all, could discharge their office but very inadequately. Yet this object is accomplished, far better than it could be by any effort of human wisdom, through the agency of men who think each of nothing beyond his own immediate interest, — who, with that object in view, perform their respective parts with cheerful zeal, and combine unconsciously to employ the wisest means for effecting an object, the vastness of which it would bewilder them even to contemplate.

"It is really wonderful to consider with what ease and regularity this important end is accomplished, day after day, and year after year, through the sagacity and vigilance of private interest operating on the numerous class of wholesale, and more especially retail, dealers. Each of these watches attentively the demands of his neighborhood, or of the market he frequents, for such commodities as he deals in. The apprehension, on the one hand, of not realizing all the profit he might, and, on the other, of having his goods left on his hands, — these antagonist muscles, regulate the extent of his dealings and the prices at which he buys and sells. An abundant supply causes him to lower his prices, and thus enables the public to enjoy that abundance; while *he* is guided only by the apprehension of being undersold. On the other hand, an actual or apprehended scarcity causes him to demand a higher price, or to keep back his goods in expectation of a rise. Thus he coöperates, unknowingly, in conducting a system which no human wisdom directed to that end could have conducted so well,—the system by which this enormous population is fed from day to day.

"I say, 'no *human* wisdom'; for *wisdom* there surely is, in this adaptation of the means to the result actually produced. In this instance, there are the same marks of benevolent design which we are accustomed to admire in the anatomical structure of the human body. I know not whether it does not even still more excite our admiration of the beneficent wisdom of Providence, to contemplate, not corporeal particles, but rational free agents, coöperating in systems not less manifestly indicating design, but no design of theirs; and though acted on, not by gravitation and impulse, like inert matter, but by motives addressed to the will, yet accomplishing as regularly and as effectually an object they never contemplated, as if they were merely the passive wheels of a machine. The heavens do indeed 'declare the glory of God,' and the human body is fearfully and wonderfully made; but man, considered not merely as an organized being, but as a rational agent and as a member of society, is perhaps the most wonderfully contrived product of Divine wisdom that we have any knowledge of." *

It is on a large induction from such cases as this, that political economists rest their most comprehensive and most noted maxim,—the *laissez-faire*, or "let-alone" principle,—the doctrine of non-interference by the government with the economical interests of society. True, these interests are in the hands of individuals, who look only to their own immediate profit, and not to the public advantage, or to the distant future. They are not only selfish; they are often ignorant, shortsighted, and unconscious of much of the work that they do. But society is a complex and delicate machine, the real Author and Governor of which is divine. Men are often his agents, who do his work, and know it not. He turneth their selfish-

* Whately's *Lectures on Political Economy*, pp. 103–110.

ness to good; and ends which could not be accomplished by the greatest sagacity, the most enlightened and disinterested public spirit, and the most strenuous exertions of human legislators and governors, are effected directly and incessantly, even through the ignorance, the wilfulness, and the avarice of men. Man cannot interfere with His work without marring it. The attempts of legislators to turn the industry of society in one direction or another, out of its natural and self-chosen channels, — here to encourage it by bounties, and there to load it with penalties, to increase or diminish the supply of the market, to establish a *maximum* of price, to keep specie in the country, — are almost invariably productive of harm. *Laissez-faire;* "these things regulate themselves," in common phrase; which means, of course, that God regulates them by his general laws, which always, in the long run, work to good. In these modern days, the ruler or governor who is most to be dreaded is, not the tyrant, but the busybody. Let the course of trade and the condition of society alone, is the best advice which can be given to the legislator, the projector, and the reformer. Busy yourselves, if you must be busy, with *individual cases* of wrong, hardship, or suffering; but do not meddle with the general laws of the universe.

The limitations of this "let-alone" principle are nearly as obvious as the principle itself. The office of the legislator is not, by his own superior wisdom, to chalk out a path for society to move in, but to remove all casual and unnatural impediments from that path which society instinctively chooses for itself. It is to give wider scope and more facile action to the principle we have just been considering, rather than to hedge and narrow it by artificial limits or petty restrictions. Human laws, if wisely framed, are seldom mandatory, or such as require an active obedience; they are mostly prohibitive, or designed to prevent such action on the part of the few as would impede or limit the healthful action of the many. Vice and crime, for instance, are stumbling-blocks in the path of the community; they obstruct the working of the natural laws, the ordinances of Divine Providence, by which society is held together, and all well-meaning members of it are made to coöperate, though unconsciously, for each other's good. To remove such stumbling-blocks, then, is not to create, but to prevent, interference with the natural order of things. Legislation directed to this end is only a legitimate carrying out of the *laissez-faire* principle.

The enforcement of justice in the ordinary transactions between man and man, which often requires further legislation than is needed for the mere prevention of open vice and crime, is another instance of the legitimate exercise of authority by the government. An individual may not erect a powder-manufactory in the midst of a populous village, nor carry on any operations there which would poison the air with noxious exhalations. His neighbors would have a right to call out to him, "Let *us* alone; you endanger our lives, and prevent us from pursuing our ordinary occupations in safety."

These are *internal* impediments to the natural action of society, and as such the government is bound to put them out of the way; its action for this purpose is widely distinguished from the enactment of sumptuary laws, the establishment of a *maximum* of price, prohibiting the exportation of specie, and other obvious infringements of the *laissez-faire* principle. But it is also the duty of the legislature to guard society against *external* dangers and hinderances. Men are separated into distinct communities, the action of which upon each other is not so much restrained by law, or by the natural requisitions of justice, as is that of individuals dwelling in the same community. The law of nations is a very imperfect code, and, from the want of any superior tribunal to enforce its enactments, it is very imperfectly observed. War is either a present evil to be averted or alleviated, or it is a possible future event, the occurrence of which is to be guarded against. For either of these ends, the action of individuals within the community may need to be restrained; for the safety of all, the freedom of all to pursue their lawful occupations without let or hinderance is not to be imperilled through the avarice or recklessness of a few. Accordingly, not mere restraints upon importation, but an absolute prohibition of intercourse, an embargo on all navigation, are among the legitimate measures, a necessity for which is created by national dissension and hostility.

Independent communities are not always at war with each other; but they are always rivals and competitors in the great market of the world. This feeling of rivalry is whetted by the different circumstances under which they are placed, by the peculiarities in the condition of each, and by the opposition of interests which often grows out of these peculiarities. The legislation of each state is primarily directed, of course, to the protection and promotion of the interests of its own subjects; and thus it often injuriously affects the interests of other nations. There is, therefore, a good deal of retaliatory legislation on the part of different governments. There is often, on both sides, a keen measure of wits in devising commercial regulations which shall affect, or render nugatory, measures adopted by the rival nation, not exactly with a hostile intent, but with an exclusive view to its own interests, and therefore frequently with an injurious effect upon the interests of others. Reciprocity treaties, as they are called, are sometimes formed, to obviate the evil effects upon both parties of this keen spirit of competition, when pushed too far. Now, such retaliatory legislation, so far as it operates upon the members of the very community from which it emanates, so far as it limits or restrains the action of all or a portion of them, is not an infringement, but an application, of the *laissez-faire* principle. It is designed to procure for them a larger liberty than they would otherwise enjoy; if it is effectual, if it answers its purpose, it removes an impediment created by a foreign state far more serious and extensive than the obstruction which it imposes. It may, indirectly and incidentally, turn industry from one channel to another, and make some changes in the investments of capital. But this change is effected only by opening one channel, which would otherwise, under the effects of foreign competition, have remained entirely closed, and by rendering it possible and profitable to turn capital to other uses than those to which it was formerly limited.

If we suppose that the application of native industry and capital is restricted in its range, not by the legislative policy knowingly adopted by a foreign state for this very purpose, but through the superior natural advantages possessed by that state, the same principle still governs the result. By submitting to a small restraint imposed at home, we get rid of a much larger obstacle to our freedom of action, created either by the commercial regulations, finer climate, more fertile soil, more abundant capital, or larger skill and experience of a rival community. The policy of states leads them to seek independence of each other in their economical, almost as much as in their political, relations; or we might better say, that political independence — that is, the enjoyment of distinct institutions and laws, chosen and established by ourselves — makes it still more desirable and necessary than it was before, that we should not be entirely dependent upon foreigners for the supply of great articles of consumption of prime necessity, — that we should have within our own borders, and under our own control, the means of satisfying all our natural and imperative wants. It is not even desirable that Massachusetts and Ohio should be rendered so far independent of each other, that each could obtain from its own soil, or by the labor of its own inhabitants, all that it can need; for these two States are *one* in most of their political relations. Members of the same great confederacy, living under the same laws, and each exercising its due share of influence in the national legislature, neither has cause to apprehend the hostile or injurious action of the other. The political ties between them are strengthened by their dependence on each other for a supply of many of the necessaries of civilized existence. But it is desirable that both should be independent, as far as may be, of the great powers of Europe, with whom they cannot be sure of continued friendly intercourse for any time beyond the present, and from whom they are always separated by a great breadth of ocean, and by dissimilarity of customs, institutions, and laws.

True independence, in an economical point of view, does not require us to forego all commercial intercourse with other nations; this would be rather a curse than a blessing. But it does require that each nation should be able to exercise, within its own limits, all the great branches of industry designed to satisfy the wants of man. It must be able to practise all the arts which would be necessary for its own well-being, if it were the only nation on the earth. If it be restricted to agriculture alone, or to manufactures alone, a portion of the energies of its people are lost, and some of its natural advantages run to waste. To be so limited in its sphere of occupation, to be barred out from some of the natural and necessary employments of the human race, through the overwhelming competition of foreigners, is a serious evil, which it is the object of a protective policy to obviate or redress. On whatever other grounds this policy may be objected to, it is surely not open to the charge of being an infringement of the *laissez-faire* principle, or a restriction of every man's right to make such use as he pleases of his own industry and capital. Its object is not to narrow, but to widen, the field for the profitable employment of industry, and to second the working of the beneficent designs of Providence in the constitution of society, by removing all artificial and unnecessary checks to their operation.

I repeat it, then, that these designs, as shown in the economical laws of human nature, (i. e. in the principles of Political Economy,) through their general effects upon the well-being of society, manifest the contrivance, wisdom, and beneficence of the Deity, just as clearly as do the marvellous arrangements of the material universe, or the natural means provided for the enforcement of the moral law and the punishment of crime. The lowest passions of mankind, ostentation and ambition, petty rivalry, the love of saving and the love of gain, while they bring their own penalty upon the individual who unduly indulges them, are still overruled for good in their operation upon the interests of society;—nay, they are made the most efficient means of guarding it from harm, and advancing its welfare. In the vast round of employments in civilized society, there is hardly one in which a person can profitably exert himself, without at the same time profiting the community in which he lives, and lending aid to thousands of human beings whom he never saw. We are all servants of one another without wishing it, and even without knowing it; we are all coöperating with each other as busily and effectively as the bees in a hive, and most of us with as little perception as the bees have, that each individual effort is essential to the common defence and general prosperity. "This dependence and combination," says McCulloch, "is not found only or principally in the mechanical employments; it extends to the labors of the head as well as those of the hands, and pervades and binds together all classes and degrees of society."

CHAPTER III.

HOW WEALTH IS CREATED, AND WHAT CONSTITUTES EXCHANGEABLE VALUE.

A DISTINCTION has already been briefly pointed out between wealth and property. *Wealth* consists of the aggregate of articles, chiefly material or tangible, though some immaterial products are ranked among them, which supply the wants and satisfy the desires of man; and the stock of national wealth "is kept in existence from age to age, not by preservation, but by perpetual reproduction. Every part of it is used or destroyed, — generally very soon after it is produced; but those who consume it are employed meanwhile in producing more," — not only enough to replace what is consumed, but to furnish a surplus, or profit. *Property* is the ownership of these articles, and often remains unchanged, or fixed, for many generations, — just as the river continues, though the water is perpetually running out of it into the sea.

As the articles change while the ownership continues, there must be evidences of that ownership, or "tickets of transfer," as I have once called them, — mere representatives of wealth, which command a price in the market, and are often sold, but which, in themselves, form no addition to the national wealth. Notes and mortgages, bank-bills, bank-stock, stock in any corporation or in the national debt, are such representatives. They are mere evidences that the person holding them is the owner of a larger or smaller portion of those articles which really constitute wealth; and their value to him consists only in the fact that they enable him, whenever he sees fit, to reclaim his property, or to take possession of those articles which actually belong to him, though for a time he has trusted them to others. The national wealth, therefore, does not consist of the land, the houses, the manufactured goods, &c., *plus* the public funds, bank-stock, and the like. These funds and stocks are not wealth in themselves, but are *certificates of ownership* of those articles which really constitute riches. Nay, if any portion of these stocks is held by foreigners, the aggregate wealth of the community does not consist even of the whole amount of those articles within its territory which are properly considered as wealth, but only of that amount *minus* the evidences of indebtedness to foreigners. If I buy $ 1,000 worth of government securities, I really lend $ 1,000 to the government, which, in return, mortgages to me a portion of its revenues, or of the sum which it annually raises by taxation. This sum is that portion of the valuable articles annually created by the labor of the community which the government appropriates to itself, as a compensation for the care and protection which it affords. What I really own, then, is this share of the useful articles annually produced by the labor of the whole people, which is transferred, first by the people to the government, and then by the government to me. The scrap of paper, called "public stock," which I hold, is of no value whatever, except as it enables me to claim without dispute my share of this annual product.

These truths are elementary and sufficiently obvious; but it was necessary to state them in order to clear the ground for the solution of the problem with which we are now concerned: — *What are the essential qualities of wealth, and how is it created?* How is it, that the national stock of wealth, which we are perpetually consuming, is yet perpetually reproduced, and that, too, with a profit, or constant enlargement, so that the stock at the end of the year is considerably larger than it was at the year's commencement?

As soon as we clearly perceive that wealth consists *exclusively* of those useful articles, chiefly material or tangible, which have been indicated, and that we have nothing to do with the intricate complications of property which arise from the dealings of men in the banks and the stock market, the answer to this question becomes very easy. Wealth is created by devoting human labor to the production and fashioning of these useful articles; — by tilling the ground and raising harvests of food and of the raw materials for manufacture; by spinning, weaving, and sewing; by erecting houses, working mines, and building ships; by any and every application of industry which is essential to the full enjoyment of these articles, or which has directly or indirectly concurred in their formation.

Human labor, whether skilful or unskilful, whether applied alone or artfully assisted by natural agents, is the means; wealth is the product. Whatever is necessary in order that the workman may apply himself more directly and successfully, and with less interruption, to his task, must be considered as a portion of the industry which concurs in the formation of the article produced by that workman.

Thus, he must feel secure in his employment, — secure against violence, robbery, or any improper or wrongful interruption of his labor. Government affords him this security, and is, to this extent, a fellow-producer with him, so that it rightfully claims a share — a very small share — of the finished product. "On the governor, and those with whom he is associated, or whom he appoints," says Mr. Senior, "is devolved the care of defending the community from violence and fraud; and so far as internal violence is concerned, and that is the evil most dreaded in civilized society, it is wonderful how small a number of persons can provide for the security of multitudes. About 15,000 soldiers, and not 15,000 policemen, watchmen, and officers of justice, protect the persons and property of the 18 millions of inhabitants of Great Britain. There is scarcely a trade that does not engross the labor of a greater number of persons than are employed to perform this most important of all services."

The coöperation which the laborer requires, in a highly civilized community, for the completion of his task, in order to present the article in a state fit for use, is far more extensive than we are apt, at first sight, to imagine. Thus, bread is a finished product, the total value of which must compensate a long line of laborers who have concurred in its formation. The tradesman who brings it to your door; the baker; the miller; the farm laborers who plough, sow, and reap; the farmer or land-owner; and all the artisans who have fabricated all the tools and instruments used by these persons, — must all have their share of the price finally paid for the bread which is fully prepared to be eaten. The extensive coöperation of employments, produced by the minute subdivision of labor, is the most striking feature of modern civilization. The object of this immense subdivision is to secure the greatest possible efficiency of labor, — that everything may be produced on the spot best suited for its production; that every step in the process of its manufacture may be taken by the person most capable of taking it to advantage, and under the most favorable circumstances; and that the article itself, when finished, may be adapted, even in the slightest particulars, to the wants, tastes, and convenience of those who are to use it. The value which may be added to the article by the numerous steps of this long process may be very great. "We should probably be understating the difference," says Mr. Senior, "if we were to say that the last price was a thousand times the first. The price of a pound of the finest cotton-wool, as it is gathered, is less than two shillings. A pound of the finest cotton lace might easily be worth more than a hundred guineas."

We gain another view of this marvellous coöperation of individuals, designed to make labor most efficient, by searching out the history, analyzing the cost, and tracing the processes of manufacture, of all the articles of our own daily consumption. We think it little to sit down to a table covered with articles from all quarters of the globe and from the remotest isles of the sea;—with tea from China, coffee from Brazil, spices from the East and sugar from the West Indies, knives from Sheffield, made with iron from Sweden and ivory from Africa, with silver from Mexico, and cotton from South Carolina, all being lighted with oil brought from New Zealand or the Arctic Circle. Still less do we think of the great number of persons whose united agency is required to bring any one of these finished products to our homes;—of the merchants, insurers, sailors, ship-builders, cordage and sail-makers, astronomical-instrument makers, men of science, and others, who must concur before a pound of tea can appear in our market. In view of these circumstances, it is no exaggeration to say, that the humble artisan, who spends his life, to adopt Adam Smith's illustration, in making the eighteenth part of a pin, and is hardly fitted for any higher employment, still taxes the industry of half the human race, and lays under contribution the four quarters of the globe, to supply his daily wants.

How is it, that while, in these days, men will not often labor for nothing, and while the artisan himself produces nothing but the fraction of a pin, he is still able to consume so great a variety of products, and to make the industry of so vast a multitude tributary to his comforts. The answer may be given in one word; — *by exchange*. As human labor is the only motive power, so capability of exchange is the sole directing agent, in the great social machine for the production of wealth. The immediate measure of the wealth, when produced, is, not its utility, but its exchangeable value; and Political Economy itself, as I have already remarked, has been denominated *Catallactics*, or the Science of Exchanges.

We come, then, to an analysis of exchangeable value, in order to find a basis for a theory of wealth. What is it that constitutes value in exchange, and why do various articles possess it in such unequal proportions? The answer is, that exchangeable value consists of two elements, — *utility*, and *difficulty of attainment*. The article valued must in some measure be useful; that is, it must be adapted to satisfy, either directly or indirectly, some natural want or artificial desire of men; and it must also be more or less difficult to be had. These elements may coexist in very different proportions; but in one degree or another they must both be present, or the article has no value in exchange. It may, for instance, be very useful; it may be an article of prime necessity, absolutely essential to the existence of man. Yet if there be no difficulty in the way of its attainment, if, like the air, the water, and the sunlight, the supply of it be inexhaustible and open to all the world, then it has no exchangeable value. It forms no part of what is usually called wealth. Supply the element which was lacking, — only make the article hard to be procured, as water is, in the midst of the sandy desert of Sahara, or as air was to Mr. Holwell and his companions in the Black Hole at Calcutta, and men will give all that they have in the world for a single draught of either. On the other hand, it may be very difficult of attainment; it may, like some of the most refined products of chemical analysis, require the labor of years, the greatest scientific skill, and an expenditure of the most costly materials, before it can be procured. Yet if it be not useful, if it do not satisfy some want or desire, however artificial or irrational that desire may be, it commands no price in the market; it has no exchangeable value.

But we do not here speak of abstract utility, or of that utility which is determined by reason and measured by a philosophical standard. Utility here means nothing but fitness or capability to satisfy any desire of men, however unreasonable, extravagant, or capricious that desire may be. If men are so foolish as to prize highly many articles which answer no purposes but of vain ostentation or gross and sensual enjoyment, it is not for the political economist, who views things only as they are, not as they ought to be, to censure their folly. He leaves this office to the moralist or the preacher. The fact that such articles are coveted, from whatever motive, is enough to bring them within his definition of wealth; which definition, it is evident, only expresses the common sentiment of mankind.

One factitious desire, it is curious to observe, is created solely by the difficulty of obtaining its object. Thus, books, coins, and shells are often prized merely from their rarity, or the difficulty of procuring duplicates of them; and in the case of books this passion has gone so far, that it has been aptly called *bibliomania*, or book-madness. An old volume, which, for all the proper purposes of a book, is absolutely worthless, since no person in his senses would ever think of reading it, if it happens to be what is called a unique copy, may command a price equal to that of a fine painting by one of the old masters. And this last instance shows also, that the want or taste which the article gratifies, and in gratifying which its utility, and consequently its exchangeable value, consists, may not be a common one, — may be shared, in fact, only by a very few persons in the community. Very few, certainly, are capable of appreciating a Raphael or a Correggio, or of seeing in it those beauties which make it command a price equal to a king's ransom.

As the words *value* and *utility* are often used in the moralist's sense, or according to their philosophical import, it is necessary to give this caution once for all; — that whenever in future they are here used, they must be understood only in their politico-economical signification. By *value*, we mean only *exchangeable value;* by *utility*, we mean only that utility which is an element of wealth, and which consists in fitness to satisfy any want or desire, however irrational, that is felt by any number of men.

This analysis of value, this explanation of what wealth *is*, leads us immediately to an understanding of the manner in which wealth is *created.* As the essence of value consists in difficulty of attainment, so the labor which overcomes that difficulty is the great means of producing value, or creating wealth; and everything which diminishes that difficulty is to be considered as labor,—is entitled to be called by that name, for it is recognized and compensated as such by the community. And here is the great paradox of Political Economy:—value depends on difficulty of attainment; the only way of creating values is to lessen or overcome that difficulty; but as soon as *all* difficulty is overcome, when there is no longer any obstacle in the way between man and the gratification of his desire, then value also disappears, and the boundless wealth, which seemed just within our grasp, is suddenly changed, as by a magical incantation, into dross or nothingness. Every step taken towards removing the difficulty is a step in advance,—a production of wealth,—an addition to our individual store and to the national opulence. But just when we have taken the last step, and reached the spot where we had fondly supposed that unbounded riches would be our reward, the vision changes, and all our supposed wealth—both that which we had hoped to gain by this last step, and that which we had previously acquired—becomes an airy nothing. Thus to poor mortals engaged in the pursuit of riches is realized the fable of Sisyphus, and an instructive moral is inculcated.

"With many a weary step and many a groan,
Up the high hill he heaves a huge round stone;
The huge round stone, resulting with a bound,
Thunders impetuous down, and smokes along the ground."

This paradox is not created merely by an abuse of abstract definitions and theoretical reasoning. The seeming contradiction is a literal fact, as may be clearly shown by a practical illustration. And that I may not be accused of bringing an obscure or far-fetched example, I will take that which, in all ages and all countries, has been recognized as preëminently an article of value, and identified with wealth itself. Gold surely possesses the highest value in exchange, and is eminently difficult of attainment. The story, first promulgated in the winter of 1848–9, that it abounded in the soil of California, caused as much excitement and agitation in this country, and indeed throughout the civilized world, as would have been created by another battle of Waterloo, or by the reappearance of Napoleon from the tomb. The story proved to be well founded; and the consequence was, that within six months tens of thousands of our enterprising countrymen were either wending their toilsome way over the great steppes of our Western desert, and through the frightful passes of the Sierra Nevada, where the route was strewed with the whitened bones of their predecessors who had perished of starvation, or were encountering the manifold perils of a four months' voyage round Cape Horn, in the hope of making their fortunes in this new El Dorado. Did it ever occur to one of them, that their hopes would be just as much frustrated by finding that the precious metal there was too plentiful, as by ascertaining that it was not to be found at all? But suppose that the most exaggerated reports had been correct, — that all the rocks of the Sierra Nevada itself were composed in great part of gold, — that there were gold mountains in California, just as there are iron mountains in Missouri. Is it not certain, that the value of gold all over the world, almost at once, would sink to about the same point with iron? Then carry the supposition one step farther, — the last step that I have spoken of. Imagine that it is not necessary to go to California for this metal, but that our own streets are paved and our gutters lined with gold, which also, in lumps, strews the whole face of the country. Is it not evident, that it would instantly become as valueless as the stones and dirt which now cover our streets and roads?

How vain, then, is it to expect that wealth can ever be created without labor, which is its natural and necessary price! Gold is now so precious precisely *because* so much labor is required to obtain it. What a pity it is that the old alchemists, many of whom were the most learned men of their times, and who wasted fortune and life in their vain pursuit, could not have foreseen that the philosopher's stone, when discovered, would be as worthless as another stone, which should have the property of turning everything it touched into granite!

The useful metals, generally, possess value just in proportion to the fewness and unproductiveness of the mines whence they are obtained, and to the labor required for bringing them to market and giving them the forms and qualities that fit them for use. Iron in this country owes nearly all its value to the labor expended in extracting it from the ore and manufacturing it; for iron ore is so plentiful, that, except in a few favorable localities, where fuel is abundant and transportation easy, an acre of ground with iron ore for its surface is worth hardly as much as the same extent of fertile land. Yet fine steel cutlery and watch-springs, which are only iron in a highly finished state, sell at a high price by the ounce. Copper, again, being more rare, and the mines of it less productive, owes its value chiefly to its scarcity, or the labor required for finding it and bringing it from a distance. The chief fear for our copper miners on the shores of Lake Superior is, lest they should find the metal too abundant. Yet it is so natural an illusion to believe that the high value of these metals in their manufactured state attaches to them also when they are in the ore, that a mining mania is more easily excited in the community than any other speculative bubble. The dupes are satisfied by the full proof which is offered them, that the ore is very abundant. They had better also count the cost of the labor required for extracting it and bringing it to market. The most productive mine which a man can work is situated on his own farm.

What I have called the paradox of political economy, like the hydrostatic paradox, is really very simple, and admits of an easy explanation. In proportion as the labor required for obtaining any useful article is diminished, and the article itself consequently becomes very common, in that proportion it approximates the character of those invaluable gifts of Providence, the air, the water, and the sunlight, which, because they are common and inexhaustible, have natural, but no exchangeable, value. They become *natural wealth*, they cease to be artificial wealth. Man does not, in the economical sense, *value* them, or consider them as wealth, because he is not able to exchange them for other things which can only be procured by labor; or in other words, he cannot purchase labor with them. The possession of them conveys no distinction, does not exalt one above his fellows, gives no power over other men. Each of them satisfies one imperative want, and in this respect is truly *in*valuable; but it does not possess that quality which is characteristic of all articles that are usually considered as wealth;—any one of these may be bartered for more or less of any article or product whatsoever that the possessor may desire. We are wont to consider *money* as the universal medium of exchange, though it is only a contrivance for facilitating it; this is a consequence of the popular delusion which confounds *money* with *wealth*. Any portion of wealth, any article of value, is, like Fortunatus's wishing-cap, a means of obtaining, *to the extent of its value*, whatever other article we may desire; — the contrivance of money rendering the process of obtaining it by exchange a very simple one. This Protean character of wealth, this capability of satisfying whatever want or whim the heart of man can conceive, is, like the ductility of gold, its most peculiar and attractive quality.

And here we perceive the explanation of the fact which has so often been a topic of complaint, that the pecuniary wages or earnings of scientific and literary men are, with a few rare exceptions, very inconsiderable. "Had the taste for study," as McCulloch remarks, "depended only on the pecuniary emoluments which it brings along with it, it may well be doubted whether it would ever have found a single votary; and we should have been deprived, not only of very many of our most valuable and important discoveries in the arts, as well as in philosophy and legislation, but of much that refines and exalts the character, and supplies the best species of amusement." The inadequacy of the pecuniary compensation of these persons "arises from a variety of causes; but principally, perhaps, from the indestructibility, if we may so term it, and rapid circulation, of their works and inventions. The cloth of the manufacturer and the corn of the agriculturist are speedily consumed, and there is therefore a continual demand for fresh supplies of the same articles. Such, however, is not the case with new inventions, new theories, or new literary works. They may be universally made use of, but they cannot be consumed. The moment that the invention of logarithms, the mode of spinning by rollers, and the discovery of the cow-pox had been published, they were rendered imperishable, and every one was in a condition to profit by them. It was no longer necessary to resort to their authors. The results of their researches had become public property, had conferred new powers on every individual, and might be applied by any one." As they can no longer be appropriated, the *difficulty of attainment*, which is a necessary element of artificial wealth, is entirely removed; they therefore cease to possess exchangeable value, and become a part of what we have called the *natural wealth* of mankind.

Observe, moreover, that it is in the highest departments of literature and science that labor is most imperfectly remunerated; in those of a lower rank, in adapting to popular comprehension and purposes of practical utility the ideas and discoveries of others, tact and industry may often reap a considerable pecuniary reward. Hence, invention is usually more profitable than discovery; a new machine may create a fortune for its inventor, whilst the discoverer of those abstract principles of science, or general laws of nature, which are applied in the mechanical improvement, or are presupposed in the construction of it, can obtain no compensation but the fame of his labors and the gratitude of posterity. No one thinks of rewarding the heirs of Franklin and Œrsted for those discoveries in electricity and electro-magnetism to which we are primarily indebted for the lightning-rod, the electrotype, and the magnetic telegraph. Ideas cannot be patented, or exclusively appropriated; but machines may be. So also in authorship, as McCulloch observes, "though a work should have the greatest influence over the legislation of the country or the state of the arts, it may redound but little to the advantage of the author. It is not so much on the depth, originality, and importance of its views, as on the circumstance of its being agreeable to the public taste, that the success, and consequently the productiveness of a book to its author, must depend. Many a middling novel has produced more money than the 'Principia' or the 'Wealth of Nations'; and in this respect, the 'Decline and Fall of the Roman Empire' has been far inferior to the 'Arabian Nights.'"

The conversion of artificial into natural wealth, an apparent loss in exchangeable value being a real gain to the whole community, may be further illustrated by an example borrowed from Mr. Senior. "If the climate of England could be suddenly changed to that of Bogotá, and the warmth which we extract imperfectly and expensively from fuel were supplied by the sun, fuel would cease to be useful, except as one of the productive instruments employed by art; [that is, in metallurgy, driving steam-engines, &c.] We should want no more grates or chimney-pieces in our sitting-rooms. What had previously been a considerable amount of property in the fixtures of houses, in stock in trade, and materials, would become valueless. Coals would sink in price; the most expensive mines would be abandoned; those which were retained would afford smaller rents. The proprietors and tradesmen specially affected by the change would lose, not only in wealth, but in the means of enjoyment. The owner of a mine whose rent fell from £ 20,000 a year to £ 10,000 would not be compensated by being saved the expense of fuel in every room except his kitchen. On the other hand, persons without fire-places or coal-cellars of their own would lose nothing, and the rest of the world would lose only in the value of their grates, chimney-pieces, and stocks of coal; and all would gain in enjoyment by being able to devote to other purposes the money which they previously paid for artificial warmth. Still, for a time, there would be less [artificial] wealth; [and there would be permanently a great gain in natural wealth.] The capital and the labor previously devoted to warming our apartments, would be diverted to the production of new commodities. The cheapness of coal would increase the supply of manufactured articles, and there would then be as much wealth as there was before the change; probably more, and certainly much more enjoyment."

As to the nature of the labor which ends in the production of wealth, it is justly remarked by McCulloch, that "all the operations of nature and art are reducible to, and really consist of, *transmutations*, that is, of changes of form and of place. By *production*, in this science, is not meant the production of *matter*, that being the exclusive attribute of Omnipotence, but the production of *utility*, and consequently of *value*, by appropriating and modifying matter already in existence, so as to fit it to satisfy our wants, and contribute to our enjoyments. The labor which is thus employed is the only source of wealth. Nature spontaneously furnishes the matter of which all commodities are made; but until labor has been applied to appropriate that matter, or to adapt it to our use, it is wholly destitute of value, and is not, nor ever has been, considered as forming wealth. Place us on the banks of a river, or in an orchard, and we shall infallibly perish of thirst or hunger, if we do not, by an effort of industry, raise the water to our lips, or pluck the fruit from its parent tree. It is seldom, however, that the mere appropriation of matter is sufficient. In the vast majority of cases, labor is required not only to appropriate it, but also to convey it from place to place, and to give it that peculiar shape without which it may be totally useless, and incapable of ministering either to our necessities or our comforts. The coal used as fuel is buried deep in the bowels of the earth, and is absolutely worthless until the miner has extracted it from the mine, and brought it into a situation where it may be made use of. The stones and mortar used in building houses, and the rugged and shapeless materials that have been fashioned into the various articles of convenience and ornament with which they are furnished, were, in their original state, destitute alike of value and utility. And of the innumerable variety of animal, vegetable, and mineral products, which form the materials of food and clothes, none was originally serviceable, while many were extremely noxious to man. It is his labor which has given them utility, that has subdued their bad qualities, and made them satisfy his wants and minister to his comforts and enjoyments."

We distinguish, then, three kinds of industry:—

1. The labor of *collecting and appropriating* natural products. This includes the work not only of the agriculturist, or tiller of the ground, but of the miner, the huntsman, the fisherman, and all others who bring together for the use of man the various products of sea and land which satisfy his wants.

2. The tasks of the manufacturer, the mechanic, and the artisan, who shape, combine, and fabricate raw materials into forms fit for use.

3. The business of the merchant, who brings together the products of various climes, distributes them among the people in proportion to their means and wants, and equalizes the supplies and prices of commodities by storing them up for future use, or carrying them where they are most needed.

Again, the commodities which constitute wealth may be divided into two classes:—1. The articles which are designed for immediate consumption, and which directly satisfy the wants of man, such as food and clothing, that are fit to be eaten and worn, the houses that shelter us, and the ornaments and luxuries that gratify our tastes. 2. The tools, implements, and raw materials, by means of which, or out of which, the former articles are made, but which, in their present shape, are not fitted for our immediate gratification or support. These last possess only a kind of secondary or derivative value, as they are prized, not for their own sake, but for what can be made out of them, or obtained by their aid.

CHAPTER IV.

THE MEASURE OF VALUE, AND THE DISTRIBUTION OF WEALTH AMONG THE COÖPERATING PRODUCERS OF IT.

Thus far it has been shown, that labor is not only necessary in fact for the creation of value, but enters into the very idea of it, so that, when the necessity for labor departs, the reality and even the conception of value vanish along with it. I now say that the labor required is a measure of the value produced. But here the word *labor* must be taken in its most comprehensive signification. I mean by it *any human exertion whatever, corporeal or intellectual, which directly or indirectly overcomes or diminishes that difficulty of attainment which we have seen to be an essential element of wealth.* The only measure of such labor is its comparative efficiency. Thus, the labor of one practised and skilful artisan is equal to that of at least three raw hands, or ordinary laborers, as they are termed; in some cases, it may equal that of many more. The labor, chiefly *intellectual*, of general superintendence and skilful direction of the operatives employed in a manufactory, may be measured by the *ordinary* labor which it saves, — that is, by the number of additional workmen, or the additional time, that would be needed if such superintendence were wanting; or it may be measured by the scarcity of the peculiar skill and tact which are required for such superintendence, — that is, by the difficulty of finding a competent superintendent.

So the value of a machine may be either the labor which it saves, or the labor which it costs. If, for instance, a manufacturer introduces a new machine, by the aid of which two men can do the work that formerly required ten men, (two more persons being required to build the machine and keep it in repair,) he will save the labor of *six* persons; and the value of this machine to him will be represented by six laborers working gratuitously. This will be the case, however, only so long as he can keep the machine a secret from other manufacturers, or enjoy the exclusive use of it. When its use becomes general, the general saving of labor, reducing the cost of the manufactured article, will also reduce its price; for that which costs the labor of but four persons will exchange for the labor of not more than four. No one will give anything more for any commodity than it would cost him to produce it for himself; and in the case supposed, any four workmen, by employing such a machine, might manufacture the article for themselves. Now, then, the value of the machine will be only the labor which it costs; the articles produced by it will represent the labor of but four persons, — two to work it, and two more to build and keep it in repair.

The general law, therefore, that the labor required is a measure of the value produced, is subject to two limitations: — the first is, that allowance must be made for the various degrees of efficiency of the several laborers employed; the second, that the maker has not the advantage of a patented machine or a secret process, which might enable him to produce the commodity by a smaller expenditure of labor than is usual. According to Adam Smith, a workman accustomed to the use of the hammer, but not accustomed to making nails, cannot manufacture usually more than 300 nails in a day; while such is the dexterity acquired by practice, that about 2,300 can be made in a day by a workman who has never exercised any other trade than that of making nails. The value of one day's labor of such a workman, in this manufacture, will be evidently equal to that of seven or eight days' labor by an ordinary smith. It is equally obvious, that the exclusive use of a machine, or a secret process, might render the articles produced by three ordinary workmen the full equivalent in value of those manufactured by thirty or forty hands working without any such advantage.

When the use of machinery has diminished the exchangeable value of certain commodities, the question may be asked, What has become of the difference between their former and their present cost? The difficulty of obtaining these commodities is diminished, the labor required to overcome that difficulty is consequently lessened, and therefore, according to the principles already laid down, less exchangeable value is created. Suppose cloth to be the commodity manufactured, and that the price was formerly ten cents a yard, while it can now be had for four cents. All of that cloth which is already in the market will now be held at only two fifths of its former value. What has become of the other three fifths? Is this amount of exchangeable value destroyed, and is the introduction of labor-saving machinery, therefore, an evil to the community?

The answer is, in this case as in the former one, that the *exchangeable* value of the commodity is diminished; but what is taken away from *that* value is added to what I have called the *natural wealth* of the people, in distinction from their artificial wealth, — to the stock of those things, like the air and the sunlight, which are of preëminent utility, but, being universal and inexhaustible, cannot be exchanged for anything. That this is true may be seen at once by putting the extreme case. Imagine that the machine, instead of saving only three fifths of the labor, should save the whole of it. Imagine that some contrivance should be hit upon for producing cloth in unbounded profusion, no labor of man being required in any part of the process. It is obvious that we should then obtain cloth on the same easy terms on which we now obtain air and light. It would be an addition to the natural wealth of mankind; but as any person could have as much of it as he wished without difficulty, he would not give in exchange for it anything which had cost him labor; it would have no exchangeable value. And as a machine which would save the whole of the labor would transform the whole exchangeable value into natural wealth, so, if it saved but three fifths of the labor, it would add that three fifths to our natural wealth.

Observe, however, as before, that this result would follow only if the use of the machine became *common*. If its inventor or first introducer could keep it to himself for a time, he could exchange the cloth which cost him the labor of only four men for articles which cost others, and would cost him, the labor of ten men; because it would take ten persons, without the aid of the machine, to produce the cloth. The value produced is measured by *the average* of the labor required for making or obtaining the commodity, and not by the greater or smaller amount of labor which circumstances may render necessary in a particular case. If any person has a monopoly granted by the government, or a secret process, or a machine which others cannot imitate, he can turn to his own exclusive advantage the value which would otherwise be added to the natural wealth of the community.

Accident, or good fortune, as it is called, may have the same effect as a monopoly or a secret process. Take the pearl-fishery, for instance. The value of the pearls obtained will be determined by dividing the whole amount procured in one day by the whole number of divers employed during that day; and by dividing the quantity obtained in the whole season by the number of days in that season;—thus ascertaining the *average cost* of the pearls in labor. But the business is a mere lottery; one diver may bring up, from his first plunge, a pearl worth a hundred dollars; another may dive for a week, and obtain little or nothing. If a capitalist should undertake the business, and pay fixed wages to all the divers on condition of receiving all the pearls which they found, his profits, or the value of the pearls, will evidently be determined by their *average* cost in labor, and not by individual and extraordinary cases. When Mr. Senior, who denies that labor is essential to the creation of wealth, asks triumphantly, "If, while carelessly lounging along the sea-shore, I were to pick up a pearl, would it have no value?" and, "Supposing that aerolites consisted of gold, would they have no value?" he might be answered, that accidents and miraculous events are supposed to be eliminated when we are reasoning upon the general principles which govern ordinary events; and that, if pearls were common enough to be often found by loungers on the sea-shore, or if showers of golden aerolites were so frequent as no longer to appear miraculous, certainly both the pearls and the gold would have little or no value.

I have dwelt at length upon the two fundamental maxims of Political Economy, that labor is the source of wealth, and that the wealth produced is in exact proportion to the labor expended, and is therefore measured by it, because, obvious and unquestionable as these truths may appear, they are yet such as the world is slow to recognize and reluctant to act upon. Here in America especially, too many people spend their time and waste their substance upon vain projects for getting rich without labor. They hope that some one of those accidents, or peculiar circumstances, which we have noticed as occasionally disturbing the regular proportion of value to labor, may fall to their lot; that is, — for it amounts to nothing else, — that they may become rich at the expense of their fellows; that they may, by some invention, or perhaps some roguery, be able to exchange four days' labor for ten days' labor. They will take shares in a copper-mine, or go to California to dig gold, or commit any other extravagance, though it should be demonstrated to them that the *average* return, the whole profit divided by the whole number of adventurers, would not keep one from starvation.

Take another instance. Three persons out of four, when the temptation is brought home to them, will buy a ticket in a lottery; though this is the only adventure ever offered to the public, in which, *avowedly*, the net result is not a gain, but a loss. For $120,000 received as the price of tickets, perhaps $100,000 are returned in prizes; that is, the adventurers expect that only five sixths of what they have invested will be returned to them, instead of getting back the whole and a profit besides. And the $100,000 returned are divided into so few prizes, that nineteen out of twenty of the ticket-holders must suffer a total loss of their investment. But one fortunate person — one out of 60,000 — must receive $20,000 for two invested. And yet lotteries are so popular, that they must be forbidden by law, in order to prevent clerks from robbing their employers for the sake of investing money in them; and the most effectual way of encouraging the fine arts in this country is found to be the establishment of an Art-Union lottery for their benefit. Sydney Smith, a veteran opponent of abuses in church and state, and one whose wit was not more remarkable than his sagacity and benevolence, strenuously opposed a scheme for reducing the monstrous inequalities in the compensation of the English clergy, on the ground that these inequalities allured more talent into the Church than would be brought thither by a much larger income equally distributed. Men, he argued, think only of the prizes, and take no account of the blanks. The chance of becoming an Archbishop of Canterbury, with £ 20,000 a year, is enough to allure over 10,000 clergymen into an Establishment one half of the livings in which produce less than £ 100 of annual income.*

Coming back to the subject of the coöperation and the compensation of labor, it may be remarked, that the seemingly complex and difficult process of dividing the ultimate value of the finished article equitably among all those who have had a share in its production, is really accomplished with ease, through the number of exchanges it undergoes at the different stages of its manufacture. At each stage, labor effects a change in its form, bringing it nearer to the state in which it is fitted for consumption; at each exchange, therefore, it has more labor vested in it, and consequently buys more labor vested in other products, the difference being the compensation of the last person who has made an alteration of its form. What regulates this difference, and causes each producer to be paid in exact proportion to the labor which he has bestowed, is the competition of other producers. Wheat, for instance, is first sold or exchanged as wheat, the price paid for it being the compensation of the farmer by whose care and la-

---

* *First Letter to Archdeacon Singleton.*

This argument, however, was not original with Sydney Smith. It was urged, more than a hundred years before his day, by the famous Dr. Bentley, the Aristarchus of English literature, in his "Remarks" upon Collins's "Discourse on Free-Thinking." I borrow the passage, which is written in the character of a foreigner, *Phileleutherus Lipsiensis.*

"I congratulated, indeed, the felicity of your Establishment, which attracted the choice youth of your nation for such very low pay; but my wonder was at the parents, who generally have interest, maintenance, and wealth the first thing in their view: till at last one of your state lotteries ceased my astonishment. For as in that, a few glittering prizes, 1,000, 5,000, 10,000 pounds, among an infinity of blanks, drew troops of adventurers, who, if the whole fund had been equally ticketed, would never have come in; so a few shining dignities in your Church, prebends, deaneries, bishoprics, are the *pious fraud* that induces and decoys the parents to risk their child's fortune in it. Every one hopes his own will get some great prize in the Church, and never reflects on the thousands of blanks in poor country livings. And if a foreigner may tell you his mind, from what he sees at home, 't is this part of your Establishment that makes your clergy excel ours. Do but once level your preferments, and you 'll soon be as level in your learning."

bor it was raised. As labor is the measure of value, a quantity of wheat which represents five days' labor must be exchangeable for a quantity of cloth which also represents five days' labor, — no more and no less; — no more, because this would induce the cloth-maker to turn farmer; no less, because the farmer would then turn cloth-maker. No man will give six days' labor in any one product for another product which he might himself raise in five days. And though it may be said, that he who has long practised a particular trade or art will be reluctant to exchange it for another, as he would thereby sacrifice the skill which he has obtained by experience, and be obliged to serve another apprenticeship to a new handicraft or profession, it must be remembered, that all employments can be kept full only by a succession of young and fresh hands constantly entering them, and these persons will choose, of course, the occupation that is most profitable. Thus the number of those who pursue the art which is underpaid will rapidly diminish, while the number in the more profitable branches of industry will increase, until an equality of gains among all these branches is reëstablished. Exchanges then regulate themselves, and must be made on equal terms. The farmer having received a fair compensation for his work, the miller next obtains the wheat, and, having converted it into flour, sells it to the flour-merchant at an advanced price, because more labor is now vested in it. In like manner, it passes successively into the hands of the retail dealer, the baker, and the consumer, at each stage acquiring an additional value in exchange just sufficient to compensate, on an average, the labor expended upon it at that stage.

Competition, then, when it is free, or competition modified by custom, determines the distribution of the value of a product among those who have concurred in its production. How far it may be modified by custom depends on circumstances. Mr. Mill justly observes, that competition has become "the governing principle of contracts only at a comparatively modern period"; and that "the relations, more especially, between the land-owner and the cultivator, and the payments made by the latter to the former, are, in all stages of society but the most modern, determined by the usage of the country." It was thus that, in many European countries, the serfs were gradually elevated, first into the condition of free tenants, and finally of absolute owners of the soil. Their original obligation, to furnish to their lords an indefinite amount of provisions and labor, was first transformed into a definite payment of a fixed amount of either; these payments in kind were next commuted for payments in money, which were established by custom at so early a period, and therefore at so small an amount, that they became mere quitrents; and the land was finally ransomed even from these quitrents by commutation on reasonable terms, so that the former serfs became absolute proprietors of the ground.

While the peasantry in most countries of Continental Europe were thus not only emancipated, but secured from want by the ownership of the ground which they formerly tilled as slaves, the agricultural laborers of England were far less fortunate. All landed property in England was equally of feudal origin; that is, the land was admitted to belong originally to the state, and the immediate vassals of the crown, or the tenants *in capite*, held it only on condition of rendering certain services and payments, that might be considered as rent. Just so, the practice of sub-infeudation being introduced, these vassals of the crown parcelled out their respective lands to a set of inferior tenants, many of whom were originally serfs, on condition, first, of certain services and supplies being rendered, next, of a definite payment in kind, and then, of an ordinary money rent. Thus the inferior tenantry were the vassals of the great landholder, in the same manner, and upon the same terms, upon which the latter was a vassal of the crown, both being still called *tenants* in the language of the law. As the prerogatives of the crown were gradually diminished, and the liberties of the people increased, the nobility and landed gentry, the original tenants in chief, gradually lessened the feudal burdens upon their land, which consisted in services and payments, and finally, in Charles the Second's time, shook off the remnant of them altogether, artfully exchanging what had become a mere land-tax for an excise on beer and ale. Thus they became absolute owners of their holdings or tenements. But they had no disposition to make the same concessions to their own tenantry, which they had themselves exacted from the crown. The English peasantry have not been able to retain their lands, even on condition of paying the full original rent for them. They have subsided into the class of *tenants at will*, ground down by rack-rents for a century or two, and at last expelled from the land altogether, to find their subsistence where they may. The feudal dues from the lands of the tenants in chief were slowly transformed into a species of land-tax, and at last abrogated entirely; while the same dues from the lands of the inferior tenantry were transformed into annual rents, augmented in amount by every improvement of the land in value, and when the peasants, from misfortune or bad management, could no longer pay them, they were ejected from the estate altogether, and became mere laborers for wages, or paupers.

The Scotch Highlanders have suffered still more grievous injustice. The Gaelic tenant was never conquered; he did not obtain his land from the liberality of his lord, but was originally a fellow-proprietor with him, or rather with his clan. The chief whom he followed to battle regarded him at first as his friend and relation, then as his soldier, afterward as his vassal, still later as his farmer, and finally as his tenant and hired laborer, whom he might employ for a time, but might banish from the estate when he had no further need of his services. Even the name of the clansmen, *Klaan*, in Gaelic signifies *children*. All their usages, all their reciprocal relations, all their affections, were founded on the tradition that they were the offspring of one family; all their rights were those of the children of a common parent to the common patrimony. The chieftain exercised, perhaps he usurped, the right of dividing the land among them, and even of frequently altering this distribution. It was a matter of public policy with the Celts, as well as with the Germans, that families should frequently, even annually, change their position in the district which belonged to them, lest they should become too much attached to the fields which they cultivated, and thus be unfitted for war, and averse to undertaking military expeditions. But though their locations were altered, the vacated places were occupied by other members of the same clan, and the chieftain could not alienate any portion of the common property. The tenure of the lands remained the same; the assessment for the public defence, the annual contribution for the chief-

5

tain who ruled them and led them to battle, were never augmented.

The first step in the usurpation was to grant the *tacks*, or portions of land, to the vassals for a fixed period of time. This appeared to be a concession, as formerly the occupants could be changed at will; but in truth it was a usurpation, for now, instead of filling the vacated places with other clansmen on precisely the same conditions, the lands came to be considered as farms, and at each renewal of the lease new terms might be imposed, and a higher rent demanded. Thus the Highland lords, who were rightfully entitled only to an invariable rent levied on the property of the clan, obtained at last an absolute ownership of the domain which paid this rent. Still they were far from believing that the time would come when they would take advantage of the renewal of the leases, not merely to raise the rent, but to expel their vassals from the estate. But the period arrived for this change also to be effected. "Since the beginning of the present century," says Sismondi, "the nation of the Highlanders or Gauls, the descendants of the ancient Celts, now reduced to 340,000 souls, has been almost entirely expelled from its home by the very persons whom it regarded as its chieftains, and to whom it had shown for so many centuries an enthusiastic devotion. The territory which they had cultivated from generation to generation, under a fixed rent, has been taken from them and devoted to the pasturage of flocks guarded by herdsmen who are strangers; their houses and villages have been razed to the ground or destroyed by fire, while the unhappy people have been forced, either to build cabins on the sea-shore, and endeavor to maintain their miserable existence by fishing, or to cross the ocean to seek their fortune in the back-settlements of America." "It is only within the last five-and-thirty years," says Mr. Thornton, writing in 1845, "that the straths and glens of Sutherland have been cleared of their inhabitants, and that the whole country has been converted into one immense sheepwalk, over which the traveller may proceed for forty miles together without seeing a tree or a stone wall, or anything but a heath dotted with sheep and lambs." And the example of Sutherland has been imitated in the neighboring counties.

The effect of custom in modifying competition has also been

seen in Ireland, where the custom of what is called tenant-right has sprung up, prevailing almost universally in the north, and gradually extending itself into the centre and west of that unhappy country. "My view of tenant-right," says Mr. Senior, "is, that it is the difference between the rent actually charged by the landlord according to the custom of the country, and the utmost competition value." In some cases, it is said to be founded on improvements made by the tenant on his farm, the beneficial effects of which are not exhausted, so that the outgoing tenant claims a right to sell them. The landlords, most of whom are absentees, and therefore unable to watch and know the changes which time produces on the annual value of their estates, have so long received an unvarying sum as the rent of each farm, and each farm has remained so long in the possession of one tenant, that the customary rent is now considered as all which the landlord is entitled to receive; and whatever the land is really worth beyond this sum accrues to the benefit of the tenant. If this tenant wishes to quit the holding, custom gives him the right to sell what we should call "the good-will of the farm" for his own benefit; that is, the incoming tenant pays his predecessor a handsome bonus for the privilege of taking the farm on the old, fixed rent, which is now much below the annual value of the ground. An enterprising landlord sometimes buys up this "right" for himself, in order that he may once again enter into full possession of his property.

Custom is here seen modifying the full effect of competition on the price of land, because the farm is not actually let to the highest bidder; and it often has equal influence on the prices of other commodities. Among the publishers of books, for example, the courtesy of the trade, as it is termed, often restrains one house from issuing a rival edition of a work unprotected by copyright before the edition published by another, who first risked the enterprise, is exhausted. So, also, as Mr. Mill remarks, "all professional remuneration is regulated by custom. The fees of physicians, surgeons, and barristers, the charges of attorneys, are nearly invariable. Not certainly for want of abundant competition in those professions; but because the competition operates by diminishing each competitor's chance of fees, not by lowering the fees themselves."

But competition is the general rule; and the effect of unrestrained competition is to distribute the value of a product equally among its various producers, leaving neither to any of them, nor to the consumer, any just ground of complaint. Each receives in exact proportion to the labor which he has bestowed; the labor of all was equally necessary to present the article in its finished state; and he who finally consumes it, therefore, justly pays all by rendering an equivalent amount of labor. I place stress upon this point, because the effect of sharp competition is, in some measure, to blind our eyes to the fact, that we are all indebted to the friendly coöperation of labor for all the necessaries, all the comforts, all the luxuries, which we enjoy. This coöperation and mutual dependence of all the arts and trades, all the branches of industry, all ranks and professions, is one of the most valuable lessons of Political Economy; and the fair rivalry which causes the distribution of values among them, in proportion to their respective industry and skill, ought not to create feelings of mutual jealousy and dislike, — ought not to give rise to the cry, that one class is taking more than its due share of the common product. It is impossible that any class, *as a class*, should be unduly favored. Individual cases there may be, where fortune, or singularly propitious circumstances, may swell one's gains beyond the common standard. But as a general rule, competition, if unfettered, must tend to reduce them to an equality. The manufacturer is no more dependent upon the agriculturist, than the agriculturist is upon the manufacturer; "the plough," says Adam Smith, "goes frequently the easier and the better by means of the labor of the man whose business is the most remote from the plough." The merchant is equally dependent upon both, and both depend equally upon him. Even the common laborer is as much indebted to his employer as his employer is to him, each rendering a peculiar service, without which the finished product could not be placed in the market or exchanged for other products.

The prejudice which prevents this truth from being generally recognized is the very natural one, which considers the value of the finished product to reside chiefly in the raw material, and, when that is bulky and cheap, to believe that the great enhancement of its price, which takes place as it passes through the hands of the manufacturer and merchant, is a needless and arbitrary thing, an injury both to the farmer and the consumer. But it is not so; in either case, a modification of the article is effected, and the difficulty which the consumer finds in obtaining it in a form fit for use is lessened; and it is easy to show, that all the modifications which it successively undergoes conduce to that end. We cannot consume or use raw cotton, corn in the husk, or unground wheat. The transformations effected by art are just as necessary preliminaries to use, and therefore produce wealth, just as much as the transformations effected by nature. Agriculture is but one branch of what has been happily termed "appropriative industry," or that which is applied merely to collecting and appropriating the articles which nature spontaneously supplies. It includes, together with agriculture, as we have said, the operations of mining, fishing, hunting, and collecting the wood and other products of the forest.

"The industry which prepares," says Colonel Torrens, "is, necessarily, in the order of time, secondary to that which appropriates the gifts of nature. But though man must originally have lived by merely availing himself of nature's spontaneous gifts, yet the very first, or, at most, the very second step towards knowledge and improvement, must have led him to the attempt of superadding to these gifts some rude species of preparation. Almost the whole of the productions of nature are presented to us in a new or rude state, and, if it were not for the application of labor to the preparing and forming of them, would be absolutely without utility. Without manufacturing or adaptive industry, therefore, our wealth would be necessarily limited to that scanty supply of necessaries which nature presents in a state fit for immediate consumption. Man would be reduced to a more destitute and helpless state than that in which he has ever yet been found, even in the most barbarous and savage countries. He would possess no species of clothing whatever; his only shelter from the rigors of the climate would be the hollows of trees and the caverns of the earth; and his only food would be fruits, roots, and the flesh of such of the smaller animals as he might, in his naked and helpless state, be able to outrun and overcome. Indeed, with respect to the supply of his wants, he would be placed far below the condition of the inferior animals; for these are clothed by the hand of nature, and are furnished with implements of admirable construction for the performance of every function necessary for their well-being.

"Again, without the coöperation of manufacturing industry, no other branch of industry can be effectually carried on. To fell the forest, to pierce the mine, and to traverse the waters, we must have the aid of appropriate implements and machines; and these can be supplied only by the manufacturer. This application of the instruments of production not only gives utility to articles which could not otherwise possess it, but also furnishes us with the power of appropriating useful materials, which, without its coöperation, would be for ever inaccessible."

Commerce, moreover, as a source of wealth, is equally productive with manufacturing and appropriative industry. The most precious fruits of the earth cease to constitute wealth when there is a superabundance of them, and when they no longer find wants to satisfy. Commerce comes to restore utility to them, to replace them among articles of wealth, by transporting them to places where they are wanted. Of what avail is it for me to know, that there is tea enough in China, and coffee enough in the West Indies; that there is cotton to spare in Carolina, and a surplus of wheat in Ohio, if some kind person will not intervene to bring these articles to my doors, and offer to me the precise quantity of each which I need, in exchange for other articles of which I may have a superabundance. To accomplish this transportation and distribution, each individual being accommodated with what he wants, as much as he wants, and where he wants, a large apparatus of means is necessary. Ships must be built and appointed, warehouses must be stocked, correspondence must be arranged, and the supplies must be nicely adapted to the wants and means of each locality which is to be provided for. The problem already mentioned, that of supplying a large city with all its necessaries and comforts, must be solved in every part, in all its complex details. Commerce is what renders possible that vast division of labor to which the industry of civilized man owes nearly all its superior efficiency over that of the savage. He who devotes a lifetime to the manufacture of one small article — needles, for instance — must accumulate an immense store of them; and the quantity needed by any one family is so small, that, if he would find purchasers for his whole stock, without the help of professed traders, he must give two thirds of his time to seeking purchasers of what he manufactures in the other third. The merchant takes up his whole stock at once, giving him its full value in whatever he most needs in return. It is a mere truism to say, that whoever converts an idle and superfluous thing into a highly useful one, creates wealth. The merchant does this, by making one man's, or one country's, superfluity supply another's wants; he does it by exchanging superfluities, and thus equalizing the bounties of Providence. By his instrumentality, the hard and rugged soil of Massachusetts, with its long winter, yields to its industrious cultivator all the fruits of the tropics, all the productions of the most favored climes. The merchant equalizes the gifts of nature in another manner, — by transportation in time as well as in space. The surplus from an unusually abundant harvest he stores up in reserve against the possible deficiency of the next season. He gives the alarm, when there is the slightest reason to fear that the next crop may be a failure, by raising the price of the stock already on hand, and thus renders the people economical in its consumption. Through all these methods his agency in the production of wealth is so important, that he richly earns the portion of it which falls to his lot in the general distribution of values.

CHAPTER V.

THE DIVISION OF LABOR: ITS BENEFICIAL AND INJURIOUS CONSEQUENCES.

The analysis of the nature of value, and of the distribution of wealth among its producers, has already brought us to the conclusion, that the coöperation of many laborers with each other is one great cause of the efficiency or productiveness of labor. Labor is divided in two ways; — first, by allotting different portions of a process to different hands, all coöperating with each other in the production of one article; as when eighteen workmen are employed in one pin manufactory, each devoting himself exclusively to one of the eighteen distinct operations into which the making of a pin is divided. The second kind of division takes place by the separation of employments, the several sets of laborers being employed at different times and places, and in distinct pursuits, so that their coöperation with each other, though real, is not so obvious as in the former case. These two modes of the division of labor, says Mr. Wakefield, "may be termed Simple Coöperation and Complex Coöperation." They tend equally to render labor more efficient.

Thus, the manufacturer is just as dependent on the miner, the agriculturist, and the trader, as the workman who makes the head of a pin is on him who cuts the wire and him who sharpens it. The services of all are needed, before all the community can obtain the article in its finished state; and therefore the ultimate and highest value of that article, the price of it when ready for consumption, is to be divided among all who have concurred in its production, each receiving in proportion to the labor he has bestowed. When is it "ready for consumption"? Not surely as soon as it has received the last touch of skill in the workshop, but only when it is offered to the person who wishes to use it, — offered, as it were, at his own door, in just the quantity that he desires, and in exchange for the only article which he is able to give for it. Here the intervention of the trader is needed; a peculiar task is to be performed, which can be done to advantage only by one who devotes himself to it altogether, without complicating it with other employments. The wholesale dealer takes off the manufacturer's whole stock, sparing him the labor of finding numerous purchasers of particular quantities; the retailers divide this stock, and circulate it through the length and breadth of the land, offering to each small villager just as little as he needs, and receiving in exchange, (sometimes through the intervention of money, and sometimes by direct barter,) whatever product the villager has to offer. The importance of the service thus rendered appears from the large portion of the ultimate value of the finished product which falls to their share; the profits of retailers in this country average from 10 to 20 per cent., or from one tenth to one fifth part of the values sold. And while competition is free, it is certain, for the reasons already explained, that this is only a fair compensation for their services; if it were not so, miners, manufacturers, and even common workmen, would turn retailers, and undersell them.

I borrow another illustration from Mr. Mill. "In the present state of society, the breeding and feeding of sheep is the occupation of one set of people, dressing the wool to prepare it for the spinner is that of another, spinning it into thread of a third, weaving the thread into broadcloth of a fourth, dyeing the cloth of a fifth, making it into a coat of a sixth, without counting the multitude of carriers, merchants, factors, and retailers put in requisition at the successive stages of this process. All these persons, without knowledge of one another or previous understanding, coöperate in the production of the ultimate result, a coat. But these are far from being all who cooperate in it; for each of these persons requires food and many other articles of consumption; and unless he could have relied that other people would produce these for him, he could not have devoted his whole time to one step in the succession of operations which produce one single commodity, a coat. Every person who took part in producing food or erecting houses for this series of producers has, however unconsciously on his part, combined his labor with theirs. It is by a real though unexpressed concert, 'that the body who raise more food than they want, can exchange with the body who raise more clothes than they want; and if the two bodies were separated, either by distance or disinclination, — unless the two bodies should virtually form themselves into one, for the common object of raising enough food and clothes for the whole, — they could not divide into two distinct parts the whole operation of producing a sufficient quantity of food and clothes.'"

The advantages of Simple Coöperation, which was formerly regarded as the only kind of Division of Labor, have been admirably illustrated by Adam Smith. Passing over, as it is so well known, his illustration from pin-making, I adopt an example of the effects produced by the division of labor that is given by M. Say, in a passage translated by Mr. Mill. It is taken from a very humble branch of industry, the manufacture of playing-cards. "It is said by those engaged in the business, that each card, before being ready for sale, undergoes no less than seventy operations, every one of which might be the occupation of a distinct class of workmen. And if there are not seventy classes of work-people in each card-manufactory, it is because the division of labor is not carried so far as it might be; because the same workman is charged with two, three, or four distinct operations. The influence of this distribution of employments is immense. I have seen a card-manufactory where thirty workmen produced daily 15,500 cards, being about 500 cards for each laborer; and it may be presumed that, if each of these workmen were obliged to perform all the operations himself, even supposing him a practised hand, he would not perhaps complete two cards in a day; and the thirty workmen, instead of 15,500 cards, would make only 60."

The business of watch-making in England is said by Mr. Babbage to have been divided into 102 distinct branches, to each of which a boy may be put apprentice, and taught to practise it exclusively, without learning to work at any other branch. "The watch-finisher, whose business it is to put together the scattered parts, is the only one, out of 102 persons, who can work at any other department than his own."

The prodigious increase in the efficiency of labor caused by division of the task is attributed by Adam Smith to three causes.

1. The increased dexterity, corporeal and intellectual, acquired by frequent repetition of one simple operation. The laborer thus acquires a *sleight of hand*, enabling him to perform his task with a rapidity which, to those who have had no experience in the work, appears truly marvellous. A child who fastens on the heads of pins will repeat an operation requiring several distinct motions of the muscles one hundred times a minute, for several successive hours. Gymnastic exercises, many feats of jugglery, and the ease and brilliancy of execution acquired by experienced performers on musical instruments, are other cases, as remarkable as they are familiar, of the rapidity and facility acquired by repetition. The same is true of operations exclusively mental; a practised accountant sums up a column of figures with a quickness that resembles intuition.

2. The saving of the time which is commonly lost in passing from one species of work to another, and in the change of place, position, and tools. Thus, says Smith, "a country weaver who cultivates a small farm must lose a good deal of time in passing from his loom to the field, and from the field to his loom. When the two trades can be carried on in the same workhouse, the loss of time is, no doubt, much less. Even in this case, however, it is very considerable. A man commonly saunters a little in turning his hand from one employment to another." "When the human hand, or the human head," adds Mr. Babbage, "has been for some time occupied in any kind of work, it cannot instantly change its employment with full effect. The muscles of the limbs employed have acquired a flexibility during their exertion, and those not in action a stiffness during rest, which renders every change slow and unequal in the commencement. Long habit also produces in the muscles exercised a capacity for enduring fatigue to a much greater degree than they could support under other circumstances." So, also, in the use of tools, time is lost in shifting from one to another; and when many implements are required for the different occupations, at least three fourths of them must be constantly idle and useless.

3. The invention of a great number of machines, which facilitate and abridge labor in all its departments. The division of labor reduces a complex operation to many simple tasks, each of which is incessantly repeated; and this is precisely what machines may be made most easily to perform. The whole of a workman's attention, moreover, being directed to one simple object, easier and readier methods of obtaining that object are more likely to occur to him, than when his thoughts are dissipated among a variety of things. I have heard that most of the improvements in machinery, which have been made of late years in the manufactories at Lowell, were first suggested by the common workmen who were engaged in tending the machines. In the first steam-engine, says Adam Smith, "a boy was constantly employed to open and shut alternately the communication between the boiler and the cylinder, according as the piston either ascended or descended. One of those boys, who loved to play with his companions, observed that, by tying a string from the handle of the valve

which opened the communication to another part of the machine, the valve would open and shut without his assistance, and leave him at liberty." Thus one of the most important steps in the improvement of steam-engines was made by an idle boy.

4. Another advantage derived from the division of labor was first pointed out by Mr. Babbage; — the more economical distribution of labor, by classing the work-people according to their capacity. "Different parts of the same series of operations require unequal degrees of skill and bodily strength; and those who have skill enough for the most difficult, or strength enough for the hardest, parts of the labor, are made much more useful by being employed solely in them; the operations which everybody is capable of, being left to those who are fit for no others." Thus, in a cotton manufactory, men, women, and children are employed on different portions of the work, and, of course, at very different rates of wages. Obviously there would be a great waste, if men were employed to perform tasks which children might do as well, or if fingers which were delicate enough for hem-stitching and embroidery, were devoted to raising heavy weights or swinging sledge-hammers. In needle-making, Mr. Babbage tells us, the scale of remuneration for different parts of the process, performed by different work-people, varies from sixpence to twenty shillings a day.

5. One of the principal advantages of the division of labor, says Mr. Senior, "arises from the circumstance that the same exertions which are necessary to produce a single given result are often sufficient to produce many hundred or many thousand similar results. The Post-Office supplies a familiar illustration. The same exertions which are necessary to send a single letter from Falmouth to New York are sufficient to forward fifty, and nearly the same exertions will forward ten thousand. If every man were to effect the transmission of his own correspondence, the whole life of an eminent merchant might be passed in travelling, without his being able to deliver all the letters which the Post-Office forwards for him in a single evening. The labor of a few individuals, devoted exclusively to the forwarding of letters, produces results which all the exertions of all the inhabitants of Europe could not effect, each person acting independently."

The extent of the division of labor must always be limited by the extent of the market. Ten workmen can make 48,000 pins in a day; but they cannot do so to advantage, unless there is a daily consumption of pins to that amount. If there be a daily demand for no more than 24,000 pins, they must either lose half the day's work, or change their occupation,—that is, lessen the division of labor by engaging in two separate tasks. Hence, the division of labor cannot be carried to its farthest limit except in the case of products capable of distant transport, and the consequent increase of consumption; or where the manufacture is carried on amidst a dense population, creating an extensive local demand. Where the population is limited, many trades, elsewhere distinct, are practised by the same individual. In a small village, the same person is surgeon, doctor, and apothecary; while, in a large city, there is separate employment for each of these practitioners, and even for subdivisions of their profession into the several occupations of dentists, oculists, accoucheurs, &c. The village grocer deals not only in groceries, but in dry goods, crockery, hardware, books, and stationery; and if a Yankee, he may also edit, print, and publish a newspaper, keep a school, and go to Congress. In large cities, the sale of a single article of grocery may form a large and lucrative business; in Boston and New York, there are shops where nothing is sold but tea. All improvements in the modes of transportation, as by roads, canals, and railways, obviously promote the division of labor, by widening the market which each locality can command for its special products.

"The division of labor is also limited, in many cases," says Mr. Mill, "by the nature of the employment. Agriculture, for example, is not susceptible of so great a division of occupations as many branches of manufactures, because its different occupations cannot possibly be simultaneous. One man cannot be always ploughing, another sowing, and another reaping. A workman who only practised one agricultural operation would be idle eleven months of the year. The same person may perform them all in succession, and have, in almost every climate, a considerable amount of unoccupied time. The combination of labor of which agricultural industry is susceptible is chiefly that which Mr. Wakefield calls Simple Coöperation; many persons employed together in the same work. To execute a great agricultural improvement, it is often necessary that many laborers should work together; but in general, except the few whose business is superintendence, they all work in the same manner. A canal or a railway embankment cannot be made without a combination of many laborers; but they are all excavators, except the engineer and a few clerks."

The advantages of the division of labor, however, we must admit, are subject to one serious drawback. Few things tend so effectually to dwarf the mind and stunt the faculties as the incessant and long-continued repetition of a very simple task, — a mechanical movement which is repeated with as little effort of thought as if it were performed by a machine. Even Adam Smith remarks, that constant application to such a task "necessarily renders the workmen as stupid and ignorant as it is possible to make a human being." And Say adds, that "a man whose whole life is devoted to the execution of a single operation, will most assuredly acquire the faculty of executing it better and quicker than others; but he will, at the same time, be rendered less fit for every other occupation, bodily and intellectual; his other faculties will be gradually blunted and extinguished, and the man, as an individual, will degenerate in consequence. To have never done anything but make the eighteenth part of a pin, is a sorry account for a human being to give of his existence." The division even of intellectual labor, however it may tend to excellence and insure success in a single department, is not without a similar pernicious result. The successful pursuit of a single art, or of the fraction of a single science, is but poor compensation for the loss of all versatility and alertness of mind, and for allowing most of the faculties to rust by disuse. One may become a good accountant, an expert mathematician, and even a skilful lawyer, without being anything more than the fraction of a man.

CHAPTER VI.

THE NATURE OF CAPITAL, AND THE MEANS OF ITS INCREASE.

Another circumstance on which the efficiency of labor largely depends is the coöperation of capital, or stock. All capital is wealth, but all wealth is not capital. The furniture of a rich man's house, for instance, — his carpets, his plate, his paintings, and much even of the food which is daily placed upon his table, — forms a portion of his wealth, but not of his capital. All these articles contribute to his enjoyment, perhaps some of them are necessary for his sustenance; but they do not directly aid him in the creation of other values. As they are consumed, or slowly worn out, they create nothing to replace them, and leave behind them nothing but the remembrance of the gratification which they have afforded. They are the fruit of previous industry indeed, having been created, as all other values are, by labor; but with the exception of the little food which is necessary to support life, they do not sustain present labor, do not aid in the production of fresh values. *Capital is that portion of wealth which is consumed, not for purposes of mere enjoyment, not for immediate gratification, but to aid in the production of more wealth.* It is still consumed, with greater or less rapidity; but its value disappears in one shape only to reappear in another. The necessity for the employment of capital arises from the fact, that man cannot labor to any good purpose with his hands alone. He must have tools, implements, machinery, raw material; if the article on which he is engaged requires time for its manufacture, he must be fed, clothed, and lodged while he is occupied in manufacturing it. *The aggregate of wealth existing in these various forms, designed either to aid the laborer in his work, or to support him while working, is capital.* It is consumed, but its value appears again in the larger amount of wealth which industry produces when thus assisted. The tools and machinery wear out; but the products which they have aided in creating enable the capitalist to replace them with a profit. Raw cotton is consumed in large quantities, and reappears as cloth; the seed-corn is buried in the earth, but in a few months, the harvest yields twenty or thirty fold.

Labor is limited by capital, because labor cannot be prosecuted to any advantage without capital. Yet this fact does not contradict our general proposition, that wealth is created by labor alone; for capital itself is created by labor, and might be called *consolidated or invested labor*. But although labor is thus limited, it is by no means proportioned to the amount of capital employed. A master-shoemaker, with a capital of not more than $ 5,000, may keep twenty journeymen and apprentices in constant employment; while a manufacturer of gold and silver plate, or a wholesale merchant, with a capital of half a million of dollars, may not pay wages to more than thirty or forty persons. McCulloch observes, that "a manufacturer's power to employ labor is not measured by the total amount of his capital, but by the amount of that portion only which is *circulating* capital. A capitalist possessed of a hundred steam-engines, and of £ 50,000 of circulating capital, has no greater demand for labor, and does not, in fact, employ a single workman more, than the capitalist who has no machinery, and only £ 50,000 devoted exclusively to the payment of wages." Boots and shoes, for instance, are at present manufactured without machinery, and with the aid only of a few cheap tools. With a lapstone, a hammer, a knife, and an awl, the journeyman can begin work; and even the raw material which he needs is so frequently "turned over," as the phrase goes, or so quickly converted from leather into merchantable boots and shoes, that, if the articles can be sold as soon as they are manufactured, a few dollars will keep him constantly supplied with sufficient stock. On the other hand, an immense capital must be vested in machinery, before the business of weaving cotton or woollen cloth on a great scale can begin.

Even in the rudest states of society, among savage nations, capital exists, though in small quantities, and performs its appropriate functions. "The wretched native of New Holland," says Colonel Torrens, "has his spear, his fishing implements, and his canoe, for the purpose of abridging his labor, — of performing operations of which he would otherwise be incapable, and appropriating productions of nature which, but for the aid of these rude instruments, would for ever have remained beyond his reach." Before he labors directly to capture the wild tenants of the forests and the rivers, he labors to prepare himself for the task by manufacturing the necessary implements; consequently, the exchangeable value of the articles which he finally obtains is measured by the quantity of labor, both direct and indirect, which was devoted to their production. No one will give labor of either sort for nothing. That which was bestowed on the manufacture of bows and arrows must be compensated just as much, and in the same ratio, as that which was given to the pursuit and killing of wild animals; otherwise, no one will make bows and arrows. The law of distribution, therefore, that the value of the completed product will be divided among its producers in exact proportion to the labor bestowed by each, is not altered by the coöperation of capital with labor. The profits of capital are the reward of labor just as much as the wages directly paid to the laborer.

Capital exists, as I have said, among savages; and it accumulates very rapidly with the progress of civilization. So rapid, indeed, is its increase, and so vast becomes its aggregation, that it constitutes the chief difference in point of efficiency between the labor of the savage and that of civilized man. The Australian or the Indian may be as muscular as the European; he often works as hard, and is even more capable of enduring hardship and privation. He also practises the division of labor to some extent, as a whole tribe often unite in the chase or in war, and make larger captures by acting in concert and parcelling out the work among each other. But their labor on the whole is miserably inefficient and unproductive, because it is aided only by a trifling amount of capital. "Ten men, abundantly supplied with capital, and skilful in the use of it, would be able to appropriate a greater quantity of fish, and of useful mineral productions, than could be appropriated by ten thousand, whose only instrument of production was the labor of their hands."

The savage does not amass capital, because he is incapable of foresight and self-denial. What he obtains is devoted to the gratification of the present moment, or is wasted. This, in truth, is the chief reason why he does not till the ground; he often has knowledge enough for this end, his powers of observation being largely developed. He notices slight peculiarities of vegetation, which escape the eye of the white man; and by this means, is often enabled to find his way through the trackless forests. He knows that edible fruits and grains are produced from seed. But he is not economical and prudent enough to reserve seed-corn for agriculture, or to lay in a store of food which will enable him to expend labor on the ground, to dig and plant, with the expectation of reaping the fruits of his labor only after an interval of some months. He is obliged to give all his toil to the necessities of the present hour, because he is not prudent enough to save, and not industrious enough to work when there is no immediate necessity for working. Though the common opinion runs the other way, I believe that man has no natural instinct for saving, no original propensity for labor; — none, at least, that is not constantly overridden by other and stronger propensities. The hardest lesson for children and savages to learn is that of economy, — the necessity of bridling the inclination or appetite of the moment, with a view to some prospective benefit. Long and hard experience has taught this lesson to the full-grown and reflecting man, and taught it so effectually, that, as is often the case, the acquired inclination overrides the original impulses, and all other passions are merged, not merely in the love of accumulation, but in that of saving. We not infrequently hear of misers who will give away thousands, while they are depriving themselves almost of the necessaries of life for the sake of saving units. Exertion is naturally pleasant, it is true; yet only when directed by the caprice of the moment, as in sport; not the long-continued and monotonous exertion which is necessary for the attainment of a future good. *That* always requires self-restraint, a contest with and a victory over our original inclinations.

This view of the difference between the barbarian and the civilized man leads directly to a knowledge of the origin of capital and the means of its increase. It begins in saving, and is enlarged only by the continued exercise of frugality. Labor creates wealth, the object of which is, as we have seen, the gratification of desire; and the portion of wealth which is saved from the gratification of our immediate wants, and reserved to aid our future labor, so that the future product may be greater, is capital. The inducement to the practice of such frugality is always strong enough in a civilized community; for the ability to save increases in a geometrical ratio with its exercise. *C'est le premier pas qui coute.* The hardest struggle, the severest exercise of self-denial, is to make the beginning, to spare a little from our daily comforts when as yet we are entirely dependent upon the fruits of our unaided labor. Afterwards, that little which was reserved works along with us, and the surplus is greater at the end of the second year, though we have practised no additional self-restraint. Soon, the aggregate of these savings produces more than our original, individual earnings, and our expenditures may come up again to the full measure of what they would have been if no frugality had been practised at the outset; and yet accumulation goes on as rapidly as if we had been able to reserve the whole original product of our labor, and subsist upon nothing. The industrial organization of society is now so perfect, that the smallest savings can be utilized, or devoted immediately to active employment as capital. This rapid progress of accumulation, operating like the constantly accelerating force of gravitation, supplies the strong motive for frugality, which operates like a charm in the swift growth of national opulence.

It is now easy to explain the difference, on which so much stress is laid, between productive and unproductive consumption. Take the case, referred to in a former chapter, of a laborer who has saved $ 100 from his yearly earnings. At the end of the year, having this sum in reserve, he may immediately expend it all in giving an entertainment to his friends, or purchasing finer clothes and furniture for his family. In neither case would the values thus consumed aid either his labor or that of any other being; in the first case, it would be consumed all at once, the wine being drunk, the music heard, the delicacies eaten, and there would be an end of his savings; in the other case, the enjoyment would only be spread over a little longer time; the clothes and furniture, in the course of a few months or years, would be worn out, and the $ 100 would then have equally disappeared without return. Such is what is termed unproductive consumption.

But let us suppose, as before, that at the end of the year he placed the money in a savings' bank, or bought a machine with it, by the aid of which his labor would produce half as much again as in the former twelvemonth. In the bank, as has been shown, it would successively and rapidly assume different forms, at each transformation aiding labor or setting it in motion, at each yielding a profit, and leaving a final profit for the benefit of him who deposited it. This share of profit accruing to the owner is comparatively small, because he has committed the management of his property, and the risk of losing it, to others, and they must be paid for the labor and hazard of its superintendence. If he chooses to use it himself, as in the case supposed of purchasing a machine with it, his yearly earnings will be much increased, and the surplus will be enough to keep the machine in repair, to buy another when the first one is worn out, and to leave a larger profit at the end of the year, which surplus, again, he may spend productively or unproductively.

In all the cases now enumerated, it is evident that the laborer's surplus earnings are consumed. In the first two cases, being consumed only to obtain present enjoyment, whether of a longer or shorter duration, they never appear again; in the last two, being consumed only for the purpose of aiding labor, they reappear in the increased product of that labor. And so it must be in every supposable case, except where the savings are obtained in the form of gold or silver money, and are buried in the earth; then, indeed, they are not consumed, because they are not used at all, either for present gratification or future gain.

We see the fallacy, then, of the common opinion, that the prodigals who waste their substance in riotous or ostentatious living, though they and their families afterwards suffer for it, are yet benefactors to the community, because their liberal expenditures keep laborers in employ, increase the profits of shop keepers, and diffuse benefits all around them. He who saves, on the contrary, appears in the light of one who hoards; saving seems but another word for keeping a thing to one's self, while spending appears to be distributing it among others.

This popular error arises chiefly from the fact, that the wasteful person consumes his income and his capital mostly on the spot where he resides, where the public eye can follow his wealth, and see it passing into the hands of laborers, tradesmen, and dependents. But these persons do not obtain it for nothing. They give services, goods, articles of luxury, in exchange; and when these services are rendered, and the articles consumed, there is an end of the prodigal's wealth. He has nothing left, and they are but little richer than before, having only made their ordinary gains, or received their accustomed wages. The community, then, is the poorer by the whole amount which the prodigal has squandered. The savings of the frugal person, on the other hand, are often withdrawn from sight of the immediate neighborhood, being quietly invested in a bank or manufactory, where they are consumed productively; that is, they are still applied to the purchase of labor or goods, and so equally keep industry in motion, though this beneficial result is not easily traced back, and ascribed to the proper author of it.

To make this point clearer, I will take a particular example. Suppose a prodigal maintains an establishment of ten menial servants, at an expense of $ 3,000 a year. At the end of the year, he has expended this portion of his capital, and the servants have received their usual wages; but as they have toiled only to pamper his desire of enjoyment, and to gratify his love of ostentation, no products of their labor remain at the end of the year, and they are no better off than they would have been if they had obtained equal wages for making boots and shoes, or laboring on a farm. Then suppose a frugal person, having an equal sum of $ 3,000 a year to spend, instead of hiring menial servants with it, should invest it in the shoemaking business or in agriculture. It is obvious that an equal number of persons might thus be employed, and at the same wages; at the end of the year, moreover, instead of nothing being left, there would be an additional stock of one or two thousand pairs of boots and shoes, or of four or five thousand bushels of corn. The capital of the frugal person and the riches of the community would thus be augmented to the extent perhaps of $ 4,000 (ordinary allowance being made for profits); and this would be a fund for the support of industry for an indefinite period, or until it came into the hands of a prodigal who should waste it in luxuries and self-indulgence.

Adam Smith happily illustrates this subject, by comparing the frugal person to the founder of a public charity, in that he establishes, as it were, a perpetual fund for the purpose of supplying indigent laborers with employment at good wages for all time to come. But the prodigal is like him "who perverts the revenues of some pious foundation to profane purposes, as he pays the wages of idleness with those funds which the frugality of his forefathers had, as it were, consecrated to the maintenance of industry."

It should be observed, that the only fund from which savings can be made, and capital thereby increased, is the annual income or revenue of the individual. If the manufacturer, for instance, at the end of the year, has merely got his capital back again, the values created exactly replacing those which were consumed, though he has preserved his property, he has effected no saving; he is neither richer nor poorer than he was before. His capital ought to be replaced *with a profit;* and the aggregate of the profits for a year, not the aggregate of all the values produced during that time, constitutes his income or revenue. This income, like the year's wages of a laborer, seems to be the fund naturally designed for his own maintenance and that of his family. A portion of it *must* be spent in this manner,—that is, must be spent unproductively; for health and strength must be kept up by food, drink, and clothing; in addition to which, in order to keep up the full vigor of mind and body, a small portion of every one's income ought to be devoted to amusement and a few luxuries. But if these personal expenditures, and the replacement of the capital consumed during the year, do not absorb the whole income, what remains is a true saving, an addition to capital, a benefit both to the individual and the community.

"It would be a great error," says Mr. Mill, "to regret the large proportion of the annual produce, which, in an opulent country, goes to supply unproductive consumption. It would be to lament that the community has so much to spare from its necessities, for its pleasures and for all higher uses. This portion of the produce is the fund from which all the wants of the community, other than that of mere living, are provided for; the measure of its means of enjoyment, and of its power of accomplishing all purposes not productive. That so great a surplus should be available for such purposes, and that it should be applied to them, is a subject only of congratulation.

The things to be regretted and to be remedied are the prodigious inequality with which this surplus is distributed, and the large share which falls to the lot of persons who render no equivalent service in return."

The wealth which is employed in creating more wealth has been divided by Adam Smith into Fixed and Circulating Capital. "There are two ways," he says, "in which a capital may be employed so as to yield a revenue or profit.

"First, it may be employed in raising, manufacturing, or purchasing goods, and selling them again with a profit. The capital employed in this manner yields no revenue or profit to its employer, while it either remains in his possession or continues in the same shape. The goods of the merchant yield him no revenue or profit till he sells them for money, and the money yields him as little till it is again exchanged for goods. His capital is continually going from him in one shape, and returning to him in another; and it is only by means of such circulation, or successive exchanges, that it can yield him any profit. Such capitals, therefore, may properly be called *circulating* capitals.

"Secondly, it may be employed in the improvement of land, in the purchase of useful machines and implements of trade, or in such like things as yield a revenue or profit without changing masters or circulating any further. Such capitals, therefore, may properly be called *fixed* capitals."

This distinction has been further illustrated by the remark, that Circulating Capital fulfils the whole of its office in production by a single use; while Fixed Capital produces its effect, not by being parted with, but by being kept, and its efficacy is not exhausted by a single use. Observe, also, that the same articles may be Circulating Capital while in the hands of one person, and become Fixed Capital as soon as they are transferred to another. A stock of finished ploughs, for instance, belongs to the former class while they are owned by the manufacturer or the merchant, who expects not to use, but to sell them, and can obtain his profit only from the proceeds of such a sale; but they become Fixed Capital when they are purchased by the farmers, who expect to retain and use them till they are worn out.

Fixed Capital, Adam Smith remarks, "consists chiefly of the four following articles: —

"First, of all useful machines and implements of trade which facilitate and abridge labor.

"Secondly, of all buildings used for the purpose of trade or manufacture, such as shops, warehouses, and farm buildings. They are a sort of instruments of trade, and may be considered in the same light.

"Thirdly, of the improvements of land, of what has been profitably laid out in clearing, draining, inclosing, manuring, and reducing it into the condition most proper for culture. An improved farm may be regarded in the same light as one of those useful machines which facilitate and abridge labor.

"Fourthly, of the acquired and useful abilities of all the members of the society. The acquisition of such talents by the maintenance of the acquirer during his education, study, or apprenticeship, costs an expense, which is a capital fixed and realized, as it were, in his person. The improved dexterity of a workman may be considered in the same light as a machine or instrument of trade, which facilitates and abridges labor.

"The Circulating Capital is composed likewise of four parts: —

"First, of the money by means of which all the other three are circulated and distributed to their proper consumers.

"Secondly, of the stock of provisions in the possession of the butcher, the grazier, &c. for the purpose of sale.

"Thirdly, of the materials, whether altogether rude, or more or less manufactured, of clothes, furniture, and building, which are not yet made up, but remain in the hands of the growers, manufacturers, or merchants.

"Fourthly, of the work which is made up and completed, but is still in the hands of the merchant or manufacturer; such as the finished work in the shops of the smith, the goldsmith, the jeweller, and the China merchant. The Circulating Capital consists in this manner of the provisions, materials, and finished work of all kinds, which are in the hands of their respective dealers, and of the money that is necessary for circulating and distributing them to their final consumers."

To this enumeration by Adam Smith must be added two classes of articles, which seem to have been excluded by him for insufficient reasons; namely, food and the other necessaries of life, and dwelling-houses. The name of *capital* has been denied to these two classes of things, because they are consumed as revenue, with a view to subsistence or enjoyment, and not as capital, with a view to production. But it may be replied, that the laborer, before he can construct or fashion anything, must not only have raw materials and tools, but must be secure of a lodging and a dinner. An expenditure for all four of these objects is necessary before he can complete his task; and the aggregate of such expenditure is therefore properly considered as an advance of capital, the means for this advance having been previously obtained by abstinence or frugality.

CHAPTER VII.

THE CIRCUMSTANCES WHICH FAVOR THE GROWTH OF CAPITAL: THE SECURITY OF PROPERTY.

The circumstances on which the rapidity of accumulation, or the growth of capital, depends, are various, and the study of them is one of the most interesting researches in which the economist or the historian can engage. Laws and political institutions generally have a vast influence in this respect, as well as differences of national character and peculiarities of geographical position. The results of the former may be traced, by the light both of theory and history, often in quarters where they would be the least suspected, the most prominent and marked effect being frequently attributable to the noiseless working, through many generations, of peculiar customs and laws, which do not attract much notice precisely because they are ingrained or deeply seated. Foremost among these silent but potent causes, which escape the attention of the superficial observer, must be ranked the legislative and consuetudinary provisions which regulate the succession to the estates of persons deceased. I believe the striking differences in the social and economical condition of the English and the American people, who are of the same blood, who speak the same language, who have many similar traits of national character, and whose political institutions in the main are very much alike, are more attributable to their different modes of regulating the succession to property, than to any other single cause whatsoever. But this subject will be more conveniently considered hereafter.

Our general question is, When is labor most energetic, universal, and effective in the creation of wealth, and by what means are the motives to accumulation from savings most strongly stimulated? I cannot attribute much importance in this respect to what are called the natural advantages of a country,—its genial climate, fertile soil, large expanse of territory, or happy geographical position. These natural advantages, as they are termed, have fearful drawbacks in the indolence and sense of security which they foster, and the luxurious habits to which the people who possess them incline, their chief luxury always being *repose*. Some of the countries of South America are as highly favored in these respects as any part of the habitable globe; but it is not to this portion of our continent that we look for instances of the most rapid growth of national wealth. "In the ancient world and in the Middle Ages," it has been well remarked, "the most prosperous communities were not those which had the largest territory or the most fertile soil, but rather those which had been forced by natural sterility to make the utmost possible use of a convenient maritime situation; as Tyre, Marseilles, Venice, the free cities on the Baltic, and the like." And that we may not over-estimate even this convenience of position, it should be remembered that Athens, Tyre, and Venice stand just where they did, though their commercial glory has long since passed away. The geographical position of Greece, with its long line of deeply indented sea-coast on a tideless sea, is precisely what it was when Greece almost monopolized the commerce and the arts of the Mediterranean. She is now the most insignificant kingdom in Europe, and with difficulty supports an ignorant and thinly scattered population.

But we need not go abroad for illustrations of this truth. At home,—here in Massachusetts,—where we are indebted to the rigor of our climate and the hardness of our soil for our only natural exports, capital has increased, and is increasing, as fast as in any portion of the United States, — faster probably than in Louisiana, with its rich staples of cotton and sugar, and its unequalled position at the outlet into the great Gulf of five thousand miles of internal navigation, — as fast as in Pennsylvania, with its inexhaustible stores of mineral wealth, and its soil so fertile that one county might produce more wheat than the whole Bay State. *Natural* wealth enervates both body and mind. Where an abundance can be had with little labor, much labor will never be practised. What seems a paradise on earth, the nearest natural semblance of a Garden of Eden, may be found in the isles of the South Pacific, or in the West Indies, where a race of white colonists seem to be fast becoming as feeble and brutish as were the natives whom they dispossessed. Here again, as in so many other instances, we are reminded that the essential quality of wealth, properly so called, is difficulty of attainment, — difficulty that can be overcome only by long and strenuous exertion.

The principal causes of the rapid growth of national opulence are moral rather than physical; a situation which shall make foreign commerce at least practicable, seems to be the only indispensable condition that is not connected with the character of the people. By moral causes alone can we hope to solve that interesting and difficult problem, the decline and fall of the opulence and grandeur of Spain. Hardly two centuries ago, Spain was what Great Britain is now, the richest, noblest, and most powerful kingdom in Europe, on whose dominions the sun never set, and whose people, distinguished alike in arts and arms, carried their flag and their renown to either pole, and encircled the earth with the golden chains of their commerce. Now, language seems hardly adequate to describe their poverty and abasement, and the wretched condition of Spain. I do not speak merely of the decline of her military strength and political influence among the nations of Europe. This is an effect, rather than a cause, of the great change which has taken place in the economical condition of her people, — of the decay of her commerce, the loss of her manufactures, the wretched state of her agriculture, and the gradual wasting away of her population. And her decline cannot be attributed to the loss of her American colonies; since it became marked at least a century before the first of these colonies threw off her yoke; and since apparently the same causes which have enfeebled the mother country, have prevented all progress among her emancipated children in the Western world. In Mexico, Bolivia, and Peru, as well as from the foot of the Pyrenees to Cadiz, the right arm of industry seems to be paralyzed, and what remains of energy, courage, and intelligence among the people is wasted in dissensions and civil broils, instead of being devoted to the golden pursuits of peace. The physical circumstances in the two cases are as unlike as possible; yet, in point of natural advantages, it would be difficult to say which is the more favored. A fairer field for the development of labor and enterprise can hardly be imagined, than that which exists on the high tablelands of Mexico and among the romantic valleys of Spain. Improved by English or Anglo-American hands, under English or Anglo-American institutions, they would become storehouses of wealth for future generations.

To return to our general question: — The moral causes which most effectually stimulate labor and frugality, and thereby make capital accumulate most rapidly, are those which secure to the laborer with the greatest certainty the fruit of his industry; which raise the kind or degree of labor to the highest practicable point; and which offer the highest reward, the largest measure of social advantages, to the holder of capital, — apportioning that reward strictly to the comparative amount which he holds, and making it most immediate and attractive. There are three points, then, which may be more fully stated thus: —

1. That the laborer shall be sure of receiving the full amount of his wages, or shall be protected in the ownership of the values which he has produced.

2. That the skill, intelligence, and education of the laboring classes generally shall be raised to the highest point, — so that, the labor of one well-trained mechanic being as effective at least as that of three raw hands or mere laborers, the working class shall contain as many as possible of the former, and as few as possible of the latter description.

3. That the savings when made, or the capital when accumulated, shall be attended with as high a rate of profit, and as large a measure of physical comfort, social consideration, and political influence as possible.

The illustrations which may be offered upon these three points are enough, I think, to prove that they are vastly more important than any measure of natural advantages, including even that on which most stress has been laid, — the inherited qualities of race, or the national, inbred inclination to labor and enterprise. I am no great believer in the natural excellences of Anglo-Saxon blood, but I have great faith in the acquired excellences of Anglo-Saxon institutions. My reason for distrust in the former case is, that time was, and that not many years ago, when the Dutch certainly, if not the Swiss, were decidedly superior to the English in industry, frugality, and the spirit of commercial adventure. In this last respect, even the Spaniards and the Portuguese were ahead of their English competitors. And here in America, where our population is a conglomerate of all the races of the earth, the first generation born on American soil, be its parents English, Irish, Dutch, French, or Spaniards, is sure to show the characteristic American trait, — a disposition to toil, to dare, and to save. Results so general can be accounted for only by some peculiarity in the air that we breathe, or in the institutions that we live under. And as the researches of chemists have proved that our atmosphere contains about the usual proportion of oxygen and nitrogen, I am inclined to refer this peculiarity altogether to our "institutions"; — understanding, however, this term in its widest sense; making it comprehend not merely our republican polity, our national and State organizations, but our republican habits, feelings, and tendencies, — our disposition to manage our own affairs in our own town-meetings, and there to allot the greatest trust to him who is distinguished above all others by this very American trait, this disposition to toil, to dare, and to save, be his race or parentage what it may.

First, then, *security* in the receipt and enjoyment of the fruits of labor is not merely the great stimulus, but the indispensable prerequisite, to general industry and frugality. "Security" means not only the absence of war, tyranny, intestine commotions, and all other causes of spoliation, interference, and undue control, but the absence of all *dread*, of all probability, or possibility, of such unhappy contingencies. Labor and enterprise are elastic, and will quickly recover from the effects of any sudden or unexpected misfortune, however great, if the workmen or adventurers *think* they have a reasonable protection against its recurrence. If the calamity is such that the country is not actually depopulated by it, the next harvest will make up the temporary scarcity of food, and less than a year's labor will replace the customary stock of manufactured commodities; for the circulating capital of the manufacturer is usually "turned over," as the phrase goes, or consumed and reproduced, oftener than once in a year; and if his fixed capital, his machines, buildings, and other improvements, require a little longer time for their *value* to be restored, (the potent influence of *credit* causing them to be actually rebuilt in a very short period,) it is still matter of certain calculation, that a few years will make up the loss. But if a dread should hang over the people, lest a similar catastrophe should soon recur, few would labor at all, and those few would put but little heart into their work; since few are willing to produce what others are to consume. The general feeling would be like that which prevails on shipboard, after all hope of saving the vessel is lost: "let us eat and drink, for to-morrow we die."

Security has been well defined by Mr. Mill as "the completeness of the protection which society affords to its members. This consists of protection *by* the government, and *against* the government. The latter is the more important. Where a person known to possess anything worth taking away can expect nothing but to have it torn from him, with every circumstance of tyrannical violence, by the agents of a rapacious government, it is not likely that many will exert themselves to produce much more than necessaries. This is the acknowledged explanation of the poverty of many fertile tracts of Asia, which were once prosperous and populous." Take, for instance, the very fertile and finely situated tract, once called Mesopotamia, from its position between the two great rivers Tigris and Euphrates, — now a parched and dusty plain, roamed over, rather than inhabited, by a few tribes of half-starved Bedouin Arabs. Yet there stood, and there now stand the ruins of, the great city of Nineveh, that "exceeding great city," of three days' journey, which probably contained over half a million of inhabitants. What a vast suburban and rural population must have existed in the immediate vicinity, in order to supply that great and wealthy metropolis with food! Over three thousand years ago, the banks of the Tigris must have been nearly as populous as are now the banks of the Seine near Paris. Their depopulation and consequent aridity, but few traces now remaining of the gigantic works by which that great plain was formerly irrigated, must be ascribed to the constant sense of insecurity arising from many changes of dynasty, predatory inroads, invasion and conquest, and the rigors of war exercised by barbarian conquerors. Yet these invasions, so far as appears from history, were not so frequent, but that the people might with ease have recovered from them during the intervals, had not the constant fear that they might recur at any day gradually paralyzed all effort, till the nation at last wasted away, and a feeble remnant sought shelter among the mountains, leaving that fertile plain to desolation.

Such are the evils of a government which cannot withstand aggression from abroad. Hardly less injurious in its effects is the government which is too feeble or indolent to protect the people against themselves; which cannot enforce the laws, or guard the community against the machinations and violence of the turbulent, the discontented, and the ambitious, so that society is a constant prey to rapine, confusion, and civil broils. Hence the present condition of Mexico and most of the South American republics, where, though the soil and climate are among the finest on earth, and mineral wealth abounds, yet agriculture is impeded, trade languishes, and manufactures cannot be established, the bonds of society being virtually dissolved, and the country wasted by anarchy and misrule.

Arbitrary exactions, uncertain in amount, and uncertain as to the time when they will be made, do vastly more injury than larger amounts taken by fixed and regular taxation. Industry will accommodate itself to heavy burdens, and even flourish under them, if the pressure be equable and constant, so that all calculations respecting the future may be made with as much certainty as if there were no weight to support. The regular tax comes to be esteemed as one of the charges, or a part of the cost, of production, — having the same effect as a more rigorous climate, or a less fertile soil, would have, in increasing the amount of labor required. The people of England, for instance, are at this moment taxed more heavily, — they pay a larger sum to their rulers, than was ever levied from a population of equal size by the most cruel and despotic government of ancient times. If it were possible to distribute the enormous weight of English taxation with perfect equality and fairness, making it bear on all interests alike, and on every individual in just proportion to his means, I should be far from considering it as any material obstacle to the prosperity of the country. But the changes which from time to time become necessary, or are thought to be necessary, in that distribution, — the great change, for instance, that was made by the abolition of the Corn Laws, the frequent changes in the sugar duties, and the uncertainty of the amount required by the Poor Laws, — are very serious evils. The change when completed in all its effects, the new law once thoroughly incorporated by time with the old ones, may be an improvement; but the transition is always injurious. Better a bad system, so that it be fixed, than a fluctuating and uncertain one. An alteration of the law, a shifting of the burden, always produces some change in the direction of labor and capital, whereby a portion of the skill already acquired by practice is wasted, a portion of the machinery already built becomes useless, and time and capital must be consumed in learning new employments and constructing new machines. This is one evil caused by change; and another is, that, most of the operations of industry in modern times being complex, and covering much time and space, people are tempted to engage in them only by the nice calculations that are made of their probable ultimate results; any uncertainty as to the manner in which these results may be affected by taxation, any probability that the law may be changed while the process is yet incomplete, may prevent the enterprise from being undertaken at all. It is not too much to say, that, in this country, for the last thirty years, there has not been a time when commercial and manufacturing enterprise was not materially retarded by the apprehension that the Congress then in session, or the ensuing one, might make some important modifications in the tariff of customs-duties.

"The only insecurity," says Mr. Mill, "which is altogether paralyzing to the active energies of producers, is that arising from the government or from persons invested with its authority. Against all other depredators there is a hope of defending one's self. Greece and the Greek colonies in the ancient world, Flanders and Italy in the Middle Ages, by no means enjoyed what any one with modern ideas would call security; the state of society was most unsettled and turbulent; person and property were exposed to a thousand dangers. But they were free countries; they were neither arbitrarily oppressed, nor systematically plundered by their governments. Against other enemies, the individual energy which their institutions called forth enabled them to make successful resistance. Their labor, therefore, was eminently productive, and their riches, while they remained free, were constantly on the increase. The Roman despotism, putting an end to wars and internal conflicts throughout the empire, relieved the subject population from much of the former insecurity; but because it left them under the grinding yoke of its own rapacity," — witness the administration of Verres in Sicily, which has been damned to everlasting fame by the eloquent invective of Cicero, — "they became enervated and impoverished, until they were an easy prey to barbarous but free invaders. They would neither fight nor labor, because they were no longer suffered to enjoy that for which they fought and labored."

"Much of the security of person and property in modern nations is the effect of manners and opinion, rather than of law. There are countries in Europe where the monarch is nominally absolute; but where, from the restraints imposed by established usage, no subject feels practically in the smallest danger of having his possessions arbitrarily seized, or a contribution levied on them by the government." These countries — Russia, for instance — are far better off in respect of security than France, where, not long ago, the institutions of government were nominally not unlike our own, but where there is great probability of a revolution once a fortnight. No government is ever wicked enough to aim directly and avowedly at the encouragement of vice, the distress of innocence, and the punishment of goodness. Even an Asiatic despotism professes, and probably intends, to punish theft, perjury, fraud, and unprovoked injury, in all cases where its own interest is not immediately concerned; that is, of course, in the great majority of cases that arise among its subjects. It may omit many of the forms and precautions that civilized nations have come to observe, as the safeguards of innocence and preservatives against unintentional wrong; it may administer wild justice, but justice is its aim; it wields the sword against unprovoked aggressions upon persons or property, and often with terrible effect.

CHAPTER VIII.

THE INCREASE OF CAPITAL AS AFFECTED BY THE ENCOURAGEMENT OF MANUFACTURES, AND BY THE CONCENTRATION OF THE PEOPLE IN CITIES AND TOWNS.

THE second of the moral causes indicated as affecting the increase of capital is, that such increase is most rapid in any country, when, from the variety of employments that exist there, most of its inhabitants may be engaged in those occupations for which they are peculiarly fitted by nature, which require most skill and intelligence, and in which, consequently, their labor is most productive.

If the labor of one practised and skilful artisan is equal to that of at least three raw hands or rude laborers, then it is very much for the economical interests of a country, that as many as possible of its inhabitants should be skilled artisans, and as few as possible should be raw laborers. We say "as many as possible"; because *some* rude labor is always needed. There must be, in every country, some hewers of wood and drawers of water, — some work that tasks a man's thews and sinews very severely, while it affords but little employment to his brains, — such work as is often performed by machines and domesticated animals, but which the circumstances of time and place sometimes absolutely require to be performed by men, — usually by men who are capable of nothing else. There is a large proportion of such work required in agriculture, where one skilful and careful farmer can profitably direct the exertions of a dozen or more hands, in such operations as ditching, fencing, making hay, and the like. Many, though not *so* many, laborers of this lowest class are also required in manufactures, where numerous skilled and expert hands require to be waited on by mere porters and hewers, in order that the valuable time of the former may not be wasted on the coarser operations that are necessary. Thus the bricklayer must have his hod-carrier; the driver of the steam-engine must have his fireman; the printing-office must have its errand-boys, technically called "devils." There is work even on board a ship at sea, which can only be performed by boys. Commerce demands a higher average of skill and intelligence from those who are engaged in it than any other of the great branches of industry; yet even here, in the various operations subsidiary to the transportation and exchange of goods, there is a considerable demand for this lowest kind of exertion. We say a "demand" for it, because the fact that laborers of this class expect only the lowest rate of wages, causes them to be sought for in preference to all others, when the work is such that they can perform it.

From various causes, there is an abundance of this kind of labor in the market in almost every country. The stinted bounty of nature, casualties that lessen the average capacity, vice, ignorance, and extreme poverty, are among the causes which here keep the supply up to the demand, and, in nearly all cases, make it go greatly beyond the demand. The only evil to be dreaded is a superfluity of this class of laborers, — a superfluity which sometimes, as at present in Great Britain and Ireland, exists to a frightful extent. Popular education, as that phrase is commonly understood, meaning the general cultivation of the intellect, though unquestionably a very powerful agent for lessening this evil, is not the only preservative against it. A man wholly uneducated in the common meaning of the word, that is, unable either to write or read, may yet become a very expert workman in the finest and most difficult kinds of manufacture. On the other hand, men may be quite well taught, and still be unable to get any but the rudest sort of work to do, or to obtain employment more than half the time even at that. The Scotch, for instance, are a very well educated people; the standard of instruction among them, *for all classes*, is probably quite as high as it is here in New England. Yet there is as large a surplus of rude labor in Scotland, in proportion to its population, as in England, — probably larger.

The loss which a country suffers by having a large portion of its people condemned to this rude labor, when most of them are capable, or may be made capable, of much finer work or more effective industry, is very great; *so* great, indeed, that I doubt whether any other single cause of national poverty can equal it. Men are differently constituted by nature, or by those circumstances which, in early youth, determine the bent of their inclinations and the applicability of their powers to one task rather than another. The labor of a people is effectually used only when the field of employment in the country offers scope for every variety of taste and talent, and when no formidable or insuperable obstacles prevent any individual from finding out and performing just that task which God and nature appointed him to do. If agriculture alone is pursued, all the mechanical skill of the people is wasted,—all their fitness for commerce, all their enterprise in trade, is wasted. If four millions are obliged to be rude laborers, when three millions of them might be skilled artisans, the labor of one of the latter being supposed to be equal in value to that of at least three of the former, then the value actually created is to the value which might be created as four is to ten; in other words, the yearly product of the national industry might be two and a half times greater than it is; and the yearly unproductive consumption need not be at all increased, since, in either case, there would be four millions of people to be supplied with food, clothing, and shelter. Of course,—and here comes the application of the principle to present circumstances,—the country could afford to pay a higher price for their manufactures, for the sake of having the articles manufactured at home. They could afford to spend more, for they would have more to spend.

For illustration, we will take the two extreme cases of Ireland and Massachusetts. To avoid burdening the memory with statistics, we shall employ the nearest round numbers. The population of Ireland, in 1851, was about 6½ millions; that of Massachusetts, in 1850, was about one million. According to the Irish census of 1841, which was taken with extraordinary pains and minuteness, the whole number of *families* in Ireland was one million and a half, of whom one million, or just two thirds of the whole, were engaged in agriculture;

and only three hundred and fifty thousand families, or a little less than one fourth of the whole, were employed in manufactures and trade. It is obvious that the agricultural population was excessive, for in England, where agriculture is carried to greater perfection than in any other country on the face of the globe, there was but one agricultural family to every thirty-four acres of arable land, while in Ireland there was one such family to every fourteen acres. In Massachusetts, according to the census of 1850, out of a free male population, over fifteen years of age, amounting to 295,300, about 194,600, or nearly 66 per cent, were employed in commerce, manufactures, and the mechanic arts, mining, and navigation, and only 84,700, or somewhat over 28 per cent, in agriculture and its subsidiary employments.* The proportions in Ireland, as we have seen, were about 23 per cent in commerce and manufactures, and 66 per cent in agriculture.

Now contrast the condition of the people in the two countries. The paupers in Massachusetts are about one in fifty of the whole population; but as nearly half of these are recent English or Irish immigrants, principally Irish, the real proportion is about one in a hundred. In Ireland, according to the Returns of the Poor Law Commissioners, the whole number of paupers who received relief in the workhouses during the year ending September 29th, 1851, added to the number of out-door poor who were assisted at the public charge, was 755,357, or nearly twelve per cent of the total population. Three years before, the number of paupers was at least thrice as great. The cost of relieving these 755,357 paupers was nearly six millions of dollars. It should be remembered, also, that during the five years preceding September, 1851, the emigration from Ireland averaged at least 200,000 persons a year,

* The numbers actually returned by the census are, 146,002, or 49 per cent, in "commerce, trade, manufactures, mechanic arts, and mining"; 55,699, or 19 per cent, in "agriculture," 57,942, or 20 per cent, in "labor not agricultural," and 19,598, or 7 per cent, in "sea and river navigation." As navigation is subsidiary to commerce, I have added the number of persons engaged in it to those returned under the head of commerce; and have also ranked under the same head 28,971 persons, or one half of those enumerated as engaged in "labor not agricultural." As the compiler of the census remarks that, although *laborers* were regarded as "non-agricultural," many of them are probably farm laborers, I have added the other half of their number to the agricultural population.

most of the emigrants being of that class who would probably have become paupers had they remained at home.

Can we, then, attribute this great, this frightful difference, to the unequal distribution of the bounty of Providence, — to the fact that the Irish are crowded together on land not broad or fertile enough to supply them all with food, while we in Massachusetts are fattening on the spontaneous riches of the earth? According to the estimate which we have already formed of the effect upon national well-being of what are termed "natural advantages," this is not very likely to be the case; but let us look at the facts. Here, where our only natural exports are ice and granite, it is notorious that we do not raise food enough for our own consumption. We import nearly all our wheat, the chief article of our bread-stuffs, and also buy from the other States large droves of cattle. But Ireland raises more food than is necessary for her sustenance, and exports annually vast quantities of provision to England. Her export of the cereal grains, chiefly oats, and of other edible products of the soil, increased, from less than seven millions of bushels in 1817, to twenty-six millions of bushels in 1845. Even in 1847, the year of famine in Ireland, nearly eight millions of bushels of grain and meal were exported; and in the following year, which was one of great scarcity, these exports rose again to sixteen millions. The exportation of beef, pork, butter, and other animal products, has also gone on increasing, though in a lower ratio. In each of the four years from 1846 to 1850, about 200,000 horned cattle and 250,000 sheep and lambs were shipped from Ireland to Great Britain. It is certain, then, that the penuriousness of nature is not the source of the difficulty; it is not fertile land which is wanting, but wealth; and the people do not produce *that*, because the field of employment is so limited that very little except rude labor is possible. There is no opening for the exertion of skill and enterprise, and whatever natural qualifications the people may possess in these respects cannot be developed.

Nearly the whole native population of Massachusetts being occupied with tasks that require skill, care, and ingenuity, we depend for a supply of rude labor almost exclusively upon immigrant foreigners. These do all the coarse work in building our railways and canals, and in the several other occupations that require nothing but muscular strength. The rude labor, to which alone they have been accustomed, has so incapacitated them for higher tasks, that it is now an established principle in our large manufactories, that the machines cannot profitably be worked if more than one third of the operatives be foreigners. It is not only more economical to pay the higher wages required by native workmen; but foreigners generally, and the Irish in particular, cannot be employed at all, except in that small proportion to the whole number of hands which will make it possible to restrict them to the lower or less difficult tasks. Because our own people are so generally trained to the finer and more productive branches of industry, new expedients are constantly invented by them for performing the drudgery by machines. The locomotive steam excavators, that are often employed on the line of a proposed railroad, and the various contrivances that have been patented for cutting and hoisting ice on our ponds, are instances of this sort of labor-saving machinery. The superfluity and consequent cheapness of rude labor in foreign countries render these expedients unnecessary, and the work is profitably done by hand.

Consider the rapid growth of capital in this State, which is the result of this most effective application of its industry, and also the immense unproductive consumption of the people,—their ample supply, not only of the necessaries, but of the comforts and luxuries of life; and contrast these with the poverty and destitution of Ireland. The productive part of the consumption leads to the increase of the national wealth; the unproductive part is an index of the general well-being of the community. In Ireland, the people are literally too poor to create a demand for anything but potatoes; and the country therefore affords hardly any market either for British or Irish manufactures. There is but little opening there for the mechanic arts, or for the many small occupations which are created by a due regard for the comforts and conveniences of life. The field of employment for skilled industry is consequently limited almost to a span, and the bulk of the people are driven back upon rude labor in agriculture,—to ditching, cutting turf, and planting potatoes; the meagre returns from such toil being hardly sufficient to keep them from starvation. The United

States, on the other hand, afford a better market for manufactured goods than any other country of equal population on the globe; because the universal prosperity of the community enables them to consume more. If the relation of cause and effect in this proposition be reversed, so as to say that the people consume more because they produce more, it will amount to the same thing, and be equally favorable for the purposes of the argument. More wealth is created, more is consumed, and the amount of enjoyment is thereby increased.

Unquestionably, we pay a somewhat higher price for our manufactured goods, as a return for the privilege of manufacturing them at home, and thereby having a field of employment for our skilled labor. But what does this tax amount to? The average duty levied by the present tariff on our chief articles of import is less than thirty per cent. But as one of the chief objects of a protective duty is to guard against the injurious fluctuation of prices in foreign markets, whereby we might be deluged with imported goods one year, and be very scantily supplied with them the next, the duty is fixed with reference to the lowest price at which they are ever sold abroad, and not with reference to the average price. The effect of a protective duty of thirty per cent, then, at the utmost, is to raise the *average* price fifteen per cent.

Whenever we have occasion for any of these small articles, we are obliged to spend a dollar for what might be obtained for eighty-five cents, if we would buy of foreigners; that is, we might save this fifteen cents, if we were willing to give up all our home manufactures, all opportunity for earning high wages by the exhibition of skill and ingenuity, and to confine the whole people to the comparatively rude pursuits of agriculture, thereby overstocking the market with food, and reducing the gains of farmers all over the country. Ireland has acted upon this rule, laid down by most political economists, — always to buy in the cheapest market, whatever may be the effect upon domestic enterprise. Grain and other provision can be raised most cheaply in Ireland, owing to the low rate of wages there; manufactures can be produced to best advantage in England, owing to the abundance of English capital. Ireland, therefore, raises food to buy English manufactures with; and the present condition of the Irish people is the consequence. They have the advantage, it is true, of the offer of the manufactured goods at prices fifteen per cent less than what they command in America;—an advantage which would be more sensibly felt, if the Irish were not too poor to purchase them at any price.

The proposition, I think, can be laid down as a general one, that a country, the population of which is chiefly or altogether devoted to agriculture, cannot become wealthy, whatever may be the fertility of its soil or the favorableness of its situation. Of course, its inhabitants must buy manufactures with food; that is, they must exchange the products of rude labor for the products of skilled labor; that is, again, they must give the labor of three persons for the labor of one person. The general principle of economical science is, to cause the industry of a country to take that direction in which it can be applied to the greatest advantage. Now the fertility of the soil is one advantage, and the capacity of the people for the higher departments of labor, their skill and enterprise, is another. There is no reason for allowing either of these advantages to remain latent or unworked; and in choosing between them, we are to be decided by their comparative amount and importance. Fortunate as this country is in the extent of its territory and the richness of its soil, this advantage is as nothing,—nay, it would turn out to our positive detriment,—if, in consideration of it, we should sacrifice the talents and the energies of our people,—if we should doom our whole population to the rude labor of turning up the earth, for the sake of the trifling advantage of purchasing our manufactured goods at a little lower price.

Even Adam Smith remarks,* that "A small quantity of manufactured produce purchases a great quantity of rude produce. A trading and manufacturing country, therefore, naturally purchases, with a small part of its manufactured produce, a great part of the rude produce of other countries; while, on the contrary, a country without trade and manufactures is generally obliged to purchase, at the expense of a great part of its rude produce, a very small part of the manufactured produce of other countries. The one exports what can subsist and accommodate but a very few, and imports the subsistence and

* *Wealth of Nations*, Book IV. Chap. IX.

accommodation of a great number. The other exports the accommodation and subsistence of a great number, and imports that of a very few only. The inhabitants of the one must always enjoy a much greater quantity of subsistence than what their own lands, in the actual state of their cultivation, could afford. The inhabitants of the other must always enjoy a much smaller quantity."

One mode in which the encouragement of skilled labor, leading to the interfusion of manufactures and commerce with agriculture, favors the increase of national capital, is, by concentrating the population in cities and towns. Agriculture is necessarily diffusive in its effects; the laborers must be distributed over the whole face of the territory which they cultivate. A few large cities spring up at great distances from each other, as an outlet for the commerce created by the exchange of the surplus agricultural products for manufactured goods and other necessaries brought from abroad. The great agricultural districts of Continental Europe, the wheat-plains of Poland and Southern Russia, find an outlet at the cities of Dantzic and Odessa; and we may remark in passing, that the poverty and general low condition of the inhabitants of these districts show the effects of confining a whole population to the rude labor of tilling the ground. It may be, that, from their low capacity, and their want of education and general intelligence, they are incapable of anything better. If so, the fact only strengthens our argument; wherever the capacity exists, if it be not developed, if a field of employment be not offered to it, the same results must follow. Manufactures and commerce, on the other hand, requiring a great division of labor, and also that the participators in the work should be near each other, necessarily create a civic population. They will only flourish in cities and towns, and they are the only means of creating cities and towns.

This principle, perhaps sufficiently obvious in itself, is strikingly illustrated by the differences among the States of this Union. Our Southern and Southwestern States are almost exclusively agricultural; and south of the northern boundary of Virginia and Kentucky, there is but one city, New Orleans, of the first class, numbering over 100,000 inhabitants, and but two cities of the second class, Charleston and Louisville, each numbering over 40,000. These cities, of course, have sprung up from the same causes which sustain Dantzic and Odessa; they afford an outlet for the surplus produce of the vast agricultural districts which depend upon them; manufactures have hardly contributed at all to their growth. If we reckon as civic population those only who dwell in cities or towns having at least 11,000 inhabitants each, Massachusetts and Rhode Island, two manufacturing States, with an aggregate population of only 1,142,059, have a greater civic population than these ten agricultural States, who number in the aggregate over eight millions. The civic population of the two manufacturing States is nearly one third of their whole number; that of the ten agricultural States is about one twenty-fifth of the whole. The cities in Massachusetts and Rhode Island have been created almost entirely by manufacturing enterprise, these States not being remarkable for surplus agricultural produce. Wherever there is a considerable fall of water, affording power to move machinery, there a new city springs up, though the soil in the neighborhood should be as barren as the desert of Sahara. But, under the demand for agricultural produce created by that city, the dry sand and the hard rock are converted into gardens of fruit and vegetables; while the plain of Eastern Virginia, once almost unsurpassed for fertility, its powers being now exhausted, is relapsing in part into its primitive wild condition.

Cities and towns are the great agents and tokens of the increase of national opulence, and the progress of civilization. The revival of effective industry, which preceded, and in part caused, the revival of learning in Europe, took place through the agency of the free towns and great trading cities, which sprang up most numerously in Germany and Italy, where they afforded a refuge for the arts and the pursuits of peace. Their establishment was the first effective blow given to the feudal institutions of the Continent. Commerce and manufactures, to which their walls afforded protection against the chances of war and the rapacity of the warlike nobles, "gradually introduced order and good government, and with them the liberty and security of individuals, among the inhabitants of the country, who had before lived almost in a continual state of war with their neighbors, and of servile dependency upon their superiors. By affording a great and ready market for the rude produce of the country, they gave encouragement to its cultivation and further improvement." The word *civilization* itself, as if to indicate the origin and home of the thing, is derived from *civis*, the inhabitant of a city. Sismondi attributes the greater humanizing and civilizing influence of the colonies of the ancients over those of the moderns to the fact that the former founded cities, while the latter spread themselves over much land. In the town, man is in the presence of man, not in solitude, abandoned to himself and his passions. The history of the colonization of the borders of the Mediterranean, he says, might also be called the history of the civilization of the human race.

The Egyptians, the Phœnicians, the Greeks, and the Romans successively formed colonies upon the same general plan. Each of these nations became in succession the leaders, the masters, of the civilized world, in refinement, learning, and the arts; and the colonies which they established were the means of diffusing these blessings among the rude tribes within whose territories the new settlements were formed. When the mother country became too populous, when the inhabitants of its wall-inclosed cities became straitened for room, detachments of them were sent out to found new homes for themselves on the coasts of other lands. The colony was to take care of itself, to be independent of the mother country, from the outset. Hence, to protect themselves against the savage tribes among whom they came to dwell, they were obliged, as the first step, to build a city and encircle it with fortifications. Within its walls they all slept; and they did not wander so far from its precincts during the daytime, but that they could at any hour hear the trumpet-call, which, like the alarm-bell of modern times, might summon them back to the defence of the walls. Hence they cultivated only a narrow territory, lying within sight of, or at a short distance from, the city; and to obtain food from this restricted space for their whole number, they were obliged to exhaust all the arts of cultivation upon it; it was tilled, and it bloomed, like a garden. For greater security, a portion of it was generally inclosed within the fortifications. This *pomœrium*, or cultivated space under the walls, was usually divided into small strips, and allotted to the several heads of families among the citizens. A portion of the colonists devoted themselves to tillage, and raised food enough, or nearly enough, for the whole city. A larger portion within the walls applied themselves to the mechanic arts and to commerce, exchanging their manufactured goods for food, either with their own agricultural citizens, or with the native inhabitants of the soil, when they could open peaceful intercourse with them, or with the denizens of other shores, perhaps of the mother country, to which they sent their ships. As they needed only a narrow strip of territory, which they often obtained by fair purchase from the aborigines, the hostility of the latter was not excited; and the mutual benefits of trade being soon felt, the natives came to regard the colonists as their benefactors and best friends. A knowledge of the arts, a taste for the comforts and luxuries of life, learning and religion, were thus diffused among them; and in their simplicity and gratitude, they often reverenced the authors of their civilization as superhuman beings, and paid them divine honors. Many, if not most, of the gods and goddesses of ancient mythology were originally only the founders of art-bringing, knowledge-and-religion-diffusing colonies, whose beneficent influence, handed down to grateful remembrance by tradition, — by the spoken, not the written word, — really seemed to admiring posterity divine. The colony, the city, was opulent and refined from the beginning; founded by the most enterprising citizens of the mother country, who brought their wealth, their cultivated tastes, and their industrious and adventurous habits along with them, it became almost at once a rival of the parent city in learning, industry, and the arts. Temples and theatres were built; the drama flourished; schools of eloquence were established; manufactures of costly and elegant fabrics were begun; and commerce started into life with all the vigor of youth and the large resources of manhood.

Brief as this sketch is, the classical reader will recognize in it, I think, the principal features of those colonies which the Phœnicians established along the northern shore of Africa, the Greeks along the coasts of Asia Minor, Sicily, and Magna Græcia or Southern Italy, and the Romans in Gaul and Spain. Carthage, the great commercial and manufacturing city of ancient times, the rival of Rome, may be taken in its history as a type of them all; and in the fanciful picture which, many years after its destruction, the Roman poet drew of its supposed origin, of the scene which it presented while the walls of the city were building, we recognize what was the idea, even so late as Virgil's time, of the mode of founding a colony.*

Modern colonies, on the other hand, are, from the outset, dependencies of the mother country, to which they constantly look for protection and support. They are often planted by those who do not intend to reside there permanently, but simply wish to gather again in a new country the wealth which they have dissipated in an old one, and then to return to their former home in order to enjoy it. Thus relieved from all fear of attack from the aborigines, their first care is to get possession of as much land as possible, this being the most obvious and plentiful source of riches. Individuals or joint-stock companies obtain grants of land measured by the league; and their rapacity provokes the vengeance of the natives, at the same time that it leads to their own isolation and defencelessness. The territory which they acquire is out of all proportion to their wants, their physical strength, or their capital; they cultivate only here and there a very fertile spot, where the powers of the soil are soon spent by a succession of exhausting crops; and in the careless style of agriculture to which they become accustomed, through their dependence on the extent and natural richness of their land, is soon lost all remembrance of the

---

* "Conveniunt, quibus aut odium crudele tyranni,
Aut metus acer erat; naves, quæ forte paratæ,
Corripiunt, onerantque auro; portantur avari
Pygmalionis opes pelago: dux fœmina facti.
Devenêre locos, ubi nunc ingentia cernes
Mœnia, surgentemque novæ Carthaginis arcem:
Mercatique solum, facti de nomine Byrsam,
Taurino quantum possent circumdare tergo.
. . . .
Jamque ascendebant collem, qui plurimus urbi
Imminet, adversasque adspectat desuper arces.
Miratur molem Æneas, magalia quondam;
Miratur portas, strepitumque, et strata viarum.
Instant ardentes Tyrii: pars ducere muros,
Molirique arcem, et manibus subvolvere saxa;
Pars optare locum tecto, et concludere sulco.
Jura, magistratusque legunt, sanctumque senatum.
Hîc portus alii effodiunt; hîc alta theatris
Fundamenta locant alii; immanesque columnas
Rupibus excidunt, scenis decora alta futuris."

agricultural art and science which they brought with them from their old home. Widely separated from each other, amply supplied with food by the bounty of nature, but destitute of the manufactured articles on which depend the comforts and even the decencies of life, out of the reach of the law, and beyond the sphere of education, they rapidly approximate the condition of the savages whom they have just dispossessed. They become "squatters," "bushmen," "backwoodsmen," whose only enjoyments are hunting and intoxication, whose only schoolroom is the forest, and whose sense of justice is manifested only by the processes of Lynch law. They are doomed to the solitary, violent, brutal existence, which destroys all true civilization, all sympathy with other men, though it increases strength of body, adroitness, courage, and the spirit of adventure. The want of local attachments, and an insatiable thirst for wandering and adventure, are, I fear, the most striking traits in the character of the whole population of our Mississippi valley. Their homes even in that fair region are but homes of yesterday; they had only pitched their camps on the banks of the Ohio and the Wabash, while on their way to the Sacramento and the Columbia. The truant disposition which carried them over the Alleghanies, hurries them onward to the Rocky Mountains. I do not go so far as an eminent thinker of our own day, who has expressed in eloquent language his fears lest these constant migrations should lead our countrymen back to barbarism; but it is certain that the "pioneers of civilization," as they have been fondly called, leave laws, education, and the arts, all the essential elements of civilization, behind them. They may be the means of partially civilizing others, but they are in great danger of brutalizing themselves.

Strangely enough, the only colony of modern times founded on the principles which governed the ancients in the establishment of their colonies is one commenced by a set of half-crazed fanatics in our own far-distant territory of Utah or Deseret. Here, as well as at their former place of settlement in Illinois, the Mormons appear to have begun their colony by founding a city, within or near which their whole population is to be collected, so that the mechanic arts and all branches of manufacture may be established at the same time that they make their first attempts in agriculture. The name of their present chief city in Deseret is New Hierusalem, and it is situated on the right bank of the Western Jordan, which empties into their Dead Sea. I borrow the following account of it from an Historical Discourse, delivered some years since, by Thomas L. Kane.

"Its houses are spread, to command as much as possible the farms, which are laid out in wards or cantons, with a common fence to each ward. The farms in wheat already cover a space greater than the District of Columbia, over all of which they have completed the canals and other arrangements for bountiful irrigation, after the manner of the cultivators of the East. The houses are distributed over an area nearly as large as the city of New York. They will soon have completed a large common storehouse and granary, and a great-sized public bath-house. One of the many wonderful thermal springs of the valley, a white sulphur water of the temperature of 102° Fahrenheit, with a head of 'the thickness of a man's body,' they have already brought into the town for this purpose."

It is remarkable, that one of the latest improvements or discoveries in economical science, Mr. Wakefield's theory of colonization, consists in the recognition of the fact, that the ancient mode of planting colonies is far preferable to the modern one. Mr. Wakefield perceived that a country cannot have a productive agriculture unless it has a large town population, who may supply the agriculturists with manufactured articles, while the agriculturists supply them with food. Both parties are thus furnished with a market for their surplus produce, and with the articles that they most need in exchange for it. He showed that the modern fashion of establishing new settlements,—"setting down a number of families side by side, each on its own piece of land, and all employing themselves in exactly the same manner,—though, under favorable circumstances, it may assure to those families a rude abundance of mere necessaries, can never be other than unfavorable to great production or rapid growth." The situation of Oregon hardly ten years ago affords a striking illustration of this truth; the settlers, for want of a market, were obliged to feed their horses with the finest wheat, while their own dwellings were nearly destitute of all the comforts of life. Wakefield's "system consists of arrangements for securing that every colony shall have, from the first, a town population bearing due proportion to its agricultural, and that the cultivators of the soil shall not be so widely scattered as to be deprived by distance of the benefit of that town population as a market for their produce." When land was plenty and free immigrants scarce in New Holland, the government found it convenient to make liberal gifts of territory; and accordingly, tracts varying in size from 10,000 to 50,000 acres were granted to various individuals. I borrow from the North American Review a brief outline of the system.

Mr. Wakefield argued thus: — "The welfare of any community depends very much upon such a division of labor as shall fill every trade, profession, and employment with good men, and not overload any of them. If land in any country is so cheap that all are able to become landholders, there will be no laborers, no farm-hands, or mechanics; a semi-barbarism will follow; no growth in wealth or civilization will take place, and the country will be stationary or retrograde. If, therefore, you would have a colony progressive and civilized, you must put your lands so high as to keep a proper proportion of the inhabitants in the labor-market seeking employment, and yet not so high as to prevent as many from buying real estate as can use it to advantage with the help of such laborers. If, then, England wishes Australia to grow in riches and goodness, let her sell the lands at a fixed price, never taking less, and in fixed quantities, never selling less; and let her apply the revenue arising from these sales to the transportation of free, honest laborers to the points where they are needed. In this way, the labor-market of New Holland will be supplied; the expense of supplying working hands will be paid by the lands of the colony; no more land will be taken up than can be worked to advantage; population will be concentrated, wealth will accumulate, and knowledge and virtue advance."

Mr. Wakefield's theory was good, but a practical difficulty obstructed its application. The government, adopting his views, put their lands up to a high price; and the immigrants, consequently, instead of purchasing them, or of remaining as laborers on the lands purchased by others, pushed farther into the interior, and "squatted" on the best land they could find, without paying anything. In those vast unsettled regions,

9

they knew very well that they were out of reach of the sheriff. Thus, the very measures adopted for concentrating them, and keeping them within the range of civilization and law, led to their wider dispersion and utter lawlessness.

It is curious that the United States system of disposing of the public lands, adopted in all its essential features as far back as 1800, has worked better than any other plan which has yet been devised. The land is carefully divided by the government surveys into townships six miles square, each of these being subdivided into thirty-six *sections*, of one square mile, or 640 acres, each. All is held at a minimum price of $ 1.25 an acre; and the sales are made at public auction, as rapidly as the progress of the population seems to require. Lands which will not bring $ 1.25 an acre at the public sale, are still held by the government subject to entry at any future time, at private sale and at the minimum price. Any person can select a quarter, or even an eighth section, — 160 or 80 acres, — wherever he can find one surveyed and not yet sold, and, by making a record of his intention to occupy and settle it himself, he can secure what is called the "preëmption right"; — a right which, partly by the force of law and partly by custom, amounts to a privilege of purchasing that land at the minimum price of $ 1.25 an acre, whenever the government shall think proper to sell it, which it will do when the settlement is so far advanced as to render it probable that most of the land in the vicinity will bring that price. Thus the actual settler in truth obtains his land on credit, though all actual sales are for cash. He has credit till the actual sale is ordered; and some years may intervene, during which he may proceed to clear and cultivate his land, and actually obtain enough from it to make up its price, secure that no one will overbid him, and that he cannot be obliged to pay more than $ 1.25 an acre for it, however great may be his improvements. Five per cent is reserved from the proceeds of the sales, to be expended, three fifths for making roads to the newly settled territory, and two fifths for the support of seminaries of learning therein.

I say this system has worked well, the only evil experienced under it being, that speculators will sometimes buy up large tracts not subject to preëmption right, at the minimum government price, and hold them for an indefinite period, hoping that, as the population gradually close up and concentrate around them, they may again be brought into market at a much advanced price. While thus held, they remain unoccupied, — broad patches of wilderness among the settlements, — obstructing communication between the surrounding lands, and barring out occupation and improvement. But there is a check to this evil in the fact, that such lands are subject to State taxation, though they are tax-free before they are sold by the United States; and the taxes being proportioned to the rise in value of the property, it is not for the interest of the speculators to retain the land a long time.

But the inhabitants of the Western States make a great mistake when they clamor for a reduction of the *minimum* price at which the public lands are now held, and even demand that they shall be offered, in limited quantities, as a free gift to actual settlers. Their object, of course, in making these demands, is to stimulate the spirit of emigration to the West, so that the population there may more speedily become dense, and the value of the lands already settled thus be enhanced. The object is a good one; but if there is any force in the considerations now adduced, the means adopted will tend rather to check than promote its attainment. It is surely not for the interest of sparsely settled States, like Indiana, Illinois, and Michigan, that the great wave of emigration, though broadened and deepened, should only roll over them, to be arrested at last by the farthest limits of Iowa and Minnesota, or perhaps to pass much farther, and, dashing against the side of the Rocky Mountains, to throw its spray over their summits into Oregon and California. But we may see that any great reduction in the price of the public lands will surely have this effect. The most eligible land in the three States first mentioned has already been taken up by individuals, that portion which yet remains in the hands of government being either less fertile, or more distant from navigable streams and other means of communication, or situated in a less salubrious or convenient region, than the tracts first selected for purchase. They have long been in the market, and have not yet found a buyer. Even now, most of the emigrants pass by them, seeking public lands which are more remote from their former homes, but which, in every other respect, are superior to these long-neglected spots, which a former generation of immigrants have avoided. Any general reduction of the government price could not affect this relative eligibility of the nearer and more distant lands. Reduce the price to nothing, — give away the lands altogether, — and the emigrant will still pass on, pushed forward by the emigrant's fond illusion, that the farther from home, the nearer to El Dorado.

Again, what is most needed for an increase of the prosperity of the West — of that portion of it, at least, which lies on this side of the Mississippi — is, not that the lands yet in the possession of government should become private property, but that the population should be concentrated on the tracts already owned by individuals, though in great part still covered by the primeval forest. To enhance the value of these broad regions, the people must be massed together, towns and cities must be established, manufacturing and commercial industry must be added to agricultural, and the hut of the backwoodsman must give place to the well-furnished abode of civilized and enlightened man. It would be an ill mode of enhancing the value of the farms of individuals, to offer lands in their immediate vicinity at a nominal price, or at no price at all. The passion for owning land, which converts nearly all the new settlers in our Western States into farmers, however ill fitted for such occupation by their previous pursuits, is as injurious to agriculture as to the other great branches of industry. The land is held by those who, from defect of experience or want of capital, are unable to develop its resources, or even to remove the forest from a tithe of their domains. Corn, fuel, and meat are abundant, because prodigal nature affords so many facilities for the production of them, that the skill, enterprise, and knowledge of the cultivator are little needed, and are therefore imperfectly called forth. But man does not live by bread alone; and when this alone is supplied, almost without labor and without stint, he learns to do without many of the requisites even of a low stage of civilization, and allows the wants of his higher nature to remain unsatisfied. The want of a market, and the consequent surplus of agricultural produce, reduce its price so low, that many families find it needless to raise more than is wanted for their own consumption.

Again, the agriculturist has usually but one or two staple

articles — perhaps wheat alone, or cotton alone, or hemp alone — which he can send to a distance and sell to foreigners. These alone are capable of transportation to a distance. But his farm cannot usually be worked to advantage unless he has a market in his immediate neighborhood, at which he can dispose of his green crops, market vegetables, butcher's meat, and other articles, which must be sold on the spot, or not at all. He needs this neighboring market, also, in order that he may purchase conveniently, and at the lowest price, his ploughs, spades, carts, and other farming tools. How is he benefited, then, though we were to grant that he could exchange his wheat for cloth to better advantage by trading with foreigners than with his own countrymen, if he should thereby prevent a manufacturing market town from springing up within a few miles of his farm, and thus altogether lose the sale of many of his products, and be compelled to purchase his tools at a much higher price, or be put to great inconvenience in obtaining them on any terms?

The difficulty is felt, though its true cause is not ascertained; and a general call is made for improving the means of communication, so as to give access to distant markets, when the real want is that of a market near home. This want can be satisfied only by bringing the people together, and turning one half of them from agricultural to manufacturing and mechanic pursuits. The farmer would then find the number of his competitors diminished, the number of buyers of his produce increased, and the articles needed for his domestic comfort cheapened in price; because most of them would be manufactured in his immediate neighborhood, and the expense of transportation from a great distance would be subtracted from their cost. As it is, the State too often bankrupts itself in the gigantic enterprise of creating a system of railroads and canals, so as to gain access to a manufacturing and commercial population on the other side of the Alleghanies, instead of laboring to create such a population within its own territory. Indiana and Illinois, whose united territory measures about ninety thousand square miles, and whose inhabitants, in 1850, numbered nearly 1,840,000, had but one city, Chicago, which contained over twenty-five thousand inhabitants, and but one other, Indianapolis, having over eight thousand. Has it been

9*

a benefit to these States, that the cheapness of the public lands has recently borne the tide of emigration onward into Iowa and Minnesota, instead of arresting it by the left bank of the Mississippi? In our opinion, the interests of these States, and of the emigrants themselves, would be most effectually promoted by raising the price of the public lands to a point which would really keep them out of the market for twenty years to come.

It is remarked by an intelligent English traveller in the United States, Professor Johnston, that "the wheat-exporting regions of North America have been gradually shifting their locality, and retiring inland and towards the West." During the middle and latter part of the last century, the banks of the Hudson and the Delaware, and the flats of the lower St. Lawrence, were the granary of America; the western part of New York, and especially the Genesee country, succeeded these; then came Ohio and Canada West; and now, a large portion of the surplus wheat, destined for exportation to Europe, is drawn from Michigan, Wisconsin, Iowa, and even Minnesota. The reasons for this change are to be found, partly in the migratory disposition of the people, and partly in their imperfect and exhausting processes of agriculture. The influx of population into the neighborhood causes the lands to rise so rapidly in value, that the deterioration of the soil, under too constant and exhausting crops, becomes comparatively of little moment. Little attention is therefore paid to manuring or to establishing a due rotation of crops. Only the cheapest system of husbandry, and that productive of the quickest returns, without regard to the effects produced by such tillage in the long run upon the inherent fertility of the ground, can enable the farmer to maintain competition in the market with the supplies poured in from the newly opened wheat-regions farther west, where the land has been obtained at a nominal price, and its virgin powers seem inexhaustible. Tired of a contest in which he is subject to a constantly increasing disadvantage, the New York farmer at last sells his farm, and himself migrates westward, secure of obtaining a larger and more fertile tract of land at a low cost. But in Iowa or Wisconsin, he soon finds that he has only bartered one disadvantage for many. The cost of transporting his wheat to market is now so great, that the price on the ground hardly pays the expenses of cultivation. Labor is dear, and difficult to be had at any price, as few will work for wages, when they can obtain farms for themselves at a nominal price and on long credit. All the evils of a residence on the frontier make themselves felt, and a remedy for them is but slowly introduced, as the means of transportation are improved, and a few of the simpler mechanic arts begin to be practised in the vicinity, and to afford a nucleus for the settlement of a town. The emigrants of a later day come forward, but, instead of settling down and completing the half-formed village, they push on and begin rival settlements farther still in the interior. Then competition begins anew, and the old contest with lessening prices and increasing expenses of cultivation must be renewed. The great evil in the Old World, especially among commercial and manufacturing nations, arises from the undue concentration of the people in cities, the improvements in the implements and processes of agriculture requiring every year a smaller and smaller number of laborers for the tillage of the fields. Here in America, the difficulty is of just the opposite character; the population is thinly dispersed, cities are found only at great distances from each other, and the processes of agriculture, as well as of most of the arts of life, tend rather to deterioration than improvement. As Professor Johnston remarks, "were the population as fond of their homes, and as stationary in numbers, as in the central regions of Northern Europe, — as quiescent in character, their labor as small in money value, and everywhere as abundant, and their institutions as repressive of exuberant energy, — this primitive condition of the agricultural practice would be both less felt among themselves, and a matter of less observation to foreign countries."

CHAPTER IX.

THE INCREASE OF CAPITAL AS AFFECTED BY THE ADVANTAGES AND REWARDS WHICH ARE HELD OUT TO THE POSSESSORS OF WEALTH.

THE next stimulus of labor and frugality which we have to consider is, the prospect that the savings when made, or the capital when accumulated, will be attended with a high rate of profit, and by a large proportion of physical comfort, social consideration, and political influence.

Necessity is the first and most effective spur to exertion. We have wants that *must* be satisfied; we must eat and drink, or we perish. But observe that labor or exertion tends only to the *production* of wealth, and that our natural desires urge us to consume the product just as soon as it is created. For the *accumulation* of capital, or the growth of national opulence, we must be willing not only to work, but to save. Now, the greatest of all encouragements to frugality is the sure prospect that our savings will contribute largely to our comfort, will elevate our position in society, and add to the estimation in which we are held in the community, and to the power which we actually wield. No man will practise self-denial for nothing; take away the chance of using his accumulations to advantage, and every one, to use the popular phrase, will spend as he goes. It is not enough to prove to the laborer, that what he does not spend to-day he will be able to spend to-morrow. There is some hazard, at least, that he may lose it before the morrow comes; and if an *equal amount* of enjoyment can be had with it *now*, he will be apt to secure that enjoyment as soon as possible. But when he sees that the enjoyment, if postponed, may be considerably increased, he will be anxious to save; and this anxiety will be greater in proportion to the probable rate of increase, and to the comforts and immunities which the use of the accumulation may bring. The greater the consideration and influence which attend the possession of wealth, the greater will be the temptation to amass wealth.

What has been called "the effective desire of accumulation," says Mr. Mill, "is of unequal strength, not only according to the varieties of individual character, but to the general state of society and civilization. Like all other moral attributes, it is one in which the human race exhibits great differences, conformably to the diversity of its circumstances and the stage of its progress." Again, "in weighing the future against the present, the uncertainty of all things future is a leading element; and that uncertainty is of very different degrees." "All circumstances," therefore, as Mr. Rae observes, which increase "the probability of the provision we make for futurity being enjoyed by ourselves or others, tend to give strength to the effective desire of accumulation. Thus, a healthy climate or occupation, by increasing the probability of life, has a tendency to add to this desire. When engaged in safe occupations, and living in healthy countries, men are much more apt to be frugal, than in unhealthy or hazardous occupations, and in climates pernicious to human life. Sailors and soldiers are prodigals. In the West Indies, New Orleans, the East Indies, the expenditure of the inhabitants is profuse. War and pestilence have always waste and luxury among the evils that follow in their train."

Improvidence may also proceed from intellectual as well as moral causes. "Individuals and communities of a very low state of intelligence," says Mr. Mill, "are always improvident. A certain measure of intellectual development seems necessary to enable absent things, and especially things future, to act with any force on the imagination and will. The effect of want of interest in others in diminishing accumulation will be admitted, if we consider how much saving at present takes place, which has for its object the interest of others rather than of ourselves; — the education of children, their advancement in life, the future interests of other personal connections, the desire of promoting, by the bestowal of money or time, objects of public or private usefulness. If mankind generally were in the state of mind to which some approach was seen in the declining period of the Roman empire, — caring nothing for their heirs, as well as nothing for their friends, the public, or any object which survived them, — they would seldom deny themselves any indulgence for the sake of saving, beyond what was necessary for their own future years; which they would place in life annuities, or some other form which would make its existence and their lives terminate together."

The various stages of civilization depend upon, or are the consequence of, the varying strength of this desire of accumulation. The remnants of Indian tribes which are found in villages upon the banks of the lower St. Lawrence are surrounded by circumstances which ought to secure to them all the comforts of life, and which would enable others to amass wealth. They have abundance of fertile land, already cleared from the forest, and manure in heaps lies beside their huts. Yet such are their apathy and improvidence that they often suffer extreme want; and from the privations thus endured, with occasional intemperance, their number is rapidly diminishing. Yet their apathy does not arise from aversion to labor; for they are industrious enough when the reward of toil is immediate. They are successful in hunting and fishing, and they work with ardor when employed as boatmen on the St. Lawrence. They will even till the ground, if the returns from such labor are speedy and large; they will raise Indian corn, which grows and ripens quickly in Canada, and yields perhaps a hundred fold. But they have not foresight enough to fence their fields, and hence, when the situation is exposed to the incursions of cattle, the culture is abandoned.

Nearly as low, in respect to foresight and prudence, are the emancipated negroes of Hayti and in the British West Indies. In a tropical climate, where little clothing or shelter is needed, and where the ground is so fertile that the labor of a few weeks will supply sustenance for a year, they are content to gain little more than the necessaries of a merely animal existence. "From five acres of land in Jamaica," says Mr. Bigelow, "a negro will supply almost all his physical wants. I have seen growing on a patch of less than two acres, owned by a negro, the bread-fruit, bananas, yams, oranges, shaddocks, cucumbers, beans, pine-apple, plaintain, and chiramoya, besides many kinds of shrubbery and fruits of secondary value." Yet where nature is thus bountiful, flour is allowed to cost from $16 to $18 a barrel, butter 38 cents a pound, eggs from three to five cents apiece, hams 25 cents a pound, and everything else in proportion. "Four fifths of all the grain consumed in Jamaica is grown in the United States, on fields where labor costs more than four times as much, and where every kind of provision but fruit is less expensive." The ease with which life is supported fosters indolence, feebleness, gayety, and *insouciance;* and even when the people pretend to labor, their work is scarcely worth paying for. "In the sugar-mills," we are told, "from twenty to thirty men and women are employed to do what five American operatives would do much better in the same time, with the aid of such labor-saving agencies as would suggest themselves at once to an intelligent mind"; and "this is but one of the thousand ways in which labor is squandered on this island." The people might supply themselves with all the luxuries of the earth; but they are content to live in a swinish abundance of the grossest necessaries, — to be fat and shining, and to sing, chatter, and bask in the sun.

Again, accumulation is rapid when the rate of profits is large. If this rate is so high, that the savings of a few years may be made to produce as much as the original income from which those savings were made, then the prospect of being released altogether from the necessity of labor will stimulate the habit of frugality to the utmost. The average rate of profits in this country is at least twice as large as in Great Britain; for the interest of money here averages over six per cent, while the English government funds yield but three per cent, and the ordinary rate for short loans often falls below that point. But the rate of profits on capital considerably exceeds the rate of interest on money; for he who borrows capital undertakes the risk and care of employing it to advantage; and, of course, he who lends his capital, because unwilling to take that risk and care on himself, will not expect so high a rate for it as he might obtain by using it himself. When a great deal can be made by the use of money, a great deal will be given for the use of it; but still not so much, but that something shall remain to compensate one for the skill and industry that are required to use it to advantage. The average rate of profits in this country may be estimated at twelve per cent a year, while the corresponding rate in England is but six per cent. I speak of the *annual* rate, because, if the dealer turns over his capital twice in a year, he can afford to sell at a profit of only six per cent, though the annual rate for borrowed money is six per cent.

Assuming, then, the annual rate of profits in the United States to be twelve per cent, and that the laborer or dealer uses his savings as his own capital, it is certain that, by postponing the period of consumption or enjoyment for a little over six years, the amount of that enjoyment may be doubled. In England, in order to double the enjoyment, he must practise abstinence for twelve years. It is obvious, then, that where there is the most need of capital, the temptation to accumulate it is strongest, the rate of profits being high, and its growth is most rapid.

In Holland, nearly two centuries ago, after a period of almost unequalled commercial prosperity, the rate of interest fell to about two per cent, the rate of profits suffered a corresponding reduction, and, as a necessary consequence, the growth of capital almost wholly ceased. Holland, in point of commercial and manufacturing enterprise, has been in a stationary, if not a declining state, for about two centuries. The springs of industry are not relaxed, for the people are still sober and laborious; but they lack the energy and the thirst for gain, which caused them, in the seventeenth century, to dot the surface of the globe all over with Dutch colonies. Few will practise abstinence and try to amass wealth, when the rate of profit is but little over four per cent.

The rate of interest in England, in Henry VIII.'s time, was limited to ten per cent, which implies that it had been higher. Under James I. it was reduced to eight, and after the Restoration of the Stuarts, to six per cent. Forty years afterwards, it was again reduced to five, and a continuance of the same causes, as we have seen, has now brought it down to three per cent. But for the enlarged intercourse with foreign lands, which has tempted English capitalists of late years to embark their funds in enterprises abroad, in Mexican mines, in Continental and American railroads, in Austrian and Russian funds, and in United States stocks, it is probable that the interest of money and the profits of stock would, ere now, have sunk to that low point at which the desire to accumulate ceases altogether.

True, "there would be adequate motives for a certain

amount of saving," as Mr. Mill remarks, "even if capital yielded no profit. There would be an inducement to lay by in good times a provision for bad; to reserve something for sickness and infirmity, or as a means of leisure and independence in the latter part of life, or a help to children in the outset of it. Savings, however, which have only these ends in view, have not much tendency to increase the amount of capital already in existence. These motives only prompt each person to save at one period of life what he purposes to consume at another, or what will be consumed by his children before they can completely provide for themselves." "There are always some persons in whom the effective desire of accumulation is above the average, and to whom less than the ordinary *minimum* rate of profit is a sufficient inducement to save; but these merely step into the place of others whose taste for expense and indulgence is beyond the average, and who, instead of saving, perhaps even dissipate what they have received."

The hope of elevating one's condition in the world tends more effectually to increase the national wealth in proportion as it affects a larger class of the people. In most civilized countries, the bulk of the population are poor, their daily wages hardly sufficing to buy their daily bread. Their savings, if it is possible for them to make any, must be in very small sums; and the inducement for them to be frugal must depend on the possibility of immediately investing such small sums to advantage. One of the great improvements of modern civilization consists in the means afforded, the machinery contrived, for collecting these driblets of wealth, and bringing them together into large reservoirs, whence they issue in abundant streams, giving efficiency and fertility to labor throughout the land. The water which falls in drops upon the desert, sinks through the sand, and leaves the ground arid and barren as before; but when collected in great tanks and cisterns, it turns a given portion of that desert into a garden. A century or two ago, if the laboring part of the population made any savings, they were in the form of little hoards of silver or gold, hid in an old stocking, or buried in the garden. But because the money thus stored was unproductive, and yielded no interest, and because it was always at hand when the owner was for a moment tempted to some indulgence and consequent expense, the number and amount of such hoards were always small. Now, through the multiplication of the branches of retail trade, and the lesser mechanic arts, and through joint-stock corporations and savings' banks, the first half-eagle which the laboring man or woman saves from the month's wages is profitably invested, and, by the end of the year, is increased by the twentieth part of itself. When this saving has reached a very moderate amount, it can be made to accumulate at compound interest, and thus to double itself in twelve years. In many cases, it soon comes to be used by the owner himself as capital; that is, it is invested in the purchase of tools or machinery, or a small stock in trade; and it may then accumulate at the rate of ten or twelve per cent a year, — that is, it may double itself every six or seven years. The result is, that he who began life as a common laborer, often drives about in his own carriage before its close.

In almost any other part of the world than New England, I should be afraid to give this sketch as an illustration of the manner in which the wealth or available capital of a nation is increased. But I presume it is a safe assertion, that at least one half of those who are usually called wealthy men, in Boston and its neighborhood, have obtained their wealth very nearly in the manner, or through the process, just described. This leads us to perceive that the aggregate of the small savings made by the bulk of the population, who have very small means, may constitute, and in this country actually does constitute, a larger annual addition to the whole amount of national capital, than the sum of the much larger savings made by the few who are usually considered as capitalists.

Mr. Farr stated, in 1852, in his evidence before a commission of Parliament, that, according to an estimate based upon the returns under the Income Tax, there are not more than 236,000 persons in Great Britain whose clear annual incomes exceed £ 200 each. This is the number, therefore, of those who may be considered as persons of wealth. Their aggregate income amounts to £ 174,810,000, being an average of about £ 740 to each. If we suppose that one half of these persons make savings to the extent of one tenth of their income, — a supposition which is a very liberal one, — the accumulations of the rich will amount to £ 8,740,500, or about

$ 43,700,000. That this may not appear an under-estimate, it should be remembered, that the customs of society in England require the style and expensiveness of living to come much nearer to the individual's whole income than is usual in this country, so that most of the nobility and the landed gentry, who have the largest incomes, do not make any savings at all, and many even run in debt, or encroach upon their capital. A nobleman who inherits an estate of £ 20,000 a year, inherits also a style of living which is costly enough to consume it. In the United States, on the other hand, a man usually begins poor, and therefore with frugal habits, and consequently hardly knows what to do with the income of a large property when he has acquired it. He has no ancestral castle to maintain in due state, and no county to contest at each succeeding election. Nay, the custom of the country, the force of public opinion, is such, that he *cannot* make his personal expenditure equal to his income, even if he wished. He must not keep a carriage and four, nor have a footman to stand behind his more modest equipage, nor clothe his servants in livery, nor adopt many other of the badges by which some persons try to convince the world that they are people of consequence. We are accused of being fond of titles, it is true; but the epithets of Major, Colonel, and Honorable *cost nothing* but civility, and so do not help a man to spend his fortune. We do not tolerate gold lace, nor cocked hats, nor tall footmen with gold-headed canes.

How great is the possible addition to the national capital from the savings of the comparatively poor, — of persons who live either upon wages, or upon incomes so small that they do not exceed the average wages of expert artisans? Great Britain and the United States are nearly equal in point of population; and the census (1841) of the former country shows that two and a half millions of male adults, or one half of the whole nation, are laborers or operatives who subsist entirely upon wages. We will suppose that only one half of these make any savings, and that the savings of each frugal and industrious laborer might amount to forty dollars a year, — a sum which the generality of English laborers certainly are not able to save, but which most prudent and laborious male adults in New England might save, since many family domestics and manufacturing operatives here actually lay aside a larger amount than this every year. One and a quarter millions of savings at forty dollars each, give an aggregate of fifty millions of dollars, as the sum which might be added each year to the national capital by the savings of the poor.

Thus far, we have only shown what *might be* accomplished; and the result throws a strong light on our general proposition, that, while wealth is created by labor, capital accumulates by the exercise of frugality. But there are many indications — here in New England, at least — that the rapid growth of capital is actually to be attributed to the industrious and frugal habits, — I will not say, of the poor, for, strictly speaking, we have no poor except the vicious, and the recent immigrants, — but of that part of our population who are engaged chiefly in manual labor. This class alone deposit money in our Savings' Banks, the accumulations in which, in Massachusetts alone, where our population is less than a million, already exceed $ 23,000,000. In England, the deposits in the Savings' Banks exceed $ 150,000,000, though no one person can deposit more than $ 750. It must be remembered also, that the reservoir always remains full to this extent, though a stream is always flowing out of it, several millions being annually withdrawn, — a portion, indeed, for unproductive consumption, but a larger portion for investment in other forms, in stocks, or capital for retail trade, or in machinery and tools. Considering that the class in our community who make use of the Savings' Banks is not only the poorest, but the smallest, and that a much larger class, composed of small farmers, tradesmen, and mechanics, find a more profitable use for their savings by immediately enlarging their own capital with them, we may well regard the proposition as established, that the national capital grows more by the aggregate of the small savings of the bulk of the people, including the poorer classes, than by the great gains of the rich.

CHAPTER X.

THE INCREASE OF CAPITAL AS AFFECTED BY THE POLITICAL AND SOCIAL ADVANTAGES ATTENDING THE POSSESSION OF WEALTH.

HAVING shown the importance of small savings effected by the bulk of the people, we come to the following inquiry: — Under what circumstances are the middling and lower classes able to save, and by what means is their inclination to frugality most effectually stimulated? I answer, that the most powerful means to this end is what may be called the *mobility* of society, or the ease and frequency with which the members of it change their respective social positions. The worst of all forms of civil polity is that which binds a man for ever to that condition of life in which he was born, be it of high or low degree, however he may have merited removal from it by his character, acquisitions, and behavior. Fixity of ranks and classes, or the existence of immunities and distinctions which money and talent can neither purchase nor remove, is a bar to the accumulation of wealth, — a bar which it is difficult to overleap just in proportion to the importance and extent of those unpurchasable privileges. If they are numerous and of great moment, if they cover the whole ground both of political influence and social consideration, what inducement is there for any one who is not born to the possession of them, either to labor or to save further than is required for the necessities of the present hour, — the point at which, be it remembered, the accumulation of capital begins? And what inducement to accumulate is there for one who is born to the possession of them, since he already enjoys more than wealth can buy, and cannot forfeit *this* enjoyment even if he should lose his wealth? The great improvement in the industrial organization of society in modern times, whereby the increase of wealth in all civilized nations has been made so rapid and so great, has been the successive breaking down and removal of these fixed and arbitrary barriers and divisions, so as to leave the whole field of promotion open to the career of skill, industry, and economy. A brief notice of a few points in the politico-economical history of different nations will illustrate this statement.

"Both in ancient Egypt and Hindostan," and to a great extent still in the latter of these two countries, "the whole body of the people was divided into different castes or tribes, each of which was confined, from father to son, to a particular employment or class of employments. The son of a priest was necessarily a priest; the son of a soldier, a soldier; the son of a laborer, a laborer; the son of a weaver, a weaver, &c. In both countries, the caste of the priests held the highest rank, and that of the soldier, the next; and in both countries, the caste of the farmers and laborers was superior to the castes of the merchants and the manufacturers." Adam Smith adduces these facts to explain why agriculture flourished in those regions far more than any other employment. He might with greater propriety have cited them to explain the peculiar, immovable, statue-like character of Hindoo and Egyptian civilization. The massive granite sphinxes, half covered by the sands of the desert among which they have rested for more than three thousand years, with their enigmatical and almost superhuman expression of mingled sweetness and severity, fit emblems of mystery, unchangeableness, and everlasting repose, aptly typify the character and the institutions of the people who chiselled them. The bodies of this people are even now drawn from the tombs in which they have lain for thirty centuries, perfect in every limb and lineament, as if they resisted change even after death. And such was their condition during life; the idea of movement, alteration, or progress seems never to have occurred to them. Institutions merely political, the will of a monarch or the decrees of a senate, could not retain society in this immovable state for ages. The power of religion was brought in to render sacred the fetters which bound it, and to take away from the minds of the common people any desire to rupture them. How much influence superstition had in building up these divisions of castes, and preserving them from violation or decay, may be conjectured from the fact, that the priests always formed the highest caste, and therefore profited most by this peculiar institution. Civilization thus embalmed and immured was safe both from progress or decay by internal causes. It might have remained to this day just as it was in the time of the Pharaohs, if invasion from abroad had not brought it to a violent death, — if the Romans and the Arabs had not successively made Egypt a prey to their thirst for foreign dominion.

Though the barriers of caste prevented the people, as individuals, from making any progress in wealth, their peculiar polity enabled the government to undertake and execute works which shame the magnificence and expensiveness of modern productions. What we now esteem the wonders of Egypt, her obelisks and pyramids, her excavations and temples, were strictly public works, performed at royal or priestly command by the multitude, who worked without pay, because labor was the function of their caste, and the part which they believed the gods designed to be their vocation. Wages and profits were words which in their ears had no meaning; all their time, all their labor, was due to the state, which was represented by the monarch and the priests. A portion of their time or of the products of their labor was granted back to them, which might or might not suffice for their subsistence. If savings were ever made, it was only with the intention of obtaining enlarged enjoyment from them at a future day, never for the purpose of aiding the individual's subsequent labors with a reserved fund, or of purchasing an easier or more elevated position with them. In the station of life in which each person was born, in that he was content to die. Of course, there was no accumulation of private wealth. Even the land belonged to the sovereign; all that was due to any person was a livelihood in the profession or caste to which he belonged, with that measure and kind of employment and comfort, of luxury or privation, which was allotted to every other member of the same caste. Immobility was the great characteristic of Hindoo and Egyptian civilization.

The freer spirit and quicker intellect of the Greeks, the pride and military ambition of the Romans, prevented these nations from sinking into apathy, or stagnating in castes. In the fierce democracy of Athens, the subtle politician and fluent declaimer often elbowed his way into the favor of his fellow-citizens, and consequently into offices of honor and profit. At

Rome, a man of plebeian origin not unfrequently vanquished the pride of the patricians, and obtained the consulship, or the command of the armies of the republic. There was freedom, there was life, in a society thus constituted. There was a path open to effort, and a motive for the exercise of industry and self-denial. In the turbulent times which preceded and accompanied the fall of the republic, individuals often amassed large fortunes, and with these purchased the honors which they had not political sagacity, or military skill and courage, enough to obtain by more legitimate means. One of the triumvirs who shared the empire of the world with Antony and Octavius, owed his political power solely to his wealth. Both these nations might have made far greater progress in opulence, if the institution of slavery, itself a caste, had not existed among them, and if the state and the affairs of government had not monopolized ambition and effort to so great an extent, that private enterprise, and the undertakings of individuals who did not profess to look to the commonwealth for their reward, were discouraged or held in light esteem. Both at Athens and at Rome, the republic was everything and the individual was nothing; and, as a consequence, in the city proper, society was composed of two great castes,—the citizens who were devoted to public affairs, and the slaves. The wealth of Rome was the wealth of the robber's den, obtained by plundering the rest of mankind. Even the populace of this great city were supported by gratuitous distributions of the corn which was levied as a tribute on the industry of the Sicilians and the Africans; and its patricians amassed their enormous fortunes from the plunder of the provinces which they had been appointed to govern.

With regard to slavery among the ancients, it has been acutely remarked by Sismondi, that because it was only an accident of the right of war, and not an industrial organization, it did not discredit labor in general. The slave was not a *mere* article of property, or a means, through his enforced toil, of increasing his master's property. He was rather a token of his owner's, or of the nation's, prowess in war. The possession of numerous slaves was more a matter of pride, a means of ostentation and magnificence, than a mode of investing capital with a view to profitable returns. Few of the slaves were distinguished by color, or any other physical peculiarity, which might serve as an ineffaceable mark of bondage or degradation. Hence, when manumitted, they at once took rank in society, and their children often rose to high honors in the state. As slaves, indeed, they were often put to servile and economical uses; but they were never treated as mere machines for the production of wealth. They did not perform all the labor, and therefore they did not discredit labor. They were a caste, and so did not accumulate property, either for themselves or others; but they were not a degraded caste; they were not considered vile, as were the Pariahs in India, or as African slaves are, in modern times.

"The unhealthy climate of many portions of Italy," says M. de la Malle, "made it necessary that the ground should be cultivated by freemen who were robust and acclimated, which the slaves seldom were; the latter, also, increased in number very slowly, as their ill health, caused by insufficient nourishment, long confinement, the want of air, and bad treatment, made them more susceptible to the impressions of climate."

The testimony of Varro, a contemporary of Cæsar and Cicero, is positive, and this fact ought to change the ordinary notions as to the kind of agriculture pursued in Italy at a time when Rome was the mistress of the world, and the number of slaves had considerably increased. "All the farms," says Varro, "are cultivated by freemen, or by slaves, or by a mixture of these two classes. Freemen till the ground either by themselves, with the aid of their children, as the small proprietors do, or by free laborers hired by the day, in the busy season, when they are making hay or collecting the grapes, or, finally, by those who are working out the payment of a debt. I speak of all farms in general, as it is more profitable to cultivate the unhealthy districts with hired laborers than with slaves, and even in the healthy localities, the great labors of the husbandmen, such as the collection of the fruits, the harvest, and the vintage, ought to be confided to free hired workmen, or mercenaries." Those who belonged to a caste, as the slaves did, and who, consequently, were not stimulated to labor by the hope of rising or the fear of falling in the world, could not be trusted with the most important work, even on a farm. Modern experience fully confirms this result, as no kind of cultivation is found to succeed, if conducted by slaves, except that of tropical products, where the laborers can be employed in gangs.

"Finally," continues M. de la Malle, "even in the time of Trajan, it appears that in the northern part of Italy, in the neighborhood of Lake Como at least, slaves were not employed in tilling the ground." Pliny the Younger says, "I never use slaves in the cultivation of my farms, nor does any one in the vicinity. This class of persons were mainly reserved for household labors in the city; and one can easily believe that the Gauls, the Germans, the Syrians, the inhabitants of Asia and Africa, when brought as slaves to Italy, would have fallen quickly under the influence of a climate so different from their own, of a pestilential air, and of the exhaustion caused by hard labor and insufficient nourishment."

"In fact, in a country and at a time when the legal rate of interest was fixed at one or one and a half per cent a year, and when the citizens were prohibited from engaging in trade, manufactures, or the mechanic arts, agriculture was the only means of keeping up or making a moderate addition to one's fortune. Landed property was much divided, and the smallness of the farms allowed them to be cultivated by the proprietor's own hands and those of his family." There were really but three classes in the community, separated by lines of division so permanent as almost to form them into castes; these were the slaves, the small agriculturists, and those who were either devoted to the service of the state, or who depended on it for subsistence. At least, this was the condition of Rome under the republic, when the severe virtues of simplicity, courage, and frugality were in request. Wealth then was not a passport to honor, and wealth accordingly was not accumulated. Cincinnatus was summoned from the plough to take the helm of state.

The empire wholly changed the face of affairs; but as this rapidly degenerated into an Oriental despotism, in which the insecurity of life and property was a sufficient bar to the accumulation of the latter, we need not dwell upon the causes of its decline.

After the fall of the Roman empire in the West, and the establishment of various tribes of barbarian conquerors upon its ruins, a great step was taken in social economy by the virtual emancipation of one large class in the community from the fetters of caste. I refer to the inhabitants of the free cities or towns, the foundation of which, in Germany, France, and Italy, was the first step towards the creation of the social polity of modern times. Their population, indeed, says Adam Smith, "consisted of a very different order of people from the first inhabitants of the ancient republics of Greece and Italy. They were chiefly tradesmen and mechanics, who seem in those days to have been of servile, or very nearly of servile, condition. They seem, indeed, to have been a very poor, mean set of people, who used to travel about with their goods from place to place, and from fair to fair, like the hawkers and peddlers of modern times." They were liable, while thus travelling about, to great exactions; they were either plundered without mercy by the arrogant and rapacious, or they paid heavy taxes and tolls as a price of protection. "Sometimes the king, sometimes a great lord, would grant to particular traders, especially to such as lived on their own lands, a general exemption from such taxes; and then, though in other respects nearly servile in their condition, they were called *free traders*." They were allowed to give away their own daughters in marriage, their children were permitted to inherit their property, they were allowed to dispose of their effects by will; in short, they were released from the most oppressive of the feudal burdens, to which, as of the lower class in society, they had hitherto been subject. "They were generally at the same time erected into a commonalty, or corporation, with the privilege of having magistrates and a town-council of their own, of making by-laws for their own government, of building walls for their defence, and of reducing all their inhabitants to military discipline by obliging them to watch and ward." The nobles despised the burghers or citizens, whom they regarded as a parcel of emancipated slaves, devoted to base mechanic arts, and whose wealth excited their envy and indignation. The king, on the other hand, favored them, as a counterbalance to the power of the nobility, whom they hated and feared; and the weakest monarchs, consequently, were most liberal in their grants of privileges to the cities and towns. Thus the prosperous cities of France and the Low Countries, the famous Hanse towns of

Germany, and the flourishing commercial republics of Italy and Switzerland, came into being.

In the country, the distinctions of caste and the consequent limitations of employment still existed. The great barons lived remotely from each other, each on his own estate, surrounded by his retainers and serfs, whose only occupations were war and agriculture, and who had no hope of improving their condition. Exposed to every sort of violence, they naturally contented themselves with a bare subsistence; for to accumulate more would only excite the rapacity of their oppressors. If one of them did make some small savings, he hoarded them with care and secrecy, till he could find some opportunity of running away to a town, where, if he could conceal himself for a year, he was free for ever. Thus a city often grew up to great wealth and splendor, while the country in its neighborhood was in poverty and wretchedness. The great lords themselves could obtain the articles of luxury which they desired only by bartering raw agricultural produce for them, at a great disadvantage, with the inhabitants of the towns. As the wealth and military strength of these municipal corporations increased, they could no longer be taxed but by their own consent; hence they were empowered to send delegates to parliament or the general assembly of the states of the kingdom, where, in connection with the clergy and the nobles, they granted extraordinary aids to the king, and had a potential voice in managing the affairs of the nation.

These cities were not merely republican; they were essentially democratic, in their origin, their institutions, their social relations, and their tendencies; and my point is to show, that this democratic character was the first cause of their rapid growth in opulence. Being originally servile, or nearly servile, in condition, the inhabitants had no distinctions of rank to begin with; their natural enemies were the nobles, from whose oppressive sway they were but recently emancipated. Trade and manufactures, being their only occupations, were necessarily held in high esteem among them; and he enjoyed their highest confidence and respect who had been most successful in these pursuits. A common interest and common perils bound them very firmly to each other; and the direction of affairs in their little state was naturally intrusted to those whose skill, prudence, industry, and economy had been already rewarded with the largest accumulations of wealth. No one was ashamed of his craft; no one had anything to be proud of but his riches. A brewer and a tanner, a weaver and a goldsmith, sat side by side in the town councils, or led the citizens to the defence of the walls, and even conducted them in armies to the field, where they often defeated the chivalry of France and Germany, and sometimes triumphed over their own monarchs. Van Artevelde of Ghent was a brewer; the Medici of Florence, though popes and kings were reckoned among their posterity, were at first only successful merchants. Wealth being thus the only passport to distinction, and all the avenues to it being in high repute, its possession was eagerly coveted, and the virtues of industry and frugality were practised to the farthest extent. With the growth and spread of opulence, and the calling forth of talent from the whole community through the absence of artificial distinctions, the rise and progress of literature and the fine arts were necessarily associated. Poetry, painting, sculpture, and architecture had their origin, in modern times, in the commercial republics of Pisa and Florence, and the free cities of Flanders.

Wealth passed freely from hand to hand. Feudalism was barred out by the city walls; and the father's property, instead of being kept together for the aggrandizement of the family in the person of the oldest son, was distributed equally among the children. If one or more of these were prodigal, careless, or indolent, they sank to that level whence the thrift of the father had raised them, and their places were filled by the more capable and industrious. These alternations of fortune, rapid and frequent, kept up in the community a thirst for gain, and kept down discontent and civil commotions. An aristocracy of wealth has this at least to recommend it, if wholly disconnected with an aristocracy of birth,—that by its fluctuations it rather encourages effort than represses it. While society stagnated among the feudal nobility and at the courts of feudal monarchs, it was galvanized into an almost unnatural activity within the precincts of the little civic republics of Italy, Germany, and the Low Countries. The proud nobles were reduced to seek aid of the fat and wealthy burghers, the painstaking artisans, whom they affected to despise. They obtained

11

loans from them, for which they gave their lands in pawn, and even sold to them outright their castles and hereditary estates. Ennobled by the possession of these, the ambition of the citizens grew by what it fed on, and not infrequently, as in the case of the Medici at Florence, they became the ancestors of a line of kings.

This sketch of the causes affecting the growth of opulence in ancient and modern times is introduced principally for the purpose of illustrating the most remarkable difference in the social condition of Great Britain and the United States. The most striking thing in the aspect of society here is the constant strain of the faculties, in all classes, in the pursuit of wealth, — the restlessness, the feverish anxiety to get on, which English writers, at least, are apt to regard only as "the disagreeable symptoms of one of the phases of industrial progress." In whatever light it ought to be viewed, they are certainly mistaken in considering it as a consequence of the recent formation of our institutions, and the recent establishment of our people on the shores of a new world, — in attributing it to our favorable position, with an abundance of fertile land, and with sources of opulence as yet fresh and unexhausted. Were such causes adequate to produce this particular effect, we should find society exhibiting the same characteristics wherever it was similarly situated, — in British America, for instance, in British Australia, and over a great portion of the South American continent. But it is not so; and we must therefore look for an explanation of the phenomenon to some cause which is peculiar to our own social state, — to some stimulus acting upon what political economists call "the effective desire of accumulation," which has full scope to operate here, while it is repressed or much restricted in all other nations, — even in England, where the character of the population in other respects is so similar to our own.

I find such a peculiar operating cause in the fact, that every individual here has the power to make savings, if he will, and almost as large as he will, — and has the certainty that the savings when made, the wealth when accumulated, will immediately operate, in proportion to its amount, to raise the frugal person's position in life, — to give him, in fact, the only distinction that is recognized among us. Neither theoretically nor practically, in this country, is there any obstacle to any individual's becoming rich, if he will, and almost to any amount that he will; — no obstacle, I say, but what arises from the dispensations of Providence, from the unequal distribution of health, strength, and the faculties of mind. In other words, there are no obstacles but natural and inevitable ones; society interposes none, and none exist which society could remove. And ours is the only community on earth of which this can be said. Here there are no castes, and not even an approach to a division of society by castes. Our whole population is in that state which I have attempted to describe as the condition of the inhabitants of a free town in the Middle Ages. The property which is rapidly gained is often quite as rapidly spent, for the sake of that consideration and influence which the reputation of riches alone can give. Hence, wealth circulates among us almost as rapidly as the money which is its representative. A great fortune springs up, like the prophet's gourd, in a night, and is dissipated by some unforeseen accident on the morrow. Every one is made restless and anxious by this exposure to sudden change; but one great good comes of it, that it keeps down permanent discontent, and stifles the jealousy that is usually nursed by social differences and inequalities of fortune. How is it possible, indeed, that the poor should be arrayed in hostility against the rich, when — to adopt a former illustration — the son of an Irish coachman becomes the governor of a State, and the grandson of a *millionnaire* dies a pauper? The consequence of the whole is an unceasing energy and activity in the pursuit of wealth, which accomplish greater wonders than all the modern inventions of science, which actually generate enthusiasm of character, and are regarded by foreigners with surprise and distrust, as the tokens of some constitutional disease in the body politic. Even the Irish immigrant here soon loses his careless, lazy, and turbulent disposition, and becomes as sober, prudent, industrious, and frugal as his neighbors. Nearly all the enormous fortunes that have been gathered in this country are the growth of a single lifetime, and therefore, even if they were more evenly distributed than they now are at the death of their founders, there would not be a smaller number of them in the succeeding generation. Consequently, they are regarded as the prizes of industry, economy, and enterprise; and the sight of them stimulates and sustains exertion, instead of chilling and repressing it, which is the effect produced by the fixedness in certain families of vast hereditary estates.

The aspect of society in England in this respect I will not say is the direct contrary of what it is here, for with regard to a very large and influential class, it is just the same. The middle class — what on the Continent would be called the *bourgeoisie*, the merchants, the manufacturers, the small tradesmen, the master mechanics — are about as busy as we are here in the pursuit of wealth; and their numbers and influence in the state gave occasion to Napoleon's sarcasm, that the English were a nation of shopkeepers. But the parallel between their condition and that of the free towns in the Middle Ages may be carried much farther; *outside of the city walls there are the nobles and the serfs.* The effect of the activity of the commercial class upon the eye of the philosophical observer is qualified by the comparative repose — the stagnation, one can almost say — of the laboring poor and of the nobility and landed gentry. These two classes, the top and the bottom of English society, are true *castes*, for nothing short of a miracle can elevate or depress one who is born a member of either. The true movement, the life, of the community in Great Britain is among those who are engaged in commerce and manufactures; here are alternations of fortune, not so frequent, perhaps, as in this country, but as sudden and as great. An Arkwright begins life as a barber, and ends it as a *millionnaire;* a Peel gives his days and his nights to cotton-spinning, and his son becomes prime minister of England. But outside of this class there is stagnation and death. One half of the whole population is composed of laborers who subsist entirely upon wages, who cannot make savings if they would, for their whole earnings barely suffice to keep soul and body together. Hopeless of rising, encouraged by no examples, among those who were born his equals, of elevation to a higher grade, the laborer has no ambition, no thought even, of changing his position in life. His condition is best described in the strong language of McCulloch, when he speaks of "the irretrievable helotism of the working classes of England." And the upper classes, the nobility and the gentry, occupy a sphere which is equally immovable. With estates locked up by entails and marriage settlements, so that they cannot squander them, with an inherited scale of expenditure proportionate to their rank and fortune, so that they cannot make savings from income, and with a measure of political influence and social consideration secured to them by the long-established habits and opinions of their countrymen, they form a *caste* almost as fixed as that of the Bramins in India.

The difference in the aspect of society and the social condition of the people between Great Britain and the United States seems to me one of the most pregnant and instructive facts which the political economist has to consider; for it shows the superiority of moral over physical causes in the growth of national opulence, and that the hope of rising in the world is the chief motive for the accumulation of capital. Great inequality in the distribution of wealth may operate either as a check or a spur to industry and frugality; it is not, then, in itself, to be deprecated. On the contrary, a perfectly uniform partition of the goods of this world, if it were possible, which it is not, would create universal torpor. Take away the fear of poverty and the hope of rising in the world, and no one would exert himself but for his own amusement. Add the power of a despot, to make such exertion compulsory, and we should have exactly that state of things which existed in Egypt and India, when the institution of castes as yet was unimpaired. If the whole population formed but one caste, from which they could neither sink nor rise by any fault or merit of their own, they would be no more inclined to labor than if they were divided into several castes. It is the *fixedness*, and not the *inequality*, of fortunes which is to be dreaded; it is the retention of them in the same families throughout many generations, which chills exertion and unnerves the right arm of toil. Wherever there is motion, there is life. Property cannot be rendered immovable, except by the effect of human institutions which are designed to counteract the laws of nature. In this instance, surely, if in no other, the political economist has a right to cry, *Laissez faire!* let alone! and do not attempt to amend the ways of Providence! We do try to amend them when we attempt to enforce, or to render permanent, either equality or inequality. Laws of primogeniture and entail, the object of which is to insure to certain families the possession of their wealth for ever, are not a whit more unnatural and unjust in their operation, than would be the schemes of the philanthropic reformers, as they call themselves, who would fain reconstruct society on the basis of making the distribution of all property equal and unchangeable.

"The laws and conditions of the production of wealth," as Mr. Mill remarks, "partake of the character of physical truths. There is nothing optional or arbitrary in them. Whatever mankind produce must be produced in the modes and under the conditions imposed by the constitution of external things, and by the inherent properties of their own bodily and mental structure. Whether they like it or not, their production will be limited by the amount of their previous accumulation, and, that being given, it will be proportional to their energy, their skill, the perfection of their machinery, and their judicious use of the advantages of combined labor. Whether they like it or not, the unproductive expenditure of individuals will, to an equal extent, tend to impoverish the community, and only their productive expenditure will enrich it. The opinions or the wishes which may exist on these different matters, do not control the things themselves. We cannot indeed foresee to what extent the modes of production may be altered, or its powers increased, by future extensions of our knowledge of the laws of nature, suggesting new processes of industry of which we have at present no conception. But howsoever we may succeed in making for ourselves more space within the limits set by the constitution of things, these limits exist; there are ultimate laws which we did not make, which we cannot alter, and to which we can only conform."

Among such ultimate laws is the tendency to an unequal distribution of the wealth that is created by human labor. A law of natural justice, which is recognized by savages quite as much as by civilized nations, assigns the ownership of a useful article to him by whose skill and industry that article was created. The game that is caught, the implement of the chase that is manufactured, belongs, by the consent of all, to him by whom it is caught or made. Nor is any alteration produced in this law because the successful person has so much strength, skill, and enterprise, that he can catch or manufacture two or three times as much as any other member of the tribe. The property is still recognized as his, for this simple reason, if for no other, — that he would not put forth his force and ingenuity, if others should deprive him of their fruits. Again, if he chooses to hold these articles in reserve, instead of immediately consuming them, if he prefers a wigwam well stocked with implements of war and the chase, and a store of food for future use, to present indolence or the immediate gratification of his appetites, still his rights of ownership are respected. His prudence and economy, as much as his strength and skill, are allowed to redound exclusively to his own advantage. There is even a stronger reason for respecting his property in this case than in the former one; for the whole community profit by his savings; they operate to some extent as an insurance to them all against famine. There is now a stock of food or implements in the tribe, which, though not common property, may still operate for the benefit of all at some future day, when the chase happens to be unproductive, because the owner will sell them to others for their services, or as a debt, or for honors which it may be in their power to bestow.

In this simple instance, we can easily see how injurious it would be to the common welfare if the rights of property were not respected, and how surely such respect tends to an unequal distribution of the goods, I will not say, of fortune, but of industry and frugality. As men are differently endowed by nature with faculties of mind and body, with indolence or energy, with improvidence or thrift, so their situations in life must differ. And it is the true policy of society to encourage the more valuable qualities; — not to dishearten frugality by depriving it of its savings, nor to foster idleness by feeding it with the fruits obtained by the persevering toil of others. In civilized society, the same principles hold. The case becomes a little more complicated, because, by the transmutations of capital that have already been explained, the property of an individual is constantly assuming various shapes. But so long as it continues *productive* property, so long, in one form or another, it must further and assist the operations of labor; and so far it must benefit others as well as the owner. The general law, that industry is limited by capital, is borne out by the obvious consideration, that without implements, machinery, raw material, and a previously accumulated stock of food and clothing, the workman cannot bestow his labor to advantage, — cannot, in fact, work at all.

Even if it were granted, that all the wealth of a nation *could* be distributed equally among all the people, and that the stock of it, by obliging all to labor alike, would for ever remain equal to all their wants, — and no more improbable supposition could be framed, — it is certain that this would be no real improvement of their condition. "Those who have never known freedom from anxiety as to the means of subsistence," says J. S. Mill, "are apt to overrate what is gained for positive enjoyment by the mere absence of that uncertainty. The necessaries of life, when they have always been secure for the whole of life, are scarcely more a subject of consciousness, or a source of happiness, than the elements. There is little attractive in a monotonous routine, without vicissitudes, but without excitement, — a life spent in the enforced observance of an external rule, and performance of a prescribed task; in which labor would be devoid of its chief sweetener, the thought that every effort tells perceptibly on the laborer's own interests or on those of some one with whom he identifies himself; in which no one could by his own exertions improve his condition, or that of the objects of his private affections; in which no one's way of life, occupations, or movements would depend on choice, but each would be the slave of all; — a social system in which identity of education and pursuits would impress on all the same unvarying type of character, to the destruction of that multiform development of human nature, those manifold unlikenesses, that diversity of tastes and talents, and variety of intellectual points of view, which, by presenting to each innumerable notions that he could not have conceived of himself, are the great stimulus to intellect and the main-spring of mental and moral progression. The perfection of social arrangements would be, to secure to all persons complete independence and freedom of action, subject to no restriction but that of not doing injury to others; but the scheme which we are considering — (that of an equal partition of wealth and of labor) — abrogates this freedom entirely, and places every action of every member of the community under command."

The rate of wages in any country is determined by the competition of the laborers with the capitalists. Which shall have the advantage in the competition will depend on the relative numbers of the two parties, and will be in an inverse ratio to these numbers. In England, certainly, the capitalists have the advantage; their immense accumulations, and the fewness of those who can compete with them when compared with the vast number of those who subsist entirely upon wages, enable them generally to dictate their own terms, and to keep wages at the lowest point which will supply the workmen with the necessaries of life. In this country, it is quite as certain that the laborers have the advantage; most of them have a little capital of their own, on which they could subsist for a time, or, owing to the great demand for labor, they can find work in other establishments, perhaps in other trades. Here, frequently, it is not the employer who discharges the workman or the domestic, but the workman or the domestic who discharges the employer.

Many kinds of production can be successfully kept up only upon a large scale; for the larger the enterprise, the further the division of labor may be carried. In order to keep such enterprises in motion, capital must be aggregated in large masses. In England, the great inequality of the distribution of wealth allows such enterprises to be managed by individuals; in most cases, a large manufacturing establishment is owned either by one person, or by a firm which embraces but a few partners. In the United States, from the comparative paucity of large private fortunes, such an establishment is generally formed and conducted by a joint-stock company, — which is comparatively a modern invention, but one that, from its democratic character, is peculiarly suited to this country, and to the wants of the age. Many small capitalists, by clubbing their means, can successfully compete with men of vast fortune, — an undertaking which would otherwise be a hopeless one, as the great capitalist can live through reverses of trade, commercial crises, and casualties, which would ruin one who had little or nothing in reserve. So consonant are these joint-stock companies to the genius of our institutions and to the circumstances of the country, that they have multiplied with astonishing rapidity. They have survived even the necessity which called them forth; for as large private fortunes have sprung up with the growth of national opulence, the owners of them have preferred to distribute their capital by taking stock in many of these associations, rather than to concentrate it upon one undertaking. The risk of a sweeping calamity is thus materially diminished. I know of nothing more irrational than the common prejudice against such corporations. They are true savings' banks, in which the common laborer not infrequently invests his modest savings, and shares the gains of his wealthy employer, instead of being crushed by competition with him. It is not unusual, I believe, for operatives to hold stock in the very manufactories in which they work for wages. At any rate, the savings' bank, to which they first confide the fruits of their economy, often invests them in such stock. These corporations allow persons of very moderate means to participate in enterprises which, in other countries, are conducted exclusively by the rich. The occasional failure of one of them does not bankrupt many of the stockholders, whose property, invested in other ways, is left untouched; and as this seems a hardship to the creditor who has lost a portion of his debt, he is apt to declaim against those who are rich, and still do not pay what they owe. But his accusation is unjust; he who allows such an institution to become indebted to him, trusts it on account of the largeness of its capital, and its supposed solvency. It is the same thing for him, whether he trusts an individual or a corporation, the ground of his confidence, in either case, being his knowledge of the fact that the person or the corporation began business, perhaps, with half a million of capital, and he knows not that this capital has been wasted or lost. If he prefers, he may trust an individual who is supposed to be worth only $50,000, instead of a corporation reckoned at ten times that sum. If he chooses the latter course, he trusts the corporation, not the stockholders; he deliberately prefers the joint-stock security to the security offered by individuals; and, consequently, has no reason to complain if the latter do not pay him.

CHAPTER XI.

THE MALTHUSIAN THEORY OF POPULATION CONSIDERED AND REFUTED.

The laws of Political Economy, for the most part, it has been remarked, are inferences from the general fact, that individuals compete with each other in the pursuit of wealth. Rents, profits, wages, prices, are determined by competition; and as we are able to foresee what the effects of competition will be, we can show how these things will vary under given circumstances. Thus, profits tend to an equality in all employments, because capitalists compete with each other, and will withdraw their capital from a business which is less profitable, to invest it in one which is more so; this influx of capital into the more lucrative employment soon reduces the rate of profit in it to a level with the profits in other employments. The price of an article, of which there is a given quantity in the market, is determined by the demand for it, — that is, by the competition of the buyers. And this demand, again, regulates the future supply of that article; for as the competition of the buyers becomes warm, the price is enhanced, the profits of those who produce the article are increased, more capital is attracted into the employment, the supply is enlarged, and the price falls again.

These principles are sufficiently obvious, and if there were not exceptional cases, if their application was not modified and restricted by a crowd of circumstances, political economy might be called a demonstrative, or even an intuitive, science. Its maxims might all be taken for granted, and men would act upon them without giving themselves the trouble of enunciating them in an abstract form. But there are numerous exceptions and modifying circumstances, which need to be carefully considered; and in this chapter I propose to examine the most important of them.

There are two things the supply of which is not regulated by the demand; and they are two very important things, —

namely, land and population. Our wants and our desires do not, in these two cases, create, or even tend to create, the means of satisfying them; those means are wholly beyond our control. We cannot increase the quantity of surface of the habitable globe; we cannot, at will, either enlarge the population, or put limits to its growth, except by transgressing the moral laws which guard the sanctity of human life. It is conceivable that the well-being of a community may be greatly affected by these two inexorable facts. With all its labor and ingenuity, it cannot materially enlarge the limits of its territory, except by robbing its neighbors; it may reclaim a little land from the waters along the margin of a river, a lake, or an ocean; but it is obvious that its power in this respect is restricted within very narrow limits. And if its population should begin to waste away, or to increase with undue and inconvenient rapidity, the will of a monarch or the wishes of a people would not suffice to arrest either its decline or its growth. Still they are dependent for food upon the products of the land, the amount of which products must finally be limited by the extent of surface of the earth; — I say, must *finally* be so limited, because improvements in agriculture, the discovery of new means of increasing the product of a given surface of ground, may continually push the limit farther off, and open the way almost for an indefinite increase of the present population of the globe.

Yet on this possible or conceivable increase of the numbers of mankind, united with the fact that the cultivable surface of the earth is determined by fixed boundaries, which cannot be overleaped, is founded the celebrated theory of Mr. Malthus, and the doctrines which that theory is usually made to support. We are not at liberty to put aside the discussion of this theory, as if it were, what at first sight it appears to be, a mere speculation, which can have no practical importance except in a contingency certainly very remote, and which *may* never be realized. It is dwelt upon and applied by nearly all the English economists as if it were a truth of great moment, immediate in its bearings, and fruitful in results. The whole subject of political economy is colored with it; it affects the doctrine of rent, profits, and wages, and leads to inferences in respect to each of them, which otherwise would be immediately rejected.

The professed followers of Malthus are somewhat dogmatic in their enunciation of the doctrine, and altogether impatient of any doubt or question as to its correctness. This positiveness arises from a perception of the unquestionable correctness of the *data* on which the theory is founded, and of the chief features of the theory itself; while the general reluctance to accept it proceeds from involuntary dread of the shocking conclusions that it has been made to support, and from disgust at the consequences of its practical application. The doctrine of Malthus is sometimes understood, in its extended sense, to comprise the whole body of these inferences from it, together with its immediate application as advice to men for the government of their conduct and the regulation of society; and it is when thus understood, that the common sense and natural feelings of mankind shrink from it with that strong aversion which the followers of the theory are apt to stigmatize as "sentimental horror." Taken in the more restricted meaning, which is always used when the theory is controverted or denied, Malthusianism contains only one or two truisms about the law of increase that is common to the human race with the whole animal creation, which have no practical importance whatever, except for the purpose to which they were first applied by Malthus himself,—namely, to confute an absurd speculation by Godwin as to the perfectibility of the social state. Upon this ambiguity of meaning depends the whole controversy as to the law of population, and its consequences upon the well-being of society.

The proposition upon which the whole theory rests is this,—that the power of increase of any race of animals, the human species included, is indefinite, or incapable of exhaustion; and *if it were exercised to the utmost, without any check from external circumstances or from the animal's power of self-control*, the earth would not be large enough, I do not say merely, to afford subsistence, but even to give standing-room, to the beings who would claim a place upon it. The capacity of increase necessarily acts *in a geometrical progression;* for each pair being capable of procreation, if the race, under certain circumstances, increases within thirty years from ten thousand to twenty thousand, a mere continuance of the same cause and the same circumstances would enlarge the number, within the next thirty years, to forty thousand; and the third period would carry it to eighty thousand. For example, a given rate of increase, in the ten years from 1790 to 1800, added but 1,200,000 to the white population of this country; but from 1830 to 1840, the same rate of increase added 3,600,000. The population was more than doubled from 1790 to 1820; it was again more than doubled from 1820 to 1850. But the former doubling added less than five millions to our numbers, while the latter doubling added over ten millions; and the next doubling, in 1880, will add twenty millions. This law of possible increase in a geometrical progression belongs to every species, both of the animal and vegetable kingdom, of which we have any knowledge; it is an immediate and logical inference from the self-evident fact, that every pair, whether of the earliest or the latest generation, whether forming part of a very small or a very numerous community, is equally capable of continuing and multiplying its kind. Its prolific power is not at all affected by the greater or smaller number of its fellow-creatures which may be already in being. If population should go on in this manner without check, it is evident that, within a few centuries, the earth might literally be overstocked with human beings; if they should stand shoulder to shoulder, as thickly as the stalks of wheat in a cultivated field at harvest-time, every plain, valley, and hill-top, the surface even of every sea and ocean, might be covered with them; and there would still be a call for room, for the next thirty years would inevitably double even this immense assemblage, which we have supposed to be already like the sands of the sea for multitude.

Observe that this law of increase by geometrical progression holds good, whether the annual rate of increase be fast or slow. In the United States, for instance, the annual rate, *exclusive of the effects of immigration*, is 2.39 *per cent*, and, as a consequence, the population is doubled in little over 32 years. In France, the annual rate is but 0.6 (six tenths of one per cent), and the population, therefore, is not doubled in less than 115 years. Still, it *will* be doubled in that time, and therefore, in 230 years, it will be quadrupled, thus following the law of increase by geometrical progression, if it increase at all. The theory of Malthus may be said to owe its plausibility, in great part, to the fact with which all arithmeticians are very familiar, that a number increasing by geometrical progression within a given period rises to a very formidable amount. Thus, McCulloch calculates that the population of the United States, *if the present annual rate of increase should continue*, in one century from this time will amount to 240 millions; and in two centuries, that is, in A. D. 2050, it will reach the very respectable sum of 3,840 millions, or nearly five times the present population of the globe. The possibility of such a result is certainly appalling, and at first sight, it may appear to justify the alarm expressed by the Malthusians.

Even without taking into view the ultimate check to the increase of the numbers of mankind that will be found in the limited extent of the earth's surface, Mr. Malthus undertakes to show, that the means of subsistence, under the most favorable circumstances, cannot increase so rapidly as the number of mouths calling for food. The race of population against food, he maintains, is like that of Achilles against a tortoise; it is too unequal, whatever may be the advantage at first possessed by the weaker party. Whatever may be the present superfluity of sustenance, or of the means of increasing sustenance, population multiplies so fast, that it must soon overtake and surpass the supply of nourishment. Looking at first only to Great Britain, he says:—"If it be allowed, that, by the best possible policy and great encouragements to agriculture, the average produce of the island could be doubled in the first twenty-five years, it will be allowing probably a greater increase than could with reason be expected. In the next twenty-five years, it is impossible to suppose that the produce could be quadrupled. It would be contrary to all our knowledge of the properties of land. The improvement of the barren parts would be a work of time and labor; and it must be evident to those who have the slightest acquaintance with agricultural subjects, that, in proportion as cultivation extended, the additions that could yearly be made to the former average produce must be gradually and regularly diminishing. That we may be the better able to compare the increase of population and food, let us make a supposition, which, without pretending to accuracy, is clearly more favorable to the power of production in the earth than any experience we have had of its qualities will warrant.

"Let us suppose that the yearly additions which might be made to the former average produce, instead of decreasing, which they certainly would do, were to remain the same; and that the produce of this island might be increased, every twenty-five years, by a quantity equal to what it at present produces. The most enthusiastic speculator cannot suppose a greater increase than this. In a few centuries, it would make every acre of land in the island like a garden. If this supposition be applied to the whole earth, and if it be allowed that the subsistence for man which the earth affords might be increased every twenty-five years by a quantity equal to what it at present produces, this will be supposing a rate of increase much greater than we can imagine that any possible exertions of mankind could make it. It may fairly be pronounced, therefore, that, considering the present average state of the earth, *the means of subsistence*, under circumstances the most favorable to human industry, *could not possibly be made to increase faster than in an arithmetical ratio.*

"The necessary effects of these two different rates of increase, when brought together, will be very striking. Let us call the population of this island 11 millions, and suppose the present produce equal to the easy support of such a number. In the first 25 years, the population would be 22 millions, and, the food being also doubled, the means of subsistence would be equal to this increase. In the next 25 years, the population would be 44 millions, and the means of subsistence only equal to the support of 33 millions. In the next period, the population would be 88 millions, and the means of subsistence just equal to the support of half that number. And at the conclusion of the first century, the population would be 176 millions, and the means of subsistence only equal to the support of 55 millions, leaving a population of 121 millions totally unprovided for.

"Taking the whole earth instead of this island, emigration would of course be excluded; and supposing the present population equal to one thousand millions, the human species would increase as the numbers 1, 2, 4, 8, 16, 32, 64, 128, 256, and subsistence as 1, 2, 3, 4, 5, 6, 7, 8, 9. In two centuries, the population would be to the means of subsistence as 256 to 9; in three centuries, as 4,096 to 13; and in two thousand years, the difference would be almost incalculable."

We cannot find much comfort in the fact, that the human race have already inhabited this globe for more than six thousand years, a period surely long enough, with the aid of a geometrical progression, even if the annual rate of increase had been very small, but regular, to have brought into being vastly more than the poor 800 millions who now stock the earth. In former times and in barbarous countries, war, pestilence, famine, tyranny, and all the other ills which uncivilized man is heir to, not only kept down the rate of increase, but often caused the population to retrograde. Practically, down to the present day, the only evil which has been felt has been, not an excess, but a deficiency, of population. Even Spain, once the head of European civilization, had ten millions of inhabitants in the middle of the sixteenth century, and one hundred and twenty years afterwards, it had only six millions. The classical scholar need not be reminded of the still more striking depopulation of Italy under the Roman emperors, and, at a still earlier day, of the provinces which now constitute Turkey in Europe. Asia Minor and the region on the banks of the Tigris and Euphrates were teeming with inhabitants twenty-five centuries ago, while they are now very sparsely populated, and probably do not increase at all. But the causes which formerly kept down the natural increase of the people have now, in all civilized communities, in a great measure ceased to act. War is, at present, an infrequent and much less destructive calamity. Epidemic diseases no longer lay waste whole provinces; remedies for them, or modes of preventing them, have been discovered. The practice of vaccination alone, by robbing that frightful disease, the small-pox, of its terrors, has added some years to the average duration of human life. The greater prevalence of cleanliness, the improvement of the diet, dress, lodgings, and other accommodations of the mass of the people, and the drainage of bogs and marshes, by which agues and marsh fevers have been prevented, with the many improvements in medical and surgical science, have materially lessened the rate of mortality, and thus caused the population to increase more rapidly.

A comparison, made by M. de Chateauneuf, of the movement of the population in most countries of Europe from 1825 to 1830 with what it was from 1775 to 1780, an interval of only half a century, supplies some striking illustrations of this point. Out of a given number of children born in Europe, only one third, says the author, now die in the first ten years, while formerly one half died within that period. Fifty years after birth, three fourths of a generation, or 75 in a hundred, had died; now, only thirteen twentieths, or 65 in a hundred, die below the age of fifty. Twenty-three in a hundred, instead of only eighteen, now reach the age of sixty. The proportion of deaths to the whole population is now as one to forty; formerly, it was as high as one to thirty-two.

These facts to most people would seem to afford great cause for congratulation. Human life has been made longer; disease has lost a portion of its power, or has been conquered by care and medical science. Population is kept up, not merely by increasing the number of births, but by lessening the proportion of deaths; thus, among a given number of inhabitants, there are fewer children; and hence the average strength and capacity, the productive power of the community, is increased. "The prevalent opinion," says McCulloch, "had been, that an increase of population was the most decisive mark of the prosperity of a state, and that it was the duty of government to stimulate its increase, by encouraging early marriages, and granting exemptions from onerous public services and bestowing rewards on those who reared the greatest number of children." Many such expedients were tried at Rome under the republic and the empire.

"But Mr. Malthus," he adds, "has set the erroneous nature of this policy in the most striking point of view. He has shown, by a careful examination of the state of countries in every stage of civilization, and placed under the most opposite circumstances, that the number of inhabitants is everywhere proportioned to the means of subsistence; that the tendency of the principle of increase is not to fall below, but to exceed, these means; and that, consequently, wherever the population is not kept down to its necessary level by the influence of moral restraint, or by the exercise of a proper degree of prudence and forethought in the formation of marriages, it must be kept down by the influence of mortality originating in vice, want, and misery."

I cannot trace out here all the gloomy consequences which

Malthus and his followers derive from his theory; it must suffice to indicate a few of them. He assumes that the population in every country in Europe has already increased to such a degree, that it is actually pressing upon the means of subsistence; and as it tends still to multiply faster than the quantity of food can be increased, the low wages of labor, poverty, disease, crime, and an average duration of life much less than it might be, are the inevitable consequences. Stop up the evil in one quarter, and it must break out in another, on account of the prolific power which is in reserve. Put an end to war, and famine, or some epidemic disease, must take its place, and carry off yearly as many victims as the war would have done. Stop the ravages of the small-pox by vaccination, and the Asiatic cholera, or some other disease, must appear to scourge mankind with an equivalent number of deaths, if they will not learn prudence enough to diminish the number of marriages and births. The vessel is already full, and it is also fed from beneath with perennial springs. Check the overflow in one quarter, therefore, and it must escape in another. I will quote Mr. Malthus's own words. "I feel not the slightest doubt," he says, "that if the introduction of the cow-pox should extirpate the small-pox, and yet the number of marriages continue the same, we shall find a very perceptible difference in the increased mortality of some other disease." Wages, it is further said, depend on the proportion between the numbers of the laboring class and the capital which is devoted to paying for labor. As the number of those seeking employment increases, —and it always tends, like a depressed spring, to increase,— the laborers compete with each other in offering to work at low prices, and wages inevitably fall. Vainly does private munificence or public liberality seek to prevent this evil. Interference, in fact, only does harm; if the laborer can look to a poor fund, or to private charity, to provide against the effects of his imprudence, he will never learn to be prudent. Leave him alone, then, say the Malthusians, to be chastised by fever, hunger, and misery, into a sense of his obligation to society to refrain from increasing the number of his class. Let not the possession of a starving family constitute an additional claim for him who begs your charity; rather let it be his punishment. To devise means for relieving the present frightful condition of the laboring poor in England and Ireland is a hopeless and insoluble problem. The best advice which the leading economist of this school can give his countrymen, in respect to this subject, is, that they should "fold their arms, and leave the *dénouement* to time and Providence."

The most effectual means of keeping down the increase of population, it is said, is to raise the laborer's ideas of what is necessary for his maintenance. Thus, says Mr. Thomson, "a laborer in Ireland will live and bring up a family on potatoes; a laborer in England will see the world unpeopled first. Englishmen have the physical capability of living on potatoes as much as other men; but fortunately they have not the habit; and though it might be wrong to say that they would starve first in their own persons, they will utterly refuse to multiply upon such diet, the effect of which on population is ultimately the same. The Englishman will not live and bring up a family on potatoes; because, though he may consent to live on them when he can positively procure nothing else, habit, custom, the opinion of those around him, have made it in his eyes contemptible, irrational, absurd, for a man to be living on potatoes when he has the opportunity of getting anything better. In his hours of prosperity, therefore, he will to a certainty solace himself upon bacon, and most probably venture upon beef; and as this absorbs a greater portion of his income in what he views as necessary to his individual existence, it proportionally reduces his disposition to burden himself with new mouths. If the Irishman had the prospect of all this bacon and beef, he would view it as convertible into potatoes for a family like a patriarch's. The Englishman thinks it but decency to swallow all, and omits the family."

I have endeavored to give as full a view as possible of the theory of Malthus and its consequences, without disguising the force of any of the considerations that may be adduced in its support. Without accusing it of any demoralizing tendencies, it must be admitted to present a very gloomy view of the condition of the human race, and of the ways of Providence with man. It justifies the stoical indifference with which many regard the woes of their brethren, and the evils of the social state, when they wish to avoid any responsibility for their continuance, or when they despair of being able to relieve them. I hope to prove satisfactorily, that the doctrine itself is a mere hypothetical speculation, having no relation to the times in which we live, or to any which are near at hand. In those facts which appear so alarming to the Malthusians, I see only indications of a beneficent arrangement of Providence, by which it is ordained that the barbarous races which now tenant the earth should waste away and finally disappear, while civilized men are not only to multiply, but to spread, till the farthest corners of the earth shall be given to them for a habitation.

I begin with the proposition, that the power of the earth to afford sustenance is now so far in advance of the actual numbers of mankind, that no probable, and in fact no possible, increase of those numbers, not even by a geometrical progression, can create a general and permanent scarcity for centuries to come. The great and palpable error of the Malthusians consists in assuming, without a particle of evidence, nay, when all the evidence tends to the contrary, that *the time has already come*, that population has reached its limits, that there is even now a deficiency of food, so that the only present mode of increasing the happiness of the lower classes is to lessen their numbers. Malthusianism in its simplest form is only the expression of a law that belongs both to the animal and vegetable kingdom, and its truth is undeniable; yet we say that it has no applicability to the present state of affairs, and we have no immediate concern in establishing its truth or falsehood. If a speculatist in natural philosophy should undertake to demonstrate that the sun was gradually but surely expending its stock of light and heat, constant drafts being made upon it in those immense floods of radiance and warmth with which it now inundates every part of the solar system, and there being no means of supplying the waste, so that the time must inevitably come, in the lapse of ages, when this now glorious orb will appear utterly dark and cold, we should listen to his evidence certainly with attention and respect, as to the announcement of a curious truth in science; but if any individual, on the strength of this supposed discovery, should preach up the instant necessity of economizing with the utmost care our fuel and oil, should advise people to go to bed at sundown in order to save candles, and to warm themselves by flannels instead of fires, his friends would reasonably be alarmed for his sanity, and would urge him to retire for a while to a mad-house.

The absurdity of talking about the necessary pressure of population upon the means of subsistence, as an explanation of the evils with which society is *now* oppressed, was well exposed, many years ago, by Colonel Thompson. "If it should be urged," he says, "that there *must always come* a time when population will press against food, and therefore there is no use in attempting to escape it; this would be like urging that there is no use in a man's escaping from murder now, because he will not be immortal afterwards. There is all the difference in the world between enduring an evil by the will of Providence, and by the act of man. Human life, in the whole, is but the procrastination of death; but that is no reason why men should die just now, for other men's convenience. There may come a time when there will be no coal to burn, no iron to make tools, and perhaps no salt left in the sea; but this is no reason why men should not make something of the interval which must intervene. The time when population will press irremediably against food must, to a great manufacturing and naval people, be almost as remote as the time when there will be no salt left in the sea. And come when it may, it must always come gradually, which is by itself no small diminution of the mischief."

The average density of population in Europe, in which quarter of the globe alone any excess of numbers is to be feared for centuries to come, does not amount to 70 persons to the square mile. The Europeans, then, on an average, are not quite so crowded as are the inhabitants of Spain, a country the population of which might be increased fourfold before it would be as thickly peopled even as England. Belgium has the densest population of any state on the Continent of considerable magnitude, the average (in 1846) amounting to at least 344 persons to the square mile. Great Britain and Ireland, in respect to which the complaints of over-population have been loudest and most frequent, had but 235 to the square mile in 1851, so that the population might be increased nearly 50 per cent before these countries would be as densely peopled as Belgium. Taking all Europe together, the population might be five times as great as it is now, before the inhabitants would be as crowded as they are already in Belgium. Supposing that the average rate of increase for all Europe were as high as it now is in France, a supposition which is certainly beyond the truth, more than three centuries must elapse before the Continent could be thus peopled, even if no allowance were made for emigration and the gradual lessening of the rates of increase as the population becomes more dense. Making allowance for these checks, the period must be increased to at least five centuries. An evil which is at least five hundred years distant from us, need not excite much alarm in the present generation. Before this period elapses, it has been calculated that the stock of bituminous coal in England may be exhausted, — an article on which British power and wealth unquestionably depend. Yet we have not heard any fear expressed on this score, nor has economy in the consumption of coal been recommended, though such strenuous efforts have been made to deter the laboring poor from forming early and imprudent marriages.

Is there any evidence, then, that Belgium is over-peopled, the country which is already in the condition that all Europe fears it will arrive at some five centuries hence? By no means. The information which shows that it is not, I derive from McCulloch, one of the ablest statisticians of Europe, and who is himself an ardent upholder of the theory of Malthus, so that his testimony can be received without question. "Although the cultivation of the earth in this kingdom is carried to a great extent, one eleventh of the surface still remains uncultivated; one eighth consists of grass lands, and the arable lands occupy one half. The very large produce obtained by the Flemish farmer is solely attributable to indefatigable industry; for the soil is naturally poor, and the climate is by no means especially favorable, the winters being longer and more severe than in England. The most fertile districts in the country were formerly alluvial morasses, which have been drained and embanked, or have been gained entirely from the bed of the ocean, against which they are now protected by dykes. The provinces of West and East Flanders and Hainault form a far-stretching plain, of which the luxuriant vegetation indicates the indefatigable care and labor bestowed upon its cultivation; for the natural soil consists almost wholly of barren sand, and its great fertility is entirely the result of very skilful management." The account of the natural condition of most of the other portions of the country is but little more favorable. "The central part of the kingdom includes much of the richest portion of the soil; but it does not, on the whole, exceed the average fertility of the inland counties of England, and must decidedly be considered inferior to the rich alluvial soils denominated the *carses* of Scotland. But taking the whole country together, the soil, artificially enriched, produces more than double the quantity of corn required for the consumption of its inhabitants, and agricultural produce is exported to a great extent." *

Looking, therefore, merely to the capacity of the earth to afford sustenance, it appears that the most densely peopled country in Europe, and one by no means richly favored in respect to the natural properties of its soil, is not yet more than half populated; and still several centuries must elapse before all Europe can be as densely populated as Belgium. Turning to America, we find the basin of one great river, the Mississippi, capable of supporting as many inhabitants as now occupy all Europe, though the actual population of the whole United States does not equal one tenth part of that number. If we add the tropical and southern portions of the great American continent, and then go to the Antipodes to look at Australia, the area of which does not fall far short of that of all Europe, — if we consider what an insignificant fraction of these vast regions is yet tenanted by civilized man, — we are obliged to give up our statistical calculations in despair; the imagination fails to grasp the possible number of human beings whom the earth might support, or the number of years that must elapse (judging from the world's history thus far) before this extent of space can be fully peopled, and there can be a just call for room.

Till this limit is approached, — that is, for several centuries yet to come, — every birth adds something, or might add something, to the possible surplus of food. If there are more mouths to feed, there are more hands to feed them with; if

* These statements are selected from the article on Belgium in McCulloch's *Geographical Dictionary*.

there is more work to be done, there are more laborers to do it. It is demonstrable that, even in Ireland, (until its population shall be thrice as great as it is at present,) since the labor of one person upon the soil must produce more than is necessary for his personal subsistence, the more hands there are employed in agriculture, the greater will be the surplus for those engaged in other occupations. That the surplus will not increase *in the same ratio* with the number of agricultural laborers, is a fact of no importance; before the growth of the population can be checked by absolute deficiency of food, there must cease to be *any* surplus, and the earth must not yield enough even for the subsistence of him who cultivates it. We may have as much dread of *this* contingency as of the sun's expending its whole stock of light and heat, or of there being no salt left in the sea.

Ireland is an instance directly in point to bring the doctrine of the Malthusians to a test. They say that the island is over-peopled, and that their excessive number is the cause of the wretchedness of its inhabitants. But in ordinary years, Ireland not only supplies food for her whole population, but her exports of the cereal grains alone amount to five millions sterling, and of meat, butter, and cheese to at least half as much more. It is absurd, then, to say that the population is here pressing against the means of subsistence; and if the doctrine does not hold true in this case, to what country in the civilized world is it applicable? Another view of the matter leads to the same result. If the land were parcelled out, and the same modes of cultivation pursued, in Ireland as in the Netherlands, the former country being naturally far the more fertile of the two, it is demonstrable that the soil would furnish abundance of food for twenty-six millions of inhabitants, instead of supporting, as it now does, little over six millions, one half of whom, five years ago, were on the brink of starvation.

Barbarous, and even half-civilized nations, it is admitted on all hands, are in no danger of multiplying too rapidly; the law of a geometrical progression is not applicable to them; they do not increase, but decrease. The aborigines of a country, wherever they come in contact with civilization, melt away as ice and snow do at the approach of summer. So it has been with the Indians of our own continent, with the natives of

Australia, the Hottentots of South Africa, the Moors of Barbary, and the natives of the Pacific isles; and so it must always be. War, disease, vice, and ignorance, which are necessary accompaniments of the savage state, are destructive of human life; they do not allow the population to increase, they seldom allow it to hold its own. Go a little higher in the social scale, and this result is but little modified. The Turks, the Arabs, the Tartars, the Hindoos, are probably not so numerous as they were a century ago. The countries which now form Turkey in Europe and Turkey in Asia were more populous two or three thousand years ago, than they are at the present day. The wasting away of such tribes may be, in some cases, the consequence of a deficiency of food; but it is certainly not the result of over-population; for the civilized men who come to occupy their places, obtain from the same soil abundance of food for a population larger than theirs by twenty or a hundred fold. The North American Indians, when their hunting-grounds generally exceeded ten square miles for every member of the tribe, and the soil was often of great fertility, were sometimes severely pinched by famine. For this reason, infanticide was not infrequent among them, and life was shortened by privation and hardship. So far, then, as the mere lack of food proves excess of numbers, the Malthusians might as well have preached abstinence from marriage to them as to the Irish. In both cases, the bounty of Providence is not exhausted, but men do not make proper use of the means that are within their reach for satisfying their bodily wants; it matters not whether they leave the soil untilled altogether, or send a large portion of its product out of the country while millions are famishing at home.

Civilized nations, let them multiply as fast as they may, do not devote their attention chiefly, or even in great part, to the supply of food, but to the pursuit of wealth. Exchangeable value in general, not the means of subsistence even in particular, is the object of their endeavors. What matters it to me, that my neighbor owns and cultivates a large extent of fertile land, while I do not own a square foot, provided that I have plenty of money in my purse? With that money, I know, I can purchase food of my neighbor, that I can even lay the fertility of both Indies and of the farthest corners of the earth under contribution to supply my personal wants. Communities and nations act, in this respect, just like individuals. If it should be more profitable to them to devote their arable lands to other purposes than those of husbandry, they will do so without hesitation, being confident that they will be supplied from other lands. The inhabitants of the island of Barbadoes, with a soil abundantly capable of supplying their wants, actually devote all their ground and labor to the cultivation of sugar, cotton, and a few tropical products, which they export, while they import all their provisions, their wheat, pickled fish and salted meat, butter, cheese, &c., from the United States. They do not, on their own ground, raise food enough for the hundredth part of their own consumption. What they do almost exclusively, all commercial and manufacturing communities do to a certain extent. They devote their energies to getting wealth, and buy food whencesoever it may come to them, being wholly indifferent whether it is raised in their own or in foreign lands. Thus, in Massachusetts, as already remarked, we do not raise wheat and cattle enough for our own consumption, while our population, as a Malthusian would say, is increasing with frightful rapidity. But should we be justified, then, in abrogating our laws for the support of paupers, on the ground that the number of the people already exceeded the capacity of the soil to sustain them, and that the poor must consequently be chastised into the system of prudent marriages?

Such a plea would appear ridiculous here; is it any more reasonable in Great Britain? Since the abolition of the corn laws, and of other oppressive charges in the British tariff, the market price of the chief articles of provision is not, and cannot be, ten per cent higher in Liverpool than in Boston; and *the supply* of these articles (which is the only point that we need consider here) is just as abundant in the former place as the latter. The farmers of Ohio, Wisconsin, and Iowa would rejoice at an opportunity to supply all England and Ireland with all the wheat that they require. A failure of the English crops, or a multiplication of the English people, is certainly no misfortune to us, though we have to supply the food which in that case becomes necessary; is it then a misfortune to the English, — a misfortune, I mean, of such a character as to justify them in complaining of the ways of Providence for sending more human beings upon the earth than the earth is capable of supporting? It is a calamity, unquestionably, *in regard to the acquisition of wealth;* for the necessity of buying so much food diminishes their store of wealth. But it is not a calamity *in regard to the supply of food,* or to the limited extent and fertility of the earth's surface. Man, not Providence, is in fault. Great Britain is obliged to buy all her cotton, an article of almost as universal consumption as wheat; yet this fact, being one to which she is habituated, is not made a subject of complaint. Cotton, however, can be produced to advantage only in a few regions, of comparatively limited extent; while the cereal grains can be raised over three fourths of the surface of the habitable globe. Should a new process of agriculture be discovered, by which cotton could be grown over all England with so much facility and profit that the yearly returns of the farmer would be twice as great as by raising wheat, it is very certain that no wheat would then be raised on English ground, and yet there would be no deficiency in the supply of that necessary article. In this case, she would raise her cotton, and buy her wheat; now, she raises her wheat, and buys her cotton.

We can now see with sufficient distinctness the two great facts which afford a complete refutation of Malthusianism. The first is, that the limit of population in any country whatever is, not the number of people which the soil of that country alone will supply with food, but the number which the surface of the whole earth is capable of feeding; and it is a matter of demonstration, that *this* limit cannot even be approached for many centuries. The inability of England alone, or of Ireland alone, to supply her teeming population with food, is a fact of no more importance in the world's history, than the inability of the city of London alone to supply her two millions of people with farming produce from her own soil. London taxes all the counties of England for sustenance; England taxes all the countries of the earth for sustenance; — I cannot see any difference between the two cases.

Then, secondly, I say that the practical or actual limit to the growth of population in every case is the limit to the increase and distribution, not of food, but of wealth. Among civilized men in modern times, a famine is created, not by any absolute deficiency in the supply of food, but because the poorer classes have no money to buy it with. As every human being is an implement for the production of wealth, a means of enlarging the aggregate national product, or the amount of exchangeable values belonging to a nation, the increase of population is not a cause of scarcity of food, but a preservative against it. It makes no difference whether the mass of the people are engaged in hammering iron, spinning cotton, or raising wheat; for the product in each of these cases either is food, or is exchangeable for food, which amounts to precisely the same thing. Commerce distributes equally all products for which there is an equal demand. In respect to the supply and the price of food, New York has no advantage over Liverpool, because there is a wide, fertile, and only half-tenanted region lying behind the former, while the latter backs upon a land teeming with poverty-stricken millions; for the supply, whencesoever obtained, is distributed between the two places in exact proportion to the demand for it in each; and if the price in Liverpool is higher because the grain must be brought thither from New York, the price in New York is higher because the grain must be carried thence to Liverpool. *Our* crops did not fail in 1847, but the price of grain, in our seaport towns, and even in our back country, rose in as great proportion as in Ireland and Scotland. But all classes of our people were still able to buy the grain, even at the advanced price; while one half of the Irish people, and perhaps one sixth of the Scotch, were too poor to obtain it at this price, and therefore they hungered, and very many of them died of starvation.

This is the true explanation of the famine of 1847 in the British Isles. The march of civilization, the extension of trade, the facilities of transport, and the consequent ease of supplying the failure of the crops in one country by the superabundance of the harvest in another, have made the recurrence of a proper famine, in modern times, impossible. By a *proper* famine, I mean such an absolute deficiency of food, and impossibility of obtaining it on any terms, as is suffered by the garrison of a besieged town, or by the crew of a wrecked ship. It is not in the scheme of Providence, as hitherto revealed to man, that harvests should fail all the world over at the same time, or even for the failure to be so general that the aggregate product should not suffice — perhaps with some scrimping and some hardship — for the aggregate want. A semi-barbarous nation in the far East, or the population of a little island separated by thousands of sea-miles from any continent, may suffer from a famine, properly so called, before the arm of Christian Europe or America can be stretched out to the rescue. But no civilized nation, either in the Old or New World, whatever the Malthusians may say to alarm them, ever fear an absolute deficiency of food; its fields may be unfruitful for a single season; but in such case, it looks with well-founded confidence to its neighbors, and even to remote parts of the earth, for a supply. In 1847, the bounty of Providence to the British Isles did not fail; ship-loads of corn were turned away from their shores for want of a market. The granaries of the two islands were filled to overflowing, not indeed from the products of their own harvests, but from the immense supplies poured into them by our ever-teeming land. Flour and meal became a drug in the English market before a sheaf of that year's wheat was cut, and many dealers in grain were bankrupted by the consequent sudden reduction of prices. If the stock of provisions had been equally distributed among the people, not a man, woman, or child among them would have suffered from famine for a single hour. The fate of the Irish and Scotch appeared the more terrible, because *they starved in the midst of plenty.* They died, not because the fields were cursed with barrenness, but because they had not wherewithal to buy food. The price of breadstuffs did not become more than double its average in ordinary years, did not rise so high by one third as in 1800 and 1801; and in those years, though there was scarcity, there was no famine; the sufferings of the poor were increased, but there was no general starvation. The year 1847 witnessed a frightful anomaly, which will long be remembered as a disgrace to modern civilization, — *a famine of which poverty was almost the sole cause.*

A fallacy pervades the whole reasoning of the Malthusians on the relation of the supply of food to the growth of the population. More grain is raised because there are more men who need it, and not more men are raised because there is more grain to feed them with. Procreation is not stopped because there is no more grain, since misery and the peril of starvation only make men reckless, and cause them to multiply faster. But agriculture is stopped when there are no more mouths calling for food; a cessation of demand causes a cessation of supply here, because the husbandman is looking only for pecuniary gain. But in the case of population, a want of demand does not occasion a want of supply; since men are urged by their natural inclinations, and not by the state of the children-market, or by the desire of profit. They do not always marry because they want children, but because they want a wife. It is true, that the call for more food, which is created by an excess of numbers, will not be an effectual calling, unless the people have the means to purchase it with;—but these they will never lack, if the wealth of the country is distributed according to the natural course of things,—that is, in exact proportion to the increase of each family, all the children sharing alike. At any rate, if the demand be rendered ineffectual from this cause, the real evil, the real check upon the population, is not the insufficient supply of food, but the want of property. Turn the matter as we may, it is not the niggardliness of nature which is the source of misery, but the devices of man and the injustice of the laws.

I have endeavored to prove, that in the most thickly populated country on earth, the number of the people is yet very far within the limit of the subsistence which the land is capable of affording, even if we look only to the capacities of their own soil, and not to the immeasurable supplies which their wealth and commerce might pour in upon them from other shores. Still further, I do not believe there is any danger that mankind, even in the lapse of future centuries, will ever multiply up to the limit which the terraqueous globe is able to contain and nourish. To adopt the favorite metaphor of the Malthusians, the weights which are now actually keeping down the spring of population—that spring which they think is always ready to fly up with the full force of a "geometrical progression"—are war, vice, unnecessary or curable disease, ignorance, idleness, bad habits, bad government, and inequality of wealth fostered by bad laws. Remove these, one by one, or in a mass, and there will be room for an almost indefinite expansion of the compressed force, and a consequent increase of human happiness, before the ultimate check, which may be considered as a weight hanging much higher up, can come into action through the absolute inability of the earth to contain and support more. In truth, it is demonstrable both from reason and experience, that population never can rise to the point where it will meet this last and insuperable obstacle. Among the lower weights to be first removed are ignorance, vice, bad government, and a virtual division of society into castes through unnatural yet fixed inequalities of wealth and condition. Take away these, and you remove along with them the widely spread misery which they foster, and which is the great cause why the population multiplies unduly, or under circumstances that are not fitted for it, because such hopeless misery renders men imprudent and reckless, and leads them to burden themselves with a family, though they are already starving, because they cannot be worse off, and there is no hope of improving their estate. To adopt the phraseology of Mr. Malthus, take away the "positive check," and the "preventive check" will come into play of its own accord, — will come into play naturally, inevitably, and without compulsion, — not as the consequence of a theory, but as the easy, beneficent, and necessary result of the laws of nature and nature's God. Whatever tends to keep men hopelessly poor is a direct encouragement, the strongest of all incentives, to an increase of population. Take away the causes of misery, remove the insurmountable barriers which now keep the various classes of European society apart, and educate the people, and there will be no fears of an excess of numbers. Take away the lower weights which keep down the spring, and it will never rise high enough to meet the upper one. The bounty and the wisdom of Providence never fail. It is not the excess of population which causes the misery, but the misery which causes the excess of population.

Dr. Whately, with great acuteness, has traced the erroneous conclusions of Malthus to an ambiguity in the meaning of a word. "By a 'tendency' towards a certain result, is sometimes meant the existence of a cause which, *operating unimpeded*, would produce that result. In this sense it may be said with truth, that the earth, or any other body moving round a centre, has a *tendency* to fly off at a tangent; that is, the centrifugal force operates in that direction, though it is controlled by the centripetal: or, again, that man has a greater tendency to fall prostrate than to stand erect; that is, the attraction of gravitation and the position of the centre of gravity are such, that the least breath of air would overset him, but for the voluntary exertion of muscular force: and again, that population has a tendency to increase beyond subsistence; that is, there are in man propensities which, *if unrestrained*, lead to that result.

"But sometimes, again, 'a tendency towards a certain result' is understood to mean 'the existence of such a state of things that that result may be expected to take place.' Now it is in these two senses that the word is used in the two premises of the argument in question. But in this latter sense, the earth has a greater tendency to remain in its orbit than to fly off from it; man has a greater tendency to stand erect than to fall prostrate; and, (as may be proved by comparing a more barbarous with a more civilized period in the history of any country,) in the progress of society, subsistence has a tendency to increase at a greater rate than population. In this country [Great Britain], for instance, much as our population has increased within the last five centuries, it yet bears a far less ratio to subsistence (though still a much greater than could be wished) than it did five hundred years ago."

It is of this ambiguous meaning of the word *tendency*, that the Malthusians avail themselves, first, when they are pressed by argument and by the statement of facts which are irreconcilable with their hypothesis, and, secondly, when they wish to apply that hypothesis to the explanation of social phenomena at the present day. In the former case, they intrench themselves in a naked statement of the fact, common alike to the animal and the vegetable kingdoms, that each species *tends* to multiply itself according to the terms of a geometrical progression, doubling itself in as short a time, and with as much ease, whether the number of individuals in the species be ten, or ten millions; — a statement which no one will think of impugning, though it affords no more ground of alarm than the kindred statement, that the earth has a tendency to fly off from its orbit at a tangent, or that man tends to fall prostrate. No sane person expects, in either of these cases, that the *tendency* will be carried out, or practically exemplified. But in the second instance, when left to themselves, in their attempt to educe from their doctrine an explanation of the misery of the working classes in Great Britain and Ireland, and of the causes of the depression of wages, the Malthusians use the word *tendency* to denote "such a state of things that the result (over-population and consequent misery) may be either immediately expected, or declared to have already taken place."

In this last case, they may be met by the counter statement that *there is no such tendency*, — that is, no instance can be adduced in which the privations or the misery of a people may be fairly attributed to their numbers having outgrown their supply of food. History does not furnish one; reason and religion alike declare such an event to be impossible. In truth, the population of the whole earth has increased very slowly, some tribes, races, and nations wasting away, while others flourish and multiply; and the excess of the increase in the latter case over the diminution in the former one is an almost inappreciable quantity, when compared with the whole number of mankind. It would be difficult to prove that the world is more populous now than it was a hundred years ago; the Europeans, it is true, are considerably more numerous; but the Asiatics and Africans have probably diminished in number, and the native tribes of America — once reckoned at sixteen millions in only the northern half of the continent — have almost entirely dwindled away. It is certain that the earth is not yet peopled up to the hundredth part of the number which it might supply with abundant food; and judging from the past only, or from what experience, our only safe teacher on such a subject, declares to be probable, its population could not multiply a hundred-fold in less than thousands of years.

The Malthusian is certainly bound to maintain, that the number of mankind is now considerably greater than it was in the middle of the ninth century. But he will not venture to assert that they are now less abundantly supplied with food. Nay, he will be obliged to admit, that the countries in which the population has advanced most rapidly are precisely those which are now most abundantly supplied with the necessaries of life. Practically, then, the experience of the last thousand years has proved, that *subsistence has a "tendency" to outrun population*, which is just the reverse of the proposition of Malthus. Thus it must always be, so long as the earth yields much less than it is capable of producing; for, in this case, all that is needed to develop its latent capacities is an additional number of hands to be devoted to agriculture, each one of whom must produce more than is necessary for his own sustenance, and must thus increase the surplus of necessaries which are seeking for a market. I have already endeavored to prove that the agricultural population of this country — which embraces two thirds of the freemen, and, if the slaves be added, more than three fourths of the whole number — is excessive; that the surplus of grain and other produce of the earth remaining for exportation is consequently too great, and its price abroad is unreasonably diminished; that a greater value in commodities might be obtained for a smaller quantity sent abroad; and that the persons thus set free from the cultivation of the earth might be more profitably employed in manufactures, in which the whole product of their toil, which, as skilled labor, would command a higher recompense, would be an addition to the present stock of national wealth.

CHAPTER XII.

THE PRINCIPLES WHICH REGULATE THE GROWTH OF POPULATION.

Having briefly considered the doctrine of Malthus, I propose in this chapter to examine the true theory of population, to inquire into the circumstances which govern its increase and distribution. The true law of the increase of numbers in a civilized society is not hard to find, though it is difficult to express all the modifications that it undergoes from a change of circumstances. The consideration which affects most strongly the inclination of people to labor and to save, and thus furnishes the chief stimulus for the accumulation of capital, also regulates in a great degree their tendency to increase in number. It is natural that it should be so; other things being equal, a man's condition as married or single, and the size of his family, are decisive of his worldly fortune. If his ambition is awakened by a fair prospect of the attainment of riches and consequent advancement in society, he will become prudent not only in his expenditures, but in contracting any relations which may become a burden to him, — which may impede his efforts to rise, and may even tend to depress him in the world. In a normal state, then, the inclination of people to marry is controlled by their opinion of the effect which marriage will have upon their position in life. If they have no fears that the additional expense thus incurred will sink them to a lower rank in society, or interfere with their hopes of rising in the world, they will follow the impulse of natural affection and desire.

The eldest son in a wealthy family, where the right of primogeniture prevails, will marry because his future is secure; whatever may happen, a fortune is secured to him beyond the effects even of his own imprudence. The miserable laborers on his estate, who do not taste meat more than once in a month, will marry because *their* future is secured in another way: they have touched bottom; nothing can sink them in the world, and no degree of prudence or self-denial can ever raise them above a laborer's estate. Their unhappy children, it is true, may starve, or die of diseases induced by insufficient or improper food; and if the theory of Malthus were true, this consideration would often operate to deter them from marriage, for they are the only class who may be said to have the fear of starvation directly before their eyes. But excessive misery creates recklessness and despair; they who have no hope or fear, cannot be expected to deny themselves the only gleam of comfort or alleviation of wretchedness of which their miserable state is capable.

The younger sons in noble or wealthy families, if the patrimony falls exclusively to the eldest, generally remain single, or marry late in life, as an early connection of this sort would be certain degradation; at any rate, they could not maintain the style of living to which they have been brought up. As the marriage of only one person out of a family cannot do more than keep up the number in the class to which they belong, and often may not effect even that, these families constantly tend to die out; and if it were not for promotions to their rank from the middle classes, the upper orders of society would gradually disappear. Of the 216 Barons who now sit in the English House of Lords, the peerage of all but 30 has been created since 1711; and 127, or considerably more than half of the whole number, have been admitted to the peerage since 1800. Royal families are still more prone to die out than the families of noblemen; from the line of succession to the English throne, the families of the Plantagenets, the Tudors, and the Stuarts have already disappeared; and the house of Brunswick, saving that branch of it the title of which is transmitted through a female, exists by a very slender tie, and will probably soon be extinct. George III. had seven sons, four of whom died without issue admitted to be legitimate by English law; and the three who married and had issue, left but five children in all, only two of whom are sons. The history of several other royal families in Europe is of a similar character; but the principle is, perhaps, most strikingly exemplified among the landed gentry of England, whose continued and increasing opulence is chiefly to be attributed to this cause; for the diminution of their numbers, of course, tends to the concentration of their estates.

In the intermediate conditions of life, the frequency of marriages still depends on the same rule, though its operation is affected by the general circumstances of the country, and by the particular position of individuals. In a newly settled region, children are a help to the parents' advancement, because labor is so valuable; hence the rapid advance of population in the frontier States of our own Union, an advance which immigration alone does not account for, though a considerable part of it is certainly attributable to this latter cause. In a more thickly populated country, children are a hinderance, from the difficulty of establishing them in an equal position of life with their parents. But even in this case, those who are in easy circumstances will marry, while those who can but just maintain themselves in the condition of life in which they were born will often remain single. This last case is that of the peasantry of many countries of Continental Europe, who cultivate their own little farms, and are perpetually admonished by the moderate size of their properties, that any increase of their number must lead, not indeed to starvation, but to the forfeiture of their position as land-owners.

Thus, in Switzerland, which is, in the main, a country of small proprietors, the population increases so slowly, that, at its present rate, it is estimated that it would not double itself in less than 227 years. In France, where also the land is cut up into very small estates, but where the peasantry are less prudent, less disposed to make calculations respecting the future, than the Swiss, the estimated period of duplication varies from 115 to 138 years. "Denmark," says Mr. Laing, "being altogether agricultural, not manufacturing, except for the home use of her own agricultural consumers, her population increases very slowly, and keeps very far behind the means of subsistence from the products of the soil. She is a living evidence of the falsity of the theory, that population increases more rapidly than subsistence where the land of a country is held by small working proprietors. There are large estates and small all over the country, estates of noblemen and gentlemen, and estates of peasant proprietors. The greater part of the land of Denmark is in the hands of the latter class. As a class, they are wealthy."

The general effect in the Old World, then, may be thus stated, — that the numbers of the poor increase most rapidly, of the middle classes more slowly, and of the upper or wealthier ones, either not at all, or by a fraction so small that the effect would hardly be perceptible. This is strikingly illustrated in Sweden, where the census and the registration of births, deaths, and marriages are taken with reference to the division of the people into three classes. The official returns for 1835 give the following results. The yearly excess of births over deaths among the persons reckoned as belonging to the class of the nobility was only one for every 1,508. For those who are described as "persons of property and station," the yearly excess was one for every 640; while for the peasantry it was one for every 107. In other words, the rate of increase for the peasantry is nearly six times greater than that of the middle class, and over fourteen times greater than that of the nobles. Among the nobility, 13 per cent of the married males were but twenty-five years of age, or under; among the peasantry, 37 per cent were married at this early age. In wretched Ireland, more than one half of the males who are over seventeen years of age are married. Thus do the laws of nature itself operate against a permanent or hereditary aristocracy.

If we compare different countries with each other, we still find, in every case, that the lowest classes increase most rapidly, and that the rate of increase diminishes as we ascend in the social scale. But we also observe, that this law becomes more prominent and conspicuous, according as these social distinctions are more fixed and unalterable, — that is, as they approach the nature of castes; and also, it becomes more marked in proportion to the degree of poverty and wretchedness of the lowest class. Thus, we can discern the operation of the law even in this country, where it is matter of common observation, that laborers, mechanics, small tradesmen, and farmers generally marry at an early age, and have large families; while educated men, members of the professions, and sons of wealthy parents often defer "establishing themselves in life," as the phrase goes, till a comparatively late period. But owing to the general well-being of all classes here, and to the frequency and rapidity of transitions from one class to another, these differences are less obvious than in the Old World. Population here generally advances in a broad wave, coming from all divisions of society. But that the "preventive check" is not inoperative here in the United States, with all our advantages of broad and fertile territories, appears from the fact brought to light by the registration act in Massachusetts, that the average age of males at the time of first marriage here is twenty-five years and nearly nine months, while in England it is but twenty-five years and a little over five months. The average age of all the males who contracted marriages in Massachusetts during the four years 1844 – 48, (either first or subsequent marriages,) was 28.27 years; the average age of all the males marrying in England was 27.30; so it appears that Englishmen marry, on an average, when about one year younger than the men who marry in Massachusetts. Of all the males who married in Massachusetts, only 1.6 per cent were under 20 years of age; in England, 2.6 per cent married at this early age. Obviously, then, if females did not marry here at an earlier age than in England, and if marriages were not more general and more fruitful, our population would not advance more rapidly than the English population; and in fact, we find from the registration returns, that females in Massachusetts are married two years earlier than females in the mother country.

In France, where the land is minutely divided, and the peasantry are vastly better off than in England, but where each person is far more strongly chained to that class of society in which he is born than is the case in the United States, the rate of increase of the population, for ten years, is only 5 per cent, while in England it is 15 per cent, and in Connaught, the sink of Irish misery and degradation, from 1821 to 1831, it was as high as 22 per cent. In the province of Ulster, the rate is 14, while in the county of Donegal, it rises to 20 per cent. "And this is precisely the county which official reports represent as forming an exception to the general condition of Presbyterian Ulster, and affording an instance of poverty little less extreme than that of Connaught. In the latter province, we find Galway and Mayo, notoriously the two most destitute counties, exhibiting, the one an increase of 27, and the other of 25 per cent." This rate, it may be remarked, is rather higher than the rate of increase, excluding the effects of immigration, in the United States; so that the two extremes, of general misery and of general well-being, produce very nearly the same effect on the movement of the population, — a fact utterly irreconcilable with the theory of Malthus.

The probable result for our own country may now be very clearly seen. So long as land continues abundant and cheap, and the wages of labor high, so long the population will continue to increase with great rapidity. Barbarous tribes will die out before its advancing wave, and the desert will be peopled. But as the country fills up, and the wages of labor fall, it will become more difficult to rise from one class of society to another, and the rate of increase will diminish. When the land becomes as thickly settled as Belgium now is, — a result which centuries will be required to accomplish, — the population will advance as slowly as it now does in Belgium. I see nothing in this prospect which need alarm even those who are most apt to be apprehensive of the future. I see no signs of what the Malthusians most dread, — the over-population of the earth.

Mr. Senior has very happily illustrated the truth, that the

preventive check upon marriages is the fear, not of lacking the necessaries of life, or of positive starvation, but of being deprived of those comforts and enjoyments, of falling below that scale of expenditure, which custom has marked out as appropriate for every condition in life, or every rank in the social scale. Hence it is, that in countries abundantly supplied with food and other mere necessaries of life, population often advances more slowly than in more populous lands, where poverty prevails, and large classes of the people are subject to severe privations. I borrow the whole passage from Mr. Senior, though it is of considerable length, as it gives a clear statement of some useful distinctions.

"Though an apprehended deficiency of some of the articles of wealth is substantially the only preventive check to the increase of population, it is obvious that fear of the want of different articles operates, with all men, very differently; and even that an apprehended want of the same article will affect differently the minds of the individuals of different classes. An apprehended want of corn would produce on the minds of all Englishmen a very different effect from an apprehended want of silk. An apprehended want of butcher's meat would affect very differently the minds of Englishmen of different classes. It appears to us, therefore, convenient to divide for this purpose the articles of wealth into the three great classes of Necessaries, Decencies, and Luxuries, and to explain the different effects produced by the fear of the want of the articles of wealth falling under each class. We must begin, however, by stating, as precisely as we can, what we mean by the words *Necessaries*, *Decencies*, and *Luxuries;* terms which have been used ever since the moral sciences first attracted attention, but with little attention to precision as to consistent use.

"It is scarcely necessary to remind our readers that these are relative terms, and that some person must always be assigned with reference to whom a given commodity or service is a Luxury, a Decency, or a Necessary.

"By *Necessaries*, then, we express those things, the use of which is requisite to keep a given individual in the health and strength essential to his going through his habitual occupations.

"By *Decencies*, we express those things which a given individual must use in order to preserve his existing rank in society.

"Everything else of which a given individual makes use, or, in other words, all that portion of his consumption which is not essential to his health and strength, or to the preservation of his existing rank in society, we term *Luxury*.

"It is obvious that, when consumed by the inhabitants of different countries, or even by different individuals in the same country, the same things may be either luxuries, decencies, or necessaries.

"Shoes are necessaries to all the inhabitants of England. Our habits are such, that there is not an individual whose health would not suffer from the want of them. To the lowest class of the inhabitants of Scotland, they are luxuries; custom enables them to go barefoot without inconvenience and without degradation. When a Scotchman rises from the lowest to the middling classes of society, they become to him decencies. He wears them to preserve, not his feet, but his station in life. To the higher class, who have been accustomed to them from infancy, they are as much necessaries as they are to all classes in England. To the higher classes in Turkey, wine is a luxury and tobacco a decency. In Europe, it is the reverse. The Turk drinks and the European smokes, not in obedience, but in opposition, both to the rules of health and to the forms of society. But wine in Europe and the pipe in Turkey are among the refreshments to which a guest is entitled, and which it would be as indecent to refuse in the one country as to offer in the other.

"It has been said that the coal-heavers and lightermen, and some others among the hard-working London laborers, could not support their toils without the stimulus of porter. If this be true, porter is to them a necessary. To all others, it is a luxury. A carriage is a decency to a woman of fashion, a necessary to a physician, and a luxury to a tradesman.

"The question, whether a given commodity is to be considered as a decency or a luxury, is obviously one to which no answer can be given, unless the place, the time, and the rank of the individual using it be specified. The dress which in England was only decent a hundred years ago, would be almost extravagant now, while the house and furniture which now would afford merely decent acccommodation to a gentleman, would then have been luxurious for a Peer. The causes which entitle a commodity to be called a necessary are more permanent and more general. They depend partly upon the habits in which the individual in question has been brought up, partly on the nature of his occupation, on the lightness or the severity of the labors and hardships that he has to undergo, and partly on the climate in which he lives. Of these causes we have illustrated the two first by the familiar examples of shoes and porter. But the principal cause is climate. The fuel, shelter, and raiment, which are essential to a Laplander's existence, would be worse than useless under the tropics. And as habits and occupations are very slowly changed, and climate suffers scarcely any alteration, the commodities which are necessary to the different classes of the inhabitants of a given district may, and generally do, remain for centuries unchanged, while their decencies and luxuries are continually varying.

"Among all classes, the check imposed by an apprehended deficiency of mere luxuries is but slight. The motives, perhaps we might say the instincts, that prompt the human race to marriage, are too powerful to be much restrained by the fear of losing conveniences unconnected with health or station in society. Nor is population much retarded by the fear of wanting merely necessaries. In comparatively uncivilized countries, in which alone, as we have already seen, that want is of familiar occurrence, the preventive check has little operation. They see the danger, but want prudence and self-denial to be influenced by it. On the other hand, among nations so far advanced in civilization as to be able to act on such a motive, the danger that any given person or his future family shall actually perish from indigence, appears too remote to afford any general rule of conduct.

"The great preventive check is the fear of losing decencies, or, what is nearly the same, the hope to acquire, by the accumulation of a longer celibacy, the means of purchasing the decencies which give a higher social rank. When an Englishman stands hesitating between love and prudence, a family actually starving is not among his terrors; against actual want, he knows that he has the fence of the poor-laws. But however humble his desires, he cannot contemplate without anxiety a probability that the income which supported his social rank while single, may be insufficient to maintain it when he is married; that he may be unable to give to his children the advantages of education which he enjoyed himself; in short, that he may lose his caste. Men of more enterprise are induced to postpone marriage, not merely by the fear of sinking, but also by the hope that, in an unencumbered state, they may rise. As they mount, the horizon of their ambition keeps receding, until sometimes the time has passed for realizing those plans of domestic happiness which probably every man has formed in his youth." *

It is this last cause, undoubtedly, which makes the period of marriage for males here in Massachusetts somewhat later than it is for males in Great Britain.

CHAPTER XIII.

THE THEORY OF RENT.

THE entire science of *English* Political Economy may be said to be built upon three leading theories; — that of Adam Smith concerning free trade, that of Malthus in regard to population, and that of Ricardo in regard to rent. They are intimately connected with each other; and a full appreciation of the mixture of truth and falsehood which they contain, would tend to clear the science of its local, English character, and to fit it for universal acceptance and utility. Having considered the first incidentally, and the second at some length, we may pass to an examination of Ricardo's doctrine; and in explaining it I shall follow the method, and, to some extent, the phraseology, of its most distinguished advocates.

The permanent or average value of everything not limited in quantity depends on the cost of its production, or on the

---

* Senior's *Political Economy*, (ed. 1850,) pp. 36 – 38.

amount of labor required to produce it. But the cost of producing some commodities cannot always be reduced to the same uniform standard; a few persons may enjoy certain facilities, some peculiar implements or patented machinery, *which other persons cannot obtain*, and by the aid of which, they can produce the article at less cost, or with a smaller amount of labor. They cannot, however, thus produce enough to satisfy the whole demand; and therefore, other persons must produce some at the expense of more labor. In such a case, the price of the commodity will be determined by the cost of *that portion which is produced with the greatest difficulty;* for, unless the price indemnified *these* producers, they would give up the business, and the necessary amount of the article could no longer be had. But the price having risen to this point, the persons producing the article more easily, by the aid of a machine or implements of which they have a monopoly, would receive an extraordinary profit. This whole extra profit may be called *rent*, a phrase which obviously includes the profits of a patentee of a useful machine, as well as those of a landholder.

The produce of land, according to this theory, is obtained under circumstances precisely analogous to those here supposed. The supply of grain or cattle may be indefinitely increased, by employing more capital and labor; but it cannot always be increased *in the same proportion* to the capital and labor expended. In the manufacture of cottons, woollens, and silks, double the capital, and you will usually double the amount produced. But in agriculture, this is not the case. The most eligible land is first taken up, — either that which is most fertile, or that which is nearest to market, or both. We will call this portion *land of the first class.* For a while, this produces enough to satisfy the demand. But the population increases, more grain is called for, and, as there is no more land of the first class to be had, the producers are obliged to take *land of the second class*, either that which is less fertile, or farther from market, or both; the demand having previously outrun the supply, the price has risen enough to remunerate them for employing capital and labor on this less promising soil. For a while, this additional supply suffices; but then population again advances, the demand for food is increased, the price rises again, and, as a necessary consequence, *land of the third class* is brought into cultivation. And so on, indefinitely. At each step, there is a necessary enhancement of price, and therefore of profit, to those who work the land of higher quality, or of more easy access. The price of the grain and cattle which are brought to market must always be high enough to pay those who work the poorest land in use; otherwise, they would quit the employment, and the land would fall out of cultivation. But this price, of course, will give a larger profit to those who hold the land of the next higher class, and a still larger one to the owners of land of the first class. And as still inferior lands come into use, these profits must become yet larger. The result is, that the amount of rent for land must always depend on the degree of superiority of that land over the least fertile, or least eligible, ground which is cultivated at all.

By the original constitution of nature, land is of various degrees of productiveness. One acre, with a certain quantity of labor bestowed upon it, will yield forty bushels of wheat; another acre, with the same amount of labor, will yield but thirty bushels; a third acre, still requiring the same labor, gives but twenty bushels. Now, suppose that these three acres of land constituted the whole stock of a family of persons living upon an island of this extent, and wholly cut off from intercourse with the rest of the world, by the intervention of a wide waste of ocean, and by their lack of ships or boats. If this family consisted of but five persons, we may suppose that one acre would furnish them grain enough, and, of course, they would choose the most productive land. There being land of this quality enough for all, no portion of it would yield any rent. But if three persons should be added to their number, there would be a necessity of cultivating the next best acre of land; and to the persons undertaking to cultivate it, it would amount to the same thing whether they took without rent the land yielding thirty bushels to the acre, or paid a rent, equal in value to ten bushels of grain, for the land producing forty bushels to the acre. The increase of population, then, rendering it necessary to have recourse to land of inferior fertility, would cause land of the first class to pay rent; and this rent would be exactly proportioned to its degree of superiority over the worst land in cultivation, which yields no rent. A farther accession of three individuals would oblige the community to till the third acre, which yields but twenty bushels; and one might have his choice between having this land without rent, or paying ten bushels a year for land of the next best quality, or twenty bushels a year for the most fertile spot. The result in either case would be the same to him. Always the worst land in cultivation pays no rent; and all other land pays rent in proportion to the degree of its superiority over this poorest land.

Natural fertility is but one of the circumstances that give value to land, or cause it to pay rent; nearness to market, or any other natural quality, operates in precisely the same way. If all the land produces the same quantity to the acre, and if the produce of one acre can be sold on the spot, while it costs the value of ten bushels of grain to carry the produce of the second acre to market, and of twenty bushels to transport that of the third acre, then the first acre will bear a rent of twenty bushels, the second a rent of ten bushels, and the third no rent at all, because it produces but twenty bushels, and the value of this product is all consumed in transporting it to market. The increased demand of towns, occasioned by the increase of their population, not only tempts the cultivators in their vicinity to improve their lands more highly, but frequently causes large portions of their supplies to be brought from a great distance. Hence it sometimes happens, that the advantage of vicinity more than counterbalances the disadvantage of comparative barrenness, so that lands of inferior fertility, in the immediate environs of a large town, yield a considerable rent, while much richer land, at a distance from good markets, yields little or perhaps no rent. As vicinity to a town is a cause of rent, so vicinity to a road, navigable river, or canal, by diminishing the expense of carriage to some great market, may have a similar effect.

Observe, also, that the theory still holds good, whether the increase of population constrains us to take poorer land, hitherto neglected, into cultivation, or to expend more capital and labor upon the land already in tillage, with a view of increasing its product. For the additional capital thus invested will not yield a return proportionally great with that capital which was first employed. If, for instance, a thousand dollars of capital spent upon a farm will cause it to yield at the rate of thirty bushels to the acre, the expenditure of a second thousand dollars upon it may raise the crop, perhaps, to forty bushels per acre; but it certainly will not double the crop, or make the yield to be sixty bushels, as it ought to do, if the second application of capital were equally remunerative with the first. Then the second application of capital will not be made till the increase of population has caused the price of grain to rise so high, that this second thousand dollars will produce as large profits as capital applied in other ways. And when this second thousand dollars will yield ordinary profits, it is obvious that the first thousand dollars, applied under circumstances much more advantageous, will yield much more than the ordinary profits. The difference between these two rates of profit is the rent of the land. Thus, always, just as there are more mouths calling for more food, either poorer land must be taken into cultivation, or more capital must be applied with perpetually diminishing returns, or at rates of profit growing successively less and less.

It is true, as the theory admits, that the necessity of having recourse to inferior lands, or of applying more capital with constantly diminishing returns, is *postponed* by the improvements that are made, from time to time, in the tools and processes of agriculture, which enable us to obtain more food from the same quantity of land without a proportionate increase of capital or industry. But the evil day is thus only postponed, not entirely removed. It is impossible that agricultural improvements should keep pace for any long time with the increase of the population; for they are limited in their nature and extent, while the prolific power of the human race is unbounded. These improvements also stimulate the increase of numbers, and thus, in one way, tend to increase the evil, which they do but partially check in another. "Improvements in the construction of farming implements," says McCulloch, "the discovery of more efficient manures, the introduction of more prolific crops, and of improved systems of management, increase, in a high degree, the productiveness of the soil, and proportionally reduce the price of raw produce; but a fall of price, though permanent in manufactures, is only temporary in agriculture. When the price of corn is reduced, all classes obtain greater quantities than before in exchange for their products or their labor; hence the rate of profit, and consequently the accumulation of capital, are both increased; and this increase, by causing a greater demand for labor and higher wages, leads, in the end, to an increase of population, and, consequently, to a further demand for raw produce, and an extended cultivation. Agricultural improvements obviate, sometimes for a lengthened period, the necessity of having recourse to inferior soils; still, however, their influence in this respect cannot be permanent. The stimulus which they at the same time give to population, and the natural tendency of mankind to increase up to the means of subsistence, are sure, in the long run, to raise prices, and, by forcing recourse to poor lands, rents also."

Mr. Malthus has ingeniously illustrated this theory of rent. "The earth," he says, "has been sometimes compared to a vast machine, presented by nature to man for the production of food and raw materials; but to make the resemblance more just, as far as they admit of comparison, we should consider the soil as a present to man of a great number of machines, all susceptible of continued improvement by the application of capital to them, but yet of very different original qualities and powers. This great inequality in the powers of the machinery employed in procuring raw produce, forms one of the most remarkable features which distinguish the machinery of the land from the machinery employed in manufactures.

"When a machine in manufactures is invented which will produce more finished work with less labor and capital than before, if there be no patent, or as soon as the patent is over, a sufficient number of such machines may be made to supply the whole demand, and to supersede entirely the use of all the old machinery. The natural consequence is, that the price is reduced to the price of production from the best machinery; and if the price were to be depressed lower, the whole of the commodity would be withdrawn from the market.

"The machines which produce corn and raw materials, on the contrary, are the gifts of nature, not the works of man; and we find by experience that these machines have very different qualities and powers. The most fertile lands of a country, those which, like the best machinery in manufactures, yield the greatest products with the least labor and capital, are never found sufficient to supply the effective demand of an increasing population. The price of raw produce, therefore, naturally rises, till it becomes sufficiently high to pay the cost of raising it with inferior machines, and by a more expensive process; and as there cannot be two prices for corn of the same quality, all the other machines, the working of which requires less capital compared with the produce, must yield rents in proportion to their goodness. Every extensive country may thus be considered as possessing a gradation of machines for the production of corn and raw materials, including in this gradation not only all the various qualities of poor land, of which every large territory has generally an abundance, but the inferior machinery which may be said to be employed when good land is further and further forced for additional produce. As the price of raw produce continues to rise, these inferior machines are successively called into action; and as the price of raw produce continues to fall, they are successively thrown out of action. The illustration here used serves to show at once the necessity of the actual price of corn to the actual produce, and the different effect which would attend a great reduction in the price of any particular manufacture, and a great reduction in the price of raw produce."

This is a brief, but, I hope, sufficiently clear and fair exposition of Ricardo's celebrated theory of rent. I call it Ricardo's theory, though aware that it was first promulgated by Dr. Anderson, of Scotland, as early as 1777. It then attracted hardly any notice, and was subsequently forgotten. It was afterwards rediscovered, almost simultaneously, by Sir Edward West and Mr. Malthus, while Mr. Ricardo has most successfully developed it, applying it to the theory of profits, and to the solution of many other problems in economical science. Malthus was certainly put upon the track of it by his own theory of population, of which it is an obvious complement. As it might be objected to the Malthusian doctrine, that the danger which it contemplated was prospective and distant, the world certainly not being over-populated *as yet* in all its parts, this theory of rent comes in to fill up the deficiency in our heritage of woe, and to prove that the increase of population, to which the human race is always tending, is *always* an evil, — that, for every new life which is created, some new restraint, privation, or loss is imposed upon those already in being. "Granted," these prophets of evil may exclaim, "that there is not as yet any absolute deficiency of food; yet every birth tends to raise the price of the stock of sustenance which we have, because it obliges us to cultivate still poorer land, and to apply labor and capital with constantly diminishing returns, — or to work at smaller wages, and apply capital at smaller profits." * Mr. Mill states the legitimate inference from these two theories of population and rent clearly and strongly, when

* Dr. Chalmers actually argues in this manner, and with characteristic earnestness. "It is thus," he says, "that, for the continued pressure of the world's population on its food, it is far from necessary that the food should have reached that stationary maximum beyond which it cannot be carried. It is enough for this purpose, that the limit of the world's abundance, though it does recede, should recede more slowly than *would* the limit of the world's population. A pressure, and that a very severe one, may be felt for many ages together, from a difference in the mere tendencies of their increase. The man who so runs as to break his head against a wall might receive a severe contusion, even to the breaking of his head, if, instead of a wall, it had been a slowly retiring barrier. And therefore we do not antedate matters by taking up now the consideration of Malthus's preventive and positive checks to population. There is scarcely a period, even in the bygone history of the world, when the former checks have not been called for, and the latter have not been in actual operation. To postpone either the argument or its application till the agriculture of the world shall be perfected, is a most unpractical, as well as a most intelligent view of the question; — for long ere this distant consummation can be realized, and even now, may the obstacle of a slowly retiring limit begin to be felt. The tendency of a progressive population to outstrip the progressive culture of the earth, may put mankind into a condition of straitness and difficulty, — and that for many generations before the earth shall be wholly cultivated. . . . . . Let the population increase to the extent of its own inherent power of increase, and it would force the existing limit of cultivation; or, in other words, flow over upon a soil inferior to that which had last been entered upon, or inferior to that which, at the then rate of enjoyment, could do no more than feed the laboring cultivators and their *secondaries* [the manufacturers who supply them with tools and wrought goods]. The consequence of such a descent is inevitable. The rate of enjoyment must fall. The agricultural workmen must either submit to be worse fed than before, or, parting with so many of their secondaries, they must submit to be worse clothed, or lodged, or furnished than before. The likelihood is, that they would so proportion their sacrifices as to suffer in both these ways; — and so there behoved to be a general degradation of comfort in the working classes of society. There is, to be sure, another way in which they might possibly extract from the more ungrateful soil, on which they had just entered, the same plenty as before. They may submit to harder labor, by putting forth a more strenuous husbandry on the inferior land; but this too is degradation. Whether by an increase of drudgery, or an increase of destitution, there may, in either way, be a sore aggravation to the misery of laborers." — Chalmers's *Political Economy*, Vol. I. pp. 35 - 37.

he says, that "a greater number of people cannot, in any given state of civilization, be collectively so well provided for as a smaller."

I do not accept these gloomy views of the course of nature and Providence. I do not believe that any increase in the number of the civilized, Christian inhabitants of the earth is an evil, or that it entails any evil upon coming generations. Recognizing the facts, which must be obvious to all, that the civilized nations of the earth are now steadily advancing in numbers, though with various degrees of rapidity, while the barbarous tribes are either stationary, or are dwindling away, some of them with fearful speed, I see in them the beneficent working of a great law of Providence, which is giving the earth to be the exclusive habitation of those who know how to develop its resources, and apply them to the noblest uses. The arts of peace, and the discovery of new means and appliances of civilization, are at least keeping pace with, if they do not outstrip, the actual increase of mankind in numbers. A nicely graduated principle of restraint, applied just where it is most needed, checks the undue multiplication of the race in certain localities, where the pressure of population on the means of subsistence just begins to be felt; and this principle, mild and beneficent in its mode of operation, like all the general laws of Providence, must become universal in its effect, at that far distant day in the lapse of ages, when, if ever, the earth shall be so fully stocked with happy human beings, that there shall not be room and sustenance for more. The social evils which unquestionably now exist, and which are traced by such economists as Malthus, Ricardo, and McCulloch to an excess of population, appear clearly imputable to defective, unnatural, and unjust institutions of man's device, and admit of remedy without shaking the pillars of social order, or impiously calling on God to send war, inundations, or pestilence, wherewith to scourge mankind into a sense of their duty to restrain their natural inclinations, and destroy the sources of domestic happiness. Having established these points against the doctrines and the calculations of Malthus, I proceed to show that there is nothing in this theory of rent which ought to shake our confidence in them.

And first, I would call attention to the fact, that both these theories are of English origin, and were first suggested, as is obvious, by observation of those evils in the social condition of England, which only within the present century have become of crying magnitude. These evils have manifested themselves in the only country in Europe in which all the land, the great food-producing machine, has come to be owned by so small a class, that the great body of the community seem to have no part or lot in it; while, at the same time, those ancient patriarchal and religious institutions, which certainly did much to mitigate the effects of an undue aggregation of landed property in the hands of a few, have entirely died out or been destroyed. It is the boast of the English, that the relations of vassal and lord, clansman and chieftain, serf and master, no longer exist among them. The English barons no longer support each an army of retainers to be their followers in war, and to keep up their feudal state. English prelates and monks no longer dispense open-handed hospitality and charity at the gates of richly endowed monasteries. These institutions of the Middle Ages have been destroyed in England, root and branch; but their fall has not, as in many parts of the Continent, caused the landed property once aggregated in their support to be parcelled out again, with great minuteness and some approach to equality, among those who were formerly maintained by it in rude plenty, though not in peace or perfect freedom. Feudal relations have been done away, but the magnitude of feudal estates has not been diminished. The Highland chieftain has banished his clansmen from their hereditary possessions and hereditary dependence on him, has compelled them to emigrate or starve, has turned his vast Highland estate into sheepwalks and deer-parks, and has himself become a wealthy English nobleman. A cool pecuniary calculation of profit and loss has induced him to take this step. The same motive has caused the great English landholders to depopulate their estates, driving the rural tenantry into the towns and manufacturing districts, where they must become operatives or paupers. The consequence of this aggregation of landed estates, and this mode of deriving the largest possible rent from them, has been a fearful increase of pauperism, and a general apprehension lest the tax for the support of the poor should become so large as eventually to beggar the rich also. No wonder that any increase of the population should be deemed an evil, when it appears from the returns, that one tenth part of that population are legalized paupers; and as not the same individuals, in all cases, receive public relief each successive year, it is probable that as many as one sixth of the whole number of the people are, or have been, dependent on public charity.

Systems and theories of political economy suggested by circumstances so anomalous and peculiar as these, or contrived with a view to explain and justify them, are not likely to be applicable to other countries, or to contain many general truths. England is the only country in the world in which the laboring class is entirely dependent on the wages of hired labor; on the Continent, in most instances, they have a small property on which they can subsist, though poorly, in seasons when they cannot obtain employment elsewhere for time not needed at home, so as to add to their scanty incomes a small amount received as wages. If they have not a little land which is entirely their own, they have a sort of prescriptive right to cultivate the land of others, on certain fixed terms, either as *metayers*, giving all the labor for a portion of the produce, or as feudal subjects bound to the soil, and having a right of maintenance from it. In neither case are they driven into the labor-market, as their only refuge from starvation, there constantly to depress wages by their frantic competition for employment, or to give up the struggle in despair by throwing themselves upon compulsory public charity.

Ricardo's theory of rent was discovered or invented with reference to this anomalous state of things. It is an attempt to establish as a law of nature the general fact, that an increase of the numbers of a people, *under any circumstances*, is an evil, because it creates an additional demand for food, which can only be met by having recourse to poorer or less advantageously situated soils, and by applying more labor and capital with constantly diminishing returns. It is abundantly confuted by facts, and can easily be shown to be unsound in principle. The assertion of Mr. Mill, "that a greater number of people cannot collectively be so well provided for as a smaller," becomes absurd when applied to an infant colony, established in a vast territory, on a virgin soil. Who can seriously maintain, that an increase of population is an evil in British Australia, or in the great valley of the Mississippi? It might as well be said that the people of Ohio, Indiana, and Wisconsin are straitened for want of room, as that their proportionate supply of food was lessened by the increase of their numbers. Among them, surely, it is apparent that an increase of population is an increase of productive power, and hence a proportionate increase of the surplus of grain and other articles of sustenance, which, after satisfying all their own wants in the amplest manner, they are able to send off to satisfy the wants of other nations. The average price of flour in Philadelphia market between 1800 and 1810, exceeded eight dollars a barrel; from 1810 to 1820, the average was about nine dollars. The population of this country in 1800 was but little over five millions; in 1820, it was somewhat less than ten millions. It is now more than twenty-three millions. And is the nation, in consequence of this vast increase of numbers, less bountifully supplied with food? On the contrary, the price of flour and other bread-stuffs has greatly diminished, and we are supplying the world with them. The average price of flour for several years preceding 1853, was less than six dollars.

Our average annual export of articles of food now probably exceeds thirty-five millions of dollars in value; and in case of any failure of the crops in Europe, it could probably be raised to seventy-five millions, without materially lessening the enjoyments of the people of this country, or raising the price of grain to a point beyond the reach of the poorest class of the population. In 1847, the year of famine in Ireland, our export of bread-stuffs actually rose to nearly sixty-nine millions, and in 1853, owing to a partial failure of the crops and to the Russian war in Europe, it was about sixty-six millions. Do these facts afford any evidence that the twenty-three millions, who now constitute the American nation, are not so well provided for as the five millions who occupied their place only fifty years ago? Are they not rather a demonstration of the principle, that the increase of numbers is an increase of productive power, and a consequent proportionate increase of the means of subsistence, — of the necessaries, comforts, and luxuries of life?

But it may be said that America is an exceptional case, and that we have no right to argue from the fortunate circumstances in which we are placed, to general conclusions which would be wholly inapplicable in other portions of the world. We answer, that the facilities afforded by commerce now really connect all the civilized nations of the earth into one great community, the supply of all articles being made everywhere proportionate to the demand and to the ability to pay for them. Grain and other articles of provision are matters both of foreign and domestic traffic; every country can obtain an abundance of them, though her own soil may be entirely barren. Great Britain has no difficulty in obtaining a supply of cotton, though the cotton-plant will not grow in the British Isles. Grain and other provisions can be purchased even with greater facility than cotton and tobacco, or coffee and tea; for these latter articles can be raised only in a few favored countries, while the market of the whole world is open for the sale of food. In fact, the markets of New York and Liverpool now regulate each other; since the abrogation of the corn-laws, the price of grain cannot rise five per cent in the latter place without a corresponding enhancement of price in New York within one fortnight, the time which it takes for a steamer to cross the Atlantic and convey the intelligence; and before another week has elapsed, ship-loads of corn are stemming their way eastward, to supply the trifling deficiency indicated even by this slight change in the market. It is no more a hardship or a disadvantage for England, than for our own State of Massachusetts, to be obliged to buy a portion of the articles of subsistence for her population; and the deficiency in our own case, it may be remarked, is relatively greater than in the mother country; for we *never* raise food enough for our own consumption, while the English crops, in ordinary years, suffice for nearly the whole English demand. In both cases, it may be said, the deficiency proceeds, not from natural causes, but from the choice of man. It is found more profitable to devote the larger portion of the labor of the two countries to commerce and manufactures, and to buy a portion of the food that is required, than to cultivate the soil to the full extent of which it is capable, and thereby raise the whole stock of provisions. If a given amount of labor employed in spinning yarn and weaving cloth will produce enough to buy two bushels of grain, while, if devoted immediately to tilling the ground, it will raise only one bushel, it is certain that the labor will be given to manufactures, and not to agriculture; and the deficiency of food thus created, (if it can be called a deficiency,) will afford no reason for impeaching the bounty of Providence, and no cause for fear lest the increase of the population should outstrip the increase of the supply of food.

We say, then, that this theory of rent, being inapplicable and unsound in the case of America, is *consequently* untrue in its application to Europe generally, and even to England. An increase of the English population *does* create a larger demand for food. But this demand does not oblige the people to have recourse to the poorer soils in order to enlarge the crops, nor even to apply more capital with less profit to the soil already under tillage; it simply obliges them to import more food from America and the countries on the Baltic and the Black Sea. And the supply which these countries may afford is indefinite; the only reason why they do not *now* send more corn to England, is that England needs no more. There is every reason to believe, that if Great Britain should altogether cease to be a grain-producing country, if it should devote all its fields to pasturage, these other countries would still keep the English market bountifully stocked with grain, and with no material enhancement of its price. The possible supply of wheat and maize from the back country of the United States defies all calculation; it is kept dammed up there now, because the producers know, if it were thrown upon the market at once, that it would sink the price below the cost of production. But because it exists in excess, if the capacity of the market were increased, the supply might be indefinitely enlarged without any material or even perceptible enhancement of price. There is no more risk that our back country will be drained of wheat, than that the great Mississippi will drain it of water. Lower the bar at its mouth, or sink the level of the broad ocean itself, and the rivers will yet continue to run, for their springs are perennial. The bounty of God feeds them. Instead of saying, then, that population presses on the means of subsistence, the true proposition would be, that the supply of food presses hard upon the increase of population. The force of the pressure being thus turned the other way, the supply of food might be indefinitely increased, without any enhancement of price from the enlarged demand.

Thus much for the contradiction of the theory by the facts in the case. The refutation of it in principle, or by abstract reasoning, is equally easy. And first, it is to be observed, that the natural fertility, or what Ricardo calls the original and inherent powers of the soil, as an element of rent, are wholly insignificant in comparison with nearness to market. The most barren soils in the world, even hard rock, pure sand, or stagnant marsh, should a populous and wealthy city spring up in the neighborhood, will yield rent, often a large rent, because they afford a field which human industry and skill can convert into a productive garden. On the other hand, soil of the greatest natural fertility, if it be far distant from any market for agricultural produce, will command no price and yield no rent. For instances of the former class, take the larger portion of the soil of Belgium and Holland, much of which has been literally reclaimed from the sea, against which it is now protected by stupendous dikes, and a still larger part was originally barren sand, on which it was first necessary to plant coarse grass, the roots of which might protect it from being perpetually shifted by the winds. Yet these broad districts of sea and sand are now the gardens of Europe, shaming even the wonders of English farming by the fulness of their crops. Two and a half acres of them yield food enough for a family of five persons. The acclivities of the Alps in Switzerland, dug out into terraces, and blooming with the olive and the vine, — and many an acre of former marsh in Cambridge and Lincoln counties, England, now forming rich corn-fields, — are other instances of land made productive and yielding rent by vicinity to a market, in spite of the greatest natural disadvantages.

For examples to corroborate the other branch of the statement, we have only to look at the remote West of our own fair land. Thousands of square miles of the most productive land in the world, in Kansas and Minnesota, are even now lying tenantless, because they will not command the government price of only $ 1.25 an acre. And even in the more thickly settled States of the great Mississippi Valley, many a broad region yet remains waste in the ownership of the government, far superior in natural advantages to the soil of Belgium in its original condition, and for which, notwithstanding, no one will give this almost nominal price. The reason is, that there is not market enough in the neighborhood to take off the surplus agricultural produce. If the population should increase in numbers, so as to require a larger amount of food, though at the same price at which it is now held, this waste land would soon be purchased and reduced to tillage.

This point being established, then, that the original fertility of the soil is an element of little or no importance in the theory of rent, we have only to consider that portion of Ricardo's doctrine which relates to comparative distance from the market. He maintains, that land bears rent in proportion to its nearness to the place where agricultural produce is needed and consumed; and that the increase of population, consequently, is an evil, because the community are obliged to send farther and farther off for their supplies. Here is the great and obvious fallacy, of supposing that *the population, as it increases, remains stationary, or on the same spot*, so that the grain must be brought to it at a price enhanced by the cost of transportation. We answer, that, *instead of the food coming from a distance to the population, the population go to the food.* The nation expands over more space as it increases in numbers. The tide of emigration sets towards the waste lands in a current, the velocity and depth of which are proportioned to the increase in the volume of the waters. The new-comers, the addition to the nation, instead of raising the price of food for themselves and their predecessors, actually cheapen it. As they spread themselves over the waste lands, and reduce them to cultivation, they not only raise food enough for themselves, but they increase the surplus which is sent to market, to be there exchanged for manufactures and the produce of foreign climes.

This is exemplified in the history of our own New England. The average rate of increase of the population here, during the last thirty years, has been about 17 per cent for every ten years, while for the whole United States it has been about 34 per cent, or twice as large. Why is this, since the excess of births over deaths is probably as great in New England as in any other portion of the country? The answer is obvious. One half of those who are born here, and survive to the age of maturity, (one half of the surplus, I mean, over those who are needed to compensate for the deaths, and thus to keep up the population to its original number,) emigrate to the West, and there take their part in the great work of settling the wild lands, and reducing them to tillage. And so successful have their labors been, that the price of grain and other agricultural produce has not risen in proportion to the increase of our numbers, as it ought to have done, if Ricardo's theory were true; the average price of food, all over the country, has fallen since 1800, though since that time our population has been quadrupled, and though our exports of provisions also have increased to an immense extent.

We come, then, to a theory of rent which differs very widely from that of Ricardo's. *Rent depends, not on the increase, but on the distribution, of the population.* It arises from the excess of the *local* demand over the *local* supply, and is therefore ultimately regulated by the expense and inconvenience of bringing the food from a distance, or by the discomforts and privations which attend the removal of a portion of the people to a new home. The migration is not necessarily directed to another country; the more remote and less populous counties or states may receive the surplus population of the metropolitan region and the manufacturing districts, and an additional supply of food will then be obtained from the agricultural labor of those who have thus found a new home. An increase in the numbers of the people may thus be followed by more than a proportional increase of the means of subsistence. The price of food, then, will not vary in proportion to the rent; on the contrary, the rent may increase indefinitely, while the price of food is diminishing. A livelihood may be more easily and cheaply obtained by commercial or manufacturing industry in a great city or a populous region, notwithstanding the considerable outlay required for rent, than by tilling the ground in a district where land may be hired for a trifling sum, or even purchased at a nominal price; and still the extension of agriculture may be so great, as the forest is cleared up and the prairie planted, that corn and flour may be bought by the inhabitants of cities more cheaply than ever. This is not mere theory, but fact; it is but a recital of the mingled experience of the manufacturing districts of New England and the border districts of cultivation in the Western States.

Not only in America, but in Great Britain and Ireland, and

indeed throughout the civilized world, it is notorious that rent is produced and increased, or, in other words, that value is given to the land, by creating a market for agricultural produce in the neighborhood of the land whence that produce is obtained; that is, by collecting a town or civic population, engaged in manufactures and commerce, who have the means to buy the wheat. By *collecting* such a population, I say; not by *creating* one, or by making the total number of the whole people larger, as Ricardo's theory requires. It is not the want of a larger supply of food, but the altered locality of the demand, and the altered habits and occupations of the people, which swell the value of the land and enhance the rent.

And, conversely, the population might be considerably enlarged, and more food consequently be required, at the very time when rents were falling throughout the country, if the process of dispersion should be going on at the same period, the people leaving the manufacturing towns and the centres of commerce, and spreading themselves over the face of the country, so that each family would come nearer the particular spot of land that feeds it. This is the evil often experienced here in America, where many towns and smaller cities upon the Atlantic coast, which were prosperous and wealthy in the latter part of the last century, and up to the close of the war in 1815, have since ceased to advance, and even retrograded, in riches and population, many of the citizens joining the great tide of migration to the Western States, because the policy of the national government was no longer favorable to manufactures, the fisheries, and commerce. Very recently, the establishment of railroads, and other local causes, have somewhat checked this tendency to dispersion; but the account here given is still applicable, in a greater or less degree, to such seaports in New England as Portsmouth, Newburyport, Salem, Nantucket, Newport, and New London, and to some formerly flourishing towns on Chesapeake Bay and the Southern Atlantic coast. Of course, as these towns dwindled, the value and the rent of farms in their immediate vicinity were also depressed, and agriculture, instead of advancing, visibly retrograded, the prices of all kinds of rural produce being kept down by the abundant supplies which began to arrive from the newly cleared regions at the West. Yet all this while the total population of the United States was increasing with unparalleled rapidity, and, if Ricardo's theory were true, rent ought to have advanced *pari passu.*

To illustrate the opposite result, the rise of rents and of the prices of agricultural produce produced by the concentration of the people in manufacturing districts and towns, I might refer to such obvious instances as the neighborhood of Lowell in Massachusetts, Manchester in New Hampshire, Rochester in New York, Pittsburg in Pennsylvania, and many others, the rapid and immense increase of which in population and wealth seems almost fabulous. It is the rapidity of this increase, indeed, which proves that the result is attributable to bringing the people together, and not to the natural growth of the total population. It cannot have been from the increased number of births, that Rochester, for instance, which had a population of only 1,500 in 1820, numbered over 9,000 inhabitants in 1830, over 20,000 in 1840, and over 36,000 in 1850; or that Lowell, whose population in 1830 was about 6,500, numbered over 33,000 in 1850. For illustrations from Great Britain, in which country alone does Ricardo's theory of rent seem even plausible, I need only bring together a few passages from an able essay recently published by a French writer, M. Léonce de Lavergne, on the "Rural Economy of England, Scotland, and Ireland," * contrasted with that of France.

Up to the time of Arthur Young, he says, "the English farmers had, like all those of the Continent, worked with little view to a market. Most agricultural productions were consumed on the spot by the producers themselves; and although in England more was sold for consumption beyond the farm than anywhere else, it was not export which regulated production. Arthur Young was the first who made the English agriculturists understand the increasing importance of a market; that is to say, the sale of agricultural produce to a population not contributing to produce it. This non-agricultural population, which up to that time was inconsiderable, began to develop, and since then its increase has been immense, owing to the expansion of manufactures and commerce. Everybody

* Translated from the French, with Notes, by a Scottish Farmer. Edinburgh and London: W. Blackwood and Sons. 1855. Chapters 11, 18, 20.

knows what enormous progress the employment of steam as a motive power has effected in British manufactures and commerce during the last fifty years. The principal seat of this amazing activity is in the northwest of England, the county of Lancaster, and its neighbor, the West Riding of Yorkshire. There Manchester works cotton, Leeds wool, Sheffield iron, and the port of Liverpool, with its constant current of exports and imports, feeds an indefatigable production."

"One third of the English nation is concentrated on these two points,—London in the south, and the manufacturing towns of Lancashire and the West Riding in the north. These human ant-hills are as rich as they are numerous. What becomes of the immense amount of wages paid to this mass of workmen every year? It goes, in the first place, to pay for meat, beer, milk, butter, cheese, which are directly supplied by agriculture, and woollen and linen clothing, which it indirectly furnishes. There exists, consequently, a constant demand for productions which agriculture can hardly satisfy, and which is for her, in some measure, an unlimited source of profit. The power of these outlets is felt over the whole country; if the farmer has not a manufacturing town beside him to take off his produce, he has a port; and should he be distant from both, he brings himself into connection with them by canal, or by one or more lines of railway."

"If Lancashire is the most productive district in the world, it is also the dullest. Let any one fancy an immense morass, shut in between the sea on one side and mountains on the other; stiff clay land, with an impervious subsoil everywhere hostile to farming; add to this a most gloomy climate, continual rain, a constant cold sea-wind, besides a thick smoke shutting out what little light penetrates the foggy atmosphere; and lastly, the ground, the inhabitants, and their dwellings completely covered with a coating of black dust,—fancy all this, and some idea may be formed of this strange county, where the air and the earth seem only one mixture of coal and water! Such, however, is the influence upon production of an inexhaustible outlet, that these fields, so gloomy and forsaken, are rented at an average of 30*s*. ($ 7), and in the immediate environs of Liverpool and Manchester, arable land lets as high as £ 4 ($ 20), an acre. There are not many soils in the most sun-favored lands which can boast such rents. At the sight of such wonders, one is almost tempted with the Latin poet to exclaim,

> 'Salve, magna parens frugum, Saturnia tellus,
> Magna virûm!'"

"If England's history as a manufacturing country is brilliant, what shall we say of Scotland? We may judge by a single example. The counties of Lanark and Renfrew, where manufactures and commerce are most active, have increased in population, in the space of a hundred years, from 100,000 to 600,000, and Glasgow alone from 20,000 to 400,000. Clydesdale, once deserted, now rivals Lancashire for its collieries, manufactories, and immense shipping trade. In 1750, the germ even of this wealth did not exist; it was English capital, combined with the plodding and frugal genius of the Scotch people, which in so short a time made that unproductive district what it now is. Strong proof this of the advantages which may accrue to a non-manufacturing country by being associated with one rich and already industrial! Scotland, as long as she remained separate from England, and dependent on her own resources, only vegetated; but as soon as the capital and experience of her powerful neighbor broke in upon her, she took a start quite equal to England. This sudden growth of manufactures has been increased, as always happens, by a corresponding advance in agriculture. In proportion as commerce and manufactures multiply men and augment wages, agriculture renews its efforts to supply food for the constantly increasing mass of consumers; and in a limited country, like the Lowlands, a population such as that of Glasgow and its dependencies causes the demand for agricultural produce to be felt over its whole extent."

In England, "the manufacturing districts *par excellence*, commencing with Warwickshire in the south, and ending with the West Riding of Yorkshire, are those in which rents, profits, and agricultural wages rise highest. There the average rent is 30*s*. per acre, and a country laborer's wages 12*s*. a week; whilst in the district exclusively agricultural, lying south of London, the average rent is not more than 20*s*. per acre, and wages 8*s*. a week. The intermediate counties approach more or less to these two extremes, according as they are more or less manufacturing, and everywhere the rate of land and wages is a sure criterion of the development of local industry.

"It is pretty generally believed, that pauperism prevails more in the manufacturing than in other districts. This is quite a mistake." It appears from the official returns, that in the manufacturing counties, "the poor's rate is about 1*s.* in the pound, or 3*s.* to 4*s.* a head, and the number of poor 3 to 4 per cent of the population; whilst in the agricultural counties, it exceeds 2*s.* in the pound, or 10*s.* a head, and the number of paupers is from 13 to 16 per cent of the population. The cause of this difference is easily understood; the number of paupers and the cost of their maintenance increases as the rate of wages becomes lower. Although the working population be three or four times more dense in the manufacturing than in other parts of the country, its condition there is better, because it produces more."

"If we transport ourselves to France, to the most backward departments of the centre and south, what do we there find? A thinly scattered population, at the most, not exceeding on an average one third that of the English, — one head only, in place of three, to five acres, — and that population almost entirely agricultural; few or no large towns, little or no manufactures, trade confined to the limited wants of the inhabitants; the centres of consumption distant, means of communication costly and difficult, and expenses of transport equal to the entire value of the produce. The cultivator has little or nothing to dispose of. Why does he work? To feed himself and his master with the produce of his labor. The master divides the produce with him and consumes his portion; if it is wheat and wine, master and *métayer* eat wheat and drink wine; if it is rye, buckwheat, potatoes, these they consume together. Wool and flax are shared in like manner, and serve to make the coarse stuffs with which both clothe themselves. Should there happen to remain over a few lean sheep, some ill-fed pigs, or some calves, reared with difficulty by over-worked cows, whose milk is disputed with their offspring, these are sold to pay taxes.

"In this state of things, as there is no interchange, the cultivator is obliged to produce those articles which are most necessary for life, — that is to say, the cereal grains: if the soil yields little, so much the worse for him; he has no choice, he must produce corn or die of hunger. Now, on bad land, there is no more expensive cultivation than this; even on good, if care is not taken, it soon becomes burdensome; but under these conditions of farming, no one thinks of taking account of the expense. The labor is not for profit, but for life; cost what it may, corn must be had, or at all events, rye. As long as the population is scanty, the evil is not overwhelming, because there is no want of land: long fallows enable the land to produce something; but as soon as the population begins to increase, the soil ceases to be sufficient for the purpose; and a time soon arrives, when the population suffers severely for want of food."

That rent depends upon the distribution, and not upon the increase, of the population, may be easily seen by putting the extreme case. Suppose the inhabitants of a country distributed with perfect evenness over its territory, each family residing upon the centre of the spot, say ten or twelve acres in extent, which feeds it. While the population is small, a district of limited extent may supply homesteads for all the inhabitants. As the people increase in number, suppose additional lots, upon the outskirts of the former settlements, to be laid out for the new families. It is not necessary that the soil should be of equal fertility throughout the land, so that all the farms should consist of the same number of acres. In the more productive districts, six or eight acres may suffice for a family; in the less favored ones, sixteen or twenty may be needed. The only essential point is, that each family should have enough land, and no more than enough, for its own wants.

Under these circumstances, it is evident, the land would not yield any rent; there would be enough for all. Monopoly, or exclusive appropriation, being impossible, a price would no more be set upon the land, than upon the air or the light. No one would think of charging rent, any more than of levying tolls for the right to cross the broad ocean. And it is conceivable, that this state of things should exist over the whole earth, and should continue for many centuries to come. Islands of limited extent, like the British Isles, might indeed be filled up, or completely occupied, the people having become so numerous that no more land could be had for the new families. In such case, the new families would have to emigrate, as they are now actually obliged to do; but they would find abundance of unoccupied land in America, Australia, and elsewhere. It has already been demonstrated, that the earth does not contain a hundredth part of the population it is capable of feeding. "Malte-Brun has said, that the soil of Europe alone could afford ample food for a thousand millions of inhabitants; being nearly five times its present number, and more by one fifth than the whole actual population of the globe." Considering that the facilities for emigration are rapidly multiplying, and that already over 400,000 human beings annually cross the Atlantic to seek a new home, it is obvious that there is no practical difficulty in dividing the increase of population among the most distant regions of the earth, or wherever food can be most easily obtained.

But if the population of one country, or of the whole globe, were thus distributed with perfect evenness, each family residing upon the spot that furnished it with food, though there would be no rent, it is obvious that there would be little or no division of labor, and, consequently, no progress in civilization and the arts, and no advancement in opulence. Mankind would begin to retrograde to a condition as low as that in which any portion of them have yet been found. The labor of far the larger portion of each family would have to be devoted to agriculture, in order to obtain the necessary sustenance from the ground; and as the labor of the remaining part would not suffice to renew and keep in repair the stock of tools, domestic utensils, and household comforts, these would soon be expended or worn out. As tools become imperfect and deficient, more labor must be given to tillage. The processes of agriculture would thus rapidly degenerate, till at last the incessant toil of the whole family would produce only a scanty supply of the coarsest sustenance, and from the want of leisure, knowledge and civilization would die out.

But experience even of the commencement of these evils would teach mankind their appropriate and easy remedy. Several families would unite, in order to obtain the benefits of a division of labor. Some would devote themselves exclusively to the manufacture of agricultural implements and household articles, while the labor of the others would supply them with food. As manufacturing operatives must work near each other, the ground originally allotted to a single family would come to be tenanted by many, and would form the nucleus of a town. But a town is necessarily a market for the sale of agricultural produce and the purchase of manufactured commodities. From the advantages which the town would thus afford, the land in its immediate vicinity, being limited in quantity, would assume a value, or, in other words, would begin to yield a rent. Upon any hypothesis that can be framed, even upon Ricardo's doctrine, the origin of rent must be traced to monopoly, — to a necessarily limited supply met by an unlimited demand. Only a small number of farms of the original size, from six to twenty acres, can have the advantage of immediate proximity to the newly formed manufacturing village; the occupants of these farms would be better furnished with tools, and more able to exchange their products for manufactured goods. The occupants of farms at a distance would be willing to purchase these advantages of them, — to offer two or three acres remote from market, in exchange for one acre adjoining a town. Thus rent would begin, not at all as a consequence of the absolute *increase* of the population, for the total population might be stationary or even retrograding while these changes were going on, but as a consequence of the altered distribution of the people over the face of the country.

Malthus and Ricardo, with their followers, perceived that the origin of rent must be attributed to monopoly; for the value of land, so far as it consists in the natural and inherent qualities of the soil, is an instance of the existence of value without labor, and therefore, according to the first principles of Political Economy, it can be explained only by a limited supply and exclusive appropriation. But they failed to perceive the causes and nature of the monopoly, or to trace the consequences of the application of their own doctrine. They imagined that the high rent of land in a given county or district is only a particular case of the over-populousness of the whole country or kingdom, — of the fact that the whole extent of territory is insufficient to meet the wants of the whole population. They supposed, therefore, that the rise of rent *properly so called* must be uniform throughout the whole country, and must also be exactly proportioned, after deducting the effects of agricultural improvements, to the increase of the total population, — two suppositions which are contrary to the facts. The notorious fact, that not even England is yet over-peopled, but is capable of supporting, *from her own soil*, a population thrice as dense as her present one, as is proved by the example of the most densely inhabited portions of Belgium, or a hundred times as dense, if we consider the supplies of food which she might obtain from abroad, — this fact, I say, they endeavored to explain away by the unfounded assumptions that the most fertile land is always the first occupied, and that the people are compelled, by every increase of their numbers, to have recourse to inferior soils, or to apply additional capital to the ground with constantly diminishing returns. Not the more fertile lands, however, but those which are nearer to cities and to populous manufacturing districts, yield the higher rent; and the highest rents of all are obtained from land that is not used at all for purposes of agriculture, but only for habitation or manufacturing purposes, within the limits of the cities themselves, — a phenomenon of which the theory of Ricardo furnishes no explanation whatever. His theory is applicable only to what may be called agricultural rents; civic rents, the ground-rents of houses and shops in crowded cities, afford the best of all instances of *rent properly so called*, as they are free from the effects of the great disturbing cause, — agricultural improvements. These ground-rents do not depend upon the magnitude of the population of the city, or upon its rate of increase; they rise and fall in different streets, under the varying demand produced by the changes of business and the mutations of fashion. In London, they have risen enormously high in Belgravia, and fallen proportionally in what was the fashionable part of the metropolis a century ago; in the most crowded portions of the city proper, they are probably no higher than they were in the time of George III., and do not certainly equal some in Washington Street, Boston, the population of which city is not one twelfth part as great as that of London. In the English metropolis, the population, as it increases in number, necessarily spreads itself over more space; and therefore it may be doubted whether the *aggregate* ground-rent of those portions of the city which were densely inhabited at the beginning of this century is any greater now than it was in 1800, though the population of all England meanwhile has doubled.

In the United States, the want of local attachments and the restless and migratory character of the population have drawn attention to the fact, that rents begin, or the land acquires value, as fast as the vicinity is peopled. The favorite form of speculation here, the easiest and most common mode of money-getting, is the acquisition of a tract of land in some neighborhood where the circumstances indicate that a new town or city must soon spring up. A fortune is thus easily acquired, as the land acquires value before any labor is expended upon it, and long before the necessities of an increasing population would require it to be inhabited, or even cultivated. In England, the more stationary habits of the population have concealed this fact, and as the land slowly rose in value with the advancement of opulence and the gradual increase in the number of the whole people, Anderson's or Ricardo's theory of rent seemed plausible enough. Their doctrine seemed to illustrate the phenomenon, otherwise apparently inexplicable, of the steady growth of the fortunes of the aristocracy and the landed gentry, who neither labor nor spin, proportionally with the increase of the wealth of the commercial and manufacturing classes, whose prosperity is attributable to their own industry and enterprise. Yet even in England, there has been a regular movement of the population, a steady drain from the agricultural counties, and a filling up of the manufacturing districts. The increase of the population during the last fifty years, in the agricultural counties of Hereford, the North Riding of York, and Wilts, has been respectively but 31, 35, and 38 per cent; while in Stafford, for the same period, it has been 151, in Durham, 160, and in Lancaster, 201 per cent. And the consequence has been the unprecedented rise of rents, already mentioned, in the counties last named, while in Wilts, Hereford, and the North Riding, it may be doubted whether the average annual value of the land, excluding the improvements effected by capital, is any greater than it was half a century ago.

The rise of rents, as thus explained, is no hardship for those who are not landholders, and does not tend to depress the laboring part of the population. Those who pay these higher rents, or the higher prices of corn which produce them, are compensated by the advantages they obtain through their vicinity to a market. In fact, the enhancement of price for the burghers or citizens is merely nominal; they obtain more, and have a readier sale, for the manufactured goods which they produce, and pay more for the corn which they consume, the one result counterbalancing the other. What matters it to the laborer, if he pays more rent for his dwelling, and a higher price for his corn and potatoes, provided that the additional wages which he receives are more than enough to meet these additional expenses? The positive gain to the community consists in the saving of transportation both ways. If the population were not concentrated, it would be necessary to transport the agricultural produce a long distance to the town where it is consumed, and to carry the manufactured goods an equal distance to the farmers who need them. Even the English economists admit, that a great saving is effected in this respect through canals, railways, and other contrivances which lessen the cost of transportation. Is it not still a greater saving to do away with the necessity of these improved means of transport, and with the cost of constructing them, by bringing the agriculturists and the manufacturers nearer to each other?

While reasoning in favor of the abolition of the corn-laws, McCulloch himself presents this point with much clearness. He argues that the repeal of these laws will not leave the English farmer destitute of protection, for he will still have an advantage over the foreign grower, consisting in the cost of importing the grain from the Baltic, the Black Sea, or America. The charges of transportation and the profits of the importer must still be added to the price of the grain at the place where it is raised, and as the risk is great in dealing in corn, this enhancement of price must be considerable. To take the nearest source of supply, for instance, he computes the cost of transporting grain from the upper provinces on the Bug to Dantzic to be from *7s.* to *9s.* a quarter; and thence to London, including insurance and profit, *5s.* or *6s.* more. If the Polish grower, therefore, receives *43s.* a quarter for his wheat, "it could not, in ordinary years, be offered for sale in this country for less than from *55s.* to *58s.* a quarter, a price more than sufficient to insure the continued progress of British agriculture." * If there were manufacturing cities in the southern part of Poland, the farmer there might obtain 33 per cent more for his wheat, an advantage which would more than compensate him for paying a protective duty of equal amount on manufactured goods.

It is as much for the interest, then, of the farmers of the Mississippi valley, as of the manufacturers themselves, that the American system of protection should be restored. At present, the value of the lands at the West is kept down by the distance of their produce from a market. The cost of transporting a barrel of flour from Cincinnati to New York amounts, at ordinary prices, to at least thirty per cent of its value at the former place; the cost of its further transportation to Liverpool, including insurance and other necessary expenses, raises this proportion to about forty per cent. Create a manufacturing population in Ohio like that which exists in English Lancashire, and the price of flour at Cincinnati would be made equal to its price at Liverpool. Free trade between England and Ohio, then, means simply that Ohio produce should be admitted into the English ports under what we may call a "transportation duty" of forty per cent; while, owing to the great value, in a small bulk, of the finer manufactures, English produce is to be admitted into Cincinnati at a duty of only fifteen per cent. In other words, the opponents of protection would persuade the Ohio farmer that it is better for him to buy English broadcloth at $ 1.70 a yard, and sell his flour at $ 5.00, than to buy American broadcloth of the same quality at $ 2.00, and sell his flour at $ 7.00. The depression in the value of Ohio produce, which took place between 1847 and 1852, is clearly attributable to the fact, that the crowds of laborers discharged from our unprosperous manufacturing establishments, and the 400,000 immigrants annually landed on our shores, have been driven into agriculture, and have so increased the annual product of Michigan, Iowa, and Wisconsin, as to undersell the Ohio farmer at his own door. The protection of our manufactures would enlarge the home market for him, through the very means which are now swelling the number of his competitors.

---

* McCulloch's *Geographical Dictionary*, Art. *Dantzic*.

CHAPTER XIV.

THE CAUSES WHICH AFFECT THE RATE OF WAGES.

THE doctrine of the English economists respecting wages may be easily inferred from their two theories, which have just been considered, respecting population and rent. Putting aside the consideration of wages reckoned in money, as these are subject to merely nominal variations, according as the value of money rises or falls, they say that wages rated in commodities, or the quantity of produce apportioned to each laborer, is determined by the ratio which the capital of the country bears to its laboring population, or to the number of those who work for hire. By capital, however, they here mean "only circulating capital, and not even the whole of that, but the part which is expended in the direct purchase of labor. To this, however, must be added all funds which, without forming a part of capital, are paid in exchange for labor, such as the wages of soldiers, domestic servants, and all other unproductive laborers."* The aggregate of capital or wealth devoted to this purpose, to the payment of productive or unproductive labor, may be termed the *wages-fund* of a country; and the share of it which each laborer receives will evidently be determined by its amount, compared with the whole number of persons seeking employment.

Thus explained, the doctrine is a mere truism. We obtain no insight into the causes which regulate the rate of wages, when we are merely told that this rate depends upon the whole sum annually expended for wages, divided by the whole number of persons who share this sum among them. But as it is intended to be understood, this proposition is merely a covert statement of the theory of Malthus. Assuming it to be impossible, by any measure of legislation or government policy, to increase the aggregate funds employed in hiring laborers, it is affirmed that a "diminution in the number of competitors for

---

* J. S. Mill's *Political Economy*, Vol. I. p. 401.

hire" is the sole means of raising wages, and that the power and responsibility are thus placed in the hands of the laborers themselves. If they will refrain from overstocking the labor market, their condition as a class may be bettered; but "every scheme for their benefit, which does not proceed on this as its foundation, is, for all permanent purposes, a delusion." "It is impossible," continues Mr. Mill, "that population should increase at its utmost rate without lowering wages. Nor will the fall be stopped at any point short of that which, either by its physical or its moral operation, checks the increase of population."

Here is the great mistake of confounding the undue relative number of a class, with a general excess of the whole population. The former evil might be corrected by portioning out society anew, through the gradual influence of altered laws, so that the divisions or castes which are too thin in number, might be recruited from those which are in excess, and the proper balance be thus restored without the necessity of adopting any measures which would affect the bulk of the people. The latter evil, if it ever really existed, could be removed only by war, pestilence, famine, or a general adoption of the doctrine of Malthus. If it were as easy in England as it is in this country for a common laborer to become a master-mechanic, or a small tradesman, or to buy a farm; or if, as in most countries on the Continent, the bulk of the laboring community possessed either peasant properties, or a kind of prescriptive right to farm the land of another "on shares," as *métayers*, there would be no need of preaching abstinence from marriage to them; they would not compete with each other in the labor market, if the rate of wages were not high enough to tempt them to forsake their independent occupations. The number of persons in Great Britain who are entirely dependent on the wages of hired labor is unquestionably much too great; the proportion of this class to the whole people is probably five times as large as in any country in Continental Europe. Diminish their number, then, by all means. But how? The Malthusian economists assume that the only mode of effecting this end is to check the natural growth of the whole population, to lessen the yearly average of marriages and births. But would it not be equally effectual, and more practicable, to recruit from them the classes which are strikingly deficient in numbers, and thus restore the proper balance of society? It is certainly an anomaly and an evil, that more than half of the people of Great Britain should be hired laborers, who have neither capital nor land; but it is equally anomalous and injurious to the welfare of the whole nation, that only about 60,000 persons should own nearly all the land,* and less than 300,000 possess four fifths of the whole property, both real and personal. If the greater part of the hired laborers in England could be converted into peasant proprietors, we should hear no

---

* Samuel Laing, Esq., the distinguished traveller, tells us that "the class of landed proprietors in Scotland does not, it is said, exceed five or six thousand individuals"; and in Ireland, before the recent proceedings of the Commission for the Sale of Encumbered Estates, *The Times* newspaper, with the best means of information, estimated the number of landholders at only eight thousand. If fourteen thousand persons own all Scotland and Ireland, it may seem extravagant to admit that there are as many as 46,000 proprietors in England and Wales. But this number includes many who own only small lots of land, sufficient for a residence and a garden; and also a few "statesmen," as they are called, in Cumberland county, who cultivate their own little farms, and are the small remains, every day diminishing in number, of the ancient "yeomanry" of England. Undoubtedly, far the greater part of the land devoted to tillage is owned by a much smaller number of persons than is here allowed. M. Léonce de Lavergne, who will not allow that property in England is so much concentrated as is commonly imagined, admits that "a certain number" of proprietors, "at most 2,000, possess among them one third of the land and total revenue; and of these 2,000, there are 50 having princely fortunes. Some of the English dukes possess entire counties, and have a revenue of millions of francs." These 2,000 families, he estimates, possess 25,000,000 acres of land, and £20,000,000 of income. The whole number of acres in the three kingdoms is 78,000,000; so that 2,000 persons own nearly one third of the land in the British Isles.

According to the census of 1851, those who returned themselves as "landed proprietors," for all Great Britain, were less than 20,000 males and 15,000 females. Of course, some were owners of land who did not return themselves in the census as such, but under the head of some occupation, as barristers, physicians, officers in the army or navy, &c. On the other hand, the rank and social importance attached to the ownership of real estate probably induced many to class themselves among the "landed proprietors," though they did not own more than a house and garden. The whole number of separate farm-holdings in Great Britain, according to the census of 1851, is 285,936. If we allow an average of six farms to an estate, which is little enough, as many noble proprietors count their tenants by fifties, we have less than 48,000 land-owners for all England and Scotland.

The estimate that less than 300,000 persons own four fifths of all the property, both real and personal, is rather vague; but as Mr. Farr, the eminent actuary, in his evidence before a committee of the House of Commons, computes from the returns under the Income Tax that there are but 236,000 persons in Great Britain who possess an income of £200 or upwards, the estimate probably errs only on the safe side.

more complaints about the lowness of wages, or the over-populousness of the country. The true mode of raising the rate of wages is to alter the relative numbers of employers and employed, not to diminish the total population.

According to the English theory, however, there are certain limits to the extent to which wages may be reduced. "The cost of producing labor," says McCulloch, "like that of everything else, must be paid by the purchasers. The race of laborers would become extinct, were they not supplied with the food and other articles sufficient, at least, for their support and that of their families. This is the lowest limit to which the rate of wages can be permanently reduced; and for this reason, it has been called *the natural or necessary rate of wages.* The market, or actual, rate of wages may sink to the level of this rate, but it is impossible it should continue below it. It is not on the quantity of money received by the laborer, but on the quantity of food and other articles which that money will buy, that his ability to maintain himself, and rear children, must depend. Hence the natural or necessary rate of wages is determined by the cost of the food, clothes, fuel, &c. required for the use and accommodation of laborers. And though a rise in the market or current rate of wages be seldom exactly coincident with a rise in the price of necessaries, they can never, except when the market rate of wages greatly exceeds the natural or necessary rate, be far separated. However high its price, the laborers must always receive a supply of produce adequate for their support; if they did not obtain thus much, they would be destitute; and disease and death would continue to thin the population, until the reduced numbers bore such a proportion to the national capital as enabled them to obtain the means of subsistence."

The standard of natural wages, however, does not always mean the smallest amount of food and other necessaries that is absolutely requisite to preserve the lives of a laborer's family. As we have seen, what are accounted *necessaries* in one country, may be esteemed in another the *decencies*, and, in a third, the *luxuries*, of life. In England, the custom of the country requires that the laborer should have beer; his family, tea; and all must have daily provision of bread, and occasionally taste meat. Only in Ireland, before the recent exodus, was the standard of natural wages generally reduced to the cost of the absolute necessaries of existence, to a few potatoes and a little buttermilk, the scantiest provision of the coarsest and cheapest food that would support life. In such case, of course, no retrenchment is possible; and whenever a partial failure of the crops, as in 1847, or any other adverse circumstance, produces the slightest enhancement of the price of these necessaries, the laborer must starve, if public munificence does not come to his relief. But in England, if wages are temporarily reduced, or if food for a short time be of higher cost, the working classes can dispense with meat, beer, and tea, and still subsist. But the standard of living being established by long custom, the laborers will not submit, or need not submit, to such a reduction of their comforts as a permanent arrangement, but will rather throw themselves, or their families, upon the poor laws for support.

Hence the importance which is attributed by the Malthusian Economists to the preservation of as high a standard of living as possible for the laboring classes. Those who work for hire, they argue, are themselves to blame, if, in their eagerness to burden themselves with families, they submit to lower wages and a poorer style of living than that established by their forefathers; they must blame themselves if they do not even take advantage of a temporary increase in the demand for labor, or a temporary reduction in the price of food, to improve their condition permanently, by refusing to go back to the low wages and diminished comforts of their former life. "Unfortunately," says Mr. J. S. Mill, "this salutary effect is by no means to be counted upon; it is a much more difficult thing to raise, than to lower, the scale of living which the laborers will consider as more indispensable than marrying and having a family. If they content themselves with enjoying the greater comfort while it lasts, but do not learn to require it, they will people down to their old scale of living. If, from poverty, their children had previously been insufficiently fed or improperly nursed, a greater number will now be reared, and the competition of these, when they grow up, will depress wages, probably in full proportion to the greater cheapness of food. If the effect is not produced in this mode, it will be produced by earlier and more numerous marriages, or by an increased number of births to a marriage. According to all experience, a great increase invariably takes place in the number of marriages, in seasons of cheap food and full employment."

It is in this way that the Malthusians justify the uniform despondency of their views, and refuse to believe that the abolition of the corn-laws, emigration, a widely spread epidemic, a destructive war, or any other cause of cheapened food or lessening for a time the number of competitors for hire, can effect any permanent improvement in the condition of the working classes. Instead of profiting by the occasion to raise their standard of living, the laborers only use it as a means of rearing more children, whose competition must eventually bring back wages to their former proportion to the price of food. The fact is overlooked, that it is the present hopelessness of their condition, the impossibility of rising above their present rank in life, or even, as they are already at the bottom of the scale, of falling below it, which renders the laboring poor reckless and improvident in respect to marriages, and which makes them consider children as no encumbrance, and relief in the poor-house as no degradation. Under a different constitution of society, which should give the bulk of the people a right of ownership in the soil, such as the corresponding classes generally possess upon the Continent, and should break down the now impassable barriers between the different classes in the community, leaving the avenues to wealth and honor as open as they are in the United States, they would become more provident and hopeful, or a large family would no longer be esteemed a burden.

Certainly, no one, under present circumstances, would advise either an English or an Irish laborer, who is entirely dependent on wages, to diminish his chance of keeping out of the workhouse by taking upon himself the support of a wife and children. What would be imprudence for an individual, would be imprudence also in the whole class or body of men to which he belongs, or whose position in life resembles his own. The English Economists do right, then, at the present time, in dissuading the laboring poor from marriage. But we do not hereby acknowledge that the actual wretchedness of this class is the consequence of their having already multiplied up to the farthest limit at which the earth will supply them with food. Much less do we accept the doctrine which tends to make the wealthier classes in Great Britain hard-hearted and indifferent at the sight of the sufferings of the poor, by teaching that their misery is their own fault, the inevitable result of their own perversity and improvidence in keeping up their numbers too high. On the contrary, the very fact, that it is now imprudent for them to marry, is what they have most right to complain of, since it is *not* their own fault, but that of the laws and the aristocratic institutions of their country. If the policy of the English law, for the last half-century, had favored the distribution of fortunes as directly as it has actually encouraged their aggregation, or if it had been only neutral in this respect, as it is in this country, and had allowed property to take its natural course of an equal division among all the children when the parent had expressed no wish to the contrary, the laboring classes of England, like the peasantry of France and Switzerland, and the inhabitants of our own land, might now be free to follow their own inclinations without incurring the charge of imprudence. Their right to do so would be established by a fact of the first importance in the eyes of a Malthusian; they would not have become as numerous as they now are. The population of France, under the law which compels an equal division of the parent's estate among his children, increases at the rate of only five per cent in ten years, while the rate for England is about thrice as great. Yet no one supposes that the Englishman is naturally more careless and improvident, or more inclined to excess, than his neighbor across the Channel.

In England, an increase of the population is, *pro tanto*, an addition to the number of laborers seeking employment, an increase of the supply in the labor-market, and therefore a cause of the depression of wages. In America it is not so. The facilities for collecting a little capital are so numerous, and the expenses of living among a rural population, especially in the Western States, are so moderate, that the class of persons who are dependent exclusively upon wages, and who form the bulk of the community in many European countries, is here very small. The bulk of our people, at least of those who are native-born, may be said to belong to the class of independent laborers or small capitalists. Either by inheritance, or the assistance of friends, or the facility of obtaining credit, or by savings made from wages earned during his minority, almost every native American may be said to have the option of "beginning life," as it is called, with a little capital. But because this capital is small in amount, the possessor of it is willing, if wages are high, to work for others for a time, either as a journeyman, a farm-laborer, a clerk, or in some other capacity, in order to increase his little store by additional savings from wages, before he commences business on his own account. To be in the receipt of wages is not in America, as it generally is in Europe, to be entirely dependent upon wages. The person employed not unfrequently lends capital to his employer, and is thus placed upon an equality with him, and saves his self-respect, though he is "working for hire." One who either owns, or has the power of purchasing, a small farm, will yet "hire himself out," as the phrase is, for a season or two, in order to obtain the means of stocking his land, or otherwise facilitating his future enterprise.

Should wages be low, however, persons of small means see little advantage in postponing their introduction to business, and are tempted to employ their own capital at once in some independent occupation. There are innumerable openings for private adventure, which require only an adventurous spirit and a very moderate amount of capital or credit. The step between the situations of a journeyman and a master-mechanic, a clerk and a small tradesman, a farm-laborer and a small farmer, is a short one and very easily taken. If nothing better can be done, there is always the resource of removing to the West, and becoming a pioneer in the settlement of government land, which is first obtained with a squatter's preëmption right, and paid for out of the proceeds of subsequent harvests, or out of the enhanced value of the land when the neighborhood begins to be peopled. The tide of emigration westward always becomes fuller and stronger in periods of commercial depression, the stoppage of manufactories, the low prices of agricultural products, and the consequent reduction of the rates of wages. A check is thus immediately applied to the fall of wages, which do not sink as low as might be expected from the general depreciation of property and diminution of the rate of profit. If wages should be considerably lessened, few operatives for hire could be had, except those of foreign origin. Many have a home in the rural districts, to which they can retire in such an emergency, and wait for a return of the prosperous times which first tempted them to leave the paternal roof, and commence work for high wages in a manufacturing town.

Again, hired laborers easily become small tradesmen or master-mechanics, because the business of the manufacturer, the merchant, and the artisan is here not so much concentrated in the hands of a few persons with large capitals as it is in England. The competition of many, each having but a small stock in tools or trade, is not so easily crushed out by the monster undertakings of large houses wielding an immense capital, who can outlive the reverses of trade or the periods of depression in the market that are usually fatal to persons of smaller means. Reverses happen and failures ensue, oftener even than in England, and to the large and small capitalists alike; but, as already mentioned, there are great facilities here for bankrupts to recover their position and try again. Profits and losses are great, speculation is rife, and great fortunes are acquired and dissipated with marvellous rapidity. Hence there is great instability, but also much life and enterprise, in trade, and in all departments of industry. I have already explained some of the causes of the peculiar mobility of society, the ease and frequency of the interchange of social position, which is one of the characteristic features of American life, and a necessary result of our political and social institutions. The particular consequence of it, to which I wish here to direct attention, is, that it keeps down the number of laborers for hire, in spite of the rapid increase of the population, and keeps up the rate of wages, or at least prevents it from falling so rapidly as it would otherwise do.

Here, also, is the explanation of the restless, migratory spirit, and the want of local attachments, which have so often attracted the attention of foreign observers. Of the population of three of our Western States, Michigan, Iowa, and Wisconsin, amounting in the aggregate to nearly one million, according to the census of 1850, only 25 per cent were born within the limits of these States in which they are domiciliated, about 20 per cent were born in foreign countries, and over 51 per cent had their nativity in other States, though still within the limits of the Union; of about 4 per cent, the places of parentage were unknown. In European countries, the bulk of the population work for hire, and are too poor to be able to change their locality; they lack rather the ability than the disposition to emigrate. But both in Europe and America, the rule holds, that, in general, only the poorer people, the laborers for wages, are inclined to seek a new home. If, therefore, within twenty years, about half a million of our people have migrated into these three States, it is a proof that the laboring class here generally have the pecuniary means for such migration, or, in other words, they have a small capital, which, if they saw fit, (and many of them actually adopt such a course,) they might employ in establishing themselves in business on their own account, in the places of their nativity, and thus ceasing to work for wages. Taking the whole population of the United States together, according to the same census, it appears that about 4,175,000 native-born white Americans, or over 21 per cent of the whole number, are now resident in other States than those in which they had their nativity.

The doctrines of the English Political Economists respecting wages, that any increase of the laboring population is necessarily an evil, as it increases the demand for the means of subsistence without proportionally increasing the supply of those means, and as it increases the competition in the labor market, thereby depressing the rate of wages; that the natural or necessary rate of wages is the smallest sum that will purchase those articles for a family which, according to the custom of the country, are regarded as requisite for the necessaries and decencies of life, or, in other words, that the only limit to the depression of wages is this conventional standard of what is absolutely requisite for the maintenance even of the poorest family, — these doctrines, I say, cease to be applicable, or to have even the appearance of truth, here in the United States. Our natural standard of wages is, not the smallest sum which will enable the temperate and industrious native-born laborer to support a family with decency, but the smallest that will enable him to do not only thus much, but to amass capital, — that will induce him to forego the independence and the other advantages of trading or working for himself. A true regard for the interests of the class to which he belongs would lead us to seek rather to lower, than to elevate, his idea of what is necessary for this end. The love of independence, the thirst for adventure, the hope of drawing one of those glittering prizes that often reward a daring spirit, though accompanied with a vast proportion of blanks, tempt far too many to abandon the safe course of slowly collecting a moderate property by savings from wages. Many a bankrupt farmer, tradesman, or master-mechanic might have safely earned independence by continuing to work for hire.

The progress of the population, unparalleled as it has been for rapidity, has been far from producing here what the English Economists regard as its necessary result, — the depression of wages. The real value of wages, or the quantity of the necessaries of life which they will purchase, may be rather said to have steadily increased in this country ever since the beginning of the present century, when our population was less than one fourth of its present amount. Neither can the phenomenon be wholly explained by the recent date of our settlements, nor by the extent of fertile, unoccupied land in our Western territory. It is only by comparison that the States on our Atlantic border, in which this phenomenon of high wages is exhibited, can be called recent settlements. Most of them are already over two hundred years old, and have long since passed beyond the stages of colonial infancy and childhood. True, the drain that is caused by the constant migration westward tends to explain the effect; but the question remains, why a similar result is not produced even in England; for, as I have already remarked, the way from Massachusetts to Iowa, Kanzas, and Minnesota, is nearly as long, and quite as expensive, as from Dublin and Liverpool to Nova Scotia and Canada. I attribute the result, therefore, to moral rather than to physical causes, — to American institutions, more than to the fact that America is still a new country, and is rich in fertile and yet unoccupied land. The mobility of society, the wider distribution of property, the absence of castes, *la carrière ouverte aux talens*, and other peculiarities created and fostered by our laws, are alone sufficient to account for the phenomenon.

The only two causes which strongly tend to a depreciation of wages in this country are the vast and constantly increasing immigration of foreigners, and the discouragement of our manufactures through the want of a protective tariff. These two causes, in a great degree, work together, and their combined action may soon produce as lamentable an effect upon wages in the United States, as other agencies have caused in Great Britain and Ireland. At present, our institutions are preserved, and general content exists among the people, because no class in the community finds itself doomed to irretrievable penury, and not one individual is without the well-grounded hope of improving his condition, and perhaps of rising even to high rank in the social scale. But let the rate of wages here be reduced to what the English Economists regard as their natural and necessary standard, — that is, to a bare sufficiency for subsistence from day to day, — and the class of laborers, who must always form the majority in any community, and who, with us, also have the control in politics, will not be satisfied without organic changes in the laws, which will endanger at once our political and social system. Our immunity thus far ought not to betray us into a blind confidence for the future. A few years have produced a marvellous alteration in our prospects, and the change has not been altogether for our advantage. The Atlantic has been bridged by steam, and the ties which connect us with Great Britain, and link our commercial and social well-being with hers, are strengthening every day. Ireland is depopulating itself upon our shores; and already the rate of increase from abroad is two thirds as great as that of the natural growth of the population at home. During the year 1854, the number of immigrant foreigners brought by sea to our shores was 427,833; the average for the last four years exceeded 400,000 annually. The annual average for the three years ending December 31, 1845, was but 121,000, or considerably less than one third of the present average. In one particular, this result is inevitable; we might as well try to dam up the Mississippi with bulrushes, as to stop this great westward migration of the nations. But we may enlarge the field of employment, and increase the number of the applications of industry, so that this immense influx shall not produce its full effect in depressing the price of labor.*

* The number of passengers arriving in the United States by sea from foreign countries, from September 30, 1843, to December 31, 1854, was as follows: —

The tide of emigration was first turned with overwhelming force upon our shores in 1847, a year of famine in Ireland and Scotland, and of great distress in several other parts of Europe. The census taken by the English government in 1851 not only affords evidence of the extent of the calamity then endured, but has brought to light another startling fact, which is without a parallel in the history of the world; — a great and fertile country, inhabited by a civilized people, enjoying a mild and equitable government, and yet, without the agency of war, pestilence, or any sudden paralysis of its industry from external causes, actually becoming depopulated by famine and emigration.

The population of Ireland in 1841 was 8,175,124. Assuming that the natural rate of increase of the Irish people for ten years is twelve per cent, which is the estimate of the Census Commissioners for 1841, it follows that the number in 1851, if it had not been diminished by the two causes just mentioned, would have been 9,156,139. But the actual population of Ireland in 1851 was 6,515,794; that is, 1,659,330 less

From	To	Males.	Females.	Sex not stated.	Total.
Sept. 30, 1843,	Sept. 30, 1844,	48,897	35,867		84,764
" 1844,	" 1845,	69,188	49,290	1,406	119,884
" 1845,	" 1846,	90,973	66,778	897	158,648
" 1846,	" 1847,	134,750	96,747	1,057	232,554
" 1847,	" 1848,	136,128	92,883	472	229,483
" 1848,	" 1849,	179,253	119,915	442	299,610
" 1849,	" 1850,	200,903	113,392	1,038	315,333
" 1850,	Dec. 31, 1850,	38,282	27,107	181	65,570
Dec. 31, 1850,	" 1851,	245,017	163,745	66	408,828
" 1851,	" 1852,			398,470	398,470
" 1852,	" 1853,	236,596	164,181		400,777
" 1853,	" 1854,	284,887	175,587		460,474
		1,666,874	1,110,492	404,029	3,174,395

From the number of arrivals here given for 1854, we should deduct 32,641, as the number of citizens of the United States returning home, leaving 427,833 immigrant foreigners, as stated in the text. A corresponding reduction should be made for the other years; but, on the other hand, this table includes only the number of arrivals *by sea*, and takes no account of those who came into the country over our inland frontier, from Canada and elsewhere. The number of foreigners entering the United States by land would be more than an offset for the number of Americans included in the preceding table among the arrivals by sea.

Of those who arrived in 1854, about 215,000 are reported as coming from Germany, 101,606 from Ireland, over 58,000 from Great Britain, and 13,317 from France. In former years, the proportion of Irish immigrants was much greater.

than it was ten years before, and considerably over two and a half millions less than what it should have been, if the natural law of increase had not been checked.*

What has become of these millions of human beings? The official returns of the total emigration from the United Kingdom for the ten years ending in March, 1851, show that only 1,741,476 persons emigrated during this period. This includes the drain from England and Scotland also; but it is probable that nearly as many Irish passed over into the sister island as would make up for the number of natives who left it to go abroad. And yet there remain about 900,000 Irish to be accounted for, — an immense loss of population, to be attributed to famine and the diseases consequent upon extreme misery and want. And the drain still continues; a panic seems to have seized the population of Ireland, and they rush to the seaports to embark for any other portion of the earth, as if the whole island labored under a curse. The emigration for 1849 and 1850, amounting to 432,491, is included in the numbers already given. But in 1851, we learn that 254,537 Irish emigrants left their native land; 224,997 left in 1852, and 199,392 in 1853; thus making a total of 678,926 persons who quitted Ireland during the next three years after the last census was taken. The population of the island at the close of 1853, therefore, cannot have amounted to six millions. The total emigration from the United Kingdom of Great Britain and Ireland, for the three years ending in December, 1853, (including the numbers already given for Ireland,) amounted to 1,033,537, a number somewhat exceeding the natural increase through the excess of births over deaths, so that the population of the kingdom actually declined during this period.

* The actual rate of increase in Ireland from 1831 to 1841 was only five per cent. But during this period, the causes had already begun to operate, which, in the succeeding decade, had so remarkable an effect in thinning the population. In the preceding ten years, 1821 to 1831, the rate was fourteen per cent, which is about two per cent lower than the corresponding rate in England for the same period. There is reason to believe that the Irish *tend* to multiply faster than the English or the Scotch; that is, that the births among them are proportionally more numerous. The Irish Census Commissioners show that their estimate, which I have adopted in the text, is a safe one, by proving from the returns that 572,464 persons emigrated from Ireland during the ten years preceding 1841, — a number sufficient to raise the proportion for that decade from five to twelve per cent.

I do not dwell upon these facts merely because they afford a spectacle and a problem which may well claim the attention of the whole civilized world. They have a peculiar meaning and pertinency for us here in the United States; they must affect our future prosperity, whether for good or ill, far more even than that of Great Britain. It is to our shores, not to those of Great Britain and Ireland, that this great Irish exodus is directed. These exiles are coming to us, mostly in a state of great destitution, bringing with them Irish habits, and Irish willingness to live in squalor upon the smallest pittance that will support life. Already they constitute, either by themselves or in connection with the Germans, almost the whole class of our menial or domestic servants in the non-slaveholding States, and of rude laborers in the construction of railroads and other public improvements. Cheapness of provisions is not the attraction that brings them here; at this moment, all the common articles of provisions are as cheap in Ireland as in the Atlantic States of this Union; many of them are cheaper. Nor is it comparative freedom from taxation which they seek; for the annual amount of Irish taxes is only about ten shillings a head, which hardly exceeds the burden of government here in America. But they come in quest of constant employment and higher wages. *These* are the tangible tokens of our prosperity, the causes of the general well-being of our people; and these have made the United States a harbor of refuge for the poor of the civilized world. And we have proof that the Irish have succeeded in obtaining in America what they came to seek, — wages which should suffice, not only to support life, but to enable them to effect considerable savings. The remittances which they are making to alleviate the misery of their relatives and friends at home, or to enable them to emigrate to this country, have reached an amount that hardly seems credible, though the statistics of the subject, collected by the British government, cannot be questioned. It appears that the amounts remitted from America to Ireland through the banks, exclusive of sums sent by private hands, amounted, in 1848, to £460,000; and that they steadily increased, till, in 1853, they reached the prodigious sum of £1,439,000, or about seven millions of dollars. It is probable that a portion of this sum is remitted for investment, a favorable opportunity being afforded for the purchase of land by the proceedings of the Commission for the Sale of Irish Encumbered Estates. Thus the Irishman comes to America as a pauper, and in a few years collects the means of returning, if he sees fit, to his native country as a land-owner.

Wages depend, as the English Political Economists are fond of remarking, upon the ratio of population to capital and employment. They ought to rise, then, as the numbers of the people diminish, though trade and manufactures should only, to use an expressive phrase, "hold their own"; and they should rise still more rapidly, if, at the same time, trade and manufactures be remarkably prosperous, and capital be steadily increasing. But it is a surprising fact, that although Ireland has lost during the last ten years over two millions of her people, being one fourth part of her whole population, and though there has been a considerable influx of capital into the country, owing to the settlement and improvement of the Encumbered Estates, "very little improvement, if any, has occurred in the rate of wages of labor in the districts most depopulated by emigration." This is the language of the Irish Poor Law Commissioners, in their Annual Report made in 1853. "In January last," they say, "we obtained returns from our Inspectors, relating to nearly the whole of Ireland, showing the comparative rate of wages in the present year and in several past years, summaries of which" are given in the Report. "In very few departments of labor does the money rate of wages appear to have been higher in the beginning of 1853 than it was in 1845, the year before the commencement of the famine." True, the condition of the peasantry had improved, as the same amount of wages would purchase a greater quantity of provisions, as employment could be more constantly obtained, and as the number of paupers was much smaller, this last result being directly attributable to the emigration. The fact that money wages have not risen, can be explained by the previous great redundancy of the laboring population, owing to the narrowness of the field of employment caused by the almost exclusive devotion of the people to agriculture. We have here a strong corroboration, then, of our previous doctrine, that a country cannot become wealthy whose inhabitants are chiefly or altogether occupied in tilling the ground, whatever may be the fertility of its soil or the favorableness of its situation.

The history of Ireland shows the inevitable consequences of free trade with a country having so vast an aggregate of capital as Great Britain, and reaping the fruits also of the skill and experience acquired during a strict enforcement of the protective policy for two centuries. The legislative union of the two countries, at the beginning of the present century, broke down the few barriers which formerly limited their intercourse, and left them to compete on what the English Economists consider as *equal terms*. Till this epoch, whatever political evils Ireland may have endured, her social state was not in any marked degree inferior to that of England. The habits of her people, it is true, were not so neat and industrious; but wages were not reduced to a starvation limit, and her cottiers generally had enough to eat and to spare. But unrestricted intercourse with England stifled the small beginnings of her manufacturing industry; for her people could purchase from the sister country even all the products of the small mechanic trades and arts cheaper than they could, at the time, manufacture them for themselves. They bought in the cheapest market, forgetting that they had nothing but the cereal grains, pigs, potatoes, and butter, to offer in exchange, and that the production of these articles would not afford employment to half the industry of the people. Manufactures could never gain a foothold among them, save in the North, where a colony of canny Scotch introduced the culture of flax, made linen, and have since kept themselves out of the abyss of poverty into which the rest of the island has been plunged. So feeble were the means of the native Irish for keeping up trade by exportation, that their consumption both of domestic and foreign goods dwindled almost to nothing. Mr. Martin, one of the latest and ablest statistical writers upon Irish affairs, cannot suppress his astonishment, that "the consumption of British manufactures in Ireland is not more than one guinea *per annum* for each inhabitant, whereas the negroes in the West Indies consume each five pounds' worth annually." But the reason is obvious enough; the negroes in the West Indies have sufficient employment for their industry in the production of sugar, coffee, and pimento, in regard to which they are not exposed to Transatlantic competition. Having enough to sell, they are consequently able and willing to buy. But the Irish have nothing to sell except the provisions which they take from the mouths of their children. So they have gone on, constantly exporting a larger share of their pigs, potatoes, and butter, till they have at last ceased to preserve any to satisfy their own hunger. "The most remarkable thing," says Mr. Martin, "is, that, even during the recent famine, there were large exports of provisions from Ireland." While this famine was at its height, upwards of three millions of persons were fed at one time by public charity.* If these are the consequences of free trade with England, and exclusive addiction to agricultural pursuits, we may well call for the restoration of a protective policy here in the United States.

But the danger in this country is still greater, owing to the immense influx of foreigners who are attracted hither by the higher wages of industry, and whose presence and competition with the native operatives are likely to effect a general and great depreciation in the price of labor. Besides the natural rapid growth of our population, an annual addition to our numbers of over 400,000 immigrants, all of them, except an insignificant fraction, being of the poorest class, cannot but produce a marked effect of some kind, even if the field for the employment of industry here were widening under the most favorable circumstances. Many of these exiles are Irish, who have been accustomed to regard six shillings ($1.50) a week as liberal wages for the father of a family, even when they could get employment only for half of the time.†

---

* "Neither ancient nor modern history can furnish a parallel to the fact, that upwards of three millions of persons were fed every day, in the neighborhood of their own homes, by administrative arrangements emanating from, and controlled by, one central office." — *The Irish Crisis*, by C. E. Trevelyan, Secretary to the Treasury.

† Seven years before the occurrence of the Irish famine, that wild genius, Mr. Carlyle, beheld the inevitable effect, upon the wages of English workmen, of the influx of the Irish into England, and thus, in his quaint fashion, wailed over it: —

"Crowds of miserable Irish darken all our towns. The wild Milesian features, looking false ingenuity, restlessness, unreason, misery, and mockery, salute you on all highways and byways. The English coachman, as he whirls past, lashes the Milesian with his whip, curses him with his tongue; the Milesian is holding out his hat to beg. He is the sorest evil this country has to strive with. In his rags and laughing savagery, he is there to undertake all work that can be done by mere strength of hand and back, for wages that will purchase him potatoes. He needs

Though the number of Irish who have crossed over into Great Britain probably does not equal one fourth of those who have found a refuge in the United States, Mr. J. S. Mill, who generally opposes the interference of government on any occasion, makes this extraordinary admission: — "If there were no other escape from that fatal immigration of the Irish, which has done and is doing so much to degrade the condition of our agricultural, and some classes of our town population, I should see no injustice, and the greatest possible expediency, in checking that destructive inroad by prohibitive laws."

But the field for the employment of industry in the United States is not widening. An alteration of the tariff in 1846 paralyzed for a time the chief branches of manufactures, and brought down the prices of bread-stuffs and other provisions, for several years, to a point which gave the farmer no temptation to raise more of them than were necessary for home con-

---

only salt for condiment; he lodges to his mind in any pig-hutch or dog-hutch, roosts in out-houses; and wears a suit of tatters the getting off and on of which is said to be a difficult operation, transacted only on festivals and the high tides of the calendar. The Saxon man, if he cannot work on these terms, finds no work. . . . . . And yet these poor Celtiberian Irish brothers, what can they help it? They cannot stay at home and starve. It is just and natural that they come hither as a curse to us. Alas! for them too it is not a luxury. The time has come when the Irish population must either be improved a little, or else exterminated. . . . . . Every man who will take the statistic spectacles off his nose, and look, may discern in town and country, that the condition of the lower multitude of English laborers approximates more and more to that of the Irish competing with them in all markets; that whatsoever labor, to which mere strength with little skill will suffice, is to be done, will be done, not at the English price, but at an approximation to the Irish price; at a price superior as yet to the Irish, that is, superior to scarcity of third-rate potatoes for thirty weeks yearly; superior, — yet hourly, with the arrival of every new steamboat, sinking nearly to an equality with that." — *Chartism*, by T. Carlyle.

Mr. De Quincey, in his "Logic of Political Economy," observes: "The true ruin of Irish pauperism to England and Scotland is not of a nature to be checked by any possible Poor Bill. This ruin lies, first and chiefly, in the gradual degradation of wages, English and Scotch, under the fierce growth of Irish competition; secondly, in the chargeableness of Irish pauperism, once settled, upon funds English and Scotch. In Scotland, the case is even worse at present than in England." At Paisley, in 1842, "the sheer impossibility of feeding adequately the entire body of claimants, coerced the humane distributors of the relief into drawing a line between Scotch and Irish. Then it was that the total affliction became known, — namely, the hideous extent to which Irish intruders upon Scotland had taken the bread out of her own children's mouths. As to England, it has long been accepted as a fair statement, that 50,000 Irish interlopers annually swell the great tide of our *native* increase"; or about half as many as now annually come to the United States, and about one eighth part of our total foreign immigration.

sumption. The effect, so far as agriculture was concerned, was suspended in 1847, and partially in 1848, by the potato-rot in Ireland, and the partial failure of the crops in England and on the Continent, which caused a large demand for American articles of food to be exported. But the demand and the price fell off again in subsequent years. In 1850 and 1851, the average price of flour in our Atlantic seaports was about five dollars a barrel, a price at which the farmers of the West cannot afford to export it at all, except for the purpose of relieving a glutted market by a sacrifice.* Meanwhile, the sale of British manufactures in this country, to the great depression of our domestic industry, rapidly increased. Our imports of the manufactures of wool, cotton, and iron, for the year ending in June, 1851, had become forty-three per cent, and for that ending in June, 1853, one hundred and twenty-five per cent, greater than they were the year before the alteration of the tariff. To pay for these extravagant importations, we were obliged to sell our agricultural products at the reduced price just mentioned, and to export an immense amount of California gold besides.

The effect upon the demand for labor in manufacturing operations in the United States may be very briefly illustrated. In Pennsylvania, the number of blast furnaces for the production of iron from the ore was 304, capable of making half a million of tons annually. Within three years after the effects of the new tariff began to be felt, 167 of these furnaces, or 56 per cent, were put out of blast, and the iron made by the remainder was 49 per cent less than the quantity previously manufactured. There were also 200 establishments for the manufacture of wrought iron, and they produced about 200,000 tons annually; within two years after the enactment of the new tariff, their product fell off 33 per cent, and the manufacture generally ceased to yield any profit, and was continued only to avoid a heavy sacrifice in the cost of the machinery.†

* The present enhanced price (1855) of American provisions and bread-stuffs does not affect this argument. A deficiency of the crops in England, the war with Russia, and the disturbing effect upon the prices of all commodities of the great influx of Californian and Australian gold, is the cause of this enhanced price, which, to a considerable degree, is merely nominal.

† To the suggestion, that these unfortunate results may possibly be attributable to

The capital invested in the 504 iron works in Pennsylvania exceeded twenty millions of dollars; and the number of persons directly employed in them, when all at work, would be 30,103. Reckoning also the hands employed in mining and transporting coal and ore to the works, and in transporting the finished iron to market, we have a grand total of 41,616 men dependent on the iron business in Pennsylvania alone. This State probably produces half of all the iron manufactured in the United States; and as the statistics now given leave no doubt that at least one half of the workmen formerly engaged in making iron were dismissed, it is certain that the new tariff threw out of employment 40,000 laborers in this business alone. Most of these discharged workmen necessarily became farmers and agricultural laborers, and, by their competition, tended to reduce the prices, already ruinously low, of agricultural produce.

This is not all. Within three years after this reduction of the tariff, the price of the imported iron began to rise rapidly, and in 1852 and 1853, it was even higher than it had been before the ruin of the home manufacture. Then, at a great cost, the old business was resumed, the deserted works were repaired, the machinery replaced, and the manufacture was again in the full tide of activity, but subject to another decline and fall with the next fluctuation in the foreign market. The injury done to American industry arises not so much from the quantity, as from the ruinous fluctuations in price, of the imported commodities. What is needed from a protective tariff in this country is, to prevent the foreign article from being frequently sent hither to be sold below its cost, in order to relieve the glutted English market. The aggregate cost of iron to American consumers, during the eight years preceding 1854, was undoubtedly greater than if the reduction of the duties through the tariff of 1846 had never taken place.

There are no means of ascertaining precisely the effect produced by the new tariff on the manufactures of cotton and

---

over-trading, and not to the tariff of 1846, the conclusive answer may be made, that, in the year when the production of Pennsylvania iron was greatest, the country imported over 50,000 tons of pig and bar iron, exclusive of chains, wrought-iron, hardware, &c. A manufacture cannot be deemed excessive which is insufficient to supply the home market.

wool. According to the census of 1850, these manufactures then gave employment to upwards of 55,000 male operatives, and to over 75,000 females, a number probably not so great by 50 per cent as it would have been, but for the reduction of duties in 1846. The vicissitudes to which these manufacturers have been exposed, have not been destructive to many works already in existence; but there has been no such development or extension of them as the interests of the country required. It is not enough for the peculiar situation in which the people of this country are now placed, that the great departments of industry should be able merely to sustain themselves, by a great effort, at the point which they had reached ten years ago. They must be developed and multiplied at a rate proportioned at least to the rapid growth of our population both from native and foreign sources. Otherwise, the profits of capital and the wages of labor must sink to the level at which they have long rested in Great Britain. The inevitable consequence of free trade and constantly increasing commercial intercourse between the two countries must be, to establish among the inhabitants of both of them the same standard of material well-being, the same measure and distribution of individual prosperity. Great Britain is now pouring upon us in a full tide both the surplus of her population and the products of her overtasked manufacturing industry. She is giving us more mouths to feed, at the moment when she is taking away from us the means of feeding them in any other way than by forcing them into agricultural industry, and thus cheapening still farther the agricultural products which alone she can receive from us in exchange. The ocean, which once separated us, steam has contracted to a span. For all purposes of free intercourse, we are now virtually two contiguous countries, separated by no mountain barriers, by no differences of race, language, or polity, by no fundamental dissimilarity of our political institutions, and governed by the same system of municipal law. We are rapidly becoming as much one people as the English and the Irish, or the English and the Scotch. To expect that, in two countries thus situated, without any special direction of public policy towards maintaining some barrier between them, the pressure of population, the profits of capital, and the wages of labor can long remain very unequal, would be as idle as to believe that, without the erection of a dam, water could be maintained at two different levels in the same pond. Throw down the little that remains of our protective system, and let the emigration from Great Britain and Ireland to our shores increase to half a million annually, and within the lifetime of the present generation, the laborer's hire in our Atlantic States will be as low as it is in England. Our manufactures would flourish then, as those of Great Britain flourish now; cheap labor is the only requisite for placing them upon the same level. It is not, then, for the sake of the capital now embarked in our manufacturing enterprises, that we would advocate a return to what has been well denominated "the American policy." But that the bulk of our laboring population should fall into that condition where they would be exposed to such evils as have visited the laboring classes of Great Britain and Ireland during the last ten years, — that the *necessary* standard of wages, as the English economists call it, should be here, as well as there, the smallest sum which will give a mere subsistence, — this we should regard as the greatest calamity which the folly of men or the wrath of Heaven could bring upon the land.

CHAPTER XV.

THE CAUSES OF DIFFERENT RATES OF WAGES IN DIFFERENT EMPLOYMENTS.

The effect of competition upon the rates of wages in different employments has been admirably illustrated by Adam Smith. It is matter of common observation, that the workmen in different arts and trades are paid very unequally, if their wages be reckoned only in money. A blacksmith usually earns more than a farm-laborer; a watchmaker more than a blacksmith; a lawyer or a physician — for these also are laborers for hire — more than a watch-maker. How can such inequalities exist, when competition, the great equalizing agent, is always at work, and tends always to bring profits, wages, and prices to a level? Why do not persons leave those employments that are underpaid, and flock into those which receive more than the average? The answer is, that laborers are paid for their services not only in money, but in the various degrees of credit or estimation in which their business is held, in the agreeableness or disagreeableness of the occupation, the ease or difficulty of learning it, and in its several other peculiarities; and that competition is often limited by circumstances, so that it is unable to produce its full effect. Competition is free only when all persons are at liberty to enter into it; and men compete for employment in different occupations according to their view, not merely of the pecuniary gains which it offers, but of the various circumstances, among which the nominal amount of wages is only one, that render it more or less desirable. I borrow with some enlargement the illustrations of this topic by Adam Smith and other economists.

First, "the wages of labor vary with the ease or hardship, the cleanliness or dirtiness, the honorableness or dishonorableness, of the employment." Thus, the work of a stevedore, that of loading and unloading vessels at the wharves, as it is more humble, dirty, and fatiguing, is more highly paid, than that of a shoemaker. "A journeyman blacksmith, though an artificer, seldom earns so much in twelve hours as a collier, who is only a laborer, does in eight; his work is not quite so dirty, is less dangerous, and is carried on in daylight and above ground. Honor makes a great part of the reward of all honorable professions." The profession of a teacher is more respectable than that of a dressmaker; and therefore many young women, here in New England, will keep school at three dollars a week, when they might earn six dollars in the same time by ministering to their countrywomen's love of fashion and elegance in dress. Occupations which can be pursued at home are not so largely remunerated as those which must be carried on within the precincts of a great manufactory. A farmer's daughter, who has what is called "slop-work" supplied to her at home from the cheap-clothing establishments, cannot earn one third as much as she would receive for tending a loom in a cotton-factory; but then she can choose her own hours for work or recreation, can rise early or late, and be free from any external control. This freedom of action is paid for by a diminution of wages. The brakeman employed on a railway must receive higher wages than the laborer employed in grading the road, as his occupation is a dangerous one; he must be paid for the not improbable event of breaking a leg or an arm, or losing his life. The laborers employed in constructing a railroad across the Isthmus of Panama received very high pay; they were compelled to go far from home into a climate so pestilential, that probably one half of their number perished while the work was in progress.

"Secondly," says Adam Smith, "the wages of labor vary with the easiness and cheapness, or the difficulty and expense, of learning the business. When any expensive machine is erected, the extraordinary work to be performed by it before it is worn out, it must be expected, will replace the capital laid out on it, with at least the ordinary profits. A man educated at the expense of much labor and time, may be compared to one of these expensive machines. The work which he learns to perform, it must be expected, over and above the usual wages of common labor, will replace to him the whole expense of his education, with at least the ordinary profits of an equally valuable capital. It must do this in a reasonable time, regard being had to the very uncertain duration of human life, in the same manner as to the more certain duration of the machine. The difference between the wages of skilled labor and those of common labor is founded on this principle."

It should be added, that all persons are not capable of learning the more difficult employments, for which a quick eye, a dexterous hand, and some natural taste or ingenuity, are often requisite. Not all common laborers, after any expense of time and training, would make good blacksmiths; nor are all blacksmiths capable of becoming first-rate machinists. The competition for employment in the more difficult trades is therefore first limited by Nature, through the various capacities which she bestows upon men; and secondly, by the necessity of education, which not all, even of those who are naturally gifted, have time, money, or opportunity to obtain. Engraving has risen to be one of the fine arts, as the talent for practising it with the highest success is as rare as that of a great painter or sculptor. An ordinary engraver may not earn more than a watchmaker; but a single copy of one of the works of Raphael Morghen, Sir Robert Strange, Bartolozzi, or Piranesi, now commands a high price in the market. In engineering, the construction of machinery, and ship-building, great natural ability, improved by education and practice, may obtain remuneration so liberal as to appear extravagant. The services of Paul Moody in superintending the erection of the machinery for the manufactories at Waltham and Lowell, and of Telford, Stephenson, and Brunel in the great works of internal improvement which they constructed in Great Britain, were paid for at rates proportioned to the magnitude of the enterprises which they directed. "In some manual employments," says Mr. Mill, "requiring a nicety of hand which can only be acquired by long practice, it is difficult to obtain, at any cost, workmen in sufficient numbers, who are capable of the most delicate kind of work; and the wages paid to them are only limited by the price which purchasers are willing to give for the commodity they produce. This is the case with some working watchmakers, and with the makers of astronomical and optical instruments. If workmen competent to such employments were ten times as numerous as they are, there would be purchasers for all which they could make, not indeed at the present prices, but at those lower prices which would be the natural consequence of lower wages."

In what are called the liberal professions, however, though a protracted and expensive education is required for admission to them, the rates of compensation, on an average, are very low, — sometimes actually lower than in the mechanic trades. In the State of Ohio, for instance, and, it may be presumed, in most of the other Western States, the salaries of the clergymen are not equal to the wages of good journeymen blacksmiths; the former do not receive an average of more than $ 500 a year; the latter readily obtain two dollars a day, or over $ 600 a year. True, some of the clergymen, especially in the Baptist and Methodist denominations, are not liberally educated men; but the great majority have completed their training both at college and in the professional schools. At the bar, also, though a few eminent practitioners make great gains, the aggregate earnings of the whole body of lawyers, if equally distributed among them, would hardly equal the average wages of the mechanics. The cause of the discrepancy in this particular case, however, will be explained hereafter. Physicians may be somewhat better paid on an average, though the aggregate earnings of their craft are capriciously distributed, an ignorant and impudent quack often obtaining more than a competent and thoroughly instructed practitioner. This is because there is no certain criterion of the physician's skill; whether the patient lives or dies, it is generally doubtful whether the result is to be attributed to nature or the doctor.

Adam Smith justly attributes the inadequate compensation of labor in the liberal professions, first, to the superior dignity or honorableness of such labor, which is an offset for the inferior pecuniary reward; secondly, to the natural confidence which every man has in his own abilities and his own good fortune, whereby he persuades himself that he shall draw one of the few great prizes in the law or the church, instead of one out of the many blanks; and thirdly, so far as literature and the sacred ministry are concerned, to the number of persons who are educated for those occupations at the public expense. The first point is too obvious to require any farther illustration than it has already received; and the second was considered (see page 45), when we were commenting upon what may be called "the lottery principle" in human nature, whereby sanguine visions, and the pleasurable excitement of a pursuit in which success is wholly uncertain, must be made our consolation for frequent failure. In respect to the last, I borrow the language of Adam Smith. "It has been considered as of so much importance, that a proper number of young people should be educated for certain professions, that sometimes the public, and sometimes the piety of private founders, have established many pensions, scholarships, exhibitions, bursaries, &c., for this purpose, which draw many more people into those trades than could otherwise pretend to follow them. In all Christian countries, I believe, the education of the greater part of churchmen is paid for in this manner. Very few of them are educated altogether at their own expense. The long, tedious, and expensive education, therefore, of those who are, will not always procure them a suitable reward, the church being crowded with people who, in order to get employment, are willing to accept of a much smaller recompense than what such an education would otherwise have entitled them to; and in this manner the competition of the poor takes away the reward of the rich."

In the United States, generally, it may be said, that, through the efforts of Education Societies and the founders and benefactors of colleges, the clergy are educated gratuitously, — a policy very well designed to prevent pulpits from becoming vacant, but not so likely to insure the respectability, the adequate compensation, or even the sincerity, of those who fill them. It is to be feared that many are bribed, through the offer of a liberal education without charge, to enter the ministry, though they have no peculiar fitness, and not even any strong desire, for the sacred calling. Nay, it may sometimes happen, that the parents of a child who is unfitted for almost any other pursuit, because weak in body and not very strong in mind, may be tempted, by this liberal proffer, to make a minister of him, being encouraged to believe, like the mother of Dominie Sampson, that "he may wag his pow in a pulpit yet," though he cannot wag it to good purpose anywhere else.

> "Olim truncus eram ficulnus, inutile lignum,
> Quum faber, incertus scamnum faceretne Priapum,
> Maluit esse deum."

In respect to the education, in part gratuitous, which is offered by the colleges as a general preparation for the other professions, though the effect is certainly to lessen the emoluments of practitioners by increasing the number of competitors, sound policy, or a regard for the best interests of the people, requires that it should be continued. Adam Smith, with his usual bias towards the principles of free trade, would have the whole matter regulated by the natural operation of supply and demand, assuming that, if more lawyers, physicians, and literary or scientific men are needed, their rates of compensation would be raised, and thus more persons would be tempted to enter these professions, even at the cost of educating themselves. But the immediate earnings of literary and scientific men, as already explained, are inferior to their merits, and altogether insufficient for their wants; while it is of the utmost importance for the interests of the public, that a numerous class of highly educated men should exist in the community, capable of appreciating each other's efforts, and of aiding the progress of letters, science, and invention. Besides, many must receive the benefits of a liberal culture, in order that the few who are able to profit by it in the highest degree may be sure not to miss the requisite preparatory training, without which even their eminent abilities may not produce their proper fruits. Many thousands must graduate at Oxford and Cambridge, in order that a possible Milton, Newton, or Bentley may not be hindered from benefiting the world by his genius. It is a commonplace remark, that "mute, inglorious Miltons" probably rest in every village churchyard. That is a short-sighted policy, which would weigh the cost of institutions of learning against only the average result upon all those who are trained at them; the value to the community at large of the services of such men as have been named is literally inestimable; it would outweigh the expense of founding and maintaining universities enough to educate the whole people. This consideration is even strong enough to justify the policy of educating most clergymen at the public charge; without it, the world might have lost the preaching of Jeremy Taylor, Jonathan Edwards, and Thomas Chalmers.

Thirdly, says Adam Smith, "the wages of labor in different occupations vary with the constancy or inconstancy of employment. In the greater part of manufactures, a journeyman may be pretty sure of employment almost every day in the year that he is willing to work. A mason or bricklayer, on the contrary, can work neither in hard frost nor in foul weather, and his employment at all other times depends upon the occasional calls of his customers. He is liable, in consequence, to be frequently without any. What he earns, therefore, while he is employed, must not only maintain him while he is idle, but make him some compensation for those anxious and desponding moments which the thought of so precarious a situation must sometimes occasion." It is easy to see that the person who can be employed only a part of the time *ought* to receive higher wages than one who has regular work and constant pay; and for evident reasons, his compensation *must* be larger. On account of the irregularity and uncertainty of his occupation, fewer persons will be disposed to engage in it; thus the competition will be less, and he will be able to raise his price, until the increased pay affords an adequate compensation for the inconstancy of the employment.

In most cases, employers take all the risk; that is, they insure regular wages to their hands, whether the work be constant or irregular, lucrative or insufficient to pay the expenses. Thus, the driver of a stage-coach receives the same pay, whether the vehicle be full or empty; and the clerk in a store must have his regular salary, though business is sometimes dull, and he has little to do. So, also, a ship must be manned by sailors enough to take care of her even in a storm; and the consequence is, that in ordinary, pleasant weather, the crew may be idle more than half of the time. Sometimes, however, the person employed takes the risk, and his wages when he is at work, must be high enough to compensate him for occasional necessary idleness. Thus, the driver of a hackney-coach is paid only a certain proportion of what he can earn during the day; and the crews of our American whaling-vessels generally "go upon shares," as it is termed; that is, they have no monthly wages, but receive the value of a fixed portion of the oil that they take. As ships sometimes come home "clean," or without any oil, so that they obtain nothing for one or two years' labor, their share of a full cargo ought to exceed, and actually does considerably exceed, the ordinary amount of seamen's wages for a voyage of the same length.

The fourth cause assigned by Adam Smith for variation in the rate of wages, is the small or great trust that must be reposed in the person employed. Thus, goldsmiths and jewellers are paid more liberally than workers in brass or iron, not on account merely of their greater skill, and in spite of their labor being more agreeable and less fatiguing, but because of the greater value of the materials with which they are intrusted. "We trust our health to the physician, our fortune, and sometimes our life and reputation, to the lawyer and attorney. Such confidence could not safely be reposed in people of a very mean or low condition. Their reward must be such, therefore, as may give them that rank in the society which so important a trust requires. The long time and the great expense which must be laid out in their education, when combined with this circumstance, necessarily enhance still further the price of their labor."

On the same principle, also, those who are intrusted with the handling of much money, such as the cashiers and tellers of banks, the treasurers and managers of manufacturing and railroad corporations, must receive high salaries. It may be thought, perhaps, that there is some degradation in being rewarded for common honesty, as men ought to be honest without being paid for it. So they ought; but what they are paid for is, not honesty, but the reputation for honesty, — that security which is found in their well-known previous lives and character, and in the general circumstances of their situation, that they will be faithful to their trust. Not all, not even many persons, are lucky enough to be well known to the community at large, as deserving full confidence in any office, however much exposed to temptation. The competition for such offices being thus restricted to a few, they are enabled to raise the price of their services. Sometimes security is taken, the persons employed being required to give bonds to a heavy amount for their fidelity to their engagements. In this case, there is no need of their integrity being well known to the public at large; it is enough that they have so far earned the confidence of a few as to be able to obtain sufficient bondsmen. The contrivance of giving bonds thus opens the competition, and tends to reduce salaries, but not to make them so low as they would be if no bonds were required.

Fifthly, says Adam Smith, "the wages of labor in different employments vary according to the probability or improbability of success in them. In the greater part of the mechanic trades, success is almost certain, but very uncertain in the liberal professions. Put your son apprentice to a shoemaker, and there is little doubt of his learning to make a pair of shoes; but send him to study the law, and it is at least twenty to one if he ever makes such proficiency as will enable him to live by the business. In a perfectly fair lottery, those who draw the prizes ought to gain all that is lost by those who draw the blanks. In a profession where twenty fail for one that succeeds, that one ought to gain all that should have been gained by the unsuccessful twenty. The counsellor at law, who perhaps, at forty years of age, begins to make something by his profession, ought to receive the retribution, not only of his own so tedious and expensive education, but of that of more than twenty others, who are never likely to make anything by it. How extravagant soever the fees of counsellors at law may sometimes appear, their real retribution is never equal to this."

The average gains of practitioners at the bar are reduced by the great number of those who enter the profession without depending upon it for support, as they have independent means of livelihood, and desire only a genteel excuse for doing nothing. Some, also, have recourse to the law, because it is not only a highly reputable business, but is an easy mode of making the transition to political life. Many thus appear to be waiting for clients, who are really on the look-out only for a chance of being elected to the legislature or to Congress. Though these two classes of persons do not enter actively into the competition for fees, their presence diminishes the chances of success for those who hope to rise in the profession; some business occasionally falls into their hands, and they increase the crowd in the midst of which merit and ability often remain hidden from the world. Hence, as Adam Smith remarks, while the ordinary income of shoemakers and blacksmiths exceeds their ordinary expenditure, it will be found that the annual gains of the lawyers, as a body, bear but a small proportion to their annual expenses. The profession is but a lottery at the best, even for those who diligently qualify themselves for it, and found upon it their only hopes of success; the splendor of a few prizes in it is apt to dazzle the judgment of many, who, by a cool calculation of the chances, would be induced to try a different occupation.

I do not mean that success is more doubtful at the bar than in any other business. In this country, undoubtedly, trade is equally uncertain, for it is said that three fourths of those who engage in it become insolvent in the course of the first five years; and of those who escape the gulf of bankruptcy, not one in ten succeeds in amassing a fortune. But "uncertainty of success," as Mr. Senior remarks, "cannot well affect the wages of common labor, since no man, unless he be to a certain extent a capitalist, unless he have a fund for his intermediate support, can devote himself to an employment in which the success is uncertain." He remarks, moreover, "that there are two sorts of uncertainty. In some cases, the hazard is essentially connected with the employment itself, and recurs, in about an equal degree, at every operation. Smuggling and the manufacture of gunpowder are instances. Experience and skill may somewhat diminish the risk; but the best smuggler and the best maker of gunpowder probably each suffers an average amount of loss. But there are employments in which success, *if once attained*, is permanent. Such is often the case in mining. That mining is generally the road to ruin is notorious in all mining countries; but there are miners who have never suffered a loss. The same may be said of the liberal professions. Granting them to be as uncertain as Adam Smith believed them to be, the evil to which that uncertainty refers is experienced only by those who fail. To those who succeed, they afford a revenue eminently safe and regular. Their uncertainty is personal. It arises from the error to which every man is subject, when he compares his own qualifications with those of his rivals. If he be found on the actual trial inferior, his failure is irretrievable; in the other alternative, his success is as permanent."

The inequalities thus far considered proceed from causes that are inherent in the employments themselves. But there are others, as Adam Smith remarks, which arise from the peculiar laws and customs of different nations, and which operate by obstructing the competition that would otherwise reduce wages and profits to a level. If other things are equal, and if persons are left to their own choice, they will flock into the occupations that are more lucrative, and will desert those which are less productive, until the increased supply of labor and capital in the former, and the diminished supply in the latter, bring about equality between the two classes. But people are not always left to themselves; hinderances often exist, sometimes created by the laws, sometimes only by the habits and feelings of the people, which obstruct the free movement of labor and capital from one occupation to another.

The most remarkable of the hinderances existing by force of law are the exclusive privileges that were granted to the corporations, or guilds of trade, which formerly existed in almost every city in Europe, but which are now rapidly dying out. All the persons practising any one art or trade in a particular city, such as the tailors, the brewers, the tanners, the goldsmiths, &c., were united into a company, which received from the government by charter the exclusive right to practise their vocation. The competition in this art or trade was thus restricted to those who had been made free of the company; and no person could become free of the trade, till he had served an apprenticeship to it, usually for seven years, and had complied with other regulations, which were often intentionally made numerous and vexatious, in order to prevent too many persons from entering the business and diminishing its profits. Thus, the number of apprentices which each master might have was often determined by law, and sometimes a heavy fee or fine was exacted, before the apprentice who had completed his term could become free of the craft. "In their greatest prosperity, these fraternities, more especially in the metropolis, became important bodies, in which the whole community was enrolled; each had its distinct common hall, made by-laws for the regulation of its particular trade, and had its common property." Membership became the principal avenue of admission to the general franchise of the municipality; and as the impediments to becoming freemen were multiplied, the management of civic affairs gradually fell into the hands of a little oligarchy. Sometimes, the royal charters expressly vested the local government, and even the immediate election of members of Parliament, in small councils, originally nominated by the crown, and ever after self-elected. But of late years, the laws requiring apprenticeship have been repealed or essentially amended, and in England, the Reform Bill, together with the Municipal Reform Act, has swept away nearly all the exclusive privileges of these incorporated trades; but many of the companies, especially in London, still exist, having the ownership and management of large funds, and some local dignities and rights, which cause membership of them to be highly prized. There are, in all, eighty-one of these incorporated trades in London, twelve of them being called the *Great Companies*, and from one of these the Lord Mayor must be chosen. They have become charitable, rather than political or trading institutions, and they expend their revenues partly in festivities, but principally in pensions to widows and decayed brethren, the support of schools, &c.*

* These incorporated trades must not be confounded with what are commonly

"All such incorporations," says Adam Smith, "were anciently called *Universities*, which indeed is the proper Latin name for any incorporation whatever. The University of Smiths, the University of Tailors, &c., are expressions which we commonly meet with in the old charters of ancient towns. When those particular incorporations which are now peculiarly called *Universities* were first established, the term of years which it was necessary to study, in order to obtain the degree of Master of Arts, appears evidently to have been copied from the term of apprenticeship in common trades, of which the incorporations were much more ancient. As to have wrought seven years under a master properly qualified was necessary in order to entitle any person to become a master, and to have himself apprentices in a common trade, so to have studied seven years under a master properly qualified was necessary to become a Master, Teacher, or Doctor (words anciently synonymous) in the liberal arts, and to have scholars or apprentices (words likewise originally synonymous) to study under him."

The ostensible purpose of the incorporated trades was like that of our modern inspection laws, to insure the good or merchantable quality of the commodities offered for sale; this end it was proposed to effect, by ordaining that the articles should be manufactured only by practised and skilful workmen, who

---

called *corporations*, instituted for manufacturing, banking, turnpike, or railroad purposes, here in America; though the similarity of name and origin has directed much unfounded political odium against the latter. The old guilds of trade were proper *monopolies*, no other persons being permitted to exercise the craft which was their special vocation. But our modern corporations have no exclusive privileges; any individual, or another incorporated company, may begin competition with them in the same town or village. Sometimes, indeed, when the object is one of great public utility, as to open a new avenue of transit and communication, a clause is inserted in the charter, that no rival company shall be permitted to build a similar road or bridge, parallel to theirs, and within a small distance from it, for a given number of years. Some such boon from the legislature may be needed to induce capitalists to run the risk of first constructing such a work for the public benefit and their own possible emolument. But such privileges are now not often granted, and are not always respected, even when the public faith is pledged for them. The charter is usually granted only to enable persons of small property to club their means, and thus to effect by combination what no individual is rich enough to do singly. Hence, as already explained, they are true democratic institutions, on the limited partnership principle, which has very recently been legalized and applied with much success both in England and America.

had served a full apprenticeship to the craft. But as Adam Smith remarks, "the institution of long apprenticeships can give no security that insufficient workmanship shall not frequently be exposed to public sale. When this is done, it is usually the effect of fraud, and not of inability; and the longest apprenticeship can give no security against fraud." The inspection-mark upon a barrel of flour, or salted meat, or pickled fish, or the name of the manufacturer printed upon a bale of cloth, is a much better guaranty of the quality of the article. Besides, long apprenticeships are not needed, as the mystery of any handicraft can be learned in less than a year, so that the operative can work, not as speedily indeed, but as well, that is, he can turn out as perfect an article, as any veteran in the business. At any rate, he will be the quickest to learn, who has the prospect of being fully paid just as soon as he can complete the article in a workmanlike manner, and who is furthermore required to pay for the tools and materials that he spoils. The real purpose of the guild was to maintain a monopoly of the trade, under the cover of which, purchasers were obliged to take what they offered for sale, at such prices as they chose to affix, or do without the commodity altogether. Individual members of the company, it is true, might compete with each other; but their competition was always subject to the by-laws enacted by the council of the guild.

Old expedients come up for renewed trial, after the lapse of centuries, with only a change of name. The modern Trades' Unions, strikes, and associations of operatives, are but the ancient guilds revived, their avowed object being to raise wages and prices by diminishing the number of competitors. Even here in America, where the utmost freedom of competition has been the life of trade, and there are fewer restrictions upon industry, either legal or consuetudinary, than in any country upon earth, at a recent strike of the journeyman printers, the Union required that only a certain number of apprentices should be employed in each office, in proportion to the number of journeymen in it, and that women or girls should not be employed to set types, though it is an occupation in which they are nearly as well fitted to excel as in the use of the needle. Mr. Laing, the distinguished traveller and political economist, seriously argues in favor of such measures, on the ground that "labor itself is a property, entitled to legal protection as much as land, or goods, or any kind of property that labor produces"; and that "the supply of the public with all the articles of handicraft, or labor of skill, [should be] confined to those who had acquired a property in that labor."

Here appears to be a confusion of thought; labor is rightly considered as property, and is most effectually protected as such, when it can be applied to any purpose, or in any occupation, which the laborer prefers. To create any impediment to the transition of labor from one employment to another, is not to protect, but to violate, the essential rights of industry. To give to any individual, or any association, the monopoly of any article or any employment, is to create in the favored class a right of property in other men's labor, — that is, a right to prevent all other persons from selecting their own occupations, and making the best use that they can of their physical and mental powers; it is also to tax the whole community for the benefit of the favored class, by compelling the former to pay such a price for the commodity, or such wages for the labor, as the latter may require. Prices are equitably adjusted, when the seller says to the purchaser, 'Pay me what I ask, or manufacture the article for yourself.' The ancient incorporated companies and the modern Trades' Unions say, 'Pay me what I ask, or do without the article altogether; you shall not have the option of manufacturing the article for yourself.' How does Mr. Laing suppose, that the operatives in any craft, whether they have served a long apprenticeship to it or not, can have "acquired a property in that labor"? Unquestionably they are entitled to prosecute it themselves; but they have no right, either natural or acquired, to keep other persons out of the same employment.

Adam Smith takes a more correct view of the subject when he says: "The property which every man has in his own labor, as it is the original foundation of all other property, so it is the most sacred and inviolable. The patrimony of a poor man lies in the strength and dexterity of his hands; and to hinder him from employing this strength and dexterity in what manner he thinks proper, without injury to his neighbor, is a plain violation of this most sacred property. It is a manifest encroachment upon the just liberty both of the workman and of those who might be disposed to employ him. As it hinders the one from working at what he thinks proper, so it hinders the others from employing whom they think proper. To judge whether he is fit to be employed, may surely be trusted to the discretion of the employers whose interest it so much concerns."

These principles, however, are not of universal application; an exception should be made in the case of the restraints that are imposed by the laws of most countries upon admission into the learned professions. Usually, the purchaser is the best judge of the quality of the goods that he buys, and the character of the person that he deals with; a regard for his own interest will protect him against fraud more effectually than any regulations which the government can devise. But it is not so, when he buys the services of a physician. Health or sickness, life or death, then depends upon the competent information and skill of the person employed by him; and of these qualities he is a very poor judge, as sickness may have been a rare occurrence in his family, as the consequences of an error may be fatal, and as the event indicates but very imperfectly the beneficial or injurious consequences of the medical treatment pursued. A plausible charlatan may easily impose upon the credulity of the public, and many valuable lives may be lost before his ignorance and presumption can be fully exposed. Most governments attempt to protect the community against such injury, by multiplying restrictions upon irregular practitioners, and extending the full privileges of the profession only to those who have completed a prescribed course of education, and have obtained a diploma, or certificate of competency, from a board of duly qualified examiners. A similar policy is usually pursued with respect to lawyers and clergymen, though the reasons in its favor are not so conclusive as in the case of physicians. Ignorance and deception at the bar or in the pulpit are more easily detected than in the sick-room.

I have already intimated that competition for employment is sometimes restricted, not only by law, but by the customs of the country, or by the habits and feelings of the people. In the United States, mobility of fortune, station, and employment is the most striking feature of society; no impediment is created by law or fashion to the most frequent and sudden changes of position and business. Thus an equalizing process is constantly going on with respect both to wages and profits; no one profession or employment can enjoy even a momentary advantage, without sharing it among a crowd of competitors. In England, it is far otherwise; a well-established and clearly defined gradation of ranks has existed so long, and has so moulded the habits and expectations of the people, that comparatively few think of stepping out of the station or the business to which they were born. The larger emoluments and superior advantages of a different position hardly attract their notice, and certainly excite no emulation or regret.

Mr. J. S. Mill has given a lively picture of this condition of things, and its consequences. "So complete," he says, "has hitherto been the separation, so strongly marked the line of demarcation, between the different grades of laborers, as to be almost equivalent to a hereditary distinction of caste; each employment being chiefly recruited from the children of those already employed in it, or in employments of the same rank with it in social estimation, or from the children of persons who, if originally of a lower rank, have succeeded in raising themselves by their exertions. The liberal professions are mostly supplied by the sons of either the professional or the idle classes; the more highly skilled manual employments are filled up from the sons of skilled artisans, or of the class of tradesmen who rank with them; the lower classes of skilled employments are in a similar case; and unskilled laborers, with occasional exceptions, remain from father to son in their pristine condition. Consequently, the wages of each class have hitherto been regulated by the increase of its own population, rather than of the general population of the country. If the professions are overstocked, it is because the class of society from which they have always mainly been supplied has greatly increased in number, and because most of that class have numerous families, and bring up some, at least, of their sons to professions." It would be more correct to say, that the learned professions are overstocked because they are recruited from every rank in society above that of the artisans; the sons of merchants being ambitious of admission to them, and the younger sons of the landed gentry and the nobility, as well as of professional men themselves, finding in them, and in the service of government, the only means which the right of primogeniture has left them of obtaining a livelihood without forfeiting the social position to which they were born. It is the fixity of the other ranks in the kingdom, and the institutions which are designed to maintain that fixity, which indirectly operate to swell the number of applicants for admission to the learned professions and to offices under government. "If the wages of artisans," continues Mr. Mill, "remain so much higher than those of common laborers, it is because artisans are a more prudent class, and do not marry so early or so inconsiderately."

In England, and, to a small extent, in some of the States of this country, an obstacle to the free circulation of labor is created by the poor laws. A town or parish is bound to support those paupers only who were born in it, or who, in various ways specified by the laws, have obtained a "settlement" within its limits. Sometimes, forty days' undisturbed residence were made sufficient for obtaining a settlement; more stringent regulations required that the person should have been assessed to parish rates and paid them, or should have served an apprenticeship there, or have been hired into service there and remained in such service for a full year. Those who have not complied with these requisites may be warned off, or sent home to the parish where they belong. Through such regulations, it is evident that there may be a superfluity of labor in one place, and considerable deficiency of it in another, and that industry may be very unequally compensated in different districts. Frequent litigation arises under the law of settlement, as the facts in each case are often imperfectly known or difficult to be proved; and cases of extreme hardship sometimes happen, as when a family reduced by poverty and sickness are forcibly removed to a distance from the place which they have chosen for their home, or are sent travelling over the whole country in search of the parish to which they rightfully belong. But as I have already intimated, the evil is not one of much moment here in America, where the wages of labor are high, and where there is but little pauperism among the native born, and that little can be supported at insignificant expense. No great pains, therefore, are taken to prevent a person from obtaining a settlement wherever he likes.

But the great influx of foreign immigrants, many of whom are extremely poor, while some were paupers at home, and have been sent over to this country by the parish authorities only to get rid of the expense of their maintenance, makes this subject one of considerable importance for the States on the Atlantic coast. The charge of foreign paupers is assumed by the individual States, as the matter does not come within the province of our restricted national government, and as no one town or district, more than another, is fairly chargeable with the support of this class of the poor. To require the ship-master who brings them over to give bonds that they shall not become chargeable as paupers, or to levy a duty on all immigrants, so as to form a fund for the support of the poor among them, are measures which, though generally adopted, are of doubtful expediency and legality. Payment of the bonds is easily evaded when any length of time has intervened, or when the foreign poor have wandered into the inland States; and the fund collected in Massachusetts or New York, under a doubtful authority, as it belongs to Congress alone to regulate foreign commerce, cannot be made available for the expenses of pauperism in Connecticut or Pennsylvania. As the evil becomes greater with the now constantly increasing flood of immigration, some comprehensive measure will probably be devised to meet it, which will require the joint action of Congress and the State legislatures.

Mr. Senior justly remarks, that "the difficulty with which labor is transferred from one occupation to another is the principal evil of a high state of civilization. It exists in proportion to the division of labor. In a savage state, almost every man is equally fit to exercise, and in fact does exercise, almost every employment. But in the progress of improvement, two circumstances combine to render narrower and narrower the field within which a given individual can be profitably employed. In the first place, the operations in which he is engaged become fewer and fewer; in a large manufactory, the man who is engaged in one of these operations has little experience in any of the others. And in the second place, the skill which the division of labor gives to each distinct class of artificers generally prevents whatever peculiar dexterity an individual may have from being of any value in a business to which he has not been brought up. A workman whose specific labor has ceased to be in demand, finds every other long-established employment filled by persons whose time has been devoted to it from the age at which their organs were still pliable and their attention fresh."

This subject is excellently illustrated by Mr. Laing, with reference to the qualifications of emigrants to perform the novel tasks imposed upon them by their change of residence. "Two hundred years ago," he says, "when the peopling of the old American colonies was going on, the great mass of the population of the mother country was essentially agricultural; but every working man could turn his hand to various kinds of work, as well as to the plough. He was partly a smith, carpenter, wheelwright, stone-mason, shoemaker. The useful arts were not, as now, entirely in the hands of artisans bred to no other labor but their own trade or art; very expert, skilful, and cheap producers in that, but not used to, or acquainted with, any other kind of work. This inferior stage of civilization, in which men were not coöperative to the same extent as now, but every man did a little at everything, and made a shift with his own unaided workmanship and production, was a condition of society very favorable to emigration-enterprise and to colonization. It continues still in the United States, and is the main reason why their settlers in the backwoods are more handy, shift better for themselves, and thrive better, than the man from this country, who has been all his life engaged in one branch of industry, and in that has had the coöperation of many trades preparing his tools and the materials for his work.

"Another advantage for emigration in that state of society which we in Great Britain have entirely outgrown, was, that the female half of the population contributed almost as much as the male half to the subsistence of a family, especially an emigrant family. . . . . . In the days of King James, and of Charles I. and Charles II., and down even to the end of the last century, the emigrant could reckon upon the household work of the females of his family as more or less profitable, and at least saving, by the production of all clothing material. In genteel families at home, all the family linen and cloth for common wear, and often some for sale in the country towns, was produced by household work. The progress of society to a higher state of material refinement has entirely superseded such family production. Coöperative labor in factories supplies the public with much better and finer goods; and the public taste is so much refined by the continual enjoyment of finer articles, that the old mode and quality of production would not satisfy it now; but that former state was more favorable to emigration than our present more advanced social condition. There seems to be a stage in the progress of nations at which they can throw off swarms with most success. A nation, like an individual, may become too refined for colonizing; its social state too coöperative; men too dependent on other men for the gratification of acquired tastes and habits, which have become part of their nature, and interwoven with the daily life even of the poorer classes." *

The case of household or home manufactures, here alluded to by Mr. Laing, is an interesting one, as it shows that, under certain circumstances, persons may be willing to work, and may find it profitable to work, for much less than the ordinary compensation of labor in their neighborhood. An agricultural family has considerable leisure time in the course of the year, the winter being a period of almost entire suspension of their customary tasks. This leisure they may profitably devote to any species of manufacture which can be pursued at home, at intervals, and without the aid of costly tools; for however poorly such labor may be compensated, its proceeds are all clear gain. The time would be entirely lost, if it were not thus employed. Thus, spinning and knitting may continue to be carried on by hand in many an humble family, long after the most perfect machinery for performing these processes has been invented, and the prices of the articles spun or knit have consequently been reduced to a very low rate. The family would not be enabled to subsist by devoting themselves entirely to these employments; but their subsistence being already secured by agriculture or some other adequately compensated labor, their leisure may be economized by such supplementary tasks, and a small addition be thus obtained to their slender income. The Swiss, a frugal and industrious

* Laing's *Observations on Europe in* 1848 *and* 1849, pp. 69, 70.

people, are noted for having carried these home manufactures to a great extent, and for maintaining them against the formidable competition of British fuel, capital, and machinery.

A similar case is presented in the wages of female labor, which are usually much lower than those of males. The reason is, that comparatively few women are solely dependent upon what they can earn for themselves; most of them have a husband, father, or brother by whom they are supported. Being fed from other sources, they can afford to perform at a very low price the few tasks that are deemed appropriate for their sex. So many of them are willing to work upon these terms, in order to obtain, not a livelihood, but the means of copying a new fashion, or of purchasing a coveted article of furniture or a bit of finery, that wages in their whole department of industry are permanently depreciated; and the few women who are unfortunate enough to be thrown wholly upon the fruits of their own industry for subsistence, are reduced to great straits. Thus, sewing is a peculiarly feminine occupation, and is therefore more inadequately paid than any other species of manual labor. Hood attracted the attention and sympathy of all England for the hard fate of the needlewomen of London; and novelists have woven many pathetic fictions out of the sorrows of governesses. The menial services of females are better paid, in America at least, than any other species of woman's industry; a good cook sometimes earns more than an accomplished teacher, and certainly finds it easier to obtain employment. The meanness, or, as most women consider it, the degrading character, of the employment, must be compensated by high wages.

CHAPTER XVI.

THE CIRCUMSTANCES WHICH DETERMINE THE RATE OF PROFITS.

CAPITAL being amassed, as we have seen, by frugality or abstinence, Profits are the reward of *abstinence*, just as Wages are the remuneration of *labor* and Rent is the compensation for the use of *land*. Labor, capital, and land are the three instruments of production; and therefore the exchangeable value of everything produced is resolvable into three component parts,— Wages, Profits, and Rent. To adopt Adam Smith's language, "In *every* society, the price of every commodity finally resolves itself into some one or other, or all, of these three parts; and in every *improved* society, *all the three* enter, more or less, as component parts, into the price of the far greater part of commodities." In the origin of society, fertile land being abundant or equally distributed, so that there is no monopoly, Rent does not exist, and the whole value of the thing is resolvable into Profits and Wages. A still earlier state of things is conceivable, though very seldom exemplified, where, no capital being as yet amassed, labor is the sole producing agent, so that the whole value consists of Wages, or, in other words, the whole produce of labor belongs to the laborer. When children pick berries in a bushy pasture, or men gather clams on the sea-shore, provided they use no implements but their hands, the whole value of what they collect is their own gain, or consists exclusively of Wages; if they use a few tools, such as baskets and spades, a very small portion of that value must be accounted Profits.

But under ordinary circumstances, or in every stage of society above the lowest degree of barbarism, all three of these elements concur to make up the value of every article produced. "In the price of corn, for example," says Adam Smith, "one part pays the rent of the landlord, another pays the wages or maintenance of the laborers employed in producing it, and the third pays the profit of the farmer. These three parts seem, either immediately or ultimately, to make up the whole price of corn. A fourth part, it may perhaps be thought, is necessary for replacing the stock of the farmer, or for compensating the wear and tear of his laboring cattle and other instruments of husbandry. But it must be considered that the price of any instrument of husbandry, such as a laboring horse, is itself made up of the same three parts, — the Rent of the land upon which he is reared, the Labor of tending and rearing him, and the Profits of the farmer who advances both the Rent of this land and the Wages of this labor.

"As any particular commodity comes to be more manufactured, that part of the price which resolves itself into Wages and Profits comes to be greater in proportion to that which resolves itself into Rent. In the progress of the manufacture, not only the number of Profits increase, but every subsequent Profit is greater than the foregoing; because the capital from which it is derived must always be greater. The capital which employs the weavers, for example, must be greater than that which employs the spinners, because it not only replaces that capital with its Profits, but pays, besides, the Wages of the weavers; and the Profits must always bear some proportion to the capital."

Still it is true, in the last analysis, as already stated, that the creation of all value can be traced to labor alone. Capital itself is created by labor, and may be called consolidated or invested labor. It consists of the economized or reserved fruits of *previous* labor, so that Profits are only the compensation of *former* industry, just as Wages are the compensation of *present* industry. What is usually called Rent, also, is, in great part, only the compensation of the labor and capital that have previously been expended upon the land, and so closely incorporated with it that the original and the acquired properties of the soil can no longer be distinguished from each other. The greater part of what is popularly termed Rent, then, is nothing but Profit, or, in other words, the Wages of past industry. As to Rent *properly so called*, or the compensation for the original and inherent properties of the soil, it is not, strictly speaking, the reward of an agent that has concurred in the production, but is only a share, appropriated on the *monopoly* principle, of the previously created value. These original properties of the soil are the free gift of Nature; like the air and the light, they cost nothing to anybody. But as they are not inexhaustible in amount, — at least in localities where they are most needed, — they are appropriated by individuals, and through the monopoly thus created, a tax is levied upon the producers of value. Thus, a portion of the value of every article of wealth is appropriated to paying Rent properly so called; but this portion is not the reward of any personal agency that has concurred in the production of wealth.

But when Profit is spoken of as the third component part of value, there is an ambiguity in the meaning of the word which deserves attention, as it is the source of several of Mr. Ricardo's paradoxes. In the ultimate distribution of the price or value, the whole share which falls to the capitalist is called Profit by Ricardo; but this includes the replacement of the capital which he originally vested in the undertaking, as well as that enlargement of this capital in the process of production which alone is usually denominated Profit. What this economist calls Wages, also, is only the share or proportion of the finished product which is received by the laborer; as what he terms Profit is the share or proportion of the same product which accrues to the capitalist. Thus, Rent being a fixed sum, to be first deducted from the total value, without any reference to the comparative amount of Wages and Profits, what remains after this deduction is to be divided between the laborer and the capitalist. Hence Mr. Ricardo was led to affirm, that "nothing can affect profits but a rise of wages"; that "whatever raises the wages of labor lowers the profit of stock"; and that, "as the wages of labor fall, the profits of stock rise." Summing up the whole doctrine in one theorem, he maintains that high wages and high profits are incompatible, since whatever is added to the one must be taken from the other. Having sliced off (say) one third of the apple for Rent, he proposes to divide the remainder into two parts, giving the name of Wages to the one, and of Profits to the other; and *if his nomenclature is correct*, the truth of his doctrine is self-evident. When a given quantity is to be divided into only two parts, it is manifest that either one of these parts can be enlarged only at the expense of the other; they must vary in the inverse ratio of each other.

But few words are needed to expose this paradox. When

words are taken in their ordinary acceptation, it is certain that high wages and high profits often go together, and tend to produce each other. The rates of both are considerably higher in the United States than in Great Britain; both are much higher in California than in New York. When a capitalist is making large profits, he is eager to extent his business, to employ more hands, and consequently he offers higher wages. A fall in wages is symptomatic of a decline in business, and a general depreciation of profits.

But it should be distinctly understood, that we here mean by wages, not the *proportion* of the finished product that falls to the laborer, but the *amount*, the quantity and quality, of the commodities which he can purchase with the results of his day's labor. If a journeyman carpenter is able to buy one fourth of a barrel of flour with his day's wages, while a seamstress can obtain only one tenth of a barrel with hers, then the wages of the former are two and a half times greater than those of the latter; and this would be true, though the carpenter received only 80 per cent of what his day's work sold for, while the seamstress was paid 90 per cent of the value of hers. In like manner, "profits are not measured by the proportion which they bear to the rate of wages, but by the proportion which they bear to the capital by the agency of which they have been produced." If a farmer, to borrow Mr. McCulloch's illustration, employs a capital amounting to 1,000 bushels of grain, paying 700 of it for wages, and 300 for seed and other expenses, then, if the return at the end of the season be 1,200 bushels, his profit is 200 bushels, and his rate of profit is 20 per cent. Mr. Ricardo would say, that the total product, 1,200 bushels, is divided into profits and wages in the proportion of 5 to 7, inasmuch as the laborers received seven twelfths of it, and the capitalist only five twelfths; — a doctrine which is correct as he understands it, but which is calculated only to mislead, if words are taken in their ordinary meaning.

Several things are usually confounded under the name of Profit, which must be clearly distinguished from each other before we can gain a clear view of the circumstances on which the rate of Profit, at any given time and place, depends. The general principle is, that Profits *tend* to an equality in all employments and in all localities. I do not say that they *are* equal, or that they must *become* equal; but an equalizing process is constantly going on; for if the gains in one department of enterprise are notoriously above the average,—if it is even suspected by a multitude of sharp-sighted observers, who are on the lookout for such opportunities, that they exceed the average,—more capital is at once attracted into the employment, till, by the competition of the capitalists with each other, the rate of Profit is reduced to the common standard in other enterprises.

But though Profits *tend* to an equality in different employments, it is equally certain that there is a great seeming inequality in them, most of which can be readily explained by a reference to the several really distinct elements which are usually confounded under the general name of Profits. Thus, among those who superintend the application of capital,—*entrepreneurs* the French call them, *managers* is the nearest English appellation, for they are not always the owners of the capital which they manage,—there is every degree of skill, enterprise, and intelligence; the gains vary, of course, in proportion as these faculties are exercised. The prudent and sagacious merchant makes a fortune out of the very business from which a dozen of his competitors may retire as bankrupts. Only those who are successful continue in the business for a long time; and the average of the gains of such persons is found greatly to exceed the ordinary rate of Profits. Obviously, however, their gains are not all to be reckoned as Profits, strictly so called; a large portion of them are to be considered rather as the Wages of labor, or as the salary paid to an unusually skilful person for managing the concern. This portion—*the wages of management*—being deducted from their total gains, it is only the remainder which can properly be regarded as Profit, and its rate compared with the rate of Profits in other employments, with which it will be found to agree. These wages for skilful management often rise to a very high point; some of the manufacturing corporations in Massachusetts have found it for their advantage to pay to their general agent or manager a higher salary than the government of the United States paid to its Minister to Great Britain, or than it now pays to the Chief Justice of our Supreme Court. If this person, instead of acting as an agent for others, should enter into business on his own account, and trade with his own capital, we ought to subtract $10,000 a year from his annual gains, before those gains are considered as any indication of the general rate of profit in his business.

Again, *the risk* incurred varies much in different employments. If, in a particular business, three ventures out of four fail altogether, or result in a loss, the gains of the fourth venture, on an average, must be high enough to compensate for all these losses, and to afford at least the ordinary rate of profit for the capital required during all the time which is consumed by all four ventures. The gains of the slave-trade between the coast of Africa and Brazil are so great, that if three ships out of four are captured and condemned, with all their slaves on board, the profit on the return cargo of the fourth ship is large enough to make the business a lucrative one to the merchant. The true rate of profit, then, must be calculated only after a large deduction is made from the total gains as an *insurance* against total loss.

But here another element comes in to modify our calculations, — an element already once mentioned as "the lottery principle in human nature." So much does the prospect of splendid gains outweigh, in the estimation of sanguine and adventurous persons, the chances of loss, that an undue proportion of capital is attracted into some very uncertain employments, and the rate of profit in them is consequently reduced to a very low point, — often, indeed, to nothing or less than nothing. There is no doubt that the average gains in a trade in which large fortunes may be made, — in our own flour-trade, for instance, or in California mining, — "are lower than those in which gains are slow, though comparatively sure, and in which nothing is to be ultimately hoped for beyond a competency. In such points as this, much depends on the characters of nations, according as they partake more or less of the adventurous, or, as it is called when the intention is to blame it, the gambling spirit. This spirit is much stronger in the United States than in Great Britain; and in Great Britain than in any country on the Continent of Europe. In some Continental countries, the tendency is so much the reverse, that safe and quiet employments probably yield a less average profit to the capital engaged in them than those which, at the price of greater hazards, offer greater gains." *

The moral character of individuals — or, at any rate, the estimation in which they are held in the community — is affected by the comparative prevalency of the gambling spirit. Here, the standard phrase for a "failure," or an act of bankruptcy, is "misfortune in business"; — that is, *fortune* only is blamed, the *individual* is pitied, and the sympathy of his companions and former rivals helps him to try again. The reason why the act is so leniently viewed is, that it is so frequent; no one can conscientiously blame his neighbor for what is so likely to happen to himself, — for what, perchance, has happened to himself more than once. I have heard it estimated on good authority, that in Boston, where the estimate of commercial honor is certainly as high as in any city of the United States, at least two thirds of the young men who commence business on their own account *fail* in the course of the first five years. No one reproaches them for this fact; for not a few even of the wealthy men of the city remember their own two or three unsuccessful trials before they finally acquired a fortune. Still, in estimating the profits of trade as compared with those of agriculture, the professions, and the mechanic arts, the number and amount of such failures must be taken into view, or our calculations will be very wide of the truth. The prevalence of this speculating or gambling spirit is undoubtedly one of the reasons why the rate of interest in this country continues so high; lenders are affected with it as well as borrowers, and will incur great hazards when tempted by usurious rates.

In England, bankruptcy is a more serious matter. The bankrupt not only loses credit; he also, to a great extent, loses caste. He is a dishonored man, whose sense of personal degradation is not infrequently so keen as to drive him to suicide. Sidney Smith wittily remarks, that an Englishman's idea of Paradise is a place where people always pay their debts. Hence the opprobrium incurred by our repudiating States was so much greater in England than in this country, and was expressed with so much bitterness as absolutely to goad and sting the defaulters into a sense of the heinousness of their act,

---

* J. S. Mill's *Political Economy*, Vol. I. p. 489.

and an attempt to retrieve their reputation. There was a time when a Mississippian or a Pennsylvanian in London ran great risk of being treated as roughly as General Haynau was in Barclay's brewery. And yet, serious and wholly indefensible as was the breach of faith on the part of the defaulting States, the complaints of the English bond-holders were exaggerated and unreasonable. They knowingly incurred a greater risk, for the sake of obtaining a higher interest; they deliberately preferred investment at considerable hazard in American funds at six per cent, to a perfectly safe investment in English government funds at three per cent, and therefore had comparatively little ground for complaint when a certain portion of their hazardous investment turned out unfavorably. Most of the American States redeemed all their obligations without delay; some others were unable for a time to pay the interest, but ultimately redeemed their credit by paying off the arrears; two or three others were hopelessly bankrupt. Considered as one transaction, and on purely commercial principles, the total investment of English funds in American stocks was a successful enterprise; the bond-holders obtained more than they would have received from an equivalent investment in the English national debt.

In France, the lot of the bankrupt is still more severe; he not only loses his social position, but the law prevents him from engaging in any other business on his own account till he has redeemed his outstanding obligations.

I have dwelt at length upon these circumstances affecting the rate of profits, because they illustrate the principle already stated, that the theory of Political Economy is but an exposition of human nature as it appears when engaged in the pursuit of wealth. The rate of profits varies according to the opinions, and habits of mind and action, of those who apply capital to productive uses. The money-getting propensity is but one tendency or phasis of human nature, and it is constantly modified and controlled by the other passions and habits of men, with which it is blended, and among which it is by no means the strongest.

Another illustration of this general principle is found in a circumstance just alluded to, — the extraordinary fluctuations of the grain and flour market in this country, — fluctuations which are so great and frequent as to put all calculation at defiance, and to make the gains of the dealers nearly as uncertain as the chance of drawing a prize in a lottery. As the results of successful speculation in this branch are very brilliant, and as bankruptcy is no disgrace, the business is probably more overdone — that is, the *average* rate of profit is lower — than in any other enterprise whatsoever. Flour may be five dollars a barrel in New York at the beginning of the season, may rise to twelve dollars in the course of the summer, and fall even below its starting-point when the next crop comes in. The effect of such changes as these on the business of a dealer who has a stock of a quarter of a million of barrels at a time may be easily seen. He may literally gain or lose one or two millions of dollars in one season. How are such fluctuations possible? At the first sight, it would appear that the price of bread-stuffs would be the most stable of all prices. The quantity needed, the number of mouths to be satisfied with food, varies by a fixed and well-known law of increase from year to year. The average crop over a country so extensive as this varies but little; a bad harvest in one State is compensated by an unusually good one in another. And should there be any marked deficiency or excess, foreign commerce stands ready, as usual, to equalize the market by distributing the aggregate product uniformly where it is most needed.

But the vast quantity of the article which is produced and consumed every year, and the fact that it is also an article of prime necessity for all classes of people, introduce a new element into the calculation. The hopes and fears of men are strongly excited in relation to a product on which not merely comfort, but life, depends, and the use of which is absolutely universal. Its price rises and falls, not merely in proportion to the deficiency or excess of the crop, but to the alarm and the spirit of speculation which are excited by that deficiency or excess. A failure of one sixth of the crop, instead of raising the value in the market only in that proportion, will often double the price; a surplus of not more than an eighth of the average annual harvest may sink the price below the actual cost of production. A mere rumor of an apprehended partial failure of the crop in England has power to raise the price of grain and flour from five to twenty per cent on the banks of the Ohio. Here, obviously, a correct statement of a law of Political Economy is a general fact in the science of human nature, a law of which we must take cognizance in the philosophy of the human mind. The sensitiveness and excitability of the American character give peculiar prominence to the operation of such laws within our nearest range of observation.

What Mr. Mill calls "the perpetual overflow of capital into colonies or foreign countries, to seek higher profits than can be obtained at home," is certainly a powerful agent in equalizing the rates of profit in different lands. But that it is not so efficient for this purpose as we might be tempted at first thought to imagine, appears from the notorious fact, that the rate of interest for money is twice as high here as in Great Britain. This difference of rate would be greater than it is, if British capital were not occasionally sent hither in large amounts. But why is not the migration sufficient to equalize the rates at once, since every man would prefer to receive six, rather than three, per cent for his money? Several answers may be given to this question. In the first place, the capitalist is not often willing to emigrate along with his capital. He is bound to his native soil by many ties of feeling and interest, which he cannot easily sever, and which, being at any rate in easy circumstances, he is under no strong temptation to break. He must be separated from his property, then, and the distance of the place of investment, other things being equal, enhances the risk; no one likes to trust his capital in operations that he cannot oversee, to individuals of whom he knows but little, or to places where it will be controlled by laws and institutions differing from those with which he is familiar. War may possibly break out between the two countries, or their peaceful relations be so far disturbed, that the profits cannot be remitted with regularity, or perhaps the principal itself may be lost. Lastly, the sentiment from which no man is entirely free, — a sentiment which may be dignified by the name of patriotism, or branded as national prejudice, — prevents the credit of foreigners from being fairly estimated. Public affairs may be more widely and accurately known than private enterprises; foreigners, therefore, usually prefer government stocks to other means of investment. Next to these, chartered companies, whose transactions are large and of a public character, enjoy a preference.

But on the whole, capital is every day assuming more of a cosmopolitan character, and the time when the rates of interest will become nearly equal in all commercial countries cannot be far distant. "The inequality in the rate of profit throughout the civilized world," says Mr. Senior, "is much less than the inequality of wages. And as the general progress of improvement tends more and more to equalize the advantages possessed by different countries in government and habits, and even in salubrity of climate, the existing inequalities of profits are likely to diminish."

Deducting compensation for risk and the wages of management, Mr. J. S. Mill considers that the rate of profits strictly so called "is measured by the current rate of interest on the best security; such security as precludes any appreciable chance of losing the principal." If he means that the current rate of profits in the narrowest sense of that term is *identical* with the current rate of interest, the proposition may be doubted. He who superintends the employment of his own capital expects to gain much more than the rate of interest; and the whole of this excess can hardly be attributed to the two elements that have been mentioned. The hazard, in the estimation of the capitalist, cannot be great, or he would not encounter it, as he has a choice among different modes of employing capital; or if there be an extra risk, it is balanced by the chance of an extra profit. And though the wages of management, as we have seen, may sometimes be very high, it should be remembered, that, if great skill, enterprise, and sagacity are needed for the successful use of capital, a command of capital is equally necessary to give full scope to these high qualities of character and intellect; and the joint effect is properly divisible between the two factors. Still, as the rate of profit unquestionably varies *proportionally* with the current rate of interest, though exceeding it by an indefinable amount, we may take the latter as a measure and type of the former, and investigate the causes which affect equally the rates of both.

In English systems of Political Economy, the theory of the circumstances which determine the average rate of profit, as well as the doctrine respecting the average rate of Wages, is a deduction from the theories of Malthus and Ricardo respecting population and rent. Indeed, ever since Ricardo's time, it has been the ambition of English writers upon the subject to erect Political Economy into the rank of a deductive science; — to begin with a few postulates or universally recognized facts; to trace these to their consequences, under the law of competition, by a course of abstract reasoning; and to make the results thus obtained square with observed facts by the method of exhaustions, eliminating, evading, or explaining away all the phenomena that do not coincide with the theory. This method has elevated some startling paradoxes into the dignity of first principles of the science; he who does not possess the key to them, or is incapable of explaining them in what is claimed to be the true scientific method, that is, by reference to the very few and simple facts which alone are admitted to be the proper data of the science, is held to be unworthy of mingling in the discussion. He is ruled out of court, on the ground of ignorance. Hence an offensive tone of assumption and dogmatism has crept into the writings of the expounders of the system, and the breach between scientific economists and practical business men is unnecessarily and injuriously widened.

Some of these paradoxes we have already reviewed, and traced them to their origin in the arbitrary assumptions, or arbitrarily limited definitions, which have been made the basis of the science. Thus, it is assumed that the growth of the population everywhere tends to outrun the increase of the means of subsistence; and the inference is, that the natural or necessary standard of wages is the smallest sum that will furnish the laborer with what his class in society regard as the necessaries of life. It is assumed that the most fertile soils are always the first to be cultivated, and that the population, as it increases, remains on the same spot; and the inferences are, that additional food is always obtained at a disadvantage, that additional capital can never be applied to the land but with constantly diminishing returns; and hence, that the increase of the population anywhere, and under all circumstances, is a great evil; — a paradox of the most startling kind, inasmuch as the common sense of mankind has everywhere taken it for granted, that the rapid growth of the population is one of the most unfailing indications of great prosperity. Profits are arbitrarily defined to be, what remains to the capitalist from a division of the whole value created between him and the laborer, rent having been previously deducted; and the inference is, that profits and wages vary in inverse proportion, or that high wages and high profits are incompatible; whereas it is a matter of the commonest observation, that they vary in direct proportion, high wages being incompatible with low profits. It is assumed that individuals are always the best judges of their own interests, that nations are composed only of individuals, and that individual and national interests are identical; and it is inferred, that, as it would be unwise to place restrictions upon trade between individuals, so it would be impolitic to put any fetters upon international commerce; but that a little kingdom like Denmark should be exposed, in every branch of her industry, to the overpowering competition of the immense capital and other resources of a great nation like England. Yet it is certain, as Mr. Rea remarks, that individual and national interests are not always identical, because individuals often grow rich by the *acquisition* of wealth previously existing, but nations by the *creation* of wealth that did not before exist; and we have already seen, (pp. 36 – 38,) that private persons may be impoverished by the conversion of artificial into natural wealth, though nations are always benefited by this process. For the case of Denmark, I borrow the language of Mr. Laing, an English Political Economist who has partly shaken off the trammels of this system, and prefers to reason from facts rather than assumptions.

"Denmark has no metals or minerals, no fire power, no water power, no products or capabilities for becoming a manufacturing country supplying foreign consumers. She has no harbors on the North Sea. Her navigation is naturally confined to the Baltic. Her commerce is naturally confined to the home consumpt of the necessaries and luxuries of civilized life, which the export of her corn and other agricultural products enables her to import and consume. She stands alone in her corner of the world, exchanging her loaf of bread, which she can spare, for articles she cannot provide for herself, but still providing for herself everything she can by her own industry. This is no unhappy condition either for an individual or a nation. This home industry of hers is protected by heavy import duties on all foreign articles which could compete with her own manufactures, and these are avowedly imposed, not for revenue, for which a lower duty would be more productive, but for protection. The object of this policy of the Danish government is simply to secure a living and occupation to that portion of the population which is not engaged in husbandry, and which, without protective duties on all that interferes with their branches of industry, would become a burden on the rest of the community, owing to the natural want of products or capabilities in the country of giving employment in manufactures, commerce, or in any branch of industry but agriculture, and the few arts and trades connected with it. This protective system in any country, and under any circumstances, would have been scoffed at a few years ago by our English Political Economists, as contrary to all sound principle; but it wears a less foolish aspect if we examine it closely, and with reference to the physical circumstances which impose it upon some countries, such as Denmark, and to the social or conventional circumstances which dispose the classes the most distant and most opposed to each other in general, to clamor for it in our own. The Danish government appears to have adopted, and always acted upon, that policy which the physical circumstances of the country — namely, the natural want of all products or means by which a surplus population could be employed in manufactures or commerce — have imposed upon it; and to have protected, as a species of property, the skill and labor of her working operative classes by heavy import duties on all articles that interfered with their industry; and to have protected them, also, against themselves, that is, against an accumulation of more labor and skill in any trade than the locality required and could subsist; and to have protected the landed interest and their laborers by a free export of their products."

But I return from this digression to a consideration of the circumstances that determine the average rate of profits. The phenomenon to be explained by any theory that may be broached upon this subject, is the gradual but sure declension of the rate of profit in all countries, as their population and wealth are augmented. The growth of national opulence resembles that of the human body. It is most rapid in infancy, the body usually doubling in weight during the first year of its existence, a rate of increase which it never afterwards equals. In early childhood, the growth is still quick, though not so rapid as at first; and it steadily declines, as the child approaches maturity, till at last it reaches its stationary point in full manhood, when, though all the corporeal powers and functions are in full vigor and activity, the body no longer increases either in stature or weight, except as a consequence of disease or other extraordinary circumstances. Adam Smith long ago remarked, that in a new colony, which is "more understocked in proportion to its territory, and more underpeopled in proportion to the extent of its stock, than the greater part of other countries," profits are very large, and the rate of interest is consequently high. "As the colony increases, the profits of stock gradually diminish"; and "in a country fully stocked in proportion to all the business it had to transact, the competition would everywhere be as great, and consequently the ordinary profit as low, as possible."

Thus, in California, soon after its cession to the United States and the discovery of its gold-washings, profits rose with unexampled rapidity, and the current rate of interest was from thirty-six to forty-eight per cent a year. These extravagant rates, however, soon began to decline, and they are now not more than twice as high as in New York. Similar changes have taken place in Australia, since the discovery of gold in its southern region. I have already observed, that the rate of interest in England, which was over ten per cent in the early part of the sixteenth century, slowly but steadily declined, till it reached its present ordinary rate of three per cent. I have also cited the case of Holland, which seems to have attained the stationary state over a century and a half ago. The rate of interest there, on government security, had then fallen to two per cent, the lowest point to be generally established through a whole country that is known in the history of commerce. For fifty years before this stage was attained, — that is, during the latter half of the seventeenth century, — the Dutch were the most active commercial and manufacturing power in the world. Their colonies were scattered over both hemispheres, and their sails whitened every sea. They had almost exclusive control of the carrying-trade, and the Navigation Laws of the English were enacted for the avowed purpose of wresting a portion of this traffic from them. They alone, for a long period, contended with England for the mastery of the seas; and during a portion of this time victory inclined to their flag. Then were executed those gigantic works of internal improvement which rescued Holland permanently from the ocean, converted her marshes into gardens, and made her canals the highways of the commerce of Europe. Having touched the zenith of their fortunes, the Dutch did not begin to decline, but simply remained stationary, while other nations, England especially, have in their turn risen to be masters of the commercial world.

And the same cause which checked the progress of Holland, which opposes a necessary limit to the growth of national opulence, threatens even now to stay the course of English prosperity. There are the same symptoms of a relaxation of the energies of the system, as the organs become distended with over-abundant wealth. The rate of interest is with difficulty maintained at a point above that where it rested in Holland a hundred and fifty years ago; the Bank of England is now often driven to discount private paper at only two and a half per cent. But for the overflow of English capital into colonies and foreign countries, and for a commercial crisis, which often sweeps away a great amount of capital to the manifest advantage of what is left, just as a gush of blood from the nose sometimes relieves a patient who is in danger of apoplexy, the tide would have turned in Great Britain some time since, leaving the people not exhausted, but satiated. During the last thirty years, the English have thrown away capital enough upon South American and Mexican mines, Spanish and Greek funds, and railroads, to serve as a good basis for the opulence of another country of equal population. Through the stubborn perseverance of the national character, the productive energies of the people seem to have outlived the motives which called them into being, and for a long time sustained them in action.

This constant downward tendency of the rate of profit is a phenomenon to be explained, for it is the opposite of the issue that we were prepared to expect. As capital accumulates, experience is enlarged and skill perfected; it would seem, then, that labor, being more abundantly supplied with all the means for its most effectual exercise, would be most successfully applied, and would be followed by the largest and most profitable results. True, the prices of commodities fall as the cost of their production is diminished. But there seems to be no reason why they should fall *more* rapidly than the cost of the articles decline; and therefore we cannot see, at the first glance, why the rate of profit should be diminished, — why it should be less than when men work at great disadvantage, under all the privations and difficulties incident to the attempt to found a new colony.

Adam Smith ascribes the fall of profits in some measure to the competition of capitalists. "When the stocks of many rich merchants," he says, "are turned into the same trade, their mutual competition naturally tends to lower its profits; and when there is a like increase of stock in all the different trades carried on in the same society, the same competition must produce the same effect in them all." But the objection is properly made, that competition can tend only to equalize the profits in different employments and different places. It can make the profits of cotton-spinning equal to those in the iron manufacture, and can reduce the gains of merchants in New York to a level with those in Boston; but it supplies no reason why the average rate of profit in all employments, and at all places, should be depressed. To produce this effect, there must be something to come into competition with capital itself, — some other agent, which shall render industry equally effective; and we have no such agent, and cannot even conceive of one.

Mr. Ricardo and his followers attempt to solve the problem by reasoning in their peculiar manner from the few facts which are all that they admit as data in the science. With them, as I have said, the doctrine of profits is a deduction from the Malthusian theories of population and rent. The value of every commodity being divisible into the three elements of rent, wages, and profits, whatever cause tends to augment the two former, or even to increase but one of them without an equivalent reduction of the other, must certainly lessen the third element, which is all that remains for profit. Such a cause is found in the necessity, created by an ever-increasing population, of constantly having recourse to inferior soils, and thereby of perpetually augmenting the rent of the lands which were previously under cultivation. But if rent is increased, there remains a smaller portion to be divided between wages and profits. Still further; there is a limit to the depression of wages, but there is none to the fall of profits. The natural and necessary rate of wages, according to these theories, as has been already explained, is the smallest sum that will supply the laborer and his family with what are believed to be the necessaries of life. As the cost of food is increased, therefore, by the necessity of cultivating inferior land, the expense of supplying the laborer with food is also increased, and his wages must rise. The portion remaining for profit is thus diminished, as it were, at both ends; as the population increases in number, from the value of every commodity a constantly increasing share must be cut off for rent, and another regularly augmented portion must be deducted for wages. Obviously but a small portion, and that perpetually becoming less, remains for profit. "In one brief formula," says Mr. De Quincey, "it might be said of profits, that *they are the leavings of wages;* so much will the profit be upon any act of production, whether agricultural or manufacturing, as the wages upon that act permit to be left behind."

The following diagram or ocular construction, also borrowed with some modification from Mr. De Quincey, may not only make this clearer to the reader, but may illustrate the peculiar character of Ricardo's reasoning,—the strict, logical deduction from a few arbitrarily assumed premises, little or no regard being paid to the modifying circumstances in a case which is obviously a very complicated one.

No. I. 100 bushels to the acre.	W		P	R'''	R''	R'
No. II. 90 bushels to the acre.	W	W'	P	R'''	R''	
No. III. 80 bushels to the acre.	W	W' : W''	P	R'''		
No. IV. 70 bushels to the acre.	W	W' : W'' : W'''	P			

Here No. I., the upper parallelogram, represents land of the first quality, yielding 100 bushels to the acre. No. II. represents the second class of soils, yielding but 90 bushels to the acre, and required for tillage as soon as the growing population has made the produce of No. I. insufficient to satisfy the demand for food. No. III. represents the third class of soils, yielding but 80 bushels to the acre, brought under cultivation under the same pressure continually increasing. No. IV. represents the poorest quality of the soil that is cultivated, yielding 70 bushels to the acre, or only enough to pay the ordinary wages of the labor, and the necessary rate of profit on the capital required for its cultivation, and therefore yielding no surplus for rent. We have only to add, that W expresses the function of wages, P of profit, w', w'', and w''' the several increments of wages, and R', R'', and R''' the several increments of rent, as they emerge successively under the series of agricultural expansions rendered necessary by the constant growth of the population.

As soon as No. II. is called into use by the increased demand for food, the increased price of that food will pay ordinary profits and wages for the cultivation of land yielding only 90 bushels an acre; and therefore R', representing 10 bushels an acre, will be left for the rent of No. I., though it yielded no rent before No. II. was cultivated. But this enhanced price of food renders necessary also an advance of wages, because the wages formerly paid were barely sufficient to purchase the necessary food for the laborer's family at the old price. Hence this increment of wages, represented by w', must also be cut off from P, which is at the same time lessened by the deduction of R'. When a further increase of the population brings into use No. III., yielding only 80 bushels, both R' and R'', representing 20 bushels, must be deducted from No. I., and R'', or 10 bushels, from No. II., for rent. So, also, w'' must be deducted for a further rise of wages. In like manner, when No. IV. is broken up for tillage, R', R'', and R''' will be paid for rent on the three classes of soils of a higher quality, and w', w'', and w''' will be the successive additions to the original rate, W, of wages. So long as No. IV. is the poorest land in cultivation, its whole produce will be absorbed in the payment of profits and wages, and nothing will be left for rent.

The preceding diagram is constructed only to show the *suc-*

cessive deductions that are made from profits to pay wages and rent. It does not represent the whole state of the case, after tillage has been brought down to No. IV.; for as there can be but one rate of wages at the same time, w', w'', and w''', or the successive increments of wages, must be deducted from the three higher classes of soils, as well as from No. IV. The following construction, then, shows how little remains for profits after No. IV. has come into use.

		a			*c*	*d*		*b*
No. I.	W	w'	w''	w'''	P	R'''	R''	R'
No. II.	W	w'	w''	w'''	P	R'''	R''	
No. III.	W	w'	w''	w'''	P	R'''		
No. IV.	W	w'	w''	w'''	P			

Here P, representing profits, extended from *a* to *b* when only No. I. was in cultivation, but reaches only from *c* to *d* after tillage has descended to No. IV.

This diminution of the rate of profits must go on indefinitely, so long as the increase of the population obliges us to have recourse to soils of constantly diminishing fertility. Rent at the same time will be proportionally augmented; the landholder will receive not only a larger portion of the total product, but the price per bushel of the whole product will be augmented. Wages, however, will be only nominally increased; the successive increments, w', w'', and w''', cannot be more than enough to pay the enhanced price of food which caused them. In fact, they will not suffice to pay the new price, but the laborer will submit to live on a smaller quantity of food, or on food of a coarser quality; for while food is becoming dearer, the constant tendency of the population to increase is adding to the competition in the labor-market, so that wages cannot rise in full proportion to the higher cost of food.

Thus far, it would seem that the new rates of wages and profits would be established only in agriculture, where alone a necessity for them appears to have been created. But a little reflection will show that they must extend equally to all employments of industry and capital. The enhanced price of food must raise wages throughout the country; and competition must equalize profits. If the returns for the employment of capital were smaller in farming than in commerce and manufactures, capital would be diverted from agriculture till the balance was restored. Furthermore, the increased cost of the raw material, which is always obtained more or less directly from agriculture, will immediately lessen the profits of the manufacturer; for instance, "even upon shoes," as De Quincey remarks, "there will be a small increase of labor, because the raw material will grow a little dearer as hides grow dearer; and hides will grow dearer as cattle grow dearer, by descending upon worse pasture-lands."

There is but one possible check upon this descent of agriculture to inferior soils, and the consequent declension of profits, augmentation of the price of food, and increase of rent. This is the progress of agricultural improvements, by means of which more food is obtained from the same quantity of land, or the same amount of food is procured by a smaller expenditure of labor and capital. In this way, the wants of an increasing population may be provided for without the necessity of bringing more land into tillage, or of applying capital with constantly diminishing returns. But this check cannot have any permanent influence; it may postpone, but cannot finally avert, the consequences of a steady growth of the population. Its influence, indeed, is self-limited; for, as McCulloch remarks, "the rise of profits consequent to every invention, by occasioning a greater demand for labor, gives a fresh stimulus to population; and thus, by increasing the demand for food, again inevitably forces the cultivation of poorer soils, and raises prices." And again, "from the operation of fixed and permanent causes, the increasing sterility of the soil is sure, in the long run, to overmatch the improvements already made in machinery and agriculture, prices experiencing a corresponding rise, and profits a corresponding fall."

It only remains to notice a corollary from this theory, in respect to the different manner in which this declension of the rate of profits affects the comparative value of commodities produced in great part by Fixed Capital, and of those produced in great part by Circulating Capital. These two kinds of capital differ chiefly in point of durability; Circulating Capital is employed for the most part in the payment of wages, and is very soon replaced by the fruits of the laborers' industry. Fixed Capital consists of tools and machines, varying in their degrees of durability, though all are consumed and replaced much more slowly than the various elements of Circulating Capital. According as Fixed Capital has less and less of durability, so far it approximates the separate nature of Circulating Capital. Some commodities are almost exclusively produced by the expenditure of capital, chiefly of Fixed Capital. Gunpowder, for instance, to avoid the hazard of human life, is manufactured by machinery moved by water-power in some retired place, the works being so contrived that the process is continued with very little superintendence, the workmen visiting the place only occasionally, to bring additional raw material, to remove the finished product, and to make a few adjustments of the machinery. Boots and shoes, on the other hand, are made almost entirely by the immediate labor of man; machines are not used in their manufacture, and the workman needs but few and simple tools.

Now, a fall of profits, as Mr. Mill remarks, "lowers in natural value the things into which profits enter in a greater proportion than the average, and raises those into which they enter in a less proportion than the average. All commodities in the production of which machinery bears a large part, especially if the machinery is very durable, are lowered in their relative value when profits fall; or, what is equivalent, other things are raised in value relatively to them." Recurring to the diagram, we see that wages rise while profits fall, though not in the same proportion, the fall of profits, owing to the deduction of rent, being more rapid than the rise of wages. For a double reason, then, as population advances, and inferior soils are brought into cultivation, gunpowder, and other articles the value of which consists mostly of profits, fall in price when compared with boots and shoes, and other commodities the value of which consists chiefly in wages. The elements of the former are declining, at the same time that the elements of the latter are rising, in comparative value. The result is otherwise briefly stated by Mr. Mill in this formula: — "Every fall of profits lowers, in some degree, the cost value of things made with much or durable machinery, and raises that of things made by hand; and every rise of profits does the reverse."

This is a brief outline of Ricardo's celebrated theory of value in relation to rent, wages, and profits. It is a masterpiece of abstract reasoning, imposing from its scientific pretensions, the boldness of its assumptions, the paradoxical character of many of its results, and the ingenuity which has been manifested in explaining these paradoxes and reconciling them with the facts of observation. In point of logic, it is unexceptionable; once admit its premises, and there is no stopping short of its conclusions. We may accept in great part the criticism of it by an eminent French economist, J. B. Say. "It is," he remarks, "perhaps a well-founded objection to Mr. Ricardo, that he sometimes reasons upon abstract principles to which he gives too great a generalization. When once fixed in an hypothesis which cannot be assailed, from its being founded on unquestionable observations, he pushes his reasonings to their remotest consequences, without comparing their results with those of actual experience. In this respect, he resembles a writer upon the mathematical theory of mechanics, who, from undoubted proofs drawn from the nature of the lever, would demonstrate the impossibility of the vaults daily executed by dancers on the stage. And how does this happen? The reasoning is unexceptionable; but a vital force, often unperceived, and always inappreciable, makes the facts differ very far from the calculations. From that moment, nothing in the author's work is represented as it really occurs in nature. It is not sufficient to begin with facts; other facts must be collected, steadily examined, and the consequences drawn from them constantly compared with the effects observed. The science of Political Economy, to be of practical utility, should not attempt to teach what *must necessarily* take place, even if deduced by legitimate reasoning, and from undoubted premises; it ought to show in what manner that which in reality *does* take place *is the consequence* of another fact equally certain. It should ascertain the chain which binds them together, and always establish from observation the existence of the two links at their point of connection."

It is unnecessary at present to examine this reasoning in detail, in order either to point out flaws in the argument, or to show that its results do not harmonize with those of observation and experience. The whole theory rests upon a few premises, which have already been examined and shown to be mere assumptions, paradoxical in appearance, and having no foundation in fact. It is not true, that the increase of the population tends to outrun the supply of food, or that it compels us to have recourse to inferior soils, or that it necessarily increases the competition of laborers for employment. Food does not become dearer, but is cheapened, by the growth of the population; the districts which are most recently brought into cultivation are not the least fertile, but are often more productive than those which have been peopled and tilled for centuries; and the capital which is applied to them generally yields a larger return than that which is employed in the old settlements. It is not even necessary, as the people increase in numbers, to send to a greater distance for food; but emigration distributes the people, and commerce distributes the food, where both are most needed, the combined result being that each generation is more fully supplied with the means of subsistence than its predecessor. The only inequality to be feared is that which is sometimes caused by human institutions, in the distribution of property; and the only famine which is possible in modern times, and among civilized nations, is produced by poverty, and not by a deficient supply of food.

The premises of Ricardo's theory being thus proved to be baseless, the entire superstructure falls. The whole is a mere exercise of logical ingenuity, a long series of deductions being obtained from a few definitions and hypotheses, which have no foundation in experience, and no applicability to the circumstances of the present time. The original phenomenon to be explained — the declension of the rate of profit as society advances in numbers and wealth — presents little difficulty, when we regard the limited extent of the field for the employment of capital. But this subject demands for full consideration a separate chapter.

CHAPTER XVII.

THE RATE OF PROFIT AS AFFECTED BY THE LIMITED EXTENT OF THE FIELD FOR THE EMPLOYMENT OF CAPITAL: THE THEORY OF GLUTS.

Mr. Wakefield was the first among English Economists to notice the seemingly obvious fact, that, in every country, the field for the employment of capital is of limited extent. The first introduction of capital into such a field is attended with very large returns; but as the amount of it increases, the rate of profit falls off; and when the limit is attained, or so nearly attained that profits have fallen to a *minimum*, accumulation ceases, there being no longer any sufficient motive for the exercise of frugality. With an evident desire to reconcile this fact to the theories of Malthus and Ricardo, with which it appears to conflict, Mr. Mill states the principle thus:—that "on a limited extent *of land*, only a limited quantity of capital can find employment at a profit." Thus enunciated, it seems to be only a corollary from Ricardo's doctrine of rent, which expressly affirms that successive applications of capital to the same quantity of land can be made only with successively diminishing returns. It will appear, however, that the extent of territory is not the only, or even the chief, limiting circumstance; but that the proper restriction is to be found in the magnitude of the wants of the people, as determined by their numbers, by the degree of civilization under which they live, and by the greater or less inequality of the distribution of property among them.

But it should be observed, that we are here speaking of a limit to the profitable employment *of capital*. Some distinguished Economists, among whom are Sismondi and Malthus, have maintained that there may be a general over-production *of wealth*, "a supply of commodities in the aggregate exceeding the demand, and a consequent depressed condition of all classes of production." We are all familiar with the fact, that there is often, in the market, a glut of a particular commodity, or of several commodities at once. Prices are adjusted, and the current of productive means and productive energy is turned from one article to another, through the indications afforded by such instances of glut or over-supply on the one hand, and of dearth or scarcity on the other. But the doctrine of these Economists is, that there may be a *general* glut, or that the disposition and the ability to produce may outrun the *ability* of the nation to consume. The *disposition* to consume, of course, is coextensive with the disposition to produce. But the ability to purchase, or, in other words, the active and efficient demand, it is supposed, may so far fall below the supply, that there will be a general depression of prices and general distress.

On the other hand, it has been contended, with great force, that a general glut is impossible; for every article brought to market is a source both of supply and demand, — the owner of it always wishing to exchange it for something else of equal value, so that his *desire to purchase* contributes to lighten the market to precisely the same extent to which he burdens it by his *desire to sell.* No man appears exclusively in the character of a seller; he is a buyer also, and he buys to the same extent to which he sells. If he brings a bale of cloth to market, for instance, it is because he wishes to exchange it, in the first place, for money. But this money he does not intend to keep in reserve, in order to increase indefinitely his store of it. He knows very well, that, if the money remains idle in his chest, it will yield neither interest nor profits. He will aim, therefore, to expend it as soon as possible, — either to buy articles of comfort or luxury for his own unproductive consumption; or to purchase raw material, tools, machinery, seed-corn, or the like, with a view to further production; or lastly, he may lend it to another, who, by investing it productively, — that is, by making purchases with it, — will be enabled to pay him interest for its use. In either way, the money is expended; purchases are made to the full extent of the original sale. If the seller chooses to lend the money to a bank, instead of trusting it to an individual, the result is the same. The bank immediately lends it over again to some person who wishes to enlarge his stock in trade by buying more commodities.

This reasoning is quite conclusive against the possibility of a general glut; but it must be applied with two important limitations. First, it goes upon the supposition, that the laws and other institutions of the country admit the freest possible interchange of all articles of wealth. If there be a monopoly of any one article, if only a few persons are privileged or enabled to produce and sell it,—and especially if this article be one of prime or universal necessity,—then there may be a glut, or over-production, of all other articles with reference to this one. To illustrate this point, I will take the most general case. All articles that are offered for sale or exchange may be roughly divided into two classes, according as they are articles of manufacture or products of agriculture. The latter are chiefly articles of food, and the demand and supply of food, as we have seen, are regulated by causes peculiar to itself, wholly irrespective of the presence or absence—the high or low prices—of other commodities. The *demand* for agricultural products depends on the number of appetites to be satisfied, and can only be enlarged by an increase of the population, or diminished by the population becoming smaller; the *supply* of these products is determined by the extent of territory capable of cultivation, and by improvements in the modes of husbandry. Neither of these sources of supply can be increased at will, or on demand; the land, in such a country as Great Britain, is all owned and occupied, and the number of acres is limited; improvements in agriculture are made by the progress of discovery and invention, and not merely because they are needed to feed the people.

Now manufactures must be exchanged for food, and consequently they may be produced in too great abundance; there is no limit to their increase, but there is a limit to the supply of the only article for which they can be bartered. And we cannot here say, as the English Economists are fond of saying in the case of a particular glut: "Transfer your capital and industry from the article of which there is a surplus to that of which there is a deficiency." In England, industry *cannot* be transferred from manufactures to agriculture; the land is all owned and held at a monopoly price, and the landlords refuse to employ more labor upon it, even if a greater amount of food should be produced by the introduction of more hands. They find, or think they find, that a greater *net* product remains to themselves when few hands are employed, than when there are many. Hence they endeavor to get rid of a portion of the agricultural laborers, instead of increasing their number. The policy of most English landlords is to depopulate their estates, to make the peasantry give place to flocks and herds, as in the North of Scotland, or to compel them, by unroofing and tearing down their dwellings, as in Ireland, to emigrate to foreign lands. Thus they imitate the system which has been practised for centuries in the Roman Campagna, which reduced the fields of Italy in the age of Pliny to a desert, and subsequently surrendered them to the Northern barbarians because there were not men enough left to defend them. The dispossessed tenantry are obliged to emigrate, or are driven into manufacturing industry; and thus the glut of manufactures is increased by the very causes which diminish the supply of food. True, food may be imported, as we have seen, even to an extent which is practically unlimited. But the very necessity for such importation, if it is found to exist in a country the agricultural resources of which are not yet developed to the utmost possible extent, proves that, in that country at least, there is already a glut of manufactures, and one which, in its effect on the rate of profits, would be very seriously felt, if there were not in other countries a glut of food. What actually exists in one nation, is possible in all nations; if there be an actual glut of manufactures in Great Britain, such a glut is possible for the whole civilized portion of mankind. And this glut of manufactured products in England is not a consequence of the stinted bounty of nature in reference to agricultural products. The amount of food produced there, from its own soil, is yet far from having attained its *maximum;* it might become as populous as Belgium, — that is, fifty per cent more populous than at present, — and yet not only feed all its inhabitants, but "produce commonly," as Belgium does, "more than double the quantity of corn required for the consumption of its inhabitants." *

In most civilized countries, at least two thirds of the working population are engaged in agricultural pursuits, and but one third in manufactures and commerce; and this proportion

* McCulloch's *Geographical Dictionary.*

existed in England itself down as late as the reign of the Stuarts. But in 1821, only one third of the English population were engaged in tilling the soil; and twenty years later, or in 1841, there were only about one fifth thus employed, — a depopulation of the rural districts to the rapidity of which there is no parallel in history.* There is no absolute deficiency either of land or food; for both can be had in abundance, as has been shown, in other countries. But as there are obstacles which impede the emigration of capital, so there are those which obstruct in a still greater degree the emigration of the indigent portion of the people. Poverty — the very cause which renders it desirable for them to emigrate — also renders emigration difficult, and often impossible.

The second limitation of the doctrine that a universal glut is impossible, is founded on the division, that I have already made (pp. 40, 41), of all the commodities which constitute wealth into two classes. *First*, there are the articles which are designed for immediate consumption, and which directly satisfy the wants of man; such as food and clothing that are ready to be eaten and worn, the houses that shelter us, and the ornaments and luxuries that gratify our tastes. And, *secondly*, there are the tools, implements, and raw materials, by means of which, or out of which, the former articles are made, but which, in their present shape, are not fitted for our immediate gratification and support. These two classes may be designated respectively as, 1. *Finished products*, and, 2. *Producing agents*. The division between them does not exactly correspond with that between capital and the other portion of

---

* The following table, taken from the official reports, shows the proportionate per cent of the British population who were engaged respectively in agricultural, commercial, and manufacturing, and all other pursuits, at four decennial periods.

	Agriculture.	Trade and Manufactures.	All others.
1811	.35	.44	.21
1821	.33	.46	.21
1831	.28	.42	.30
1841	.22	46	.32

The census of 1851, though it presents a more minute classification of the occupations of the people, unfortunately does not enable us to divide the population into three classes, so as to continue the foregoing table. But according to the best estimate that can be framed from it, the agricultural portion of the British population in 1851 was a little less than 20 per cent of the whole.

wealth which is not capital. All *producing agents* are capital, it is true; but all *finished products* are not excluded from the definition of capital. A merchant's capital, for instance, often consists exclusively of commodities that are completely manufactured and ready for use; a retailer's stock is generally of this character.

It is evident that all wealth of the second class, all *producing agents*, possess only a kind of secondary and derivative value; they are prized, not for their own sake, but for what may be made out of them, or produced by their aid. And it is equally evident, that if the demand for commodities of the first class, *finished products*, is not coextensive, if it does not keep pace, with the demand for the second class of objects of wealth, or *producing agents*, then there must be an excess of supply, or a glut, of the former, and a consequent fall of prices and diminution of profits. No one buys a plough or a loom for its own sake; for in itself, it gratifies no feeling and satisfies no want. The one is valued only because it helps us to raise corn, and the other, because it enables us to manufacture cloth. The only effect of the purchase of either, then, is, not to relieve the market already glutted with corn and cloth, but to furnish prospectively a greater supply of both, and thus to increase the glut.

We may admit, then, the force of the common argument, so far as it goes, against the possibility of a glut; and we may still deny that it covers the whole ground, or that it demonstrates the impossibility of any such excess of supply of one class of articles, as cannot be remedied by diverting the sources of production from those commodities which are in excess to those which are deficient. We admit, that a capitalist who wishes to sell also wishes to buy; for to sell is to exchange, and the seller's disposition to part with one product is exactly measured by his disposition to obtain another of precisely equivalent value. We admit, also, that he does not wish to sell or exchange for money alone, so as to create a scarcity of that one article; for though he receives money in one half of his transaction, or as a seller, he pays it in the other half, as a purchaser. So far as money is concerned, then, his operation leaves the market in the same state in which he found it, — not glutted by the number of sellers of goods, nor "tightened," as the phrase is, by the want of money.

But though he buys as much as he sells, is it true that he always relieves the market by the former operation just as fast, and to the same extent, that he burdens it by the latter, so that the balance of transactions remains as it would have been, if he had not entered the market at all? We can easily see that he does not, in any one case of two articles corresponding to each other as *finished product* and *producing agent*. Suppose the market, for instance, to be already amply furnished with grain. One who brings to it an additional thousand bushels of grain to sell, occasions a glut of this article, and certainly does nothing towards relieving this glut by expending all the money which he received for grain upon the purchase of ploughs and other implements for clearing and breaking up more land, and thus producing a larger harvest the next year. Or if cloth enough is already offered for sale, the sellers of it will certainly occasion a glut of this article, if they exchange the whole stock of it for power-looms, and thus double or treble the quantity of cloth which will be offered for sale the next month. The same reasoning is applicable to any other two commodities that are related to each other as finished product and producing agent. It is equally evident that it is applicable to all such cases, taken together; or, in other words, a general glut *of finished products* is possible, and such a glut cannot be relieved by diverting capital to other employments. There is no other employment for it, as every use of capital is, directly or indirectly, to increase the amount and value of finished products. Then a superabundance of capital, in reference to the field for its employment, is possible; and the inevitable result of such a surplus is a diminution of the rate of profit.

Thus far, I have only proved that a glut of finished products is *possible*. The probability of its actual occurrence, I have already said, will depend upon the magnitude of the wants of the people, as determined, 1. by their numbers, 2. by the degree of civilization which they have obtained, and, 3. by the greater or less inequality of the distribution of property among them.

First, it is obvious enough, that the consumption of finished products in any country, other things being equal, will depend upon the number of its inhabitants. The demand for food is necessarily in proportion to the number of appetites to be satisfied; and the other articles which are absolute necessaries of life must follow the same measure. Even the demand for luxuries will be determined in the same way, if the tastes and the abilities of the people remain the same.

Secondly, it is equally plain that the extent of the demand for finished products will be affected by the degree of civilization which the people have attained, and that, other things being equal, it will advance with the progress of refinement among them. The wants of the natives of the South Pacific Isles, when they were first visited by Europeans, were almost entirely supplied by the bread-fruit and cocoa-nut trees, and by yams and bananas. The bread-fruit tree alone supplied them with food, clothing, and the material for huts. When they learned from foreigners the existence of other comforts and luxuries, their wants rapidly multiplied; the knowledge of the uses of iron alone opened a wide field for the industry that it created. Intercourse with China has created a demand all over the world for tea; the discovery of America added tobacco, the potato, and many other articles, to the list of our wants. It would be difficult to estimate the number of trades that have been created, and the number of persons who have found employment, through the diffusion of a taste for the fine arts.

Thirdly, as an effectual demand is created only by the coexistence of the disposition and the ability to purchase, its extent will depend upon the equality of the distribution of property. The two circumstances already mentioned affect only the magnitude and prevalence of human desires; and in the present state of civilization in Europe and America, it may be said that these desires are unbounded; the gratification of some desires appears to have no effect but that of exciting others. But the ability to satisfy these desires exists in very different degrees. If this ability were equally diffused, no such thing as over-production would be possible; the consumption of an individual, or a family, possessing a very moderate amount of wealth, certainly exceeds the productive power of such a person or family. On the other hand, the consumption of much the larger part of the population of Europe is limited to mere necessaries, or to what the custom of the country regards as necessaries. If the demands of all were thus restricted, there would be a great surplus of productive power; in the present state of invention, and with the present accumulation of capital, mankind might be idle probably more than half of the time. It is the luxury of the rich which offers the only vent for all finished products that exceed the definition of necessaries. This fact does not furnish any apology for such luxury; for a more equitable division of the goods of this world would cause the surplus of productive power — all that is not needed for the creation of necessaries — to be expended in providing a multitude of what may be called comforts and decencies for the bulk of the nation. But when property is very unequally distributed, the luxury of a few must make up for the forced abstinence of many, or there will be a constantly increasing surplus of capital, which will manifest itself either by the forced emigration of such capital, or by such a diminution of the rate of profit as will take away all temptation to make additional savings.

This doctrine seems plain enough, though it is vehemently opposed by all English Economists of the Adam Smith and Ricardo school, who insist upon the paradox, that, not consumption, but production, creates a vent or market for products, and that the only means of dissipating an *apparent* glut is to stimulate production. Their chief reason for insisting upon this theory is the admitted fact, that no one ever finds any difficulty in bartering a finished product for some other finished product, provided he will allow the purchaser to fix the terms of the exchange. Certainly, exchange is always *possible;* the only question is, whether it is always *profitable.* And this question seems to be answered by another admitted fact, that as a country becomes wealthy, and capital accumulates, producers find that the only exchanges which they are able to make become less and less profitable, or, in other words, that profits decline, and are only prevented from ceasing altogether by a stop being put to the process of accumulation.

All will allow, that the productive power of every civilized nation already exceeds what is requisite for providing all the people with a stock of mere necessaries. Any excess beyond this point — whether such excess be created by the invention of new machinery, or by the accumulation of fresh capital —

must be directed towards the production of comforts and luxuries. It is a mere evasion, as we have seen, to say that it may be directed to the purchase or construction of more productive agents. Such additional agents will only increase the amount, perhaps already too great, of comforts and luxuries in the form of finished products. But when they have reached this form of finished products, they must either be consumed, or they will lie idle and rot; no other use can be made of them. They are no longer *agents* for anything but the gratification of taste and desire. Consumption, or rotting unused, is their only possible destination. Now, I have admitted that, if property — or *purchasing power*, which is the same thing — is pretty equally distributed among the people, the aggregate desire will take off and consume the aggregate product of comforts and luxuries, without causing any great declension of profits. On an average, each family would be inclined to consume all the products which, under a perfectly equal distribution of property, it would be able to produce; and this would be enough to prevent profits from falling at all; the only effect of the invention of new machinery and improved processes of manufacture would be to increase the stock of luxuries which each family might thus consume, or to give them more leisure time, which is in itself an additional luxury. Some would consume more, and some less, than this; but the prodigality of the former would be balanced by the frugality of the latter, and the only effect would be the inequality of property that would thus be gradually induced.

But suppose property to be very unequally distributed, only one hundred families now having all the wealth, and the whole remaining population being limited to the bare necessaries of life. As we suppose the productive power of the community to be unaltered by this change in the distribution of property, there will be the same amount of comforts and luxuries to be consumed as before, and it is evident that they must be consumed solely by the one hundred wealthy families. Now, suppose one of these families to be disposed to make savings, and thus to increase its productive power: it may be proved that both the act of saving and the employment of the savings will tend to create a glut and to lower profits. The act of saving will leave the luxuries formerly distributed among one hundred, to be consumed by only ninety-nine families; and this diminution of the demand will depress prices and profits. And the employment of the savings as capital, though it will give wages to an additional number of poor families sufficient to procure necessaries for them, and will furnish these necessaries through their labor, will leave also an additional margin of profit, which must be devoted, as before, to the creation of luxuries; and thus a larger supply of luxuries will be forced upon the market in which the ninety-nine wealthy families are the only purchasers. A second depreciation of prices must be the consequence.

The intention of Providence seems to be, that the time and labor economized, through the use of machinery and improved modes of production, in the production of necessaries, should be devoted to the creation of luxuries for very general use, — for most of the working families, as well as for a few persons of wealth; or, supposing that there are already luxuries enough for all, that the time, the immunity from the necessity of labor, so obtained, should be distributed among the people with some approach to equality, nearly all having a portion of leisure each week, to devote either to recreation or mental improvement. When the distribution, not of wealth indeed, but of the opportunities for obtaining wealth, is equalized, or made to approach equality, there will be no possibility of creating too many labor-saving machines, producing too much, reducing the rates of profit too low, being oppressed with a surplus of population, or glutting the market of the world. Those whose ambition is limited and whose wants are few, will not enter into the strife as rival producers, but will devote the surplus of time and wealth which they have earned to the gratification of their tastes and to a quiet enjoyment of life.

I have already noticed the fact, that Ireland, where the inequality in the distribution of property is extreme, is, in proportion to her population and wealth, one of the poorest markets for manufactured produce in the world; while in the United States, as there is a near approach to equality in everything, there is the largest demand for such produce. From their inability to purchase the cheaper products of the English manufactories, the peasantry of Connaught, of some parts of Munster, the county of Donegal, and the western counties of

Leinster, "usually make their own clothing, consisting of linen, knitted stockings, a coarse but very serviceable flannel for women's clothes, and a good frieze for men. The fleece of his own sheep, spun and woven in his own house, at seasons which would otherwise have been unemployed, enabled the cottier and peasant farmer to provide comfortable clothing for his family, which it was hardly possible for him to obtain in any other way."* In the United States, on the other hand, notwithstanding our home manufactures are already very considerable, the importation of cotton and woollen goods alone, in 1853 and 1854, after deducting the reëxportation, exceeded in value an annual average of 58 millions of dollars, or nearly three dollars a head for the total white population. These large imports consist for the most part of commodities which may be accounted as comforts and luxuries; the cheaper articles, which come under the head of *necessaries*, are now almost exclusively of home production.

In the business of production, capital—which may be called *embodied labor*, because it consists of the reserved fruits of previous industry—must bear a certain proportion to *free* or *immediate labor*, which is the direct application of human strength and skill. Embodied and free labor have each a task to perform; neither can be effectually applied without the aid of a due portion of the other. The industry of man is of little avail, if it be not assisted by tools, implements, and machines, the accumulated results of his previous toil or earnings. Even the savage cannot hunt without his weapons, nor fish without appropriate implements; and in order to rise in the scale of civilization, he must have industry and foresight enough to get together an accumulated stock of necessaries, so that he may be able to execute prolonged tasks, and to wait till they are completed before he can enjoy their fruits. On the other hand, at the opposite extreme of the social scale, when the arts are carried to perfection, and machinery exists in its most costly and complicated forms, wherewith to abridge human labor, there is still a necessity for some free labor to superintend and aid its operation. There may be an excess, as well as a defi-

* *The Condition and Prospects of Ireland, and the Evils arising from the Present Distribution of Landed Property*, by Jonathan Pim, (Dublin, 1848,) p. 111.

ciency, of the implements and machines with which any community performs its work. Between these extremes, the field of employment for capital, and the consequent demand for it, vary to every conceivable degree; and according as the supply of such capital falls short of, or exceeds, the demand, the profits are large or small.* This can be best illustrated by a glance at the successive stages of progress of an infant settlement formed by civilized men in a country hitherto unoccupied, or inhabited only by savages.

In the infancy of such a settlement, the demand for capital is urgent, for the capacities and wants of the settlers far exceed their means. The sources of its prosperity as yet are latent, and need to be developed. Clearings are to be made in the forests, buildings are to be erected, roads are to be opened, tools to be provided, and nearly the whole of the complex machinery through which an organized society applies its energies is to be created out of the raw materials afforded by the land, the sea, and the forest. Luxuries as yet do not exist; there is hardly any opportunity for unproductive consumption, beyond that of the mere necessaries of life. The people are frugal by compulsion; the fruits of nearly all their toil, then, become capital, or are converted into means for the future more advantageous application of industry. The profits of what capital there is are also, of necessity, very great; one tool must be applied to many purposes, and is therefore constantly in use. The axe for a time must do its own work, and that of the hammer, the saw, and the plane. The possession of this one instrument must, then, be a source of great gain to its owner; he can buy the unaided services of his fellows, the only payment they have to offer, for a long time, by the loan

* Dr. Chalmers states this reasoning very clearly in the form of an *argumentum ad hominem* for the Malthusians. "As surely as there might be too many ploughmen," he says, "so there might be too many ploughs. If, in virtue of the excessive number of ploughmen, all cannot find employment without forcing an entrance upon soils that would return inadequate wages for the labor, so, in virtue of the excessive number of ploughs, all cannot find employment without a like return of inadequate profit for the capital. . . . . . What is true of the living, is true of the inanimate instrument; both might be unduly multiplied. As there might be too many men, so might there be too many machines, — too many power-looms, as well as too many weavers at hand-looms, — too many cotton-mills, as well as too many cotton-spinners." — Chalmers's *Political Economy*, Vol. I. pp. 93, 94.

of it. And in a similar way, every other item which constitutes capital in such a community will be productive of large gains.

After the hardships and privations of the first season are surmounted, each laborer probably finds himself provided with tools, so that the profits on this branch of capital are lessened, and, as an opening has been made in the forest, the operations of agriculture can begin. There is now a great demand for seed-corn, for the natural fertility of the land will return a hundred fold, if the settler has only what is requisite for planting. He can safely promise to return three bushels of grain in the autumn, for one bushel lent to him in the spring; in other words, he can offer the capitalist a profit of two hundred per cent for seed. But after the first harvest is successfully gathered in, so bountiful is the product of the virgin soil, that very probably grain cannot be sold at all in the infant settlement, the supply altogether exceeding the colonists' own wants, and the means of transportation and export not being yet provided; that is, no profit can be made on food till the means are obtained for sending this food to market. Capital is now required to construct roads and furnish shipping; and as the commodity is to be carried from a place where it has little or no value, to one where it will command a ready sale and a high price, the gains of the merchant engaged in this transportation will necessarily be immense. For the first few seasons after American farmers had established themselves in the Oregon Territory, it is an historical fact that they fed their horses with the finest wheat, no market being within their reach for the sale of this product. California was then suddenly peopled, almost in a single season, after the gold-deposits and auriferous sands were found there; and the gold-seekers being too eager in their proper pursuit to find time for planting grain for themselves, the agricultural products of Oregon suddenly rose to a high price. The farmers on the banks of the Willamette found that they could obtain California gold more cheaply by raising maize and wheat on their own farms, than by going to the country to dig it for themselves. The discovery of gold in the neighboring Territory, instead of tending to the depopulation of Oregon, as was at first apprehended, was the great source of its prosperity, as it furnished a market, and indirectly supplied the country with capital.

After a country is once sufficiently stocked, as it would seem, with capital, the progress of invention may suddenly create a great additional demand for it, by calling for the construction of new machines and improved implements, the use of which soon supersedes the old ones. Thus the invention of railways, and the application of steam to the purposes of land conveyance, have occasioned, both in England and America, during the last twenty years, an immense demand for the investment of capital, some of the old forms in which it was embodied being rendered useless or unproductive. Turnpikes cease to be productive property, and canals are less profitable than before. For a time, floating or circulating capital is in great request, as it is needed for conversion into this form of fixed capital; and accordingly, the rate of interest rises. But when the improvement is completed, this demand ceases, the returns from the new processes are very great, floating capital accumulates more rapidly than ever, and the rate of interest falls again. The railway improvement in England and in the eastern portion of the United States may now be said to be completed; only the great Valley of the Mississippi, and the lines of communication with the Pacific coast, still call for additional investment on roads to be traversed by the agency of steam.*

But I need not trace further these successive steps in the progress of opulence and the accumulation of capital. It is evident that the rapidity of its increase depends on the rate of profit, which is necessarily high in a new country, where the people are frugal and industrious. The rate gradually diminishes, both as the primary and most imperative wants of the community are satisfied, and as artificial tastes and an ap-

* According to Mr. Porter, (*Progress of the Nation*, p. 330,) up to the end of 1849 there had been constructed in Great Britain and Ireland 5,996 miles of railway, representing a capital of £197,500,000. Over 14,000 miles of railway have been completed in the United States; and if those be added which are in process of construction, the sum will be 17,146. Taking the average cost of construction and equipment at $25,000 per mile, which is a very low estimate, the capital vested in these American roads will be $428,750,000. The capital of the British railways, reckoned in our currency, being about $975,000,000, we have a grand total of $1,403,750,000, as the sum which the English and American people have converted into this one form of fixed capital during the last thirty years. What effect would have been produced on the rate of profit, if this immense sum had remained in the form of circulating capital, seeking investment?

petite for luxury and unproductive consumption are diffused among the colonists. Yet floating capital is soon acquired in sufficient quantities for the ordinary purposes of industry and traffic. In such countries as England and Holland, however, immense sums gradually take the form of fixed capital, being vested in making land-improvements of the largest and most expensive character; in constructing docks, harbors, and canals, erecting dikes, and furnishing manufactories with costly machinery. Vast as the field is which such works open for the investment of capital, it needs but a glance at the present condition of England and Holland to satisfy us, that this field is all occupied, and the work of fixed capital is done. What farther savings from income are made, must go into the market as floating capital, seeking investment, seeking borrowers who will take it offering undoubted security, and a very moderate rate of interest. There is great competition of the lenders with each other in the English and Dutch markets, — a competition which is most strikingly shown when the government appears as a borrower, and puts up a large loan at what is virtually an auction, to be sold in shares to the highest bidder.

A diminished rate of profit tends to throw the great branches of manufacture and commerce exclusively into the hands of large capitalists, and thus to increase that inequality in the distribution of wealth which was one of the original causes of a fall of profits. Hence it is that, in such countries as Holland and England, where a low rate of interest has prevailed for a long period, there is as great an inequality of fortune among manufacturers and merchants, as among land-owners. "It is in the nature of trade and manufacture," says Mr. Laing, "that great capital drives small capital out of the field; *it can afford to work for smaller returns.* There is a natural tendency in trade to monopoly, by the accumulation of great wealth in a few hands. It is not impossible, that, in every branch of trade and manufacture in Great Britain, the great capitalist will, in time, entirely occupy the field, and put down small capitalists in the same line of business; that a moneyed aristocracy, similar to that in Genoa, will gradually be formed, the middle class of small capitalists in trade and manufacture become gradually extinguished, and a structure of society gradually arise in which lords and laborers will be the only classes or gradations in the commercial and manufacturing, as in the landed, system. An approximation, a tendency towards this state, is going on in England. In many branches of industry, — for instance, in glass-making, iron-founding, soap-making, cotton-spinning, — the great capitalists engaged in them have, by the natural effect of working with great capital, driven small capitals out of the field, and formed a kind of exclusive family property of some of these branches of manufacture. Government, by excessive taxation and excise regulation, — both of which have ultimately the effect, as in the glass and soap manufacture and the distillery business, of giving a monopoly to the great capitalist *who can afford the delay and advance of money these impediments require*, — has been hitherto aiding rather than counteracting this tendency of great capital to swallow all the employments in which small capital can act. It is not an imaginary, nor perhaps a very distant evil, that our middle classes with their small capitals may sink into nothing, — may become tradesmen or small dealers, supplying a few great manufacturing and commercial classes with the articles of their household consumpt, and rearing supernumerary candidates for unnecessary public functions, civil, military, or clerical; and that in trade, as in land, a noblesse of capitalists, and a population of serfs working for them, may come to be the two main constituent parts in our social structure." *

I shall afterwards have occasion to show, that it is the abundance of floating capital seeking investment, the competition of lenders with each other, and the consequent depression of the rate of interest, that is the great incentive to those wild and ruinous speculations which usually precede a commercial crisis, and are commonly, though improperly, attributed to some defective regulation of the currency. The state of the currency, it is true, is an index of this perilous condition of things. The currency feels the first whispers of the approaching storm; and it is by a judicious management of the banking system of the country that the force of the tempest may be somewhat checked. But the real origin of the difficulty is situated farther back, and is attributable to the imprudence of capitalists

---

* *Notes of a Traveller*, ed. of 1854, p. 187.

rather than bankers, who are mere agents of those who have the real power to control the market.

But my present point is sufficiently illustrated, which is, that when a sufficient amount of wealth has taken the form of fixed capital to satisfy all the real wants of the country, — that is, when the whole establishment or fabric of agricultural, manufacturing, and commercial industry is completed, — then, if savings from income continue to be made, they must be pushed into market as circulating capital seeking investment; and the rate of profits and interest must decline from the competition which ensues. This is already the state of affairs in England; and if we are still distant from it in the Atlantic States of our own Union, it is because the new settlements which are constantly forming in the West operate as a drain upon our capital as well as our population; and also because the field open for the productive investment of fixed capital in the gigantic improvements required in our immense territory is so vast, that centuries must elapse before it is fully occupied.

The stationary state of wealth, which we thus see at the end of a long vista of years, is not a consummation to be dreaded. When capital enough has been accumulated to afford an income sufficient for all our wants, the only requisite for general happiness is, that it should be distributed with some approach to equality; — not the visionary and perfect equality which the brain-sick schemers of France are vainly endeavoring to realize; but the necessary approximation to it which is consistent with entire regard for the rights of property, and which must result from the mild and beneficent operation of laws which leave every man at liberty both to spend and to save, and which, at the decease of the first owner, distribute his inheritance equally among his natural heirs.

CHAPTER XVIII.

THE THEORY AND USES OF MONEY.

A HISTORY of the opinions of men respecting money, and the precious metals that are the material of which money is made, would be almost a complete history of the progress of Political Economy. The errors to which we are liable on a superficial consideration of the subject are so natural, so liable to be entertained by persons of ordinary judgment and ordinary means of information, that we cannot wonder at their having seriously affected the course of legislation in most countries and the general policy of nations. The true theory of money, when nakedly stated, seems like a string of paradoxes, which are contradicted by the common sense of mankind. Yet the truth of this theory is now so clearly established, and the course of events in the commercial world has contributed so largely to illustrate it, that its fundamental principles have come to be regarded as axioms, which no one thinks of contesting. A review of the mistakes which men committed in reasoning upon the subject in former times, of the causes which led to them, and of the very serious evils which were their inevitable consequences, would be a curious and instructive chapter in the philosophy of the human mind. I can notice but a few of these blunders,—those only, in fact, the confutation of which will help to establish and illustrate the doctrine that I wish to propound.

As money is the universal medium of exchange, and as wealth itself subsists, or is continued in existence, only through an interminable succession of exchanges, all wealth must, more or less frequently, appear as money, and be reckoned or estimated as such. Money is the universal form or garb which all the items or commodities that constitute wealth occasionally assume. At any one time and place, it is a universal measure of the comparative value of those commodities, and a common denomination, to which, when we wish to ascertain their aggregate or sum total, they are all reduced. If a man is reduced to the necessity of borrowing, he borrows, not the particular articles that he actually wants, but the money wherewith he can purchase those articles. If he pays a debt, he does not return the very articles that he borrowed, or an equivalent amount of a perfectly similar kind, but he pays a proportionate amount of money. The children in the house of an opulent trader, (to use once more Mr. Senior's happy illustration,) having all the necessaries and comforts of life supplied to them with mechanical regularity, without any effort or sacrifice on their part, may never inquire into the machinery by which these effects are produced. But if their attention should be turned to the subject, finding that their father often talked of the difficulty of getting money, and seldom of the difficulty of spending it, — that he generally spoke of his fortune as consisting of the money he was worth, and that the motive which he generally assigned for refusing them any luxury was, that he had not money enough to afford it, — they would conclude that money alone was wealth, or the solitary means of obtaining everything which is desirable; that their enjoyments depended on the money which their father received, and were lessened by every other occasion he had for expending money; and that their abundance, in truth, depended on the amount of money, for the time being, in his strong-box, and would be increased indefinitely, provided that this amount could be indefinitely augmented and retained.

This now seems to us as the reasoning of children; yet it was precisely thus that the legislatures and governments of the most civilized nations reasoned, down certainly to as late a period as the beginning of the last century. The most stringent, even sanguinary, laws were made to prevent the exportation of the precious metals; and bounties were held out to favor the exportation of other commodities, for which, it was supposed, these metals would be received in exchange. Even so distinguished and sensible a philosopher as Mr. Locke argues thus: — "All other movable goods are of so consumable a nature, that the wealth which consists in them cannot be much depended on; and a nation which abounds in them one year may, without any exportation, but merely by their own waste and extravagance, be in great want of them the next. Money, on the contrary, is a steady friend, which, though it may travel about from hand to hand, yet, if it can be kept from going out of the country, is not very liable to be wasted and consumed. Gold and silver, therefore, are the most solid and substantial part of the movable wealth of a nation"; and to multiply these metals ought, he thinks, upon that account, to be the great object of its political economy. Many worthy persons, even at the present day, though they do not reason quite so absurdly as this, are accustomed to deplore an unfavorable turn in our exchanges with foreign countries, not because it is an index of a real evil, — that we have been overtrading, or buying foreign goods on credit to an extent beyond our wants and our means, — but because it tends to drain the country of its precious metals, to lessen the specie basis on which our banks are trading, and thereby to diminish the security of our currency.

In attempting to refute these errors, I shall speak first only of *money properly so called*, and not of its substitutes. In other words, I shall consider the currency as if it consisted exclusively of specie, or of coined gold and silver, and shall speak of the circumstances which determine the value of such specie, of its utility as one of the bases of its value, and of the manner in which its use as money affects the value of the bullion from which it is made.

I say, then, that money is merely a contrivance for diminishing the friction of exchange; and though a safe and convenient, it is also a very costly, contrivance for this end. It is absolutely unproductive except for this purpose; it is a portion of the wealth of the country, it is true; but it is a portion of our unproductive wealth, not of our capital. We are the poorer by the loss of profit or interest on all of it which we are obliged to keep on hand. Money (paradoxical as the assertion may seem) yields neither profit nor interest. It is only the goods or commodities that are transferred or exchanged by means of money, which yield profit; and this profit or interest, as we have seen, depends on the mutations or changes of form that they undergo. The very reason which Locke adduces for the high estimate put upon money in comparison with other objects of wealth, — namely, its durability, or the fact that it cannot be consumed, — is the cause why it is not productive. The specie which a merchant or a banker holds in store, to provide against daily calls or sudden emergencies, is the only unproductive portion of his capital; he is subject to a loss of interest on the whole amount thus retained. It has been already proved, that it is only through the constant transformations of capital, through its repeated consumption and reproduction, that it is made to yield a profit. And even as an article of unproductive wealth, it may be said of money that it gratifies no taste, and, in its capacity as money, apart from its character as a portion of wealth, it yields no enjoyment. The coin which a man keeps in his pocket does not, like his shoes or his hat, contribute to his comfort; it is a convenience to him only as it supplies immediate means for making small purchases or satisfying small demands.

Thus it answers a useful purpose; for, as I have said, it facilitates exchanges. In this respect, it corresponds perfectly, if I may adopt Adam Smith's illustration, to the land which is used for roads and other avenues of passage and transportation. The land thus appropriated affords no rent; it cannot be used for the purposes either of agriculture or building. We cannot do without the roads, any more than we can do without money; but the necessity of devoting much land to this use is a tax upon the community, and a tax to a serious amount; for it yields no profit, and it costs a considerable sum for keeping it in repair. So the cost to a community of the money which it needs is a serious drain upon its resources. For money also needs to be kept in repair; the loss by abrasion, by actual rubbing down through much handling, is considerable. The deficiency in weight of the old, worn coins, when they are called in to be recoined, has to be made up by the public. An operation of this kind in William and Mary's time, recoining all the specie currency of Great Britain, and issuing it again of the proper weight, cost the government about two and a half millions sterling, or twelve millions of dollars. McCulloch estimates the whole loss from abrasion, and from such accidents as shipwrecks, fires, and forgetting the places where hoards of it have been buried or otherwise concealed, at one per cent a year; estimating, as Mr. Senior does, the whole metallic currency of England at thirty millions sterling, or 150 millions of dollars, the annual cost of maintaining this currency in repair is about a million and a half of dollars.

This, however, is not the heaviest charge which the possession of a large amount of coined money entails upon the nation. The loss of profit or interest may be estimated by regarding the specie currency as so much unproductive wealth, which, if it were turned into active capital, would increase the national income by a large annual profit. The whole gold and silver currency of France, for instance, is estimated at 400 millions of dollars; considering the rate of profit in that kingdom to be only six per cent, the annual expense of keeping so much money within the limits of the country is twenty-four millions; add one per cent as the cost of keeping the coin in repair, and the total expense is twenty-eight millions of dollars, or more than half the sum which would defray the whole expense of our national government in a time of peace. We cannot estimate with much precision the amount of currency here in the United States; but the returns of all the banks in the Union, made to the Secretary of the Treasury in May, 1854, indicate that the average circulation of bank-notes is now about 200 millions of dollars, founded on specie reserves held by the banks, of sixty millions. The gold and silver in the treasury depositories of the United States at the same period amounted to twenty-five millions. If we suppose that forty millions of gold and silver coins are in the hands of individuals and other corporations than banks, an estimate certainly not too large, we have 265 millions of dollars as the total of our circulation. The average rate of profit throughout the United States is at least as high as ten per cent; add one per cent for the loss by abrasion, and by shipwrecks, fires, &c., and we have over twenty-nine millions for what would be the annual cost of our currency, did it consist exclusively of specie. In fact, a large portion of it consists of bank-notes, a cheap substitute for coin; so the actual cost is but eleven per cent on 125 millions of specie, or a little less than fourteen millions a year.

I should be unwilling to introduce these statistical computations, if they did not contribute more powerfully than other arguments to overthrow the old popular errors, that coined silver and gold alone constitute national wealth, or that they possess material advantages over every other commodity which is admitted to be wealth. There is no occasion to undervalue the real service that is rendered by money; it is just as essential in every civilized, nay, in every barbarous community, as a system of roads or other means of transportation. Our only point is, that it is a very expensive servant, and that the true policy of nations is to get along with the use of as little of it as possible. We need a certain amount of money, proportioned to our population, the extent of our territory, and the magnitude of our commercial operations; to attempt to amass a larger amount than this, would be as great a folly as to lay out a greater number of roads than is necessary, and to build more carriages than are needed to carry the freight and passengers. Because specie is costly, there have been invented of late years a great variety of cheap substitutes for it, chiefly various forms or sorts of bank-notes, some of which are very useful, and others very mischievous expedients. The great advantage that gold and silver money possesses over them all is the perfect security that it affords; the great disadvantage is its expensiveness.

The utility of such a universal medium of exchange as money is very clearly and briefly explained by Adam Smith. "When the division of labor has been once thoroughly established, it is but a very small part of a man's wants which the produce of his own labor can supply. He supplies far the greater part of them by exchanging that surplus part of the produce, which is over and above his own consumption, for such parts of the produce of other men's labor as he has occasion for. But when the division of labor first began to take place, this power of exchanging must frequently have been very much clogged and embarrassed in its operations." One man may have hats that he wishes to sell, and another person may wish to buy one. But the latter may have only bread to offer in payment, an article with which the former may be already provided. "No exchange can in this case be made between them. In order to avoid the inconveniency of such situations, every prudent man must naturally have endeavored to manage his affairs in such a way, as to have at all times by him, besides the peculiar produce of his own industry, a certain quantity of some one commodity or another, such as he imagined few people would be likely to refuse in exchange for the produce of their industry." If the whole community should select and agree upon some one article for this purpose, every person in it would gladly accept this commodity in exchange for anything that he had to sell; he would receive it, not because he wished to use or consume it, but because he intended to buy something else with it; and he knows that the person who has this other thing to sell, will readily part with it in exchange for that commodity which all had agreed to accept. This is just the case with money; every one is willing to receive it, not because he intends to use it as a thing to be consumed, but simply because he knows that every one else is willing to take it in exchange. He receives it because he intends to part with it as soon as possible in exchange for something that he does desire to consume. The first requisite, then, for an article that is intended to be used as money, is the willingness of everybody to receive it in exchange for anything that he wishes to sell; and the characteristic quality of money is that it is not intended, and in fact is not fit, to be used for any purpose but that of being passed from hand to hand. It is simply a ticket of transfer, a medium of exchange.

It would seem, then, that almost any commodity might, by common consent, be used as money; and, in fact, different nations have employed a great variety of articles for this purpose. The North American Indians used wampum, or small shell beads strung together as ornaments; and our Puritan fathers, having very little silver and gold, gravely adopted this Indian money, and conducted their own traffic with each other, as well as with the savages, in wampum. Afterwards they used Indian corn, their staple product, as currency. Some African and East Indian tribes use cowries, another kind of small ornamental shells strung together; the inhabitants of Newfoundland adopted dried cod for this purpose, and the Abyssinians rock-salt.

Some considerations of convenience, however, have generally inclined civilized nations to adopt one or more of the metals for use as money. "Metals can not only be kept with as little loss as any other commodity, scarce anything being less perishable than they, but they can likewise, without any loss, be divided into any number of parts, and by fusion these parts can be easily reunited, — a quality which no other equally durable commodities possess, and which renders them peculiarly fit to be the instruments of commerce and circulation." The quantity of metal can be proportioned to the precise quantity of any other commodity which we have occasion to purchase. The weight and purity of a lump or bar of metal can also be determined, once for all, with great exactness; and when determined, they can be made known by a stamp, proper precautions being taken against this mark being counterfeited, and the stamp being made to cover the whole surface of the piece, so that no portion of it can be abstracted without the loss being readily perceived. The trader is thus relieved from two very considerable inconveniences, — the trouble of weighing and of assaying every piece of metal which he receives. The qualities which recommend the metals for use as currency indicate with sufficient clearness the second requisite of money, — namely, that it shall be a good common measure of value, so that an exact equivalent can be offered in it for any amount or quantity of value which we wish to exchange.

The importance of this requisite appears from the experience of the ancient Greeks, who seem to have used cattle as money; Homer tells us that the armor of Diomede cost only nine oxen, whilst that of Glaucus cost one hundred. "But cattle," says Colonel Torrens, "must have been a most inconvenient instrument of exchange. The person who wished to purchase a supply of cloth, and who had nothing to give in exchange for it but a sheep or an ox, would be obliged to buy cloth to the value of a whole sheep or a whole ox at a time. He could not buy less, because his medium of exchange, his money, could not be divided without loss; and if he wished to purchase more, he would for the same reason be obliged to take double or treble the quantity, — the value of two or three sheep, or two or three oxen. Now, it is evident that a medium so bulky, so unportable and indivisible as cattle, would frequently obstruct the interchange of commodities. Finding it often difficult, and sometimes impossible, to exchange by means of cattle the surplus products of their respective industry for the precise quantity of other articles which they might require, the inhabitants of the country in which cattle formed the only acknowledged measure of value would, on many occasions, be compelled to supply their various wants by combining in their own persons a variety of occupations. The divisions of employment would therefore be very imperfectly established; the productive powers of industry would be checked, and the country withheld from the acquisition of that general opulence which, if it possessed a more perfect instrument of mercantile industry, it would be capable of acquiring."

In fact, the want of a convenient medium of exchange increases in a direct ratio with the progress of the division of labor, and the consequent development of commercial industry. In the earliest stages of society, when each family raises and manufactures nearly all the commodities which it consumes, and therefore needs to effect but few exchanges, and can generally transact these by directly bartering its superfluities for necessaries, a very rude medium of exchange will be sufficient, or the people can do without money altogether. But when the division of labor is so far advanced that one man manufactures only a part of a knife-blade, or the fraction of a pin, and the industry of his neighbor is equally limited, some article must be selected for use as money, which will be a convenient and universally acknowledged measure of value, and possess all the other attributes requisite for effecting exchanges with quickness and facility.

Various metals have been used at different times for this purpose. The Spartans adopted iron, the ancient Romans copper, the Russians, at one time, platinum; but modern nations, with great unanimity, have preferred silver and gold. One reason for this preference is, that they have great value in proportion to their weight and bulk. Silver, of course, is less convenient in this respect than gold; to pay a debt of a quarter of a million of dollars would require the transfer of about five tons of metal. But the capital consideration in favor of these metals is, that they are less subject to fluctuations in value than any other commodity whatsoever. Not to be liable to sudden changes in value, nor as far as possible to any changes at all, is the third great requisite for money. From the time when the precious metals were first generally adopted for this purpose, up to the year 1848, they underwent only one great change in value, — that which followed the great increase in the supply of them consequent upon the discovery of the mines in Spanish America. This event, in the course of a century and a half, caused a depression of their value to about a fourth part of what it had been; that is, an ounce of silver or gold in 1650 would purchase but one fourth as much food as could have been obtained for it a century and a half earlier. With this exception, and excepting also the change which the influx of Californian and Australian gold is now effecting, the precious metals have been very steady in value; their quantity cannot be suddenly diminished; and the demand for them is so great, that any unusual productiveness of the mines cannot speedily lower their value.

The other articles which have been used as money are subject to sudden and great variations in value. An unusually abundant harvest may depress the price of corn one half in a single season. No one would be willing to accept in payment a commodity which might lose a large portion of its value while in his possession. Cattle cannot be preserved, or transported from one place to another, without considerable trouble and expense; and owing to a difference in their qualities, one ox might be worth two or three oxen of a different species. Salt, shells, and fish are equally liable to objection; the values of equal quantities of them differ considerably; some cannot be divided, and others cannot be preserved or transported, without some expense.

For obvious reasons, two or three metals are generally used together, for different denominations of money, in the same country. Gold, which contains the most value in proportion to its bulk, is most convenient for large payments; it is not so well adapted for "making change," as it is called, or settling the fractional parts of an account, even the gold dollar which is coined in the United States being inconveniently small. For sums varying from five cents to a dollar, silver is the most convenient medium, copper being used when even a silver piece would be too minute in size. Copper coins, however, are employed only as tokens, being rated from 75 to 100 per cent above their real value. The privilege of issuing them at this nominal valuation is confined to the government, and they are made legal tender only to the amount of the smallest silver coin. In France and some other countries, a compound of silver and some baser metal is sometimes coined, which not only represents, but is actually worth, the small sums for which copper is used elsewhere.

"Whatever may be the advantages attending the use of coined money," says McCulloch, "and they are great and obvious, it is necessary to observe that its introduction does not affect the nature of exchanges. Equivalents are still given for equivalents. The exchange of a quarter of corn for an ounce of pure, unfashioned gold bullion, is undeniably as much a real barter, as if it had been exchanged for an ox or a barrel of beer. But supposing the metal to have been formed into a coin, that is, marked with a stamp indicating its weight and fineness, it is plain that circumstance could have made no change in the terms of the barter. The coinage saves the trouble of weighing and assaying the bullion, but it does nothing more. A coin is merely a piece of metal of known weight and fineness; and the commodities exchanged for it are always held to be of equal value. And yet these obvious considerations have been very generally overlooked. Coined money, instead of being received in the same light as other commodities, has been looked upon as something quite mysterious. It was said to be both a *sign*, and a *measure*, of value. In truth, however, it is neither the one nor the other. A sovereign is not a *sign;* it is *the thing signified.* A promissory note, payable at some stated period, may not improperly be considered as the sign of the specie to be paid for it; but that specie is itself a commodity, possessed of real exchangeable worth. It is equally incorrect to call money a *measure* of value. Gold and silver do not measure the value of commodities, more than the latter measure the value of gold and silver. Everything possessed of value may either measure, or be measured by, everything else possessed of value. When one commodity is exchanged for another, each measures the value of the other. If the quartern loaf were sold for a shilling, it would be quite as correct to say, that a quartern loaf measured the value of a shilling, as that a shilling measured the value of a quartern loaf."

To ascertain the relative value of different commodities *at any one time and place*, I have already said that money is the best measure, simply because a silver dollar or a gold sovereign is a well-known and convenient unit of measurement;

when the coinage is in a perfect state, any one dollar or sovereign is precisely equal in weight and fineness to any other dollar or sovereign; and every article of value is more frequently exchanged for money than for any other one commodity. Tell a shoemaker that a certain house is worth *so many dollars*, and the information will be definite and intelligible to him; for he has been accustomed to barter shoes for dollars, so that, knowing what is the relative value of these two things, he can know by inference the relative value of the house and shoes, — the article that he is best acquainted with. But tell him that the house is worth *so many oxen*, and the information will probably be of little use; for he has not been wont to exchange shoes for oxen, and he knows that oxen differ widely from each other in value.

To ascertain the relative value of commodities *at different times*, especially if a long lapse of years has intervened, a bushel of wheat is a better unit of measurement, though still an imperfect one, than a dollar. The discovery of new mines or deposits of the precious metals, or the exhaustion of old ones, may have so far affected the value of bullion, that an ounce of it at the later date may purchase only half as much, or twice as much, as at the former one. The quantity of silver contained in a dollar in 1650, for instance, would buy only one fourth as much grain or meat as in 1500. But it cost about the same amount of labor to raise a bushel of wheat at one of these periods as at the other; and the whole quantity of wheat raised in England bore about the same proportion to the whole number of persons to be fed. The value of wheat, then, for long periods, is more stable than that of gold and silver. Still it is but an approximation to the ideal standard of value, which should be absolutely invariable. The corn-rents of lands in England which are let on very long leases have depreciated in value much less than the money-rents. A still nearer approximation to a fixed standard of value might be obtained by taking the average prices of a dozen of the most necessary articles in common use, wheat being one of them, and sheep, oxen, hides of leather, wool, tallow-candles, soap, &c., being added. In the average of many, the effect of accidental circumstances in varying the price of any one of them for a few years would be less a source of error.

The relative value of commodities *at different places*, as well as at different times, cannot be determined with any accuracy. Owing to differences of soil and climate, and the variety of articles that are used for human sustenance, the cost of food varies widely in different parts of the globe. The value of the precious metals in different lands will depend upon the extent of the use which is made of them, and upon the distance of the mines that produce them, and the ease or difficulty of communication with the mining regions. Perhaps the nearest approach to a standard in such cases may be found in the value of an ordinary day's labor of a person of average strength and health. But it can be easily shown that this is only a rude approximation to the truth. According to Mr. Senior, "the average annual wages of labor in Hindostan are from one pound to two pounds troy of silver a year. In England, they are from nine pounds to fifteen pounds troy. In Upper Canada and the United States of America, they are from twelve pounds troy to twenty pounds. Within the same time, the American laborer obtains twelve times, and the English laborer nine times, as much silver as the Hindoo." This prodigious difference cannot be explained by the difference in the value of silver in the three countries; for owing to the facilities of commercial intercourse between them, and the small cost of transporting silver from New York or Liverpool to Calcutta, an inequality of this sort could not exist; dollars would be transported to Calcutta, if they would purchase commodities of much greater value there than in England or America. Neither can the whole difference be attributed to the only cause of it which is assigned by Mr. Senior; namely, the greater diligence, energy, and skill with which English and American labor is applied, the latter being assisted, moreover, by superior fertility of soil and greater extent of territory in proportion to the population. Unquestionably some effect is thus produced; but as only rude labor is in question, it would be extravagant to assume that twelve Hindoos can accomplish only as much as one American. The inequality must rather be attributed in great part to the undue depression of the laboring classes both in England and Hindostan, arising from the very unequal distribution of wealth in the two countries, the great bulk of the population thus consisting of laborers for hire, who are solely dependent upon wages, and are constantly competing with each other for employment. In Hindostan, this effect is very much increased, of course, by the low standard of living, and the cheapness of rice and cotton cloth, which, in that climate, are almost the only necessaries of life. In America, the laborer must have thicker and better clothing, more fuel, a more perfect shelter from the weather; and he also expects a greater amount, variety, and delicacy of food. He is enabled to obtain these additional comforts, because the class to which he belongs is not so numerous in proportion to the rest of the community, because there is consequently not so much competition for employment, and because, if wages are not high enough to satisfy him, he will leave the class of laborers, and become a small landholder, or enter into trade or manufacture on his own account.

Adam Smith long ago distinguished the *real price* of commodities from their *nominal price.* Their real price, he says, is the labor which it costs to produce them. So it is; but when they are once produced, their real *selling* price is the amount of the necessaries, conveniences, or amusements of life that can be obtained in exchange for them. Every man is rich or poor, according to the degree in which he can afford to enjoy these things; and the real value or price of all the commodities which he possesses, therefore, is the amount of these things which his commodities will purchase. On the other hand, the nominal price of his goods is the money — the number of shillings or dollars — which they will bring. This price is called nominal, because for two reasons it is uncertain in amount; it varies with the fluctuations in value of the precious metals, arising from the larger or smaller supply of them obtained from the mines, and it varies with the higher or lower price of the commodities which we wish to purchase with the money. The price may be nominally the same, that is, it may be represented by the same number of shillings or dollars; but it may purchase a larger or smaller amount of commodities than before. Thus, wages and salaries have generally risen in the United States during the last five years, the amount of the increase being, on an average, at least fifteen per cent; but the rise is only nominal, as $115 will not now purchase any more necessaries and comforts than could be bought for $100 in 1850. A portion of the rise is directly proved to be nominal by the fact, that the dollar does not now contain so much pure silver as it did before 1853 by about seven per cent. Only 345.6, instead of 371.25, grains of pure silver are now coined into a dollar.

It has already been said, that money is not a sign of value, because it possesses value in itself; it is the thing signified. It is custom and the general consent of the community, not the authority of government, nor the stamp upon the face of the coin, which causes money to pass current, like other commodities, and to be received in exchange for them. The stamp is a convenience, as we have seen; for it saves the trouble of weighing and assaying every piece which the seller receives. But if government should affix the stamp which now belongs to a silver dollar to a piece of copper of similar shape and size, and should call this base coin a dollar, it could not oblige the people to receive it as such, or to give their goods in exchange for it at its nominal valuation. It is not the stamp, nor the authority which affixes the stamp, but the known value and weight of the metal which receives the impression, that renders money universally acceptable, or gives it currency. In this matter, as in many others, the government even of a despotic state cannot govern, except by respecting the wishes and preferences of its subjects. If there was good reason to believe that any other commodity — wheat, for instance — would pass more currently in exchange for the various articles which are needed, people would not give their goods for dollars, but would demand wheat, which would then be invested with all the properties of money. And this, as M. Say remarks, has sometimes occurred in practice, when the authorized or government money has consisted of paper which has lost public confidence. The business of coining money, or of dividing the precious metals into pieces of a convenient shape and size, and affixing a convenient stamp, is usually retained exclusively in the hands of the government, to secure the advantages of uniformity, undivided responsibility, and public confidence. If individuals were allowed to assume this office, we should be perplexed by a multitude of coins of different denominations, and we could never be sure that the stamp correctly indicated the weight and fineness of the metal.

Seigniorage is a charge made by government to defray the expenses of the mint, or the cost of converting bullion into coined money. The machinery for coining money is now brought to such perfection, that the actual expense of this process is but trifling; it is computed to amount to one half of one per cent (.005) for gold coins, and one and a half per cent (.015) for silver coins. Some governments, among which, till recently, were those of Great Britain and the United States, performed this work gratuitously, or took upon themselves the expense of the coinage. Any person might carry any amount of gold and silver bullion of the requisite fineness to the mint, and, after the time required for coining so much metal had elapsed, or as soon as the demands of previous applicants were satisfied, he was entitled to receive an exactly equivalent weight of gold or silver coins. But the time required for the process, or to satisfy previous comers, involved the loss of a small amount of interest; and it was therefore provided in the United States law, that the owner of the bullion might receive an equivalent weight of gold and silver coins for it immediately, with a deduction of one half of one per cent, as an indemnification to the mint for the delay caused by the coinage. At present, however, the law of 1853 provides that the depositor of gold bullion shall always pay this charge of one half of one per cent, and the government reserves to itself the privilege of issuing as much silver coin as the public seem to require, at a profit of about five per cent. The French government levies a seigniorage of only $\frac{1}{3}$ per cent on gold and $1\frac{1}{2}$ per cent on silver, — hardly enough to defray the actual expense of the process. Governments in former times attempted to convert their mints into sources of revenue, by charging a seigniorage of 10 or 15 per cent. This form of taxation, for it is nothing else, would not be practicable in our day, as private coiners would enter into competition with government, being stimulated by the large profits that would accrue from the manufacture of good coin. Their operations would flood the country with a depreciated currency; the prices of other commodities would rise in the same ratio with the over-valuation of money.

Some writers have contended that the state should not make any charge for coining money, but that the expenses of the mint should be defrayed by the public. They have an indefinite impression that the quantity of precious metals in the country might thus be increased, persons being encouraged to bring them hither by the opportunity of having them manufactured, or coined, gratuitously. Of course, this liberal offer of the government would tempt them to bring more bullion here to be coined; the only question is, whether it would stay here after it was coined. It is difficult to see that the country would gain anything by having fifty millions of dollars annually brought hither in bullion for the sole purpose of receiving the government stamp, and then immediately exported to Europe, without paying our mint anything for the process, which costs over half a million of dollars. During the five years beginning in January, 1850, the United States mint and its branches coined over 260 millions of dollars in gold. Hardly one third of this great amount of coin was needed for our own use; in fact, the custom-house returns during this period show that about 170 millions in specie were shipped from this country to Europe. What possible advantage can there be in bringing hither more gold than we want, transporting it first from San Francisco to New York, thence to Philadelphia, coining it there gratuitously at a heavy expense, carrying it back to New York, and then shipping it off immediately to London or Paris, where it will be melted up as soon as possible, and converted into English or French coins? Why should it not be shipped immediately to the place where it is needed, thus saving the entire expense of coinage, the cost of much unnecessary transportation, and the interest on the whole amount for at least two months' needless delay? It must not be supposed that England will obtain the gold, either as bullion directly from San Francisco, or as coin by way of New York, without rendering a full equivalent for it in other commodities; or that the United States suffer any loss by allowing the miner to exchange his gold for other goods. Gold is only an article of merchandise, like copper, tin, and iron; and, like them, it must be sent to the market where it is most wanted, and where, consequently, it can be sold to the greatest advantage. Would it be good policy, in order to increase the stock of copper in this country, to enact that the pig metal should be manufactured into sheets, plates, and rods at the expense of government, without charge to the owner, who should also receive a free gift of the interest on the whole value of the copper during the time required for its manufacture? Such a law would doubtless bring all the Chilian copper hither, to be put into a form fit for use, and England and France would then obtain their share of it without any charge for the transformation it had undergone. As McCulloch remarks, "those who contend that the state ought to defray the expense of the coinage, might, with equal cogency of reasoning, contend that it ought to defray the expense of manufacturing gold and silver teapots, vases, &c. In both cases, the value of the raw material, or bullion, is increased by the cost of workmanship. And it is only fair and reasonable that those who carry bullion to the mints, as well as those who carry it to the jewellers, should have to defray the expenses necessarily attending its conversion into coin."

"But there are other reasons," continues McCulloch, "why a seigniorage, to this extent at least, ought to be exacted. Wherever the expenses of coinage are defrayed by the state, an ounce of coined gold or silver, and an ounce of gold or silver bullion, must be very nearly of the same value. And hence, whenever it becomes profitable to export the precious metals, coins, in the manufacture of which a considerable expense has been incurred, are sent abroad indifferently with bullion," and even in preference to it, as the latter must be weighed and assayed when it reaches its place of destination, while the coins bear the evidence of their weight and fineness on their face. "Admitting, however, that it were possible, which it most certainly is not, to prevent, or at least materially limit, the clandestine exportation of coins, it is conceded on all hands to be quite nugatory to attempt to prevent their conversion into bullion. In this there is almost no risk. And the security with which their fusion can be effected, and the trifling expense attending it, will always enable them to be melted down and sent abroad whenever there is any unusual foreign demand for the precious metals. This exportation, however, would either be prevented or materially diminished by the imposition of a seigniorage or duty, equal to the expense of the coinage. The coins, being by this means rendered more valuable than bullion, would be kept at home in preference; and if, as Dr. Smith has observed, it became necessary on any emergency to export coins, they would, most likely, be reimported. Abroad, they would be worth only so much bullion; while at home, they would be worth this much, and the expense of coinage besides. There would, therefore, be an obvious inducement to bring them back, and the supply of currency would be maintained at its proper level, without its being necessary for the mint to issue fresh coins."

An alteration in the relative value of gold and silver, or, indeed, between any other two media of exchange which are united in one currency, produces immediately a marked effect. The one which is over-valued, or of which the nominal exceeds the real value, at once displaces or pushes out the other, and takes the whole circulation to itself. As fast, for instance, as gold becomes depreciated in consequence of the influx of that metal from the deposits recently discovered, silver will disappear, or cease to be used as currency, if measures are not taken to obviate this effect by putting a smaller amount of silver into a dollar. The reason is obvious. Suppose this depreciation to amount to only five per cent, or that silver in that ratio should become more valuable than gold. Then, every one who makes a purchase or pays a debt in silver, pays five per cent more than if he used gold. Silver would generally be sold, or exchanged, for gold, in order to obtain the premium, or difference in value; and because, if used as coin, it could only pass at par with gold, it would be melted up, and devoted to the other uses to which it is subservient, — as to the manufacture of plate, — or it would be sent out of the country.

Hence the great inconvenience that is experienced, when, in a country where both specie and bank-notes are current, the latter become depreciated in consequence of the failure of the banks to redeem them in specie. The immediate effect is, that the smaller coins, which supply "change," as it is called, at once disappear, being gathered up by the money-changers, and either melted, or sent out of the country to some place where the depreciated notes will not pass current. The only mode of stemming this current is for the banks to restrict their issues, till the necessity for having a certain amount of value to fill the ordinary channels of circulation raises the value of the depreciated notes again to par. Another cause tends to increase the drain of gold and silver under such circumstances. Money being the universal medium of exchange, its value operates reciprocally against prices; that is, as money rises in value, prices fall; and as money is depreciated, prices of all other commodities rise. Of course, in the latter case, goods are imported in large quantities, to take advantage of this rise in price. These goods must be paid for, and as they come from foreign countries, where the depreciated money will not pass, gold and silver must be collected to discharge the debt. In this manner, even the smaller coins are gathered and sent off, till it becomes impossible to obtain "change" for the smallest bank-note. The necessity of having some money of a small denomination then gives currency to some remarkable substitutes for coin. Omnibus tickets, pieces of bank-notes, and tokens, or "shin-plasters," as they are vulgarly termed, — certificates of value to a small amount, issued by municipal authority, and receivable in payment for taxes, — all circulate as money, and supply the place of "change."

The principle, that money which is depreciated in real value, though to a very slight amount, always drives out, and takes the place of, the sounder portion of the currency, received a remarkable illustration from the operations of the banks in Massachusetts about thirty years ago. Up to that time, the bills of the country banks were redeemed only at their own counters, in various parts of the State. The operations of trade brought large amounts of their bills into Boston, where they circulated as currency. But the banks in Boston would not receive them, either on deposit or in payment of notes; for they could not afford to sort them into parcels, and send one little parcel into Berkshire, and another to Nantucket, bringing back from each place a corresponding amount of coin, with all the expense of transportation. These country bank bills, consequently, not being redeemable in the place where they circulated, were naturally depreciated, or became subject to discount, in comparison with the bills of the Boston banks, which were redeemed in specie on the spot. The discount was very small, varying from one to two per cent, according to the distance of the bank from Boston. What was the consequence? These depreciated and so far dishonored bills drove the good Boston bills almost wholly out of the market, and, so to speak, took the circulation to themselves. The law which I have spoken of, that a depreciated or over-valued medium of exchange will drive away the sound currency, was fully exemplified. How this result was effected can be easily explained. Every merchant who had dealings with the Boston banks laid aside or reserved all the Boston bank-bills that he received, for the sake of making deposits or paying his obligations at the banks. The country bank-bills that came into his hands he paid out again, either in change to his customers, or in payment for articles purchased. Thus the depreciated country bank paper was maintained in circulation; the good bills, not subject to discount, were returned to the banks as soon as issued. Every one knows that the profits of a bank, other things being equal, depend on the amount of their paper which they can keep in circulation. The country banks, therefore, profited by the dishonor of their paper; the Boston banks suffered by keeping up the credit of their bills. This injustice and loss could not be tolerated. Most of the Boston banks entered into a combination, headed by the Suffolk Bank, to compel the banks in the country to make provision to redeem their bills, not only at their own counters, but also in the metropolis, where often they had a larger circulation than in the locality where they were issued. Each of these banks was to be compelled to maintain on deposit with one of the Allied Banks, a sum in specie large enough to redeem immediately any amount of their own notes which might be offered to any or all the banks in Boston. Then the Allied Banks could afford to receive country bank paper at par. They would no longer be subject to discount, and would consequently keep only their share of the circulation. If any country bank should refuse to enter into this arrangement, and refuse to make the specie deposit in Boston, the Allied Banks would still receive its paper at par, till, having accumulated a large amount of its notes, they would suddenly, without warning, cause the whole sum to be presented at once at its counter for payment, a measure which would infallibly break the recusant bank.

This was the famous Allied Bank, or Suffolk Bank system, the object of so much discussion and obloquy at the time, but now so fully vindicated, and still in successful operation. It was represented as a high-handed act of oppression, a warfare of the strong against the weak, of the rich Boston corporations against their feeble but honest brethren in the country, — an attempt to compel the country banks to redeem their paper in two places at once, and to lend large sums in specie without interest to their oppressors in the metropolis. But when the subject is fully understood, nothing can be clearer than the abstract justice and expediency of the course then adopted and still pursued. So great are its advantages even to the parties who at first fancied themselves oppressed by it, that other country banks, not within the range of the system as first proposed, have petitioned to be admitted into it. It is both the duty and the interest of every institution that issues bills to serve as currency, to preserve these bills from depreciation in every place where they circulate to any extent. If, by any strange chance in the course of trade, the bills of our Boston banks should come to circulate in London, strict justice and sound policy would require them to make provision to redeem their paper in that city.

But this is a digression, which I have entered into only for the purpose of explaining the manner in which two media of exchange, like gold and silver, united in the same currency, affect each other. The government at any time may cause either to predominate, or nearly crowd the other out of circulation, by causing the preferred metal to be a little overrated in its relation to the other. It is made legal tender at a rate a little above its market value as bullion; or what would amount to the same thing, the metal which the government desires to drive out of circulation is made legal tender at a rate a little below its market value. Till within five years, France, preferring silver, underrated gold coin a little, so that silver circulated almost exclusively in that country, and gold coin could be obtained there only by paying a little premium. In Great Britain, on the other hand, till 1816, silver was underrated in proportion to gold, so that the latter metal circulated by preference, except in change for small sums; and though, at the period spoken of, this state of things was reversed, yet in order to prevent the overvalued silver currency from driving the gold out of the country, it was enacted that silver should be legal tender to the extent of forty shillings only, and private persons were prohibited from coining it. Silver, consequently, in

Great Britain occupies merely a subordinate place in the currency, just as copper does in that country and elsewhere. In the United States, till the Gold Bill of 1834 was passed, gold was underrated, and therefore had disappeared from the circulation, — the product even of our own gold mines in Carolina and Georgia being sent to England for coinage. To remedy this evil, the Gold Bill was passed, requiring the eagle, which was rated at ten silver dollars, to contain only 232 grains of pure gold, instead of 247, which were formerly put into it. Of course, 23.2 grains of gold, or 371.25 grains of silver, passed indifferently for one American dollar; these two numbers are in the relation to each other very nearly of one to sixteen, which was, up to 1850, about the true relation of the market values of the two metals; and they therefore circulated indifferently in this country, till the discoveries in California and Australia again changed their relation to each other.

Not many years ago, our small-coin currency was flooded with old Spanish *pistareens*, as they were termed, — a much worn coin, worth about 18½ cents. They had come into circulation as of the value of 20 cents; and in consequence of this over-valuation, amounting to nearly 8 per cent, nearly all of these coins which were in existence found their way hither. To drive them out, it was resolved at the post-offices and the banks, that they should be received only at the valuation of six to a dollar, or 16⅔ cents, — a point as much below their true value as the former estimate had been above it. The effect was almost instantaneous; the coins were either melted up or sent out of the country, and a pistareen is now rarely to be seen. Whenever it is judged expedient to drive out the old Spanish eighths and quarters of a dollar, most of which have lost from 6 to 8 per cent of their value by abrasion, a similar course must be adopted.

The precious metals have an inherent value of their own, wholly apart from their use as money. They are used in the arts, in fabricating plate and jewelry, and thus bear a price in the market like any other commodity, founded on the uses which they subserve, and the difficulty of obtaining them, or the amount of labor which must be expended for their production. It is a knowledge of this fact, that they have an independent value, less liable to fluctuation than that of any other

26

commodity, which gives them currency as money, which causes individuals to receive them with confidence that their value will not be depreciated while in their hands. And it is important to observe, that their adoption to serve as money considerably augments their intrinsic value, or their worth as an article of commerce. It is equivalent to the discovery of a new utility of these metals, and a consequent enlargement of the demand for them, while the supply is left as it was before. The employment of a great part, the half, or perhaps three fourths, of the whole stock of them on hand, as money, necessarily renders the whole more scarce and dear. In a word, the employment of the precious metals in manufacture makes them scarcer and dearer as money; and in like manner, their employment as money makes them scarcer and dearer in manufacture. I dwell upon this point, because, when we once see that the precious metals derive a part of the value with which they are invested solely from their use as money, we shall be better prepared to admit, what I shall afterwards have occasion to prove, that other articles, of little or no intrinsic value, may be used as money, and, in consequence solely of such use, may receive a very high value.

There is a larger demand for silver in the arts and for purposes of ornament, than for gold; and this larger consumption of silver makes its value higher in comparison with gold than it would be if their respective values were determined solely by the comparative quantity of each which is produced or can be obtained. Silver plate, in greater or less quantity, is in almost universal use; gold plate, from its greater expensiveness, is hardly at all in use, except by crowned heads, or persons of immense fortunes. Silver-plated ware is also manufactured in great quantities, while comparatively few articles are coated with gold, except in the form of gold-leaf, which is very cheap on account of its marvellous tenuity and fragility. Silver spoons are to be found in almost every house; and the consumption of this metal for watches and trinkets is also very great. The consequence is, that, though 45 times more silver than gold existed, and was annually produced from the mines, the value of silver was to that of gold, not as 45 to 1, but as 16 to 1. Its cheapness enlarged its use; and the extensiveness of its use, on the other hand, counteracted its cheapness, or rendered it dearer.

If we apply this principle to the depreciation of the value of gold, which is now taking place on account of the recently enlarged supplies of that metal, we see at once a new limit to that depreciation, or a reason why it cannot go so far as it otherwise would. To double the present amount of gold bullion in the market would not be to sink gold coin to half of its present value. As its value fell, the use or consumption of it would be greatly increased. Gold plate would become fashionable, gold trinkets would be far more common, and gold would even be applied to certain purposes in the arts, for which it is admirably fitted by its ductility, great specific gravity, and power of resisting oxidation or corrosion, — uses from which it is now excluded by its high cost. The discovery of America increased the supply of gold and silver tenfold; but they were thereby reduced, not to one tenth, but only to one fourth, of their former value.

The most important quality of money, when considered as an engine of commerce, and even as a means of civilization, is its stability of value. If money is depreciated in value, every creditor in the community, during the time of its depreciation, suffers loss and wrong to the full extent of the fall in value; he has lent, we will suppose, a thousand dollars, at a time when that sum was equivalent to two hundred barrels of flour, or a proportionate amount of any other commodity; and he is paid when the sum will no longer purchase more than one hundred and fifty barrels: and what he unjustly loses, his debtor, of course, unjustly gains. If the value of money rises, this process is reversed; the creditor now gains, and the debtor loses, both in proportion to the enhancement of value. In former centuries, governments, when heavily in debt, often had recourse to a depreciation of the coin, as a means of relieving themselves from their embarrassments. It was beyond their power to effect an actual change in the market value of gold and silver bullion, such as would result from an enlarged or diminished supply of these metals from the mines. But their debts were contracted under a certain denomination, just as a debtor at the present day is bound to pay a certain number of *dollars*, under an implied, but not an express agreement, that the dollar shall retain its present, or rather its former, amount of metal, — that is, 371¼ grains of silver, or 23.2 grains of gold.* If the government should decree that the dollar in future should contain only 186 grains, he might nominally release himself from his debt by paying only half of what he had really contracted to pay. This is a very rude expedient, — an actual license of universal bankruptcy, all claims being released on a payment of 50 per cent. It has not been tried in modern times, for even the courts of law would afford a remedy against so gross a fraud. But it was frequently resorted to in the Middle Ages, and a curious monument of the fact is preserved to us in the names of certain coins. The English pound sterling, in the time of Edward I. contained a pound-weight of silver of known fineness; and the English *penny* was then a real *pennyweight* of silver, — the twentieth part of an ounce, or the two hundred and fortieth part of a pound. Even the word *shilling* seems to have been originally a denomination of weight, or another name for an *ounce*. By successive depreciations of the coin, the pound, shilling or ounce, and pennyweight of money have come to contain only a third part of the silver which their names indicate. A pound sterling contains less than four ounces of silver. The Scotch pound has only a thirty-sixth part, and the French *livre*, or pound, only a sixty-sixth part, of their original weight of silver.

This mode of depreciating the *metallic* currency was called, by a singular abuse of language, "raising the standard." It has not been tried in modern times, as I have said, because it is so palpable a fraud that the courts of law would probably afford a remedy against it. But these courts give no redress, as we all know, against a depreciation of *paper* currency precisely similar in its character and effects. In May, 1837, all the banks in the United States suspended specie payments; and the immediate consequence was a depreciation of their paper, or a rise of specie to a premium, differing in amount in the various States according to the various degrees of solvency of their respective banks; but of which the average for the whole country was at least as high as 12 per cent. The natural consequence followed, that all specie disappeared from the circulation, and all obligations were discharged in paper, —

* The silver in the dollar was diminished in 1853 to 345.6 grains, for reasons to be explained hereafter.

that is, by the payment of 88 cents on the dollar. If a person lent $ 1,000 in April of that year, to be repaid in June, he lent what was in fact 1,000 silver dollars, each worth 100 cents, and he received back only 1,000 paper dollars, each worth 88 cents. This event, of course, was an act of national and universal bankruptcy; every creditor received only about seven eighths of what was due to him, for an entire discharge of his debt. The government of the United States alone, in the exercise of its prerogatives as the sovereign, refused to submit to this loss, and obliged all its debtors to pay specie; — an act of strict justice, it is true, but one which caused it a greater loss by bad debts than it would have suffered by consenting to share the misfortune equally with the community; and which was farther so unpopular, that it was the chief cause of the overthrow of the then existing administration.

This general bankruptcy was not the only evil, or the only injustice, caused by the suspension of the banks. The community had to undergo another shock when specie payments were resumed, though the burden was reversed in reference to the class of sufferers. The debtors now suffered wrong, the creditors were unjustly benefited. If, for instance, a man obtained a loan of $ 1,000 while the depreciation was at its height, he received only what was equivalent to one thousand times 88 cents in specie; and if the day of payment came after the resumption, he was obliged to pay 1,000 times 100 cents. But the 88 cents in one case, and the 100 cents in the other, being both *called* a dollar, — so great is the deceptive power of mere names, — most persons probably were not sensible of the wrong they actually suffered. Yet to suppose that the dollar was the same thing in the two cases, would be as great an error as to imagine that the pound troy weight of silver was the same thing as the pound sterling of modern times.

26 *

CHAPTER XIX.

THE DISTRIBUTION OF THE PRECIOUS METALS THROUGHOUT THE WORLD: SUBSTITUTES FOR MONEY: BILLS OF EXCHANGE: THE COURSE OF INTERNATIONAL TRADE.

METALLIC currency, or money properly so called, it was shown in the last chapter, is a safe, but a costly, means of effecting exchanges. It is safe, because it is not subject to such ruinous fluctuations of value as took place in the paper currency of this country between 1836 and 1843. It is costly, because the expense of keeping it in repair, and the loss of profits on so large an amount of what may be called "dead capital," amount, in this country, to at least eleven per cent. It then becomes important to know what are the substitutes for its use, — substitutes which we may expect to find less safe, but also far less expensive, than metallic money. And as a preliminary to this inquiry, we wish to know how much currency is needed in each country, — or rather, since its numerical amount cannot be ascertained with any precision, how the quantity needed is affected by the growth of the population, the extension of commerce, the progress of opulence, and the general state of civilization; and also, by what law the whole quantity now in existence is distributed among the various nations of the earth, and in what way it preserves its equilibrium among them. To these inquiries the present chapter will be devoted.

In every exchange, the two values which are exchanged for each other are supposed to be equal. Every exchange is a barter of a quantity of merchandise for a certain sum of money which is its equivalent. But it does not follow that there must be in the community as much money as there is merchandise; for as the money is not consumed by effecting this exchange, it is ready immediately to effect another purchase. The same piece of money may be exchanged successively for any number of articles of merchandise of the same value; or, in other words, any sum of money can purchase successively a quantity of merchandise worth an infinitely larger sum.

The circulation of money and of merchandise bears some analogy to the *momentum* spoken of in physical science, which is composed of the velocity multiplied by the mass; the *momenta* are equal, though the velocity should be increased tenfold, provided that the mass is but one tenth part as great. So, also, the *momentum* of wealth is its value multiplied by the rapidity of its circulation. As money circulates far more rapidly than merchandise, it is evident that (the number of exchanges on both sides being equal) there must necessarily be less value in the money than in the merchandise, and as much less as the circulation of the money is more rapid than that of the merchandise. If the value of the merchandise which changes hands in a country in the course of a year amounts to a thousand millions, and the circulation of the money is ten times as quick as that of the merchandise, a hundred millions of money will effect all the exchanges. Let the quickness of the money circulation be doubled, and fifty millions will suffice.

Mr. J. S. Mill has stated this point very clearly. "If we assume the quantity of goods on sale, and the number of times those goods are resold, to be fixed quantities, the value of money will depend upon its quantity, together with the average number of times that each piece changes hands in the process. The whole of the goods sold (counting each resale of the same goods as so much added to the goods) have been exchanged for the whole of the money, multiplied by the number of purchases made on the average by each piece. Consequently, the amount of goods and of transactions being the same, the value of money is inversely as its quantity multiplied by what is called the rapidity of circulation. And the quantity of money in circulation is equal to the money value of all the goods sold [including all the resales as additional goods], divided by the number which expresses the rapidity of circulation."

Stating the matter algebraically, we have

$$g\,s = m\,r;$$

where $g =$ quantity of goods on sale;

$s =$ number of times the goods are resold;

m = quantity of money in circulation;

r = number of purchases effected by each piece of money.

Of course, any three of these quantities being given, the fourth can be deduced from them. Thus,

$$m = \frac{g\,s}{r};$$

which is the principle just enunciated. It is also evident, that the value of money will be inversely as its quantity; for if we suppose the quantity of money to be doubled, we still have

$$g\,s = 2\,m\,r;$$

whence, $$2\,m = \frac{g\,s}{r};$$

that is, 2 m is worth only the same value which was formerly represented by m.

This calculation, however, excludes all exchanges that are directly effected by barter, or into which money does not enter; and these, as we shall afterwards see, really constitute a large part of mercantile transactions. The formula represents only *money* purchases. Direct exchange of one commodity for another, by the process vulgarly called "swopping," is evidently not affected by any valuation, however arbitrary, of those commodities in money; though the two are usually represented in money, at the current market price, for convenience of calculation and intermixture with other accounts.

"The phrase, 'rapidity of circulation,'" continues Mr. Mill, "requires some comment. It must not be understood to mean, the number of purchases made by each piece of money in a given time. Time is not the thing to be considered. The state of society may be such, that each piece of money hardly performs more than one purchase in a year; but if this arises from the small number of transactions,—from the small amount of business done, the want of activity in traffic, or because what traffic there is mostly takes place by barter,—it constitutes no reason why prices should be lower, or the value of money higher. The essential point is, not how often the same money changes hands in a given time, but how often it changes hands in order to perform a given amount of traffic. We must compare the number of purchases made by the money in a given time, not with the time itself, but with the goods sold in that same time. If each piece of money changes hands on an average ten times while goods are sold to the value of a million sterling, it is evident that the money required to circulate those goods is £ 100,000. And conversely, if the money in circulation is £ 100,000, and each piece changes hands by the purchase of goods ten times in a month, the sales of goods for money which take place every month must amount on the average to £ 1,000,000.

"*Rapidity of circulation* being a phrase so ill adapted to express the only thing which it is of any importance to express by it, and having a tendency to confuse the subject by suggesting a meaning extremely different from the one intended, it would be a good thing if the phrase could be got rid of, and another substituted, more directly significant of the idea meant to be conveyed. Some such expression as 'the efficiency of money,' though not unexceptionable, would do better; as it would point attention to the quantity of work done, without suggesting the idea of estimating it by time. Until an appropriate term can be devised, we must be content to express the idea by the circumlocution which alone conveys it adequately, namely, *the average number of purchases made by each piece in order to effect a given pecuniary amount of transactions.*"

As a nation increases in opulence, the value of the merchandise it circulates also increases; and consequently it has need of more money. But this need does not increase in the same proportion with its wealth. In rich countries, the activity of the circulation enables the people to effect their exchanges with a smaller quantity of money. A given sum will suffice for ten exchanges, when in a poor country it might have effected but one. Besides, it is in wealthy countries that credit most easily takes the place of money. Not only bank-bills, but all sorts of private obligations, — drafts, bills of exchange, sales on credit, and *clearances*, (terms which will afterwards be explained,) — all become substitutes for money.

But confining ourselves for the present to the distribution of *coined* money among the various nations of the earth, I observe, that the amount which is needed by any country, and which actually circulates among its inhabitants, does not depend in the least upon the quantity which the government of that country sees fit to coin, or upon the activity of its mint. International exchanges bring the coin of one country to circulate in another; sometimes it is melted up and coined over again for this purpose, sometimes it circulates, or is held in reserve, under its original stamp. Often the larger portion of the specie reserves held by our banks consists of English sovereigns. During the sixteenth and seventeenth centuries, Spain and the Spanish colonies had the first coinage of nearly all the precious metals which found their way into circulation in Europe, simply because Spain owned the most productive silver and gold mines. The value of the money annually coined in our own United States mints, from 1841 to 1846, varied from two millions to eleven millions. In 1847, it rose to nearly twenty-three millions, much English coin and bullion being brought hither in payment for the immense quantity of bread-stuffs which we exported that year, because the crops in Europe were deficient; in the following year, it fell again to about six millions. From 1850 to 1854, the influx of Californian gold raised it to an average of fifty or sixty millions annually. Of course, the quantity actually in circulation could not have varied thus rapidly and largely. The fact is, — and I crave attention to the statement as an important and pregnant one, — that the quantity of the precious metals retained in circulation as coin, for the whole world, regulates itself through the aggregate amount of money actually needed by all mankind to effect their exchanges, — regulates itself wholly irrespective of the efforts made by one government, or by all governments, to increase or diminish its amount. If more money is coined than is thus needed to supply the aggregate want, it will infallibly be melted up again; if the mints are not active enough to supply this want, a pressure will be felt somewhere, which will compel them to quicken their action, or private coiners will somewhere take the business out of their hands.

And it is just so with the distribution of this aggregate amount of coin among various countries. No one nation can, either by the efforts of its government, by its laws, or by concert among its individual members, increase or diminish the quantity of money that circulates among them; — by no efforts directly looking towards this end, I should say; for, unquestionably, a tyrannical or foolish government, or an unwise course of legislation, may paralyze the energies of commerce, root out manufactures, or blast the hopes of the agriculturist, and thus lessen the amount of money needed, by destroying many of the enterprises and exchanges in which money is employed. But no laws prohibiting the exportation of specie, or making it penal to melt up the current coin, — no laws designed to foster one branch of trade more than another, under the belief that this particular traffic brings more coined money into the country than any other, — no such laws, I say, can ever permanently increase the amount of money in circulation. The currency distributes itself among different nations, in due proportion to the circumstances of each, just as easily as water finds its level in a pond; and such legislation as I have just adverted to can have no more effect upon such distribution, than would be produced upon the level of the pond by dipping up water in a bucket from one part and pouring it into another.

It is possible, to be sure, to displace a portion, or even the larger part, of the specie currency, and make paper currency, or some other substitute, take its place; and the specie thus displaced will either go abroad or be melted up. But the total amount of the currency will remain just as before; the value of the paper and the precious metals taken together will be just what the specie alone would be, if paper were not used. Suppose, for instance, that the currency of the United States consists of 200 millions of dollars, of which three fifths are paper money, and two fifths are specie. We might destroy all the paper portion, and specie enough would flow in from abroad to make up the currency to 200 millions again; or we might add so much to the paper, that all, or nearly all, the specie would leave us and go abroad. But the impassable limit to the real value of the paper issued would even then be 200 millions of dollars. If 300 millions of paper dollars were stamped and issued, the inevitable consequence would be, that it would sink in value, or become subject to a discount of one third, so that the aggregate *real* value would remain as before.

This self-adjusting power of the currency is a fact which it is difficult to establish directly, because the amount actually needed varies from day to day with the varying opulence of the country and the varying activity of commerce and circulation. If 200 millions be the amount now wanted, 220 millions may be needed next month, as a consequence either of our increased wealth within that time, or of a check to our prosperity and a diminished activity of circulation, growing out of a general want of confidence, and a disposition on the part both of banks and of individuals to hold larger sums in reserve. The practice of hoarding, though most common in the Asiatic states, where it is a precaution taken by individuals against arbitrary exactions by a despotic government, is not unknown in the most civilized communities of Europe and America. In times even of general prosperity and quiet, many persons of the lower and more ignorant classes keep by them a little fund in specie, stored away, perhaps, in an old stocking, as a precaution against a rainy day; and though the establishment of Savings' Banks has greatly diminished the number and amount of these little hoards, there are still enough of them, in the aggregate, to keep a considerable portion of the metallic currency, as it were, in a state of abeyance. If the currency be a mixed one of paper and specie, and if some event should happen to disturb public confidence, such as the bursting of a commercial bubble, or the discovered mismanagement of two or three banks, then commences what is called "a run upon the banks" generally, the effect of which is greatly to increase the number and amount of these hoards. To provide against the possible recurrence of such panics, the banks are obliged to keep much larger amounts of specie in reserve than would suffice for their ordinary transactions. The quantity of specie required as a basis and security for the circulation of the banks is like the thickness of timber and planking in the sides of a ship; it must suffice not merely for ordinary fair weather, but for possible storms and squalls, and now and then a sand-bank. The gold and silver coin thus stored up by banks and individuals is not a part of the circulation proper; the whole currency of the country may be divided into two portions, only one of which is active, or is daily employed in effecting exchanges; the other for a time is latent. This last portion is somewhat arbitrary in amount, depending upon the character of the people and their mood for the time being; it is only the active portion of the currency which has the self-adjusting power that I have spoken of.

In respect to the varying amounts of specie thus held in reserve by the banks, and so not entering into active circulation, Mr. Tooke justly observes, that "transmissions of the precious metals might and would take place occasionally between [Great Britain] and other countries to a considerable amount, (five or six millions *at least*,) without affecting the amount or value of the currency of the country from which or to which the transmissions were made; and without being a cause or a consequence of alteration in general prices." The stock of specie and bullion in the Bank of England, which, before 1848, used to average only about eight or nine millions sterling, in the summer of 1852 rose to twenty-two millions, or more than double the amount which the law regards as a safe basis for its circulation. But the amount of bank-notes in active circulation was not thereby increased; it was not materially greater than it had been six years before. At least twelve millions of this large bank reserve might have been sent to foreign countries, to import corn or any other needed article, without withdrawing a sovereign from the active currency, or affecting in the slightest degree the prices of other commodities. In fact, since 1852, about six millions have actually been withdrawn from the reserve, which now does not exceed sixteen millions; and yet prices generally, far from receding, have considerably advanced.

Every export of the precious metals, therefore, is not to be regarded as a contraction of the currency properly so called, nor is every import of them an enlargement of it. At the present time, in consequence of the large supplies from California and Australia, large amounts of bullion are *in transitu*, — wandering about, as it were, from one country to another, to find where they will be of most value, — before they pass into active circulation as currency. The stock of bullion in the hands of goldsmiths and silversmiths, ready for conversion into plate or jewelry, and, still more, the stock of it which already exists in the form of plate, the setting of jewels, lace, gilding, &c., might surely be exported in part, or altogether, without affecting the money market, or lowering the prices of commodities generally. But at least eight millions sterling out of the specie reserve in the Bank of England is as dead for all purposes of circulation, or for any effect upon prices, as if it existed only in the form of plate; for the reserve has not fallen below eight millions for the last thirteen years, and we have only the word of the bank officers for our assurance that this sum still exists in the vaults, where it has remained undisturbed at least since 1842. It is only when the demand for the precious metals to be exported has so far reduced the stock of specie in the banks as to alarm the latter for their own safety, and thus to cause them to diminish their discounts and their circulation, that the self-regulating power of the active currency shows itself.

The power of the currency thus to determine its own amount, arises from the reciprocal action of the quantity of money in active circulation and the prices of commodities. All exchange, as I have said, is a barter of merchandise for money; and the quantity of money which an article of merchandise will command in the market is termed its *price*. If I barter directly one article of merchandise for another, without the intervention of money, the quantity of that other article which I can obtain will depend upon the whole quantity of it in the market, when compared with the demand for it. Should there be more of it than there is needed or asked for, I can obtain a larger quantity of it in barter for the goods which I have to offer; should there be less than is wanted, I can obtain but little. Now money is that which is offered in exchange for all commodities; and the price of all articles depends upon the quantity of money, or active currency, which exists in the country. Increase that quantity, and the price of all articles inevitably rises; diminish it, and the price as certainly falls. The whole process of exchange may be compared to the operation of weighing with a well-poised balance, the money and the merchandise being placed on the opposite arms of the lever; increase the weight on the money side, and the merchandise is sure to rise. The whole operation was exemplified on the largest scale in the sixteenth century, after the discovery of the rich gold and silver mines on this continent. The quantity of coined money was increased by this discovery fourfold; and the prices of all articles rose all over the world to four times their former amount. This was called a *nominal* rise of prices, and it was nominal; for as there was no circumstance which could affect the real value of all the articles of merchandise at once, it was, in truth, not the merchandise which rose in value, but the money which fell. The fact, then, is a proof of my first position, that the real value or true amount of all the currency in the world cannot be increased or diminished at pleasure, but regulates itself; increase the quantity of it, and its true value falls in the same proportion.

We can now easily see why this fixed amount of currency for the whole world distributes itself, by its own laws, among all nations, according to their respective wants. If by any means one nation should obtain a larger portion of the whole currency of the world than falls to it by the regular course of trade, all articles of merchandise belonging to that nation must rise in price; they must be exchanged for a larger quantity of money. Articles of foreign growth and manufacture would be irresistibly attracted thither by this alteration of values. A single article might possibly be excluded by prohibitory legislation. But no arbitrary enactments can so clip the wings of commerce as to prevent it from seeking a market in a country where the prices of all commodities have risen above their average value all the world over. Foreign goods must necessarily be imported in such a case, whether by open trading or by smuggling; and being imported, they must be paid for. Money is the only redundant article in such a community, the only one which can be offered in payment; for all other goods are, by the hypothesis, of a higher price with them than in any other country, and cannot be sent abroad but by a sacrifice. Money, then, would be exported, in spite of all coast guards, and even of the penalty of death; and the currency would thus be reduced to its natural level.

The irresistible tendency of money to go abroad from places where it exists in excess, was well illustrated in 1852, both in San Francisco, California, and in Melbourne, Australia. In consequence of the immense influx of gold from the "diggings" in the neighborhood of these places, the prices of all commodities there rose to an extent which seems almost incredible. Flour was $30 a barrel; the wages of ordinary labor were $8 a day; $60 a ton was paid for coal.* Of course,

* Mr. Howitt gives the following list of prices of poultry and dairy produce in Melbourne, as late as May, 1854, after the excitement had somewhat subsided. "Turkeys, 20*s.* to 25*s.* each; geese, 20*s.* to 30*s.* each; domestic ducks, 20*s.* a pair; fowls, 16*s.* to 18*s.* a couple; and eggs, 3*s.* to 4*s.* a dozen. Fresh butter is bringing from 4*s.* to 5*s.* a pound; and sweet milk from 1*s.* 6*d.* to 2*s.* a quart."

these prices caused a prodigious importation of foreign goods. "While in 1850, the year before the gold discovery," says Mr. Howitt, "the imports of the whole colony amounted to only £ 744,925, for the year ending April 5, 1854, the declared value of imports at the port of Melbourne alone had reached the enormous sum of £ 17,675,472." The markets were quickly glutted by this rush of goods from abroad, a reaction took place, and prices fell almost as suddenly as they had risen. Whole cargoes were sold at auction, and did not bring enough to pay the expenses of freight and insurance. Meanwhile, however, the gold had been shipped off to pay for the imported commodities which had been sold at extravagant rates; and the further supplies obtained from the auriferous districts ceased to appear in the market as money, where they would have a disturbing effect on prices, but were reckoned as bullion, or an ordinary commodity for export, and sent to the ports where it could be sold on the most favorable terms.

Californian and Australian experience is rich in instruction on some other points in the theory of money, which are but imperfectly understood by most persons. Thus, when the rates of interest are very high, it is generally said that there is a scarcity *of money;* and conversely, when these rates are low, money is thought to be abundant or cheap. But the truth is, paradoxical as it may seem, that the abundance or scarcity of money, or currency, has nothing to do with the rates of interest, which rise or fall in proportion only to the quantity of floating capital which happens to be in the market seeking investment; and what is usually termed the "*money* market" is more properly called the *loan* market. So, at the period just referred to, both in Melbourne and San Francisco, *money* was marvellously plentiful and cheap, as was indicated by the extravagantly high prices of all commodities. At the same time, the rates of interest at those places were exorbitant, varying from 36 to 48 per cent a year; these rates prevailed because profits were very high, and there was a great deficiency of *capital*, notwithstanding the extraordinary abundance of *money*.

So, also, the severe reverses which attend a period of wild speculation, terminating in a "commercial crisis," are usually imputed to the bad management of the banks, which are said to deluge the community with their "paper money," as it is reproachfully called, at one moment, and at the next, are compelled to withdraw their excessive issues, and to raise the value of money as suddenly as they had lowered it, greatly to the detriment of the mercantile community, who suffer equally by each extreme. To restrict the issue of bank-notes, and to recur to a "hard currency," is the measure usually recommended at such periods to prevent the return of the calamity. But the fact is, that neither paper money nor coined money has anything to do with these injurious alternations, which usually proceed from the opening of a new source of business, supposed to be attended with immense profits, the rush of capitalists into this new employment, the extravagant rates of interest which they are tempted to pay from their anticipation of extravagant profits, and the inevitable recoil or disappointment of their hopes, either from the new business being overdone, or from the detected fallacy of the original representations concerning it. No commercial crisis was ever more severe than that which occurred in California in 1853–4, and in Australia in 1854–5; and these surely were not attributable to any improper action of the banks, for there were then no banks of issue in those countries, and the "hard currency" which had always existed there did not avert the storm. Not the abundance of money, but the excessive profits which resulted from the anomalous state of trade there, first created the fever of speculation which was the original source of the evil; and the scarcity *of money* was so far from being the cause, or the characteristic feature, of the recoil, that hard money continued to be throughout the crisis, what it had been in the preliminary period, the staple article of export to other lands.

But this is a digression, and I return to the subject of the equalization of the currency. We have seen what will be the turn of trade when money is redundant. In the other case, if the currency of any nation should fall below the average proportion to its wants, the prices of all merchandise would fall, they being exchanged against a smaller amount of money. There would be a tendency, then, to export all commodities, since a profit could be made by the sale of them in foreign countries rather than at home. And in payment for the commodities thus sent abroad, money must be returned till the equilibrium of the currency is restored. Thus the equal distribution of specie among all countries, in proportion to the wants of each, takes place through the inevitable tendencies of trade, all goods invariably seeking a market where they can be sold to the best advantage. The equalization of money is but another name for the equalization of prices. The general principle has been clearly stated by Mr. Ricardo, who has shown "that redundancy and deficiency of currency are only relative terms; and that, so long as the currency of a particular country consists exclusively of gold and silver coins, *or of a paper immediately convertible into such coins*, its value can neither rise above nor fall below the value of the currencies of other countries by a greater sum than will suffice to defray the expense of importing foreign coin or bullion, if the currency be deficient; or of exporting a portion of the existing supply, if it be redundant."

Regarding this principle as established, that the currency is of a fixed amount or value, I come now to consider the various practices and expedients by which the necessity of filling up the whole of this currency with so costly a material as gold and silver coin is obviated. Some of these may properly be viewed, not as substitutes for the precious metals, but as practices which have grown up in commercial countries, whereby commercial transactions are really completed without the intervention of any money. Such are what are termed *accounts current*, opened between merchants who have frequent dealings with each other. If, for instance, A has occasion, in the course of a year, to make a hundred different purchases of B, and B to buy as frequently and about as largely from A, were each transaction to be completed and settled by itself at the time, two hundred transfers of different sums of money from one to the other must be made in a twelvemonth. But if each party chose to allow the other credit till a fixed time for settlement, then the whole amount of purchases on one side might be deducted from the whole amount on the other, and only the balance be paid in money. If nine tenths of an account are thus settled by offsets, and only one tenth by cash, it is evident that nine tenths of the trade has been a direct barter of one kind of merchandise for another, just as if money, or a universal medium of exchange, had never been invented. It is by practices analogous to this, rather than by increased rapidity of circulation, as I believe, that a nation's want of currency does not increase in as rapid a ratio as its population and its opulence. Even when the sales are all made by one of the parties, a person who has credit with him may adjust by a single payment in cash several hundred different purchases made at various times since the former settlement. It is important to remember such familiar facts as these, when an attempt is made to attribute all the evil of over-trading to an undue expansion of paper currency, and a scarcity of specie. We see that over-trading may take place to any extent, without the intervention of any currency whatever, whether paper or metallic.

Another mode of avoiding the frequent transfer of specie is the transfer or sale of debts. If a merchant has a sum of money due to him by one person, A, while he owes an equivalent sum to another, B, he can cancel both obligations at once, without having the money pass through his own hands at all, by simply giving B an order upon A for the amount required. Here, one operation — one transfer of currency — evidently takes the place of two; instead of A paying the given sum to the merchant, and the merchant immediately paying it over to B, A pays it directly to B, and the account is squared all round. If the merchant does business in New York, while A and B are both resident in London, such an order is called a bill of exchange, and the saving of trouble and expense that is effected by it is very obvious; without such an order, A must pay his debt by shipping the required amount of specie from London to New York; and then the merchant, in order to pay *his* debt to B, must immediately ship the specie back again to London. There would then be a loss of time enough for making two voyages across the ocean, a loss of interest on the money during this time, and the cost of freight and insurance on the amount during two voyages. All this expense and inconvenience are saved by the simple expedient of a bill of exchange, or an order for the transfer of a debt.

It may happen that the merchant, though he has a debt due to him in London, does not himself owe any money in that city; still, he will not be obliged to have the specie sent to him by sea, if he can find another merchant in New York who does owe a debt in London to precisely the same amount. The first merchant, C, will then sell his debt to the second merchant, D, or in other words, sell him a bill of exchange, which, when paid in London by A to B, at once cancels A's debt to C, and D's debt to B. Two payments of money, the one from A to B, who are both in London, and the other from D to C, who are both in New York, evidently cancel four obligations, two of which, one from A to C, and another from D to B, are eliminated, or set off against each other, their direct adjustment being inconvenient, because the respective parties to them reside in different cities.

We can now understand what is meant by the course and par of exchange. All the merchants in New York who have debts *due to them* in London, draw bills of exchange for the amount of these debts, and go into market to sell these bills to other New York merchants who have debts *to pay* in London. If the former set have a larger amount to sell than the latter have occasion to buy, — or, in other words, if a greater amount of debt is due from London to New York, than from New York to London, — the competition of the selling merchants with each other will lower the price of these bills a little, or subject them to a small discount. A bill of exchange for one hundred dollars may not bring in the market more than 98½ dollars; the exchange is then said to be 1½ per cent against London, or 1½ per cent below par. It *cannot* fall much lower than this, for the merchant, rather than take 98 dollars for his bill, will cause the 100 dollars to be sent over to him by his London debtor in specie; the freight, insurance, and other charges, cannot amount to more than two dollars. Whenever, then, the exchange falls about 1½ per cent below par, we may expect that shipments of specie from England to America will begin. On the other hand, if a greater amount of debt is due from New York to London than from London to New York, then there will be more buyers than sellers of such bills in New York market; and the competition of these buyers with each other may cause a bill for $100 to sell for $101.50. The difference cannot be much greater than this, or it would cause specie to be shipped from America to England. The exchange is then said to be against New York, or 1½ per cent above par.

In order to simplify this explanation, I have supposed the

metallic currency of the two countries to consist of the same denomination of coin, — namely, of dollars. But this is not the case; the New York merchant who has a debt due to him in London, draws a bill of exchange, not for so many dollars, but for so many pounds sterling, or sovereigns. Now the American dollar, or the tenth part of an eagle, contains, as we have seen, 23.2 grains of pure gold, and the English sovereign has 113 grains and a small fraction. These two numbers are to each, very nearly, as 1 to 4.87. The exchange, then, is really at par when a bill on London for 100 pounds sterling sells in New York for 487 dollars. This, I say, is the *real* par; the *nominal* par, established in 1789, and ever since retained in exchange operations, made the dollar equal to 4*s.* 6*d.* sterling, and the pound sterling, therefore, worth only $ 4.44. The present value of the pound sterling, $ 4.87, is about 9½ per cent more than this; and therefore the exchange is really at par, when, according to the prices current, it is 9½ per cent above par. The expense of shipping specie either way being about 1½ per cent, when the exchange nominally rises to about 11 per cent, specie will be shipped from New York to London; when it nominally falls below 8 per cent, specie will be shipped from London to New York. As the quoted price of exchange at New York is for bills on London at sixty days' sight, allowance must be made for interest for this time.

It is easy to see that the par of the currency of any two countries means, among merchants, the equivalence of a certain amount of the currency of the one in the currency of the other, supposing the currencies of both to be of the precise weight and purity fixed by their respective mints. Thus, according to the mint regulations of Great Britain and France, the same quantity of pure gold which in London is coined into one pound sterling, in Paris is coined into 25 francs and 20 centimes; and accordingly, this is said to be the par between the two countries. The exchange between the two countries is said to be at par when bills are negotiated on this footing; that is, when a bill for £ 100 drawn on London is worth 2,520 francs in Paris, and conversely. As we have already seen that $ 4.87 in New York equals one pound sterling in London, it follows that $ 4.87 also equals 25 francs 20 centimes in Paris; or, what is the same thing, one American dollar is worth 5 francs 17 centimes and a small fraction, which is the par of exchange between France and the United States.

From the explanation now given, it appears very clearly that bills of exchange represent the items in the account current between England and America; and the specie shipped either way is the cash balance that is struck on the adjustment of the account. Bills of exchange are not drawn against air; they represent real transactions. The New York merchant cannot draw bills on London unless he has debts *due to him* there, which debts have been contracted for cotton, flour, tobacco, and other American products, which he had sent thither to be sold. On the other hand, a New York merchant cannot have debts *to pay* in London, except in return for manufactured goods, whether of cotton, silk, woollen, or iron, which he has received from England, and consumed or sold in America. And in the long run, it is evident that our exported goods must exactly pay for our imported goods, or the two sides of the account must balance each other. If they did not balance, if our exports were not equivalent in value to our imports, the deficiency would have to be made up by sending specie abroad; and a continued drain of specie, according to what has already been demonstrated, would raise the value of the money left behind, and, in consequence of raising the value of money, would lower the prices of goods in America; and the influx of specie into England would lower the value of money there, and raise the prices of goods. Erelong, then, the tide would turn; more goods would be sent from America, where they are *lower* in price, to England, where they are *higher* in price; and in payment for these goods, the current of specie would set in the opposite direction, till the value of money in the two countries was equalized again.*

* There is a curious feature in the management of the trade between England and the United States, which is in marked contrast with the course of mercantile transactions between England and all other commercial nations. For some inexplicable reason, the bills of exchange are all drawn one way. In Boston and New York, bills can always be purchased on London or Liverpool; but neither London nor Liverpool is supplied with any bills on Boston or New York. When cotton or flour is purchased in America for the English market, the seller draws bills of exchange on the consignee of the goods for the proceeds of the sale, and disposes of these bills in the New York market. But when manufactured goods are bought in Great Britain for the American market, the seller, instead of drawing directly on the New

The exports of any country must exactly balance its imports, for the same reason that, when two individual producers of different articles trade exclusively with each other, they must really barter merchandise for merchandise, exchanging equivalent values of different kinds; money serving no purpose between them but that of facilitating the exchanges of goods; — and this is, in fact, the only office that money, as such, ever performs. It is oil that diminishes the friction of exchanges. If, for instance, a hatter trades exclusively with a shoemaker, the former can buy no more shoes than he can sell hats with which to pay for them. He may, indeed, run in debt for a large stock of shoes at once; but that debt he will be obliged ultimately to pay by restricting his purchases of shoes, and enlarging his sales of hats. So, this country, trading with all the rest of the world, can buy no more foreign products than it has domestic products with which to pay for them. Money and bills of exchange cannot help us to pay our debts; they only facilitate and represent the operations out of which those debts have grown. Thus, in the fatal year 1836, the imports into the United States were about 190 millions of dollars, and the exports were less than 129 millions, — apparently a balance of 61 millions against us; a sum much too large to be accounted for by the ordinary profits of trade and charges of transportation. We ran deeply in debt that year, and had to suffer for it afterwards. In 1838, the balance was 5 millions, and in 1839, it was 41 millions, the other way. The sum of these two, or 46 millions, probably paid off, or

---

York merchant to whom the goods are consigned, draws on a banker in London, and the bills so drawn are accepted by the banker on commission for the American purchaser, who undertakes to make provision for them before they become due by making remittances of English bills which he purchases in New York. Of course, the London banker, by accepting the bills before remittances are made to meet them, becomes responsible for their payment, and charges an extra commission for assuming this responsibility.

In reference to this anomalous course of business, Mr. W. J. Lawson, the author of a "History of Banking," remarks: "To place the trade of America on the same footing as that of all other commercial nations has long been a desideratum. Numerous appeals, in the shape of pamphlets and other publications, recommending the adoption of a course of exchange between the two countries, have brought conviction to the mind of almost every mercantile man; yet, strange to say, no step has yet been taken to effect the object; it is an evil which must ultimately work its own cure."

nearly paid off, the balance contracted the other way, in 1836, of 61 millions. For it is important to state, that, although we must really pay for our imports with our exports, the former must always exceed the latter in nominal amount, if we take the home valuation of both. This may easily be perceived by attending to a single voyage of one ship. Suppose a merchant sends a cargo of oil to Russia, and brings back a ship-load of duck, iron, hemp, and other Russian products. If his venture be a successful one, it is evident that the aggregate value of the return cargo must so far exceed that of the outward cargo as to pay the charges of transportation both ways, and afford a reasonable profit on both parts of the transaction. Estimate the values in the Russian port, and it will appear that our general proposition holds true; the oil exactly paid for the duck, iron, and hemp, — the exports just balanced the import. Estimated in the American port, the duck, iron, and hemp exceed in value the oil enough to pay the charges of the voyage and leave a profit.

I borrow another striking illustration of this law from a speech by the great Senator of Massachusetts. Many "years ago," says Mr. Webster, "in better times than the present, a ship left one of the towns of New England with seventy thousand specie dollars. She proceeded to Mocha on the Red Sea, and there laid out these dollars in coffee, spices, drugs, &c. With this new cargo, she proceeded to Europe; two thirds of it were sold in Holland for one hundred and thirty thousand dollars, which the ship brought back, and placed in the same bank from the vaults of which she had taken her original outfit. The other third was sent to the ports of the Mediterranean, and produced a return of twenty-five thousand dollars in specie, and fifteen thousand dollars in Italian merchandise. These sums together make one hundred and seventy thousand dollars imported, which was a hundred thousand dollars more than was exported"; and yet, in each foreign port which the ship visited, equal values were exchanged. In those ports, the imports exactly balanced the exports; but in the New England harbor, the imports exceeded the exports by this large sum, which, minus the charges of transportation, was all profit.

This illustration brings us to an important qualification of the principle as first stated, and to an explanation of another purpose, or office, of bills of exchange. To simplify the matter, I supposed at first that the United States traded with England alone, that bills of exchange facilitated our transactions with her; and we were thus led to the general proposition, that foreign trade is really a barter of merchandise for merchandise, equal values being exchanged, and money playing only a very subordinate part in the affair. But foreign trade is only a long and heavy *account current* of one nation with all the rest of the world, charges on one side being *set off* by charges on the other, and the account being finally adjusted by the transfer of a comparatively trifling sum in cash to represent the balance. Our trade is not confined to England; it extends to every nation of the earth, and to every isle of the sea. The account is not balanced with each nation separately; far from it. In the case of China, our purchases very much exceed our sales; in the case of the British kingdom, our sales very much exceed our purchases. We set off one case against the other; we pay our debt to China by transferring to her a portion of the debt owed to us by Great Britain, — bills of exchange enabling us to transfer debts not only from one individual to another, but from one country to another. We annually buy tea and other Chinese products to the amount of 10½ millions; we export directly to China less than four millions. The balance, which is evidently too great to be accounted for solely by charges of transportation and profits of trade, we pay by sending to China bills of exchange on London. On the other hand, our annual exports to the British West Indies are from four to five millions, while our imports from these islands seldom exceed one million. We may receive pay for the balance by bills of exchange on London; that is, the West India planters pay us for the articles of provision that we send to them, by transferring to us a part of the debt due to them for the sugar, molasses, spirits, &c., which they have sent to England. These very bills of exchange, emanating from the British West Indies, we might use in paying our debt to China for tea. One article of merchandise is really paid for with another, though the one is obtained from Canton, and the other is sent to Jamaica. Very little money is used in the whole circle of transactions; a single shipment of half a million of dollars may suffice to balance an immensely long account, opened with England, the continent of Europe, China, and both Indies, amounting in the aggregate to sixty or seventy millions.

If we examine the facts as they are given in the official returns, we find that they agree with the theory. The reports, for instance, for the year ending June 30, 1844, show that the imports entered for consumption, exclusive of specie, amounted to more than 96 millions of dollars, while the coin and bullion we sent abroad that year was but $ 5,454,214. Our total exports of domestic produce for that year exceeded 99 millions, while the specie we received from abroad was but $ 5,830,429. The actual cash balance that year, of course, was the difference of these two sums of specie; that is, only $ 376,215. And this was the balance of an account current of the United States with all the world, which had 96 millions on one side, and 99 millions on the other. Again, if we take the year 1846, we find the imports amounting to over 110 millions, while the specie sent abroad was less than 4 millions; the exports were nearly 102 millions, and the specie received was a little more than 3¾ millions. In other words, a remittance of $ 127,536 in cash would have settled an account in which 102 millions were sold, and 110 millions purchased.

If we examine the returns for a series of consecutive years, and anywhere find an apparent departure from this rule, either by an excessive importation or excessive exportation of specie, we also perceive a corresponding excess of exports or imports, proceeding from some peculiar causes affecting the course of trade for that year; and we find, moreover, a recoil the following year, produced by that self-regulating power of the currency which has been explained. Take, for instance, the following table, which I have compiled from the Secretary of the Treasury's Report for 1854.

Year ending	Imports entered for consumption.	Coin and bullion exported.	Domestic produce exported.	Coin and bullion imported.
June 30, 1844	$ 96,390,548	$ 5,454,214	$ 99,531,774	$ 5,830,429
1845	105,599,541	8,606,495	98,455,330	4,070,242
1846	110,048,859	3,905,268	101,718,042	3,777,732
1847	116,257,595	1,907,024	150,574,844	24,129,289
1848	140,651,902	15,841,616	130,203,709	6,360,224
1849	132,565,168	5,404,648	131,710,081	6,651,240

Here we find, for 1847, a great excess of specie imported,

amounting to 24 millions, the average for the other years being only 5 millions. The reason for this excess appears in the amount of domestic produce exported that year, which was 150 millions, or at least 35 millions more than could have been anticipated from the natural rate of increase of our exports. This sudden enlargement of the exports was caused by the great amount of bread-stuffs, (68 millions, or more than double the average quantity,) shipped from our ports that year, to make up for the famine in Ireland and the dearth throughout Western Europe. This large amount of coin and bullion received made our currency redundant, and we perceive that an effort was made the next year to get rid of the superfluous money. But no action of the government, no combination of individuals, was requisite for this purpose; the matter regulated itself. England had sent away a considerable portion of her currency, and therefore the prices of her commodities fell; the United States had received what England had lost, and therefore prices in America rose. Thus it became profitable to purchase goods in England and sell them in the United States; and thus our imports in 1848 suddenly rose to 140 millions (an excess of 16 millions over the average of 1847 and 1849); and, to pay for these goods, we exported nearly 16 millions of coin and bullion, which restored the balance of the currency. A severe commercial crisis in England was the consequence of this drain of specie, in 1847, caused by the necessity of buying food, though the effect was probably somewhat aggravated by excessive investment in railways. But the mismanagement of the banks, or an excessive circulation of bank-notes, was certainly not the cause of the evil, the act of Parliament passed three years before being an insuperable obstacle to any extension of the paper currency. On the contrary, Mr. Tooke rightly argues, that a moderate increase of the amount of bank-notes in circulation might have obviated the calamity in part, or altogether, by filling up the vacuum in the currency created by the exportation of specie.

When, in the course of international trade, one country becomes indebted to another, the question whether the deficiency shall be made up by remittances of money or of goods, is one that determines itself, on the same principles which usually cause one commodity to be preferred to another as an article of export. The merchant will send the one which he thinks is less valuable at home, and more valuable abroad, than any other commodity. If coin and bullion answer this condition, — that is, if other commodities are dearer at home than abroad, — then coin and bullion will be sent. But, as Mr. McCulloch remarks, "though the premium on foreign bills should increase, so as to equal the cost of exporting the precious metals, (for it cannot *exceed* this sum,) it does not by any means follow that they would therefore be exported. That depends entirely on the fact, whether bullion be, at the time, the cheapest exportable commodity; or, in other words, whether a remittance of bullion be the most advantageous way in which a debt may be discharged. If a London merchant owe £ 100 in Paris, he sets about finding out the cheapest method of paying it. On the supposition that the *real* exchange is two per cent below par, and that the expense of remitting bullion, including the profit of the bullion merchant, is also two per cent, it will be indifferent to him whether he pay £ 2 of premium for a bill of £ 100 payable in Paris, or incur an expense of £ 2 by remitting £ 100 worth of bullion directly to that city. If the prices of cloth in Paris and London be such, that it would require £ 103 to purchase and send as much cloth to Paris as would sell for £ 100, he would undoubtedly prefer buying a bill or exporting bullion. But if, by incurring an expense of £ 101, the debtor be able to send as much hardware to Paris as would sell for £ 100, he would as certainly prefer paying his debt by an exportation of hardware. By doing so, he saves one per cent more than if he bought a foreign bill or remitted bullion, and two per cent more than if he exported cloth. It follows, then, that the balance of payments might be a hundred millions against a country, without depriving it of a single ounce of bullion. No merchant would remit £ 100 worth of gold or silver from England to discharge a debt in Paris, if he could invest £ 98, £ 99, or any smaller sum, in any other species of merchandise which, exclusive of expenses, would sell in France for £ 100. Those who deal in the precious metals are, we may depend upon it, as much under the influence of self-interest, as those who deal in coffee or indigo. But who would attempt to discharge a foreign debt by exporting coffee which cost £ 100, if he could effect the same object by sending abroad indigo which cost only £ 97? No person in his senses would export a hat to be sold for 20*s.*, provided he could sell it at home for a guinea; nor would any person export an ounce of bullion, if its value were not less in the exporting than in the importing country, or if there were any other commodity whatever that might be exported with greater advantage."

Bills of exchange, or the transfer of debts, may take the place of money to an almost incalculable extent. The instances thus far adduced relate only to *foreign* bills of exchange, or the adjustment of our trade with other countries. But *domestic* bills of exchange are also drawn to vast amounts, to represent and balance the items in our account current with the other States and cities of this Union; they are not, indeed, always called by this name; they generally appear under the form and appellation of *drafts* and *checks*. But they all amount to the same thing; they are really *bills of exchange*, because they are written orders for the transfer or sale of debts. They are distinguished from paper currency, properly so called, or bank-bills, by this single circumstance, — that a proper bill of exchange, draft, or check must usually be indorsed by each party through whose hands it passes, and every person who indorses it incurs a modified responsibility for its payment; while bank-bills, as we all know, pass from hand to hand without any indorsement.

And this leads us at once to an explanation of the true nature of a bank-bill; like a bill of exchange, it is simply evidence of a debt, which debt is transferred from hand to hand, or exchanged for merchandise. The bank which pays out one of its own bills, simply acknowledges that it is indebted for a specified amount to the person who receives it, or to any other person to whom he may transfer it; and it promises to pay this debt on demand in specie. If the politicians who, at various times, have given themselves so much trouble about the repression of the banks, and the establishment of an exclusively metallic currency, had known how little difference there is between bank-bills and the various forms of bills of exchange, the two really performing the same functions, they might have saved their labor. I hazard nothing by the assertion, that, if the circulation of bank-bills in this country should be entirely stopped by law, the number and value of these other evidences of debt —(less convenient, indeed, than bank-bills, because they require indorsement) — would be so largely increased, as to prevent the necessity of importing a much larger amount of specie. Already, in England, where the circulation of bank-bills of a lower denomination than five pounds sterling, or twenty-five dollars, is prohibited, numerously indorsed bills of exchange have come to circulate to an immense amount as currency. They are drawn to as small an amount as ten pounds sterling, are used by the country farmers in making their purchases of merchandise, and often come into the hands of the person in London by whom they are finally payable, with no less than forty indorsements upon them. The average amount of them in circulation at any one time was calculated by Mr. Leatham, an eminent banker, to be over 132 millions sterling, — say, 640 millions of dollars. Imagine the loss of interest, and expensiveness in other respects, of an attempt to replace this amount of what is virtually paper currency by silver and gold!

And it is a curious circumstance, that these domestic bills of exchange are finally paid off, or cancelled, without occasioning the transfer of more than an insignificant fraction of money. They are made payable by some one of the numerous banking-houses in London, and when they approach maturity, they are paid into, or left to be collected by, some other banking-house. "But the convenience of business," says Mr. Mill, "has given birth to an arrangement which makes all the banking-houses of the city of London, for certain purposes, virtually one establishment. A banker does not send the checks and bills, which are paid into his banking-house, to the banks on which they are drawn, and demand money for them. There is a building called the Clearing-House, to which every city banker sends, each afternoon, all the checks and bills on other bankers which he has received during the day, and they are there exchanged for the checks on him which have come into the hands of other bankers, the balances only being paid in money. By this contrivance, all the business transactions of the city of London during that day, and a vast amount besides of country transactions, represented by bills which country bankers have drawn upon their London correspondents," — amounting in the daily aggregate nearly to fifteen millions of dollars, —

"are liquidated by payments of money not exceeding on the average one million." The process is so convenient, and saves the handling of so much money, that Clearing-Houses have recently been established in the cities of New York and Boston, where the various banks effect their settlements with each other by exchanging bank-bills as well as checks, and paying off only the balances in cash.

As the territory of the United States is very extensive, and different portions of it have their peculiar staple products, the dealings of our merchants in drafts or domestic bills of exchange are necessarily very heavy. The extent of the transactions in these bills must be proportioned to the number and value of the commodities which are interchanged. The South furnishes cotton, rice, sugar, and tobacco, for consumption at the North, and for export to foreign countries; and she needs in return the manufactured goods of the North, and the foreign commodities which are imported chiefly into the Northern ports. The West sends to the Atlantic States her surplus product of bread-stuffs, beef, pork, hemp, and lead, and also receives manufactured and foreign goods in exchange. It is easy to see, that this immense internal traffic takes place in great part without the intervention of money, whether in the form of coin or bank-bills. Drafts or domestic bills of exchange are here the great instruments of commerce, or the circulating medium that facilitates the interchange of commodities. The farmer in Illinois or Michigan forwards by railroad his wheat and Indian corn to a miller at Rochester or a merchant in New York, and *draws* upon him for the value of the consignment at current prices. This draft he transfers to his neighbor, a Western merchant, in payment for articles of household use and other commodities, with which he has been supplied throughout the year; and the merchant, when he goes to New York to purchase a fresh stock of foreign and manufactured goods, gives up this draft to pay for them. The whole series of transactions, representing all the complex interchanges of commodities between the East and the West, might be completed without the intervention of a bank-bill or a piece of coin in any part of the business, except perhaps to "make change," or settle a small fractional part of an account. The business of the Southern planter is managed nearly in the same way: though the larger part of his produce is shipped to a foreign market, the transaction is settled for him by a draft on a merchant in New York or New Orleans; and this draft, after its acceptance, can be directly used in the purchase of commodities. It usually commands a small premium, or is worth more than cash; for the currency of the neighborhood, being supplied by local banks, is not available for purchases at a distance, and the transportation of specie is burdensome and expensive. A draft is really the safest and most convenient form of money; for as it is indorsed over from one person to another, the danger of its value being lost or stolen is entirely obviated. In this commerce of the different States and other portions of the country with each other, as in international trade, commodities are really purchased with commodities, and the amount of sales must, in the long run, equal the amount of purchases; otherwise, the course of exchange would turn against the State or district which bought more than it sold, and the deficiency would have to be ultimately made up by a remittance in specie, or by diminishing purchases and increasing sales.

I have been compelled to anticipate to a considerable degree the explanation of the next substitute for metallic money in effecting exchanges and payments. I refer to the establishment of what are called *banks of deposit*, or to one branch of the business performed by the ordinary banks in this country, which have in truth three separate functions, — being banks of *issue*, *discount*, and *deposit*. Banks of deposit as first instituted, at Amsterdam, Hamburg, and elsewhere, were places "where private merchants could lodge any amount of local national coin, of bullion, or of foreign coin reckoned by the bank as bullion; and the amount so lodged was entered, according to its value, as so much money of the national standard. At the same time, the bank opened an account with each merchant, giving him credit for the amount of his deposit. Whenever a merchant wanted to make a payment, there was no occasion to touch the deposit at all; it was sufficient to transfer the sum required from the credit of the party paying to that of the party receiving. Thus values could be transferred continually by a mere transfer on the books of the bank. The whole operation was conducted without any actual transfer of specie; the original deposit, which was entered at its intrinsic value at the time of making it, remained as security for the credit transferred from one person to another; and the specie, so lodged with the bank, was exempt from any reduction of value by wear, fraud, or even legislative enactment."

It was presupposed by this arrangement, that all the merchants of the city made their deposits and kept their accounts at one and the same institution; and it answered, of course, only for their dealings with each other, and not with the merchants of other cities or of foreign lands. Banks instituted exclusively for this purpose have died out, I believe, even in the places where they originated. It has been found more convenient to combine this office with the other functions exercised by banks. It is performed by the bankers in London, who are associated into partnerships, from two to six individuals usually forming one house, and by all the American banks. In England as in America, "it is chiefly in the retail transactions between dealers and consumers," says Mr. Mill, "and in the payment of wages, that money or bank-notes now pass, and then only when the amounts are small. Not only the merchants and larger dealers, but persons of fortune, and all shopkeepers of any amount of capital or extent of business, deposit their spare cash reserved for immediate use in a bank, and make all payments, except very small ones, by checks. If all did business at one bank, as we have seen, no actual transfer of money would be necessary, but only a transfer of credit on the books. In London, the institution of the Clearing-House does virtually combine all the banks into one for this purpose, the checks being very seldom directly paid in money, and the accounts of the bankers with each other being adjusted once a day. In this country, till recently, the checks were directly paid by the institution on which they were drawn; but all checks to any considerable amount were paid in bills of a large denomination, with the expectation that these would not pass into general circulation, but would merely be carried a few steps in State Street or Wall Street, to another bank, where they would either be taken in payment of a note or be lodged on deposit; often, indeed, they were not carried out of doors at all, but were only transferred from the paying to the receiving teller of the same institution. Such bank-bills form no part of the currency properly so called; they are mere orders from one institution to another for the transfer of credits.

It will be observed that I have not, thus far, entered into any consideration of proper bank currency, viewed as a substitute for gold and silver coin; that topic, from its extent and importance, must be reserved for another chapter. Yet we have seen that the largest operations of domestic and foreign trade are carried on with the intervention of very little money; that the most important exchanges are effected without any transfer of the precious metals; and we have already abundant reason to believe that, in these modern times, the proper sphere of money is in retail transactions, and in answering frequent petty demands. We thus gain a more correct idea of the comparatively limited functions of money, which common persons are led grossly to exaggerate, merely because, at any one time and place, it is a common measure of value, a universal denomination of account. All wealth, all commodities, are estimated in dollars, francs, pounds sterling, and the like; and it is by the aid of such estimates that all exchanges are made. Thus, the *idea* of money aids us, when the *reality* is seldom employed. As pounds sterling were a universal denomination of account for a long period, during which there was no such coin as a pound sterling in existence, so the idea, or abstract conception, of numerical values expressed in coin would be a convenient, even an essential, implement or contrivance in mercantile transactions, though all exchanges should be made by direct barter of one commodity for another. Without such a contrivance, the merchant could not keep his books of record intelligibly, or preserve his accounts with individuals in his large and complicated business. Money is even now only a hypothetical or abstract medium of exchange in all the larger transactions of commerce. I almost anticipate the time, in the progress of invention and the discovery of new expedients and facilities in commerce, when it will become so universally; when, at any rate, so costly and useless a realization of the idea as gold and silver coin will be entirely done away. Only practical difficulties, or what may be called difficulties of detail, even now obstruct this desirable consummation.

CHAPTER XX.

THE FUNCTIONS OF BANKS AND THE NATURE OF BANK-NOTES: THE OPERATIONS OF CREDIT.

WHILE treating of banks and bank currency, the subjects of the present chapter, I shall, in order to avoid confusion, refer only to the banking system established in this country, and especially here in New England; at any rate, the references to the Bank of England and other foreign institutions will be only incidental, to elucidate the operations of our own banks. It has been said that our banks have properly three functions, or that they are banks of *deposit*, *discount*, and *circulation*. I have briefly explained the first of these three offices, — that of deposit, and have shown the benefits resulting from it. Through this function of the banks, dealers are released from the necessity of counting over large sums of money in order to make or receive payments, and from the risk of keeping such large sums by them in their own establishments, where they would be exposed to thieves, fire, and other casualties. They are enabled to make and receive large payments by mere slips of paper, which are only orders for the transfer of credit, on the books of the bank, from the account of one person to that of another. Their money, being useless to them except for the purpose of effecting these transfers of credit, is left undisturbed in the vaults of the banks; and these institutions, being able to calculate the average amount thus left with them continually, are enabled to use it over again, or to lend it to their customers; for credits can be equally well transferred on the bank books, whether the money represented by these credits is actually in the bank safe, or in the hands of a person to whom the bank chooses to lend it, and who may be regarded for this purpose as its agent or cash-keeper, — the bank, of course, being responsible for him, or engaging to repay the money, if he does not.

I find, by the latest returns of all the banks in Massachusetts, that the sums thus deposited with them amount to little less than twenty-two millions of dollars, and that the banks, in fact, let out every dollar of this sum to other persons, receiving interest therefor; I say the banks let out *all* the deposits, because the specie actually held by these institutions in their vaults is more properly regarded as a security for their circulation than for their deposits. Observe, now, the economizing effect of the banks in regard to the use of money. It appears that the merchants and other capitalists of this State, in order to be prepared for sudden calls and daily emergencies, find it necessary to keep sums of money by them or on hand, which amount in the aggregate to twenty-two millions of dollars. If there were no banks, this great sum of gold and silver, divided into many parcels, must remain, disused and rusting, (if the precious metals did rust,) in safes, tills, and drawers. There would be a loss of profit or interest on the whole amount. Through the machinery of the banks, these many parcels are collected together, and while their owners have just as much the benefit of them as ever, — that is, can effect all their payments equally well, and save the trouble of counting the money to boot, — the banks put all the money into profitable use, or convert it from dead into active capital. The saving thus effected to the State of Massachusetts, reckoning it only at the rate of legal interest, is six per cent on twenty-two millions, or $ 1,320,000 a year. In places where there are no banks, — in Valparaiso, South America, for instance, — there is more than one large mercantile firm which, on account of the extent of its transactions, is obliged to keep, on an average, at least $ 100,000 in gold coin constantly in its safe; this is so much subtracted from its active capital, and the annual rate of profit there being at least as high as ten per cent, the annual loss to such a house equals ten thousand dollars.

The *discounting* operations of the banks, which are their chief function in this country, lead directly to an explanation of the system of *credit*, — a system which plays so important a part in the theory of wealth, and in all mercantile transactions, that it needs to be very plainly and fully set forth. "The functions of credit have been a subject of as much misunderstanding, and as much confusion of ideas, as any single topic in Political Economy. This is not owing to any peculiar difficulty in the theory of the subject, but to the complex nature of some of the mercantile phenomena arising from the forms in which credit clothes itself; by which attention is diverted from the properties of credit in general, to the peculiarities of its particular forms."

Credit may be briefly defined as a means of putting capital into the hands of those who, for the time being, can use it to the best advantage, though they are not the owners of it. The utility and profits of capital depend, as we have seen, upon its activity, upon the speed, skill, and judgment with which it is consumed and reproduced. The capitalist himself may be deficient in all the important requisites for managing his own property; he may have inherited it, and therefore have had no experience in the mode of acquiring and using it; or from the very fact that he is a capitalist, or a man of fortune, he may not be willing to give time and labor to its superintendence, preferring to consult his own ease and amusement; or his capital may be so large, that, although in active business himself, he may not be able to superintend or manage the whole of it, but may feel obliged to lend a large portion of it. From these various circumstances, there is always, in every wealthy community, a vast amount of capital to lend, — much more than is generally supposed. For capitalists, banks, and other lending institutions are commonly thought to manage and superintend their own property, when they simply direct its investment, or determine to what persons or institutions they will by preference lend it. But not so. The real *manager* of capital is he in whose hands it exists, not in the form of money, stocks, or other securities, but in the form of goods, — whether of raw material to be manufactured, or of tools and machinery for manufacture, or of ships and other means of transport, or of merchandise for transport and sale. There may be half a dozen applications of credit, half a dozen lendings, between the proper *owner* and this *manager* of the capital. For instance, the owner may prefer to lend his capital to, or invest it in, a bank; the bank may lend it to a broker; the broker may employ it in buying up a promissory note; and the original giver or promisor of this note is probably he in whose hands the actual property represented by all these transactions is really placed, for the time being. *He* is the *manager* of the capital, whose true *owner* is not probably known to him even by name.

And here we must again remark, that the true *subject* of credit, that which is lent, and for which interest is paid, is not money, but merchandise, or some one of the myriad forms of material wealth. Money, as such, it has been demonstrated again and again, bears no profit, and therefore yields no interest. What the merchant or other needy person actually borrows, is not the little slip of paper, called a *check*, that he carries to the bank; nor yet the bank-bills which he receives in payment of the check; nor even the gold and silver coin, which, if he chooses, he can obtain for the bank-notes. The proof that these things are not what he really borrows for six months, a year, or some other period, is, that he endeavors to get rid of these things as soon as he can; if possible, on the very day on which he received them. He no more thinks of keeping the bank-notes or coin on hand, than of retaining the check in his possession. What he really keeps for the six months or year, and therefore what he really borrows and pays interest for, is the goods which he purchases with the bank-bills. A capitalist's property, though it may exist under his own eye only in the shape of notes, bank-bills, stocks, and other representatives of wealth, does not actually consist in them, but in merchandise, or articles of material wealth, which, in many cases, he has never seen; and these are what he lends upon interest. There is always a vast amount of such capital in being, which is not *managed* by its proper owners.

On the other hand, as Mr. Mill remarks, credit is "the means by which the industrial talent of the country is turned to most account for purposes of production. Many a person, who has either no capital of his own, or very little, but who has qualifications for business which are known and appreciated by some persons of capital, is enabled to obtain either advances in money, or more frequently goods on credit, by which his industrial capacities are made instrumental to the increase of the public wealth; and this benefit will be reaped far more largely, whenever, through better laws and better education, the community shall have made such progress in integrity, that personal character can be accepted as a sufficient guaranty, not only against dishonestly appropriating, but against dishonestly risking, what belongs to another." Every act of legislation, which, however benevolent in design, really diminishes the security of creditors, is an act inflicting hardship and wrong on the very class of persons whom it is intended to benefit, — the class who have not so much capital as capacity to use it, and who must, therefore, depend on credit as the only means of turning their talents to account.

Another occasion for giving credit arises from the varying demands for capital in different employments. One who has capital enough for the *average* demands of his business may find, owing to the fluctuations of trade, that, at one period, half of his whole capital would remain useless for some months, if he could not, during that time, lend it to another; and at another period, that the productiveness of his own stock would be greatly enhanced if he could increase it by one half for a few months. In other words, in order that his business may be most profitably and most economically managed, he must have the power of varying the amount of capital engaged in it from one month to another.

Now, it is the chief function of banks in this country to promote and facilitate these operations of credit, and thereby to economize both the capital and the industrial talent of the nation, allowing no portion of either to remain unemployed even for a few weeks. They bring borrowers and lenders together; they allow an individual to borrow this month and to lend the next, — nay, to borrow to-day and to lend to-morrow, according to his varying occasions, necessities, and inclinations. They do not, in this part of their office, directly add to the productive wealth of the country; but they keep what there is in the highest possible activity, and cause it to be applied constantly to the best advantage. Credit, however enlarged, cannot increase capital, cannot *create* wealth, whether productive or unproductive. It can only transfer from one hand to another the wealth already in being. "Credit has a great, but not, as many people seem to suppose, a magical power; it cannot make something out of nothing. If the borrower's means of production and of employing labor are increased by the credit given him, the lender's are as much diminished. It is true that the capital which A has borrowed from B, and makes use of in his business, still forms part of the wealth of B for other purposes; he can enter into engagements in reliance on it, and can even borrow, when needful, an equivalent sum on the security of it;

so that, to a superficial eye, it might seem as if both B and A had the use of it at once. But the smallest consideration will show, that, when B has parted with his capital to A, the use of it *as capital* rests with A alone, and that B has no other service from it than in so far as his ultimate claim upon it serves him to obtain the use of another capital from a third person, C. All capital, (not his own,) of which any person has really the use, is, and must be, so much subtracted from the capital of some one else."

We are now prepared to explain the nature and functions of a bank; and I will take, for this purpose, one of the simplest cases, — a bank established in one of our New England country towns, with a capital of not more than $100,000. We will suppose that this town, originally without any institution of the kind, has gone on increasing in population, manufactures, wealth, and trade. There are now a number of persons in it, of easy circumstances, who still make savings from income, but have not the inclination, or perhaps the capacity, to employ these savings profitably in any active business. These have capital to lend; and there are others in the town, young tradesmen and manufacturers, who have not capital enough to give full scope to their industry, talents, and enterprise, and who are therefore eager to borrow. But the borrower may often have much difficulty in finding a lender who has to spare just the sum that he wants, and for the time that he wants it; and even the lender may often have a portion of his spare capital lying idle for weeks, and even months, before he can find borrowers who will take it all on good security, and pay interest for it at short periods. Still further, the traders in the town, as we have seen, may have frequent occasion both to lend and to borrow, according to the varying demands of their business. When their stock is low, they may have a considerable sum on hand or unemployed, which they would be glad to let out at interest if they could be sure of obtaining it again as soon as needed, or whenever a favorable opportunity offered for purchasing an additional stock of goods. But it would be difficult, if not impossible, to find a borrower who would take it upon these terms; for interest can be paid only out of profits,

---

* J. S. Mill's *Political Economy*, Vol. II. p. 36.

and capital cannot be put to a profitable use without engaging it in some occupation from which it could not be withdrawn at a moment's notice. The traders, however, would be willing to lend their surplus capital for a fixed period, say three or six months, if there were some institution in the town from which they could be sure of obtaining a loan to an equivalent or greater amount, if any occasion should arise for the use of the funds before the period of three or six months had elapsed.

It will be for the convenience of all parties, then, to have a central office in town, where all can come who wish to borrow, and whither all capital may be carried which craves investment in this form. The lenders and traders, therefore, obtain a charter of incorporation as a bank, as they find that, by clubbing their means, they can raise a capital of $ 100,000. They are willing to put all the capital they can possibly spare into such an institution, because, their stock in the bank being transferable, they can readily borrow money elsewhere, or at the bank itself, by offering this stock as security, or they can sell the stock if they desire to regain their whole capital. Having procured a banking-room, and a competent person as cashier, they can commence operations by lending every dollar of their capital, which was paid in only for the purpose of being lent. They gain a trifling advantage, also, by letting their capital only for short periods, from two to six months; thus obtaining compound interest a part of the time, the money received for interest being often let out as well as the capital, before the time arrives for the semiannual payments to their stockholders.

This small gain, however, would not by any means defray their expenses for banking-room, cashier, &c.; and if the bank had no other source of revenue, it could not divide six per cent a year to its stockholders; for it only receives a trifle over six per cent on the capital, and the banking expenses must be deducted. But, for reasons already explained, all persons in town, having cash on hand for their daily emergencies, are ready and eager to deposit this cash in bank, the institution undertaking to keep it safely, and with it to manage all their payments for them, and to return it on demand. Such deposits, therefore, though always coming and going, may amount on an average to $ 25,000, or one fourth of the bank capital.

The bank pays no interest on this sum, but receives interest for it; for it is able to let out the whole, only taking care to let it for short periods, so that it may be within reach, as it were, if suddenly called for. Thus far, then, the bank, with only $ 100,000 of capital, receives interest on $ 125,000, and is thus in a fair way to pay its expenses, and still yield six per cent to its stockholders. It should be observed, that the whole amount of its deposits cannot be suddenly called for, nor even a considerable portion of them. These deposits consist in great part of the funds which the various customers of the bank are constantly transferring from one to another, in the settlement of their accounts with each other; and these transfers are made upon the bank-books, as already explained, without any necessity of ever withdrawing the sum from the custody of the institution.

The usual mode in which banks lend their capital and other funds to their customers is, by discounting promissory notes. We shall, therefore, gain a clearer view of their second function, as banks of discount, by looking closely into the origin and character of such notes. It is usual in every trade to give a certain length of credit for goods bought, — six or eight months, or even a year, according to the custom in the particular trade. This length of credit is virtually offered to the purchaser as an inducement to him to pay a higher price for the goods bought; he is offered either six months' credit, or a discount of five per cent from the price demanded, though the usual rate of interest for six months is but three per cent; and in nine cases out of ten, the purchaser decides to take the credit rather than the diminished price. The seller offers this credit, though he is in truth not able to offer it, but needs his capital returned immediately. He offers it, however, because he knows he can sell this note to the bank, or transfer the debt to it, receiving the amount *minus* the interest for the time it has still to run. It might seem to be a less circuitous and less costly mode of transacting the business, if the purchaser of the goods, instead of paying five per cent for six months' credit, should himself obtain a loan from the bank of the necessary sum at only three per cent, and thus be enabled to pay for his goods with ready money. But then the bank, for its own security, requires two persons to become responsible for the repayment of the loan, these two usually being the signer and an indorser of the note. The buyer can only offer his own personal security, which is not enough; the seller can offer a note signed by the buyer, and indorsed by himself, so as to complete the requisite guaranty. The real nature of the transaction, then, is as follows: the seller, in order to enable a customer to buy his goods, obtains for him from the bank a six months' loan of the purchase-money, charging him two per cent for this service and for guaranteeing the repayment to the bank.

It is the chief function of the banks to discount or buy such notes, which are called *real* or *business* paper, to distinguish them from another class of notes, which are denominated *fictitious* or *accommodation* paper, because they are not grounded on any debt previously due from the promisor to the indorser. "*Real* notes (it is sometimes said) represent actual property. There are actual goods in existence, which are the counterpart to every real note. Notes which are not drawn in consequence of a sale of goods, are a species of false wealth, by which a nation is deceived. These supply only an imaginary capital; the others indicate one that is real." *

But there are no good grounds for this distinction and preference. A loan obtained by a purchaser, on a note indorsed by a friend, may be applied to the purchase of goods, just as much as if the note were indorsed by the person who sold those goods. Then there may be actual commodities or values corresponding to the accommodation or fictitious paper, as well as to real notes; the wealth is no more fictitious, nor are the pretences on which the loan is obtained more unfounded or fraudulent, in the one case than in the other. Again, though all the notes should be given as the results of actual sales of commodities, it is by no means certain that these commodities are equal in value to the whole (aggregate) amount for which the notes are given; for the same goods may be sold over and over again by successive purchasers, so that there may be many notes, each representing the whole value of one and the same parcel of goods. For instance, A may sell $ 1,000 worth of merchandise to B, and receive therefor B's note at six months;

* H. Thornton's *Inquiry into the Nature and Effects of Paper Credit.*

within a week, B may sell the same goods to C, and receive *his* note for the same sum; C may soon dispose of them in like manner, and receive a third note. Before six months have elapsed, there may be a dozen such notes in being, all of which may possibly be discounted at the same bank; yet only one of them represents any actual property.

Up to this point, be it observed, there has been no mention of bank-notes, or of the issue of a substitute for specie currency. The bank might exist, might exercise the two functions now explained of deposit and discount, and pay dividends of a reasonable amount to its stockholders, though the currency of a country should consist exclusively of gold and silver. The establishment of the bank would lessen the amount of these two metals required for making exchanges,—would limit them in great part to the retail trade, or to transactions between dealers and consumers,—the business of dealers with each other being adjusted almost exclusively by checks transferring deposits. But it now becomes a question whether the precious metals may not be dispensed with, even for this service. They are used only to be passed from hand to hand; their material and specific qualities—their hardness, weight, &c.—are not needed to fit them for such transfer. A scrap of paper would answer just as well to be passed about, provided only that the receiver of it felt secure that it would not diminish in value while in his keeping, or that his neighbor would always be willing to receive it on the same valuation upon which it had come into his own hands. Instead of effecting a purchase with five hard and weighty silver dollars, it would be even more convenient to effect it with a scrap of paper, which the holder is sure of being able to exchange at any moment, and without difficulty, for that sum in specie. The bank, having relieved the large dealers from the necessity of using specie through its system of checks and deposits, may now relieve the smaller ones, and the community generally, from such necessity, by issuing its own notes for small sums, payable on demand in gold or silver at its own counter. In its immediate vicinity, such notes would evidently be preferred to coin, on account of their superior convenience; beyond that vicinity, they would not circulate, because the distance would oppose an obstacle to their *immediate* conversion into cash, and because the circumstances and solvency of the bank could not be so well known at a distance.

To return to the bank with $100,000 of capital, which was taken as an example to illustrate the theory of these institutions; we have seen that its capital and deposits combined would enable it to make loans on interest to the amount of $125,000. If we suppose that it can raise its circulation to $50,000 by keeping only 10,000 specie dollars in reserve, it is evident that $40,000 will be added to its productive means; or that it will now be able to lend on interest $165,000. It can then easily pay its banking expenses, pay 6 or 7 per cent on its capital to the stockholders, and still have a small surplus to meet the contingency of some loans made by it not being repaid, — or, in other words, to make up for bad debts. *How* this excess of circulation over the specie held in reserve is so much added to its productive means, appears very easily on a little reflection. After it has lent out all its capital and all its deposits, it can still lend its own notes, or its own promises to pay specie on demand, which will circulate as readily as hard money, and for which, therefore, the borrower will pay as much interest as for hard money.

Under ordinary circumstances, it is certain that one dollar in specie held by the banks is a safe basis for the circulation of three or four dollars in paper; for paper being equally available with specie for all domestic purposes, and far more convenient, it would be strange indeed, if the inhabitants of any town or the people of any country should suddenly have occasion to send abroad, or out of their own precincts, a sum in specie equal to one third or one fourth of their whole paper circulation. Such an export from the United States would amount perhaps to sixty or seventy millions in specie, — a drain upon the currency quite sufficient to so far raise the value of what money remained behind, that the prices of all commodities would inevitably fall much below the average, and there would consequently be an irresistible temptation to export merchandise and import bullion.

But the great danger to the circulation of the banks arises, not from the possibility of a sudden demand for a great amount of specie to be sent abroad, but from the occurrence of one of those panics among the people, which are not infrequently caused by commercial crises, or by the failure of one or more large banks through the gross mismanagement or fraud of their directors, — a failure which, among the ill-informed, of course excites suspicions as to the soundness of all the other banks. Against such panics, in truth, there is no adequate protection, except the diffusion among the people of a knowledge of the theory and practice of banking, — a knowledge which would teach them that, by yielding to the excitement, and joining in the run upon the banks, they are acting directly against their own interests, which are not otherwise in jeopardy. An anecdote is told of an eccentric banker, who, when a great crowd had collected about his doors, in consequence of one of these unreasoning excitements, came out and pushed them away with great violence of gesticulation, exclaiming, "Go away, you foolish people! or I will break, and ruin every man among you." He was quite right; in every bank that is managed, I will not say, with common ability and discretion, but with common honesty, the capital and other resources so largely exceed the circulation, that it is impossible for the notes to fail of being *ultimately* redeemed in specie. In the case of the bank which has been taken as an example, the assets are, the notes and bills of individuals, which it has bought or discounted to the amount of $ 165,000, and $ 10,000 in specie, making an aggregate of $ 175,000, as a fund for the redemption of only $ 50,000 in its own paper. If less than one fourth of these notes of individuals are duly paid at maturity, the bank-notes cannot fail to be redeemed in full; and without a breach of honesty, it is certainly impossible that the directors of any institution should let out their own money and that of others in such a manner as to lose more than four fifths of it. But a great panic may bring home upon the bank more than one fourth of its circulation in one day, each holder of its notes being anxious to secure himself, and careless of the effect upon others. In this case, the bank would be obliged to suspend specie payments, its notes would be dishonored and consequently depreciated, merchants would be deprived of their deposits and customary facilities at the banks, in consequence of which they also would fail to redeem their own notes due to the bank, and a general sacrifice or destruction of property would ensue.

There is one rule for the proper management of a bank, by which the danger of such a catastrophe is very much lessened; I refer to the rule for not discounting any but what is called "short paper," or not buying any notes which have more than a few months to run. If the bank lends all its available means for a period as long as six months, the receipts and loans being pretty equally distributed through all the business days of those months, it is evident that the daily receipts from loans repaid would be equal to the whole amount lent divided by the whole number of days for which it was lent; that is, in the case of the bank we have taken for an example, $165,000 ÷ 180, or about $916, for the daily receipts. If two months were the limit fixed, then the whole capital would be turned over, or paid in and let out again, once in every sixty days; and the daily receipts would be about $2,748. If, on the other hand, a year was the limit, the receipts each day would be only $458. Now, if we suppose that a run takes place upon such a bank, it would probably take two days to exhaust its stock of specie, $10,000, which was held in reserve. During the continuance of the run, the bank's daily receipts would also continue, but it would make no new loans; all the cash paid in would be held in reserve for the great emergency that had arisen. If it had adopted the two months' limit, the receipts during the two days' run would exceed $5,000; it would thus be prepared for a third day, and probably for a fourth, as the amount of its own notes brought in each day would rapidly diminish after three days' run. The bank would weather the storm. But if a year were the limit it had adopted, the receipts during the first two days would be only $916,—not enough to carry it through the third day. The bank must stop payment. We see an obvious reason, then, why the banks feel obliged to curtail their issues or discounts during the existence of a panic, though by so doing they increase the distress of the community. The bolder policy sometimes adopted, of increasing rather than diminishing the discounts at such a crisis, in order to lessen the distress, and thereby stop the panic, resembles the plan of crowding all sail on a ship in a storm, in the hope thereby of keeping off a lee-shore, though the increased strain thus put upon the vessel may leave her a dismasted hulk on the waters.

In order still further to provide for its own safety, a bank ought not to make very large loans to individuals, but should have the whole amount of its disposable funds divided into loans of moderate size to a considerable number of persons, and so distributed that the payments or receipts may be equalized throughout the year. Otherwise, it is obvious that the failure of one large debtor might seriously cripple the resources and shake the credit of the institution; or a run might be made upon it at a period when very few notes were becoming due, so that the receipts would not be adequate to make good the drain of specie. Simple as these rules may appear, it is upon the strict observance of them, almost as much as upon the caution exercised in making discounts only to solvent and responsible traders, that the security of the bank in times of emergency, or during a commercial crisis, will be found to depend. On occasions of this sort, private banks in England, and even the Bank of England itself, have been obliged to scrape together as many sixpences as could be found, in order to gain time by the delay inseparable from payment in such diminutive coin, until a part of the notes in its possession had fallen due.

The proper function of a bank is to supply funds for use only as Circulating Capital, the process of production being comparatively a short one, and the value of the completed product soon serving to replace the advances which were necessary for wages, raw material, &c., while the work was going on. Thus it can lend to a farmer in the spring enough to buy seed-corn and to pay the wages of his laborers, and the proceeds of his crop at harvest-time will serve to repay the loan. It can lend a retail-dealer enough to purchase an additional stock of goods, if there is a reasonable prospect that the goods will be sold, and the money be received for them, in season to meet the payment of the note which has been discounted. But the bank cannot safely aid agricultural, commercial, or manufacturing enterprise, by supplying funds for the construction of ships and machinery, for the digging of mines or canals, for the bringing of waste lands into cultivation, or for any long-winded speculation; in short, it cannot supply funds to be employed as Fixed Capital. The values invested in any of these forms can be but slowly replaced, or only after considerable intervals of time; the ship or the machine which will last twenty years before it is worn out, can pay for itself only out of the accumulated profits of nearly twenty years. The builder, indeed, may safely obtain a bank loan to enable him to finish his work, if it is his intention to sell the ship or the machine as soon as it is completed. In such case, he needs the funds for use only as Circulating Capital; it is the purchaser, or the person who intends to employ the ship or machine, who really needs the use of funds as Fixed Capital. Money lent for such purposes can be repaid, when due, only by other notes, which have a further term to run, and are negotiated with the deduction of discount. When these fall due, they are met by a third set payable at a still later date, and discounted in like manner. The operation is only an expedient for borrowing of the bank in perpetuity, or for an indefinite series of years.

Land-banks, as they are properly termed, have been instituted at various times in England, France, and even in some of the States of this Union, on the principle of lending capital upon the security of real estate, in order to make improvements upon the property. In such cases, the security, indeed, is unexceptionable; but if the bank currency thus issued is returned to the institution to be redeemed in specie, there will be only mortgages to be offered for it, and the bank will be obliged to refuse payment. Consequently, the history of such banks has been uniformly disastrous. As a general rule, the currency will not absorb bank issues, or prevent them from being soon returned for redemption in specie, if those issues have not furnished a means for the immediate creation of fresh values, the proper circulation of which requires an additional amount of money. If bank-bills amounting to one million of dollars, for instance, are lent to supply the manufacturers with Circulating Capital, additional manufactured goods will be brought into market, in the course of a few months, to the value, probably, of $ 1,200,000, allowing 20 per cent for profit; and the numerous exchanges occasioned by this quantity of merchandise will require additional currency, not amounting, it is true, to one million of dollars, the original amount of the loan, but still sufficing to keep back a considerable portion of the bills from being presented for redemption at the bank counter. On the other hand, if the same amount of bills should be lent to furnish the manufacturers with Fixed Capital, the additional goods brought to market in the course of the next year might not exceed $ 150,000, and but a small portion of the bills would therefore be absorbed into the currency.

If the paper issues of the banks at any time exceed the demands of circulation, there follows a perpetual reflux of the bank-bills, which will soon drain the specie reserves, and can be checked only by a limitation of the issues. It is not necessary that the bills should be actually presented at the counter with a demand for their redemption in coin. They may also be returned by the customers of the banks, who make deposits with them, or return them in payment for their notes which have been discounted and have fallen due. For illustration, we may go back to the case of the supposed bank, with $ 100,000 of capital, $ 25,000 of deposits, and $ 50,000 of circulation. We may suppose the daily receipts at such an institution to amount to $ 6,000, one half of this sum being lodged on deposit, and the remainder being received in payment of the advances which it has made, or the notes which it has discounted. If its circulation be excessive, the state of the money-market not requiring so large an amount of its bills, the greater part of this daily receipt, say $ 5,000, may be in its own bills, and only $ 1,000 in specie and in the bills of other banks. It will then have only $ 1,000 to meet the demands upon it the next day, and cannot safely make any additional loan; for a further amount of its own bills has meanwhile been paid into other banks, either on deposit or in the discharge of loans, and in its settlement with these banks, these bills must be redeemed, either by the payment of specie, or by the return of bills which they have issued. If, on the other hand, the circulation be not already glutted with its own issues, five sixths of the daily receipts may be in specie or the bills of other banks, and only one sixth in its own paper; then, a small sum being reserved for exchange of bills with other banks, the institution may not only lend over $ 4,000 out of the former day's receipt, but may safely make an additional loan, say $ 2,000, in its own notes.

It is only in a period of excitement, during a commercial

crisis, or an alarm for the solvency of one bank or of all the banks, that its notes are directly brought to its counter for redemption in coin. In ordinary times, the real limit upon the circulation of any one bank is found in the daily settlement of its accounts with other banks. In the Clearing-Houses recently established by the banks both in New York and Boston, every bank each day presents all the bills of the other banks which it has collected in the day's transactions, and offsets with them its own bills which have been paid into those banks; only the balance, which is comparatively a small sum, is settled by the transfer of specie. Any redundancy of its own issues is sure to be followed by the presentation at the Clearing-House of a larger amount of its own bills than it has bills of other banks wherewith to redeem them, and the consequent necessity of paying the difference in gold or silver coin. Checks drawn upon it against deposits must be met in the same way. When a bank discounts the note of an individual, it does not necessarily pay out its own notes. The borrower may only desire the amount to be placed to his credit on deposit. But the next day, perhaps, he has to redeem or pay off another note, discounted some months before at another bank. He pays this last note by a check on the bank from which he has just obtained a discount; and this bank must account for the amount of the check in its account current with the other bank, or at the Clearing-House, — must perhaps pay specie for it. Hence we perceive the necessity to which the banks are subjected, in times of alarm and of the depression of credit, of contracting their loans and discounts in order to diminish the amount of their bills in circulation. It is not an arbitrary restriction; if they did not diminish their loans, their bills would be returned to them so rapidly as to exhaust their specie reserves.

Through these necessary dealings of the banks with each other, they become the guardians of each other's solvency, and are connected together by the closest ties of mutual dependence and guaranty. The question which was formerly much debated in this country, whether the banking business of the community would be more safely transacted by one great national bank, resembling the Bank of England or the Bank of France, or by numerous small banks of comparatively private character and limited resources, as in the present American system, is one of no substantive importance. As our small banks necessarily deal with each other, by receiving each other's bills and settling their mutual accounts every day, they are virtually bound together into one institution; if the issues of any one of their number become excessive, the others are the first to perceive it, and are the first losers by its insolvency. This remark applies to them, however, only in their single function, as banks *of circulation;* their other two functions, of receiving deposits and making discounts, may be, and often are, exercised by private merchants and capitalists, just as well as by the banks themselves. And these two functions constitute far the larger part of the banking business. In those States of our Union where, as in South Carolina and Missouri, there is but one State bank, which monopolizes the issue of bank-bills, there are numerous private bankers, as they are termed, who perform the greater part of the banking and exchange business. These bankers are under very few legal restrictions; their business is just as open to the community as any other branch of commerce. The office of issuing bank-bills, which are to become a part of the currency of the country, is certainly a more delicate and important one; but it is not easy to see that it would be more safely performed by one institution, than by many. If the transactions of one great bank are more publicly known and closely scrutinized, and if it can be managed by a few persons of high reputation for probity, wealth, and intelligence, so the consequences of its failure would be more general and more disastrous. It would not be watched by any rival institution deeply interested in an early detection of its insolvency. Massachusetts has 169 banks, with an aggregate capital of over 58 millions, and an aggregate circulation of less than 23 millions. If all this business were concentrated in the hands of one institution, even the rumor that it was in danger would create a panic that would paralyze the business of the whole State, and its actual failure would occasion almost universal bankruptcy. But under the present system, the unsoundness of one bank is quickly detected, and the rotten member is easily lopped off without shaking public confidence, or doing more than slight injury to very few individuals. The average circulation of a

Massachusetts bank is but little over $135,000, and that of the largest banks does not equal half a million. There are many private merchants whose liabilities greatly exceed this amount, and whose failure would be a more serious shock to public credit. And the cases of insolvency are proportionally more numerous among the merchants than among the banks; of the latter, there have not been more than half a dozen failures during the last fifteen years.

Nothing can be more erroneous than the common opinion that the banks are able to increase their loans, and augment their circulation, at pleasure, or according to their own ideas of what is safe and expedient. There are no other funds from which loans can be made but (1.) the capital, (2.) the average amount of the deposits, and (3.) the excess of the circulation over the specie reserve. The first of these is a fixed quantity, determined by the charter and the nature of the case. The amount of the second depends upon the number of the customers of the bank, and upon the nature and extent of their business; the deposits are made up by those who need to have money at hand, or within call, as it were, but have no immediate occasion to use it, and though their deposits are continually being withdrawn and replaced, or transferred from one person's credit to another's, their average amount is nearly a fixed quantity, and, after a little experience, can be easily determined. The third fund, though generally supposed to be variable, is in truth as much a fixed quantity as either of the others. We have seen that a reflux of the bank issues is always steadily going on, not through their presentation for specie, but through the receipts in deposit and in payment of the loans and discounts which have come to maturity. The bank can do nothing to lessen or retard this reflux, except by diminishing the issue of the bills. If it should suddenly and incautiously enlarge its issues to-day, there would be an equivalent augmentation of the reflux to-morrow; for as the community was previously supplied with currency enough for its usual exchanges, the additional amount of money thus thrown into the market must come into the hands of persons who would have no immediate occasion to use it, but would lodge it on deposit in the banks, and it would thus be immediately returned to the source whence it came.

Experience as well as theory confirms this statement. The doctrine which "denies to banks any power of increasing their circulation except as a consequence of, and in proportion to, an increase of the business to be done," is supported, says Mr. J. S. Mill, "by the unanimous assurances of all the country bankers who have been examined before successive Parliamentary committees on the subject. They all bear testimony that, in the words of Mr. Fullarton, 'the amount of their issues is exclusively regulated by the extent of local dealings and expenditure in their respective districts, fluctuating with the fluctuations of production and price; and that they neither can increase their issues beyond the limits which the range of such dealings and expenditure prescribes, without the certainty of having their notes immediately returned to them, nor diminish them, but at an almost equal certainty of the vacancy being filled up from some other source.'" Thus Mr. Anderson, manager of the Glasgow Union Banking Company, when asked by a Parliamentary committee, if the extraordinary advances made by the banks in a season of pressure did not increase the circulation of the country generally, answered, "*Those notes which we pay out, do not remain out;* they must be paid back, either to us or to some other bank, in the shape of deposits, till they are to be used, and they do not increase the permanent circulation of the country unless for a day or two, scarcely even for a day." As a bank cannot issue its own bills to any great extent without making additional loans and discounts, it cannot take advantage of the fact that the bills must remain out at least a day or two, before they find their way back; for if they were returned even on the third or fourth day, the bank would have nothing wherewith to redeem them except the notes which it had just discounted, and which have still from two to six months to run.

Accidental circumstances, indeed, sometimes enable a bank to pay out a considerable amount in its own bills, taking in return, not notes or drafts which will mature some months hence, but securities that are immediately convertible; a bank, for instance, is sometimes requested to furnish small bills, of the denomination of $10 and under, in exchange for a single $1,000 note of another bank. These bills of a low denomination, being needed to effect small payments, pass almost immeliately into the hands of retail dealers, who are consequently enabled to collect and deposit an equivalent amount, either in these very bills or in others of the same tenor. These dealers may deposit in several different banks, and the result will be, that a portion of the bills will be immediately returned to the bank which issued them, while the remaining portion will drive out of circulation, or force back upon their issuers, an equivalent sum in the bills of other banks. The operation will increase to some extent the circulation of one bank at the expense of the others; it will not augment the general circulation of the country.

The doctrine which I have endeavored to establish, may be summed up in the two following propositions.

1. The currency of any commercial nation, whether it consists exclusively of specie, or of a mixture of specie with bank-bills redeemable in specie on demand, is a fixed quantity, determined by the extent of the trade and the population, and by the perfection of the financial arrangements of commerce, as compared with the trade, population, and financial arrangements of all other commercial nations; the necessary equalization of the prices of all commodities in different countries, through the operations of international trade, is at once the result and the proof of this equal distribution of the total currency of the commercial world among all commercial nations, in exact proportion to the wants and circumstances of each. In the same manner, and under the operation of the same laws, prices are equalized through the various cities and towns of any one nation, and each city and town is consequently supplied with its due proportional share of the total currency of that country. This distribution of money is a self-adjusting process, not requiring any interference of legislation, or any efforts of individuals or associations specially directed to the purpose. *Laissez faire.*

2. In any mixed currency consisting of specie and convertible bank-bills, the amount of bank-bills of any given denomination which remains in circulation is determined exclusively by the convenience, the feelings and preferences at the time, of the people among whom they circulate, wholly irrespective of the regulations and the efforts of the institutions which issue these bills, — provided only that they issue them freely, or do

not arbitrarily keep the supply below the amount which the community is willing and desirous to receive. The banks may create a deficiency, but they cannot create an excess, in the circulation of such bills. In the numerous payments which are daily made at the banks, either in deposit or in liquidation of notes, that element of the currency, be it specie or bills, which is least in demand, least adapted to the present wishes and convenience of the people, will predominate, and will thus be quickly eliminated from the active circulation, till the ratio of the two branches of the currency is reduced to that point which the popular will requires. As the daily payments *into* the banks must, on an average, just equal the daily payments *out* of them, no effort or contrivance of the bank managers can avert this result. They *may* pay out, they usually *do* pay out, nothing but bills, and therefore, as a general rule, only bills are paid in; and thus the proportion of bills to specie continuing in circulation remains unaltered. But if a panic respecting the solvency of the banks should be created, besides the usual payments in deposit and in liquidation of notes, bills will be presented at the counter to be cashed, or redeemed in specie; and thus the proportion of coin in active circulation is rapidly augmented. After the panic has subsided, finding that so much coin is inconvenient, on account of its weight and bulk, and the trouble of counting it, specie will be freely paid in on deposit; and then the bank payments in bills will quickly restore the usual amount of paper to the currency.

The conclusion of the whole matter may be thus stated: — that the total amount of the currency is determined by the exigencies of international trade, or by the equalization of the prices of commodities throughout the commercial world; and the proportion of bank-bills to specie in a mixed currency is determined by the convenience and the wishes of the community at large.

Mr. Tooke, the able advocate in England of what is called "the banking principle," in opposition to "the currency principle," states a portion of his conclusions in the following manner: —

"That it is not in the power of banks of issue, including the Bank of England, to make any direct addition to the amount of notes circulating in their respective districts, however disposed they may be to do so. In the competition of banks of issue to get out their notes, there may be an extension of the circulation of some one or more of them in a large district, but it can only be by displacing the notes of rival banks.

"That neither is it in the power of banks of issue *directly* to diminish the total amount of the circulation; particular banks may withhold loans and discounts, and may refuse any longer to issue their own notes; but their notes so withdrawn will be replaced by the notes of other banks, or by other expedients calculated to answer the same purpose.

"That neither the country banks nor the Bank of England have it in their power to make additional issues of their paper come in aid of their banking resources. All advances by way of loan or discount, when the circulation is already full, can only be made by banks of issue in the same way as by non-issuing banks, out of their own *capital* or that of their depositors." *

In explanation of the only exception to the truth of these principles, I borrow again from Mr. Tooke's able pamphlet. "The only plausible argument," he says, "that I have met with, for a distinction between issuing and non-issuing banks, in their tendency to issue *money* in excess, (meaning, if translated into correct language, 'to make advances of *capital* in excess,') is, that in the competition, either of new banks of issue to get a portion of the existing circulation, or of established banks to get an increased share at the expense of neighboring banks, they are induced, with a view of getting out their notes, to make advances to an undue extent, and upon insufficient securities. This, I think, may be admitted as true to some extent; and to this extent there may be sufficient ground for making whatever regulations should be thought advisable to guard against malversation of banks generally, more stringent as against banks of issue." † But the object of the regulations adopted for this purpose would be, not to diminish the amount of bank-bills in circulation, but to confine the issue of them to solvent and well-regulated institutions conducted upon sound banking principles.

The greatest abuse of the banking system here in America

---

* Tooke *on the Currency Principle*, p. 122. † *Ibid.*, p. 95.

consists in the unrestricted competition of the banks with each other in the attempts made by each one to force its own bills into circulation. To understand the artifices adopted for this end, we must revert to the distinction already explained between the peculiar office performed by bills of a high, and by those of a low, denomination. The smaller notes, not exceeding the value of $ 10 each, circulate chiefly in the transactions of the consumers with the retail dealers and with each other, in the payment of wages, and in the thousand petty transactions which make up the whole business of life for those who are not engaged in large commercial operations. These small bills often pass from hand to hand, effecting a multitude of small payments, and remaining out of the bank a long time, before they are at last collected by some small dealer, and returned to a bank on deposit, often in a dirty and worn condition. The larger notes, on the other hand, embracing nearly all that exceed $ 10 each, circulate only among dealers, the largest of all only among wholesale dealers, and generally do not effect more than one payment before they are returned to the bank; often they are only carried from one bank to another, and then they are exchanged in the first settlement at the Clearing-House, and do not properly pass into circulation at all. It is only through the small-note circulation, then, that a bank can keep out any considerable amount of its bills. The extent of this circulation would properly depend upon the comparative population of the district to which the bank belongs, and not upon the amount of business transacted in that district, except it be business of a particular kind. Thus, manufacturers and other persons employing a large number of operatives have occasion to pay out weekly a considerable sum in wages, and, needing small bills for this purpose, can usually obtain a discount at the bank on very favorable terms, or when all other applicants would be refused. The officers of railroads, and others who have occasion to receive a great number of small payments, can distribute many small bills in "making change" for the larger bills which are tendered to them; and these also can obtain discounts on easy terms, sometimes on doubtful security. Some banks will even make loans to applicants from distant places, on express condition that the bills received shall be carried away, and not be paid into any bank at the first instance, but be distributed in small sums as occasion may arise. As only applicants of doubtful credit or in straitened circumstances would consent to buy the favors of the banks on such terms, it is obvious that such practices can be carried on only at great hazard.

The difference between the large-note and small-note currency may be further illustrated by the difference between metropolitan and country banks, in respect to the amount of their bills which they are able to keep in circulation. Here in Massachusetts, the Boston banks, with an aggregate capital of nearly thirty-three millions, have a circulation of only seven millions; the banks out of Boston, with a capital of only twenty-six millions, have a circulation of 15½ millions. More precisely, the Boston banks have one dollar in circulation to every $ 4.58 of capital; for the country banks, the proportion is one to every $ 1.66. The reason for this great difference is, that the Boston banks supply a small-note currency for a population of only 150,000; the country banks for a population numbering at least 835,000. The contrast would be still more striking, if the returns enabled us to distinguish large notes from small ones; it would probably be found, that the larger part of the country-bank currency consists of bills not exceeding on an average $ 10 in value, while most of the Boston circulation is in bills of $ 20 and upwards. So small an amount of active currency for so great a commerce as that of the metropolis of New England is enough to prove the correctness of Mr. Tooke's statement, that "the great bulk of the wholesale trade of the country is carried on and adjusted by settlements or sets-off of debts and credits, the written evidences of which are in bills of exchange, (including in that term all promissory notes payable to order after date,) while current payments for what are called cash sales are mostly made by checks; the ultimate balance only, arising out of the vast mass of such transactions, requiring liquidation in a comparatively small amount of bank-notes.

The banks in England cannot issue bills of a lower denomination than five pounds sterling, or nearly $ 25; the Bank of France issues none below 500 francs, or nearly $ 100. In both those countries, therefore, the currency which is in the hands of the common people, and by which all small payments are effected, consists exclusively of gold and silver; bank-notes are confined to the operations of trade, chiefly of the wholesale trade, and to the expenditures of the government and of persons of considerable fortune.

It may well be doubted whether a similar policy ought not to be generally adopted in this country; whether, at any rate, the circulation of bank-bills of a lower denomination than $ 10 ought not to be prohibited by law. It is evident from what precedes, that I regard a well-regulated bank currency, convertible into specie on demand, as a cheap and convenient substitute in part for the use of the precious metals, and as a necessary instrument of commerce; and that the evils commonly attributed to it, of being liable to issue in excess, and thereby of causing violent expansions and contractions of the total currency, and ruinous fluctuations in prices, are imaginary, no such issue in excess being possible so long as the banks continue to redeem their bills in coin. But a small-note currency cannot be well regulated; the profits resulting from its issue being considerable, there is a keen competition among the banks to obtain as large a share as possible of the business, and this competition leads to injurious and hazardous practices, whereby the solvency of these institutions and the stability of the whole system are perilled. Such a currency is safe only when it is backed by sufficient specie reserves; but as there is a loss of interest on such reserves, there is a great temptation to reduce them to narrower limits than prudence would warrant. The circulation of some of the country banks in Massachusetts is to the specie in their vaults as more than forty to one. It is true, that a portion of the specie which is the guaranty of their circulation is lodged in the Boston banks; but the aggregate bank circulation of the State is to the aggregate specie reserve as more than five to one, a proportion which is hardly consistent with the safety of the whole, and which, as this reserve is very unequally distributed, is certainly pregnant with danger to many. Each bank, looking only to its own safety, and not to the safety of the whole system, relies upon the aid of the other banks, in case of specie being suddenly demanded of it to any considerable extent; it issues, for instance, $ 100,000 in bills, when it has less than $ 3,000 in coin, because it knows that, if an emergency should arise, it could easily obtain $30,000, either in coin or bills, from the neighboring or associate banks. So it could, if the emergency were a limited one, that perilled only its own safety. But if there were a general run upon all the banks, such as might easily be produced in a time of pressure by the reported insolvency of two or three of them, each one would be obliged to take care of itself, and could render no aid to its correspondents or neighbors. Though the run, then, might not be extensive enough to appear serious in the outset, it might still suffice to break half of the country banks in the State; and the alarm being thus quickened into a panic, the demand for coin would so rapidly increase, that a general suspension of specie payments would inevitably ensue. It was thus that all the banks were compelled to suspend in May, 1837. At that time, most of the banks in New England, and many of those in the other States, were in what would be usually considered as a perfectly sound condition; they had suffered no extraordinary losses, their capitals were unimpaired, and their specie reserves bore the ordinary ratio to their circulation. But it was a time of great financial distress, — the reaction from a speculative fever that had reached its crisis. While the public mind was in this excited state, the failure of a few really insolvent banks in the Middle States gave a direction to the panic, and an immediate and total suspension became inevitable. As fast as the news spread, the banks, conscious of their inability to meet a storm, closed their doors before the run upon them could begin. Though perfectly provided for ordinary fair weather, they were unable to withstand the first gust of a tempest. But the act was only a suspension; it was not insolvency. After the alarm had had time to subside, the banks reopened their doors, and, here in New England at least, not one in fifty of them failed to redeem every penny of its obligations.

In reference to bank currency, what the public need to be guarded against is not the occasional mismanagement or fraudulent conduct of a few institutions; against these, the watchfulness of the other banks, and the general severity of the laws against fraud, are a sufficient protection. The great evil is the general insecurity of the whole system in a time of pressure; and this evil cannot be obviated so long as there is a bounty upon the diminution of the specie reserve, and upon the extension of the small-note currency. Our present system throws the bulk of the circulation into the hands of the community in general, — that is, of persons who have no concern with the banks in their ordinary transactions, who have little to do with commerce, who know nothing of the circumstances on which the safety of the currency depends, who are peculiarly liable to panic, and are apt to adopt, when alarmed, only such measures as will increase the danger. There is a saving of expense, as we have shown, in the substitution of bank paper for gold and silver coin; but this is not a saving of expense for the body of the people. It accrues exclusively to the benefit of the banks, and of the customers of the banks, — that is, of the trading community and the capitalists. It is a saving made *through* the people, but not *for* the people, who do not profit by it, except in some small measure, by an increase of convenience in the use of a currency which is not burdensome by its weight and bulk. Common justice requires, then, that the people should be protected against the slightest risk in the use of this currency. It should be made to them as secure as the coin which its circulation deprives them of; and this is obviously impossible, so long as the occurrence of a financial pressure may at any time drive all the banks in the country, however well managed, to a suspension of specie payments. Banks are now instituted where the exigencies of commerce do not call for them, — in small towns, where there is little trade and little surplus capital, — in order only to profit by the circulation of small bills, which can be put forth in large amounts in such neighborhoods. They are country banks only in name and ostensible location, their capital being generally furnished by merchants and bankers from a distance, and often lent out again in large sums to the stockholders themselves. Cut off the small-note currency, and such institutions, which are established on false pretences, even if they are not fraudulent in intention, would cease to exist; and the banking business proper would be conducted only in cities and large towns, by that portion of the community who are directly interested in it, and who alone would be affected by its fluctuations. Banks would no longer be the objects of popular jealousy and dislike. They would be regarded as exclusively commercial institutions, whose operations no more concern the public at large than those of the stock exchange.

The great obstacle in this country to the prohibition of a small-note currency is the independent legislation of the different States. If Massachusetts, for instance, should forbid the issue of bills for a less sum than $10 by its own banks, its currency would immediately be flooded by small notes from the other New England States, the banks in which, being relieved from competition, would be able to send out a much larger amount of such notes than before. The Federal government having no power under the Constitution to interfere in such a case, the circulation of small notes could be effectually prohibited only by concert among the individual States; and this would require greater unanimity of action by the different legislatures than can reasonably be expected.

All the expedients which have been devised for the security of a small-note circulation are insufficient, because they are not directed against the quarter from which there is any real apprehension of danger; they are fortifications of a point which is not seriously menaced. They are expedients, not to lessen the amount of the small-note currency, nor to provide against a general suspension of specie payments by the banks, and a consequent depreciation of the whole currency, but to obviate the risk of insolvency by one or more banks, and to provide for the ultimate redemption of their bills even when they become insolvent. This last purpose would be sufficiently answered by merely giving a priority of payment to the bill-holders, as in all ordinary cases, the assets of an insolvent bank are large enough to redeem its circulation, though not to pay off its deposits and other liabilities; and extraordinary cases are provided for by the penalties enacted against fraud.

The Safety Fund system, as it was called, was a kind of mutual insurance by the banks of each others' circulation; all were compelled to contribute a small proportion of their capital to form a general fund, out of which the bills of an insolvent bank were to be redeemed. This was a tax imposed upon the well-regulated institutions to make up for the frauds or malpractices of their rivals; it offered no security against the occurrence of a general panic and a general suspension.

Another expedient, now adopted in many States, is to authorize any association for banking purposes to issue notes of any denomination, from one dollar upwards, on condition of making a deposit with the State authorities of public stocks, mortgages, and other good securities, to an amount, at their present market value, equal to that of the notes which they propose to circulate. This deposit is a guaranty for the *ultimate* security of their issues, which sort of guaranty, as we have seen, is not at all necessary. What is needed is security for the *immediate* convertibility of bank currency, without which, in a general panic, it may undergo great depreciation, though there is positive assurance that the notes will *ultimately* be redeemed in full. To allow mortgages of real estate to form a portion of this State deposit is especially unwise; for mortgages, as we have seen, because the sums for which they are granted cannot be realized till after long delay, do not form a safe basis on which the banks could make ordinary discounts. As to the State stocks and other public securities, Mr. Gouge properly observes, "The mischief is, that they are least available when they are most wanted; the very causes which might prevent the banks from redeeming their issues promptly, would cause a fall in the value of the stocks and mortgages on the ultimate security of which their notes have been issued." In a commercial crisis, or after a general suspension of specie payments, many such stocks and securities might become entirely unsalable.

The Sub-Treasury system, as it is called, adopted by Congress in 1846, as a means of divorcing the fiscal operations of the Federal government from the banks, and of contributing to the establishment of a currency consisting exclusively of gold and silver, is ludicrously insufficient for this last purpose, to effect which it begins at the wrong end. It is the rude and operose plan of requiring all payments to or by the United States to be made entirely in specie. The balance which remains at any time in the hands of the government must consist exclusively of coin, and be deposited in vaults and safes, under the strict injunction that it must not be put to any use, or applied to any beneficial purpose whatsoever. In what manner this sum, varying during the last few years from 20 to 25 millions of dollars, thus lying dead and unproductive, guarded by thick walls and iron grates, can promote or expedite the general adoption of a specie currency, it is difficult to imagine. The mere necessity of keeping up this idle deposit, which is liable to sudden and great fluctuations in amount, under the varying ratio of the government receipts to the government expenditures, would of itself be a formidable obstacle to the safe establishment of a metallic currency; the money-market would be subject at any time to a dangerous expansion or contraction from the involuntary movements of the national treasury. Besides, the fiscal transactions of the government are necessarily on an extensive scale; it deals in very large sums, such as most easily and naturally assume the shape of paper evidences of debt, transfers of book credits, and other modes of settling accounts and effecting current payments without the necessity of moving, or even counting, large amounts of specie. It is in the numerous petty transactions of ordinary life among common people, that the weight and bulk of gold and silver coin cease to be an encumbrance, and that the want of the perfect security which it affords is seriously felt. A metallic currency would be a boon to the lower classes, but is an intolerable burden to the State. According to the admission of its most zealous advocates, the Sub-Treasury has occasioned only a very limited circulation of gold and silver, — "chiefly from the public depositories to the banks, and back again from the banks to the public depositories."

In spite of numerous and jealous restrictions in the law, large sums will be received and paid out by the same office, on the same day, in some more easy and compendious form than by a double transfer of coin, or by rolling kegs of specie out of the door, and then rolling them in again; and the business of exchange between distant portions of the country will be conducted without the actual transportation of the precious metals, except to a very limited extent. The law requires, for instance, that all sums should be received and paid in gold or silver; but the law cannot prevent A, a creditor of the United States, who has just received a draft for $ 10,000 on the Sub-Treasurer in New York, from selling that draft to B, a merchant who has occasion to pay the government that sum on account of the duties on a cargo of goods, and who finds it more convenient to deliver the draft than to employ a horse and dray to carry the specie. In respect to such transactions, the Sub-Treasury is only a convenient *deposit bank* for the creditors of the United States, and the government drafts upon it are unexceptionable evidences of debt, or certificates of deposit, which, being indorsed over from one person to another, may effect many settlements of accounts between individuals, before they are finally paid into the treasury as ordinary receipts of custom-duties. Nay, the government itself, for its own convenience in transporting funds from one part of the country to another, has been obliged, in order to avoid the delay, risk, and expense of the actual conveyance of specie, to drive a traffic in these drafts, thus performing a service for others while receiving a favor for itself. "For example," says Mr. Gouge, "a person in Washington city wishes to pay a sum of money in New York. He deposits the gold or silver in the treasury office at Washington, and receives an order in return for an equal amount of gold and silver on the assistant treasurer at New York. In this way, the government is saved the expense of bringing gold and silver from New York to Washington city, and private individuals the expense of carrying gold and silver from Washington city to New York." In fact, the practice was soon instituted "of assigning transfer drafts to bankers, brokers, and others, and allowing them the use of the money for such time as, it may be supposed, will compensate them for the expense of transporting specie from one depository to another. . . . . . At the commencement of the system, some seventy or eighty days were allowed for carrying money from New York to New Orleans; but the time was gradually prolonged, so that from 100 to 135 days were consumed in transporting the public money from the depository at New York to the depository at Washington." The transfers thus made within a period of twenty-eight months exceeded fifteen millions of dollars, and the money was out of the treasury depositories on an average about sixty days. In respect to this function of transfer, the Sub-Treasury is only a great *exchange bank*, though it performs gratuitously the services for which other exchange brokers charge a premium. Instead of divorcing the treasury from the banks, therefore, the institution is itself a bank, — a very ill-constituted one, however, performing in a bungling manner two banking functions in spite of itself, but reaping no profit from them, and only deranging the transactions of other banks by its abnormal interference and competition.

It really performs to a certain extent a *third* banking function, by supplying a considerable amount of paper currency; when the government draws upon it, there is nothing to prevent the person in whose favor the draft is made from indorsing it *in blank*, as it is termed, (that is, without naming the indorsee,) and then it is a bank bill, which, without further indorsement, may be transferred successively to many different hands, and effect as many payments, before it is finally presented for payment, or paid in, at the particular Sub-Treasury on which it is drawn. True, the law requires the Secretary of the Treasury "to enforce the speedy presentation of all government drafts for payment at the place where payable, and to prescribe the time, according to the different distances of the depositories from the seat of government, within which all drafts upon them respectively shall be presented for payment." But this provision is wholly indefinite, and cannot be made otherwise than indefinite, as more or less time may be necessary under different circumstances, and within a very short time many transfers of the draft would be possible.

These facts illustrate the general principle, that large pecuniary transactions cannot be effected on the rude and burdensome plan of an actual transfer of specie at every payment. The various commercial expedients, of deposits, transfers of credit, sets-off, bills of exchange, and other forms of paper currency, will intrude themselves, however they may be forbidden by law, in order to save the parties concerned the intolerable annoyance of counting out, or weighing out, large amounts in coin, of carrying tons of specie to and fro over great distances, and of employing a horse and dray every time that it is necessary to pay or receive a few thousands. We might as well seek to do away with gas-lights, steamboats, and railroads, as attempt to prohibit these labor-saving and time-saving contrivances. What is wanted is not prohibition, but regulation, of a paper currency. Take away the small notes, and the large ones will regulate themselves, because they will circulate only among merchants, bankers, and capitalists, who understand the principles on which they are issued, and will most easily detect any mismanagement in relation to them, by which they would be themselves the first and greatest sufferers.

I have already borrowed from Adam Smith the ingenious illustration, that "the gold and silver money which circulates in any country may very properly be compared to a highway, which, while it circulates and carries to market all the grass and corn of the country, produces itself not a single pile of either." He carries out the comparison still further. "The judicious operations of banking," he remarks, "by providing, if I may be allowed so violent a metaphor, a sort of wagon-way through the air, enable the country to convert, as it were, a great part of its highways into good pastures and corn-fields, and thereby to increase very considerably the annual produce of its land and labor. The commerce and industry of the country, however, it must be acknowledged, though they may be somewhat augmented, cannot be altogether so secure, when they are thus, as it were, suspended upon the Dædalian wings of paper money, as when they travel about upon the solid ground of gold and silver. Over and above the accidents to which they are exposed from the unskilfulness of the conductors of this paper money, they are liable to several others, from which no prudence or skill of those conductors can guard them."

Among such accidents is the possible occurrence of a panic, or the reaction from a speculative fever, which may cause a drain of specie sufficient to exhaust the reserves of the banks. The mere presence of a reserved fund of coin and bullion in the country is no safeguard against such a calamity, if it be locked up as in the vaults of the Sub-Treasury, whence it will not be forthcoming to meet a drain, whether that drain be caused by a demand for export growing out of previous excessive importation, or by a general propensity to hoard coin stimulated by alarm for the safety of the banks. The fund so locked up might as well, for any practical purpose, be on the other side of the Atlantic.* It is said, indeed, that the neces-

* "Any addition of specie," says Mr. Webster, "in order to be useful, must either go into the circulation as a part of that circulation, or else it must go into the banks to enable them the better to sustain and redeem their paper. But this bill [to establish the Sub-Treasury] is calculated to promote neither of those ends, but exactly the reverse. It withdraws specie from the circulation and from the banks, and piles

sity of keeping up this fund occasions frequent calls upon the banks for coin, and to meet these calls they are obliged to fortify themselves with larger specie reserves than they would otherwise deem necessary. So they are; but the additional funds are thus provided to meet the demands of the treasury, and not to be a safeguard of the bank issues; the additional danger exhausts, and probably a little more than exhausts, the additional protection.

The only use to which this idle treasury fund could be put, with a view to the improvement of the currency, would be to make it the basis for an issue by the government of an equivalent sum in small notes, designed for general circulation. As such notes would rest upon the faith of the Federal government, would be represented, dollar for dollar, by coin actually in the treasury, for which, at any time, they could be exchanged, and would have a general instead of a local character and currency, they would be preferred to the small bills issued by the banks, which they would soon displace and drive out of circulation. Being issued, moreover, only for small sums, never exceeding five, or, at the utmost, ten dollars, they would only form small currency for the bulk of the people, and would be used but to a very small extent in wholesale trade or large financial operations, so that they would not enable government to interfere with the ordinary course of traffic and exchange. As they would be issued only in payment of government debt or in ordinary expenditure, the treasury would still have the use of all its funds, while preserving intact in its vaults an amount of specie equal to the whole amount of its notes in circulation. Such a currency, if limited to an amount somewhat below that of the probable circulation of small bills, would have all the convenience of paper and all the security of coin; no panic could shake public confidence in it, or subject it to a depreciation. There would, indeed, be no

it up in useless heaps in the treasury. It weakens the general circulation, by making the portion of specie which is part of it so much the less; it weakens the banks, by reducing the amount of coin which supports their paper. The general evil imputed to our currency, for some years past, is, that paper has formed too great a portion of it. The operation of this measure must be to increase that very evil. I have admitted the evil, and have concurred in measures to remedy it. I have favored the withdrawing of small bills from circulation, to the end that specie might take their place." — Webster's *Works*, Vol. IV. p. 457.

economy in its adoption, as a corresponding amount of specie would lie idle in the treasury. But it lies there idle now, while the injurious and unsafe portion of the bank currency circulates freely. The only object in issuing this paper would be to displace the insecure small-note circulation of the banks, and to provide a perfectly safe and convenient currency for the community at large, who are not engaged in trade or banking.

But as political considerations would probably be an insuperable obstacle to the adoption of this plan, or of any other scheme for doing away with the small-note circulation of the banks altogether, the question remains, if there are not some means of lessening the quantity, and adding to the security, of that circulation. A judicious application of the taxing power might have this effect. Here in Massachusetts, and in several other States, a heavy tax is laid on bank capital as such, and individuals are also taxed for the bank stock which they may own, as well as for their other property. Thus, capital invested in banks is taxed twice over, — an injurious and unreasonable distinction, as its effect, so far as it goes, is to raise the rate of interest, increase the difficulty of borrowing money, hinder capital from passing into the hands of those who will use it to the best advantage, and prevent the industrious and enterprising classes from obtaining the means of applying their industry and enterprise in such a way as to obtain the largest possible results. I have already shown at some length, (*vide ante*, pp. 8 – 12,) that wealth is *not* locked up when placed in banks, but rather that it is thereby released from a state of inactivity, and "made to do its full part in supplying the lungs of industry, keeping it alive and active, and making all the parts of the body politic and social contribute to the sustenance and growth of the whole." A widow, for instance, who could make no use of her little property if it remained in her own hands, invests in a bank, which lends it to industrious tradesmen and mechanics, and they obtain additional tools and goods with it, and thus labor to better purpose, sharing their increased gains with the owner of the capital, who thus obtains income from it without diminishing the principal. "The declaration so often quoted," says Mr. Webster, "that 'all who trade on borrowed capital ought to break,' is the most aristocratic sentiment ever uttered in this country. It is a sentiment which, if carried out by political arrangement, would condemn the great majority of mankind to the perpetual condition of mere day-laborers. When we abolish credit, we divorce labor from capital; and when we divorce labor from capital, capital is hoarded and labor starves."

Instead of imposing a double tax upon the banks, *so far as they are institutions of deposit and discount*, they ought rather to be released from taxation altogether. A bounty rather than a penalty should be enacted for taking capital out of the hands of those who either cannot use it or will not use it, and confiding it to those who will unite it with industry, and thus make it active in the great business of production. The double tax has been imposed from an indistinct perception of the fact, that the banks in their third function, as issuers of bank currency, and especially of the small-note circulation, obtain profits which do not properly belong to them, and subject the community thereby to very considerable hazard of loss for the sake of their own advantage. If paper currency is to be substituted for metallic currency, the profits of the substitution ought to accrue for the benefit of those who make it, — of those who are willing to give up coin, and accept paper with all its attendant risks. The act of substitution is the act of the community at large; to be the agents in this act is a usurped function of the banks, in no wise connected with their other and proper offices. It belongs to the state, and ought to be exercised for the benefit of the tax-payers, — that is, of the persons who, by giving up coin and accepting paper, make a saving of the precious metals, and ought to profit by that saving. Especially is this reasoning applicable to the case of the small-note circulation. In respect to bills of a higher denomination than $10, it may fairly be urged, that they circulate generally among merchants, bankers, and capitalists, who therefore ought to be allowed, through the banks, to control the issue of them, so far as it can be controlled consistently with maintaining their convertibility into specie on demand, and to reap the benefit of their circulation. But not so with regard to the small bills, which are the money of the bulk of the people. Here, the whole risk rests with the persons who use the notes; and if any profit is to be derived from that use, this also should belong to them. Otherwise, a serious hazard is imposed upon them for the benefit of others, who can show no good title to the gains which they usurp. "It is quite idle," says Mr. T. Tooke, a zealous advocate of the banks, "it is quite idle to say that the lower classes have the option of refusing to take the country notes; practically, in the great majority of instances, they have not and cannot have any such option. But if there is any object more important than another, for which the government of every state has been invested with the privilege of coining money, it is that of protecting the lower classes of society, who are little competent in this particular to protect themselves, from the risk of loss in receiving their stipulated wages or other payments."

Take off the tax of one per cent on bank capital, then, and impose a tax of five or ten per cent on the circulation of all bills below the denomination of $10. The amount of small notes would thus be very much diminished, and as the state, through the tax, would reap nearly the whole profit from those remaining in circulation, it could well afford to guarantee their immediate convertibility into specie. Such a measure would be even preferable to the one adopted in England, after the failure of so many private banks of issue in 1825. The circulation of one-pound notes at that time was computed at upwards of five millions sterling. So many of them became valueless, or were greatly depreciated, by the failure of the issuing banks, that Parliament the following year entirely suppressed this class of notes. However it may be regretted, adds Mr. Tooke, "that the holders of private country bank-notes, being now of the denomination of £5 and upwards, should occasionally be exposed to loss by failure of the issuers, it will hardly be contended that their case is so important and so clearly distinct from the case of depositors, and other sufferers by the failure of banks, as to justify, with the view of protecting them, an alteration of the whole system of issue."

CHAPTER XXI.

PAPER MONEY, AND ITS USE AS A REVOLUTIONARY CURRENCY.

We have still to speak briefly of the circulation of *paper money*, properly so called, or of bills which do not profess to be immediately convertible into specie. These are sometimes issued by the state, in cases of great emergency, and are then usually called *bills of credit*. In this form, they are forbidden by the Constitution of the United States, which declares that "no State shall coin money, emit bills of credit, or make anything but gold or silver coin a tender in payment of debts." Bank-notes, also, after the banks have suspended specie payments, so that their notes are no longer convertible into coin on demand, become bills of credit, or paper money. Thus the currency of Great Britain consisted of paper money from 1797, when the Bank of England suspended payment, till 1819, when it resumed. The distinguishing characteristics of such money are, that it is inconvertible, and its circulation is compulsory. Thus, to take the more common form of this currency, which is issued by the authority of the state, when the government has no longer the means of meeting its pecuniary engagements, it begins to make purchases and to pay its debts by issuing, not coin, nor bills immediately convertible into coin, but its own promises to pay at some future time. These "promises to pay" are made *legal tender*, — that is, creditors are compelled to receive them in satisfaction of their demands. Their circulation is compulsory, then; but the very fact that they are receivable in payment of debts gives them a conventional value. To any person who has money to receive, it matters nothing whether the money possesses intrinsic value or not, or whether the "promise to pay" which it bears upon its face is ever redeemed or not, provided he is sure that he can make payments with it, and cancel his own obligations. Even if the money is undergoing a rapid depreciation, as he does not expect to retain it any time in his possession, but intends to pay it away again the next day, or even the next hour, he knows that it cannot lose much value in his hands, but that it will be worth nearly as much when he parts with it as when he received it. Paper dollars are as good as silver ones, so long as they will cancel debts and effect purchases equally well.

Paper money of this kind was issued by nearly all the American Colonies before the period of their separation from England; and from the various degrees of its depreciation in different parts of the country arose the different value of the *shilling*, which is still with us a popular denomination of account, though not an actual coin, and not recognized in the legal currency. The shilling was the denomination used in the Colonial paper money; and when the shilling had its par value, 4*s.* 6*d.* were equal to a silver dollar. But paper shillings became depreciated, so that, in New England, *six* shillings came to pass for a dollar; in New York, *eight*, and in Pennsylvania, *seven* shillings had this value. The *names* of these "shillings" and "pence" have remained for nearly a century after the disappearance of the reality, and still create much confusion in the popular mode of reckoning money.

But the most remarkable experiment of paper money here in America was the Continental currency, as it was called, issued by authority of Congress during the American Revolution. The epithet "Continental," like *National* or *Federal* now-a-days, marked the distinction between what was done by the government of the whole Union, and the acts of the separate Colonies or States. In June and July, 1775, to meet the expenses of the war which was seen to be inevitable, and in fact had already commenced at Lexington, Congress, having no other funds, issued three millions of dollars in these bills of credit, with a promise that they should be redeemed in four annual instalments, to commence at the end of four years. The burden of redeeming them was distributed among the several Colonies, in the ratio of their supposed number of inhabitants. The bills were issued in the purchase of provisions and munitions of war, and in the payment of the troops. In November of the same year, the issue of three additional millions became necessary; the annual instalments for redeeming this sum were to begin in eight years. Specie, which had been scarce before, had now almost entirely disappeared from the country, and the "Continental money" was considerably depreciated. So rapidly did this depreciation and the exigencies of the war increase, that in the course of the following year, 1776, fourteen millions more had to be issued. After the issue of the first six millions, no time was fixed for the redemption of the bills. Of course, the depreciation, aggravated by large local issues of the several Colonies, soon became alarming, and futile attempts were made by Congress and the Colonial legislatures to check it. The New England Colonies tried to regulate by law the prices to be paid in this currency for labor and commodities; and Congress resolved, that the bills ought to pass for the same value as Spanish dollars in all dealings and payments, and that all persons who should refuse to take them at this valuation, ought to be considered as "enemies to the United States," and to be punished with forfeitures and other penalties. But the necessary laws of exchange and trade were not to be counteracted by legislative enactments or the patriotism of the people. Additional issues continued to be made, and the paper continued to depreciate, until, in 1780, the amount in circulation was about 200 millions, and 500, even 1,000, dollars in this currency were offered for one in silver.* Then finally the bills ceased to circulate, and became entirely worthless, as dealers would not accept them on any terms.

No attempt was subsequently made to cancel the original obligation by redeeming the bills, either in full or in part; for as the depreciation had been gradual, while the bills were rapidly circulating in the community, it had obviously become impossible to measure the exact loss which each holder of them had suffered. To pay the last holder in full would only have aggravated the injustice, by giving him much more than was his due, and leaving his predecessors without any compensa-

---

* John Adams, in a letter to the Count de Vergennes (June 22, 1780), gives some curious particulars respecting the enormous prices which were paid for commodities in America in 1779 and 1780, in consequence of this depreciation of the currency. "Bohea tea," he says, "forty sous a pound at L'Orient and Nantes, sold for forty-five dollars. Salt, which costs very little in Europe, and used to be sold for a shilling a bushel, was forty dollars a bushel, and, in some of the other States, two hundred dollars at times. Linens, which cost two livres a yard in France, forty dollars a yard. Broadcloths, a louis d'or a yard here, two hundred dollars a yard. Ironmongery of all sorts, 120 for one. Millinery of all sorts, at an advance far exceeding. These were the prices at Boston. At Philadelphia and in all the other States, they were much higher." — John Adams's *Works*, Vol. VII. p. 199.

tion whatever. It was justly remarked, that the depreciation of the paper money ought to be considered as a tax, inasmuch as the paper was first issued only to relieve the people from the necessity of paying a tax. Each person through whose hands the money passed parted with it again at a loss, proportioned to the quantity he held and the time he held it. As the currency circulated among the whole people, the rich and poor holding it, and suffering by its depreciation, in proportion to the respective amounts of their cash purchases and sales, the whole loss was divided among them very nearly in just proportion to their ability and liability to pay a tax. The payment of the whole value borne on the face of the bill to one who had received it, perhaps, at the rate of a hundred for one, could have been made only by a second tax on the same persons who had already been fairly and heavily taxed by its depreciation.

The history of the paper money issued in France, in the course of the Revolution which commenced in 1789, is perfectly similar to that of the corresponding experiment in America. The French bills of credit, however, as their name (*assignats*) indicates, were nominally issued upon a basis of real property. The national domains, as they were termed, or the confiscated estates of the crown, the clergy, and the emigrants, were made over, or sold in mass, to the municipalities or towns in which they were respectively situated. These municipalities, not having funds to pay immediately, received the property on long credit, binding themselves to pay in instalments, as fast as they were able to make sales of the estates without sacrifice. The creditors of the state then obtained their dues by receiving orders or assignments (*assignats*) on the municipalities for a portion of the debt thus due to the state. The holders of these orders might, if they saw fit, immediately obtain the value of them, by becoming the purchasers of the estates which the municipalities had to sell, and paying for them in *assignats*. If they preferred to wait, they still had the value of the national domains, and the obligations of the municipalities, as securities for the ultimate payment of the debt. Meanwhile, the *assignats* themselves were transferable property, which might be exchanged for commodities, or assigned in payment of debts; and to aid the negotiation of them, they were made transferable without indorsement, and constituted legal tender; that is, they were converted into paper money, and as the issue of them increased, they displaced the sounder portions of the currency, and became the universal medium of exchange.

As the expenditures of the state were heavy, through the war in which it was involved, and as it was an easy process to stamp and issue *assignats* in satisfaction of all demands, the issue of this paper money soon became excessive, and the inevitable consequence followed, its rapid and great depreciation. This fall in value could not be checked by the sale of the confiscated estates, for, as the currency depreciated, the prices of the national domains, as well as of all other property, rose in the same proportion. The issue began in 1790; and as early as 1793 one franc in silver had come to be worth six francs in *assignats*. The arbitrary government of the Jacobins, who were then in power, having put in forced circulation the anticipated proceeds of the property, now undertook to sustain the value of its currency by penal enactments. They might as well have enacted laws to prevent the sun from setting at the close of the day. Six years' imprisonment was denounced against any one who should exchange any amount of silver or gold for a greater nominal value of *assignats;* and a *maximum* of price was established for bread and the other necessaries of life. The only consequence was, that the owners of grain and other commodities refused to bring them to market at all, and thus what was a scarcity became a famine. The starving people then became furious; the severities formerly exercised only against the nobles, the clergy, and the royalists were now turned against the rich, the farmers of the public revenue, the traders who were accused of monopolizing food and holding it back from sale, &c., and these were sent in crowds to the guillotine. But all the terrors of that period which was emphatically called "the Reign of Terror" were not enough to arrest the depreciation. Bread rose to 22 francs (nominally over $4) a pound, and the prices of other commodities were in proportion. The issue of *assignats* amounted, in 1796, to the enormous sum of 45,000,000,000 of francs. But the state receipts from taxes, loans, the sale of the national domains, and other causes, had reduced the amount actually in circulation to about

24,000,000,000. These were exchanged, at the rate of thirty for one, for *mandats*, another species of paper money, the holder of which was entitled to take any portion of the confiscated estates not yet sold, by paying in this new currency 22 times the rent which the property brought in 1790. The *mandats* were also receivable in payment of government taxes and loans. In this way, the stock of paper money in circulation was greatly diminished; but the issue of *mandats* still being excessive, they finally became as much depreciated as the *assignats* had been before them, and by a spasmodic effort, both the government and the people reverted to a specie currency. The final result of the experiment in France, as in America, was, that through the depreciation of the currency, the people paid a very heavy tax for the success of the Revolution, — a tax somewhat irregularly and unequally imposed, but yet approaching as near to equity as could be expected from any public measure which had its birth in the exigencies and turmoil of a great civil war.

Paper money was also issued by the revolutionary authorities of Hungary and Rome in 1849; but the speedy restoration of the former government in both cases prevented the experiment from being worked out to an end. In fact, experience has proved, what might have been demonstrated from the theory of the subject, that this kind of money is a proper *revolutionary currency*. It is usually first issued amid the commercial disasters, and the destruction of public and private credit, which are among the first consequences of the overthrow of an old government, and the outbreak of a civil war. The way is prepared for the introduction of it by a violent contraction of the old currency, consequent on the general disappearance of the gold and silver coins, which everybody at such a crisis is disposed to collect and hoard, or to send out of the country. This gap or vacuum in the circulation manifests itself by the extraordinary low prices of all commodities, the difficulty of effecting sales of any kind of property, the consequent impossibility of meeting commercial engagements, and general bankruptcy. Some kind of money — it hardly matters what — is needed to fill up this gap; and it turns out, by a happy coincidence, that the issue of some sort of conventional currency is the only financial resource of the revolutionary government. At the trivial expense of stamping bits of paper with a vague "promise to pay" at some future date, the insurgent authorities, otherwise penniless, find their exchequer as well supplied for a time, as if, to adopt Mr. Ricardo's illustration, a gold mine had been suddenly discovered within the precincts of the public treasury. In such cases, it is thought to be the enthusiastic patriotism of the people which, for a while, sustains the credit of the new currency, and preserves it from any material depreciation, till a very considerable amount has been issued. But the truth is, that the gap produced in the circulation, by the causes already explained, creates a pressing want of something to fill it up, and restore prices to their former level. Any kind of money, though the feelings of the people were against rather than in favor of the issuers of it, would have this effect, provided only that it be made legal tender, or an instrument for discharging debts. So long as the new currency is not more than sufficient to fill up the vacant space in the old one, its value will remain nearly at par; — *nearly*, I say, because gold and silver coin, being capable of exportation, which paper money is not, will always command a slight premium. And the difference indicated by this premium will act still further in favor of the new currency; because, for reasons already explained, the depreciated or overvalued money will drive out even what remained of the perfect and sound currency, and take the whole circulation to itself.

Suppose, for instance, that the currency of the country in its normal condition is equal to 200 millions. If, then, in the panic created by a revolution, 80 millions should be hoarded or sent abroad, the insurgent government will be able to issue 80 millions in paper at once, which will circulate at a discount of not more than 2 or 3 per cent. As every person will then prefer to pay his debts and make purchases with paper rather than coin, inasmuch as he will thereby save 2 or 3 per cent, the remaining portion of the sound currency will be gradually collected and sent abroad, and the new government will be enabled to issue 120 millions more in specie, without doing any other injury than raising the prices of commodities 2 or 3 per cent, — a difference too slight to be noticed.

Any revolutionary government, therefore, though it should inherit, as is most probable, only an empty treasury, may at once obtain funds equal in amount to the whole circulation of the country, by merely issuing paper money to this extent. Still further: this issue, coming immediately after a period of violent contraction of the currency, and of consequent low prices, inability to realize property or collect debts, general want of credit, and widely spread bankruptcy, will have the effect to raise prices again, to restore credit, to animate commerce anew, and to diffuse through the whole country the glow of returning prosperity. All this will operate to the advantage of the new government, and the revolutionary fever of the people will rise higher than ever. Yet again: as this paper money, now in universal use, depends solely upon the faith of the revolutionary government, whose engagements, it is feared, would not be respected by the former authorities, should they be restored to power, every person in the country has an interest in resisting such a restoration, and supporting the cause of the insurgents. It is thus that a heavy national debt and a large depreciated paper currency, such as exist in Austria at the present day, though to a superficial glance they may appear as sources of weakness in the government, are in truth the pillars of its strength. Every capitalist, every person who has any property to lose, under such circumstances, will resist a revolution to the death, fearing that the successful insurgents would wipe out the debt with a sponge, and obtain room for a new batch of paper money by repudiating the former issue. Without its enormous national debt, it may be doubted whether even the government of Great Britain would have resisted as successfully as it did the political convulsions of the memorable year 1848. As it was, every stockholder and every shopkeeper in London armed himself as a special constable, to resist the ragged army of proletaries who assembled on Kennington Common in April of that year.

Could the revolutionists stop here, then, in their issue of paper money, all would be well. Unfortunately they cannot stop. There is a necessity of lavish expenditure in a revolution, especially if the exigencies of a civil or foreign war are added to the other demands on the treasury. Having put forth paper money enough to fill up the whole circulation of the country, and being intoxicated with the brilliant success of this measure, the needy government finds itself compelled, not unwillingly, to issue more; and then, inevitably, marked depreciation ensues. John Adams stated the theory of this subject with perfect correctness seventy-five years ago, when his own country was affording a striking illustration of the truth of his doctrine. "The amount of ordinary commerce, external and internal, of a country," he says, "may be computed at a fixed sum. A certain sum of money is necessary to circulate among the society in order to carry on their business. This precise sum is discoverable by calculation, and reducible to certainty. You may emit paper or any other currency for this purpose, until you reach this rule, and it will not depreciate. After you exceed this rule, it will depreciate; and no power or act of legislation hitherto invented can prevent it. In the case of paper, if you go on emitting for ever, the whole mass will be worth no more than that was which was emitted within the rule." *

In the case already supposed, of the ordinary currency amounting to 200 millions, should paper money be issued to the extent of 400 millions, the certain result will be a depreciation of fifty per cent; that is, no greater value will remain in the hands of the community than 200 millions, though the government has nominally paid off twice as much. Here, then, taxation begins; by issuing 400 millions when only half as much was needed, the government has really taxed the community to the extent of 200 millions, less the depreciation to which each portion of this sum was subject at the date of its emission. If, for instance, 40 millions of this sum were issued before the depreciation began, a second 40 millions when the depreciation was at 12½ per cent, a third 40 millions when it was at 25, a fourth at 37½, and a fifth at 50 per cent, the tax really levied upon the people amounted to 150 millions. As the depreciation goes on, moreover, the necessity of issuing more paper rapidly increases; and hence it is, that, when the fall in value has once begun, it seems to continue and enlarge with frightful rapidity. When the depreciation, for instance, is at 50 per cent, the prices of all commodities are doubled; government must pay twice as much in wages and salaries, and for provisions and munitions of war, and must therefore

* John Adams's *Works*, Vol. VII. p. 195.

pay out 200 millions to do the work which 100 millions did before. At the same time, its resources are diminished; all payments to it, being made in the depreciated currency, are worth but half their nominal amount. When the currency has fallen to one fourth the value of coin, 400 must be issued where 100 formerly sufficed; and the deficit in the receipts being added, the proportion may be even five or six for one.

It must not be inferred, however, that this rapid depreciation of the currency will seem to impede traffic or to paralyze industry. On the contrary — at least until the depreciation has become extreme, say 500 for 1 — commerce and labor will be galvanized into unnatural activity, and a deceitful glow of animation and success, like the flush of a fever, will appear to pervade the nation. Prices rise, of course, as rapidly as the currency falls; property which was sold for 100 to-day, will command 500 or 1,000 to-morrow. At the same time, money is superabundant, and those who were once too poor to buy can now easily obtain the means of purchase. The pressure of debt is also lessened; obligations are cancelled by paying back what is actually but one half, one fourth, or a still smaller fraction, of the real value which was due. Ease in getting rid of old debts only creates a thirst for contracting new ones. Commerce is thus stimulated, while the basis on which it rests is every day becoming less secure. A reckless spirit of speculation, akin to gambling in its character and results, appears to have seized the greater part of the community. The circulation of Continental money in America, in 1779, as we are told by a writer of that day, was "never more brisk and quick, than when its exchange was 500 for 1." And M. Thiers, speaking of the depreciation of the French *assignats* in 1795, says, that to the horrors of famine were added the scandals of reckless speculation and stockjobbing, the sale of merchandise which had no existence, as the pretended traffic was only betting upon prices, and the diffusion of a taste for luxury, dissipation, and excess, which is the invariable concomitant of sudden mutations of fortune.

We are now prepared to explain the great difference between convertible bank currency and inconvertible bills, or paper money properly so called, — that the latter is liable to issue in excess, and consequent depreciation, while the former is not. We have seen that the former is necessarily liable to perpetual reflux upon the institutions which issue it, the amount remaining in active circulation not depending at all upon the wishes of the banks, but upon the convenience of the public. This reflux takes place in three forms, through lodgements in deposit, the repayment of loans and discounts, and actual presentation at the counter for redemption in coin. These are but three forms of payment *to* the banks, and in the long run, they must equal, and for a time, they may easily exceed, the payments *out of* the banks. It is for the public, and not for the banks, to decide what portion of this reflux shall consist of bills and what of specie, and, consequently, what portion of each shall remain in circulation. The banks can do nothing to affect this result. Let them pay out their own bills as fast as they may, and in what quantities they may, the inflowing stream will be of corresponding depth and volume. And they peril their own safety even by a slight tendency to excess; for as they can issue their bills, in the majority of cases, only by discounting the notes of individuals that will not mature for some weeks, while their own bills may be brought back the next day, the reflux of any excessive issue might easily exhaust their specie reserve, and oblige them to suspend payment. And the public are sure to decide rightly what portion of the reflux shall consist of bank-bills, and when the reflux itself shall be augmented. If the currency has become redundant because trade for a time has languished, and less money is needed to effect the fewer exchanges which take place, then spare funds will accumulate in the hands of the dealers; and these funds, because there is nothing else to be done with them, will be lodged on deposit in the banks. But if the currency be redundant because there has been a speculative fever, which has raised the prices of commodities, and therefore called for more money wherewith to circulate them, then there will be a demand for specie to send abroad, where commodities can be had on cheaper terms; and there will be a reflux of the bills in order to obtain the specie. Those who fear an excessive issue of convertible bank-bills, might as well apprehend that Lake Erie would overflow its banks and flood all the surrounding country, because it is constantly receiving the surplus waters of the three upper lakes and of innumerable tributary streams. They forget that the average level of the lake depends, not upon the quantity of water flowing into it, but upon the quantity that flows out of it over Niagara Falls; and that no cause could affect the level except by raising or lowering the bar at the opening of Niagara River, which regulates the rate of the efflux.

But with paper money it is not so. In this case, there is no reflux and no occasion for repayment, so that the quantity in circulation depends exclusively upon the quantity emitted. The currency that is supplied with inconvertible paper is like the Dead Sea, which receives the waters of the Jordan, but has no efflux; augment the flow into it, and the level must rise. The government pays out its bills of credit, or paper money, in discharge of its debts, in the purchase of commodities, and in the payment of wages and salaries; in neither of these cases does it create any necessity for repayment, so as to bring the bills back again. True, the paper money is receivable by the state in payment of taxes and other government dues; but then there will be no necessity of issuing it at all, unless the expenditures largely exceed the receipts; and it is the amount of this excess, or the extent of the annual deficit, — very large in a revolutionary period, or in case of a civil war, — which determines the amount of the annual addition to the inconvertible paper currency. As this currency is not available for remittances abroad, no diminution of it is possible through the purchase of commodities in foreign lands. Every exit and channel of reflux being thus dammed up, the emission of every additional bill must advance the period when depreciation will begin, or increase the rate of that depreciation. To adopt Mr. Tooke's language, the distinction between bank currency and government paper money is, that the latter is "*paid away* and is *not returnable to the issuer*, whereas the bank-notes are only *lent*, and are *returnable to the issuers*." Because the paper money cannot be returned, it remains in circulation as an agent to raise prices, so that it "will constitute a fresh source of demand, and must be forced into and permeate all the channels of circulation."

If the banks suspend specie payment, their bills become inconvertible, and are thus far assimilated to paper money. Still, though *one* channel of reflux is thus dammed up, the bills being no longer presentable for redemption in coin, they can still be returned to the banks on deposit, and in repayment of the loans and discounts. *Bank* paper money is thus distinguished from *government* paper money, this last not being returnable at all. It is expended in the purchase of naval and military stores, in building ships, in constructing public edifices, and in the payment of services performed for the state, no means being usually taken to insure its ultimate return to the exchequer. The bank issues, on the other hand, being made only in the discount of approved promissory notes of short date, naturally return after a short interval, even if they are not redeemable in specie. So long, then, as the banks confine themselves to their proper functions, and do not squander their funds, or let them out on doubtful security, there is no reason why, even after a suspension, their currency should be depreciated, except to a very small extent. Thus, the Bank of England suspended specie payments in 1797, but its notes remained at par, or within two per cent of par, till 1801. Then, indeed, a heavy demand for gold to be exported, on account of the large purchases of corn which were rendered necessary by the failure of the English crops, and of large expenditures by the British government in prosecution of the war, made specie rise to a premium, or, what is the same thing, the bank-notes to be depreciated seven or eight per cent. These disturbing causes being removed, the currency rose again in 1803, and continued at a point only 2½ per cent below par till 1809.

It is unnecessary to dwell upon this point, however. A suspension of specie payments by the banks is not likely to be again sanctioned, either by law or public opinion, for any long period. It is enough to have shown, that government expenditure and the issue of government paper money are the chief causes of a depreciation of the currency, and that the banks cannot contribute much to this result except by becoming the agents of government, or by misconduct which proceeds rather from fraud than ignorance or involuntary error.

I return to a view of the consequences of an excessive depreciation of paper money, and of the measures which then become necessary for restoring the currency to a specie standard. As soon as the bills have fallen considerably in value, two prices are established for commodities, one in specie and

33

the other in paper currency, the difference between the two marking the rate of depreciation. When this difference has become inordinate, the progress of the depreciation is most rapid, the value of the currency fluctuating so suddenly and largely, that most persons are unwilling to receive it on any terms. The rate to-day may be 500, and to-morrow 600, for 1; under these circumstances, also, the rate will be found to vary in different localities, and be variously estimated by different tradesmen. So much confusion and uncertainty are thus created, that, by a spontaneous movement of the whole community, the paper currency is discarded altogether, the price in specie is the only one that will be received in payment for commodities; and if the paper has not already ceased, through the action of the legislature, to be legal tender, acknowledgments of debts are made with an express stipulation that the payment shall be in specie, or some other commodity of fixed value. Such a restoration of the standard seldom requires any action of the government; it is the voluntary and united act of the whole people, having been dictated by the necessities of the case.

The immediate consequences of this reversion to a specie currency are in striking contrast with the results, already noticed, of the first issue of paper money and its gradual depreciation. The latter seemed to animate industry and commerce to relieve the pressure of debt, and to supply abundant funds for enterprises which must otherwise have been abandoned; but the former seems to carry the community back, by a cruel revulsion, to worse evils than those from which it had apparently been rescued. It is the state of collapse that sometimes follows the excitement and delirium of a fever. It is now seen that the issue of paper money is really a desperate measure, that the relief which it promises is but temporary, and that the prosperity which it causes is wholly fallacious. As money rises from a low valuation to a higher one, wages are depressed, prices fall, trade stagnates, and bankruptcies become numerous; and these evils are the more serious, as the depreciation was great, and the revulsion sudden. Formerly, it was the creditors who were injured, being obliged to receive payment in a currency less valuable than the one in which the debt was contracted; now the debtors, who are more numerous and less able to bear losses, must suffer harm and wrong, being required to pay more than they received, and to do this at a time when, from the depression of wages, the abandonment of industrial and commercial undertakings, and the fall of profits, they are least able to bear an additional burden. All these hardships are summarily attributed to one cause, more frequently spoken of than understood, — "a scarcity of money"; it means only a higher real value of money, the prostration of credit, the consequent inactivity of capital, and general despondency.

As the prosperity growing out of the earlier part of the experiment with paper money strengthened the hands of the revolutionary government, so the disasters and suffering attendant upon its close create a reaction, and weaken the cause of the insurgents. The popular discontent thus generated tends either to the reëstablishment of the old form of government, or to anarchy.

It was so at the close of the Revolutionary war in this country, when both the people and the army, exhausted by the efforts and sacrifices which they had made, bankrupt in fortune, and seeing no resources open to them, were for a while on the point of turning their arms against each other. Nothing but the moderation, wisdom, and firmness of their great Commander-in-chief saved the country from the horrors of a military usurpation. The establishment of peace seemed only to render matters worse. The courts then began in earnest to enforce the settlement of accounts and the payment of debts; and the property seized for this purpose being sold at a great sacrifice, its former owners found themselves homeless and penniless, and still burdened with the greater part of their pecuniary obligations. The unthinking multitude then began to clamor for "stop-laws," or enactments to delay process and execution after judgment had been obtained for debt; for "tender-laws," compelling the creditor to accept in satisfaction of his claim any property of the debtor at a fixed valuation or appraisement, instead of offering it at auction for cash, when it would bring but a trifle; and above all, for a new and large issue of paper money, the rapid depreciation of which would enable debtors to get rid of their obligations on very easy terms. Several States were weak enough to yield to these demands, and thus only prolonged the period of uncertainty, confusion, and suffering, besides aggravating the evil by injustice. Massachusetts resisted, seeing that really the best and easiest mode of escaping present difficulties was to adhere resolutely to a specie currency, and to enforce a speedy settlement of all outstanding claims, so that industry and commerce might at last revive, without further impediment or drawback from the past. The consequence was, that a formidable rebellion broke out in this State in 1786, the avowed object of the insurgents being to close by violence the courts of law, thus putting a stop to legal measures for the collection of debts, and to compel the government to make a fresh issue of depreciating currency. The insurrection was suppressed with difficulty, and the terror which it inspired had this indirect good result, — that it animated and strengthened the general effort which was then made to create a stable government for the whole Union. This effort led to the adoption of the Federal Constitution, one article of which, as already noticed, prohibits the emission of "bills of credit" and the enactment of "tender-laws."

In France, the final abandonment of the depreciated *assignats* and *mandats*, and the difficulties in which the government was thus involved, had consequences equally serious. The sufferings of the people exasperated them alike against the Revolution and the authors of it, whom they had so recently followed into the wildest excesses of Jacobinism. A reaction took place in favor of the ancient dynasty, which was so general, that the royalists obtained the command of the elections, and seemed likely to obtain their end by a peaceable vote of the two Councils or legislative assemblies. The Directory, indeed, aided by the army, which was still republican in sentiment, prevented this result through the *coup d'état* of the 18th Fructidor, 1797; they seized the leading royalist deputies, and sentenced them to deportation. But the triumph was dearly bought, as it marked the ascendency of military power, and foreshadowed the dominion of Napoleon.

It follows from this whole review of the subject of paper money, which I have intentionally based, as far as possible, upon historical facts rather than abstract reasoning, that the depreciation of it is attributable solely to excess in its issue.

If this excess could be prevented, that is, if the amount of paper currency could be kept precisely equal to what the amount of metallic currency would be in case there were no paper in circulation, then there would be no depreciation of the paper; nay, the paper might even command a premium over coin, if the aggregate value of it were made less than what the coin would amount to, and if it were also possible to prevent the importation of specie. Money acquires the power of exercising its functions, not from any intrinsic qualities that it possesses, but solely from convention. To adopt Mr. Mill's language, "convention is quite sufficient to confer the power, since nothing more is needful to make a person accept anything as money, and even at any arbitrary value, than the persuasion that it will be taken from him on the same terms by others." The value of paper money, not depending at all upon its cost of production, is regulated solely by its quantity. A certain determinable sum of money is needed in every nation to effect its current exchanges, and to maintain prices at an equilibrium with the average prices of commodities throughout the commercial world. Coin being banished, if the issue of paper money is less than this sum, the paper will command a premium; if greater, it will be at a discount.

The difficulty is, that this sum is a varying quantity, depending upon the state of trade, of public confidence, of the foreign exchanges as affected by the relative amounts of the exports and imports, and other circumstances which cannot easily be determined. The difference in value between the coin and the paper money is usually taken as a measure of the depreciation of the latter; and so it is, if the value of gold and silver be taken as the standard. But it should not be forgotten that this standard itself may vary, not only in accordance with the greater or less productiveness of the mines whence the precious metals are obtained, but also according to the varying demand for gold and silver in different localities. A general war in Europe, causing large sums of specie to be moved about in the military chests of great armies, and impeding the intercourse by sea which is the only means of equalizing prices; the consternation produced by revolutionary movements that tend to anarchy, or by the progress of invasion from abroad, causing large amounts of money to be hoarded; and a great failure of the crops, making heavy importations of grain necessary, which must be paid for in specie, — these and other circumstances may raise the value of specie in different places much above its average, and retain it at the advanced valuation for a considerable time. It is the opinion of Mr. Tooke and other well-informed writers, that the difference between Bank of England notes and bullion from 1810 to 1817, amounting at times to 25 per cent, "was not greater than the enhancement in value of gold itself, and that the paper, though depreciated relatively to the then value of gold, did not sink below the ordinary value, at other times, either of gold or of a convertible paper." There was certainly no excessive issue of bank-notes at that epoch enough to account for their depreciation; the circulation of the Bank of England, indeed, was increased, but no more so than was necessary to fill up the gap in the currency caused by the destruction of a large amount of country bank paper, and to accommodate the rapidly increasing business of the country.

Reasoning upon these principles, Mr. Ricardo published, in 1816, his "Proposals for an Economical and Secure Currency." The plan was, to supersede the use of gold *coin* altogether, by requiring the Bank of England to redeem its notes by the payment, not of coin, but of gold bars, or bullion, of the standard purity, at the mint price of gold (£ 3 17*s*. 10½*d*. an ounce), or at such other price as Parliament should determine. These gold bars, or ingots, not being fitted for circulation as currency, would not be called for except when they were needed for exportation; but if the issue of bank-notes ever became excessive, so that they tended to depreciation, the gold would be then needed for export, and the issue would be checked, or the notes be poured back upon the Bank. Thus the heavy expense of a metallic currency would be saved, and full security would be given that the value of the paper currency would always correspond with that of gold.

Government adopted this scheme as a portion of its plan for the gradual resumption of specie payments. The act for this purpose, commonly known as Peel's Bill, was passed in 1819. It required the Bank, from the 1st of February, 1820, to the 1st of October in the same year, to pay its notes in bullion of standard fineness, at the rate of £ 4 1*s*. per ounce. From the

1st of October, 1820, to the 1st of May, 1821, it was to pay bullion at the rate of £3 19*s.* 6*d.* per ounce; and after this last date, it was to redeem its notes in bullion at the old mint price of £3 17*s.* 10½*d.* an ounce. Two years afterwards, it was to pay *coin* at this price, the resumption being then complete. But as the Bank had abundance of coin in its vaults, and as the forgery of the one-pound notes, a large amount of which it was necessary by this scheme to keep in circulation as a substitute for guineas or sovereigns, caused much trouble and uncertainty, the Directors anticipated the operation of the act by beginning to redeem the notes in coin at the full price some time before the date specified.

The plan of gradual resumption by successive steps is a good one, as it relieves commerce from the violent shock which it would experience, if the currency were suddenly raised from a state of considerable depreciation to par. Should another suspension of specie payments by the banks of this country unhappily take place, the best policy for the legislature would be, to sanction the depreciation at its actual amount for the current month, on condition that the banks should immediately pay specie for their notes at this depreciated rate, and advance it two or three per cent each successive month, till it was brought again to par. Confidence would thus be immediately restored, further depreciation would be impossible, a time would at once be fixed for resumption, while the run upon the banks would cease almost entirely, as each holder of the notes would perceive that he would gain two or three per cent a month by delaying their presentation.

CHAPTER XXII.

THE DECLINE IN THE VALUE OF MONEY.

It is now generally admitted that a great revolution is taking place in the commercial and monetary world, caused by a considerable decline in the value of money, — a revolution the like of which has not occurred for more than two centuries, and of which there is but one parallel in all history. The two precious metals, after maintaining a nearly uniform value for a very long period, are now, owing to a sudden and immense increase in the supply of gold, undergoing a great change, not only in their relation to each other, but in their value as compared with that of all other commodities in the world. This change is not to be a merely nominal one. It might seem, indeed, that, as the precious metals are a universal measure of value, any depreciation of them would amount only to a general rise of prices, all commodities being affected in precisely the same ratio, so that their relation to each other would remain unaltered. This is true; such a change would not benefit or injure any one. But all stipulations for the payment of money at a future day will be really affected to the full extent of the change which the precious metals may undergo while the contract is outstanding. A single instance will enable us to see the vast importance, in this respect, of a depreciation in the value of money. The national debt of Great Britain, — that great incubus which has been supposed to be immovably fixed upon the shoulders of the nation, and which has been properly regarded as putting the English people under very heavy bonds to keep the peace, as any considerable enlargement of it by other wars would make the burden of paying its annual interest well-nigh intolerable, — this mountain of debt must shrink comparatively into a mole-hill. It may all be paid off in a few years, with as little effort as it now costs to pay merely the interest. A revolution which will have this effect, and a proportional one on all other contracts to deliver money at a future day, may well be deemed a momentous one.

The first points to be considered are, the probable extent of the depreciation, and the time within which it may be expected. Fortunately, there is one example on record of a perfectly similar change, the study of which will enable us to see the true nature and probable limits of the present revolution. I refer, of course, to the effect produced in Europe by the great supplies obtained from the American mines in the sixteenth and seventeenth centuries.

We do not need to know the whole amount of gold and silver actually in use in the world, either as coin or plate, before the discovery of America. It is a well-ascertained principle, that the permanent or average value of a commodity depends, not on the larger or smaller stock of it already in being, but on the average cost of its production. If a pound of iron is worth only one-thousandth part as much as a pound of silver, it is not because there are a thousand times as much iron now in use as silver, but because it requires a thousand times as much labor to raise an additional pound of silver from the mines, as it does a pound of iron. If the stock already in use be ever so large, the value of it cannot *permanently* fall below the cost of production; for as the labor of obtaining more would not be remunerated, no more would be produced; and the constant consumption would steadily diminish the stock, till the value of what remained would rise high enough to pay the laborer for the effort of procuring a fresh supply. On the other hand, if the stock is ever so small, no one will pay more for any portion of it than it would cost him to raise or manufacture the article for himself. The steady average value, then, the point about which the price oscillates, never departing from it far in either direction, is the cost of production; and a tolerably accurate measure of this cost, so long as the demand remains the same, is the quantity annually produced.

It is important to recollect this, as many persons have been led to believe, because the very great addition made by the Californian and Australian washings to the stock of gold did not immediately and sensibly affect the value of that metal, that no future depreciation of it is to be expected. But till it is ascertained that this is a *permanent* increase of supply, and that the newly discovered auriferous districts will continue for many years to yield, not probably as much as they have done, but enough to make the former sources of supply appear comparatively insignificant, and thus to diminish the *average* cost of production, the change of value will be too small to be generally appreciated.

Down to the time of Columbus, the average annual supply of the two precious metals certainly did not exceed three millions of dollars.* How much was this increased by the supplies from America during the sixteenth and seventeenth centuries? Humboldt is here the only authority generally relied upon; and as he made very extensive and laborious investigations, was well acquainted with all that had been written upon the subject, had ready access to official sources of information unknown to former writers, was well versed in the theory and practice of mining, and critically examined some of the most celebrated mines, it is probable that his statements are a very near approximation to the truth. He tells us that the annual supplies of the precious metals obtained from America were as follows.

America discovered in 1492.	Dollars a year on an average.
From 1492 to 1500	250,000
" 1500 to 1545	3,000,000
" 1545 to 1600	11,000,000
" 1600 to 1700	16,000,000
" 1700 to 1750	22,500,000
" 1750 to 1803	35,300,000

Hence it appears, if we suppose the Old World continued to furnish as much as before, that in the first half of the sixteenth century the supplies from America had doubled the annual product. In the latter half of this century, they rendered it nearly five times as large. In the seventeenth century, it became over six times, and in the eighteenth, over eleven times, larger than it was before 1500. The great increase in the latter half of the sixteenth century was owing to the discovery of the mines of Potosi, which were first systematically worked in 1545.

How great and how rapid a depreciation of the value of money was caused by this vast increase of supply? Here,

* Humboldt estimates that all the European and Asiatic mines, as late as 1800, did not yield annually more than five millions of dollars.

again, the means for forming an opinion are very imperfect, being chiefly an extensive and laborious comparison of the prices, at different periods, of certain leading commodities, which are in uniform and perpetual demand. The staple articles of food, such as grain and meat, are the best for this purpose, as it may be presumed that they are not often produced in larger quantities than are wanted, and as nearly the same amount of labor is required for the production of a given quantity of them in one century as in another. If a genuine record can be obtained of the prices actually paid, at one place, for such articles, for a long series of years, the variations, if any, in the value of the precious metals during those years may be deduced from it, allowance being made, of course, for any alterations of the quantity of pure metal passing under the same denomination of coin, and for the state of the coinage, whether worn and clipped, or fresh and perfect. Such a record is found in the accounts of Eton College, and in the lists of prices collected by Bishop Fleetwood and M. Dupré de St. Maur. The conclusions deduced by various writers from these accounts do not agree very well; but the variations do not materially affect the result for the purpose which we now have in view. We select the computations made by Adam Smith, as they were made with great care and knowledge of the subject, and have been generally accepted by later writers on Political Economy.

Adam Smith says the American mines do not seem to have produced any effect upon prices till after 1570, though the mines of Potosi had then been actively worked for a quarter of a century. Between 1595 and 1620, silver fell to about one third of its former value; and about 1636, it had fallen to one fourth part of that value, where it has remained with little variation almost to the present day. Before 1570, a quarter (eight bushels) of wheat of middle quality was sold in England, on an average of a long period of years, for about *two* ounces of pure silver; about 1600, (still taking an average of many years, so that the very good and very bad crops may offset each other,) the price had advanced to a little over *six* ounces; about 1636, it had risen to nearly *eight* ounces. The average value of a quarter of wheat in England, from the repeal of the Corn Laws up to 1852, did not vary much from forty-three shillings, which contain almost exactly eight ounces of pure silver.

Comparing these results with the table already given of the annual product of the precious metals, we find, — 1. *That doubling the annual product of money for half a century had no effect on its value, or did not raise prices at all;* 2. *That making the annual product five times as great had no effect upon its value for* 25 *years, after which time, however, the value gradually fell to one third of what it had been;* 3. *That about* 36 *years after the annual product had become six times as great, the value had fallen to one fourth of its former amount;* 4. *That from* 1636 *to* 1848, *or* 212 *years, the value of the precious metals underwent no material alteration, though meanwhile the annual supply of them had become eleven or twelve times greater than what it had been before the discovery of America.**

These facts satisfactorily support two general conclusions: — 1. That a very considerable increase of the supply may take place without any perceptible change in the value; 2. That the alteration, when it does occur, is very slow and gradual, the variation from one year to another being hardly perceptible.

Such was the result of the only experiment recorded in history, which enables us to form any conjecture as to the probable effect upon the money-market of the vast addition which has been made to the annual supply of gold within a few years by the discoveries in Russia, California, and Australia. To make the comparison clear and obvious, I have stated the results in their broadest form, or with the fewest limitations and doubts. There will afterwards be considerations to suggest which will modify the conclusions to be drawn from these statements.

Let us now see how great have been the changes in the annual supply during the present century. About the year 1800,

* According to J. B. Say, however, whose conclusions are based upon the lists of prices collected by M. Dupré de St. Maur, though they do not appear to have been so carefully worked out as those of Smith, silver fell to one half of its former value as early as 1536, and to one fourth of that value as early as 1602, remaining unchanged at this point till 1800. But I cannot find any satisfactory evidence that the value of silver was at all affected until the mines of Potosi for a considerable period had been pouring out their vast supplies, — that is, for some years after 1545.

the annual supply of gold amounted to $ 12,648,000, and of silver to $ 36,289,008; making a total of $ 48,937,008. There is reason to believe that the large portion of this product which was furnished by the American mines was rather increased than diminished up to 1810, when the contest began which finally produced the independence of the Spanish American colonies. The revolutionary troubles, and the proscription of the old Spanish families to whom the mines chiefly belonged, caused the works in many cases to be abandoned, and there was a great falling off of the product. Mr. Jacob estimated, that, for the twenty years ending with 1829, they did not yield annually over $ 20,000,000, or considerably less than half of their former product. But he evidently exaggerates the falling off; and the estimate which Mr. McCulloch formed in 1834 may be safely extended to the whole period, making the annual supply from all parts of the earth to be $ 30,000,000. Soon after 1834, the gold product of the Russian mines and washings began to swell the amount very rapidly, so that Mr. McCulloch affirmed, in 1845, that, if the supply from this source should continue a few years longer, it would cause a fall in the value of gold as compared with silver and with everything else. In 1847, it had raised the annual supply from all parts of the world to $ 67,000,000, making it nearly one third larger than it had been in 1800. But what was this to the astounding results produced by the discovery of the Californian and Australian gold washings? The gold obtained in Australia alone, in 1852, was estimated at 330,000 pounds Troy; and the supply from California that year is believed to have been 252,000 pounds Troy. It has turned out, indeed, that 1852 was far the most productive year, and there has been a considerable falling off since, especially in Australia. Still, it is safe to estimate the total product of these two countries, in 1854, at 350,000 pounds; and if the supply from Russia and other sources be added, the aggregate is nearly 482,000 pounds, or about $ 119,536,000. By a curious coincidence, the annual supply of silver from the Mexican and South American mines has been largely augmented during the last ten years, the total for the whole world being one third larger in 1850 than it was in 1845; the aggregate amount mined in the former year was nearly $ 44,000,000. Putting these two sums together, we have the value of gold and silver obtained from the mines in 1854 equal to $163,536,000.*

The results now obtained may be put into a tabular form for the purposes of comparison.

	Annual product of the two precious metals.
From 1800 to 1810	$ 49,000,000
" 1810 to 1836	30,000,000
1847	67,000,000
1854	163,536,000

The supply for 1854, then, was five and a half times larger than the annual product twenty years ago, and about three and one third times larger than the greatest amount obtained in any one year before 1840. Unless new gold fields should be discovered, however, of which there seems little probability at present, it is certain that the maximum supply was obtained in 1852, and that there has since been a very rapid and considerable falling off. While 718,000 pounds Troy were obtained in 1852, only 597,000 pounds formed the supply in 1853, and 482,000 pounds was the estimate, probably an exaggerated one, for 1854, the diminution in two years being nearly 33 per cent. In 1855, the supply was probably not more than half as great as in 1852. The falling off was even more sudden and marked in Australia than in California. In respect to silver, on the other hand, the supply is steadily but slowly on the increase, the most cautious estimates making the increase at least 2½ per cent a year. The annual product of this metal is now estimated at very nearly $50,000,000, the chief portion of the increase being from Mexico and Chili.

The great difference between the experiment which was tried two or three centuries ago, and that which is now in progress, is, that in the former case far the greater part of the addition which was made to the world's stock of the precious metals was in silver, while most of the present increase is in gold. And this is a very important difference, as regards the

* The estimates in this paragraph, except that I have sometimes used the nearest round numbers, are taken from J. D. Whitney's "Metallic Wealth of the United States described and compared with that of other Countries," (Philadelphia, 1854,) a work which contains a great deal of original information of much interest, and a careful digest of all the statistics of the subject that could be gleaned from recent publications of good authority both in Europe and America.

question of the probable long continuance of the enlarged annual product. Silver is obtained by mining, and the veins which are worked are most frequently found to grow richer as they are followed into the bowels of the earth. The expense of working them increases as we descend, but the steadily increasing product is generally more than an offset for this enlarged cost. Gold, on the other hand, is generally obtained by washing from a superficial deposit of gravel and sand. It is chiefly found in what the geologists call "the drift," and in a stratum of it of no great thickness. Being thus spread out over a great extent of ground, and lying at or near the surface, almost any number of persons can be engaged in obtaining it without impeding each other's operations. If, also, as is the case in California, and to a great extent in Australia, the land in the auriferous district has been but imperfectly, or not at all, appropriated either by individuals or the government, — if it is, in the main, open to all comers, as the Great Bank is to all fishermen, — then, large as the district may be, it is soon covered with gold-hunters. The most promising localities are quickly exhausted; and then, every year, the labor of gathering the shining dust will increase, and the returns will diminish. The experience of California is conclusive on this point. There can be no doubt that the whole amount obtained was considerably diminished after the number of washers was largely increased. True, the first search is generally imperfect, and a second washing of the same gravel, with more care and method, may afterwards yield a fair profit. So, also, the solid rock, though it be tough quartz, in which the gold spangles now found in the drift were originally imbedded, may be crushed and ground by heavy machinery, and a supply of auriferous sand and gravel be thus obtained by artificial means, in addition to that which natural agencies have spread out over the surface. We may not anticipate, then, that the gold-fever will subside as rapidly as it rose, or that the gold-bearing districts will ever be *completely* exhausted. Still, two processes must always be more laborious and expensive than one, and the ground will no longer be open to every comer, though he has no other capital than a stout pair of arms, and a great capacity of enduring fatigue. When the business is all reduced to pounding up primary or metamorphic rocks with machines which are yet to be invented, and to washing gravel for the second time, it is reasonable to expect, that, although capitalists may get a fair return for their enterprise, the steam-ships will no longer bring home gold at the rate of three or four millions a month.

Taking all these considerations into view, together with the fact that we have now three great gold-bearing regions to depend upon, so distant from each other as Russia, California, and Australia, it will not be deemed incautious to anticipate, that *the annual supply of the two precious metals will not fall below a hundred millions of dollars for many years, and that, within a quarter of a century, this supply will depreciate money to one half or one third of what was its value before* 1850.

In respect to the relative amounts by weight of the two precious metals, it appears from the statistics already given, that, at the beginning of the present century, the annual product of gold was to that of silver as 1 to 43. In 1845, the supply from Russia having largely increased the quantity of gold, and the quantity of silver being somewhat less than in 1800, the ratio was only as 1 to 17. In 1852, the supply from the Californian and Australian gold-fields having obtained its maximum, the ratio of the two metals was as 1 to 4; in other words, if the annual product of the two metals had continued to be in this proportion, silver would have risen certainly to one fourth, and probably, considering the more extensive use of the cheaper metal, to one half, of the value of gold. But the proportion has not been continued; the amount of gold obtained in each year has rapidly fallen off, while that of silver has steadily increased, so that, in 1854, the ratio is probably as 1 to 6. The following table exhibits in one view these sudden changes in the relative quantities of the two metals, the figures indicating the weight in pounds Troy.*

	1800.	1845.	1852.	1854.
Silver	2,337,300	2,183,500	2,958,296	3,106,210
Gold	54,000	129,250	717,950	482,000
Ratio	1 to 43	1 to 17	1 to 4	1 to 6¼

In the sixteenth and seventeenth centuries, while the Mexican

* In this table I have adopted the estimate of the well-informed City correspondent, or commercial editor, of *The Times,* that since 1850 the annual product of silver has been increasing at the rate, at least, of 2½ per cent a year.

and South American mines were pouring out their treasures of silver, gold rose, from a comparative value only ten times as great as that of silver, to that which it had in 1848, of nearly 16 to 1. Only three years ago, then, it appeared reasonable to believe that the sudden and great increase in the annual product of gold, the annual product of silver being then supposed to be nearly stationary, would carry back the relative value of the two metals, not merely to its former point of 10 to 1, but perhaps, as already mentioned, of 4, or even 2, to 1. It was even thought, that the rise in the comparative value of silver would be a tolerably exact measure of the depreciation of gold. Acting under this expectation, the government of Holland demonetized gold, and made silver the standard of value, thinking thereby to avoid the threatened decline in the value of money. But as the annual supply of gold is now rapidly falling off, while that of silver is steadily increasing,* it appears probable that the relative value of the two will not be much affected, — that it will not become less than 10 or 12 to 1, — while there will be a regular progressive diminution in the value of both. We cannot expect, then, that the whole decline in the value of money, or even a considerable portion of it, will be indicated by the variation in the relative values of gold and silver.

Very good reasons have been given why the discovery of the

---

* Humboldt declared, forty years ago, that the mines of New Spain contained silver enough to deluge the world. A recent observer, M. Dupont, who has published an excellent work on the production of the precious metals in Mexico, adopts the views of Humboldt, and adduces much additional testimony in confirmation of them. He describes several formations of rock, in which silver is almost sure to be found, and says, that although these formations are rare in the neighborhood of the city of Mexico, as we travel further northward they become of frequent occurrence, and, on crossing the principal chain of mountains towards the Gulf of California, the whole western slope of the Sonora Cordillera is composed of them. Improved methods of mining, also, have produced great results in some of the old localities, where the works had been given up for years, under the belief that it could not be continued with profit. Thus the Frasnillo mine, described in 1827 as an abandoned property, from which no hopes could be entertained, now yields more than $2,000,000 in silver annually. From another locality, in Zacatecas, which was thought to be exhausted about 1800, there was extracted, between 1827 and 1839, about 150 million francs' worth of silver. If an efficient government and a race of energetic emigrants should ever be introduced into Mexico, — as in case of its probable annexation to this country, — a revolution would take place in silver mining, and a fall in value of silver would be inevitable.

American mines, in the sixteenth century, and the influx intc the market of eleven times as much of the precious metals as before, did not reduce their value in the same proportion, but only in the ratio of 4 to 1; and why, when the ratio of the quantity of silver to that of gold was as 45 to 1, the ratio of their values was only as 1 to 15. It has already been observed that in commerce and the arts, chiefly on account of its inferior cost, silver has been far more generally in use than gold. It has supplied much the larger portion of the currency of all nations. With some nations of the East, the Chinese for instance gold is not used at all for this purpose. Even on the continen of Europe, silver is, in many cases, the only legal tender, gold being merely an article of merchandise, which is sold at an *agi* that fluctuates from week to week, though, of course, few peo ple will refuse to receive it in payment. Silver must always be used for the smaller pieces of money, at least until gold ha fallen much below its present value. Our gold one-dollar piece is inconveniently small, and will not probably come into genera circulation, unless there should be some alteration in its form.

The general principle is, that the value of money falls in precisely the same ratio in which its quantity is increased. I the whole money in circulation should be doubled, price would be doubled; if it was only increased one fourth, price would rise one fourth. This is not the case with commoditie generally, the value of which does not vary in the same ratio with the excess or deficiency of the supply; because the desire being for the thing itself, may be stronger or weaker, and th amount of what people are willing to expend upon it, being always limited, may be very unequally affected by the diff culty or facility of attainment. But money is desired as th means of purchasing everything, and the demand for it, there fore, consists of everything which people have to sell.

The principle, however, even in the case of money, hold good only under the supposition that the quantity of commod ities, the number of exchanges, and the number of people hav ing occasion to effect exchanges, remain unaltered. Othe wise, if there be an increase in either of these respects, th quantity of money being unchanged, the value of that mone will rise; or if money is increasing, the increase in these oth respects may neutralize, wholly or in part, the depreciation that money. This was the case after the discovery of America. There was an immense enlargement of commerce and manufactures at that period, and a great improvement in the modes of living. The discovery of America itself, and of the passage round the Cape of Good Hope, and the colonization of the West by Europeans, greatly enlarged the demand for money. Before 1500, vastly the larger portion of the people were engaged in agriculture; they raised most of the articles which they needed by their own labor, and obtained many others by direct barter. Afterwards, many were diverted into commercial and manufacturing pursuits, and the consequent division of labor greatly increased the number of proper mercantile exchanges. The middle classes now first came into notice as a distinct power in the state. As wealth advanced, luxury grew apace. The actual consumption of the precious metals, by abrasion of the coin, the wear of plate, lace, and trinkets, by plating and gilding, and by losses through shipwreck or fire, became considerable.

It is easy to perceive why, under such circumstances, the supply having become eleven times as great, the value fell only to one fourth of what it had been. On the other hand, why the value did not advance again, in the century during which the supply was nearly stationary, though commerce, wealth, and luxury were still rapidly increasing, is a point which requires explanation. But as society advances, means are discovered for economizing the use of money. The vast extension of credit; the establishment of banks, and especially of Savings' Banks, which bring together and keep in active use a vast number of small sums, which would otherwise be hoarded or lie dormant in the hands of individuals; the circulation of bank-notes, checks, and bills of exchange, which perform nearly all the functions of money; and, more than all, perhaps, the introduction of accounts current among traders, by which purchases are set off against sales, and commodities are thus virtually bartered for commodities, money being needed only at the final settlement, and then only to a trifling amount, — all are expedients for completing exchanges without the actual transfer of coin. Only the rapidly extended use of these expedients could have prevented a considerable rise in the value of money, and consequent fall of prices, between

1810 and 1830, when the annual supply of the precious metals was much diminished, and the operations of commerce greatly enlarged.

Is it probable that the effect of the present vastly increased supply of the precious metals will be, to any considerable extent, retarded or neutralized by an increased demand for money, through the growth of luxury and trade? We see no circumstances likely to produce this result, except the colonization of the gold-bearing regions themselves; and even this can have comparatively little influence. These countries, it is true, are very distant from the world's great centres of commerce and wealth, and their population grows with marvellous rapidity. In all distant colonies, and especially in those formed under the excitement of searching for gold, the various expedients for economizing the use of money are slowly introduced and imperfectly developed. Time is needed to import the machinery of banking and all the refinements of trade, and especially for the establishment of confidence in the community, so that large operations can be conducted upon credit. For many years, at least, California and Australia must use chiefly a hard-money currency, while large amounts of bullion, as I have already remarked, will be *in transitu*, — wandering about, as it were, from one country to another, to find where they will be of most value, — before they pass into active circulation as currency. But these circumstances can impede the result only for a few years; they cannot materially lessen or weaken it. Perfect as the machinery of trade now is, and perfectly as it is understood, no country which is colonized by commercial nations can remain far behind the mother land in the use of money-saving expedients. In respect also to the use of the precious metals for articles of luxury and ostentation, M. Chevalier finds reason to believe that it is rather diminishing than increasing. The official returns, both in England and France, show that there was a larger manufacture of gold and silver plate in those countries before 1830 than there ever has been since, if we except the last three or four years, during which time, as might have been anticipated, there has been a moderate additional consumption of gold in the arts. "The luxury of our days," says Chevalier, "has democratic features; it is very calculating and economical. It is lavish of gilding and silvering, but requires few massive articles in silver, and still fewer in gold." It seems most probable, then, that the general principle will hold, that the value of money will fall in the same ratio in which the average annual supply of it is increased.

Leaving all these preliminary considerations, then, we come to the main question, — Is there anything in the prospect of a great decline in the value of money to create serious uneasiness and alarm? We suppose that the decline will be gradual, that it will be spread over many years, that at least a quarter of a century must elapse before it can be completed. There will be a rise in the prices of all commodities, with a corresponding increase in wages and salaries. Labor will be higher paid, both because it will be more productive, or, in other words, the articles it produces will have a greater nominal value, and because the cost of living will be greater, so that, if wages and salaries did not rise, the labor could not be had. The rise of prices being general, will consequently be only nominal; that is, one commodity may be bartered for another on just the same terms as before. If, when flour is five dollars a barrel, it takes five barrels of flour to buy one coat, after money has fallen to one half of its value, the coat can still be had for five barrels of flour; but it will then be said to be worth fifty dollars, and the flour to be ten dollars a barrel, instead of five. In this narrow view of the subject, therefore, or so far as this effect extends, no one will be directly benefited, and no one directly injured.

With respect to outstanding obligations, or contracts to deliver money at a future day, the case will be different. If I borrow one hundred dollars at a time when that sum will purchase twenty barrels of flour, or an equivalent amount of other commodities, and am not called upon to repay it till money has so far fallen in value that the sum will buy only ten barrels, the debt is really cancelled by returning only one half of the value which was borrowed. To this extent, therefore, every one will be benefited so far as he owes money, and will be injured so far as he has money to receive. But in either case, he will be affected only by the amount of the depreciation which takes place in the interval between the contraction of the debt and its payment. If twenty-five years elapse before the depreciation is completed, and if it take place uniformly, or at the rate of two or three per cent a year, then all promises to pay, which have not more than a year to run, will not be affected to the extent of more than two or three per cent. Now, vastly the larger number of contracts that are made in the ordinary course of business are completed within the year; they will not be so much affected by the general decline in the value of money as they often have been by the common fluctuations of interest, and by changes in the price of particular commodities. Often, within the last ten years, money has been borrowed when the current rate of interest did not exceed five per cent a year, and the time of repaying it has come when it could with difficulty be had at one per cent a month. We may say, generally, then, that all the common transactions of business will not be sensibly affected by the great change which is in prospect.

But all fixed money payments which are now contracted for, and have many years to run, will be seriously affected by the coming alteration; that portion of them which extends over a full quarter of a century, will experience the full effect of it. All government stocks, and other stocks yielding a fixed rate of interest, and not bearing any obligation to be paid off in a few years; all bank stock, and other permanent investments of money yielding income only under the form of interest; and all property let on long leases at a fixed annual rent, must decline in value with the money which they represent. Such stocks, and the property also, if the lease be a perpetual one, when the depreciation is complete, will possess only half their present *relative* value. The nominal income yielded by them will remain the same, but it will only purchase half as many commodities as before. There will be no actual loss to the community, for what one loses, another gains. The British tax-payer, for instance, will profit by the whole amount of the British fund-holders' loss. As the depreciation goes on, taxation may be extended *pari passu*, without throwing any additional burden upon the community; and a sinking-fund, formed out of the surplus thus obtained, would pay off the national debt in less than one generation. As such stocks, moreover, are transferable, and frequently pass from hand to hand, the total loss upon any portion of them will seldom fall on one person; it will be divided among many, and thus be distributed among the wealthier portion of the community, who, profiting in their capacity as tax-payers by the depreciation which occasions this loss, will have no great reason to complain. Life-annuitants, persons who have insured their lives, mortgagees on long periods, and those who have let property on permanent or long leases, will be almost the only class compelled to bear the loss without any direct compensation or means of escape. The funds of public institutions and of individuals, which exist in the form of floating capital, or what is usually called "money at interest," will, of course, suffer the full effect of the depreciation; but, as the ownership of real estate is commonly connected with the possession of such funds, and as the value of real estate will rise even in a higher ratio than the prices of commodities, owing to the general eagerness to secure the only form of permanent investment which will not be affected by the decline in the value of money, the loss in this case will not be generally without compensation.

The rates of interest cannot be directly altered by the change. If gold sinks to half of its present value, the $100 of principal, and the $6 of annual interest for it, will be affected in precisely the same ratio; both sums will purchase but half as much of any given commodity as can now be obtained for them. Being affected in the same manner, and to the same degree, their relation to each other will remain unaltered. Indirectly, however, a slight diminution in the rates of interest may be produced. The great addition to the stock of the precious metals will appear, at first, in the form of floating capital, seeking investment; it will swell the specie reserves of the banks, making them eager to extend the circulation of their notes. Thus, until the prices of commodities begin to be sensibly affected, there will be more lenders than borrowers, and money will be offered at a lower interest. It was so in 1852. In consequence of the influx of gold, the specie reserves of the banks were distended to repletion. The Bank of England had the enormous sum of twenty-two millions sterling in its vaults, or nearly 110 millions of dollars, which is about double the amount that is usually considered a safe basis for its circulation. On the strength of this large reserve, its charter allowed it to issue in bank-notes thirty-six millions of pounds sterling;

but all its efforts could not raise the active circulation over twenty-three millions. It consequently reduced the rate of interest, first to $2\frac{1}{2}$, and then to 2, per cent a year, — the lowest rate at which it had ever discounted bills. Consols, moreover, or government three-per-cent stock, rose to par and above, and the ministry, therefore, formed a plan for reducing the rate of interest on the national debt. The Bank of France, also, had specie to the amount of 120 millions of dollars, or far more than it needed. The accumulation in our own Sub-Treasury, or government exchequer, was about seventeen millions; and the coin in the New York banks exceeded the amount of their notes in circulation. Supported by these heavy amounts of specie in their vaults, the banks of England, France, and America might safely have increased their issues of notes to a very great extent; and they did endeavor to increase them, as otherwise their profits would have been much diminished. Accordingly, they pressed more accommodation upon their customers, and money was offered at very low rates. Everywhere there appeared to be a superfluity of currency, or of money seeking investment, which did not fail soon to produce its usual results.

It has already been said, that it is only the coin in active circulation which operates directly upon prices. What is in the vaults of the banks is dormant in this respect, its office being only to guard the really active portion of the currency against frequent and sudden fluctuations. The effects of an influx or efflux of the precious metals are first felt on these bank reserves, which so far retard or deaden the shock, that it is not even perceptible by the community at large till the increase or drain has become very serious. Then, even the banks begin to feel the pressure. After an unnatural inflation of prices by a speculating fever, the heavy importations of goods, and consequent heavy exportations of specie, so far diminish these specie reserves, which are the ballast of the banks, that they find they must furl sail, or contract their paper issues, if they would not be thrown on their beam-ends. On the other hand, an anomalous state of things, like that which existed in 1852, creating an immense influx of specie, they find their ballast so much increased, that the motion of the vessel has become sluggish, and they cannot force their way through the water unless they spread more sail, or induce their customers to borrow a larger amount of bank-notes.

It may seem strange, that, as the spirit of speculation has usually been rife when but slight temptation was offered, it should have shown itself so dull, when there was a moral certainty that there would soon be a general rise of prices. But the prospect of a general and gradual rise of prices does not tempt men into hazardous enterprises so strongly as the chance of a sudden and great enhancement of the price of one commodity or several. The report of a war with China may double or triple the price of tea in a month; or a rumor of the potato-rot and a failure of the crops in England may create a fever almost at once in the flour-market here in America. But a gradual enhancement in the money value of all commodities does not quickly induce people to purchase largely on borrowed capital. There may be brief and violent fluctuations in the relative value of particular commodities, while the great movement is silently going on which slowly enhances the value of all. It is conceivable, and even probable, that one effect of the abundance of capital seeking investment, and the consequent diminution of the rate of interest, will be to lower the prices of many commodities, instead of raising them, because these circumstances aid and stimulate production. More cotton will be spun, because it will be more easy to obtain capital wherewith to build manufactories and keep them in operation.

Still, the loan of capital could not be so generally offered at very low rates of interest without producing, sooner or later, its proper result, — a disposition to speculate and a general inflation of prices. This effect began to be manifest towards the close of 1852, and became very conspicuous the following year. Commodities generally rose in price, to the extent, on an average, probably of 15 or 20 per cent beyond what was obtained for them in 1850; and in the case of breadstuffs and some other articles of provision, a partial failure of the crops in Europe in 1854 made the enhancement of price much greater. As a necessary consequence of the increased cost of living which was thus produced, there was a general rise of wages and salaries, amounting to at least 15 per cent. These results were attended by considerable speculation, it is true;

as loans could be easily obtained, and there is always a strong temptation to buy on a rising market. Thus, the very lucrative trade with California and Australia, stimulated by the extraordinary disturbance of values which was created by the discovery of the gold deposits in those two countries, was soon carried to excess, and a reaction ensued which ruined many adventurers. A reaction followed throughout the United States in 1854, which extended to England and France the following year. Many persons had traded beyond their means, and therefore found great difficulty in meeting their engagements. The rate of interest rose to its highest point, and loans were difficult to be obtained on any terms. The rate of discount at the Bank of England was fixed at six per cent at the close of 1853, and seldom fell below this point during the two following years. In short, there were all the features of a commercial crisis, except a fall of prices, which was prevented by the steady influx of gold, diminished in amount, it is true, but still sufficient to maintain prices and wages at the elevation which they had reached. It has become manifest, then, that this is a permanent elevation; having withstood a general pressure in the loan-market, which continued for an unusual period and with extraordinary severity, there is no reason to believe that it will give way when ease and prosperity return. No one expects that prices will return to the level at which they were in 1850; money has depreciated in value within five years about fifteen or twenty per cent.

The question will naturally be asked, What has become of the large amounts of gold, which were deposited in the banks of England, France, and the United States in 1852? The answer is easy; it has been absorbed by this very rise of prices, or depreciation in the value of money, assisted in some degree, perhaps, by the exigencies of the war with Russia, which has caused large amounts of specie to be transported to Constantinople and the Crimea. If, as has been estimated, the whole amount of coin circulating in the commercial world before 1850 was 400 millions sterling, and if prices have risen generally 20 per cent, 480 millions are now needed to effect the same amount of exchanges as before. The depreciation has taken place because 80 millions sterling, or nearly 400 millions of dollars, have been added to the active specie currency of the world. This amount was first accumulated in the banks, there being no demand for it in open market till the disposition to make purchases was excited, which at last produced the rise of prices. But the addition to the bank reserves, as we have seen, necessarily created this disposition to buy; loans being offered in large amounts, and on very easy terms, the purchases were made, prices rose, and the money was absorbed into the active circulation, instead of being thrown back upon the banks. The continued influx of the precious metals from the mining countries prevented prices from receding again, and the depreciation in the value of money is thus established. The reserve in the Bank of England has now fallen to less than half of its amount in 1852; that in the Bank of France has been reduced so low as to create alarm for the safety of the institution.

The experience which we have now had enables us to predict with some confidence the future course of the depreciation in the value of money. It will not stop here; the continued influx of at least 100 millions of dollars a year from the silver mines and gold deposits must again raise the prices of commodities, within five or six years, another 15 or 20 per cent. As farther supplies are received from California and Australia, the specie reserves of the banks will again be distended, the rate of interest will again be reduced, loans and discounts will be freely offered, and, as a necessary consequence of the larger amount of money thus thrown into the market, prices will rise still higher, or, what is the same thing, the value of money will be still further depreciated. That a speculating fever should also ensue, many persons being encouraged by this abundance of money and enhancement of price to make purchases beyond their capital, is a natural, but not a necessary, consequence of this alteration of value. It is evident that the change *might* take place by a steady and gradual process, each annual receipt of the precious metals from the mines operating upon the market to raise prices to an extent almost too slight to be appreciated; if so, there would not be even a fluctuation in the rate of interest to indicate the change which is going on. But it is more probable that the revolution will not be thus uniform in its progress, but that it will advance, so to speak, by hitches and starts, a single year being marked by a considerable rise in prices, which will be followed by two or three years of seeming quiescence, and then another rise will ensue. Such has been our experience thus far. The principal effect upon the market was produced in 1853, the receipts from California and Australia having reached their highest point the previous year. Since 1853, there has been no general advance; prices have only been maintained,—those of some commodities have even fallen off.* In a year or two, we may expect another start, if the annual supply from the mining countries should not be suddenly and largely diminished.

One reason why money does not sink in value slowly and uniformly, but by starts, is to be found in the time which is required for equalizing prices throughout the world. After they have risen in the chief commercial countries, such as England, France, and the United States, the effect must be transmitted to the East, to British India and China. The price of opium, tea, silks, and other Eastern products, must also rise, and large amounts of gold and silver will be transmitted to pay for these commodities at their enhanced valuation. The East has always required more metallic currency in proportion to the extent of her commerce than the West, as it has fewer banks and other expedients for economizing the use of money.

It may be readily inferred, from what precedes, that, far from regarding a considerable decline in the value of money, when produced by natural causes, as a calamity, we consider it as a blessing. It will greatly alleviate the burden of taxation in many states that are now oppressed by a heavy national debt. Private debts, as well as public, will become easier to bear; they will be subject to a steady process of abatement, too slow, and compensated in too great a variety of ways, to occasion any serious loss to the creditor, and still affording a sensible relief to all who have payments to make. The greater proportion by far of fixed payments are made by those who are engaged in business or industrious undertakings, to those who are enjoying leisure and wealth. Thus, the

* Breadstuffs may be thought to be an exception; but these ought not to be taken into account, except on an average of a considerable number of years. A very short or very abundant harvest will affect the price of flour much more than any advance or decline in the value of money.

relief and the encouragement come to the more active and industrious classes, while the loss, small in proportion, falls upon those who are most able to bear it. The increasing abundance of money, and the steady rise of prices, stimulate all forms of industry and enterprise. As the operations of trade and manufacture are quickened, wages tend to rise even in a higher ratio than the prices of commodities. Thus the condition of laborers is ameliorated, and the inequality in the distribution of wealth, which is the great misfortune of the most prosperous nations, is slowly diminished. Hume, long ago, remarked that, "in every kingdom into which money begins to flow in greater abundance than formerly, everything takes a new face; labor and industry gain life, the merchant becomes more enterprising, the manufacturer more diligent and skilful, and even the farmer follows his plough with greater alacrity and attention. But when gold and silver are diminishing, the workman has not the same employment from the manufacturer and merchant, though he pays the same price for everything in the market. The farmer cannot dispose of his corn and cattle, though he must pay the same rent to his landlord. The poverty, beggary, and sloth that must ensue, are easily foreseen." Even so cautious and conservative a writer as McCulloch fully admits the truth of this view, though he adds the obvious and just qualification, that the fall in the value of money, which is to be advantageous to a country, must proceed from natural causes, and not be an intentional reduction by the authority of the state. Apart from the obligation to act with good faith and equal justice to all classes, which is incumbent upon every government, it is obvious that any measure, having this end in view, would occasion a great shock to public and private credit, and cause a large amount of capital to be transported to other lands as to places of security.

Those who were apprehensive that a decline in the value of money, produced by the increased supply of the precious metals, would derange the operations of business, and destroy large amounts of wealth, may console themselves by remembering that England, France, and the United States have, at no remote period of their history, passed, without any very serious consequences, through crises similar in character, but more violent and sudden than that which is now in prospect.

In May, 1837, when all the banks in the United States suspended specie payments, specie rose to a premium amounting, on an average, to at least 12 per cent, and therefore disappeared from the circulation, all obligations being discharged in paper, — that is, by the payment of 88 cents on the dollar. This alteration in the value of the currency was far more violent, and more sweeping in its effects, than that which we are now experiencing. It was a depreciation of 12 per cent, and as it took place at once, it literally affected *all* debts which came due while it continued. But a gradual depreciation of two or three per cent a year has scarcely a perceptible influence on the great bulk of business transactions, which involve obligations to pay that have only a few months to run. It is more important to observe, that the suspension itself, or the acknowledgment of the depreciation of the currency, which, in truth, had already taken place, was felt as a relief. It had been preceded by a period of advancing prices, great activity in commerce and manufactures, and universal prosperity. These high prices could not be maintained, because the inflation of the currency had been unnatural, and was, therefore, temporary. The suspension came, not because the currency had expanded, but because it could not expand any further, — because there were not gold and silver enough to maintain it at the point which it had reached. The distress was caused, not by the decline in the value of money, but by its advance, — by the contraction of prices, and the restoration of things to the old standard. It was felt, not when a debt of 100 dollars could be paid off by 88 dollars, but when a debt contracted by receiving virtually only 88 dollars had to be discharged by paying 100. As no such reaction or collapse can follow, when the rise of prices has been occasioned by a natural cause, that is, by the augmented supply of the precious metals, we shall have, in the case before us, the period of prosperity, and a long one too, without being obliged to pay bitterly for it afterwards.

It was just so during the suspension of specie payments by the Bank of England, that began in February, 1797, and continued till 1819. The depreciation, which was very slight for a few years, rose suddenly, in 1810, to 13 per cent, and attained its maximum in 1814, when it was 25 per cent. The ministry, who at first regarded the suspension with great anxiety, came afterwards, it is said, to be as much delighted with it as if they had found a mountain of gold. And well they might be delighted. It was this depreciation of the currency which carried England triumphantly through the war, — which enhanced rents and profits, gave unprecedented activity to manufactures and commerce, kept the laboring population employed, and therefore quiet, enabled the government to raise enormous loans without difficulty, and made the people bear, with ease and cheerfulness, an amount of taxation which they can now hardly contemplate without shuddering. "It is undeniable," says a very well-informed writer, "that during the greater part of that period (from 1793 to 1814) the trade of the country was in a state of unexampled prosperity. In no twenty-two years of our history, of which we have authentic accounts, has there ever been so rapid an increase of production and consumption, as in the twenty-two years ending with 1814." It is not going too far to say, that, without the high prices of those years, Wellington could not have driven the French out of Spain, or triumphed at Waterloo. The dark hour came, when, after the close of the war, it was thought necessary to take measures to contract the currency, restore the former value of money, and submit to the consequent fall of prices. "In whatever degree minor circumstances may have coöperated, the great and mighty source of the distresses felt by all classes of producers has been the transition that took place at the termination of the war, — the transition from an immense, unremitting, protracted, effectual demand for almost every article of consumption to a comparative cessation of that demand." "There was," adds Mr. Tooke, "from 1814 to 1816 (a period of rapid contraction of the currency) a very general depression in the prices of nearly all productions, and in the value of all fixed property, entailing a convergence of losses and failures among the agricultural, and commercial, and manufacturing, and mining, and shipping, and building interests, which marked that period as one of most extensive suffering and distress."

By a very natural association of ideas, the years marked first by a great decline, and then by a rapid restoration, of the value of money, come to be remembered only as one period, or complete cycle, of great prosperity followed by still greater depression and distress; and men naturally shrink from so cruel an alternation. They forget that the prosperity alone is consequent on the depreciation of the currency, and if this depreciation could continue, or become permanent, no reaction, no distress, would succeed. It was such a permanent decline in the value of money which caused the marvellous development of the wealth and material prosperity of England, that took place during the reign of Elizabeth; and it is to a decline equally permanent, and perhaps equally great, that we have now to look forward. Surely, there is nothing in such a prospect to create agitation and alarm. We know not what political troubles may grow out of this grand monetary revolution, or that it will have any political effect whatever; but industry, commerce, and the arts have nothing to fear from it, but everything to hope.

Coming down again to particulars, it was generally expected that the decline in the value of money would be indicated by a variation in the relative values of gold and silver, as the increase in the annual supply was thought to be almost exclusively of the former metal. Such a variation would enable the legislature, from time to time, to determine the amount of the depreciation which has taken place, and, by such enactments as the Gold Bill passed in 1834, and the law enacted by Congress in 1853, to adjust the state of the currency to the new values of the precious metals. But we have already shown that, owing to the unexpected increase of the annual product of silver, and the sudden diminution of that of gold, the change in the relative value of the two metals will probably be much less than was anticipated. The variation will indicate *in part* the decline in the value of money, but it will not be a measure of the *whole* depreciation. Silver, for instance, is now only two per cent dearer in comparison with gold than it was in 1848, while the depreciation in the value of both metals, or of money generally, is from 15 to 20 per cent. One reason, perhaps, why the change in the proportional value of the two has not become more manifest, may be found in the change which has taken place in the currency of France. The circulation in that country was almost exclusively metallic, as the only bank-bills were of a very high denomination; and, till recently, it consisted for the most part of silver, gold bearing an *agio* of about seven in a thousand, and therefore not coming into general use. But the influx of gold from Australia and California has reversed this state of things. The French mint has coined a very large amount of gold during the last five years, which has entered rapidly into circulation, displacing an equivalent amount of silver coin, which has been melted up and sent abroad. It is estimated, by well-informed French and English writers, that the silver thus set free in France alone amounts to thirty millions of dollars. To this was added for a time a very considerable supply from this country, obtained in a similar way, — as we know that before the law was altered, in 1853, our American silver coins, of full weight, had generally disappeared, their place, for purposes of change, being supplied by the worn and clipped Spanish pieces. About fifteen millions in silver were thus set free in the United States for a year or two; but the new law of 1853 called it all back into circulation.

But *any* alteration, though a small one, in the relative value of the two precious metals, will be an inconvenience in every country where there is a double standard, or, in other words, where both gold and silver are a legal tender for the discharge of debts; for according to the law already explained, the metal which is overvalued in relation to the other will push that other out of circulation, and thus become the sole medium of exchange. A change must be made in the mint regulations, therefore, as we cannot do without silver for purposes of "small change," and it would be inconvenient to do without gold in making large payments. The question then arises, — and it is a very important one, — how the alteration in the coinage shall be made. Shall it be by adding to the quantity of gold, or by diminishing the quantity of silver, which now passes for a dollar? If the former course be adopted, the value of money will decline only in proportion to the depreciation of silver, the greater depreciation in the value of gold being obviated by the increased quantity of it which passes under the old denomination. If the latter course be preferred, money will fall in value as rapidly as the worth of gold is depreciated. In either case, several successive changes of the mint regulations will be necessary. If, for instance, gold is now worth two per cent less, when compared with silver, than it was four or five years ago, the quantity of gold contained in an eagle must be increased two per cent, or the quantity of silver contained in a dollar must be diminished two per cent. In either case, the relative value of the two precious metals still tending to change, the operation in a year or two must be repeated. The matter might be simplified, it is true, by giving up the double standard, and using in future but one metal for coinage. Thus, we might coin gold only, and at the present rate, putting 232.2 grains of pure gold into an eagle, or 23.22 grains into a dollar, and allow silver to be bought and sold only as bullion, or at whatever rate it might command in the market per ounce, Troy weight. Or, gold coins might be dispensed with, and only silver allowed to circulate as currency, and at its former rate, of 371.25 grains to a dollar. In this case, as so much more silver would be needed if all money was to be composed of it, its absolute value would probably be enhanced; it would be worth more, not only in relation to gold, but in relation to all other commodities.

The question which we are now considering is not one of mere convenience or expediency; we must also see what abstract justice requires in all dealings between debtors and creditors. Those who are in favor of increasing the quantity of gold, rather than of lessening the quantity of silver, which now passes for a dollar, may argue very plausibly, that a debt ought to be cancelled only by the payment of money equal in value to that in which it was contracted. If I have borrowed one thousand silver dollars, or something which could readily be exchanged for one thousand *silver dollars*, I ought not to be allowed to cancel the debt by paying one thousand *gold dollars*, after gold has fallen to one half of the value which it had when I obtained the loan.

This argument is plausible, but it is insufficient. All mercantile contracts must be construed literally, or must have a specific performance. The law never undertakes to guard either party against the evil consequences to himself of a change of values which he has not foreseen. Such changes are very frequent in mercantile transactions, and the maxim, *Caveat emptor*, applies to them all. If I pay one thousand dollars now, for one hundred barrels of flour to be delivered three months hence, and if the price of flour falls meanwhile to eight dollars a barrel, I must not expect that one fifth of the purchase-money will be paid back to me; and if the price, on the other hand, rises to twelve dollars, the seller cannot require me to make up the difference. Each party must bear the consequences of his bargain, and of his own want of foresight. In like manner, if a landholder leases an estate for twenty years, at an annual rent of five hundred dollars, he cannot rightfully demand compensation, nor can the lessee ask an abatement, if, in the course of those twenty years, the value of the dollars should be altered by circumstances over which neither party had any control. According to the state of the law before 1853, when we suppose the lease was made, the annual payment was to be *either* five hundred times 23.22 grains of pure gold, *or* five hundred times 371.25 grains of pure silver. It was a part of the contract, that the lessee should have the option of paying his rent in *either* of these forms, the two metals in these proportions being both legal tender. It is the misfortune of the lessor, but certainly not the fault of the lessee, if, when the rent becomes due, the 23.22 grains of pure gold will no longer purchase so many commodities as before. The latter cannot, therefore, be obliged to pay silver; for he bargained to pay gold, if he saw fit. If, indeed, the government should arbitrarily "raise the standard," as it is termed, or decree that the dollar should in future contain only 200 grains of pure silver, instead of 371.25 grains, then equity, if not law, would require the lessee to pay his rent in coins of the old standard, or their equivalent; for the spirit, if not the letter, of his covenant is, not to pay what *may be called a dollar* at any future time, but what is really accounted to be a dollar at the time when the bargain was made. It is but another application of the same rule of equity to say, that he shall not be held to pay 40 grains of pure gold for a dollar, when he covenanted to pay only 23.22 grains.

Apart from all considerations of expediency, then, it would be an obvious violation of justice, in any country where a double standard exists, to seek, by altering the regulations of the mint, to prevent the present and the expected depreciation in the value of gold from affecting the value of all money to the full extent of such depreciation. In other words, it would be wrong to alter the law on any other principle than those on which it was altered in 1853. The bill on that occasion was prepared in conformity with an able report from the Director of the Mint, and it passed both houses of Congress by a large majority. It provides, that the silver half-dollar, instead of 206¼ grains of *standard* silver, one tenth being alloy, which was its former weight, should contain but 192 grains of such silver, — the quarter of a dollar, dime, and other silver coins, being reduced in the same proportion. In other words, the silver dollar now contains only 345.6 grains of *pure* silver, instead of 371.25 grains, as formerly, the reduction being about 6.91 per cent. Thus the ratio of gold to silver in our coins, instead of being nearly 1 to 16, as before, is now as 1 to 14.884. The former ratio undervalued silver about two per cent; the present one overvalues it about five per cent, so that there will be no occasion to make any further change, till gold has fallen more than five per cent below the present ratio of its value to silver. At the same time, to prevent the new silver coin from driving the gold coin out of the currency, the law provides that the new coin shall be legal tender only to the amount of five dollars. As the silver bullion which can be purchased for $100 is coined at the mint into $105, the law prohibits silver from being deposited for coinage except by the Treasurer of the Mint, under the authority of the United States; and care is taken that no more of it shall be coined than is needed for the purposes of circulation, as otherwise the coin might be depreciated in the market to the extent of this five per cent.

The necessity for passing this law arose from the fact, that, in 1852, gold having fallen two per cent below its relative value to silver as established by the mint regulations then in force, — that is, 23.22 grains of pure gold having fallen two per cent below the value of 371.25 grains of pure silver, though either of these sums was legal tender for a dollar, — all the former silver coins of full weight had been melted up or exported, and the public were thus exposed to great inconvenience from the want of "small change." The only small coins in circulation were the worn and defaced Spanish pieces, which had lost, by abrasion or clipping, from five to ten per cent of their nominal value; and as there were not enough even of these for the purposes of the currency, it had become very difficult to effect small purchases, or to obtain "change" for a dollar.

A profit of two per cent is enough to tempt the bullion-dealers to gather up the silver coin very eagerly and send it abroad. On every million of dollars thus sent, — and we were then remitting millions to Europe every month, — they made a gain of $ 20,000, if they could collect the sum in United States silver coin. Obviously, no gold would be sent so long as silver coin could be had; and though, since 1789, the mint had issued over 77 millions of dollars in such coin, in less than six months it had become so scarce that an American half-dollar of full weight was seldom seen. The question was not, then, whether we should fall from a silver coinage containing 371.25 grains of pure silver in the dollar, to one which is nearly seven per cent inferior to it in value, but whether we should rise from a worn and insufficient Spanish currency, which had lost nearly 10 per cent of its value, to one that is degraded only about five per cent. The new law did not by its own efficacy debase or depreciate any kind of money; it only recognized a depreciation that had already taken place, from natural causes, over which human legislation had no control, — a depreciation of gold caused by the great increase in the annual supply of that metal, and a depreciation of silver money produced, so to speak, by its *contact* with the depreciated gold. The new law was a measure to prevent the necessary or inevitable decline in the value of money from proceeding in an irregular manner, or throwing our currency into unnecessary confusion. At present, the government obtains a considerable profit from the manufacture of silver coin; its over-valuation, amounting to five per cent, is also enough to prevent it from being exported or melted up, but is not so large as to afford any temptation to the counterfeiter.

The object of the new law was to introduce into this country the system of coinage which has been tried in England for over thirty years, and has been found to answer excellently well, especially during the last four or five years, when it has obviated the difficulty that would otherwise have arisen from the varying ratio of gold to silver. The English system is explained by McCulloch as follows: —

"From 1666 down to 1817, no seigniorage was charged on the silver coin; but a new system was then adopted. Silver having been underrated in relation to gold in the mint proportion of the two metals fixed in 1718, heavy silver coins were withdrawn from circulation, and gold only being used in all the larger payments, it became, in effect, what silver had formerly been, the standard of the currency. The act of 56th George III., regulating the present silver coinage, was framed, not to interfere with this arrangement, but so as to render silver entirely subsidiary to gold. For this purpose, it is made legal tender only to the extent of 40*s.*; and 66*s.*, instead of 62*s.*, are coined out of a pound Troy, the 4*s.* being retained as a seigniorage, which, therefore, amounts to $6\frac{14}{31}$ per cent. The power to issue silver is vested exclusively in the hands of government; who have it, therefore, in their power to avoid throwing too much of it into circulation, and, consequently, to prevent its fusion, until the market price of silver shall have risen to above 5*s.* 6*d.* an ounce."

"Under these regulations," adds McCulloch, in another place, "silver has ceased to be a standard of value, and forms merely a subordinate or subsidiary species of currency, or change, occupying the same place in relation to gold that copper occupies in relation to itself. This system has been found to answer exceedingly well." Our copper coins, like those of England, are rated about 75 per cent above their real value; but as the government alone determines how many of them shall be issued, and as they are legal tender to the extent only of the smallest silver coin, this over-valuation is not productive of any bad effect. As no more of them are issued than are needed, they do not tend to fall below their nominal valuation, they cannot be exported or melted up without great loss, and the coinage of them affords a considerable profit to the government. About $ 1,300,000 worth of them have been issued in this country, nearly three fourths of which sum is clear profit.

It has been objected to the law of 1853, that, by making gold the sole measure of value, it will enable "the debtor to pay in gold perhaps worth only as one to ten [in silver], when *he contracted to pay worth as one to sixteen.*" But the misstatement here is obvious. *The debtor has not contracted to pay gold which shall be worth sixteen times as much as silver;* no such obligation is expressed, none is implied, in his contract. He has simply bound himself to pay as many times 23.22 grains of pure gold as he owes dollars, be the worth of that gold more or less. The law under which he made his contract, and which still exists, declares that the coin containing 23.22 grains of pure gold shall be legal tender for a dollar. Accordingly, to increase the quantity of gold in a dollar, — to declare, for instance, that it should in future contain 30 grains, — unless the declaration were accompanied with a proviso that all debts previously contracted might be discharged by payment of the old coin or its equivalent, would be to violate that clause in the Constitution which forbids the passage of any law impairing the obligation of contracts. A debtor no more insures the future value of the dollars which he promises to pay, than the grain-dealer insures the future price of a cargo of flour, which he sells before it has yet come into port. The contingency of a rise or fall in the value of the article is what the buyer knowingly takes upon himself.

There are some particular reasons why a decline in the value of money, such as is now taking place, should not be regarded with apprehension in this country, but rather as a great addition to the future sources of our national well-being. As has been mentioned, those countries which have a large national debt are most likely to be benefited by the change. The burden of taxation will be essentially diminished, while the loss sustained by the fund-holders will fall on shoulders that are most capable of bearing it, and will also be distributed among many, and over a long period of years, the frequent changes in the ownership of the stocks, moreover, tending to render their real depreciation almost imperceptible. For this reason, the present revolution in the monetary world seems to be contemplated without terror in Great Britain; at any rate, no one hints at the expediency of giving up the present exclusive gold standard, which exposes the currency to the full shock of the alteration. There are few advocates there of the plan of making silver the standard, and gradually increasing the quantity of pure metal in the gold coins. Our national debt, it is true, is but small, and what little there is will quickly be extinguished. But the debts of the individual States are large, amounting in the aggregate to over two hundred millions of dollars, a large portion of which is owned in Europe. There are also stocks to a very large amount, issued by cities, railroads, and other corporations, in which English capitalists have made large investments; while there are no foreign stocks owned in this country. The rate of interest being higher here than in the Old World, European capital has been attracted here in so large quantities, that our annual remittances for interest already constitute no small portion of our exports. We do not call these remittances "a drain upon the resources of the country," as they are often denominated by the unthinking; for the transactions on which they are founded have swelled those resources far beyond the limit which would otherwise have bounded them. Still, it is satisfactory to remember, that, as the monetary revolution will operate exclusively to the benefit of the indebted party, our own land will derive as much benefit from it, in proportion to our means, as any other country on earth.

CHAPTER XXIII.

EFFECT OF SPECULATION UPON PRICES.—THE THEORY OF A COMMERCIAL CRISIS.

Having considered at length the nature and uses of money, we are now prepared to explain the adjustment of prices in the market, and especially the causes of fluctuations of price. The price of a thing may be defined to be its *present market value*, or temporary exchangeable power *reckoned in money*. Its permanent or *natural exchangeable value*, as I have already shown, depends on the *cost of its production*, and is the pivot about which the price, or immediate market value, is perpetually oscillating, never departing from it far, or for any considerable length of time, in either direction. If the price falls below the cost, a smaller quantity of the article will be produced, and therefore the price will soon begin to rise; if it considerably exceeds the cost, production will be stimulated, more of the article will be offered in the market, and then the price will fall.

The general principle is, that the price so adjusts itself that the demand shall be just equal to the supply. If the supply be too great for the present demand, if the market be overstocked with the article, a fall of price must ensue, and this diminished price will bring the commodity within the means of a larger class of consumers; that is, the demand for it will be increased enough to take off the quantity which was a drug in the market at the higher price. For instance, when flour is ten dollars a barrel, it is beyond the means of a large class in the community, who will then be obliged to live on corn-meal and potatoes. We will suppose that 600,000 barrels of flour can be disposed of at this price, because this quantity will satisfy the wants of all who are able to pay ten dollars a barrel. But if the price should fall to five dollars, the poorer class can purchase flour, and a million of barrels may consequently be disposed of. On the other hand, if the supply should not be equal to the demand, — if only 500,000 barrels should be brought to market, — the competition of the buyers with each other will cause the price to rise (say) from ten to twelve dollars; and this enhancement of price will lessen the number of those who are able to purchase, so that now only half a million of barrels are required. Thus the fluctuations of price are the means through which the demand is always made just equal to the supply.

But there is one remarkable exception to the principle, that cheapening the price will increase the demand, or augment the number of consumers. It is not true that purchasers will always buy what they can buy cheapest. If the pursuit of wealth, or, what is the same thing, the desire to make savings, were always the ruling motive, the principle would hold good. But it is not so; in many instances, the ruling motive is, notoriously, not the love of gain, but the love of display. Through the rivalry of individuals in the display of wealth, some articles are prized only on account of their high cost. Cheapen them, and the demand will not be enlarged, but diminished, for the consumption of them will then be abandoned by this class of persons, who will immediately seek out other and more costly articles with which to gratify their love of ostentation. Render them very cheap, and they will go out of use altogether. If pearls were as common as oysters, pearl bracelets and brooches would never be manufactured. If equally serviceable articles of intrinsically higher cost cannot be found, the aid of that capricious goddess, Fashion, will be called in to create a factitious enhancement of the price of certain commodities. The demand for these commodities is then increased by the addition to their price; when cheap, they were neglected; when they have become scarce and high in price, they are eagerly sought after, and persons even of moderate means will submit to considerable sacrifices in order to obtain them. And the cases are neither few nor unimportant, in which the rule is thus inverted. Most of the finer manufactures of cotton, wool, and silk, together with fine cutlery, expensive pieces of furniture, and nearly all the fancy articles which become articles of desire because they are fashionable, belong to this class. Lower their price, and the demand for them is diminished.

What Political Economists term *the demand*, consists of two elements, — the ability to purchase, and the desire for the thing itself, or the disposition to purchase. These two must coexist in order to constitute an *effectual* demand, and thus affect the price. In the case of the poorer classes, including persons of moderate means, it is the want of the former element, the ability, which limits the demand. In this case, then, lower the price, and the consumption is increased. But for people of wealth, it is the lack of the second element, the desire or disposition, which restricts the demand; to diminish the price will not increase their consumption of the commodity, but in most cases will lessen it, as the possession of the article will no longer be a token of wealth.

The price is usually said to vary in inverse ratio with the supply, or to diminish as the supply increases, and *vice versa*. But not all the commodity which is in being, not all even of that portion of it which is intended sooner or later to be sold, constitutes what is properly termed *the supply*. This term is restricted to that portion of the article which is already in the market, or is *now* offered for sale. The quantity which is held in store by speculators, awaiting an expected rise of price, has no more effect on the present market, than the quantity which is already purchased and held in store only for consumption; as when the government has purchased sufficient stores for the army six months in advance.

And even in reference to what is *now* offered for sale, it should be observed that the price does not vary *in the same ratio* with the deficiency or excess of supply. This depends upon the nature of the commodity, or rather upon the nature of the desire to possess it, — whether it be a natural and imperative want, or only an artificial one. If the article be a mere luxury, or desired only for purposes of ostentation, a deficiency of one third in the amount offered for sale will not make the price one third larger; rather than purchase it at a cost so much enhanced, many persons will do without it altogether. If the annual supply of diamonds from the mines were reduced one half, it is not probable that the price of them would be doubled, or even that it would be materially increased; as they are of little use except for purposes of display, persons would gratify their ostentatious feelings by purchasing some other commodity at a price nearly equivalent to what they formerly paid for diamonds. Large pearls, or other gems of high cost, would answer just as well. On the other hand, if the article is a necessary of life, so that people will submit to any sacrifice rather than resign it, and especially if it be of such a nature that an apprehended scarcity of it operates strongly on the fears of the multitude, a deficiency of one third may double, triple, or quadruple the price. "The price of corn in England," says Mr. Tooke, "has risen from one hundred to two hundred per cent, when the utmost computed deficiency of the crops has not been more than between one sixth and one third below an average, and when that deficiency has been relieved by foreign supplies."

To what point, then, will the enhancement of price in either case — whether of luxuries or necessaries — be carried? "To that point," says Mr. Mill, "whatever it be, which equalizes the demand and supply; — to the price which cuts off the extra third from the demand, or brings forward additional sellers sufficient to supply it." It appears, also, contrary to what might have been anticipated, that articles of high cost, and therefore in comparatively limited demand, are most steady in price; while those of prime necessity and in general use, such as breadstuffs and other provisions, are liable to sudden and violent fluctuations.

The influence of mercantile speculations on price has been

well explained by McCulloch. "It rarely happens," he says, "that either the actual supply of any species of produce in extensive demand, or the intensity of that demand, can be exactly measured. Every transaction in which produce is bought that it may be afterwards sold, is, in fact, a speculation. The buyer anticipates that the demand for the article he has purchased will be such, at some future period, either more or less distant," or at some other place, either in the same country or across sea, "that he will be able to dispose of it at a profit; and the success of the speculation depends, it is evident, on the skill with which he has estimated the circumstances that will determine the future price of the commodity. It follows, therefore, that in all highly commercial countries, where merchants are possessed of large capitals, and where they are left to be guided in the use of them by their own discretion and foresight, the prices of commodities will frequently be very much influenced, not merely by the actual occurrence of changes in the accustomed relation of the supply and demand, but *by the anticipation of such changes*. It is the business of the merchant to acquaint himself with every circumstance affecting the particular description of commodities in which he deals. He endeavors to obtain, by means of an extensive correspondence, the earliest and most authentic information with respect to everything that may affect their supply or demand, or the cost of their production; and if he learned that the supply of an article had failed, or that, owing to changes of fashion or to the opening of new channels of commerce, the demand for it had been increased, he would most likely be disposed to become a buyer, in anticipation of profiting by the rise of price, which, under the circumstances, could hardly fail of taking place; or if he were a holder of the article, he would refuse to part with it unless for a higher price than he would previously have accepted. If the intelligence received by the merchant were of a contrary description, — if, for example, he learned that the article was now produced with greater facility, or that there was a falling off in the demand for it, caused by a change of fashion, or by the shutting up of some of the markets to which it had previously been admitted, — he would act differently; in this case, he would anticipate a fall of prices, and would either decline purchasing the article, except at a reduced rate, or endeavor to get rid of it, supposing him to be a holder, by offering it at a lower price. In consequence of these operations, the prices of commodities, in different places and periods, are brought comparatively near to equality. All abrupt transitions, from scarcity to abundance, and from abundance to scarcity, are avoided; an excess in one case is made to balance a deficiency in another, and the supply is distributed with a degree of steadiness and regularity that could hardly have been deemed attainable." *

All commerce, then, may be said to consist in speculation, if we leave out of view those operations which are more properly regarded as subsidiary to commerce than as forming a part of it; such as the actual transportation of commodities from one place to another, and breaking bulk, or selling by retail for the greater convenience of consumers. The rest is only buying or selling with a view to profit from an expected change of price; and the success of the dealer will depend upon the correctness of his anticipations. Speculation, then, as McCulloch remarks, "is only another name for foresight." It plays an important part in those beneficent arrangements of Providence through which the cupidity and selfishness of individuals are made to minister to the general good. To recur to an instance already cited, it is through the speculations of private merchants that the inhabitants of a great metropolis are supplied with food and all other necessaries of life, without wastefulness and yet without stint, each family receiving every day just what it wants, and as much as it wants, and being admonished through the price to limit or economize its consumption of any one article, whenever a failure in the harvest or other mode of supply, or even the prospect of a failure, renders such economy essential.

The common prejudice against speculation arises, first, from confounding it with gambling, to which we must admit that it is very nearly allied, as the two operations run into one another by imperceptible degrees. A stock-jobber, for instance, agrees to purchase at a future day a particular amount of government stock at a certain price, expecting that the market price will rise before the day comes, so that he will make a

---

* McCulloch's *Principles of Political Economy*, 4th ed., pp. 336, 337.

profit by the bargain; the jobber who contracts to sell him the stock at that time, and on those terms, expects that the market price will fall in the mean time. But the party who agrees to sell has really no stock to dispose of, and he who agrees to purchase does not expect to receive the stock, but only to receive or pay, on the day appointed, the difference between the actual market price and the price agreed upon. Obviously, this is only betting upon the rise or fall of stocks within a given period, and is therefore properly denounced as "gambling in the stocks." On the other hand, a flour-merchant agrees to purchase, at a fixed price, a cargo of flour which has not yet arrived in port, because he has been led to believe that the price will rise, while the person who sells it to him expects it will fall; and this is admitted to be fair speculation, or a legitimate operation of trade.

How can these two cases be distinguished in principle, so as to prove that the one is censurable and the other praiseworthy? McCulloch says, "That may be termed a gambling adventure *in which the contingencies are unknown, or in which they are nearly equal*"; for instance, if a bet is to be decided by a throw of dice, it is gambling, because the utmost sagacity cannot determine how the dice will turn up. But if a flour-merchant contracts to purchase or deliver flour at a future day, he relies upon the information which he has obtained respecting the amount of the crops, and the probable extent of the demand, and his action, as it is thus based upon calculation and foresight, is a fair exercise of skill in trade.

It would seem to follow, then, that if one of the betters knew beforehand that the dice were loaded, and could thus anticipate how they would turn up, he would not be a gambler, but an honest man. But the common sense of mankind decides directly the other way. It may be said, indeed, that the criminality here consists in the deception, the one party using information, or having knowledge of facts, which the other party was not aware of. But then the flour-merchant often acts in the same manner, as he may have ascertained some circumstances which will probably affect the future price of grain, and he bases his action upon this knowledge, carefully concealing the facts from the person whom he deals with; and however such conduct may be viewed by strict moralists, it is sanctioned by the almost universal custom of merchants, and is regarded as a fair exercise of activity in getting early information, and of sagacity in profiting by it.

Speculation can be accurately distinguished from gambling, as it seems to me, only by taking into account the different motives and intentions of the parties. The gambler, acting from the love of excitement almost as much as from the thirst for gain, makes bets, or forms contracts which amount to bets, with reference to the doctrine of chances only, having no regard to the effect which his transaction will have upon markets by equalizing prices and supplies. The upright merchant, excluding as far as possible all consideration of mere chance, forms no bargain if his calculations do not assure him that it must lead to a favorable result, barring only all unforeseen contingencies; his transactions are all real, or based upon the actual transfer of merchandise, with reference to the effect of such transfer upon the markets in removing a surplus from one time or place, and supplying a deficiency in another. Accidents that could not be foreseen may falsify his calculations, and bring failure and loss; but he engages in no enterprise that bears hazard upon its face, regarding this as the province of the gambler. Failure, therefore, always takes him by surprise, and he shuns danger, while the other courts it, or deliberately weighs the probability of loss against that of gain.

Another prejudice against legitimate speculation in trade has arisen from its supposed effects in creating an unnecessary enhancement of price, to the detriment of the consumers. This is a mistake; the speculator cannot raise prices unnecessarily, without injuring himself more than those who buy of him. To prove that he cannot, I will take the strongest case, and one in which he is most frequently exposed to popular odium, the grain and flour trade. It is for the interest of the community that each crop should be distributed equally throughout the country and throughout the year. The business of the grain-merchant is to equalize the supplies, and the more equal and perfect that he makes this distribution, the larger is his profit. His interest, then, even in years of the greatest scarcity, is exactly coincident with that of the consumers. If the deficiency be very great, he sends to foreign countries for an additional supply, and thus contributes effectually to lower the price. If the harvest, on the other hand, has been unusually abundant, he exports a portion of the surplus, and thus prevents injury and discouragement to the agriculturists from the price falling too low, and guards the people against the formation of wasteful and improvident habits in consuming a cheap commodity. True, if he has a large stock on hand when the scarcity begins to be felt, he makes immense profits from the rise in price; and he sometimes holds back his stock in expectation of a further rise, though meanwhile the poorer classes are actually suffering from hunger. But in so doing, as Adam Smith remarks, he only treats the people in the same manner as the prudent master of a vessel often treats his crew. "When he foresees that provisions are likely to run short, he puts them upon short allowance. Though, from excess of caution, he should sometimes do this without any real necessity, yet all the inconveniences which his crew can thereby suffer are inconsiderable, in comparison of the danger, misery, and ruin to which they might sometimes be exposed by a less provident conduct. If he raises the price unnecessarily high, he becomes himself the greatest sufferer, as he runs the risk of losing a portion of his stock, by the natural decay of so perishable a material, and of being obliged to sell what remains of it at a much lower price than he might have obtained some months before. The profit which he makes when the price unexpectedly rises from a failure of the crops, is only a fair compensation for the loss which he must suffer when the price unexpectedly falls. The average rate of profit cannot be higher in this trade than in any other, as the business is free to all, and as competition brings profits everywhere to a level."

In fine, says Mr. Buchanan, "those who still imagine that corn is artificially raised in price, would do well to consider, that, as the supply of provisions is liable to great variations, there must be some provision in the economy of nature for making a smaller supply last as long as a larger supply; that there is no way of thus regulating the consumption but by the price; and that it is, accordingly, in reference to this great object that the price is invariably fixed. It neither can be lowered nor increased, but for the sake of more exactly suiting the daily and weekly waste to the supply of the year. If we suppose, for example, that the supply falls in one year one twelfth below the level of an average crop, (which we know frequently happens,) it would, if consumption were to go on at the ordinary rate, be consumed in the course of eleven months, leaving the last month wholly unprovided for. But this, we know, never happens, and it is only prevented by a rise of price, which measures the consumption by the deficiency of the crop; and whether, therefore, there is an abundant, middling, or scarce crop, a suitable allowance is sure to be measured out to the consumer by a low, a middling, or a high price. The corn-dealer, indeed, thinks nothing about all this; his object is to sell his commodity at the highest price; and in a scarcity, he takes his full advantage; but while he is thinking only of himself, while he is only playing his own paltry game, he is a mere instrument in the hands of Him who brings good out of evil, and who turns the little passions of man to the purposes of His own benevolence and wisdom. There is really nothing in nature more wonderful than that great law of society by which subsistence is measured out in due proportion to the supply of the year; and the more deeply it is considered, the more worthy will it appear of profound and rational admiration."

It is not denied, that in the corn-trade, as in other branches of commerce, prices are sometimes raised or lowered unnecessarily by the operations of speculators, who have been misled by wrong reports, or have erred in their estimates of the effects which would be produced on the market by political changes, the breaking out of a war, new inventions and discoveries, or the stoppage of some sources of supply. Merchants as well as other persons are sometimes mistaken in their calculations. But the mistakes thus committed soon correct themselves; they are usually of small extent and short duration, and they injure none so much as those who make them. When the error is discovered, the market experiences a revulsion, and prices for a time are depressed as much below their proper level as they were formerly, without due cause, elevated above it, so that the average result to the consumers is the same as if no disturbance had happened. When war was expected between England and China, in 1839, it was believed that the supply of tea would be almost entirely cut off; the whole supply in the market was therefore eagerly bought up by dealers and speculators, and prices advanced 100 per cent and upwards. But in less than three months, it was ascertained that the supply, by means of indirect shipments, cargoes being transhipped from American and Dutch to English vessels, would probably be as large as ever, while the consumption had been much diminished by the high price. There was, consequently, a violent reaction in the market, consumers obtained their tea cheaper than ever, and most of the speculators became bankrupts; they had injured nobody but themselves.

Such a speculative movement as this, affecting the price of only one commodity, can seldom be of much importance to the whole body of consumers, or the community at large. In fact, there is but one article, wheat and the flour which is made of it, the consumption of which is so vast, on account of its being in universal use, that any enhancement of its price, not connected with a general rise of prices, is a matter of national concern. But in this case, fortunately, the sources of supply are as numerous as the consumption is great; and owing to the differences of soil and climate, an unusually poor harvest in one district or country is usually offset by an unusually good one in another. In 1847, there was a more general failure of the crops in Western Europe than had been known for many years; but the harvest in the United States was abundant, and the unavoidable enhancement of price, as already explained, having limited the consumption, the aggregate supply for the whole world was sufficient for the aggregate demand. On account of the immense quantity of wheat and flour that is constantly in the market, speculation has a comparatively limited effect upon its price. "Not only its value," says Adam Smith, "far exceeds what the capitals of a few private men are capable of purchasing, but, supposing they were capable of purchasing it, the manner in which it is produced renders this purchase altogether impracticable." It is produced all over the country, and is necessarily divided at first among an immense number of owners, some of whom supply the consumption in their immediate neighborhood, while others send their produce to distant markets. "The inland dealers in corn, therefore, including the farmer and the baker, are necessarily more numerous than the dealers in any other commodity, and their dispersed situation renders it altogether impossible for them to enter into any general combination. If in a year of scarcity, therefore, any of them should find that he had a good deal more of corn upon hand than, at the current price, he could hope to dispose of before the end of the season, he would never think of keeping up this price to his own loss, and to the sole benefit of his rivals and competitors, but would immediately lower it in order to get rid of his corn before the new crop began to come in. The same motives, the same interests, which would thus regulate the conduct of any one dealer, would regulate that of every other, and oblige them all in general to sell their corn at the price which, according to the best of their judgment, was most suitable to the scarcity or plenty of the season." *

But apart from those mistakes of speculators which affect the price of only one or two articles, experience tells us that far more general errors are sometimes committed; that a fever of speculation appears at times to seize upon the whole mercantile community, producing for a while an unnatural inflation of the prices of nearly all commodities, and then, with a sudden reaction, carrying them back to a point much below their former average, and thus causing general distress, loss of confidence, and bankruptcy. These violent changes from a period of great activity and seeming prosperity of trade, to one of marked depression of prices, stagnation in business, and general inability to meet pecuniary engagements, are called commercial or monetary crises, and are among the most striking phenomena in the history of commerce. The state of trade, says Lord Overstone, (formerly Mr. Jones Loyd,) "revolves apparently in an established cycle. First, we find it in a state of quiescence, — next improvement, — growing confidence, — prosperity, — excitement, — over-trading, — convulsion, — pressure, — stagnation, — distress, — ending again in quiescence." Experience does not seem to teach caution, or instruct merchants and speculators how to avoid a recurrence of the evil. These crises are not of infrequent occurrence. Both in England and the United States, they come round, on an average, about once in every seven or eight years. Sir

* *Wealth of Nations*, p. 234.

Robert Peel, speaking in 1844, says: "Within the last twenty years, there have been, I think, four such periods, — in 1825, in 1832, in 1835-36, and in 1838-39." Since the date of his speech, there have been two others, — in 1847, and in 1855. In the United States, there was a very violent monetary crisis in 1837, when all the banks in the country suspended specie payments. Another followed in 1841, when there was a partial suspension by the banks, and a third in 1854.

When it is expected that circumstances will cause some commodity to rise in price, dealers in it enlarge their purchases, in order to profit by the alteration; and these additional purchases tend to increase the effect to which they have reference, or to raise the price still higher. Other speculators are then attracted into the business, and their operations cause a further advance. The price thus obtains an unnatural elevation, much above what would have been produced by the circumstances which first tended to raise it; and those who have accumulated a large stock of the commodity now become anxious to sell. This is the *turning* of the tide; the price ceases to advance, and even begins to decline. The holders rush into the market to avoid further loss, and their eagerness to sell carries down the price more rapidly than it rose. The lessons of experience are of little use under such circumstances; for though it be generally perceived that the rise is merely speculative, and the reaction be foreseen, each dealer still wishes to hold back till the advance has reached its maximum, and to sell only when the decline is about to begin. A few succeed in choosing the right moment for disposing of their stock; but the sanguine wait for the tide to rise still higher, and are caught by the suddenness of the revulsion. A concurrence of circumstances may affect the price of several commodities at once; and then, partly from sympathy, partly from the excitement produced by seeing great fortunes quickly accumulated by the few who made large purchases at the right moment, the rise becomes general, and a fever for buying and selling almost any article appears to pervade the whole community. Many of those who press so eagerly into the market when any new channel of commerce is opened, or when any considerable rise of price is anticipated, are not merchants, but persons engaged in other business, or living perhaps on fixed incomes, who speculate in the hope of suddenly increasing their fortune. "In speculation, as in most other things," says McCulloch, "one individual derives confidence from another. Such a one purchases or sells, not because he has any peculiar or accurate information in regard to the state of the demand and supply, but because some one else has done so before him." The interference of persons not experienced in business tends, of course, to fan the excitement, and, when the recoil comes, to render the catastrophe more general and more ruinous.

Two opposite theories prevail respecting the nature and causes of a commercial crisis. The first attributes nearly the whole evil to an unnecessary expansion of the currency, caused by the mismanagement of the banks, and undertakes to find a preventive or a remedy by placing very heavy restrictions upon the issue of bank-notes. The other regards the banks as necessarily passive in the matter, as they have nothing to do with buying or selling commodities, and finds the characteristic feature of the phenomenon in a great extension of the system of credit, which cannot be prevented by legislation, and which might take place, and, in fact, often has taken place, in countries where only a metallic currency was in use. The one party maintains that an expansion of the currency always precedes a commercial crisis, and that it is this expansion which produces the rise of prices; the other affirms that it is the rise of prices which produces what there is of an expansion, but that this increase of the currency, at the most, is inconsiderable; — that it is one of the attendant circumstances or consequences of the crisis, but is not its cause. Their doctrine is, that prices rise first, and that there is a slight increase of the circulation some time afterwards.

I have already endeavored at some length to prove, that a *convertible* paper currency *cannot* be issued in excess; that the whole amount of money needed by the country is a fixed quantity, and it is not in the power of the banks, however disposed they may be to do so, to make any direct addition to the aggregate of notes circulating in their respective districts. I shall now proceed to show that an expansion of the currency cannot produce the fever of speculation and the unnatural rise of prices which lead inevitably to a commercial crisis.

The currency theory is really founded upon the old error, so difficult to be entirely exploded, which confounds all wealth, and especially all capital, with money; which regards every debtor as a person who has borrowed money, and every creditor as an owner of money which is temporarily in the possession of another; and which therefore considers any excess in the contraction of debts as resulting from the abundance of money, and any general difficulty in the payment of debts as arising from the scarcity of money. The theory may be confuted, then, by a recurrence to first principles, which teach us, that what any person borrows is really not money, but the merchandise which he purchases with money; that what he pays is, in truth, only a certificate of the ownership of property, which is made over or transferred to his creditor; and that any general difficulty in the payment of debts arises from the fact, that many persons have contracted to deliver property at a future day, and have been deceived in their expectations of obtaining the property in season to fulfil their engagements. Money plays a very insignificant part in the whole circle of these transactions, being, in truth, only a means of effecting these transfers of property with somewhat greater facility; all the transactions might take place, though in an awkward and clumsy way, not only if the currency were exclusively metallic, but if there were no money whatever in circulation, so that all commerce should be reduced to barter. The same specific sum of money — that is, the same coins or bills — may be used to effect several payments in the same day; and if there was not money enough in the country to perform this office quickly and conveniently, the deficiency might, in great part, be made up by causing what money there was to do more work in a given time, or to effect, on an average, six instead of three payments a day; in other words, greater quickness of circulation might be made to compensate for any deficiency in amount. The office of money, then, in facilitating the *exchange* of merchandise and other values, is precisely analogous to that of carts and horses in effecting the *transportation* of merchandise. It would be absurd to affirm, that a superabundance of the means of transportation tempted merchants to transport more commodities than were needed, or that, in the present advanced state of the arts, there could be any serious difficulty in fulfilling contracts for the delivery of merchandise arising from a want of carts and horses.

The doctrine which attributes all the evils of excessive speculation to the mismanagement, or excessive issues, of the banks, may be all summed up in the oft-repeated assertion, that "it is only the money in circulation that affects prices."* Now it is certain and obvious, that the power of making extravagant purchases, and thereby enhancing prices and contributing to bring about a commercial crisis, does not at all depend upon the quantity of money, whether coin or bank-notes, that is in circulation. It might be exercised, as I have already said, to any extent, though the currency were exclusively metallic, and even though there were no currency, so that all debts should be contracted, and all payments made, in kind, or by the delivery of specified amounts of particular merchandise.† An individual may purchase by giving in exchange either his own notes, or bank-notes; that is, he may buy with his own promises to pay, or with the bank's promises to pay. The *former* promises may be issued in great excess; there is, in fact, no limit to their amount. The *latter* cannot be issued in excess. There is a check — an instantaneous and decisive check — on the issue of bank-notes; specie or actual value may be demanded for them at any time at the bank counter; and such a demand is a certain consequence

---

* *Currency or Money; its Nature and Uses, and the Effects of the Circulation of Bank-Notes for Currency,* by a Merchant of Boston. 1855. p. 60. This pamphlet contains a clear and able statement of the currency theory, by one of its most earnest advocates.

† Of course, when there is a currency, whether paper or metallic, it is not denied that, *if the amount of that currency can be increased,* prices will rise as a consequence of such augmentation. My only points are, first, that bank or convertible currency *cannot* be issued in excess, and, secondly, that an increase of the currency is not the *only* means of affecting prices, for prices might be raised, as is asserted in the text, though there were no circulation. A metallic currency can be augmented, as California and Australia have already taught us, and prices have risen in consequence. So, also, paper money *properly so called*, or inconvertible paper currency, can be issued in great excess, and prices rise enormously in consequence, as is proved in a preceding chapter. The great mistake of the currency doctors consists in obstinately confounding bank currency with paper money, though hardly any two things can be more unlike. Thus, in the pamphlet just cited, by "a Merchant of Boston," the instances given to prove that bank currency may be issued in excess are the paper roubles of Russia, the Continental money of the American Revolution, and the circulation of the Bank of England from 1797 to 1819, — all being instances of paper money.

even of a slight excess in the issue. There is no check on the excessive issue of the notes of any private person, because they are given on time, — for six months, a year, or more. Specie cannot instantly be demanded for them.

Over-trading, or excessive speculation, arises from an abuse of the purchasing power, which every man possesses in a greater or less degree. "The amount of purchasing power which a person can exercise," says Mr. Mill, "is composed of all the money in his possession, or due to him, and of all his credit. He is tempted to exercise the whole of this power only under peculiar circumstances; but he always possesses it; and the portion of it at any time which he *does* exercise is the measure of the effect which he produces on prices." In fine, credit as much exceeds currency in its influence on prices, as the number of purchases on credit exceeds the number of purchases for cash; and in the dealings of merchants with each other, every one knows that this ratio is at least as one hundred to one. Under ordinary circumstances, most traders find no difficulty in extending their credit, so far as the purchase of goods is concerned, to any extent that they may think desirable. They may not be able to borrow or hire capital directly, but they can purchase merchandise on credit, as it is termed, with no other check than their own judgment of what is honest and safe. Even in England, where a far more rigid rule of credit is applied than in the United States, Mr. Tooke says, "a person having the reputation of capital enough for his regular business, and enjoying good credit in his trade, if he takes a sanguine view of the prospect of a rise of price in the article in which he deals, and is favored by circumstances in the outset and progress of his speculation, may effect purchases to an extent perfectly enormous compared with his capital. The conditions requisite are, that the market should be a large one, and the article susceptible of great fluctuation of price from political or physical causes; and in fact, it is only articles of this description that are the subject of speculations sufficiently extensive to attract notice." Thus, when the difficulties with China, in 1839, produced a speculation in tea, one dealer was known, "who, having a capital not exceeding £1,200, which was locked up in his business, had contrived to buy 4,000 chests, value above £80,000"; and this was done without the outlay of actual capital or currency in any shape. Another example given is that of an operation in the grain market between 1838 and 1842. "There was an instance of a person who, when he entered on his extensive speculations, was, as it appeared by the subsequent examination of his affairs, possessed of a capital not exceeding £ 5,000, but being successful in the outset, and favored by circumstances in the progress of his operations, he contrived to make purchases to such an extent, that, when he stopped payment, his engagements were found to amount" to over half a million sterling. These are English examples; I need not quote American ones, as the memory of any of our merchants will supply instances quite as striking as any that have been mentioned.

But to this doctrine, that credit may be indefinitely extended without any expansion of the currency, it may be objected, that credit is necessarily limited by the amount of disposable capital in the country; for no more capital can be borrowed than there is capital to lend. Exactly so; but then the instances given are, *nominally*, not loans, but purchases; and consequently, the limit to them is, not the amount of capital which is seeking a borrower, only interest being expended for it, but the amount of merchandise which is seeking a purchaser, and on which profits are expected. To buy on credit is only to borrow on the hard condition of paying for the sum borrowed, not merely the rate of interest, which is but six per cent, but the rate of profit, which equals at least ten or twelve per cent. Hence a merchant who would immediately refuse to lend a brother merchant $ 5,000 on interest for six months, will very readily sell him $ 50,000 worth of goods on six months' credit. Thus there is literally no limit to the expansion of credit; the whole amount of merchandise offered for sale, both in this country and in foreign lands, may be sold on credit, under the temptation of the high prices, and consequent expectations of large profits, which are caused by a speculating fever; and having been sold once in this manner, the purchasers may then sell them again to another set of speculators, and again, till their value is indefinitely multiplied. What a mountain of indebtedness may thus be created, without the intervention, at least before some months have elapsed, of one dollar of currency, or even any demand upon the banks for additional loans! Large importations are only one mode of obtaining credit, or "borrowing money," as it is termed; and commercial crises are oftener produced by them than by any other means.

Here in the United States, there is a peculiar fund for speculation, and a means of creating fictitious values to any extent, without any alteration, for the time, of the quantity or value of money. I refer to the sale of the public lands by the national government. Up to June, 1853, about 235 millions of acres of these lands had been sold, or granted away for schools, military bounties, and internal improvements; and there remained about as much more to be disposed of, exclusive of the immense regions comprised within the limits of Oregon, California, Utah, New Mexico, Kanzas, and Nebraska. As the great tide of emigration constantly rolls westward, these lands assume value according as the region in which they are situated promises to become more or less populous. I have already explained, in treating of the theory of rent, that the value of the lands is determined by the distribution of the population; and this distribution is determined either by nature or the works of man, according as one spot is more fertile, more salubrious, better supplied with water and timber, or better situated with reference to navigable streams, railroads, and great lines of communication between different districts. Obviously, there is great room for the exercise of sagacity and foresight in determining how soon and how quickly any particular district will be peopled, or for enterprise in executing the public works which will draw emigrants thither. There are numerous instances in which a populous village or city has sprung up within ten years upon lands which, at the beginning of that period, were unoccupied forest or prairie, and could be obtained at the government price of $ 1.25 an acre. Reckoned as village or town lots, this land may be worth one or two thousand dollars an acre. Here, then, in the possibility of buying land in the wilderness at a merely nominal price by the acre, and selling it within a few years at a high valuation by the square foot, is an unbounded and most attractive field for speculation; and the records of the Land-Office show how far it has been carried. Between 1840 and 1850, the average number of acres sold by the government each year was less than two millions; and even this probably exceeded what was actually required for the increase of the population. But in 1835, twelve millions, and in 1836, over twenty millions, were thus disposed of. At what average price the purchasers from the government either sold, or expected to sell, the land to those who were to buy of them, it were vain to conjecture. But if they anticipated only a tenfold return, which is a very low estimate, it follows that their operations, during the two years, created speculative or fictitious values amounting to 320 millions of dollars. In 1854–5, in consequence of the rapid extension of railroads at the West, and the large grants of land by Congress in aid of these improvements and for military bounties, these speculations have been renewed and extended even to a greater amount than before; and owing to the decline in the value of money, and to the almost incredible amount of the immigration from Europe, it is probable that the expectations of the speculators have been in a great measure fulfilled.

All these immense operations might have been carried on without creating any perceptible increase of the circulation. The government, indeed, sold land only for cash; but then its price was very low, and most of the land was not purchased of it, but received as a gift, in grants for the extension of railroads and in bounties; and the grantees and original purchasers sold again on long credit, receiving their pay in annual instalments distributed over so many years as not to occasion at any one time any pressure upon the loan market. In respect even to the amounts received from the government sales, it may be observed, that, as they fell very far short of the aggregate annual expenditure by the government, they might have been all defrayed or offset by the payments due to public contractors and for military and naval services, without occasioning the transfer of a single dollar in coin or bank-bills. In fact, many payments for land were thus made by drafts upon the Sub-Treasury which had been issued in the ordinary course of government expenditure.

Enough has been said to demonstrate the possibility of speculative purchases being made to any extent, and of prices being consequently enhanced to the highest point which they have ever attained before a commercial crisis, without any perceptible expansion of the currency. Sufficient evidence may be cited to prove, also, not only that this is the possible operation of the market, but that it has been the actual result. The opinion prevails very generally, both in England and this country, that the amount of the circulation is very much increased when a speculative fever is at its height, and that prices rise only in consequence of this increase; but nothing can be further from the truth. "It may help us to form some judgment on this point," says Mr. Mill, "if we consider the proportion which the utmost increase of bank-notes in a period of speculation bears, I do not say to the whole mass of credit in the country, but to the bills of exchange alone.* The average amount of bills in existence at any one time is supposed considerably to exceed a hundred millions sterling. The bank-note circulation of Great Britain and Ireland is less than thirty-five millions, and the increase in speculative periods at most two or three" millions, — evidently not enough to raise general prices one per cent, and hardly to produce a perceptible effect upon the price even of any one commodity of large consumption, such as cotton, flour, sugar, tea, or any other that is liable to be affected by speculative movements.

The published returns of the Bank of England, which give the average amount of the circulation for every week in the year, afford curious proof of the correctness of our position. In 1847, there was a monetary crisis in England, which, with one exception, that of 1825, was severer than any that had been experienced since the commencement of the century. There were two periods of stricture or panic in the course of the year, the one occurring towards the end of April, and the other in October, the intervening period being one of comparative quiescence. "The effect of the severe contraction of accommodation," says Mr. Tooke, "was to paralyze nearly all transactions on credit throughout the country." Every description of property, (food only excepted, as the crops had been deficient,) rapidly fell in value to a very great extent. "It would not be easy," remarked Lord Ashburton, "to estimate this depreciation, extending over all merchandise, stocks, rail-

* Bills of exchange, it should be observed, perform the same office in England which promissory notes do in this country, their number and amount indicating to some extent, though not entirely, the extent of the purchases that have previously been made upon credit, and the returns from the Stamp-Office making it possible to estimate very nearly the average amount of them in circulation at any one time.

road shares, &c.; it probably would not have been overstated at from ten to twenty per cent; but what was worse, it paralyzed this property in the hands of the possessors, rendering it unavailable towards meeting their engagements, and thus produced, in many cases, pecuniary sacrifices much beyond the mere depreciation of the value of the property itself." Yet it is a curious fact, that the average amount of the notes of the Bank of England, and of all the banks of issue in the United Kingdom, in the hands of the pnblic, was greater during the stricture than in the intervening period; and was very nearly equal to the average of the circulation in the years 1845 and 1846, when the speculation in railroad stock, which was one of the chief causes of the crisis, was at its height.* Mr. Danson says: "During those months in which the purchases and sales of railway property were most numerous and extensive, while everybody was buying and selling shares, and the current rate of interest was only 2½ per cent, that portion of the circulating medium which consisted of Bank of England notes was but slightly, if at all, increased; and it reached its greatest amount when the prices of shares were lowest, when everybody had ceased to speculate, when the number and amount of current transactions were reduced to the lowest point by discredit, and when the current rate of interest for first-class bills had risen from 2½ to 4½ per cent."

The experience of the United States agrees perfectly with that of England, in proving that the circulation of bank-notes is not perceptibly expanded in periods when commerce is brisk, speculation rife, and the rates of interest are low, — in one word, when it is usually said that "*money* is plenty"; and that it is not restricted, but usually somewhat increased, when a crisis ensues, and the rates of interest are raised to the highest

* The average of the Bank of England circulation for the six weeks ending August 14, 1847, (a period of quiescence,) was £19,600,000; and in the six weeks ending November 20, (a period of panic,) it was £20,900,000. The aggregate bank-note circulation of the United Kingdom for the month ending August 14, amounted to £34,500,000, and in that ending November 6, to £36,700,000. For the four weeks ending April 24, (the first period of panic,) the Bank of England circulation was 21 millions, and that of all the banks of issue was 38.9 millions. The average circulation for 1846, which the currency doctors would call "the year of expansion," was, for the Bank of England, 21.1 millions; for all the banks, 39.6 millions. See the table appended to Tooke's *History of Prices from* 1839 *to* 1847 *inclusive*, p. 448.

point, and when, on account of the great difficulty of meeting pecuniary engagements, bankruptcy is frequent. It will be generally admitted, that 1853 was a year of the former character, being a period of advancing prices, few failures, general speculation in railroad stocks and other securities, and having all the usual signs of commercial prosperity. The aggregate circulation of all the Massachusetts banks in September of this year was about $ 21,200,000. The following year, 1854, was of the opposite character, being a time of great financial distress, which steadily increased, till, in December, it amounted to a panic. Now the total circulation of the Boston and the country banks in this unlucky year never fell below 23 millions of dollars; in July, it amounted to 25 millions, and early in December, when the crisis was at its height, it was 24⅓ millions. A period of quiescence began in the spring of 1855, and continued nearly to the close of the year; speculation was repressed, but the rates of interest were low, and it was easy to obtain loans. Yet in April of this year the circulation had fallen off to about 21½ millions, and early in September it was less than 23 millions.*

It is not, then, the want of *money* which occasions distress and bankruptcy in a commercial crisis, or when the rates of interest are very high; for the returns show that the amount of the circulation is usually increased at such periods, though the difference, whether of excess or defect, is too slight to have any perceptible effect upon the markets. But the real cause of the distress is the insufficiency of the *disposable capital* in the market to meet the sudden increase in the demand for loans, which is occasioned when the time arrives for paying off the excessive purchases on credit that have been made during the fever of a general speculation. The notes of hand and bills of exchange, which were so freely and thoughtlessly given when prices were advancing, and when it was expected that they would advance still higher, must come to maturity, usually in six months or less; and then come the pressure and

* As the law now requires a weekly report from the Boston banks, and a monthly report from the banks out of Boston, to be made on oath to the Secretary of State, and published in the newspapers, we have the means of ascertaining their condition at any period, which formerly was impossible. See *American Almanac* for 1855 and 1856.

the panic. As it was the unusual amount of these private "promises to pay," and the extravagance of the purchases in which they originated, that first produced the enhancement of prices, so now the demanded fulfilment of them causes prices to recede, and makes speculators eager to sell, and multiplies the applications to banks and usurers for loans. The whole distress is then imputed to "the tightness of the money market," though the amount of money in circulation is just as great as ever, probably greater, and though money has been as passive, or has played as insignificant a part in the matter, as the carts and ships in which the merchandise that was bought on speculation is transported. The speculator who makes an eager appeal to a bank for assistance, does not ask that the circulation, or bank issues, shall be increased for his sake; he does not want coin or bank-notes particularly, but will be entirely satisfied with a check which will suffice to take up his note, and the only effect of which will be to transfer, either at that bank or another, a certain amount of the deposits from the credit of one person to that of another, without adding a dollar to the circulation. Every one knows, that, in a large commercial city, nearly all promissory notes are paid in this manner, or, if bank-notes are used, it is only to be carried across the entry, or across the street, to another bank, without remaining an hour in circulation. In such case, a bank-note for $ 100 or $ 1,000 is only a substitute for a check, and is hardly entitled to be called "money"; it is only a ticket for the transfer of credit, and has no effect whatever on prices.

When, in a period of financial pressure, a complaint is made of "the scarcity of money," it means only that capital is wanted on credit, or, in other words, that there is a greater demand for loans than the banks and other dealers in loans can supply. There is always a certain amount of disposable capital in the market, seeking investment in loans. It is accumulated chiefly by savings from income, which are made by persons who are unwilling or unable to manage their capital for themselves by engaging in industrial enterprises, and therefore seek to lend it to others. A considerable portion of this floating fund is accumulated in the banks, making up both their capitals and deposits, and thus constituting far the larger part of what they are able to lend to their customers. Hence it is, that what are called the "loans and discounts" of the banks so largely exceed the amount of their circulation. Cut off altogether their power of issuing bank currency, and their ability to make loans would not be diminished, on an average, more than one fifth. The aggregate loan by the Massachusetts banks amounts almost precisely to one hundred millions, and their average circulation, as we have just seen, is only about twenty-three millions; and from this last sum must be deducted about three millions for the specie reserves, which are kept only for the security of their circulation, and would come into active use, or be disposable for loans, if that circulation were taken away.

And here we can see another reason why the banks are unable to increase or diminish at pleasure the issue of their notes. It is only by reducing their loans and discounts immensely, that they can be sure of acting at all upon their outstanding circulation; cut off thirty millions, for instance, from the loans and discounts by the Massachusetts banks, and as seventy millions would still remain in the hands of their customers, the larger part of the twenty-three millions of their notes might continue to circulate; in other words, the portion of the loan which was withdrawn might be paid back to them almost exclusively in coin or the notes of banks in the neighboring States, or by transferring a large amount from their deposits. On the other hand, when they are not diminishing, but extending their loans, their circulation may come back upon them in spite of themselves.

Hence, also, if the complaint against the banks for undue "expansion" in a speculating period, and undue "curtailment" when the crisis comes, means anything, it means an expansion and curtailment, not of bank currency, but of bank loans and discounts. There would be some truth in this statement, though it may still be said, that the difference in the amount of the loan is not large enough to have any considerable effect on prices. The loan from the Massachusetts banks, which a little exceeded ninety-three millions early in December, 1854, when the financial pressure was at its height, rose to over ninety-nine millions in September, 1855, when the market was quiescent and the rates of interest low. The difference was only six per cent, and the amount of six millions could not raise general prices more than one or two per cent. And even this difference is not to be laid to the fault of the banks, but of their customers, who, when the demand for loans was greatest, withdrew five millions from their deposits, and over one million from their specie reserves. The banks, who only play the part of brokers in this matter, bringing borrowers and lenders together, made smaller loans because less capital was placed at their disposal.

The other portion of floating or disposable capital, which is in the market for borrowers at varying rates of interest, but does not get into the banks, or is only lodged there temporarily on deposit, is much more fluctuating in amount, and is the real agent or subject of that "expansion" and "contraction" which are so much complained of. During the period of quiescence which follows a commercial crisis, people go on quietly making savings from income, and, having learned from recent woful experience the folly of new speculations and hazardous investments, they prefer not to engage in any enterprise on their own account, but only to lend their surplus funds on good mortgages or first-rate personal security, and, in this last case, only for short periods. But as almost everybody at such a time is afraid of speculation, new enterprises are not started, trade is quiet, and there is not, consequently, much demand for loans, and that little demand is fully supplied by the banks from their regular funds. Lenders then compete with each other, and strive to tempt merchants and manufacturers to borrow by offering the use of capital at low rates of interest. Even the banks, under such circumstances, are sometimes compelled to reduce their rates of discount, in order to find borrowers and keep their capital employed. Purchases of approved stocks already for some time in the market, whether of national or State funds, banks, manufactories, or railroads, have no effect in diminishing the amount of disposable capital in the loan-market, but only transfer the ownership of portions of it to other individuals. If A, who seeks to invest $ 50,000, cannot find a borrower who will take it on good security and pay him a satisfactory rate of interest for it, and finally decides to buy Reading Railroad bonds, or New York State stocks, he only transfers his $ 50,000 to B, who sells him these bonds or stocks, and who will now come into the loan-market to find a borrower for the funds which he has received. The supply of disposable capital, then, will be just the same as before. If, however, a State, a city, or a railroad comes forward to contract a new loan, and thus issues an additional amount of stocks or bonds, the capital which it receives is permanently taken out of the loan-market, and expended, perhaps in constructing water-works, new roads, or other internal improvements.

I have already explained the phenomena of the gradual declension of the rate of profit, which takes place in every country as it advances in opulence and gradually extends its enterprise over the whole field for the profitable employment of fixed capital. This declension is soon manifested in the loan-market, steadily operating against the rate of interest, and causing it, though with many fluctuations, to move slowly downwards. The savings from income, which at first, for the most part, were invested as soon as made, either in constructing roads, docks, and canals, or in furnishing manufactories with costly machinery, are finally driven more and more into the market as floating capital, seeking borrowers, because it is found that the work of fixed capital is so nearly completed, that no farther application can be made of it except at great hazard, or with a prospect of very small dividends. After the loan-market becomes gorged, however, and the losses experienced in former speculations are gradually forgotten, the low rates of interest and the facility of obtaining loans again allure the multitude into hazardous enterprises. New schemes are brought forward, and old ones resuscitated. Docks, copper-mines, new railroads, laying out new cities, cutting lumber, driving tunnels through mountains and under rivers, opening trade with Australia, and many similar undertakings, are proposed as excellent means of investing capital and obtaining large returns. Merchants catch the infection, and make large importations of goods. The scale of expenditure is enlarged, as people are tempted to spend in proportion to their expected gains; and thus prices begin to rise. The merits of every new scheme are so loudly trumpeted, that those who first invested in them are enabled to sell out their shares at a high profit. The plethory of the loan-market is so far relieved, that the rates of interest rise, and the cautious and prudent capitalists are as much delighted as the daring speculators.

After a time, the period of payment arrives. The notes

which have been given for heavy purchases on credit, come to maturity, and anxious borrowers find to their dismay that the tide in the market has turned, and there is now very little floating capital to be had, and that only at high rates. There is an immense increase in the demand for loans, and a great diminution of the supply, as many capitalists have caught the infection, and preferred to speculate with their funds, rather than to lend them on interest. The banks, indeed, continue to lend as usual, as their capital exists for no other purpose; but their means are strictly limited, and they can only supply the ordinary amount of accommodation to their customers, whose wants are sadly increased. They are besieged with applications which they cannot grant, and are then blamed for having first contributed to heighten the excitement, by offering loans at low rates some months before, and now refusing to lend except in small sums and on harder terms. The charge is wholly unjust, for by furnishing a steady supply to the loan-market, not enlarged in a period of speculation nor diminished in a time of pressure, their operation is like that of the balance-wheel in a machine, tending to deaden the shock of transition, and to moderate both extremes. The difficulties which the speculators labor under compel them to make forced sales of their shares or of the merchandise which they have bought at inordinate prices; and this eagerness to sell creates suspicion, and soon leads to an exposure of the rottenness of many of the schemes in which they have engaged. These fictitious values are destroyed, and their fancied wealth disappears like a dream. Public confidence being thus shaken, a general desire to *realize* property, as it is termed, or to convert mere evidences of debt into coin or other actual possessions, ensues; and then follow many failures, and general agitation and distress.

The cycle of events which I have described, is so far independent of any action of the currency, that it might all occur in such a city as Amsterdam was, when it had but one bank, and that one only a bank of deposit, in which the merchants lodged all their surplus funds, and effected all payments among themselves by a mere transfer of credit on the books. There, also, a period of quiescence in trade might cause an accumulation of floating capital, and a consequent facility of obtaining loans on low rates, which would finally induce reckless speculation; and this is sure to be followed by all the phenomena of a commercial crisis. To expect that men will learn wisdom from the frequent recurrence of these evils, so as to be able to avoid them in future, would be to expect that they would cease to make savings from income, or that the accumulation of floating capital thus produced would no longer reduce the rates of interest, or that no persons would be found willing to engage in hazardous undertakings when they can make unlimited purchases on credit, and are importuned to accept loans on easy terms.

It must not be supposed, however, that reckless speculation is the only cause of disturbance in the loan-market, rendering the supply for a while inadequate to the demand. Physical or political causes, a failure of the crops, the breaking out of a war, or the return of peace, may create a sudden demand for capital to be sent abroad, which will so far lessen the quantity usually offered to borrowers as to occasion them serious inconvenience, and even to create a panic. For illustration, I need only borrow in part Mr. Mill's account of the crisis of 1847. "It is not universally true," he says, "that the contraction of credit characteristic of a commercial crisis must have been preceded by an extraordinary and irrational extension of it. The crisis of 1847 belonged to another class of mercantile phenomena. There occasionally happens a concurrence of circumstances tending to withdraw from the loan-market a considerable portion of the capital which usually supplies it. These circumstances, in the present case, were great foreign payments, (occasioned by the high price of cotton and the unprecedented importation of food,) together with the continual demands on the circulating capital of the country by railway calls and the loan transactions of railway companies, for the purpose of being converted into fixed capital and made unavailable for future lending. These various demands fell principally, as such demands always do, on the loan-market. A great, though not the greatest, part of the imported food was actually paid for by the proceeds of a government loan. The extra payments which purchasers of corn and cotton, and railway shareholders, found themselves obliged to make, were either made with their own spare cash, or with money raised for the occasion. On the first supposition, they were made by withdrawing deposits from bankers, and thus cutting off a part of the streams which fed the loan-market; on the second supposition, they were made by actual drafts on the loan-market, either by the sale of securities, or by taking up money at interest. This combination of a fresh demand for loans with a curtailment of the capital disposable for them, raised the rate of interest, and made it impossible to borrow except on the very best security. Some firms, therefore, which, by an improvident and unmercantile mode of conducting business, had allowed their capital to become either temporarily or permanently unavailable, became unable to command that perpetual renewal of credit which had previously enabled them to struggle on. These firms stopped payment; their failure involved, more or less deeply, many other firms which had trusted them; and, as usual in such cases, the general distrust, commonly called a panic, began to set in."

An occasion to make large foreign remittances may arise either from a sudden increase of imports, or from a sudden diminution of exports. In the United States, as we may always raise more food than is necessary for our own consumption, it is more likely to proceed from the latter cause; in Great Britain, where the crops in the most fruitful seasons are hardly sufficient to feed the people, and are liable to frequent though partial failures, the former cause is most likely to operate. Here, a financial pressure is occasioned by an excess of food, or a want of demand in Europe for our surplus crops, so that we are called upon to remit gold instead of exporting provisions; there, it arises from a scarcity or dearth, which compels the people to buy grain of other nations. But in either case, a remittance of gold is not a necessary or a characteristic feature of the phenomenon. In the long run, commodities are always purchased with commodities; we pay for our imports with our exports. But the call being a sudden one for the remittance of actual values, and not having anything else to send abroad except at a great sacrifice, we send bullion or coin, and the drain comes upon the bank reserves; but the next year, we have to buy the specie back again, by either restricting our imports, or increasing our exports. The bank reserves being lessened by this abstraction of coin, those institutions usually diminish their discounts, in order to provide for their own security. But in 1847, the Bank of England, though £ 7,000,000 in coin had been taken from its coffers to send to America and the Baltic for food, adopted the bolder policy of increasing both its discounts and its circulation; or rather, the latter was increased in spite of itself, in order to fill up the vacuum both in the loan-market and the currency which had been created by these foreign remittances.* The financial pressure would otherwise have been much greater; and in fact, it was at last stopped entirely by an announcement from the Bank, under the sanction of the government, that it was prepared to make further advances, though at a high rate of interest.

And generally, it may be observed, that the drain of specie, by falling upon the bank reserves, though it should produce a slight decrease of the circulation, is not so great an evil as it would be if it were all subtracted from the active circulation, or if domestic commodities should be immediately sent abroad at a great sacrifice to pay the debt, through our inability to make the remittance in bullion. These reserves, being locked up in the vaults, have no effect whatever on prices, and a large portion of them might be sent abroad without the loss being perceived at the time, — certainly without its being indicated by any change whatever in the market. True, the money must all be bought back again, ultimately, to provide for future emergencies of the banks of a different character; and it will all be bought back again within a year, either by restricting our imports or increasing our exports, so as to make up for the temporary excess of the former, which first produced the drain of specie. We send abroad the money at first, only as a convenient article to serve for a sort of pledge or security that we will soon pay our debts in commodities. When the promise

---

* Mr. F. Baring stated in Parliament, December 3, 1847, that "the amount of bullion in the Bank on September 12, 1846, was £ 16,354,000, and that, on April 17, 1847, it was reduced to £ 9,330,000, being a diminution of £ 7,024,000. Now I take the same dates with respect to the circulation of notes, and I find that, on September 12, 1846, the amount was £ 20,982,000, and on April 17, 1847, it was £ 21,228,000, being an increase of £ 246,000. Perhaps it was impossible, before the bill [of 1844] was in practical operation, to see how the reserve of notes would operate; *but it certainly never entered into the contemplation of any one then considering the subject, that* £ 7,000,000 *in gold should run off, and yet that the notes in the hands of the public would rather increase than diminish.*"

is fulfilled, the pledge is returned. We wanted what the financiers call "an extension," in order that we might have time to raise the flour, cotton, and tobacco wherewith to pay our debts; and by sending the specie as a pledge, we obtain the delay that we wanted.

The result of this whole discussion may be summed up in the following proposition: — *that the function of money as a means of effecting exchanges is entirely distinct from its function as a standard or measure of value.* For the former, which is its chief purpose, the relative abundance or scarcity of money is a matter of no importance whatever. If we have more money than we need, a portion of it will lie idle, either in the vaults of banks or in the pockets of individuals. If we have less money than might seem necessary, we can get along very well with substitutes, and can even dispense with the use of money altogether. In other words, money is a convenience, but not a necessity. Thus, if we have no gold or silver coin, bits of paper, called bank-notes, will do just as well; if we have not even bank-notes, then checks, bills of exchange, book-credits, transfers of credit on the books of a bank or a clearing-house, will enable us to purchase goods, and to make or receive payments; and if we have not even these contrivances, we can still barter commodities directly for commodities, as we already do, to a considerable extent, through the institution of mutual *accounts current.* Turn the matter as we may, we cannot impute all the evils in the commercial world to money as the universal scape-goat, or hope to get rid of them by tinkering the currency. Trade is an exchange of merchandise; and money plays as insignificant a part in it, to recur to a former illustration, as the carts in which the merchandise is transported. If we have not carts enough, we can carry the goods on our backs; if we have not money, we can still exchange, though with some additional trouble. When we spend, we consume, not money, but commodities that gratify our tastes and appetites. When we contract debts, we borrow, not money, but the goods which we purchase with the money. And when we find any difficulty in paying our debts, the scarcity of money is not at fault, but the want of capital, and this want arises from our own improvidence.

The other function of money, that of serving as a standard

or measure of value, is performed through a delicate comparison of the value of all other commodities with that of the two precious metals, for the purpose of ascertaining, not so much the relation of merchandise to specie, as the relation of all the different articles of merchandise to each other. It is useful to know that a barrel of flour is worth ten dollars, and a coat twenty dollars, not because it is a fact of any practical importance that a barrel of flour will buy ten times 345.6 grains of pure silver, or that a coat will buy twenty times this quantity, because very few persons have occasion to buy silver at all; but as the tailor and the farmer most frequently barter coats for flour, it is convenient for them to know the exact relative values of these two commodities. For this latter purpose, the amount of silver in a dollar might be increased or diminished to any extent, and it would answer the end equally well. Consequently, in relation to this function also, the abundance or scarcity, the high or low value, of the precious metals, concerns us very little. For the purposes of trade between different nations, or for comparison of international values, moreover, this alteration of the quantity of gold and silver passing under a given name is a matter of no importance, as the bullion-merchants take care, by equalizing their distribution, that these two metals shall have the same relative value to other commodities all over the commercial world. It is only, as we have seen, for transactions extending over long periods of time, that it is necessary to ascertain if this relative value has undergone any alteration.

CHAPTER XXIV.

THE DOCTRINE OF INTERNATIONAL EXCHANGES; THE POLICY OF ENCOURAGING DOMESTIC MANUFACTURES BY LAYING DUTIES ON IMPORTED GOODS.

The explanation which has been given in former chapters of the circumstances which determine prices, and of the course of exchange with foreign countries, has prepared the way for a fuller consideration of the general question between free trade and the protective system. I have already endeavored at some length to show,* that the general doctrine of free trade is perfectly reconcilable with the policy of granting protection under special circumstances; that it does not conflict, for example, with the system of imposing for a time duties on imported goods in order to foster the manufacturing interest here in America, which cannot flourish, or even subsist to any great extent, without such favor. I now resume the subject, in order to consider more particularly the effects of such a system upon our intercourse with other nations. This brings us at once to an explanation of the theory of international values and exchanges, — a recent and valuable addition to the science of Political Economy, and one which has lately compelled the old-fashioned advocates of free trade to make numerous and very significant concessions to their opponents. It has struck away the great prop of the universality of their system, and has compelled them to acknowledge that the importation of foreign manufactures may be excessive, even for a long period of years; and that the inevitable consequence of such excess is to depress the prices of our exports in all foreign markets, and thus to neutralize all our natural advantages for producing these articles of export, by compelling us to exchange them for foreign goods upon the most disadvantageous terms.

Hitherto, the evil of excessive importation has been held to be, that it caused a drain of specie from the country, or what

* See *ante*, pp. 25 – 27, and Chapters VIII. and XIV.

was technically called "an unfavorable balance of trade." To this unwise argument the reasonable answer was, that a drain of specie to any injurious extent is impossible; for an unnatural efflux of money must raise the value of what is left, and thereby lower the money price of all goods which are exchanged for it. The fall of prices thus occasioned would inevitably tempt foreigners hither to make their purchases, and the goods thus bought must be paid for by remittances of coin or bullion, so that the current of specie would be turned the other way. Money is a self-distributing commodity, which always apportions itself among commercial nations in exact proportion to the wants of each.

In theory, this reasoning is perfectly sound; and though many attempts have been made to refute it, we know of none which have had even the appearance of success. Practically, however, as all intelligent merchants will admit, very large importations are found to be attended with very great evils. Experience has proved that they tend to depress the prices of domestic products, to paralyze domestic industry, and even to bring on commercial crises, which are equally disastrous to our agricultural, commercial, and manufacturing interests. To account for these facts, which are inexplicable upon the narrow principles of Adam Smith and McCulloch, we must go back to first principles, and, after gaining clear ideas of the nature of commercial exchanges in general, must see how the aggregate of our own exchanges with other nations is effected.

In the preceding chapter, it has been shown that prices are determined by the relation of the demand to the supply, and that an extension of the market, or an increase of the demand, can be obtained only by submitting to a fall of prices, so as to bring the article within the reach of a greater number of consumers. In any market, only a certain quantity of goods at a given price can be consumed; if more goods are forced upon the market than it naturally requires, the price must fall, and then the consumption may be very much increased.

It has also been proved, in treating of bills of exchange, (pp. 319 – 329,) that we really purchase commodities with commodities, — that we pay for our whole imports with our whole exports, — that if, in our traffic with any one country, (China, for instance,) our imports much exceed our exports, then we pay the balance, not in money, but by transferring to that country the debt due to us from another country, (England, for instance,) with which our trade is such that our exports exceed our imports. It is only the balance of the immensely long "account current" of our trade with all foreign countries whatsoever, which is struck in money; and this cash balance cannot be more than an insignificant fraction of either side of the account. The advocates for free trade have always insisted, that we must buy merchandise of England, not only to induce, but even to enable, England to buy merchandise of us, — that we must buy of any country in order to sell to her, and must buy as much as we sell. But it is not so. It is not necessary that we should take of English manufactured goods enough to pay us for all the cotton, tobacco, and wheat which we sell to England; — England is able, though of course she is not very willing, to pay us the balance in tea from China, coffee from Brazil, hemp from Russia, or whatever other article, from whatever other country, we see fit to require. We can *compel* her to pay us in whatever commodities we may select; for the articles which we sell to England — cotton, tobacco, and wheat — are of prime necessity to her, and most of which she cannot obtain elsewhere. As our exports must pay for our imports, the only point to be considered is, *how we can dispose of the exports to most advantage, or obtain for them the largest return of the imports.*

The cost to us of our *domestic* products is, the labor that is expended upon their production. But the cost to us of *foreign* products is, not the labor which has been expended upon *their* production, but the labor which we must expend upon the articles that are given in exchange for those products.

"The advantage of an interchange of commodities between nations," says Mr. Mill, "consists simply and solely in this, — that it enables each to obtain, with a given amount of labor and capital, a greater quantity of all commodities taken together. This it accomplishes by enabling each, with a quantity of one commodity which has cost it so much labor and capital, to purchase a quantity of another commodity, which, if produced at home, would have required labor and capital to a greater amount. To render the importation of an article more advantageous than its production, it is not necessary that the foreign country should be able to produce it with less labor and capital than ourselves. We may even have a positive advantage in its production; — but if we are so far favored by circumstances as to have a *still greater* positive advantage in the production of some other article which is in demand in the foreign country, we may be able to obtain a greater return to our labor and capital by employing none of it in producing the article in which our advantage is least, but devoting it all to the production of that in which our advantage is greatest, and giving this to the foreign country in exchange for the other. It is not a difference in the *absolute* cost of production, which determines the interchange, but a difference in the *comparative* cost."

The inhabitants of Barbadoes, for instance, favored by their tropical climate and fertile soil, can raise provisions cheaper than we can in the United States. And yet Barbadoes buys nearly all her provisions from this country. Why is this so? Because, though Barbadoes has the advantage over us in the ability to raise provisions cheaply, she has a still greater advantage over us in her power to produce sugar and molasses. If she has an advantage of one quarter in raising provisions, she has an advantage of one half in regard to products exclusively tropical; and it is better for her to employ all her labor and capital in that branch of production in which her advantage is greatest. She can thus, by trading with us, obtain our breadstuffs and meat at a smaller expense of labor and capital than they cost ourselves. If, for instance, a barrel of flour cost *ten* days' labor in the United States, and only *eight* days' labor in Barbadoes, the people of Barbadoes can still profitably buy the flour from this country, if they can pay for it with sugar which cost them only *six* days' labor; and the people of this country can profitably sell them the flour, or buy from them the sugar, provided that the sugar, if raised in the United States, would cost *eleven* days' labor. This is a striking example to show the benefit of foreign trade to both the countries which are parties to it. Tte United States receive sugar, which would have cost them eleven days' labor, by paying for it with flour which costs them but ten days. Barbadoes receives flour, which would have cost her eight days' labor, by paying for it with sugar which costs her but six days. If Barbadoes produced both commodities with greater facility, *but greater in precisely the same degree*, there would be no motive for interchange.

Now let us apply these principles to the trade between England and the United States. We will suppose, what is the fact, that this country has a very considerable advantage over England in the production of cotton, flour, and tobacco; while England has *some* advantage (a comparatively trifling one) over us in manufactured goods; — we say, a comparatively trifling advantage, because cotton and tobacco cannot be cultivated in England at all, and one of these articles (cotton) cannot be purchased by her in sufficient quantities from any other country than the United States; while we *can* manufacture all the goods that are now manufactured in England. Some of them (the coarser cottons, for instance) we can even manufacture more cheaply than the English; but most of the finer fabrics, unquestionably, owing to the lower profits of capital and the lower wages of labor, can be more cheaply manufactured in England. To simplify the matter as much as possible, we will take but one article, *flour*, as the representative of *all* the commodities that America sells to England; and but one article, *cloth*, as the representative of *all* the goods which England sells to America; — that is, we will suppose the trade between the two countries to consist exclusively of these two articles. As it has been proved, that, in foreign trade, we barter directly commodities for commodities, we can fortunately leave *money* out of the case altogether, and estimate the value or cost of the two only by comparing them with each other. We will suppose, on account of the respective advantages possessed by the two countries, that the production of one barrel of flour in England costs as much labor and capital as would suffice for the manufacture of *ten* yards of cloth; while in America, one barrel of flour can be produced for three fifths of its cost in England, — or, in other words, for as much labor and capital as would, *in England*, manufacture only six yards of cloth. Whether this state of things proves that, in America, the cost of flour is less, or the cost of cloth greater, than in England, is a point of no importance. We can simplify the matter still further, then, by supposing that cloth can be manufactured to equal advantage, or with the same amount of labor and capital, in both countries. Our supposition is, that, so long as each country produces both commodities for itself, the American price of a barrel of flour will be *six* yards of cloth; while the English price of a barrel of flour will be *ten* yards of cloth.

Now, if a system of free trade between the two countries be established, the two commodities will be exchanged for each other at the same rate both in England and America. The price will be equalized between the two countries; but at what point will it be equalized? Shall the English price be established in America, or shall the American price be established in England? Or shall a price intermediate between the two be established? Either of these three suppositions is possible. The Englishman can afford to give *ten* yards, for it will cost him that amount of labor and capital to produce the flour in his own country, or for himself. On the other hand, the American can afford to sell the flour for *six* yards, because this quantity of cloth, if produced in his own country, would cost him as much labor and capital as a barrel of flour. Suppose that, by the higgling of the market, the price in both countries is fixed at *seven* yards. The advantage of the trade is then shared between the two countries, but it is shared unequally. America gains *one* yard on each barrel, as she now receives seven yards of cloth for the labor which formerly produced but six; England gains *three* yards on each barrel, for the flour now costs her but seven yards a barrel, while it formerly cost her ten. We will suppose that, at these rates, America sells 100,000 barrels of flour to England, and receives in exchange, of course, 700,000 yards of cloth. The demand on each side must be just sufficient to carry off the supply received on the other. So long as England wants only this amount of flour, and the United States only this quantity of cloth, the interchange will continue at this rate, giving three fourths of the profit to Great Britain, and only one fourth to this country.

But suppose the demand to vary in one of the two countries; suppose that England, on account of the increase of her population, now needs 150,000 barrels of flour, which America is perfectly able and willing to furnish. But England can pay for this larger purchase only by sending over more cloth; the

United States, however, by the supposition, are fully supplied with the 700,000 yards which they received before; they cannot buy any more at the old rate of seven yards for one barrel. How, then, is England to obtain the additional quantity of flour that she needs? She has but one course to pursue; she must offer her cloth at a reduced price, knowing that this reduced price will bring it within the reach of a larger class of consumers, who will take off the increased quantity that she needs must sell. Instead of *seven*, she will now offer *nine* yards of cloth for a barrel of flour. At *this* price, the Americans may be willing and able to buy 1,350,000 yards of cloth, which will furnish the 150,000 barrels of flour required by England; or, if we do not need this large quantity of cloth, England has only to sell this quantity *at the reduced price* to other countries, and obtain in exchange for it tea, coffee, sugar, and other products, which (*at this reduced price again*) we *do* need. If we do not receive the benefit of the change of price in *cloth*, we shall receive it in other commodities.

There is, indeed, one other mode by which England might obtain the additional quantity of flour required without lowering the price of her cloth. Suppose that the demand of the United States for cloth had been kept down to 700,000 yards by a protective tariff, the revenue from which paid the expenses of our government, though it somewhat enhanced the price of cloth to our people. Suppose, further, that our government, learning that England was inclined to purchase more flour of us, in order to favor that inclination, should determine to abolish the tariff, and admit cloth duty free, or at a nominal duty. Then, indeed, the demand for cloth might be so far increased, that England might obtain her 150,000 barrels of flour by paying for it at the rate of seven yards to a barrel. We should, indeed, sell the increased quantity of breadstuffs, but receive in payment only 1,050,000, instead of 1,350,000, yards of cloth. By this wise act of legislation, also, we should be obliged to pay the expenses of our government by direct taxation, should have our domestic manufactures ruined, and the profits of our agriculturists much diminished by the influx into their business, and the consequent competition, of the disbanded workmen from our manufactories.

Those who have followed the reasoning thus far will have perceived, that our *suppositions* all along have been only disguised statements of recent facts. The great increase of the English population in consequence of the misery of that population, the policy of the English landlords in depopulating their vast estates by driving the peasantry into the towns, thus substituting manufactures for agriculture as their employment, and the deficient harvests of 1846 and 1847, — all these causes combined, created an evident necessity for a much enlarged importation of breadstuffs into Great Britain. These facts were recognized almost simultaneously by the leading English statesmen of both parties, — by Lord John Russell and Sir Robert Peel; and they led, first to a partial, and in a very short time to a total, abolition of the corn laws, — those laws which had existed for over thirty years, avowedly to check our sale of provisions to England, and thereby to enhance the price of English manufactures in America. But under the American tariff of 1842, a much enlarged supply of grain from this country could not be obtained without a corresponding material reduction in the price, not only of English manufactures, but of all the other foreign products needed in this country which had been purchased for us with English manufactures. The English, therefore, were eager to procure the repeal or modification of this tariff, and succeeded in persuading American statesmen that such a step would be only a fair return for the abolition of the corn laws, and that, in fact, it was necessary, in order to induce and enable the English to buy more grain and flour from us. This argument would have had more force, if it had been shown how they could avoid making this enlarged purchase at any rate. But these representations were successful; Congress did substitute the tariff of 1846 for that of 1842; and this lowered the price of English manufactures in this country so far, that our increased consumption of them paid for the whole enlarged supply of breadstuffs needed by Great Britain. The result was, that a conjuncture of events, which ought to have operated greatly to the advantage of the United States, and to the disadvantage of England, really paralyzed our domestic manufactures, almost destroying those of iron, and greatly injuring those of cotton and wool, while the English manufactures have never been more prosperous than since the abrogation of the corn laws. Why should they not be? The demand for their products in the United States has greatly increased, while the reduction of price, through which alone this increase of demand could have been effected, has really taken place, not through the English manufacturers receiving less for their goods, but through our own modification of our tariff. We have thereby just thrown away the benefit that would naturally have accrued to us from the increased English demand for our provisions, and we have nearly crushed our own manufactures into the bargain.

I have now stated the doctrine of international values in the most precise manner, carefully analyzing each step of the process, in order to show that there was no gap in the reasoning. But as the theory of the matter is necessarily complicated and abstruse, I will now state it over again in a more general way, in order to be more fully understood.

America produces chiefly raw material, because she has the advantages of a more extensive territory, and a more fertile soil; England produces chiefly manufactured goods, because she has the advantages of more capital, longer experience, and cheaper labor. (I must now use numbers and measures almost at random, for convenience of brief calculation; but any numbers and denominations will answer equally well to illustrate the principle with.) In consequence of their respective advantages, we will suppose that England must give the labor vested in *ten* pounds of manufactured goods for one hundred-weight of raw material; while the labor vested in *six* pounds of such goods would raise or buy one hundred-weight of raw material in America. Now the doctrine of free trade, (which is in itself a perfectly sound and just doctrine, if applied to two countries which are similarly situated in every respect,) if applied in this case, would teach the Americans to give themselves exclusively to the production of raw material, and the English exclusively to manufactures, on the ground that each could purchase of the other what it would then need, more profitably than it could produce that article for itself. Let us suppose that the Americans adopt this advice, and raise nothing but raw material. What will be the consequence?

As every civilized nation must consume more value vested in manufactured goods than in raw material, (without reckoning tea, coffee, and tropical products, which *must* be brought from abroad,) it is evident that we must be constantly pressed to purchase from foreign countries *more* than we can easily pay for by selling to them raw material. In order, then, to enlarge the foreign market for our cotton, tobacco, and flour, — in order to bring them within the reach of a larger class of consumers, — we must offer them on the most favorable terms. We must offer them at the *American* price, (of one hundred-weight for *six* pounds of manufactures,) rather than at the *foreign* price, which they would otherwise naturally assume, of one hundred-weight for *ten* pounds. At this last price, it may be assumed that we could dispose of only one thousand tons of the raw material; and for this amount we should procure only 200,000 pounds of manufactured goods; — not enough to supply our wants. But in order to *obtain* more, we must be able to *sell* more; and in order to sell more, we must offer the raw material at a lower price, so as to enable a greater number of foreigners to purchase it. If we offer it at the rate of six pounds to the hundred-weight, we might be able to sell, not merely one thousand tons, but ten thousand; and this, at the price mentioned, would give us 1,200,000 pounds of manufactured goods, which might perhaps be sufficient. The principle is, then, that whichever nation is under the strongest temptation or necessity to buy from others,— whichever needs to buy more value than it can readily sell of its own products to pay for, — *that* nation labors under a disadvantage in the traffic, and must offer its own commodities at the lowest possible price.

"At the lowest price which is possible," we say; for the theory shows clearly, that there are limits beyond which the price can neither be elevated nor depressed. We cannot sell for less than six pounds, because the labor and capital expended in producing a hundred-weight of raw material would, with all our disadvantages in manufacturing, enable us to manufacture six pounds of such goods for ourselves. Neither can we obtain more than ten pounds, because the English labor and capital bestowed on ten pounds of these goods would enable the English, in spite of their disadvantages in regard to raw produce, to raise one hundred-weight of raw material for themselves. Within these limits, then, is the sphere of operation of a protective tariff; beyond them is the sphere of free trade. Prohibitory duties are always unwise; for the object is to check consumption, not to destroy foreign trade. / The purpose of a protective tariff is to secure to each nation the use of its own natural advantages; or rather, to prevent it from throwing these natural advantages away, by too assiduous and exclusive cultivation of them, the effect of which would be, that the other arts and branches of industry would perish by neglect.) An analogy may here be traced between the true policy of a nation in developing all its resources, and the true system of education for cultivating all the mental faculties of a man. One faculty of a child, the memory or the imagination, may be developed by accidental circumstances to an inordinate extent. An unwise parent, like the injudicious partisans of free trade, would foster and enlarge this inequality, instead of striving to diminish it; and would thereby not only leave the other faculties to die out by disuse, but would make the one talent preternaturally developed a curse rather than a blessing. A community cannot prosper by devoting all its energies to the cultivation of but one of the three great branches of industry. Devoted to agriculture alone, or to manufactures alone, or to commerce alone, it makes no difference; — in either case, it will have but one class of articles to sell, while it will have two classes of articles to purchase; — in either case, it will have a greater surplus *of one kind* to dispose of, than other nations will be willing or able to purchase, except at the lowest possible price; — and to sell at the lowest possible price, as we have now demonstrated, is just to sacrifice the whole of the natural advantage with which we are endowed by Nature, and to put ourselves on a par with other countries in this respect, while we are below them in every other respect.

On this point, the history of England is as full of instruction as that of our own country. The English peasantry have been driven away from their natural pursuits and mode of life in the fields, and have been forced to become operatives in the towns. English manufactures have thus been developed to a prodigious extent; and the consequence is, that England is importuning every government in the world to throw down its barriers of protection, and to receive manufactured goods at a marvellously cheap price, — a price much below their natural cost of production, if English labor were remunerated at a fair rate. But it is not thus remunerated; the wages of English operatives have, of late years, been reduced to the point where starvation is ever imminent; and bewildered by the lamentable consequences of this state of things, astonished to find general misery where their theory of free trade led them to expect general prosperity, the English economists have had recourse to such doctrines as those of Malthus and Ricardo to explain away the failure of their prognostications, and have actually discovered that all the evil must be attributed to an inevitable cause, — to the over-population of the earth. What has been the fate of England in regard to manufactures, may be our own condition in respect to agriculture, if we do not become wise in time.

That I am not here advocating a protective policy to an extent which will impeach the truth of all the leading doctrines of Political Economy, as that science is usually taught, must appear from the limitations of the theory which have been already laid down, and from the fact that this theory is frankly accepted even by those English economists who are the stoutest advocates of the general doctrine of free trade. For proof, I quote from John Stuart Mill.

"If it be asked," he says, "what country draws to itself the greatest share of the advantages of any trade it carries on, the answer is, — the country for whose productions there is in other countries the greatest demand, and a demand the most susceptible of increase from additional cheapness. In so far as the productions of any country possess this property, the country obtains all foreign commodities at less cost. It gets its imports cheaper, the greater the intensity of the demand in foreign countries for its exports. *It also gets its imports cheaper, the less the extent and intensity of its own demand for them. The market is cheapest to those whose demand is small.* A country which desires few foreign productions, and only a limited quantity, while its own commodities are in great request in foreign countries, will obtain its limited imports at extremely small cost, — that is, in exchange for the produce of a very small quantity of its labor and capital." *

* Mill's *Political Economy*, Vol. II. p. 131.

Consequently, he argues, "the opening of a new branch of export trade; or an increase in the foreign demand for our products, either by the natural course of events, or by an abrogation of duties; or *a check to our demand for foreign commodities by the laying on of import duties at home*, or of export duties elsewhere; — these, and all other events of similar tendency, would make our imports no longer a balance for our exports; and the countries which take our exports would be obliged to offer their commodities (specie among the rest) on cheaper terms, in order to reëstablish the equation of demand; and thus we should obtain money cheaper, and acquire a generally higher rate of prices. Incidents the reverse of these would produce effects the reverse, — would reduce prices." *

It appears, then, that it is even more for the interest of American planters and agriculturists, than of the manufacturers themselves, that duties should be laid on the importation of foreign manufactured goods, so as to restrict the amount of such importation. We thus purchase our imports more cheaply, or, what is the same thing, as commodities are actually bartered for commodities, we sell our exports at a higher price. The effect of the duty is, not to raise the price of the imported articles, but to cheapen them, the duty actually falling in great part upon the foreign manufacturer. During the year ending June 30, 1854, for instance, we sold to other nations, cotton to the amount of 93 millions of dollars, tobacco to the amount of 10 millions, and vegetable food nearly equalling 66 millions; the total exports of the produce of the United States that year, *excluding gold and silver coin*, were about 215 millions. Our total imports retained for consumption during the same period (deducting what was reëxported) amounted almost exactly to 276 millions. The difference between these two sums, 61 millions, being evidently too much to be attributed to the profits of trade and costs of transportation, we ran in debt for a considerable portion of the balance, and had to pay the debt by exporting over 38 millions of California gold. The average duty imposed on all the articles that pay any duty is about 25 per cent.

Now let us see what would have been the probable effect of

* *Ibid.*, p. 145.

doubling the duty upon all the imported articles which come in competition with American manufactures. The value of such articles probably did not exceed 100 millions; the other imports, amounting to 176 millions, are of such commodities — tea, coffee, drugs, raw materials, and the like — that we should be obliged, under any circumstances, to purchase them of foreigners. To double the duty on the former articles would probably reduce the amount imported from 100 millions to 50 millions, so that the revenue of our own government would not be affected by the alteration. But England, from whom we obtain most of the goods which come in competition with our home manufactures, would still need to obtain from us as much vegetable food, meat, and tobacco, and nearly as much cotton and California gold,* as ever; and her sale of her own manufactures to the United States being diminished to the extent of 50 millions, she would be obliged to offer to all nations, the United States included, these manufactures, and other commodities also, at lower prices. Compelled to seek an extension of the foreign market, or, in other words, to create an increased demand in other countries, for whatever she has to sell, to the extent of over ten millions sterling, she must submit to a reduction of price, which will bring her commodities within the reach of a larger class of consumers. American consumers, for instance, would not take even half as much as before, if the price in this country were enhanced to the full extent of the additional duty, — that is, 25 per cent. England would have to bear probably 15 per cent of this duty, or to reduce her prices in this proportion, leaving the American price to be enhanced 10 per cent, which would be encouragement enough to set additional manufactories in motion in the United States, so as to produce at home the 50 millions' worth cut off from our imports.

Already, then, we see the fallacy of the oft-repeated assertion by the advocates of free trade, that a protective duty raises the price both of the home commodity, and of the foreign one which continues to be imported, to the full extent of that duty.

* I say, nearly as much gold as ever, because the United States, having become perhaps the greatest gold-producing country on earth, must continue to export that metal, and other countries must continue to receive it from her, till money and prices are equalized all over the commercial world.

If the impost be not so great as to be virtually prohibitive, — in which case we admit it would be impolitic, — the home price cannot be increased to the extent of more than one half, seldom more than two fifths, of the duty. Everywhere the inequality in the distribution of wealth is such, that the class of persons having an income, for instance, of $2,500 a year, is not, as we might be tempted by a superficial glance at the subject to believe, only 25 per cent less numerous than the class having $2,000 a year, but is probably not more than half as great. If, then, the price should rise to the full extent of the duty, say 25 per cent, the total consumption would not be more than half as great, as only those would buy who have an income at least one fourth larger than the smallest income possessed by any of the former purchasers; but a portion of what is consumed being now of home production, the importation of the foreign article would fall off considerably more than 50 per cent.

This reasoning, it is true, applies only to the somewhat finer and more costly articles of manufacture, for which alone a protective duty is needed. In respect to breadstuffs and other articles of prime necessity, we have already seen that a very considerable enhancement of price is needed in order materially to lessen the consumption. The sale of the cheaper and more common products of manufacturing industry, also, may not be much checked by an addition of 20 or 30 per cent to their price, as their cost forms but a small part of the total expenditure of any class of persons. But the principle holds true in the only cases in which we need to apply it.

Thus far, however, it would seem that the American consumer is injured to a certain extent, being compelled to pay at least 10 per cent more for the article, whether of home or foreign manufacture, than he paid before the additional duty of 25 per cent was imposed. But the principles now established prove, that he is compensated for the increase of price in this instance, by a necessary reduction of the price of other commodities. In order to pay for the American products which she *must* obtain, England must be able to make up, in other commodities, for the 10 millions sterling worth of her manufactures which we will no longer take. But our market being already fully supplied with these articles at their present prices, she must tempt us to take more of them by reducing their price. She must sell her manufactures cheaper, not only to the United States, but to China, Java, Brazil, and Cuba, and thus obtain more tea, coffee, and sugar, which she can offer to us at rates so low as to increase our consumption of them to the required extent. These articles being in universal use, the reduction in their cost to us will be more than a compensation for the additional 10 per cent which we must pay for cotton, wool, and iron manufactures. Our domestic manufactures being thus restored to a prosperous condition, and many additional hands being required, as well as more capital, to prosecute them, the competition in agriculture will be slackened, and the price of our agricultural exports will naturally rise. Our sale of raw cotton will not be diminished, because the reduced price of cotton manufactures in Europe will increase the consumption of that article there more than enough to make up for a slight reduction of the quantity sold in the United States.

The statement of these principles may seem novel; but a little reflection will satisfy us, that we have long been familiar with the operation of them on a large scale. How is it that England has been able to extend her manufacturing enterprise to its present vast dimensions, except by reducing the price of its products so low as to cut off by competition the rival manufactures of every country in Europe, Asia, and America, that has not been wise enough to foster its domestic industry by a protective tariff? While her own industry and skill were not developed enough to enable her to defy rivalry, she maintained as rigid a system of protective and prohibitive duties as was established in any country on earth. One of the just complaints which ultimately produced the American Revolution, was, to adopt the language of Lord Chatham, that "England should not suffer her colonies to manufacture even a horseshoe for themselves." She then obtained the raw products of her own colonies on easy terms, by prohibiting them from selling to any other customer than herself; and those of other countries she bought at prices almost as low, by carefully keeping her purchases from them within the narrowest possible limits, so that they were compelled to sell cheap in order to sell enough to pay for their imports. Afterwards, when so much capital and skill were embarked in her manufactures that they no longer dreaded competition, her protective system was abolished; after her defensive armor was no longer needed, she put it off, and endeavored to persuade other nations, whose education in skill and industry had hardly begun, to do the same, consoling them for the consequent ruin of their domestic enterprises, by the assurance that she could manufacture for them cheaper than they could manufacture for themselves. The only point forgotten in this argument was, that their purchase of English manufactures would be thereby so much increased, that they would be obliged to sell their own raw products on the lowest possible terms in order to pay for them.

I borrow from an English authority a clear statement of the limitations under which alone the theory of free trade is applicable. "If all the countries of the globe were actually, or were ready to become, constituent portions of one and the same great family, the theory of the free-traders might seem plausible. But the plain truth is, that the whole analogy is forced and unnatural. By treating the human race as one great family, we are not following, but departing from, the apparent design of Providence, as indicated in the dispensations which everywhere present themselves to our observation. In these we are totally unable to discover any trace of this ideal incorporation. Separated by natural and defined boundaries, often by broad tracts of ocean; differing even in physical organization; inhabiting portions of the earth's surface varying in temperature from the fervid heat of the torrid zone to the almost unendurable cold of the arctic reigons; above all, absolutely unintelligible to each other by variety of language; — the Deity seems to have stamped on the features of nature and of humanity, in unmistakable characters, that nations shall remain separate and distinct, each pursuing, under the restraints only of moral obligations and just laws, its own separate interests; and thus, in beautiful harmony with the similar arrangements among individuals of the same nation, each, however unconsciously, contributing to that general good which is but the aggregate of the separate good of its parts." *

* *Quart. Review*, No. CLXXI. p. 86. It would be easy to quote many similar admissions made by those who supported the policy of Sir Robert Peel in abolishing the English corn laws. Thus, the Hon. G. Smythe, in a speech at Canterbury in 1847,

The situation of the United States is so peculiar, that arguments drawn from European experience for the guidance of our conduct are apt to be wholly fallacious and unsound. We can more profitably go for a lesson to the other side of the habitable globe, — to a country even more widely separated than we are, by a waste of ocean, from the arts and industry of England and her European rivals; — I mean, to British India. There we find a deficiency of capital, an abundance of fertile territory, a consequent surplus of agricultural produce, and a lack of that skill in manufacture which can only be gained by long experience under a strict protective policy, such as England has enjoyed for nearly two centuries; — all these circumstances strongly reminding us of corresponding features in our own condition. Now, the Governor-General of India, in a correspondence with the East India Company on the subject of the Dacca weavers, makes this statement: — "Some years ago, the East India Company annually received of the produce of the looms of India to the amount of six to eight million pieces of cotton goods. The demand gradually fell, and has now ceased altogether. European skill and machinery have superseded the produce of India. Cotton piece-goods, for ages the staple manufacture of India, seem for ever lost; *and the present suffering to numerous classes in India is scarcely to be paralleled in the history of commerce.*"

I have introduced this example especially because it throws light upon another reason, already urged in another place (pp. 191, 192), for the establishment of a protective policy, in America as well as in India; — I mean, the great difference in the cost of transportation between raw materials and manufactured goods, which operates greatly to the advantage of the country producing the latter, because manufactures have much the greater value in the smaller weight and bulk. Rice, wheat, cotton, and sugar are among what might be called the greatest natural exports of India, as they are produced there very

remarked: "I cannot quit this subject of Free Trade without expressing my opinion on its abstract principle. I by no means hold that the principle of Free Trade is absolutely true, or that it is of universal application. If I were an American, the citizen of a young country, I should be a Protectionist. If I were a Frenchman, the citizen of an old country with its industry undeveloped, I should equally be a Protectionist."

cheaply in great abundance. The average price of wheat at Calcutta is less than fifty cents a bushel; but the freight and other charges of transporting that bushel to England, and selling it there, amount to about eighty cents. England, therefore, though she has abolished her corn laws, enjoys a virtual protective duty against wheat from India, amounting to 160 per cent. The cost of transporting English manufactured goods to India cannot, on an average, exceed 40 per cent of their value. The difference between these two rates, amounting to 120 per cent, is, of course, really prohibitive in its effects; and India wheat is not brought to England at all. The difference in the cost of transporting raw materials and manufactured goods across the Atlantic is certainly not so great as in sending them round the Cape of Good Hope; but it is enough to give a very important advantage to the traffic to England. Our chief article of export, raw cotton, is a very bulky one; and even breadstuffs and tobacco are more expensive, both for land and sea carriage, than the cheapest manufactures of the loom. I speak of the carriage by land as well as sea, because the greater part of the raw material that we export is raised far in the interior, and the cost of bringing most of it to the Atlantic coast far exceeds that of carrying it over the ocean. On the other hand, our chief articles of import from Great Britain, with the possible exception of pig and bar iron, are of the finer species of manufacture, and therefore contain great value within little weight and bulk. It would be difficult, if not impossible, to estimate the average charges of transportation of so many different articles; but it would be perfectly safe to consider the difference as twenty per cent on the whole value of the goods in favor of England; that is, as an English protective tariff to that extent. In other words, if we send a million of dollars' worth of raw material to England, we must pay thirty per cent on its value for carriage, before it is admitted; while, on a million of dollars' worth of fine manufactured goods received in exchange, the English have to pay but ten per cent. Consequently, on the very principles of free trade, which means nothing but trade with equal advantages to the two parties, we ought to levy a general protective duty of twenty per cent.

One other consideration in favor of what may be called the American system must be mentioned, because it affords an answer to an argument frequently and strenuously urged on the other side. It is said that a protective duty raises the cost to the consumer, not only of those goods which are imported, and which therefore pay the duty, but of those also which are manufactured within the country, and sold at an enhanced price, because they are in a great measure protected against foreign competition. I have already alluded to two facts, which do away with most of the force of this argument; — namely, first, that a protective duty, being designed as a check to injurious *fluctuations* of price, is graduated with reference to the *lowest* price at which the foreign commodity is ever sold, and not with reference to the *average* price. Thus, a duty of thirty, may not raise the average price more than fifteen per cent, and this last may be the whole amount of *real* protection that the American manufacturer needs; but to secure this protection at all times, the duty must be fixed at thirty per cent, because circumstances may sometimes force the foreign commodity upon the market at a price fifteen per cent below its ordinary value. And secondly, it has just been shown that the English manufacturer, in order not to lose altogether his hold upon the American market after the duty is imposed, is obliged to lower his price, so that, in fact, he pays from one half to three fifths of the duty, instead of throwing the whole of it upon the American consumer.

But further, this expression "forcing upon the market" points to another fact of frequent occurrence in trade, which demonstrates the necessity of placing a check upon excessive imports. The reaction of a commercial crisis in England, making dealers there eager to get rid of a large quantity of goods at almost any price, — or the beginning of such a crisis in America, when the speculative fever tempts importers to accumulate stocks to a ruinous extent, — may cause a glut in our market of many commodities at once, depressing the value of the whole exchangeable produce of the country to a degree far beyond the proportion which the stocks of those commodities bear to the aggregate of that produce. We have seen that the abstraction of a third part of the ordinary supply may double the price, or fail to raise it more than one sixth, according as the article is one of prime necessity, or one which people can easily do without. So the addition of a third to the ordinary stock of goods on hand may sink the price, not merely in proportion to that increase, but to one half of its former amount. The whole stock, then, both of foreign and domestic products, must be sold at this ruinous sacrifice.

I have already explained one important exception to the general rule, that the effect of cheapening commodities is to increase the sale of them, by bringing them within the reach of a larger body of consumers; and this exception has an obvious bearing upon the present subject. Mr. Mill very fairly states the point as follows, though he does not seem to be aware of the whole force of the concession. "When a thing is bought, not for its use, but its costliness, cheapness is no recommendation. As Sismondi remarks, the consequence of cheapening articles of vanity is, not that less is expended on such things, but that the buyers substitute for the cheapened article some other which is more costly, or a more elaborate quality of the same thing; and as the inferior quality answered the purpose of vanity equally well when it was equally expensive, a tax on the article would really be paid by nobody; it would be a creation of public revenue by which nobody would lose." *

Obviously, then, in respect to all articles which are used only for purposes of ostentation and display, the only strong argument against a protective tariff, that it operates as a tax upon consumers by slightly increasing the prices of the commodities on which a duty is imposed, ceases to have any weight whatever. If the duty were removed, consumers would save nothing, for they would abandon the use of the cheapened commodity, and seek out one of higher cost, not because it is of superior quality or convenience, but because its high price renders the possession of it a token of wealth. If silks are so high in price that fine cottons content the love of display, the additional amount of labor required for the production of silks is saved. An expensive cotton fabric gratifies the spirit of ostentation, of rivalry, of showing one's self as well off as one's neighbors, just as effectually as a cheap silk. Taxes upon this class of luxuries, then, *cost the community nothing*; the proceeds of such taxes are an absolute saving. Even if the finest

* Mill's *Political Economy*, Vol. II. p. 442.

American cottons were fifty per cent dearer than English goods of the same quality, a duty of fifty per cent on the imported commodity would be no tax upon the consumer. *With the duty*, he would buy the American or the English article at $1.50 a yard, and it would answer his only purpose, — would fully gratify his love of display. *Without the duty*, despising the cheaper article, he would purchase an English or French silk at $1.50 a yard, and would be no better off than in the other case; while the government would lose the whole proceeds of the tax, American manufactories would be stopped, and American workmen thrown out of employment.

I am no advocate of sumptuary laws for their own sake. But taxation itself being essential for the support of government, such an apportionment of the indirect taxes among various commodities as will discourage idle, wasteful, and luxurious consumption, is clearly expedient and just. For the aggregate amount expended all over the country for any article of luxury is increased by diminution of its price, and lessened by augmentation of that price. If, for instance, the number of diamonds should be so much increased, that the price should fall one half, people would purchase more than twice as many of them. There would then be no real saving to the community, but an actual loss; for the aggregate expenditure of the country in diamonds would be increased by the whole amount bought by those who should be more than enough to make up twice the former number of purchasers. On the other hand, double the price, and there would be less than half the former number of purchasers, and consequently a real saving to the community. If, then, we make the more costly manufactures for ourselves, instead of obtaining them from abroad, their price will be somewhat enhanced, there will be a smaller aggregate expenditure upon them, the purposes of luxury and ostentation will be equally well answered, and the prices obtained in foreign markets for our exports will be increased by the diminution of our imports, and to the full extent of that diminution. Silks, very fine cottons and woollens expensive cutlery, articles of *virtu* and *bijouterie*, and the like are necessarily consumed unproductively; we gain nothing we even lose, by cheapening them. If the wages of labor can be kept up by raising the prices of such articles, we gain all round.

But our view of this subject would be incomplete, if some notice were not taken of the common arguments against laying restraints upon importation for the encouragement of domestic manufactures. Nearly all of them may be summed up in the often-quoted maxims, that, as a community is made up only of individuals, what is most for the interest of individuals is also best for the community; that individuals better than the government can determine what is most for their own advantage; and "that the maxim of buying in the cheapest market, and selling in the dearest, which regulates every merchant in his individual dealings, is strictly applicable as the best rule for the trade of the whole nation."

That this argument may be pressed too far is very evident; for if individuals were always the best judges of what their own interest requires, many of them would refuse to pay any taxes for the support of government, and nearly all would claim a large reduction of the taxes which are severally imposed upon them. Comparatively few have sagacity and foresight enough to perceive for themselves the truth, however they may be disposed to yield a passive assent to it from custom and a respect for the authority of others, that government, which is throughout a system of repression and restraint, exists only for the common good; that in its administration, it is often necessary to sacrifice the interests of individuals to the general welfare; that private property, for instance, must often be taken for public uses; that sometimes persons must be taken away from their own occupations, and be compelled to serve on juries, or in the army or navy, or to testify in courts of justice, or to expose property and life to the hazards of war, perhaps of a war which they consider impolitic or unjust, and to do a thousand other things which they regard as vexatious and detrimental to their private concerns. The best government rests much more upon prescription and the tacit assent yielded only from the force of habit, than upon the intelligent convictions of its subjects. No one's consent is asked, as soon as he arrives at years of discretion, whether he will submit to the laws which he has had no hand in making; his submission is taken for granted, and he can withhold it only at the expense of imprisonment or exile. Peace and war must be made without consulting him, or asking how they will affect his private welfare; often the best excuse that can be offered for making either is, that it will promote the interests of the greater number, though some must suffer.

But this remark is too general to meet the whole force of the argument for free trade, and is introduced here only to show that the alleged identity of individual with national interests, upon which this argument is based, is not a truth of universal application. We may gain a better view of the applicability of the maxim in this particular case, by considering one of Adam Smith's ingenious illustrations of it, which has been so frequently cited as to appear almost a truism.

"To give the monopoly of the home market," says Smith, "to the produce of domestic industry, in any particular art or manufacture, is in some measure to direct private people in what manner they ought to employ their capitals, and must, in almost all cases, be either a useless or a hurtful regulation. If the produce of domestic can be bought there as cheaply as that of foreign industry, the regulation is evidently useless. If it cannot, it must generally be hurtful. It is the maxim of every prudent master of a family, never to attempt to make at home what it will cost him more to make than to buy. The tailor does not attempt to make his own shoes, but buys them of the shoemaker. The shoemaker does not attempt to make his own clothes, but employs a tailor. The farmer attempts to make neither the one nor the other, but employs those different artificers. All of them find it for their interest to employ their whole industry in a way in which they may have some advantage over their neighbors, and to purchase with a part of its produce, or, what is the same thing, with the price of a part of it, whatever else they may have occasion for. What is prudence in the conduct of every private family, can scarce be folly in that of a great kingdom." *

But this comparison between individuals and communities is often a faulty and deceptive one, and is particularly so in this case. Certainly it would be unwise in an individual to be his own weaver, tailor, carpenter, and blacksmith; he would thus lose all the advantages of a division of labor, and would not become skilled in any department. But this objection does

* *Wealth of Nations*, p. 200.

not hold in the case of a community, which has only a fictitious unity, and is really made up of many individuals, who may distribute among themselves all the employments which are requisite for the production of all the commodities that the society needs. No one person is thus required to practise more than one art, and the division of labor among these individuals is as perfect, as if the same number of trades were partitioned out among so many distinct communities. Still more; as communities are separated from each other often by broad tracts of sea or land, should each one confine its industry to the production of a single commodity, and purchase whatever else it needs from rival states, all its articles of consumption but one would come to it burdened with a considerable cost of transportation; and the sale of its own single product everywhere but at home would be impeded by an addition to its cost from the same cause. All the advantages of a division of labor result from a separation of employments among individuals, and become disadvantages in the case of distinct states, counties, and even towns. To one who is a blacksmith, it is no help, but rather a hinderance, that his next-door neighbor is a blacksmith also; he has thus a competitor in satisfying the wants of his own village, where every mechanic finds his best and most profitable customers; and as blacksmiths' work is heavy, he cannot carry his wares for sale even to the next county or town without lessening his profits. The inhabitants of every country town understand their own interests much better than Adam Smith did. Instead of forming themselves into a settlement composed exclusively of artisans of one trade, each community has its own mason, shoemaker, carpenter, shopkeeper, lawyer, doctor, and clergyman, and is thus not obliged to send a dozen or twenty miles in order to have a horse shod, a chimney built, a tooth pulled, or a marriage celebrated.* A Yankee farmer with half a dozen

* I am not detailing imaginary cases. Mr. Rae, who lived a long time in Canada, says: "I knew two brothers whose farms or estates lay in one of the interior districts of that country, in the midst of its forests, and consequently at a considerable distance, perhaps twenty or thirty miles, from artificers of any description. Having each of them large families and productive farms, they had occasion for the services of various artificers, and had the means of paying them. Nevertheless, they very rarely employed them; almost every article they required was made by some one of the two families. As they were prudent and sagacious men, of which they produced the best

stout sons, acts upon the same principle, in not educating them all to his own employment, but making a mechanic of one, a merchant of another, a sailor of a third, sending a fourth to college, and keeping only one at home to be his own successor upon the farm. As all occupations are precarious, he knows that, by this course, he multiplies the chances of success, or reduces the chances of failure, for the whole family, besides suiting each member of it with an employment best adapted to his peculiar powers and inclination.

Adam Smith's illustrations are fallacious, because they are drawn from extreme cases, in regard to which no one would think of denying the correctness of the maxim, and are then applied as if it were correct in every instance, though the universality of the principle is the only point in question. Thus he argues: "By means of glasses, hot-beds, and hot-walls, very good grapes can be raised in Scotland, and very good wine, too, can be made of them, at about thirty times the expense for which at least equally good can be brought from foreign countries. Would it be a reasonable law to prohibit the importation of all foreign wines, merely to encourage the making

---

evidence in the general success of their undertakings, and the prosperity of the settlement of which they were at the head, I think it likely that, in this also, they had turned their means to the best account. In fact, as they who are familiar with the details of beginning settlements in North America will admit, by this plan they in a great measure obviated the two chief drawbacks on the prosperity of new and remote settlements, — the excessive dearness of every article not produced there, from the great expense attending the transport of the raw produce and retransport of the manufactured goods, and the serious inconvenience arising from the difficulty, in such situations, of supplying, when necessary, unforeseen but pressing wants.

"Among other things which they got made on their own farms were boots, shoes, and leather. That they might get this done, they were at the pains and expense of sending one of the young men to some distance, to make himself sufficiently master of those trades for their purpose. They thought, however, that the cost they were thus put to was repaid, thrice over, by the saving of time and expense which it effected for them, in enabling them to make, out of leather which cost them very little, numerous articles that they must otherwise have been constantly sending for to a great distance, by roads that were almost impracticable a great part of the season."

A Free-Trader, continues Mr. Rae, would certainly have remarked to these two heads of families: "You are in want, you say, of some pairs of shoes; surely, then, it is best for you to purchase them at the place where you can get them cheapest. But by the plan you are taking, of going to a great expense to have them made at home, they will certainly cost you more when made there, than if bought at the place where you have hitherto purchased shoes."

Any one can judge whether such advice would have been sound.

of claret and burgundy in Scotland?" Certainly not. And it would also be manifestly absurd to attempt to raise tea, coffee, pineapples, and other tropical products, in New England. We here labor under natural disabilities, arising from peculiarities of soil and climate, which time and practice can never remove or essentially diminish. But Americans can profitably raise and manufacture iron, steel, wool, cotton, flax, and silk, for the production and fashioning of which we have as great advantages as the English, and even greater, skill and capital alone excepted. We can therefore profitably spend time, labor, and money in the acquisition of that skill and capital; that is, we can profitably submit, for a certain number of years, to an additional tax for this purpose, appearing in the additional price which we must for a while pay for the domestic products.

We may turn Adam Smith's favorite mode of illustration against himself, by asking if it be not as reasonable for a nation, as it confessedly is for an individual, to enter upon a course of education, or serve an apprenticeship, — though, during the period of discipline, the gains will be small, the labor severe, and perhaps the expenses heavy, — for the purpose of acquiring an art or handicraft which may afterwards be exercised with great profit. We suppose that the art is one for which the individual or the nation is sufficiently qualified by nature, so that merely the tact and dexterity which can only be acquired by practice are wanting. The common answer of the advocates of free trade to this question, 'that when the proper time has arrived, and sufficient capital has been accumulated, manufactures will introduce themselves, without the aid of protective duties,' is evasive and insufficient. It goes upon the supposition, that want of capital is the only obstacle to the immediate commencement of manufacturing enterprise, whereas skill is also requisite; capital, we admit, may be accumulated in agriculture and other pursuits; but skill can be acquired only by actual experiments in manufacture, and those experiments can be tried only at considerable sacrifice. Individuals cannot be expected to submit to these sacrifices, when the results of the experiment, if successful, will not accrue to their exclusive advantage, but will be open to all. In truth, the acquisition of manufacturing skill is a national advantage, though it invariably occasions a loss to the individual who, first in his nation, attempts to acquire it; it is therefore justly paid for at the national expense, or by a protective duty, which insures the beginners for a limited time against overwhelming competition from abroad.

Even in Great Britain, where free trade may now be said to be the fashionable doctrine, though it has become so only within the last fifteen years, and in every other civilized nation, these principles are carried into practical application through the encouragement afforded to authors and inventors, by securing to them for a limited period the exclusive right to sell their respective writings and discoveries. Patents and copyrights, which no one thinks it improper to grant, are signal instances of the successful application of the principles of the protective system. They are strict monopolies, no one but the author or inventor, and his agents, being allowed to manufacture or sell the particular book or machine which is thus protected. Consequently, they are prohibitive rather than protective duties; any price can be set upon the articles which the owner of the patent or copyright sees fit to demand. And the public cheerfully pay the addition thus made to the natural cost of the commodity, knowing that, without such encouragement, few good books would be written and few useful machines invented, and that, at the expiration of a limited time, (in England and the United States, fourteen years for a patent and forty-two years for a copyright,) the right to make and vend the work will become general, and the community will then be the richer by the whole value of the original proprietor's genius and labor. But he who first introduces a particular art or manufacture into a country is as great a public benefactor, as one who subsequently invents a new process or a new machine for executing the work at less cost. In fact, it is only through the enterprise of the former that the latter acquires a field and an occasion for the exercise of his inventive genius. To the capitalists who built the city of Lowell, is fairly attributable much of the merit of the inventions which have been made in it, or have there first been reduced to practice; and these are probably more numerous and valuable than have been made within the same time in any manufacturing city in the world. According to the census of 1850, the introduction of the cotton manufacture into the United States has given employment to nearly 100,000 persons, and that of iron to more than 60,000. What single invention made within the limits of this country has had equally important results, or has been carried out at equal hazard and sacrifice?

The reasonableness of granting patent rights and copyrights is thus frankly admitted by an able advocate of free trade, Mr. J. S. Mill. "The condemnation of monopolies," he says, "ought not to extend to patents, by which the originator of an improved process is permitted to enjoy, for a limited period, the exclusive privilege of using his own improvement. This is not making the commodity dear for his benefit, but merely postponing a part of the increased cheapness which the public owe to the inventor, in order to compensate and reward him for the service. That he ought to be both compensated and rewarded for it will not be denied; and also, that if all were at once allowed to avail themselves of his ingenuity, without having shared the labors or the expenses which he had to incur in bringing his idea into a practical shape, either such expenses and labors would be undergone by nobody, except by very opulent and very public-spirited persons, or the state must put a value on the service rendered by an inventor, and make him a pecuniary grant. This has been done in some instances, [as when Parliament offered a reward of £ 20,000 for a method of finding a ship's longitude at sea], and may be done without inconvenience in cases of very conspicuous public benefit; but in general, an exclusive privilege of temporary duration is preferable, because it leaves nothing to any one's discretion, because the reward conferred by it depends upon the invention's being found useful, and the greater the usefulness the greater the reward, and because it is paid by the very persons to whom the service is rendered, the consumers of the commodity.*

Having conceded thus much, Mr. Mill finds himself obliged by consistency of reasoning to make the following additional admission, which really covers the whole ground usually claimed by the advocates of a protective system in the United States. "The only case," he says, "in which, on mere principles of Political Economy, protecting duties can be defensible,

* Mill's *Political Economy*, Vol. II. p. 497.

is when they are imposed temporarily, (especially in a young and rising nation,) in hopes of naturalizing a foreign industry in itself perfectly suitable to the circumstances of the country. The superiority of one country over another in a branch of production often arises only from having begun it sooner. There may be no inherent advantage on one part, or disadvantage on the other, but only a present superiority of acquired skill and experience. A country which has this skill and experience yet to acquire, may in other respects be better adapted to the production than those which were earlier in the field; and besides, it is a just remark, that nothing has a greater tendency to promote improvements in any branch of production, than its trial under a new set of conditions. But it cannot be expected that individuals should, at their own risk, or rather to their certain loss, introduce a new manufacture, and bear the burden of carrying it on, until the producers have been educated up to the level of those with whom the processes are traditional. A protecting duty, continued for a reasonable time, will sometimes be the least inconvenient mode in which the nation can tax itself for the support of such an experiment." *

Now with reference to the great manufactures of cotton, wool, iron, flax, and silk, no one affirms that Great Britain has any natural and inherent advantages for prosecuting them which are not enjoyed, in an equal or greater degree, by the people of this country. The English have "only a present superiority of acquired skill and experience," resulting from the fact, that, in some of these branches of production, they had over two centuries the start of us, and in all the others, they had been at least fifty years in the field before manufacturing enterprise began in the United States. Even their larger command of capital is needed only for the purpose of supplying foreign markets, the resources of our countrymen in this respect being fully adequate for the home supply, and the exclusive control of the home market is all that can be given by protective duties. We have vastly larger supplies of iron ore and coal, and at least equal facilities for raising wool, flax, and silk. Cheap land and abundant water-power are also important natural auxiliaries of manufacturing industry in this country.

---

* *Ibid.*, pp. 487, 488.

In respect to the cotton manufacture, we enjoy an obvious natural advantage over Great Britain, as the raw material must be exported to that country, and then brought back again in the manufactured state, and sold here at a cost enhanced by the expense of twice carrying it across the ocean; here, it may be spun and woven on the spot where produced. For the coarser cottons, also, our period of apprenticeship in the art of producing them is finished; we can export them, as already mentioned, and undersell the English in all foreign markets. This branch of industry was first introduced into the United States under the protection afforded by the war of 1812–15, when, our ports being virtually closed by blockade, the manufacturer really had a monopoly of the home market. After the peace, as it was apparent that the infant manufacture would be entirely destroyed by foreign competition, Congress passed the tariff of 1816, which imposed a duty of twenty-five per cent on all cotton fabrics, requiring also that they should be taken at a *minimum* valuation of twenty-five cents a square yard. By the acts of 1824 and 1828, this minimum valuation was advanced, first to thirty, and then to thirty-five cents the square yard, and so continued with little modification till 1834, when the reduction of the duty commenced. But before the tariff of 1842 was enacted, the cheaper cottons had ceased to need any protection, and began to be exported. In the course of only thirty years, the infant manufacture had grown to maturity, and ceased to need the aid of government. What is more, the same fabrics which, thirty years ago, were held at a *minimum* valuation of thirty-five cents the square yard, are now sold at from five to eight cents, and the annual exports of them in 1853 amounted to nearly nine millions of dollars. There is every reason to believe, that an equally efficient protection, rendered for an equal period, to the manufactures of wool, flax, and iron, would produce a similar effect. These great branches of industry, also, if carefully nursed during the period of their growth, might subsequently repay the country tenfold the cost of their temporary protection.

Against the favorite dogma of Adam Smith and his followers, that individual and national interests are identical, I have already quoted the decisive remark of Mr. Rae, that "individuals grow rich by the *acquisition* of wealth previously existing;

nations, by the *creation* of wealth that did not before exist." Laws which simply permit private persons to amass wealth, or which favor the aggregation of property in a few hands, without opening any new sources of *national* wealth, — as by favoring invention and discovery, and introducing new arts and new processes in those formerly established, — are positively injurious. There has been an immense emigration from Great Britain and Ireland during the last eight years, and it has doubtless been much to the advantage of those who have joined in it; but who can question that their removal has been a serious loss to the country which they have abandoned, and if the drain should continue, and even increase, as it has done, that it would dry up all the sources of English strength and prosperity. Yet it is the opinion of the wisest English statesmen and economists, that nearly all the sufferings of Ireland, which have led to this unparalleled exodus of her people, might have been avoided if other manufactures than that of linen could have been established there, so as to provide employment for all classes of the population. But Irish manufactures, unluckily, with the single exception that has been mentioned, are of later date than those of England, and, without the shield of a protective tariff, have never been able to advance beyond a stage of sickly infancy. Ireland has been reserved as a market for English manufactures, and condemned to pay for them in agricultural products, while her own children were starving. Her present weakness and misery may justly be regarded as a consequence of free trade with her over-powerful neighbor.

"Invention," says Mr. Rae, "is the only power on earth that can be said to create. It enters as an essential element into the process of the increase of national wealth, because that process is a creation, not an acquisition. It does not necessarily enter into the process of the increase of individual wealth, because that may be simply an acquisition, not a creation. The assumption, therefore, that the two processes are perfectly similar, is incorrect." Hence, the most frequent cause of the increase of national wealth is the increase of the skill, dexterity, and judgment, and of the mechanical contrivances, with which the national labor is applied. Poland is not so rich a country as England, not on account of any deficiency of labor, for a Polish or Russian serf probably works as hard, and as many hours in the day, as an English artisan; but he does not work to so good purpose. His toil, being that of mere tillage, taxes his muscles, but not his brains. "When we are told that an individual this year employs in agriculture double the capital which he employed last year, the conception which most readily presents itself to us is, that he now farms double the land which he then farmed, owns double the number of horses, cattle, farming utensils, &c., and has double the number of barns and other necessary buildings. When we are told that a country has double the agricultural capital which it had a century ago, we cannot, of course, conceive that its farms are double the extent they then were; neither do we conceive that its farmers have simply double the number of barns and other buildings, of cattle, ploughs, harrows, and other farming utensils, which they then had. We conceive a change in the mode in which its fields are laid out and tilled; in the form and qualities of the stock; in the construction of all the implements of husbandry; in the size and arrangement of the barns and other buildings; and that, through these changes, the national agricultural labor produces at least double the products it formerly did. It is this change necessarily involved in our conception of the process by which nations increase their capitals, and not necessarily involved in the process by which individuals increase their capitals, that constitutes the difference between them." *

This view is illustrated by the account already given (Chapter XVII.) of the necessary restrictions upon the growth of capital arising from the limitations of the field of employment. Even according to Ricardo's theory of rent and profits, the great preventive of a constant deterioration of the condition of society, arising from the diminished fertility of the soils to which it is compelled successively to resort, and from the consequent fall of profits, is the progress of improvement; and it matters not whether this improvement takes place through the invention of new processes and new machines, or the introduction of new arts and manufactures from abroad, the condition of the former being the offer of satisfactory rewards to the inventors,

---

* Rae's *New Principles of Political Economy*, p. 13.

and of the latter, a temporary safeguard of the introducers against foreign rivalry by a protective tariff. Here again I borrow the substance of an illustration from Mr. Rae. We are much richer than our fathers, because we have threshing-machines where they had only flails, power-looms where they had only hand-looms, reaping-machines where they had only sickles, &c. Now the wealth which can be accumulated in the form of flails, hand-looms, and sickles, is very limited, since no more of any of these implements can be profitably manufactured than are wanted for specific and limited purposes. On the other hand, the wealth which can exist in the form of threshing-machines, power-looms, and reaping-machines, is very considerable; — not unlimited, it is true, but vastly greater than the capital formerly vested in the simpler implements. Hence the efforts of the legislature can be profitably directed towards promoting the progress of science and art, and favoring the introduction of manufactures, which can be prosecuted only by complex and costly machinery. Government efforts are needed for these ends, because, as a general rule, inventors and pioneers in new enterprises are poorly compensated by the public.

"Individuals as well as nations," argues the same author, "acquire wealth from other sources than mere saving of revenue; skill is as necessary, and consequently as valuable, a coöperator with the industry of both, as either capital or parsimony; and therefore the expenditure which either may be called on to make, to attain the requisite skill, is very well bestowed. But though skill is valuable both to nations and to individuals, there are many circumstances that render it more so to the former than to the latter. In the first place, it is more durable." The skill of an individual dies with him, while that of the community endures as a permanent possession. "If it be worth while paying a considerable apprentice fee for the acquisition of an art which can be probably exercised only for twenty or thirty years, it must be better worth while to pay for one, the advantages derived from the possession of which may be retained for hundreds or thousands of years." Again, the future skilled labor of an individual cannot be mortgaged or sold, except the laborer sell himself along with it, — a transaction which is not sanctioned in modern times. "On the contrary, any portion of the future revenue yielded by the skilled industry of a nation may be sold, and consequently an addition to the national skill gives a proportional addition to the command of national resources, to meet any sudden emergency. The produce of the general industry of Great Britain stands mortgaged for a sum which it would have appeared, a century ago, utterly impossible to conceive that industry could sustain, because, a century ago, it was impossible to conceive the vast increase which has been made to the skill, dexterity, and judgment with which it was then directed." *

The considerations that have now been presented tend to show, that the tax imposed upon a community by any protective duty that falls short of a prohibition, is a very light one, as a considerable portion of it is paid by the foreign producers, and reappears in the additional price received for exports; that it keeps up the rate of wages, and enlarges the field for the employment of capital; that it prevents the business of agriculture from being so overdone as to render raw material the only article of export, and to depress the price of this so low that, though the people have a rude abundance of food and other mere necessaries, they are deprived of most of the comforts and elegances of life; that so far as the duty bears only upon articles of luxury and ostentation, the tax is really paid by nobody, but is a creation of public revenue out of a mere change in the fashions and tastes of the rich; that a protective system is needed only while the people are going through a period of apprenticeship in manufactures, and can be removed as soon as the necessary skill and experience have been obtained, when the cost of the commodities will be less than it would have been if the duty had never been imposed; and that its general effect is to stimulate invention, to multiply the productive arts, and to enlarge the sources of national opulence.

But on this great question between free trade and a protective policy, these arguments relating only to pecuniary loss or gain do not merit so much notice as the considerations which were mentioned in the eighth chapter of this work, respecting the devotion of the greater part of the people to

---

* Rae's *New Principles of Political Economy*, pp. 61, 62.

skilled or rude labor, and their consequent collection in towns and cities, or wide dispersion over the face of the country. Viewed in this light, I confess, the question seems to be one between progress in civilization and the arts, or a gradual return, I will not say to barbarism, but to that very imperfect stage of civilization which exists in all countries where the population are almost exclusively devoted to agriculture. The best legislative policy is that which will most effectually develop all the natural advantages of a country, whether mental or material. It is as wasteful, to say the least, to allow mechanical skill and inventive genius to remain unemployed, as it would be to permit water-power to run without turning mills, or mineral wealth to continue in the ore, or forests to wave where cotton and grain might grow luxuriantly. If the rude labor of husbandry is to form the principal employment of the people, the higher remuneration of skilled labor in the arts must be sacrificed; and this would be as bad economy as to turn our richest soils into sheep-pastures, or to feed cattle upon the finest wheat. The dispersion of the inhabitants over vast tracts of territory in the isolated pursuits of agriculture, the great majority of them being doomed to work which would not tax the mental resources of a Russian serf or a Feejee-Islander, must be fatal, not only to the growth of wealth, but to many of the higher interests of humanity. The hardships and privations of a life in the backwoods are a fearful drawback upon that bounty which confers as a free gift a homestead farm with a soil that reproduces the seed a hundred-fold. To give full scope to all the varieties of taste, genius, and temperament; to foster inventive talent; to afford adequate encouragement to all the arts, whether mechanical, or those which are usually distinguished as the fine arts; to concentrate the people, or to bring as large a portion of them as possible within the sphere of the humanizing influences and larger means of mental culture and social improvement which can be found only in cities and large towns;—these are objects which deserve at least as much attention as the inquiry where we can purchase calicoes cheapest, or how great pecuniary sacrifice must be made before we can manufacture rail-road iron for ourselves. I see not how these ends can be obtained in a country like ours, which is, so to speak, cursed with great advantages for agriculture, emigration, and the segregation of the people from each other, without throwing over our manufacturing industry, at least for half a century to come, the broad shield of an effective protecting tariff. We shall need this shield only while we are passing through the term of our pupilage and apprenticeship, which, for a nation, of course, is always a protracted one; we shall need it, to adopt Burke's phrase, only while we are in the gristle, and have not yet hardened into the bone, of manhood. When we have enjoyed, as England has already enjoyed, the benefit of a strict protective policy for over a century, for the purpose of completing our education in manufactures, then we shall be ready to do what England at last has done, — to throw down all barriers, and to invite the world to compete with us in the application of industry and skill to any enterprise designed to satisfy the wants of man.

CHAPTER XXV.

THE DISTRIBUTION OF PROPERTY AS AFFECTED BY THE LAWS REGULATING THE SUCCESSION TO THE ESTATES OF PERSONS DECEASED.

THE question respecting the distribution of property, which has chiefly been discussed only in the abstract by politicians and Political Economists, has now become one of practical interest and of the gravest importance. The sacredness of the institution has been generally recognized. That the accumulation of wealth in the hands of individuals was indispensable, in order that the aggregate property of the nation might increase, and for the maintenance of order, the prevention of endless disputes, the encouragement of industry and enterprise, and the promotion of all the higher interests of society, was a fact that few were bold enough to deny. The inheritor of an estate usually claims it even as a natural right; he seldom thinks of defending his possession of it merely on the ground of general expediency. He holds that he is indebted for it, not to government, or legislation, or the general consent of the community, but to those general principles of morality and natural law which protect his person and insure him the free use of his faculties and his time. Consequently, he invokes the aid of the law, the assistance of society, whenever he is molested in the enjoyment of his property. His doctrine is, that government did not give it to him, but that government is bound to take good care that he be not unjustly deprived of it.

Yet nothing is more certain than that all *inherited* property is actually enjoyed by the gift of law and the consent of society. A natural right is not limited by the boundaries of states; yet a second son in France claims an equal share of his parent's real estate, in the same manner, and for the same reason, that the eldest son in England claims the whole. An American is entitled to dispose of his whole property by will, according to his own judgment or caprice; he may endow a college or a cat with it, if he sees fit, to the total exclusion of his natural heirs. But this posthumous privilege, this *post-mortem* enjoyment of wealth, is strictly limited in France; if a testator has one child, he can dispose of but half of his property; if he has two children, only a third, and if three, only a fourth, of his estate is subject to his own will. The respective shares of the sons and daughters are accurately determined, and a man cannot, even by gift during his lifetime, do anything to contravene the effect of this law. Now, as most of the wealth of a country, in the course of a single generation, must descend by inheritance or bequest, and as this descent is everywhere regulated by legislation, it follows that inherited property is the creature of law; its distribution is effected by government, or by the general consent of society, and is regulated by considerations of expediency alone. It sounds strange, but it is true, that the same authority which in England upholds the right of primogeniture, and in Scotland gives the privilege of perpetual entail, and in France deprives a testator of the power of giving away more than a small fraction of his property by will, might, *with equal justice*, decree that a man's whole estate on his decease should escheat to the state, or come under the disposal of the legislature, to be applied equally for the benefit of the whole nation. The legislative power does not enact that the whole people shall be equal and joint heirs of all property which is vacated by death, simply because it believes that it is more for the interest of the whole people that the estate should be inherited only by the children of the deceased, or should descend exclusively to the oldest son. The law which disinherits five children out of one family for the benefit of the sixth, is surely competent to deprive the sixth also of his inheritance; if it leaves but one fourth of the estate to the caprice of the testator, it may destroy the efficacy of wills altogether.

It is true, that some considerations of justice and natural right come in to limit the general authority of law. The property which a man does not inherit, but actually creates by his own industry, seems to be his own by a higher and stronger title than any which society can confer. But it is no infringement of his right to say, that his power over the valuable article thus produced by him shall cease at his death; for the only superiority of his title consists in the fact that he, the possessor of the property, was also its creator, and one who only inherits it from its first owner cannot urge this plea; to defend the absolute right of the heir, would be to maintain that a right by inheritance is equal to one by creation, and thus to destroy the original claim of superiority of title. Absolute ownership, however sacred for the time, necessarily terminates at the death of the individual; society deprives him of nothing that is his own, when it refuses him testamentary power, because nothing that belongs to earth can be enjoyed beyond the grave, and he who has nothing can be deprived of nothing.

Again, the rightful authority of the legislature over the descent of property is limited by the trusts and expectations that have been created by immemorial usage and the previously existing state of the law. The conduct, the hopes, the calculations of men, are regulated by the customs of the country, by the assumed sanctity of prescription, and by long established institutions. The laws which regulate the descent of property are fundamental in their character; they are classed with the first principles of the constitution, like those which determine the form of the executive government, whether it shall be republican, aristocratic, or monarchical; and, excepting insignificant changes of forms and details, they are never altered but on grand emergencies, or after a stormy revolution. A person of fortune adapts the education of his children to their presumed future enjoyment of his large estates; and although his own absolute right to his lands and goods certainly terminates at his death, these children suffer flagrant wrong, if their honest expectations are deceived, and they are compelled to adopt a course of life for which they were not trained. Society is under an implied contract with all who are members of it, not to make sudden or wanton changes in its own fundamental statutes, on whose presumed inviolability great hopes have been cherished, and plans devised the execution of which was to extend through future generations. Thus, if the French law of descent were suddenly introduced into this country, a great outcry would be raised, not merely against the policy, but the justice, of the measure; though no one thinks of impugning the law, as it actually exists in France, on any higher ground than that of expediency. The right of regulating the descent of property by will, of rewarding a favorite child, and disinheriting a stubborn or vicious one, has come to be considered here as a necessary incident of ownership; it would be urged, that the government might as well rob a man directly of his wealth, as deprive him of the power of giving it away as he sees fit, whether the gift is to take effect during his lifetime or after his decease. Yet nothing can be more clear, than that a man necessarily abandons his earthly property at the grave; and if any wrong is done in the distribution of it, that wrong is not suffered by the deceased, who is beyond the sphere of injury from his fellow-man, but by those whom he leaves behind. If his nearest of kin have any absolute right to it, beyond the limits of prescription and positive statute, in preference to all other persons in the community, and to the community itself, we have yet to learn on what foundation this right is based, and by what civilized nation, or in what code of laws, it has ever, to the full extent, been recognized. There is an implied contract between society and the individual, that he shall be protected in the exclusive enjoyment of his earnings, the fruits of his own labor, so long as he is capable of enjoying them; when that capacity ceases, the contract is dissolved, the obligations of society have been fulfilled, and what is left behind without a natural owner comes into the common stock, to be distributed, or appropriated in mass, solely from a regard to the greatest good of the greatest number.

These considerations are applicable to all inherited property, whether real or personal; but they are most conclusive in the case of the ownership of land. Without going into the question respecting the manner in which territory was first parcelled out and appropriated to exclusive use, or whether the original division took place by express compact, or by silent sufferance which gradually became prescriptive right, there is no doubt that the land first belonged in common to all men, and the appropriation of it by individuals is now admitted to be equitable only because it is believed to be expedient. The earth was given to be the habitation, and to provide for the subsistence, of all men, and it was at first enjoyed in common. The ocean and the air are so used even now; the former is the common highway of nations, because its vast extent affords room for all; while the right of navigating straits, narrow seas, and inlets into the land, is sometimes limited, under the pretext that one government must have the entire control of them in order to prevent interference and disputes, or to provide for its own safety, or to repay itself for disbursements required in order to make the navigation of them safe for all. These are reasons of mutual convenience; and perfectly similar reasons are alleged to justify the division of land, and the appropriation of it by individual owners. That appropriation of it in the first instance was certainly a usurpation, for it must have taken place without the consent, and even without the knowledge, of the vast majority of those who, up to that period, had enjoyed it in common, each one of whom had consequently as good a right to it as he who first fenced it in. If it could be proved that this division did not promote the general welfare, or that it produced on the whole more harm than good, every person might claim either a share of the land, or the privilege of cultivating the whole of it in common with others, as his natural birthright. In fact, a portion of the land is always given up for general use as a highway, because it is for the common advantage that all should have the privilege of passing over it. The farms contiguous to the highway could not equitably be held as private property, except from a similar regard to the common interest.

Two considerations, however, must be admitted to modify the inferences which might otherwise be drawn from this statement. The first may be given in the language of Mr. Mill. "If the land derived its productive power wholly from nature," he says, "and not at all from industry, or if there were any means of discriminating what is derived from each source, it not only would not be necessary, but it would be the height of injustice, to let the gift of nature be engrossed by a few." But this is not the case, for "though land is not the produce of industry, most of its valuable qualities are so. Labor is not only requisite for using, but almost equally so for fashioning, the instrument. Considerable labor is often required at the commencement, to clear the land for cultivation. In many cases, even when cleared, its productiveness is wholly the effect of labor and art. The Bedford Level produced little or nothing until artificially drained. The bogs of Ireland, until the same thing is done to them, can produce little besides fuel. One of the barrenest soils in the world, composed of the material of the Goodwin Sands, the Pays de Waes in Flanders, has been so fertilized by industry, as to have become one of the most productive in Europe. Cultivation also requires buildings and fences, which are wholly the produce of labor. The fruits of this industry cannot be reaped in a short period. The labor and outlay are immediate, the benefit is spread over many years, perhaps over all future time. A holder will not incur this labor and outlay, when his successors, and not himself, will be benefited by it. If he undertakes such improvements, he must have a long period before him in which to profit by them: and he cannot continue always to have a long period before him, unless his tenure is perpetual."

Again, land usually does not long continue in the possession of the person, or even of the natural heirs of the person, who first appropriated it, or took it out of the common stock. He sells it to another, who pays a price for it out of the accumulated fruits of his previous industry, these fruits being his own property by the highest title under which property is ever held. Society cannot reclaim the land, then, without stripping the present owners of their rights, which they have acquired in the most unexceptionable manner. Whatever claim the community may have, is good only against him who first wrongly appropriated what was not his own, and not against one who now possesses nothing that he has not fairly paid for out of the proceeds of his previous industry and frugality, and who has vested his wealth in a purchase of land under the tacit sanction of the public, who cannot, at this late day, retrieve the consequences of their previous neglect without gross injustice.

Little reasoning is needed to confute the theory of the Communists, who propose an equal division of goods as a remedy for nearly all the evils with which society is afflicted. They are not aware, or do not reflect, that the sight of the two extremes of opulence and poverty, — the hope of rising to the one and the fear of falling into the other, — is the constant stimulus which keeps up that energy and activity of the human race, through which alone these goods are created. Make men secure of a provision for all their wants, take away from them all objects of ambition, destroy both anxiety and emulation, — and these are the certain results of an enforced equality of property and condition, — and after a few years, even if there remained anything to be divided among them, (which there would not, for their wastefulness under such circumstances would equal their indolence,) they would become useless and discontented drones, devoured by ennui, or eager for wrangling and fighting with each other, as the only means of relieving their otherwise stagnant existence.

But the theorists tell us, that the necessity of laboring for the good of the community would be a motive to action, which would supply the place of the necessity which every person now feels of laboring for himself. We answer, that the common adage, "what is everybody's business is nobody's," is enough to show the folly of this supposition, which implies great ignorance of the dispositions of mankind. The commonest observation proves, that, to make a man industrious, you must show him that the fruits of his industry will be wholly his own; if he is to share them equally with a thousand others, who have not shared the particular effort which produced them, he will throw aside his implements of labor in disgust, or relinquish them on the first approach of weariness. The motive to exertion must be immediate, or it will not be sufficiently pungent. It matters not, if you prove to him by a demonstration, that his individual welfare is inseparably connected with the interests of the whole community. Men do not act from such far-sighted calculation as this; they look first to their own interests at the present moment. Practically, each one will argue thus: 'I am but a unit in a vast multitude, and the effect which my idleness or industry at this time will have on the general welfare, will be a quantity too small to be appreciated; and little as the general stock will be diminished by my refusal to work, my personal share of that diminution or loss, being the quotient after another division among the whole multitude, will be an infinitesimal of the second degree, an atom that I cannot distinguish, — while the effort to overcome my present unwillingness to labor will be considerable. I will remain idle, then.' This is very selfish and short-sighted reasoning, it is true; but it needs very little knowledge of human nature to convince one, that it is the only way in which the bulk of mankind will reason, and very little calculation of consequences to see what would be the result, if every member of the community should thus think and act.

Of course, we shall be told that men must be educated, and taught to act with more foresight and less selfishness, and from considerations of duty and benevolence, instead of blindly following the impulses of the moment. Certainly, let them be educated, and their moral condition be improved, by all means; when they have become universally intelligent, philanthropic, and industrious, and are no longer actuated by selfish motives, property may well be abolished, and society may exist under any form, for the social state cannot then fail to be a happy one, however constituted. Meanwhile, as this work of improving the character of the whole race will probably be a slow and tedious one, and as the new institutions will not be practicable till it is completed, it might be well to commence with the opulent classes alone, who are comparatively few in number, and who, when converted and made purely benevolent and unselfish, will need no persuasion, no new framework of society, to induce them to share their goods equally with their less fortunate brethren. Human nature, as it is now constituted, it is evident, is not compatible with the maintenance of your new institutions; any such improvement in it as might render it fit for their support, would take away the necessity of making any change.

The general advantages of the institution of property are so obvious, that it may be said to exist by general consent. Without it, mankind would relapse into barbarism, — nay, into the condition of the wild beasts; for even a tribe of savages cannot live together without exclusive ownership of their rude tools, arms, clothing, and habitations. No one would submit to the labor of tilling the ground, because others would have an equal right with him to reap the harvest. No man would even erect a hut, if his neighbors could claim possession of it as soon as it was completed. Prudence and frugality would be impossible virtues; no provision for the future would be made, if those who wasted and spoiled were allowed to enjoy that provision as well as those who saved it. No society could be organized; for the only bond of association is the possession of certain property and rights, from the enjoyment of which those who are not members of the society are excluded. Universal want would lead to universal war, and that condition of mankind which Hobbes imagined as the inevitable result of the evil principles of human nature, when not checked by despotism, would become a fearful reality.

To guard against these tremendous evils, the sacredness of property is recognized, government is instituted for its protection, and laws are made to facilitate its increase, to regulate its use, and to provide for the distribution of it, when the death of its producer or former owner leaves it to the disposal of his survivors. The rule almost universally adopted in the last case is, to distribute it among those who are nearest of kin to the deceased, though in very different proportions, according to the different policy of the law in different countries. A man's nearest relations are commonly said to be his natural heirs, not because they have any natural or indefeasible right to his estates, but because they are nearest to his affections, and, if his will were to be consulted, they would generally succeed to the ownership. The strongest *natural* claim to property thus left vacant is surely that of the community at large, to whom, if it be land, it originally belonged, and under whose protection and by whose aid, whether it be real or personal, it was accumulated. Their claim, in fact, is universally admitted, as they assume the power of giving the property away by designating the persons who shall inherit it, and the proportions which they shall respectively hold. And there is no doubt that society acts wisely in consulting the wishes of the original proprietor, by limiting the succession to his own family or his nearest connections. Industry and economy are thus promoted, as every one is encouraged to labor and to save up to the close of his life, since those who are dearest to him are to have the sole benefit of his accumulations. If he had only a life interest in his estate, if society at large, or individuals who were entire strangers to him, were to be his heirs, his exertions would be limited to the attainment of a fortune barely sufficient to supply his own wants. He would spend both income and principal, and be reckless of the future, so that he had enough left for the necessities of his own declining years. Family ties, also, would be weakened or destroyed by a law giving the inheritance to strangers; children would have less motive to reverence their parents, who could not labor to promote the welfare of their offspring, except for the brief remaining period of their own existence; and as the admirable constitution of our moral nature is such, that we always love those most upon whom we have conferred the greatest benefits, parental affection under these circumstances would be very sensibly diminished. Besides, such a law could be executed only very imperfectly. Invention, stimulated by affection, would be constantly on the rack to evade it, by fraudulent transfers and sales effected during the lifetime of the first owners; and the attempt to prevent such practices would lead to intolerable inquisition into private and domestic concerns, and to endless litigation.

It is from the wisest reasons, therefore, from the most judicious regard to the general welfare, that the law gives the property of a person deceased intestate to the nearest of kin. Still, there is room for a wide discretion in determining the principles on which the estate shall be divided among those who stand in the same degree of relationship to the first proprietor. Shall any regard be paid to the wishes of the deceased in this respect? Shall all share alike? Or what preference shall be shown to the sons over the daughters, or to the first-born over his brothers and sisters? These are grave questions, and on the answers to them, more, we had almost said, than on all other causes united, the form of government and the welfare of the people, the whole political and social framework of society, in every country, must ultimately depend. Notwithstanding their immense importance, these questions have not, till of late years, been much discussed either by legislators or political economists. "I am surprised," says M. De Tocqueville, "that ancient and modern jurists have not attributed a greater importance to the laws of inheritance. It is true, they belong to civil affairs; but they ought, nevertheless, to be placed at the head of all political institutions; for, while political laws are only the symbols of a nation's condition, those which determine the descent of property exercise an extraordinary influence over its social state. They operate in a uniform and certain manner. Man acquires through their means a kind of preternatural power over the destiny of unborn generations. When the legislator has established the laws of succession, he may rest from his labors. The machine is a self-acting one, and when once put in motion, it will advance steadily, as of its own accord, towards the previously appointed end. Adjusted in one manner, it brings together, concentrates, and heaps up property first, and power afterwards, in the hands of a few; it causes an aristocracy, so to speak, to spring out of the grouud. Adjusted on different principles, and turned another way, its action is still more rapid; it now breaks up, pulverizes, and disseminates wealth and power. It crushes or shatters every obstacle that is found in its path; it rises and falls upon the ground with repeated blows, till there is no longer anything to be seen but an impalpable and moving dust on which democracy is seated."

And long before De Tocqueville, in an address delivered at Plymouth in 1820, Mr. Webster said: "A republican form of government rests, not more on political constitutions, than on those laws which regulate the descent and transmission of property. Governments like ours could not have been maintained where property was holden according to the principles of the feudal system; nor, on the other hand, could the feudal constitution possibly exist with us. Our New England ancestors brought hither no great capitals from Europe; they were themselves, either from their original condition, or from the necessity of their common interest, nearly on a general level in respect to property. Their situation demanded a parcelling out and division of the lands; and it may be fairly said, that this necessary act fixed the future frame and form of their government. The character of their political institutions was determined by the fundamental laws respecting property. The laws rendered estates divisible among sons and daughters. The right of primogeniture, at first limited and curtailed, was afterwards abolished. The property was all freehold. The entailment of estates, long trusts, and the other processes for fettering and tying up inheritances, were not applicable to the condition of society, and seldom made use of. On the contrary, alienation of the land was every way facilitated, even to the subjecting of it to every species of debt. The establishment of public registries, and the simplicity of our forms of conveyance, have greatly facilitated the change of real estate from one proprietor to another. The consequence of all these causes has been, a great subdivision of the soil, and a great equality of condition; the true basis, most certainly, of a popular government.

" A most interesting experiment of the effect of a subdivision of property on government is now making in France. The law regulating the transmission of property in that country now divides it, real and personal, among all the children equally, both sons and daughters; and there is, also, a very great restraint on the power of making dispositions of property by will. It has been supposed, that the effect of this might probably be, in time, to break up the soil into such small subdivisions, that the proprietors would be too poor to resist the encroachments of executive power. I think far otherwise. What is lost in individual wealth will be more than gained in numbers, in intelligence, and in a sympathy of sentiment. I would, presumptuously perhaps, hazard a conjecture, that if the government do not change the law, the law, in half a century, will change the government; and this change will not be in favor of the power of the crown, as some European writers have supposed, but against it." *

In just ten years, this remarkable prediction was fulfilled by the revolution of 1830; and in less than twenty years more, by the still more democratic revolution of 1848.

---

* Webster's *Works*, Vol. I. pp. 35 - 37. I have condensed the extract.

That the extremes of opulence and destitution should exist side by side, a few revelling in the enjoyment of immense fortunes, while millions around them are suffering from the want of all the comforts, and even of the necessaries, of life, is the great reproach of modern civilization. Men have acquiesced in the evil only because they believed it to be irreparable. Any attempt to remove the inequality of property was supposed to threaten the security of the institution itself, and thus to lead immediately to the dissolution of society and government, and to the destruction of all the higher interests of the human family. The subject would not bear to be tampered with; the sensibility of the community upon this point is feverish in the extreme. To excite their fears, to shake their confidence in the permanency of the institution as it exists, is enough to break the springs of industry and enterprise at once, and to cause nearly as much mischief as a complete social revolution. Changes in the laws affecting the distribution of wealth, therefore, are seldom proposed, except in the course of some great political convulsion, when the foundations of society are broken up, and the whole fabric is to be placed on a new basis, and erected anew.

Sudden changes, then, are out of the question; they would only enhance, or render universal, the evils which we seek to remedy. The only inquiry is, whether causes may not be set to work which will tend slowly but irresistibly to the equalization of wealth, without exciting alarm, or affecting the present enjoyment of property, or injuring any vested rights, or lessening to any appreciable extent the motives for accumulation. If the diffusion of capital, the division of estates, and the consequent approach to equality of condition, when thus gradually effected, should act with resistless force upon the institutions of the state, and change the nature of the government, we need not deplore the result. In these modern days, political influence gravitates towards property, as in former ages it was always united with military strength. Riches are but another name for power, either in a republic, a monarchy, or a despotism; and as the possession of them, when fairly earned, not inherited, is usually coupled with sobriety, prudence, industry, and good sense, and, above all, with a distrust of innovation and a love of order, it is well that they should have the command or the leading influence in the state. A due regard for equality of rights, then, only requires that wealth should be open to the attainment of all, that it should never be made inalienable or indivisible by its present holder, never be locked up by legal proceedings which bind future generations, but be left to circulate freely as air, and to find its natural level, as water does, by diffusion in broad seas and oceans. The acquisition of it will thus be a natural test of character, ability, and intelligence, and political power can nowhere be more safely lodged than in the hands of its possessors. In a country where no one is poor except by his own fault, where misery is not as necessarily inherited by one class as immense wealth is by another, where pauperism never exists except as a consequence of folly, indolence, or crime, the holders of property may justly claim the exclusive control of the state. They will not need to have this power expressly given to them by laws and constitutions; it will naturally and inevitably fall into their possession, — so much of it, at least, as they shall deem necessary for their own security and happiness.

Admitting these general principles, then, that property ought to be made inviolable, that it should descend only to the family or kindred of the deceased, and be distributed among them from a regard, not to their private interests, but to the welfare of the whole community, (though these two ends in the long run will be identical,) we come to inquire into the policy of the different laws by which, in different countries, this distribution is effected. We take it for granted, that great inequality of wealth in any country is a great national evil, to be avoided or lessened by the use of all just means which are consistent with the security of property itself. If such inequality be permitted to continue or increase, except from inevitable necessity, the conduct of the legislators who foster or permit it becomes criminal in the extreme; upon their heads are justly chargeable the privation and wretchedness, the moral and intellectual degradation, the famines and plagues, which it brings upon millions of their fellow-beings.

The only systems of law regulating the succession to property which need here be considered are those which obtain respectively in England, in the United States, and in France; and the social condition of the people in these three countries may be taken as a guide to the effects of these laws, and of the customs and institutions which are encouraged or created by them, and with which they are necessarily connected. The general policy of the law is sure to direct the inclinations and habits of the people, so that the law is justly chargeable with the effects, not only of what it directly enjoins, but of what it permits, exemplifies, and fosters.

Thus, in England, the right of primogeniture applies only to the real property of intestates; but the effect of the example and sanction of the law is, to induce even those who make wills to devise the larger share of all the property, and very often the whole of the real estate, to the oldest son. Entails are allowed during the lifetime of any number of persons actually in being, and till the first unborn heir shall be twenty-one years old;* and further, any heir of entail may grant leases which will be good against the future owners of the estate for three lives. Numerous other impediments are created to the sale or division of real estates, and the people are thus encouraged to carry out the policy of the law by settlements, trust processes, and other legal devices; so that, at any one time, the real property of the kingdom is as safely tied up and guarded against the extravagance or wilfulness of the actual possessor, as if perpetual entail were permitted there, as it was till recently in Scotland. It is estimated, that more than one half of all the real estate in the latter country was thus protected for ever against division or alienation from particular families. In France, on the other hand, where the law requires the larger portion of the property to be distributed equally, the people readily acquiesce in the principle, and very seldom exercise their power of increasing the share of a favorite child by the small portion which they are allowed to give according to their own judgment or fancy; if we may judge from the Paris returns, not more than one person out of seven makes a will at all, and but one in eighteen of these testators gives the reserved portion to one of his legal heirs, so as to lessen the number of

* "An English gentleman," says McCulloch, "may entail an estate on any heir, or series of heirs, during the longest life of certain parties named or clearly specified in the deed, and alive when it was made, and till twenty-one years after the death of the last surviving nominee. It is immaterial whether the parties taken as nominees be parties on whom the estate may or may not devolve."

parts into which the estate is divided, the others preferring to bestow it upon strangers. In both countries, then, the consent of the people carries out the general policy of the law, favoring or preventing the distribution of property, just as the legislature determines in those cases which are settled by the law alone, without regard to the wishes of the owners.

Here in America, the law takes the middle course between the English and the French policy. The custom of gavelkind is the rule, unequal distribution is the exception. Entails are generally more restricted than in England, perpetual entails being never allowed; and all minor restrictions on the division or sale of landed estates being taken away, the partition or transfer of real property is effected about as easily as that of movables. On the other hand, the law does not oblige a parent to distribute his property equally, but he may make what distinctions he chooses, and may virtually disinherit all his children, if he sees fit. But the custom follows the law; many persons do not make a will, but allow the law to take its course. A testator seldom makes a very unequal distribution among his children; but if he is childless, he often disposes of his property according to fancy, the expectations of more distant heirs not being much regarded.

From the operation of these laws in the three countries, we might naturally expect that there would be monstrous inequalities in the distribution of wealth in England, while in France and this country, property would be as nearly at a level in the community as it can be brought by the influence of legislation. It is true, that the several systems must have time to operate before their full effects can be perceived. The French system did not come into full effect till the revolution of 1789; it was one, and the most effective of all, of the sweeping measures adopted at that epoch for the sole purpose of breaking the power of the feudal aristocracy. Only two generations having elapsed since that time, it might be supposed that the splitting of landed estates and the general subdivision of property have not yet been carried out there to their full extent, but that the equalization of wealth is destined to go much further.

This may be doubted; here in New England, where the law of equal partition, applied directly only to the property of intestates, but governing in fact the descent of nearly all property, has been in force for more than two centuries, the land is by no means so much subdivided as in France; and we have probably more persons of large fortune, in proportion to the whole population, than can be found in any department of that country. If the farm is already so small that it will not support more than one family with the average degree of comfort among landholders of the same class, one of the heirs will buy out the others, who will use the price of their shares as means for establishing themselves in some non-agricultural employment, or in some other locality. In truth, it is demonstrable that there must be this limit to the division of estates; for if the ground owned and cultivated by a small proprietor be insufficient for the support of his family, his poverty will oblige him to sell it, and the purchaser, of course, must be a person more wealthy than himself. It is idle, then, to talk of the risk of the whole country falling into the hands of a set of pauper proprietors; the first symptoms of pauperism will oblige them to alienate their lands, and capitalists will reunite the farms which had been injured by excessive subdivision. The ability to purchase can never be wanting, as all the natural causes of inequality of wealth operate without check during each complete generation; for during this period, they are not counteracted by laws regulating the succession to property. We can, therefore, readily admit the conclusion which has been drawn from statistical evidence,* that the smaller properties in France have not sensibly diminished in size during the last thirty years. Possibly these small estates may increase in number through the breaking up of larger ones; but they will not be

* M. Legoyt, in an article published in the "Dictionary of Political Economy," in 1854, says that he has examined the state of the case for 122 cantons belonging to twenty-seven departments, taken indifferently from the north, south, east, west, and centre of France, and has established the following results. Forty-eight cantons, belonging to eleven different departments, were divided, in 1815, into 2,754,885 estates or separate properties; and in 1847, they had only 2,438,062 such estates, being a diminution of thirteen per cent in thirty-two years. In the seventy-four other cantons, belonging to sixteen departments, there were 2,846,971 separate properties in 1815, and in 1847 there were 3,096,235, being an increase of less than nine per cent in thirty-two years. Taking the aggregate for the 122 cantons, which comprise nearly a third part of all France, it appears that there were 5,601,856 estates in 1815, and only 5,534,297 in 1847, being a diminution of over one per cent. It is very evident, then, that the *morcellement* or subdivision of landed property in France has reached its limit, and has probably begun to decline.

more contracted in dimension, for, if smaller, they would not support a single family.

Among the ancients, as a general rule, all property, on the death of the owner, descended as a matter of course to his children, or, if he had none, to his nearest relatives. In Athens, Solon confined the privilege of making a will to such as had no children; before his time, the estate was necessarily divided among the nearest of kin. In Rome, for a long period, children could be disinherited only by a will made in an assembly of the people, so that the act was not so much that of an individual as of the legislature. In the later ages of the Empire, the law required all the children of the testator to be named in the will, and if any one of them was disinherited, that special reasons should be given for such treatment. And the heir thus excluded might bring an action to test the validity of these reasons; if they were found insufficient, the will was set aside, and the disinherited child was admitted with the others to what the law termed their "legitimate portion" of the paternal estate. Before the Code and the Pandects were compiled, this portion amounted to one fourth of the whole. Justinian decreed, that, if there were not more than four children, they should succeed as of right to a third part of the property; if more than four, they received at least one half. Among the Germans, also, as we are informed by Tacitus, the children were protected in their natural heirship, and the right to devise property away from them was not allowed. Hence it appears that the French law of compulsory partition is no innovation; the voice of antiquity generally is in its favor, as consonant with reason and the natural sense of equity.

The right of primogeniture, and the privilege of entailing estates, or devising them to a series of heirs, any one of whom has only a life-interest in the property, without the power of alienating it or burdening it with debt, had their origin in the feudal system. Before the rise of feudalism, it is true, males were in some instances preferred to females, and the eldest son had some advantages over his brethren; thus, according to the Jewish law, he had a double share, a peculiarity which was borrowed from the Mosaic code for a short time by the first settlers of New England. In Anglo-Saxon times, even in Old England, all the property, whether real or personal, was divided equally among the sons, if there were any; if not, among the daughters. "The green network of hedges spread over the face of England, that peculiar charm of English land," is attributed by Mr. Laing to this circumstance; it could have been formed only by a nation of small proprietors, among whom the land was partitioned off by these enclosures into fields of very moderate extent. In Scotland, France, and Germany, where the feudal system gave the original law of real property, these small enclosures do not exist; the face of the country is not marked by permanent lines of division, but expands in broad and unenclosed districts. In England, even down to the time of Henry II., personal property or movables were divided into three equal portions, one of which went of right to the widow, another to the lineal descendants, and the direction of the third only was left to the will of the testator; if there were no children, the widow took one half, and the other half might be disposed of by testament.

But generally, at the time of the Norman conquest, the principles of the feudal system were introduced into the kingdom, and an entire change was made in the rules which determined the succession to the estates of persons deceased. The system which was then established in England, though it has undergone some changes of form, has continued, on the whole, with fewer alterations on essential points than in any other country in Europe. It was eminently favorable to the nobles and the gentry, and its continuance has kept up the power and real influence of the aristocracy in Great Britain, while almost everywhere else, especially during the present century, it has rapidly declined. The aggregation of real property into immense landed estates, and a very unequal distribution of movable goods, have been the economical results of this preservation of the principles of the feudal system relating to the succession, after every other trace of that system had disappeared. England is now as much an aristocratic country, is as much under the dominion of her great barons, as it was in the days of Warwick, "the King-maker"; only the power of the nobles now rests, not on their arms, but on their wealth. In France and most other kingdoms on the Continent, the triangular contest between the people, the nobles, and the sovereign terminated in a partial union of the people and the crown, which made the latter practically absolute, and enabled it either to crush the aristocracy, or to render it entirely subservient to the throne. But in England, the barons and the gentry wisely espoused the popular cause, and took the lead in wresting from the crown the Great Charter, the Statute of Treasons, the Petition and the Bill of Rights, and the other time-honored muniments of English freedom. Thus they have been more than a match for the crown, and have never entirely lost the support of the people. They have never become unpopular as a class, but have preserved their vast estates and their social weight and influence along with them. Their political privileges have been from time to time abridged; but their "weight in the country," to adopt a phrase which is peculiarly English, is now as great as ever. The aristocracy of France, on the other hand, is extinct, that of Spain is effete, that of Germany and Italy hardly exists except in name. Its influence in these countries has not been great enough to preserve the laws by which alone great landed estates could be kept together and preserved through successive generations; and without such estates, political power is an accident, and titles are an idle distinction. In fact, titles have usually multiplied as the power of the nobles has declined.

Feudal estates were held, for the most part, on condition of rendering military service, and therefore could not pass into the possession of females, except when the male line was extinct. There were obvious inconveniences, also, in the partition of such estates; for in military arithmetic, the sum of all the parts is not equal to the whole. A great baron, who could bring a thousand armed retainers to the wars, was a match for at least twenty of the inferior nobles, each of whom could not muster more than a hundred followers. "The security of a landed estate," says Adam Smith, "the protection which its owner could afford to those who dwelt on it, depended on its greatness. To divide it was to ruin it, and to expose every part of it to be oppressed and swallowed up by the incursions of its neighbors. The law of primogeniture, therefore, came to take place, not immediately indeed, but in process of time, in the succession of landed estates, for the same reason that it has generally taken place in that of monarchies, though not always at their first institution. That the power, and consequently the security, of the monarchy may not be weakened by division, it must descend entire to one of the children. To which of them so important a preference shall be given, must be determined by some general rule, founded, not upon the doubtful distinctions of personal merit, but upon some plain and evident difference which can admit of no dispute. Among the children of the same family, there can be no indisputable difference but that of sex and that of age. The male sex is universally preferred to the female, and when all other things are equal, the elder everywhere takes the place of the younger. Hence the origin of the right of primogeniture, and of what is called lineal succession." Fortunately for the English nobility, also, the law of England, unlike that of most kingdoms on the Continent, caused the title as well as the property to descend only to the oldest son; the younger children were mere commoners, and therefore did not make hereditary honors cheap by multiplying them, or uniting them with poverty. The younger branches of the family found their own importance enhanced by ministering to the greatness of the head of their house. If they acquired wealth and reputation for themselves, they buttressed the strength of the main trunk in their family pedigree; if they were poor and weak, they were lost in the crowd, and cast no shade on the splendor of the house whence they originated.

But it is not enough to satisfy the pride and ambition of the nobles, that the estate should be kept together, and in the possession of one person. Means must be devised also to prevent it from being alienated, or passing out of the family altogether. The eldest son might be a sot, a spendthrift, or a simpleton, from whose witless grasp the broad paternal acres might slip into the hands of parasites, gamblers, and creditors. To obviate such a misfortune, the property was entailed on a succession of heirs, no one of whom had a right to spend more than its annual income, or to burden it with debt. Besides, attainder for treason or felony might cause a forfeiture of the estate to the crown; but if the present possessor held only a life-interest in it under an entail, the property would pass at his death, in spite of the attainder, to the next heir, whose rights could not be impaired by the criminality of a previous life-holder, any more than by that of a steward or a tenant.

The property was not his, either to be forfeited or to be alienated by sale or debt. Of course, it was for the interest of the crown to prevent entails, but of the nobles and other great landholders to multiply them, and to render them strict and perpetual. Under Edward I., when the power of the barons was nearly at its height, they succeeded in passing the statute entitled *De donis conditionalibus*, which established a system of perpetual entail, each successive heir receiving the land only *under condition*, as the lawyers say, of not alienating it, but of transmitting it unimpaired to his successor. Such laws, as Adam Smith remarks, "are founded upon the most absurd of all suppositions, — the supposition that every successive generation of men have not an equal right to the earth and to all that it possesses; but that the property of the present generation should be restrained and regulated according to the fancy of those who died, perhaps, five hundred years ago." But the statute of Edward's parliament remained in force for over two centuries, which was more than enough to manifest its injurious results. "The inconvenience thereof was great," says Lord Bacon; "for by that means, the land being so sure tied upon the heir as that his father could not put it from him, it made the son to be disobedient, negligent, and wasteful; often marrying without the father's consent, and to grow insolent in vice, knowing that there could be no check of disinheriting him. It also made the owners of the land less fearful to commit murders, felonies, treasons, and manslaughters; for that they knew none of these acts could hurt the heir of his inheritance. It hindered men that had entailed lands, that they could not make the best of their lands by fine and improvement, for that none, upon so uncertain an estate as for term of his own life, would give him a fine of any value, nor lay any great stock upon the land, that might yield rent improved. Lastly, those entails did defraud the crown and many subjects of their debts; for that the land was not liable longer than his own lifetime; which caused that the king could not safely commit any office of account to such whose lands were entailed, nor other men trust them with loan of money."

These inconveniences, and the decline of the power of the nobles under the Tudors, enabled those arbitrary monarchs to do away practically with the law of perpetual entail; though not repealed by the legislature, it was nullified by a contrivance of the lawyers and the courts, which enabled the party in possession, by a fictitious suit, to bar the entail, and part with the estate by an ordinary conveyance. This method of destroying perpetuities has been simplified and extended by acts of Parliament during the last quarter of a century, so as to establish the law of entail on its present footing, the owner of real estate being allowed, as already mentioned, only to tie it up during any number of lives already in being, and for twenty-one years after. In Scotland, however, the nobility and gentry having suffered much from forfeiture during the seventeenth century, a law was passed in 1685, authorizing landholders to entail their estates in perpetuity; and five years afterwards, another statute expressly exempted entailed estates from confiscation, on the ground that every man ought to "suffer for his own fault, and not the innocent with or for the guilty." Under these acts, more than half of all Scotland was fettered by strict entail for ever;* and though the manifest evils of such restraint caused the statesmen and lawyers of the kingdom to make several vigorous efforts to change the law, the land-owners successfully resisted them till a few years ago, when Parliament passed an act which carried into Scotland all the important features of the English system of entail.

As political power and social influence in England have always followed the ownership of real estate, all the contrivances of legal ingenuity have been brought into play to prevent the division or alienation of landed property, and to preserve

---

* But the Scotch mode of regulating the distribution of personal property offers a strange contrast with this custom of tying up the real estate. "The law of Scotland," says McCulloch, "in regard to the devising of movables, is at present nearly identical with the old law of England. In the former, if a father die leaving a widow and children, whether of the last or any former marriage, the children succeed to a third part of his movable property as *legitim* (from the *legitima pars* of the Romans), and the widow to another third part. If there be no widow, or if she have renounced by her marriage contract the *jus relictæ*, the *legitim* of the children amounts to half the personal estate. And it is further to be observed, that the right of the children to claim their *legitim* cannot be defeated by testament; though it may be defeated by the father converting his movable into fixed property, and by his executing a *de presenti* conveyance of his whole movable estate to others."

This is very nearly the French law of compulsory partition, though applied only to personal property.

the nominal ownership in the family, even after the substance has been dissipated, or the estate so heavily burdened with mortgages and other encumbrances that the ostensible proprietor can derive little or no income from it. Since the right of primogeniture takes effect only in case of intestacy, so that it can be defeated by making a will, and as an entail is valid only for a limited period, it would seem that the property must be frequently liable to pass out of the family. It is possible to make entails effectual for a century or more; but McCulloch says, "this is not often done, and fifty or sixty years may, perhaps, be assumed as their usual average duration." But the aristocratic feeling prevails so generally through successive generations, that no sooner is one deed of entail discharged, than it is renewed by the parties interested in the estate; and thus, with the aid of marriage settlements, trust deeds, and other similar devices, nearly all the landed property in England, at any one moment, is as effectually tied up as if it were subjected to perpetual entail.

Mr. Byles, an English sergeant-at-law, remarks, "estates are kept in families, not by the law of entail, but by the power which exists of creating life-estates." When a land-owner marries, he wishes to make provision for his wife and the issue of the marriage after his death; and to do so, he makes over his estate to the children of the marriage successively, reserving only a life-interest in the property for himself; in legal phrase, "he becomes tenant for life, his son tenant in remainder. As soon as the eldest son comes of age, he can make way with his interest, just as his father could before him; or father and son may join, and sometimes do join, in alienating the estate altogether. But in practice, the more usual course is this: the son is about to marry, and is advised, or chooses, to settle a life-estate on himself, and to provide, after his death, for his wife and the issue of the marriage. He resettles the estate"; that is, he takes it out of the market again, by tying it up against division or alienation for another generation. "And so, in fact, estates are kept together and resettled every generation, by the voluntary act, or, if you please, the family pride, of their owners, and not by the law of entail. Indeed, personal property may be settled by means of life-estates as effectually as landed property, and the fund may be, and often is, tied up just as long; although such a thing as an estate tail in personal property never existed at any period of our law."

In one respect, indeed, this mode of keeping the property together and preventing it from going out of the family by a perpetual series of marriage settlements, trust-deeds, entails, and other legal devices, is more injurious in its consequences than the mode of tying it up once for all, and for ever, by a perpetual entail. In the latter case, unless power is granted by a special statute for the purpose, there is no power of burdening or encumbering the estate by mortgages, rent-charges, rights of dower, settlement of annuities, long leases at low rents purchased by a heavy payment outright at the commencement of the lease, and other modes of consuming the income in advance, while the estate is nominally intact. When the heir under a perpetual entail comes into possession, he finds that, though he cannot divide or sell the estate, or make any provision from it for his widow or unportioned children, he has, at least, the whole income of it undiminished for his lifetime. He does not find himself in the mortifying and embarrassed condition, of nominally owning an estate of £10,000 a year, with an establishment of corresponding splendor and magnitude to be kept up, while his actual income does not exceed one or two thousand pounds. But this is too frequently his case, if the estate, instead of being under perpetual entail, has been settled and resettled again and again; if one set of fetters upon it has been removed every generation or two, only to make room for another. For at each period of renewal or settlement, there have been debts to be secured, wives to be dowered, daughters and younger sons to be provided for, and loans to be obtained on mortgage in order to erect buildings or effect other improvements. Family pride prevents these charges from being met in the natural manner, by selling a portion of the estate; the whole number of acres must be retained, but under an encumbrance which annually subtracts a fixed sum from the income. At each successive period, as a general rule, the number and amount of these encumbrances are increased, till they at last absorb the greater part of the income. "Nor is even this all," says Mr. Byles; "men like to round their estates. They buy up and engross the little neighboring properties, and charge the whole estate with money to pay for the new purchase. Thus the complication of settlements and charges embraces and corrupts even the sound parts, like the hideous roots of a cancer." * In respect to one's worldly prospects, the greatest misfortune which can happen to a man in Great Britain is, to be born heir to a large and heavily burdened estate.

A strict system of perpetual entail opposes an almost insurmountable barrier to making improvements upon the land, since each holder of a life-interest in the estate is unwilling to expend any portion of the income upon it, because the beneficial consequences of such expenditure will be reaped chiefly by his successors. Leaseholders for short terms, also, cannot be expected to make permanent improvements, the advantages of which will be chiefly experienced by the owners of the property, and by those who may come after them under subsequent leases, with whom they have no tie of a common interest, affection, or kindred. These evils of the Scotch system being great and notorious, Parliament applied a partial remedy, first in 1770, and again in 1824. The former act authorized the life-holder, in spite of any prohibition in the deed of entail, to grant leases for ninety-nine years of small patches of ground, not exceeding five acres, for the purpose of building; it also empowered him to burden the estate to the amount of six years' rent, for agricultural improvements and the erection of a mansion-house, provided that he contributed out of his own income towards these objects one fourth as much as was charged upon the estate. The act of 1824 made a still greater innovation; it allowed the possessor, notwithstanding any prohibition in the deed, to make provision out of the estate for his widow and younger children; and the limit of the encumbrances thus authorized, under both acts, was fixed at two thirds of the net annual income. Thus, as McCulloch remarks, "the income of the heir in possession of an entailed estate may be reduced to a third part of its net rental; and out of this portion, he has to keep up the mansion-house, and to defray the whole expense

* Few readers can have forgotten the saddest story in all literary biography, — that of Sir Walter Scott virtually killing himself by over-exertion, and reducing the finest genius since Shakespeare's day to idiocy, in the vain attempt to pay off vast encumbrances on the large landed estate which he had imprudently collected, in the hope of "founding a family" that could hold its place for all time among the landed gentry of Scotland. And that family, though he left four children, two of whom were sons, — where is it?

of managing the estate, including the losses incurred by the failure of tenants, and such like contingencies. Hence it follows, that the free disposable income of an heir of entail in possession of an estate of £ 12,000 a year may not, and sometimes does not, exceed £1,500 or £ 2,000 a year." No wonder, then, that Parliament came at last to believe, that a system of perpetual entail leading to such consequences was not worth keeping up, and abrogated it by the law of 1848, which permitted all perpetuities to be broken, and assimilated the Scotch to the English system of entail.

Two peculiar circumstances tended to increase the burdens upon real estate in Ireland. Far the larger portion of the island had been confiscated since the reign of Henry VIII., and the crown had granted immense estates out of the forfeited lands to courtiers, military officers, and noblemen, who preferred to live in England, and to let their property on long leases to others, who assumed all the care of management. In Great Britain, property can be leased only for a limited period of years; but in Ireland, it has been the custom to grant a lease for a certain number of lives, with a covenant for perpetual renewal, on the payment of a moderate fine on the fall of each life. Thus the lands are virtually leased in perpetuity, and the amount so leased, says Mr. Pim, "is very great, perhaps as much as one half of Ireland." This is not all; the first leaseholder on a perpetuity again lets out the land to others, who in their turn underlet it in smaller portions, an increased rent being charged at each remove. These intermediate landlords, or "middlemen" as they are termed, and perpetual leases, are two peculiar encumbrances upon Irish estates, in addition to the marriage settlements, mortgages, heavy annuities, and family charges, with which they are as heavily burdened as English or Scotch property.

The impoverishment of the land, the decline in value of real estate, the distress of the landlord, and the misery of the tenantry, are the inevitable results of this condition of things. The present landlord has no interest in its improvement, except so far as he may wish to benefit the heir at law who is to succeed him. If, as is generally the case, he has daughters and younger sons to provide for, whatever savings he can make from income he will not expend upon the land, but will invest in other forms, where they will be subject to his control by will. Thus the fences and buildings are allowed to decay, drainage is neglected, the ground is scourged with exhausting crops, and the tenants in possession are oppressed with the heaviest possible rents, the object being to obtain the utmost present gain from the estate, at whatever injury to the future value. Mr. Pim describes a "by no means uncommon case," in which the heir comes into possession of a deeply encumbered estate, when already "burdened with debts of his own, contracted on the faith of his inheritance, and borrowed on terms of usurious interest proportionate to the risk incurred. In what difficulties is he at once involved, this owner for life of a large tract of country, with a long rent-roll, but in fact a small property! He cannot maintain his position in society without spending more than his income; debts accumulate; he borrows on the credit of his life-interest, and insures his life for the security of the lender. He lets to the highest bidder, without regard to character or means of payment. His object is immediate income, not the future value of the property. If the tenants are without leases, he raises their rents. If leases fall in, he cannot afford to give the preference to the last occupier." He cannot sell a part of the property, though the proceeds of such sale might greatly improve the value of the remainder. "Perhaps, with all his exertion, he is unable to pay the interest, or put off his creditors. Proceedings are commenced against him, and the estate passes, during his lifetime, under the care of the worst possible landlord, — a receiver under the Court of Chancery." "In very many cases," says a respectable witness, "where encumbered estates have fallen under the management of law courts, the district has usually rather resembled one which has been plundered by an enemy, than one under an enlightened government, in a country long exempt from the calamities of war."

These evils having become intolerable, Parliament at last applied a remedy, in 1848, by creating by statute the commission for the sale of encumbered estates in Ireland. Under this act, an encumbered estate, by consent of the owner, or on application of the mortgagees or other creditors, might be at once released from all burdens by the high authority of Parliament, and sold to the highest bidder, with an indefeasible title good against all the world. The proceeds of the sale are paid into the Court of Chancery, to be distributed by that court, as equity may require, between the owner, his creditors, the various encumbrancers, the heirs at law, and all other interested parties. Thus the process was an easy and simple one; the legal burdens were all taken off the land, and applied only to the money which was received from the sale of it, the estate itself being sold to the greatest possible advantage, because free from all encumbrance, resting upon the best of all titles, a parliamentary one, and being divided into such portions as would best suit the convenience of the purchasers. Before this act was passed, the mortgages and other burdens covering the whole property equally, and even rendering, through their complication, the title to it very doubtful, it was impossible to sell a portion of the property; it could only be disposed of as a whole, and with a title so uncertain, and law expenses so heavy, that it would bring but a small part of its real value.

The proceedings under this statute afford curious evidence of the extent to which real property in Ireland had become encumbered. Up to October, 1854, upwards of two millions of acres had changed hands under the authority of this commission; it had sold 1,152 estates to 5,613 purchasers, for £13,509,303. Of these estates, 364 had been in Chancery over five years, 167 over ten years, 17 over thirty-five years, and 9 over fifty years. In about five years, more than one tenth of all the landed property in the island had passed through the hands of this commission. How much more is to undergo the same process, it is impossible to tell; but the proceedings have been delayed, in order to avoid crowding so much land upon the market at once as to depress the price. One of the most significant facts that appear from these returns is, that the land sold has been divided into about five times as many distinct estates as before. The amount of the encumbrances was such, that only a small portion of the proceeds of the sale of the property remained for the benefit of its former nominal owners.

I have entered into this detailed account of the state of landed property in Great Britain and Ireland, as affected by the tenure of land and by the laws regulating the succession to the estates of persons deceased, because it seems to me to afford almost a complete explanation of those striking peculiarities in the social and economical condition of the people of that country, by which they are distinguished from all other nations, and which have suggested those theories in political economy that affect the whole aspect of the science as it is taught by the English authorities upon the subject. Such theories as those of Malthus upon population, Ricardo upon rent and profits, Adam Smith upon free trade, and McCulloch upon this very matter of the succession to property, must have originated from experience in an anomalous state of society, from observation of the laws of wealth as exemplified in their operation under very peculiar circumstances. Any refutation of them would be insufficient which did not point out the phenomena by which they were suggested, and offer some explanation of these phenomena which should be consistent with general principles and facts of universal experience.

The avowed objects of the English laws which regulate the descent of property are, the concentration of wealth in the hands of a few, and the support of an hereditary territorial aristocracy. These ends have been obtained. The inequality in the distribution of wealth in England is greater than in any other civilized nation; and her nobility and gentry are wealthier, more intelligent, more highly cultivated, more influential, and more secure in the possession of their power and property, than the corresponding classes now existing, or that ever have existed, in any country in the world. Five noblemen, the Marquis of Breadalbane, the Dukes of Argyle, Athol, Sutherland, and Buccleuch, own perhaps one fourth of all Scotland.* I have already quoted the assertion of M. de Lavergne, that 2,000 proprietors possess among them one third of the land

* The estate of the Duke of Sutherland comprises about 700,000 acres, or considerably more than 1,000 square miles. The domains of the Marquis of Breadalbane, says M. de Lavergne, "extend one hundred English miles, or forty leagues, in length, and reach nearly from sea to sea." Both of these immense estates have been cleared of their ancient inhabitants, and the Highland clans by which they were not only occupied, but *owned*, have ceased, properly speaking, to exist; they have been driven into exile, or have been exterminated by privation and hardships. A few remnants of them inhabit some miserable fishing hamlets on the sea-shore, and swell the bulk of the destitute classes in the great cities. "By far the wealthiest proprietor in the Lowlands is the Duke of Buccleuch," whose estates extend over several counties, and whose palace at Dalkeith is an establishment of regal magnificence.

and total revenue of the three kingdoms of England, Scotland, and Ireland. It is admitted that, up to 1848, there were not more than 5,000 Scotch, and 8,000 Irish land-owners; and good reasons have been adduced (page 195) for the opinion, that there are only 46,000 who should be classed as landed proprietors in England. About 60,000 families, then, own all the territory which is occupied by over 27 millions of inhabitants.

In France, on the other hand, under the laws requiring the equal partition of the property of persons deceased, the aristocracy have virtually ceased to exist, and out of a population of about thirty-five millions, at least five and a half millions are landholders. Considering these as heads of families, and allowing on an average four persons to a family, we find that twenty-two millions, or nearly two thirds of the whole population, are owners of the soil. Making the same allowance for the families of British landholders, we have but 240,000 individuals, or about the 112th part of the people, who share among them the total rental of the United Kingdom, which amounts to more than sixty millions sterling. In France, it is estimated that there are two and a half millions of proprietors whose estates do not exceed an average of ten acres each, and three millions of others whose properties average about thirty acres.

These results of a comparison of the two countries in respect to the distribution of landed property are very startling, and would almost exceed belief, if it were not evident that the policy of the law so strongly favors aggregation in the one case, and partition in the other, that such consequences, sooner or later, are inevitable. A race of husbandmen living on their own small properties, and constituting what was called the yeomanry of the land, were formerly the principal cultivators in England and Wales. The larger portion of the population were then engaged in tilling the ground, which then produced more than enough for the national consumption, and there were no complaints that the country was over-peopled. But the race of small proprietors is now extinct; large estates and large farms have absorbed the small ones, and the agriculturists, who were once two thirds, now form but one fifth, of the whole population. The doctrine of the dominant school of

English economists is, that farming must be carried on like every other trade; that large farms, like large machine-shops, large cotton-mills, and large iron-works, can produce cheaper than small ones, and therefore, very properly, supersede and obliterate them. Whatever may be thought of the correctness of this doctrine, it has certainly been carried out in practice. According to the census of 1851, there are in Great Britain, 1,132 farms containing each 1,000 acres and upwards, and 2,816 others which are over 600 acres in extent. There are but 190,573 farms of less than 100 acres each, while in France, as we have just seen, there are two and a half millions which do not exceed ten acres.

The chief argument in favor of this "monster-farm" system is, that it economizes labor, and admits the application of capital on a large scale, so that machinery can take the place of human beings, great operations in draining and manuring can be effected, and the most improved processes of agriculture can be carried out in their full perfection. It may be so, if by rent we understand only that portion of the produce which accrues to the exclusive benefit of the landlord. In many cases, his estate will give him a larger income if devoted to pasturage than to tillage; for in the former case, only a few herdsmen are required to perform all the labor that is needed on a thousand acres. But it does not produce so much food; it does not afford sustenance to so many people. He who turns his land into a sheep-pasture or a deer-park, acts on the same principle as the Dutch, when, having a monopoly of the trade in spices, they destroyed a portion of what they imported in order to enhance the price of the remainder. It behooves the landholders who reason in this manner to ask themselves, if they do not lose as much by the increased cost of pauperism as they may possibly gain by the enhancement of their rents. In England alone, the amount levied for the poor rate in 1850 exceeded seven and a quarter millions sterling (about $36,000,000); the average number of paupers receiving relief on any one day was almost exactly one million; and the whole number of different persons relieved during some part of the year, was three millions.*

* Pashley *on Pauperism and the Poor Laws,* (London, 1852,) pp. 8 – 12.

The proper object of all cultivation is to increase the quantity of the marketable produce of the land, and this is what the interest of the community, especially in such a country as England, requires; the object of the land-owner who does not till the ground himself, but lets it out to others, is to reserve as much as possible of this produce for himself. He may often obtain a greater net return by diminishing the gross amount of produce. If fifty laborers upon his estate, for instance, will enable him to send 1,000 bushels of grain to market, the price of 800 bushels being needed to pay the wages of these laborers; while ten laborers will produce 500 bushels for sale, and require only 160 bushels for wages; his rent in the former case will be only 200, while in the latter it will amount to 340 bushels. It is for his interest, then, to employ the smaller number of laborers, and thereby to produce the smaller quantity of food, especially since the inadequate supply in the market will then enhance the price of the grain. It may be, that 500 will sell for as much as could, under the other supposition, be obtained for 1,000 bushels. But it is certainly not for the interest of the public, in a country teeming with population and deficient in the supply of food, that he should adopt this course. Here is another instance, then, of the fallacy of the often quoted maxim, that individual and national interests are identical. Only half a century ago, the most profitable use which the farmers of Ohio and Western Pennsylvania could make of their grain was to distil it into whiskey; for in this highly concentrated form alone would it bear the expense of transportation to the eastward. The interests of the individual here prompted him to deprive the grain of its nutritious properties and convert it into a poison; the interests of the public required a very different proceeding.

That a larger *gross* product of food may be obtained from the land when it is divided into small properties than when it is held in large farms, is a fact which no English traveller on the Continent can think of disputing. "In Flanders," says Mr. Laing, "the face of the country resembles a carpet, little patches of gound being covered with a great variety of crops of different shades and hues, not separated from each other by enclosures, and all blooming like a garden from the care and skill of the cultivator. Not a bit of ground is allowed to run to waste, every nook and corner, every patch in the angle of a fence, being searched by the spade and hoe, and weeded by hand." The wonders of English farming are accomplished on a large scale, with high finish indeed, but with much necessary neglect or slighting of the nooks and corners, which cannot be tilled by machinery, but will yield returns only to manual labor. Spade-husbandry, of course, is less profitable, and even less productive, than husbandry by the plough, wherever land is cheap and labor is dear. But where only the nobility and gentry own the land, while a large portion of the people are constantly in want of employment and food, precisely the reverse holds; cultivation by the spade is then true economy, and husbandry on a large scale is criminal wastefulness of the bounties of Providence. The utmost amount which land is capable of producing can be estimated only on the small patches of ground, in the neighborhood of a large city, which are cultivated by the market gardeners. Here, every clod is broken, every shovelful of earth is raked and sifted, every pebble and weed is carefully removed by hand, and an abundance of hoarded manure being applied, while every accident of rain or sunshine is economized or averted, the crops are immense out of all proportion with the little space that is cultivated. Usually two or three crops of different kinds of vegetables are raised from the same land in one season. If the cultivator is also the owner of the soil, he works with a degree of diligence, earnestness, and care which can never be obtained from a hireling. The land is then, to adopt Mr. Laing's happy illustration, his Savings' Bank, in which he invests the labor of what would otherwise be his spare minutes; for though such labor may not perceptibly increase the amount of the next crop, it will add to the value of the ground. Even the little household refuse, which would otherwise be wasted, though really valuable as manure, is economized and applied to the land. The common description of a farm which is worked to the utmost is, that it is cultivated "like a garden"; and what is a garden but a small farm? A whole country divided into small properties is a constant succession of such gardens. In England, the large farmer, who often pays a rent of a thousand pounds a year, is in fact a commercial speculator on a grand scale. He cannot afford to pay much attention to minutiæ; a too jealous and closely calculated economy, by leading him to fritter away on details the care and thought which are required for the general management, might ruin him. There is always considerable waste in large enterprises; it will not do for the manager of them to cultivate corners and patches. The large farmer wields a heavy capital with great skill and science, economizes human labor by the introduction of costly and powerful machines, and may either make or lose a fortune in one season. His operations are of a sweeping character, and his returns are counted in the gross. He often makes more money by raising a smaller amount to the acre. To turn all his land into a kitchen garden would require a whole army of laborers, whose wages would eat up all his profits. The laborers would be fed, but he would sacrifice his capital. The method which he pursues has an opposite effect; he makes large profits, while the laborers are driven off the estate, and too often become dependent on public charity. Large farms economize human labor, it is true; but it depends on circumstances whether this is a benefit to the nation. Here in the United States, indeed, it would be a real saving, equivalent to the production of more wealth; but it is difficult to see what advantage it could bring to a country like England, where, in 1850, there were over 300,000 able-bodied male paupers.*

But this question respecting the comparative advantages of large and small farms can be best determined by observing the results of the two systems in actual operation, side by side. The following is taken from Mr. Laing's "Notes of a Traveller," First Series.

"Why should the physical and moral condition of this population [that of Tuscany] be so superior to that of the Neapolitans, or of the neighboring people in the Papal States? The soil and climate and productions are the same in all these countries. The difference must be accounted for by the happier distribution of the land in Tuscany. In 1836, Tuscany contained 1,436,785 inhabitants, and 130,190 landed estates. Deducting 7,901 estates belonging to towns, churches, or other corporate bodies, we have 122,289 belonging to the people, — or, in other words, 48 families in every 100 have land of their

---

* Pashley *on Pauperism and Poor Laws*, p. 19.

own to live from. Can the striking difference in the physica and moral condition, and in the standard of living, betwee the people of Tuscany and those of the Papal States be as cribed to any other cause? The taxes are as heavy in Tus cany as in the dominions of the Pope; about 12*s*. 6*d*. sterlin per head of the population in the one, and 12*s*. 10*d*. in the other But in the whole Maremma of Rome, of about 30 leagues i length by 10 or 12 in breath, M. Chateauvieux reckons only 2 factors, or tenants of the large estates of the Roman nobles From the frontier of the Neapolitan to that of the Tusca state, the whole country is reckoned to be divided into abou 600 landed estates. Compare the husbandry of Tuscany, th perfect system of drainage, for instance, in the strath of Arno by drains between every two beds of land, all connected wit a main drain, — being our own lately introduced furrow tile draining, but connected here with the irrigation as well as th draining of the land; — compare the clean state of the growin crops, the variety and succession of green crops for fodderin cattle in the house all the year round, the attention to collec ing manure, the garden-like cultivation of the whole face o the country; — compare these with the desert waste of the Rc man Maremma, or with the Papal country, of soil and prc ductiveness as good as that of the vale of the Arno, the countr about Foligno and Perugia; — compare the well-clothed, bus people, the smart country-girls at work about their cows' fooc or their silkworm leaves, with the ragged, sallow, indolent po ulation lounging about their doors in the Papal dominion starving, and with nothing to do on the great estates; na compare the agricultural industry and operations in this lan of small farms with the best of our large farm-districts, wit Tweedside, or East Lothian, — and snap your fingers at th wisdom of our Sir Johns, and all the host of our book-make on agriculture, who bleat after each other that solemn saw c the thriving-tenantry-times of the war, — that small farms a incompatible with a high and perfect state of cultivation. Sco land, or England, can produce no one tract of land to be con pared to this strath of the Arno, not to say for productivenes because that depends upon soil and climate, which we have nc of similar quality to compare, but for industry and intelligenc applied to husbandry, for perfect drainage, for irrigation, fc garden-like culture, for clean state of crops, for absence of all waste of land, labor, or manure, for good cultivation, in short, and the good condition of the laboring cultivator. These are points which admit of being compared between one farm and another, in the most distinct soils and climates. Our system of large farms will gain nothing in such a comparison with the husbandry of Tuscany, Flanders, or Switzerland, under a system of small farms."

In the isle of Guernsey, where the agricultural population is twice as dense as in England, the average wheat crop is at least 32 bushels to an acre; while the average English crop — with all the advantages arising from the application of immense capital, scientific husbandry, and agricultural machines, on which the advocates of large farms lay so much stress — is but 21 bushels. An English cultivator, with his family, it is estimated, consumes one fifth of the product which he raises; then, if there were three cultivators where there is now but one, and if their united exertions should make the crop only two fifths greater than it was before, there would still be as great a surplus to send to market, though the number of families supported upon the land would be three times as great. In other words, as one cultivator raises 100 bushels, of which he is able to sell 80, so, if three cultivators can produce 140 bushels from the same land, they can still send 80 to market, and feed themselves and their families with the remainder. This is the case in Guernsey, where the average crop exceeds the average English crop by more than two fifths.

Large estates still more than large farms diminish the aggregate product of the country, because the owners of them devote so much land to purposes of mere ornament, ostentation, and luxury. When the territory is divided among small proprietors, as in France, Prussia, and the Netherlands, almost every acre of it is employed productively; it is all given to tillage, pasturage, gardening, or the growth of fuel and timber. But in Great Britain, large portions are reserved for parks, lawns, the chase, and preserving game. If land were abundant and cheap, indeed, there would be no reason to regret that many acres should be appropriated to such uses. But when complaints are made that the country is over-peopled, that population tends to outrun the means of subsistence, and that its

45

increase drives down agriculture successively to poorer and poorer soils, it is reasonable to inquire whether the gifts of Providence are improved to the utmost, or whether the scarcity of food be not owing to the luxury and wastefulness of the rich. Among other results of that systematic compulsory depopulation of the Highlands of Scotland which has been repeatedly mentioned, M. de Lavergne alludes to the "skilful turning to account of the wilderness, through the extraordinary profit derived from its game. Ptarmigan, blackcock, all kinds of water-fowl, and especially grouse, breed upon these moors in great plenty; fallow and red deer have also been artificially propagated upon them. *Fashion has given great value to these sports.* A hill stocked with game lets for £50 for the season. Shooting-lodges, built in the most retired spots, are let, including the right of shooting over the adjacent hills, at £500. What is called a *forest* — that is to say, several thousands of acres, not exactly planted with trees, but reserved for deer to the exclusion of all kinds of cattle — brings an extravagant rent. The large Scotch proprietors, following the example of William the Conqueror, have laid out many of these forests upon their estates. Gentlemen go there at great expense, to enjoy the sport of shooting the fleet monarchs of these wilds in their precipitous retreats."

The parallel here suggested is a very significant one. William, in the stern exercise of his rights as a conqueror, resolved to make a new forest near Winchester, the usual place of his residence, that he might enjoy the pleasures of the chase; and for this purpose, says Hume, "he laid waste the country in Hampshire for an extent of thirty miles, expelled the inhabitants from their houses, seized their property, even demolished churches and convents, and made the sufferers no compensation for the injury." What he did under the rights of war, these Scottish lords have done under color of the rights of property. They have banished the inhabitants of several counties in the North of Scotland, from the homes which, according to the Celtic law and usage, belonged to them as much as to their chieftains, and have turned one portion of the district into a sheep-walk, and another into a wilderness, that they might enjoy the pleasures of the chase. The region thus depopulated is fifty times as large as that which the Norman converted into the New Forest.

M. de Lavergne apologizes, though rather faintly, for this proceeding. "People are beginning to murmur," he says, "against these last vestiges of ancient feudalism, contending that the deer are too few in number profitably to occupy the vast tracts set apart for them, and that it would be better to use them for feeding sheep. I can understand such an argument when the question concerns England, where certain wealthy proprietors still persist in keeping waste for their shootings large tracts of land in the middle of populous districts, that might otherwise bear crops; such, for example, is Cannoch Chase in Staffordshire, which contains nearly 15,000 acres; but in the Highlands of Scotland, I can scarcely believe that the loss is very great. A few thousands of sheep, more or less, would be no great addition to the national food; and then, again, the last remains of savage nature in Great Britain would be gone. To rob the country life of all its poetry, is going rather too far even in the interests of farming."

If the question were only between deer and sheep, as the inhabitants of this vast district, we might agree with M. de Lavergne, that it does not matter much which way it is decided, especially if we are to take his account of the condition of Sutherlandshire, whence a Highland clan has been driven to make room for flocks. "The depopulated lands," he says, "were divided into twenty-nine large sheep farms, averaging twenty-five thousand acres each. The hills serve for summer pasturage, and the glens or valleys for the winter. As for human inhabitants, there are none. If the sound of the bagpipe is heard among the rocks, it is no longer the gathering-call of warlike mountaineers, but the more peaceful amusement of a shepherd, who, in place of war and pillage, devotes his time to the care of sheep, and receives wages from a neighboring farmer. This is all that remains of an extinct race. One of these shepherds can look after five hundred sheep. There may be four or five hundred such upon these eight hundred thousand acres." In order to effect this improvement, "three thousand families were forced to quit the country of their fathers, and were transplanted into the new villages upon the coast. When resistance was shown, the agents of the Marchioness demolished their miserable habitations, and in some instances, in order to effect this more speedily, the huts were set on fire."

These striking instances of the arbitrary depopulation of large districts are not adduced to throw odium upon the authors of them. The fault is not imputable so much to the great proprietors in England, Scotland, and Ireland, who have effected these wholesale "clearances" of their estates, as to the system, — the policy of the law, the course of legislation, and the state of public opinion, — which has caused such an accumulation of real property in the hands of a few, and has authorized such a use of it. These are the necessary results of a system which is upheld by English theologians and political economists, as well as by English statesmen, for the avowed purpose of sustaining a splendid aristocracy. "It is not true," declares Dr. Chalmers with his wonted earnestness, "that, in virtue of elegance, and luxury, and leisure being the inheritance of a few, *there is not a blessing in the present system of things to the whole mass of society.* Under the opposite system, there would be nearly one unbroken level, the whole of which behoved, in time, to be as sunk and degraded as is the state of our present laborers. Now, it is a level rising into frequent eminences of greater or less height [a very remarkable *level*, indeed], and of radiance more or less conspicuous. And what we affirm is, that, *from this higher galaxy of rank and fortune, there are the droppings, as it were, of a bland and benignant influence on the general platform of humanity.*"

May Heaven shield every other nation from the droppings of such "a bland and benignant influence" as have rendered the Highlands of Scotland, and the dreariest hills and bogs in the sister isle, more wild and desolate even than Nature's hand had left them, because the blackened walls of many a roofless hut now tell us that man once lived there, but that he has been dispossessed and exiled in order to make room for the ptarmigan, the red deer, and the fox, and thus to afford new hunting-grounds for a magnificent aristocracy!

The system has been carried out, not merely by such princely proprietors as the Duchess of Sutherland and the Marquis of Breadalbane, and the great absentee landlords of Ireland, but by nearly all the owners of real estate in the United Kingdom. There has been a systematic depopulation of all the rural districts, as the necessary consequence of the national policy of favoring the aggregation of landed property for political purposes, or to keep up aristocratic institutions. Large estates are naturally divided into large farms, both because it is easier and safer for the owners thus to manage them and collect their rents, and because the aggregate of rent thus obtained is more considerable, though this increase of net income is procured by diminishing the gross product.

The fact that most Irish estates, till within a few years, were parcelled out into a great number of very small holdings, is only an apparent contradiction of this statement. Irish landlords, as well as English and Scotch, did in fact lease their property in a few immense farms; but the practice of underletting being sanctioned by law and custom in Ireland, while it is entirely prohibited in the sister isle, the lease-holders found it more convenient, as well as more profitable, to let out the land again in smaller parcels, and thus to become "middlemen" instead of farmers. They thus retained a higher social position, and were able to make greater profits by rack-renting the inferior tenantry, than by carrying out the most scientific processes of husbandry. The absenteeism of the landlords, and the practice of granting perpetual leases, favored this result. The middlemen under these circumstances differed but little from actual proprietors, though they held the estate under a heavy encumbrance, and were therefore more extortionate in demanding heavy rents, and rigidly exacting all their dues. Few of the kindly relations existed between them and their tenantry which generally sprang up in England between a resident landlord and a tenant family, which, in many instances, had occupied the same farm for several successive generations. The land, and all that was connected with it, were not endeared to the lease-holder by the indefinable charm which springs from absolute ownership; he was, after all, only a great speculator, and, in one sense, a hireling. Hence one of the peculiar aggravating causes of the wretched condition of Irish property, and the destitution of Irish tenants.

Abundant evidence has now been adduced, that the larger net income accruing to the landlords from leasing their estates in large rather than in small farms, arises from diminishing the quantity, and enhancing the price, of the products of the soil, instead of increasing its productiveness by improved processes of husbandry. Here, surely, the gains of the individual are a loss to the nation; such gains are the result of the *acquisition* of wealth, not of its *creation*, for they are extorted from the consumers by raising the price of food. The Scotch Highland lords, who also have immense estates in England, would not so readily convert their property at the North into sheep-walks and game-preserves, if they did not find that, by raising more grain, they lowered its price so much that their aggregate receipts would be diminished. In truth, it may be demonstrated that it is for the interest of English landlords always to keep the home supply a little short of the demand, so that some importation of food shall be necessary. Suppose, for instance, that the consumption exceeds one million of quarters by only 40,000 bushels, and that, if this additional 40,000 bushels are raised at home, the price averages fifty shillings a quarter. But if only one million of quarters should be grown in England, then, before the 40,000 bushels can be imported, the price of the whole must rise enough to defray the cost of importation, which amounts, on an average, to at least twelve shillings a quarter. By keeping the supply thus far short, therefore, they will be able to sell one million of quarters at sixty-two shillings, which will produce £ 3,100,000; whereas, if the extra quantity be produced at home, they will have 1,005,000 quarters to dispose of at only fifty shillings a quarter, which will amount to but £ 2,512,500; so that the farmers will lose £ 587,500 by their imprudent increase of production.

This is not all. Large estates and large farms impoverish the country, not only by enhancing the cost of food, but by lowering the rate of wages, and increasing the number of those who are solely dependent upon wages for their support. I have already shown, in the chapter on this subject (pp. 199–201), that wages are higher in the United States than anywhere else, chiefly because almost every native American has the option of beginning life on his own account, as a small tradesman, an independent mechanic, or a small landholder, and that he can be tempted to forego the superior independence and respectability of such an occupation, and the greater chance that it offers of making a fortune, only by the offer of comparatively high wages. Any considerable reduction of the rate of wages is sure to be followed by a great diminution in the number of those who are willing to work for hire. Mr.

Laing happily illustrates the same principle, while accounting for the higher *real* wages that are paid in many parts of the Continent than in England. "It is the possession of property," he says, "that regulates the standard of living in a country, and this standard regulates the wages of labor. People who have at home some kind of property to apply their labor to, will not sell their labor for wages that do not afford them a better diet than potatoes and maize; although, in saving for themselves, they may live very much on potatoes and maize. It is want of the necessity or inclination to take work, that makes labor scarce, and, considering the price of provisions, dear, in many parts of the Continent where property in land is widely diffused among the people."

Now the whole civilized world affords no parallel to the condition of the people of Great Britain in these respects. The concentration of landed property, as we have seen, is such, that only one person out of every 112 has any proprietary interest in the soil; and the large-farm system, with the consequent reduction in numbers of the agricultural class, has been carried so far, that only one in five has anything to do with the cultivation of it. Thus the whole ground of independence of the laboring classes has been taken away; they have been obliged to offer themselves as laborers for hire, or to starve. While two thirds of the whole French population are owners of land, full two thirds of the whole British people are hirelings, solely dependent upon wages for a livelihood.* The

---

* Mr. Morrison, one of the latest English writers on the "Relations between Labor and Capital," and a very candid and judicious reasoner, understates the contrast when he says, that, in France, "the class of manual laborers living on wages received from capitalists is seen to be only a minority, and not even a large minority, of the nation"; they certainly do not form more than one sixth of the whole. "But in England and Scotland," he says, "the classes living by wages form the majority of the population," and, according to the best estimate that can be formed from the last census, a very considerable majority.

Mr. Morrison states one of the consequences of this contrast very fairly, when he says, in reference to the mad proceedings of the Provisional Government in France, in 1848, which had raised an alarm about the safety of property, "the great mass of the nation, the peasant proprietors and others, who were neither payers nor receivers of wages, and had a great and direct interest in the preservation of the right of property, intervened before the mischief had gone very far." But in England, he adds, "not only is the division of the nation into a minority of possessors of property, and a majority of workingmen having little or no property, more complete than in France or most Continental countries, but both the wealth and the labor are col-

field for the employment of labor is not unbounded; its limits are as fixed as those of the field for the use of capital. According to the natural distribution of industry, agriculture ought to be the occupation or the chief resource of a majority of the people. The production of food is the first and greatest want of the human race; as it must be carried on over the whole face of the country, it does not admit of the division and the economy of labor so much as the other two departments of industry. Every square mile, every acre, must be cultivated by itself, wholly irrespective of the work which is done upon the neighboring mile or acre. Improvements in the processes of husbandry may enable us to raise more products from the land, but cannot materially lessen the number of tillers of the ground, or the proportion which they bear to the other classes of society, without diminishing at the same time the gross produce. The facts here are in accordance with the theory. In the whole civilized world, except Great Britain, there is not probably one country which employs less than half of its population in cultivating the soil; the usual proportion is from two thirds to three fourths. The improvements in manufacture and commerce have been proportionably so much greater than in agriculture, that one third of the people can supply the aggregate want of the nation in the two former respects, more easily than two thirds can supply its want of food.

In the extrusion of four fifths of the English people from the pursuits of agriculture, and from any connection with the soil, we find the cause of so large a class of the population being entirely dependent upon wages, of the consequent depression of wages, the extraordinary increase of pauperism, the unnatural development of manufacturing enterprise, and the other peculiar circumstances of the present social condition of Great Britain. In this single fact, we find a sufficient explanation of those social phenomena which first suggested the theories of Malthus and Ricardo respecting population, wages, and rent.

lected into great masses in a greater degree than elsewhere. Hence, if the improvement of the relations between capital and labor by the authority of government should ever become a practical political question, it will assume dimensions unknown in most other countries. It will be a direct appeal to the interests and passions of the majority of the whole nation against a minority; and there will be no third party capable of holding the balance between them."

Deprived of all other means of support, a majority of the population are driven to compete with each other for employment, by offering to work for the smallest amount of wages that will furnish the necessaries of life. Hopeless of any improvement in their condition, they become reckless as to the future, and too often burden themselves with families when their gains are hardly sufficient to preserve their individual existence. Manufactures were the only branch of industry in which any great numbers of them could find employment; and thus labor was rendered so cheap, that manufacturing enterprise has been unduly stimulated, and the persons concerned in it have offered no opposition to the proceedings of the landholders, whereby the towns have been glutted with the surplus of the agricultural population. Great Britain is in the anomalous position of not raising food enough for her own consumption, and still glutting the market of the world with the products of her manufacturing industry. No nation can compete with her in this respect, except by raising a barrier against the influx of her cheap goods, or by allowing its own laboring classes to fall into a condition as dependent and miserable as that of English operatives.

So long as the laws regulating the succession of property remain unchanged here in America, we have a guaranty of the permanency of our republican institutions, and a safeguard against the worst social evils which affect the Old World. Whatever may be the rage of parties or the temporary violence of faction, there is no danger of revolutionary violence, so long as the bulk of the people are either satisfied with their present lot, or believe ease and competency to be within their reach, if they are only willing to use industry and self-denial enough to gain them. The blessings of our peculiar institutions, I suspect, are rather social than political. We ought to prize them, not so much because they guard us against oppression and anarchy, which may be regarded as obsolete evils for an Anglo-Saxon race, as because they foster no inequalities of social condition, but open the avenues to fame and fortune alike to all. The great merit of our government is, that it lets things alone; that it allows matters to take their natural course; that it permits property to change hands as often as caprice or speculation dictates; that it offers no obstacle to enterprise in the accumulation of a fortune, however great, and no hinderance to the dissipation of it during the lifetime of the owner, or to the equal partition of it after his death among his natural heirs. Under this system of non-interference, it is true, as the English economists urge, that we cannot have permanent family estates or an hereditary aristocracy; and our consolation is, that we are able to get along very well without them.

The English economists who favor the aggregation of landed estates, ought to have more regard to their own favorite maxim, *laissez faire*. In respect to the distribution of property, more than in any other case, is there good reason for not interfering with the natural constitution of society, and the wise arrangements of Providence. As already stated, it is not the mere *inequality* of fortunes, but the *fixedness* of them in a few families, which is to be dreaded. There are natural causes enough which favor the former, and obstruct the latter, if their operation be not impeded by laws of man's device. Thus, it is a natural law, that wealth favors the growth of wealth, and poverty tends to generate poverty. In explaining the causes of the diminished rate of profit as a nation advances in opulence, it was mentioned, that large capitals tend constantly, more and more, to crowd small ones out of employment, because the owners of the former can afford to work for smaller returns, and can sustain greater reverses. This is well explained by M. Passy. "Other things being equal," he says, "the profits of each capitalist decrease in the same ratio in which the national capital increases. The little capitalist thus finds himself obliged, on account of the diminution of his income, to break in upon his capital; while the great capitalist, finding in the mass of his profits an income still superior to his wants, constantly adds to his riches by new savings. Besides, who does not know, that, being able to use the most costly machines, to carry to the utmost the division of labor, and to reduce the general expenses to the lowest point, the great capitalist can produce more cheaply than the smaller ones, and thus make himself absolute master of the market?"

Other natural causes tending to the same result are, the differences existing among men in point of natural endowments; the occurrence of unforeseen events; and the law of population itself, which makes the destitute classes multiply with great rapidity, because misery renders them reckless, while the rich tend to decrease in number, and, from the lack of male heirs, estates come to be united by marriage and collateral inheritance. Thus there will always be inequality enough in the distribution of property to allow those enterprises to be carried out which require great accumulations of wealth, and to operate as a spur to the industry and frugality of the community, by manifesting the comforts and luxuries, the higher social position, which riches alone can give.

On the other hand, in the order of Providence, there is a natural check or limitation to the excessive accumulation of property in the hands of a few, and to the consequent debasement and misery of the multitude; and this natural corrective, when not interfered with or rendered powerless by unwise laws or a bad government, tends so rapidly and effectually towards an equalization of wealth in the community, that no considerable number of persons can possibly be brought to extreme destitution, — certainly, cannot be exposed to the danger of perishing with hunger, — except by their own obvious fault. Such a check, we maintain, exists in the very circumstance or cause to which the English school of political economists are fond of attributing the whole evil, — *the natural multiplication of the human species.* Property in the hands of an individual unquestionably tends to accumulate; one who has both money and industry can make greater gains, other things being equal, than his competitor who is obliged to depend on industry alone. But from the shortness of human life, an individual can hold this property only for a brief period of years; when he dies, it descends to his offspring; and by the law of nature, as they are all equally near to him, it is equally divided among them. When this law is not abrogated by human legislation, it causes so frequent a distribution of estates as effectually to overcome the tendency of capital to accumulate, or to continue in a single line of heirs. No sooner is wealth heaped up than it is parcelled out again, and a constant movement or circulation is thus maintained, which sends the lifeblood of capital into every part of the body politic. This distribution tends as powerfully to political as to social equality, for the former, indeed, depends upon and is regulated by the latter; hence it is the safeguard of republics, and the bane of aristocratic governments.

The faster the population increases, the more rapidly does this great corrective of the accumulation of property operate; the greater the number of heirs, the more minute is the division of the parent's wealth.

I have already remarked at length (Chap. X.) on the tendency of frequent mutations of fortune, of numerous and sudden changes from poverty to opulence and the reverse, to keep down popular discontent, to increase the security of property, and to incite the activity and enterprise of the community. These results are displayed here in America to an extent which excites the never-ending astonishment of foreigners. The English system has precisely the opposite effect. So far as it extends, it chills exertion by hemming it round with barriers which no effort can overleap. In the case of real property, these impediments are such that partition or alienation in most cases is impossible, and the land is permanently placed *extra commercium*. The dignity and other advantages of a landholder's position may be inherited by the accident of birth, but cannot often be bought. Land in small parcels is seldom brought into market, as the stamp duties for the transfer are high out of all proportion with those which are charged for the conveyance of large properties; and as there is no registration of deeds and mortgages in England, the expense of investigating the title is very great, and just as heavy for a small estate as a large one. Personal property is not so well guarded; but the causes which have been mentioned, the policy of the law and the general desire to secure the possession of wealth to one's descendants, tend powerfully to heap it together; waste is possible, but natural causes, aided by legal provisions, tend strongly towards accumulation. Small capitals find a constantly increasing difficulty in competing with larger ones; industry alone, unaided by inherited wealth, has little chance in the strife. The consequence is, that the mass of the people, the laboring classes generally, sit down, not contented, but sullen and reckless, in their poverty; the great aim of life for them is reduced to the attainment of a mere subsistence.

Isolated facts give only a vague conception of the great inequality of fortune, the frightful extremes of opulence and misery, which deform the social aspect of Great Britain. The knowledge thus gained is very partial and indefinite; and it leads to no certain conclusions, because, in every country on the globe, we meet with similar afflicting instances of extreme indigence and almost unbounded wealth, the contrast between them being heightened apparently by their close juxtaposition. Everywhere it is but a short walk from the palace to the hovel; at the gate of every Dives sits a Lazarus, and the dogs come and lick his sores. But the number and extent of these frightful contrasts are vastly greater in England and Ireland than in any other nation upon the earth, and the history of all former ages affords no parallel to them. Its people are the manufacturers and bankers of the civilized world; their accumulated capital, finding no sufficient employment at home, is carried abroad, with every wind that blows, to the remotest lands and the farthest isles of the sea, everywhere setting industry in motion, supplying means for great national enterprises, and creating immense yearly returns to increase the surplus of wealth at home. But the destitution and misery of the larger portion of the people increase even more rapidly than the riches of the prosperous class. Almshouses and jails are multiplied as fast as the palatial abodes of the nobility and gentry, or the immense mills and workshops of the rich manufacturers. Noblemen, whose annual incomes exceed half a million of dollars, complain of the heavy taxes which they are obliged to pay for the support of over a million of paupers. Finally, a panic seems to fall upon the whole Irish nation, and they fly from their native home, which is noted for its fertility and abounding in wealth, with more fearful haste, and in larger numbers, than if it were scourged with a pestilence, or wasted with the sword. It is in the magnitude of these numbers, in this terrible *preponderance* of misery, that the lover of his race sees reason to doubt, whether the preservation of property, as it is now constituted in Great Britain, be not rather a curse than a blessing.

The principal argument in favor of the monstrous inequality of fortunes to which the policy of English law has given rise is, that it is absolutely necessary for the preservation of an hereditary aristocracy. This will be satisfactory to all who believe, that the few who are born to the certain possession of vast estates are more likely to be virtuous, intelligent, and capable than any other persons in the community. It does not agree very well, however, with Dr. Johnson's apology for the custom of primogeniture, when he said that it had the merit of making "only one fool in a family." Nor is it quite consistent with what Mr. McCulloch himself remarks in another connection, that, "if you would develop all the native resources of a man's mind, you must make him aware of his inferiority in relation to others, and inspire him with a determination to rise to the same or a higher level"; and that "it is not to those placed by their fortunes at the head of society, but to those in its humbler walks who have raised themselves to eminence, that mankind are indebted for the greater number of those inventions and improvements which have made such vast additions to the sum of human happiness." But we do not need to discuss the merits of aristocratic rule in the abstract; the practical question is, whether the blessings it confers upon the country at large are enough to make up for the misery which it entails upon the lower classes; whether the support of the dignity and influence of a House of Lords is a fair offset for an Irish famine and exodus, and for seven millions sterling annually expended on the English poor. Doubtless, it is desirable to have a body of fifty thousand wealthy landed proprietors in the state, many of whom are accomplished gentlemen and fit to be hereditary legislators; but they cannot be had without bringing with them over a million of paupers every year, and reducing the rate of wages, on which half of the nation are entirely dependent, to the lowest point that will sustain life on the poorest and scantiest fare.

But it is feared that the motive for accumulation will not be strong enough, if it is not stimulated by a sight of the splendor and luxury in which the great landlords live, and of the influence and consideration which they enjoy. To this Mr. Mill's answer seems sufficient, that, "in America, there are few or no great hereditary fortunes; yet industrial energy and the ardor of accumulation are not supposed to be particularly backward in that part of the world." Economists generally make a great mistake, when they put so much stress upon the necessity of keeping up the incentives for people to get rich. Human nature requires no urging in this respect. Wealth is coveted originally, no doubt, for some ulterior motive, — for the enjoyments that it will bring; but it soon comes to be loved for its own sake, the passion and the habit of money-making leading to the sacrifice of every object for which riches at first seemed desirable. The certain and undisturbed possession of a fortune for one's own lifetime is motive enough for exertion; we do not believe that the springs of industry and economy would be sensibly relaxed, if a man's power over his wealth should cease entirely at his death, the state then dividing it equally, as in France, among his children.

However this may be, Mr. McCulloch is wrong in supposing that the sight of great estates tied up perpetually in the same families, is so effectual a stimulus to industry, as if the same amount of wealth were more equally distributed, and passed frequently from hand to hand, the alternations of fortune being frequent, and the chance to every individual of being successful sooner or later being consequently increased. To induce men to buy tickets in a lottery, there must not only be great prizes in the wheel, but some chance, however small, of drawing one within a definite period. Every lawyer who begins practice, may hope one day to become Lord Chancellor, for as that splendid office is not handed down by hereditary descent, some member of the bar must obtain it; and this hope, slight as it is, is one of the springs which keep up the activity and learning of the profession. But a country gentleman with a thousand a year, sees no possibility of his becoming a Duke of Buccleuch with an income two hundred times as great; and therefore the country gentleman usually does nothing but hunt foxes and go to Newmarket. To take great estates out of the market, as was done in Scotland, tying them up for ever in the same families, making alienation, division, — and, we may add, improvement, — alike impossible, is in fact to lessen the number of the prizes of industry, and so far, while rendering one man improvident, wasteful, and idle, to lessen the hopes and deaden the exertions of all others. Go to the other end of society, and you find the same cause working out similar results. What hope has an Irish cottier, a Tipperary boy, exert himself as he may, of ever obtaining more generous fare than buttermilk and sodden potatoes? and who can wonder that, without such hope, he should become the reckless, lazy, and quarrelsome beggar that he is? What encouragement is it to him, that, from the door of his mud cabin, he can see the magnificent but deserted abode of his absentee landlord, who comes over, once in a year or two, to look after his Irish estates, which yield him an income of £ 20,000 a year? It shows the almost indomitable energy of the English character, that the sight of these extremes of opulence and misery descending in the same lines from one generation to another, the accident of birth alone determining who shall continue in them through life, has not long ago extinguished ambition and effort, and rendered society torpid and motionless. In the learned professions, indeed, and in manufactures and trade, there is some room for changes of fortune, and therefore some incitement to activity. But even here, the deadening influence of a fixed hereditary transmission of employment and social condition is felt. I have heard of one family in London which has sold tea at retail, on the same stand, through five generations. The institution of castes among the Hindoos affords the only parallel to such a social state, though even the Pariahs might compassionate "the irretrievable helotism of the working classes" in Great Britain.

This comparison of an aristocratic and a republican polity, of a system of laws which favors the aggregation of property, with one which aims at its distribution, is not instituted in any boastful spirit; for it is not the character of our people, but of our social and political institutions, that we wish to defend. No comparison could be a fairer one; for the two systems are represented as acting upon two equally enlightened and industrious nations, who are mainly of the same blood, and speak the same language, and whose respective situations are as nearly alike as those of two great nations ever can be. Too great stress has been placed by English economists upon the advantage that Americans enjoy in their abundance of fertile territory; the immense colonial dominion, and greater wealth of England, go far towards balancing this supposed advantage. Many of the British colonies afford ample proof, that the inhabitants of a country do not rapidly increase in numbers and opulence merely because they are abundantly supplied with the necessaries of life. In the character of the people and of the institutions which they live under, and not in any imaginary or real advantages or drawbacks of territory, soil, and climate, are found the true causes of national decay and national prosperity. Capital and land are not mere instruments for the production of wealth, in which light alone they are too frequently regarded by economists; they are also necessary means for the support and happiness of the whole nation; and in this capacity, like rain and other fertilizing agents for the soil, they produce the more effect the more evenly they are distributed.

Foreigners who satirize that eagerness in the pursuit of wealth, which seems to them a prominent trait in the American character, either overlook or forget the great liberality with which this wealth is here expended for public objects. Rapid alternations of fortune do not lead to contracted views of the use of riches, or to penurious habits; we may be a speculating, but we are not a miserly people. A fortune which has been speedily won, and is liable to be quite as speedily lost, is usually held very freely, or with an open hand, while it is in the individual's possession; that which has been slowly amassed from very small savings, and by the practice of rigid economy through a long period of years, is commonly hoarded with a jealous and sordid care. In a country like England, if the founder of such a fortune has had any other motive than a mere love of pelf, it is, probably, that his hard-earned wealth might be held undivided and inalienable in his own family through future generations. An object so remote as this seldom enters the mind of an American, and if it did, he would see but little chance of its attainment; he is more likely to covet immediate applause, and the transmission of his name with honor to posterity, through the endowment of a public institution or the furtherance of some scheme of general utility. The most natural and sensible way of deriving personal gratification from newly acquired wealth, and of making a show of it in the eyes of the world, is to give largely to public charities. The sums which are contributed here by individuals for the support of schools, colleges, churches, missions, hospitals, and institutions of science and beneficence, put to shame the official liberality of the oldest and wealthiest governments in Europe. A New England button-maker, the architect of his own fortune, endows most munificently an academy, and founds two or three college professorships, during his lifetime, scorning to make only a tardy provision for them in his will, out of wealth which cannot be carried beyond the grave. The benefactions of the inhabitants of Boston alone, a city which had a population of only 25,000 in 1800, though it is now about six times as large, amounted, during the first half of the present century, to over six millions of dollars. And it is a remark which can be very easily verified, that the most numerous and magnificent gifts and bequests are made, not by men who have inherited their fortunes, but by those who have amassed them by their own exertions.

THE END.